THE AVEBURY LANDSCAPE

I0892387

THE AVEBURY LANDSCAPE

aspects of the field archaeology of the Marlborough Downs

edited by

Graham Brown, David Field
and David McOmish

with illustrations by Deborah Cunliffe

Oxbow Books

First published in the United Kingdom in 2005. Reprinted in 2016 by
OXBOW BOOKS
10 Hythe Bridge Street, Oxford OX1 2EW

and in the United States by
OXBOW BOOKS
1950 Lawrence Road, Havertown, PA 19083

© Oxbow Books, Graham Brown, David Field, David McOmish and the contributors, 2016

Paperback Edition: ISBN 978-1-84217-152-3
Digital Edition: ISBN 978-1-78570-384-3 (ePub)

A CIP record for this book is available from the British Library

All rights reserved. No part of this book may be reproduced or transmitted in any form or by any means, electronic or mechanical including photocopying, recording or by any information storage and retrieval system, without permission from the publisher in writing.

For a complete list of Oxbow titles, please contact:

UNITED KINGDOM
Oxbow Books
Telephone (01865) 241249, Fax (01865) 794449
Email: oxbow@oxbowbooks.com
www.oxbowbooks.com

UNITED STATES OF AMERICA
Oxbow Books
Telephone (800) 791-9354, Fax (610) 853-9146
Email: queries@casemateacademic.com
www.casemateacademic.com/oxbow

Oxbow Books is part of the Casemate Group

Front cover: West Kennet Avenue, stone pair 35 viewed from the east on 19 December 1999 (NMR: AA000884 © English Heritage).
Back cover: West Kennet Avenue, one of stone pair 36, shrouded after vandalism in December 1999 (NMR: AA000883 © English Heritage).
Photographs taken by Ian Leonard

for Desmond Bonney

Contents

List of Contributors

Michael J Allen Wessex Archaeology, Old Sarum Business Park, Portway, Salisbury, Wiltshire

Stephen Allen University of Reading

Martyn Barber Investigator, Aerial Survey, English Heritage, NMRC, Kemble Drive, Swindon, Wilts SN2 2GZ

Mark Bowden Senior Archaeological Investigator, English Heritage, NMRC, Kemble Drive, Swindon, Wilts SN2 2GZ

Graham Brown Archaeological Investigator, English Heritage, NMRC, Kemble Drive, Swindon, Wilts SN2 2GZ

Jon Cannon Hillside, Ogbourne St George, Marlborough SN8 1SU

Rosamund Cleal Curator, Alexander Keiller Museum, The National Trust, Avebury, Wiltshire

Simon Crutchley Senior Investigator, Aerial Survey, English Heritage, NMRC, Kemble Drive, Swindon, Wilts SN2 2GZ

Andrew David Head of Archaeometry, English Heritage, Fort Cumberland Road, Eastney, Portsmouth, Po4 9LD

David Field Archaeological Investigator, English Heritage, NMRC, Kemble Drive, Swindon, Wilts SN2 2GZ

Isobel Geddes 1 School Close, Keevil, Trowbridge, Wilts BA14 6SB

Graeme Kirkham Historic Environment Service, Cornwall County Council, Percival Building, Old County Hall, Station Road, Truro TR1 3AY

Carenza Lewis Corpus Christi College, Cambridge

David McOmish Senior Archaeological Invesigator, English Heritage, 24 Brooklands Avenue, Cambridge, CB2 2BU

Joshua Pollard Lecturer in Archaeology, Department of Archaeology, University of Bristol,
43 Woodland Road, Bristol, BS8 1UU

Andrew Reynolds Senior Lecturer in Medieval Archaeology, Institute of Archaeology, University College, Gordon Square, London

Hazel Riley Archaeological Investigator, English Heritage, 5 Marlborough Court, Manaton Close, Exeter, EX2 8PF

Julie E Scott Jackson PADMAC Unit, Pitt Rivers Museum, Donald Baden Powell Quaternary Research Centre, University of Oxford, 60 Banbury Road, Oxford

Nicola Smith Archaeological Investigator, English Heritage, NMRC, Kemble Drive, Swindon, Wilts SN2 2GZ

Helen Walkington PADMAC Unit, Pitt Rivers Museum, Donald Baden Powell Quaternary Research Centre, University of Oxford, 60 Banbury Road, Oxford

Preface

It is over one hundred years since the publication of the wide ranging archaeological field investigation undertaken on the Marlborough Downs by the Rev A C Smith. Smith, a prominent Wiltshire naturalist and antiquarian who lived in the rectory at Yatesbury, near Avebury and spent much of his time traversing the downs on horseback, recording the visible archaeology as he did so. His work *Guide to the British and Roman Antiquities of the North Wiltshire Downs in a Hundred Square Miles round Abury* was originally published in two volumes in 1884 by the Marlborough College Natural History Society, the maps being bound separately from the text. Unfortunately, a fire at the printers destroyed all but 286 copies of the 500 copy print-run leaving many subscribers, not to mention members of the interested general public, without copies. Fortunately 300 copies of the map were retrieved and together with reprinted text, were bound, this time into a single volume and published in 1885 by the Wiltshire Archaeological and Natural History Society. As in most works of inventory the volume has certainly stood the test of time and is still one of the basic reference texts for students of the area. Since then, apart from a few notable exceptions, archaeological literature about the area has been largely site-based and there has been little concerning the Marlborough Downs as a whole. Instead, most writing has concentrated on the prehistoric monuments of the Avebury World Heritage Site. In order to try and redress this perceived imbalance, a day conference was organised in April 2002 and held at the University of Bath in Swindon, where it was possible to acknowledge and mark the ongoing validity of Smith's work and where a number of papers on various aspects of recent research on the Marlborough Downs were presented.

The results of the conference are presented in this volume, together with a number of other commissioned contributions from individuals who have undertaken research in the area during the last decade or so. In particular, by the Royal Commission on the Historical Monuments of England (RCHME) – now merged with English Heritage – work that otherwise may have become archive material and overlooked. The volume aims to complement the excellent recently published work by Peter Fowler, Joshua Pollard and Andrew Reynolds, and by the Avebury Archaeological Research Group. Each essay stands alone, but they are connected by a common theme, that of the land and how it has changed over millennia. They should not, however, be seen as the last word on the respective topics, for as each author will readily acknowledge, so much remains to be done and this is merely a signpost.

Graham Brown, David Field and David McOmish

Acknowledgements

We would like to express our thanks to Philip Jones and the University of Bath at Swindon for hosting the day conference. Humphrey Welfare, then Director of Archaeological Projects Division at English Heritage, for providing warm support for the venture and Paul Everson, Head of Archaeological Survey at English Heritage, who also provided continued encouragement throughout. Also, our thanks go to English Heritage for the financial support that made this volume possible. Deborah Cunliffe organised the graphics and, except for the illustrations in Chapters 4, 8, 10, 16, and 19, prepared the illustrative material. Elaine Davidson prepared Figure 2:9; Jane Brayne figures in Chapter 8. Except for those in Chapters 4, 8, 10, 16 and 19, which are copyright of the respective authors or separately acknowledged, all figures are © Crown Copyright NMR, or © Crown Copyright English Heritage. Roads and buildings indicated on plans are based on Ordnance Survey mapping and is © Crown Copyright. A number of staff of the former RCHME not mentioned by name in the following pages including Morag Brown, Paul Pattison, Valerie Wilson, Louise Barker and C Lewis also participated in field survey on the Downs over the years, some on sites not presented here, and their contributions are acknowledged. Thanks are due also to the various landowners who have kindly allowed access to their property.

Foreword

It is a privilege, a pleasure and an opportunity to be invited to introduce a stimulating and curious – in the John Aubrey sense, of course – volume about an area of England which people tend to travel past rather than to; particularly as I was not invited to the seminar in 2002 from which the volume stems. Someone is now being magnanimous.

Situated roughly halfway between London and Bristol, the Marlborough Downs, topographically, historically, tenurially, historiographically and certainly archaeologically on the evidence here, seem amoeba-like in size and shape (Fig 1). Their boundaries bulge and contract irregularly; their shape changes through time, with specialism and by author. This volume continues that tradition. It never quite makes up its mind how far they stretch in any direction except the north where Swindon is clearly the portal to another world. Burbling south to Marlborough, the River Og, whose name suggests it flows from that other world, is mentioned as the study area's eastern boundary; yet lands east of it, verily even unto the meeting of Kennet and Thames, feature albeit spasmodically as the amoeba pulses. This is a strength.

Ranging widely over central southern England, then, most

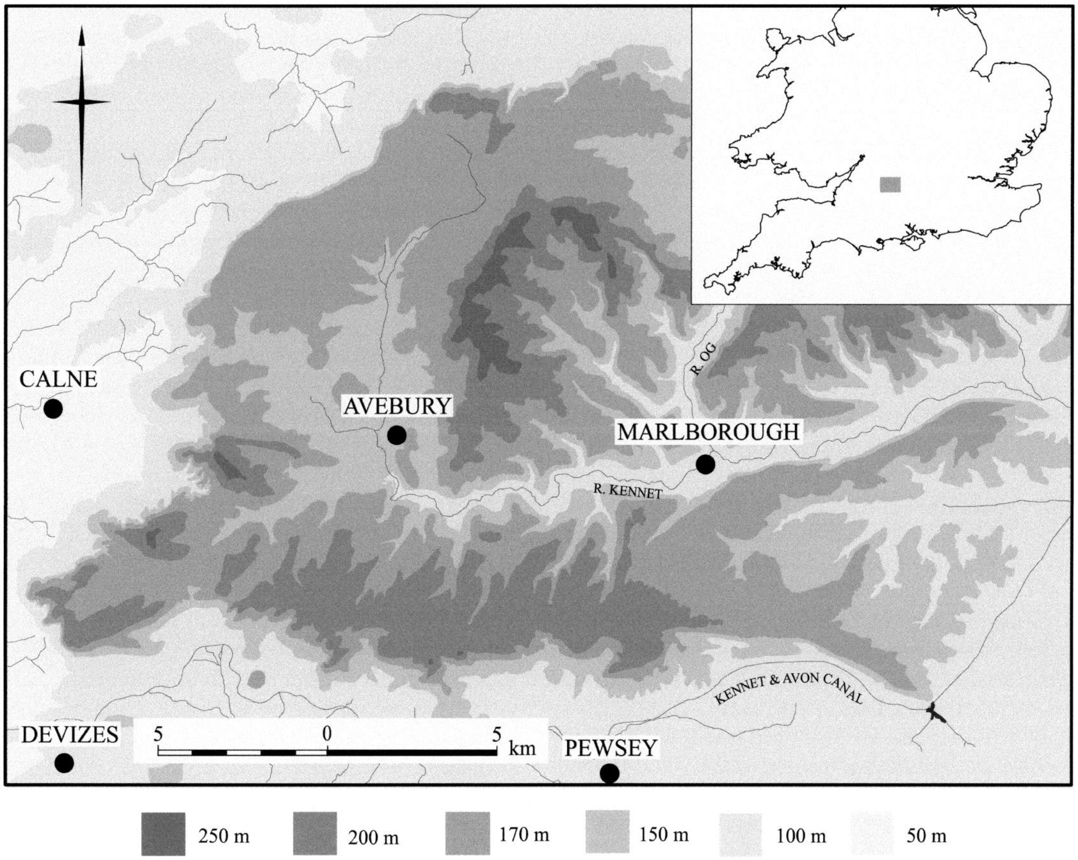

Fig 1 Location Map

among the nineteen essays in this volume nevertheless ratchet down to west of Og and north of Kennet. Some close in specifically on the landscape immediately around, and indeed of, Avebury itself. But even such well-defined concepts heave and convulse in size and shape in a most interesting way on the ground. Is Avebury High Street, for example, a micro-landscape of long-forgotten affairs? As a macro-landscape, is the Rev. Smith's (1885) rigidly geometrical 'hundred square miles around Abury' a sensible study-area? – it certainly worked for him and his wife as the basis for an inventory of past rather than pastoral interests and, in a sense acknowledged by the editors, four generations later this volume is their great-great-grandchild. In our contemporary academic and bureaucratic perception, is the 'Avebury landscape' only the space defined by the great monuments immediately around (visible from?) the henge itself, is it the area defined by the boundaries of the World Heritage Site, or does it extend more widely to include not only more distant monuments like Knap Hill – one of the earliest landscape structures in Britain – but also non-monumental, ancient agrarian landscapes as on All Cannings and Fyfield Downs?

For present purposes, no single definition is needed. Each author defines his or her area as it best fits the topic being discussed. Yes, the volume consequently lacks a sharp geographical focus but its time-span and its thematic diversity – and its consequent stimulating buzz – are such that its content is far better unconstrained by a precise spatial straight-jacket. How uncomfortable the regional Palaeolithic, medieval religious land-holding and aspects of early 21st century hippiedom would be in the same one together. The last item there, incidentally, is the core of the last, and best, chapter in the book, and no reader is allowed undeserved reward by reading it before its due turn. Its author, Jon Cannon, remarks on the non-conformist, now United Reform, chapel so provocatively placed, unlike the externalised St. James's church, close to the geometrical centre of Avebury henge. As a preacher in it might well have urged, self-mortification best precedes a tad of pleasure.

In fact the volume is (mostly) a good read rather than a cross-country punishment. I can vouch for that as I read the whole of it, in the correct sequence, between an early breakfast and a late supper on the same day – and slept well thereafter. For the Marlborough Downs, however defined, it is without doubt a significant book. Collectively, if variably, it really does take understandings of Avebury and its environs forward. It joins a contemporary, academic, literary florescence about both. Cannon begins his 'New Age' with a book (Dames 1976), apparently influential beyond academia, which when published I personally regarded as silly – as, while now more sympathetic, I still do. My own sense of an intellectual 'new age' in Aveburiana began when, a generation on from Isobel Smith's (1965) publication of Keiller's excavations, Peter Ucko and colleagues' (1990) extraordinary volume suggested the start of an academic renaissance. The last decade plus has rather borne that out. Previously standard works like Burl (1979) and Malone (1989), for example, hardly figure here, while major works of data and percipience since Gingell (1992), and a flood of scientific papers, have flowed from a new generation of seriously good scholars like Allen, Gittings, Pitts, Pollard and Reynolds. Perhaps above all, two Cardiff professors, John Evans and Alasdair Whittle, have stayed with the area longer than most and illumined some of its seemingly intractable aspects (*see* the bibliographies throughout this volume, *passim*).

Largely as a result, Avebury, after years of playing second fiddle to Stonehenge, now to a marked extent dances to its own tune, notably as sung, more or less from the same hymn sheet, by its own choir. This is prosaically called the Avebury Archaeological and Historical Research Group (AAHRG). A changing membership, including some soloists, tries to embrace everyone who is seriously researching, or contemplating archaeo-historical research, in the area. It is entirely voluntary, and it has no powers; yet it commands peer respect and so comments, criticises, prompts, sets standards, takes initiatives, encourages co-operation and, perhaps most importantly, thinks. It recently produced a world-first, a research agenda for the World Heritage Site published as a substantial academic report in its own right (Chadburn and Pomeroy-Kellinger 2001). That agenda is reflected in this volume.

Yet this volume glows with far more than an AAHRG halo. The 'Avebury landscape' may lack geographical focus but it commands a tremendous focussing of resources in the pursuance of its eternal verities. Some of those verities, and the enthusiasm and commitment they inspire, are pursued, so I understand, through largely emotional means and expressions; they lie beyond my consideration here of resources for scientific endeavour. Yet the intellectual attraction essentially creating the concentration of talented and highly-committed individuals who choose – that is the operative word – to devote their academic skills, time and energies to this area is but another facet of the magnetism that is Avebury. It is one kind of response to the pull that simultaneously brings secular tourists all the time, poets and painters on days of scudding clouds, hundreds of leather-clad motor-cyclists on Wednesday evenings, and latter-day pagans to cuddle stones on specific dates.

Behind most of the individual scholars, however, lie supporting institutions, the main national ones, English Heritage and the National Trust, half a dozen universities or so, and national and local archaeological societies. All, to a greater or lesser extent, are supported in some sense by the public, notably the tax-payer, even pagan ones. Yet such organisations are not in any formal sense contributing to a single, defined *grand projet*; there is no overall 'Avebury research design'. Individually, each is probably pursuing one or more of its own, internally-conceived programmes: the origins and execution of this volume itself lie in several such within the former Royal Commission on the Historical Monuments of England, now merged with English Heritage which wisely continues such work. Collectively, these institutions bring a *gravitas* and resources of expertises, people and equipment, massively so in the case of English Heritage; they can at least open doors to funds. Together they create a synergy through which scientific and intellectual research is pursued and on the results of which, by and large, management of the overall resource and 'Avebury and its landscape' is based.

Yet the results and effect of the research effort are, to a large extent, serendipitous. This volume is a monument to serendipity, one of the long-term strengths of the English fieldwork tradition. Eleven of its papers come from current staff of English Heritage characteristically writing, I think I dare say, in a mode fusing official work and personal research interest. Five papers have university associations; two come from professional organisations; one is from the currently unassociated Mr. Cannon of Ogbourne St. George. The Avebury landscape as represented here was not conceived as an entity worthy of the collective research of these organisations (and Mr. Cannon); yet it has emerged. In unity may indeed lie strength, as the many working relationships specified and implied here illustrate. As far as archaeological research is concerned, however, particularly field archaeology it would seem, diversity, flexibility, opportunism, an ability to respond to a circumstance, a happening and an idea, are all desirable qualities important to encourage rather than lose, for example in bureaucratic procedures or over-institutionalised human resource management. All those qualities are apparent in the Avebury of our mind-sets of the early 21st century. Unintentionally, a happy and intellectually productive circumstance has created itself rather than been created at Avebury, in part reflected in this book. We can hope that, arriving by chance, it may survive by chance; but of course the temptation is to manage it.

This volume, however arrived at, addresses some of the major issues in the archaeology and history of the Marlborough Downs area. It divides into almost equal halves: 10 papers are essentially inventories or descriptions of current work; 9 are primarily discussions (though of course the former include discussions and the latter are based on data). The former will tend to be used for some time; the latter are essential to keep ideas on the move. Among the substantial essays which present both an effort of consolidation and mark a departure point for the next phase of work are four on periods hardly yet well-represented in the Avebury bibliography: the Palaeolithic, the Mesolithic, the early medieval centuries, and one aspect, the archaeology of monastic land-holding, of the medieval period. A fifth and sixth, both on the Bronze Age, are perhaps chronologically and materially more familiar in an Avebury/Marlborough Downs context, but nevertheless both represent important works of consolidation and synthesis, one about the Early Bronze Age, the other about metalwork.

Outstanding issues remain. The volume signposts some. It brings forward a lot of new evidence, not least in the form of Royal Commission-type plans and maps; yet the needs of academic understanding are unquenchable. Most authors unite in demanding not just more data but better-quality data, whether they be Palaeolithic flints or environmental evidence or air photographs or documented places on the Downs. Yet it would seem that in some respects we have a surfeit of evidence, even allowing for evidential redundancy but judging by examples of information not used in some chapters and not referenced in some bibliographies. Meanwhile, on the unstated premise that peoples' behaviour separated by 4000 years is comparable, Jon Cannon offers another approach which does not require the permanent curation of millions of artefacts, photographs and records. It is a tempting, and cheap, scenario, but even were behavioural comparison scientifically valid across the millennia, unfortunately modern hippies do not think or do most of the things necessitated by the life-style of our prehistoric ancestors. Hard physical labour in the landscape, day after day, comes to mind. So, overall, despite its interesting hints of possibilities, there is no escape down that route.

Nevertheless, this volume overall marks a significant stage in the development of our intellectual understanding of Avebury and its context. Drawing on the inspiration here, and my own understanding, I suggest that moves towards the next stage might well include attention to the following matters (there are of course many others – *see* for example, Chadburn and Pomeroy-Kellinger 2001). I limit myself to five headings, with a brief selection of suggestions under each:

i. Avebury henge monument itself: why here (and not elsewhere)? We really have to find out about – nature, function, date – the early phase(s), of earth, timber and doubtless stone arrangements before those fossilised by Keiller in the 1930s. Specifics include answering the question begged by the presumably absolutely accurate new plan published here which suggests the present henge earthworks consist of two unequal parts: a western arc of ditch and bank on a smaller diameter than a bigger eastern, flattened arc. If so, which was added to which? And when? Further, where is the archaeology of the site for the last two millennia BC; where is 'Roman Avebury'. And how do we best set about testing Reynolds' early medieval burghal and urban hypothesis? We do not even know whether the present settlement form reflects expansion of a henge-bound settlement outside its enclosing earthworks (if so, when?); extension of a settlement outside the henge into the (empty?) interior; or familiar medieval 'settlement shuffle' essentially along the banks of the Winterbourne almost irrespective of the henge itself (*see* the new plans with Chapter 2)

ii. The immediate Avebury landscape: have we completed the discovery of all the major monuments? – given the discoveries of the 1980s–90s, probably not, but where and of what sort are the potential missing pieces of the 'Neolithic map'? Are we certain there were not 'avenues' to east (likely in my view) and north (unlikely?). Can we sharpen up our knowledge of what the avenues were for? How do we do that if essentially their function was mnemonic as suggested by Pollard here (megalithic formalisation of ethnogenesis)? Was Neolithic Avebury a landscape of big structures alone, with nothing in between them? Even if there was nothing, were the blank areas of a ritual significance in their nothingness? Or were there (a few? some? many?) other things (what? – natural vegetation? sacred groves? totem poles? corpses? excarnation platforms? observatories? the equivalents of the 'stations of the Cross' for a ceremonial progress around the area? preaching points? assembly areas? middens? deposits of the Neolithic equivalents of Cannon's plastic 'crystals' and/or bits of rag tied to bushes? wooden houses? fields? tethered stock? animal pounds? tented-camp-sites for workers and/or pilgrims? priestly ghettoes?) in the apparent 'blanks'? Another concern is that basic dating is still flabby, with too many 'floating' components in a series of landscapes. Even limited to its Neolithic phase, 'the Avebury landscape' nevertheless saw many changes: more precise contemporaneity in that landscape needs to be established, for its own sake and as the basis for observing change. Furthermore, what was the nature of, and where was, the Neolithic economic and demographic support base for an enormous expenditure of human energy on construction, and then maintenance? – was it indeed even in the 'immediate Avebury landscape'? More specifically, where are the habitation sites pre-1500 BC? And indeed between 5th–1st century BC and the 5th–10th century AD?

iii. Chronological issues: what happened to/in:

a. the Palaeolithic?
b. the Mesolithic?
c. the middle Neolithic?
d. the middle Iron Age?
e. 100 BC–AD 100?
f. AD 400–1000?
g. 'Other periods': overall, explore the concept that the material evidence of 'other periods', so often noted of sites after recognition of their original date and main phase of use, may not be of merely peripheral interest but indications of considerable and long-term significance

iv. The Marlborough Downs, topographically: five straightforward suggestions:

a. what, if anything is characteristic or special about the highest areas of the downs – the truly local 'uplands', – especially the caps of Clay-with-Flints?
b. ditto *valley sides* or, more technically, *valley slopes*, particularly along the Kennet and Og valleys (against a background of archaeological attention tending to focus on the downs or the valley floors)
c. exploit the *archaeo-environmental potential* of deposition in combes/dry valleys/winterbournes (as per Mike Allen's paper, and especially the 'Piggledean model')
d. examine critically the model of *'persistent places'* and especially the idea of *'nodal points'* in the landscape, both in relation to routes and other long-term lines of communication and boundaries; and in particular to 'nail' once and for all such key lines in the Marlborough Downs landscape as the 'Ridgeway' and 'herepath'
e. use the excellent historical research in *The History of Wiltshire, Victoria County History* series as a base to resolve in topographical and archaeological terms *landscape issues of the modern period* not discussed at all in this volume, notably the mid-16th to early-18th century (post-Dissolution), mid-18th to early 19th century (Enclosure), 19th to mid-20th century ('industrialisation'), and mid-20th century – present ('commodification')

v. Conservation: there is a pressing need of constant study of how we ourselves treat the past, not just its monuments but the conceptual matrix in which we enfold and present them and their landscape. Its audience changes too, its consumers' expectations vary. Avebury has a good World Heritage Site management plan (English Heritage 1998), with a professional mechanism for its quinquennial review (current), but it does not of course embrace the bulk of the area under discussion here. The designation of the Marlborough Downs as part of an 'Area of Outstanding Natural Beauty' does that, but cultural conservation is not its prime objective. Currently various minds are grappling with the creation of a 'statement of significance, required for both the World Heritage Site and the National Trust 'Avebury estate' (different areas, different institutional needs, different concepts of significance). Such mechanisms are good but are they enough and of the right sort? What is the right sort? Are they appropriate? How are they being applied in practice? What is the effect of such practice? Is it physically preserving the site? Is it enhancing life-style in the village, the local economy and visitors' appreciation of their experience? How do we assess and give value to such matters? From critical analysis to impressionistic assessment, management in the widest sense of Avebury and its landscape needs continuous self-examination and external review. Both processes can draw on many sources but theoretical and practical research across a range of academic disciplines is essential in their support. Unlike some academic research, it is unlikely to happen serendipitously. It has to be conceptualised, commissioned and completed.

It would be nice to believe that an awareness of the need to research conservation management, and the means to carry out such research, was as well appreciated as the need to carry out archaeological and historical research into Avebury and its landscape. With this landmark volume now in our hands, it will certainly be interesting to see whether any of the sort of research suggested above is carried out sooner rather than later. New ideas will be forthcoming – my very list of suggestions alone should spark some; serendipity will doubtless be influential. We should also be able to judge how well an improving knowledge and an increasingly well-informed management march together as this volume's successor evolves over the next decade.

Peter Fowler
1 September, 2003

1

Some observations on change, consolidation and perception in a chalk landscape

David Field, Graham Brown and David McOmish

Introduction

Even now Avebury is a sacred place – a temple to some – a mysterious part of Britain's past to others – to many a place of modern pilgrimage. Visitors come in their thousands. Even on Christmas Day people can be seen walking around the rim of the henge, and at certain times of the year, midwinter, midsummer, etc., the place is a veritable magnet for those seeking an alternative spiritual path. Druidic weddings and other ceremonies are commonplace. The village is never without visitors. People touch the stones, draw the stones and photograph them from every conceivable angle. The faithful leave flowers within niches and crevices in the sarsens and purchase metal coat hanger dowsing rods to test the mysterious powers of the place. Diviners survey the entrances with crystals. Surprisingly few picnic or play football. For most it is necessary to perambulate the embankment of the monument – procession-like. Even the elderly and infirm seem to manage at least one quadrant. Unlike Stonehenge where many uninterested visitors prefer to stay on the coach at its obligatory stop *en route* for the West Country, visitors here walk around the site and experience its visual, and perhaps its spiritual delights, and return home with interesting memories in addition to a few snaps and souvenirs. Unlike Stonehenge where visitors follow the defined pathway listening to handsets that provide anecdote and detail, but gaze through museum space at the sanitised monument, Avebury is real. You can feel it, experience it, and be part of it.

Visitors can easily get 'lost' in the great henge at Avebury because the 'monument' is of a scale that is difficult to comprehend without the aid of modern maps, plans and aerial photographs. But also as a result of the piecemeal presentation and the interruptions in viewlines imposed by building development within the interior. It is true that this sheer scale drives visitor expectations and, ultimately, understandings – in comparison to Stonehenge, where even the briefest of visits allows one to immediately (and philosophically) 'capture' the stones and their setting. This is not possible at Avebury where the very scale demands that in order to gain an understanding of the monument, its construction and its landscape setting, people *must* walk around the perimeter. Why do we always end up walking along the crest of the bank? It clearly derives from the desire for as full an experience as is possible when coming to the site – almost as if in order to comprehend its layout, scale and setting, we must perambulate the enclosure. There is obviously a strong aesthetic dimension at play as the henge sits in a perfect location from which to observe the beauty of the surrounding Downs as well as the intimate relationship with a medieval village. The bank is a good viewing platform within the modern-day 'experiential package' but this must surely find resonance with much earlier patterns of use and understanding. During our survey of the henge, it became apparent when talking to a number of tourists, that the massive external bank was not recognised as a constructed feature (i.e. there was an assumption that it was 'natural'!). This is extraordinary, but we could then ask what sort of knowledge are people armed with before and after a visit to the henge? It speaks volumes about the importance of observation from high points in order that we mentally encapsulate our environment, divide it into levels and spatially arrange it – and it could be suggested that these were, similarly, important themes in the history of Avebury.

Part of the attraction may be that it is a living village, with its own farms, school, post office and petrol station. For while isolated in the secluded Wiltshire countryside, miles from the nearest town, the busy A361 road is a constant reminder of the hectic communications necessary in the 21st century, as articulated lorries manoeuvre the chicane and narrowly miss the large Swindon Stone at the northern entrance.

What the monument is and why it should be placed there remains a matter of speculation, and while archaeological investigation has clarified detail on construction techniques and chronology, it is the non-mainstream archaeological press that has attempted to synthesise the material and analyse the landscape. Michael Dames (1992; 1996), for example, brought together elements of geography, folklore and ethnography, to provide narrative of the role of monuments within their landscape; Terrence Meadon (1999) considered the stones themselves in great detail, while it was left to Wakefield (1999) to suggest that the chambered tomb at West Kennet might be interpreted as an ancestral womb. This book seeks to redress this imbalance, furthermore, moving away from a site-centred analysis towards a fuller understanding of the multi-period landscape contexts on the Marlborough Downs.

Antiquaries

While very recent publications (Gingell 1992; Fowler 2000; Pollard & Reynolds 2002) have considered part of the area, the last mainstream archaeological publication dealing with the North Wiltshire Downs was actually published in 1884. This was the important work by the Rev A C Smith who spent 30 years recording all the archaeological information that he could muster within a 25 mile radius of Avebury (Smith 1884). He lived in Yatesbury, the neighbouring village to Avebury on the west, where little more than 4km separate one church from the other. Yatesbury sits on the Lower Chalk bench and is a useful base from which to explore the chalk downland of North Wiltshire. Smith, who was primarily interested in Natural History, had been riding over the Downs since his youth and when, in 1852, he was appointed the Rector of Yatesbury, he found himself well placed to pursue his interest in antiquities. In a similar manner to those earlier archaeological pioneers of Wiltshire, William Cunnington and Richard Colt-Hoare, he extensively explored the Downs in company with his wife and kept a mapped record of all his findings. Observing the changes to arable farming on the Downs and the numerous earthworks that were being levelled, he resolved to record them before their complete destruction. Recording directly onto an enlarged 1 inch Ordnance Survey map, he covered *'nearly every yard'* of ground traversing *'up and down and across and across'* (Smith 1884, ix, xi). As Rector, he was well placed to borrow and study the best available large-scale maps (those made for the Tithe Awards) from colleagues in neighbouring parishes, and noted and interpreted appropriate field names from them and elsewhere.

In marked contrast to their efforts in the south of the county, Cunnington and Colt Hoare carried out little practical work on the Marlborough Downs, for it was too far from home and they restricted most of their activity to observation and survey. Smith had neither the manpower nor the means of carrying out any significant amount of excavation himself, and so relied on others to provide detailed archaeological information. He did, however, carry out some small-scale work at the 'kistvaen' in Temple Bottom and at Avebury itself.

But there were earlier explorers, including Aubrey, a frequent visitor to Avebury during the 17th century. The famous story of how he introduced Charles II to the site while they were out riding has been well covered elsewhere and equally his remarkably fine plan prepared on a plane table – the earliest documented survey of the monument – has also been discussed in detail by others (Welfare 1989). Stukeley, too, spent much time around the Avebury landscape, particularly between the years 1718–24, observing, sketching, and making plans of the stones, and perhaps more than anyone since, developing an intense appreciation of the landscape. Starting with a clean sheet and without the benefit of accurate modern maps, he had to work out the curves, contours and lie of the land for himself, and the errors and corrections are there for all to see in his manuscript drawings. Although mainly remembered for his plans of the henge itself, his great achievement lay, in fact, in studying and depicting the archaeological landscape around it and placing it in a context with other monuments. Stukeley studied the wider landscape of the Marlborough Downs too; the prehistoric enclosures at Oldbury and Martinsell as well as the Marlborough Mount, were all recorded in astute detail.

Whereas Cunnington and Colt Hoare had investigated the barrows of Salisbury Plain during the earlier part of the 19th century, those in the north of the county were largely left to Thurnham to unravel some decades later. Thurnham, a surgeon and superintendent of Wiltshire County Mental Hospital at Roundway, Devizes, often appears to have been more interested in the skeletal material, particularly skulls, than in the detail of the structures investigated. Having re-excavated some of the barrows already dug by Cunnington on Salisbury Plain, he dug into a number on the Marlborough Downs, such as Alton Priors 1 (Adams Grave), Avebury 22 (West Kennet), Bishops Cannings 44 and 65 (Kitchen Barrow and Easton Down barrow. On the basis of the field evidence and artefacts recovered from the various barrow types, as well as the evidence of the skulls found within them, Thurnham concurred with Colt Hoare in the belief that long barrows were earlier than round examples.

Perhaps the most damaging episode of this early fieldwork was that of Merewether, Dean of Hereford Cathedral. Born at Ramsbury near Marlborough, he had spent his childhood on the Downs and so knew them well. He returned in advance of the meeting of the Archaeological Institute of Great Britain & Ireland at Salisbury in 1849 and carried out a single frenzied campaign of barrow investigation. Between 20th July and 15th August 1849 he opened 35 barrows, all in less than four weeks. Most of these were in the Avebury area, including four on Windmill Hill, four others nearby at Yatesbury, a series along the foot of the Middle/Upper Chalk escarpment on Avebury and Monkton Downs, but also in the south of the area in a group situated close to Wansdyke (Merewether 1851).

Archaeological investigation continued apace with H St G Gray excavating extensively at Avebury, demonstrating for the first time the immense proportions of the henge ditch. Later, Alexander Keiller, the marmalade magnate and resident at Avebury Manor, undertook research at the henge and carried out restoration work on it. In response to proposals to erect a radio mast on Windmill Hill, Keiller purchased the site in a grand philanthropic gesture, though modern-day residents of the area might now feel justified in asking 'where was the modern counterpart when similar monstrosities were erected on Morgans Hill nearby'? O G S Crawford, a contemporary of Keiller, investigated widely, but published sporadically. His investigations of Wansdyke and his work with Keiller (Crawford & Keiller 1928) confirmed the relative chronology of Dyke and Roman road.

In more recent times the henge and surrounding monuments have acted as a magnet to an international archaeological community. Stuart Piggott excavated for the Ministry of Works at West Kennet. Isobel Smith analysed Keiller's unpublished excavations on Windmill Hill and within the henge, but Vatcher's important excavations remain unpublished. This is most unfortunate as they provide interesting data that demonstrates an earlier core to the henge bank, as well as a Saxon settlement outside the bank adjacent to the village school (archives in A Keiller Museum, Avebury).

With the emergence of New Age philosophies, Avebury and its surrounding landscape have become re-energised. Many may scoff at this and, indeed, there is outright hostility from a number of professional archaeologists, but few can argue that the 'monuments' now have a revitalised importance to a growing community. The major monumental foci are certainly important nodes where this new awareness is played out and this is bringing with it its own particular tensions between those whose job it is to safeguard the historic fabric and those for whom it is now entwined within their spiritual world. The stones, monuments and natural topographical features mean many things to many people. Meaden (1999), for example, sees zoomorphic shapes in the stones and geographers and archaeologists reach to the landscape for answers (Dames 1992; 1996). Who knows what the inhabitants of Oldbury hillfort thought of the henge and its stones, built 2000 years earlier? Perhaps these ancient features would have been written into the mythological world of the ancestors, and incorporated in some form of social ritual or celebration. Monuments change 'meaning' – this is clear in a number of cases where pre-existing features have been re-built and altered and subsequently re-used within a ritual dimension, perhaps most famously witnessed at Stonehenge where repeated change and reformation took place over a long period of time. Why then should we feel uncomfortable with the current activity at the sacred sites on the Downs when clearly this is part of a sequence of use and abandonment stretching back through time? What we, ultimately, can't deny is that the Avebury landscape has become re-activated and is now relevant to a diverse public.

Genesis: The Solid and the Calabrian Sea

The ground beneath, the result of the deposition of marine organisms on the bed of the sea 75–80 million years ago, is gleaming white chalk of considerable thickness. Different levels can be distinguished by the component fossils within it and by the nature of the chalk at different levels (discussed by Geddes and Walkington below): at the base the Lower Chalk, above this the Middle Chalk, and overlying them the Upper Chalk. Within this are layers of flint, hard siliceous material formed in burrows around sponges and other creatures by chemical replacement. Dark, brittle and glassy, this couldn't contrast more with the soft white material that surrounds it.

Throughout the study area both Upper and Middle Chalk have been dramatically eroded or planed off leaving an extensive bench or plateau of gently undulating Lower Chalk stretching for some 8 kms from north to south, and 7 kms from west to east. Thought to have resulted from the presence of a marine incursion during the Calabrian (Clark *et al* 1967), the Downs are bounded by a steep escarpment in the west and north overlooking Compton Bassett, Clyffe Pypard and Swindon. To the east, the limit of this

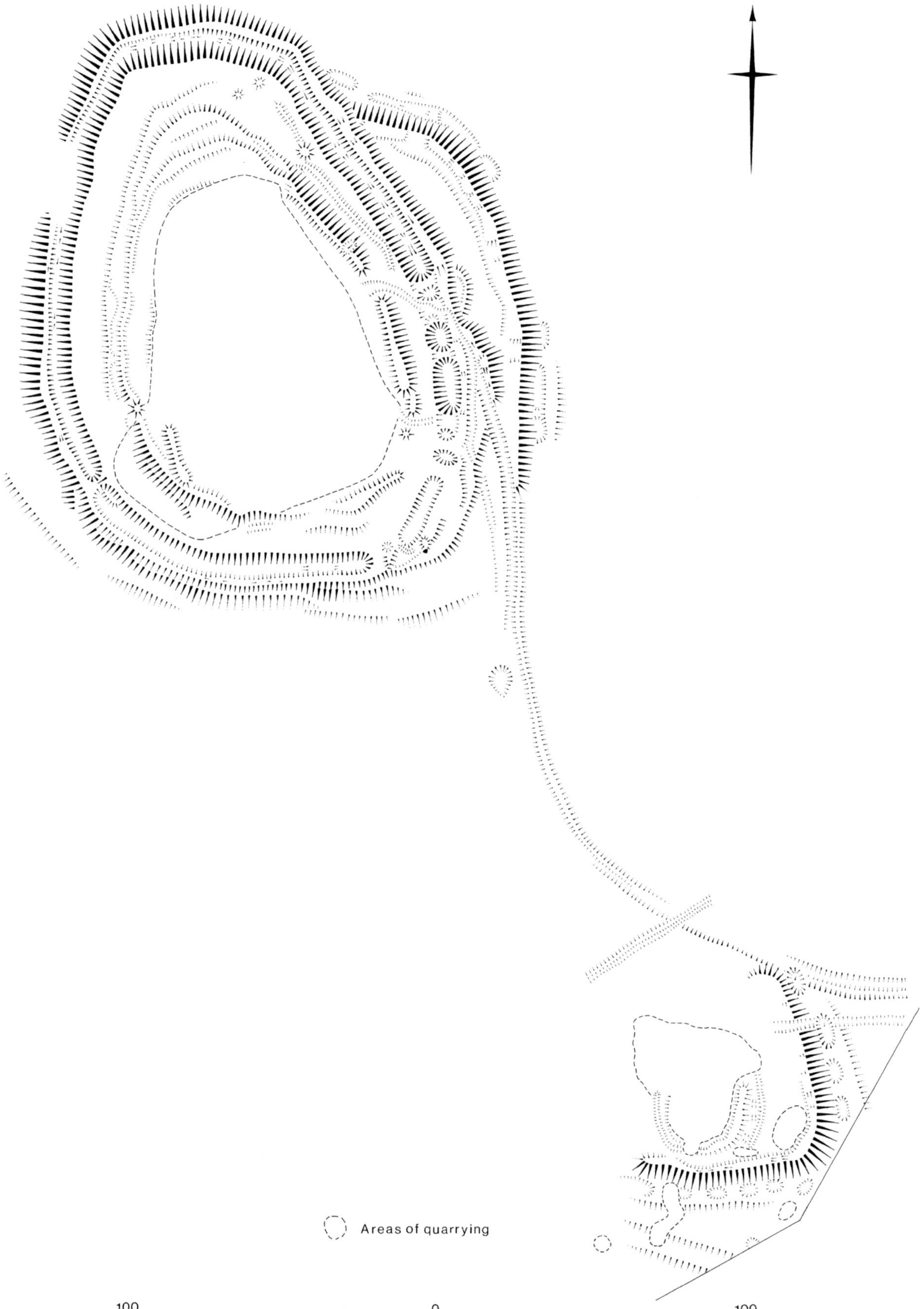
Areas of quarrying
100
0
100
METRES

Fig 1:1 (Opposite page) Plan of Rybury: Situated on the southern escarpment of the Marlborough Downs overlooking the Vale of Pewsey, the earthworks at Rybury occupy two knolls, c *180m apart, both of which have been extensively quarried, destroying earthworks. In plan, the main enclosure is approximately cordiform and it is overlain by a later construction, though a break of slope a few metres outside the later enclosure bank in the south and west, indicates its course. Where the natural escarpment is steepest, however, the bank appears more of a lynchet and the ditch as a mere ledge. At least seven causeways are present in the ditch and there are six corresponding breaks in the bank. A trench cut across the ditch by Desmond Bonney of the RCHME in 1963 revealed that it was flat bottomed and 2.1m deep, the silts containing over 600 flint flakes (Anon 1964, 185). Traces of a potential inner circuit exist on the summit of the knoll. Its outline preserved as a series of lynchet like scarps. Partially overlying the causewayed enclosure is an unusual hillfort-like enclosure with its bank outside the ditch. It might be compared to Wolstenbury in Sussex and perhaps dated to the Bronze Age. A detached part of the site lies on Clifford's Hill, a heavily quarried knoll 180m to the south-east of the first that stands proud of the surrounding downs by up to 5m. The enclosure has been set around the base of this. It is angular in outline, with straight stretches in the south and east of up to 50m, and comprises a causewayed ditch with causeways up to 4m in width. A bank 4m wide is visible in places, but this appears to have mostly eroded down the sides of the steep knoll into the ditch. © Crown Copyright. NMR.*

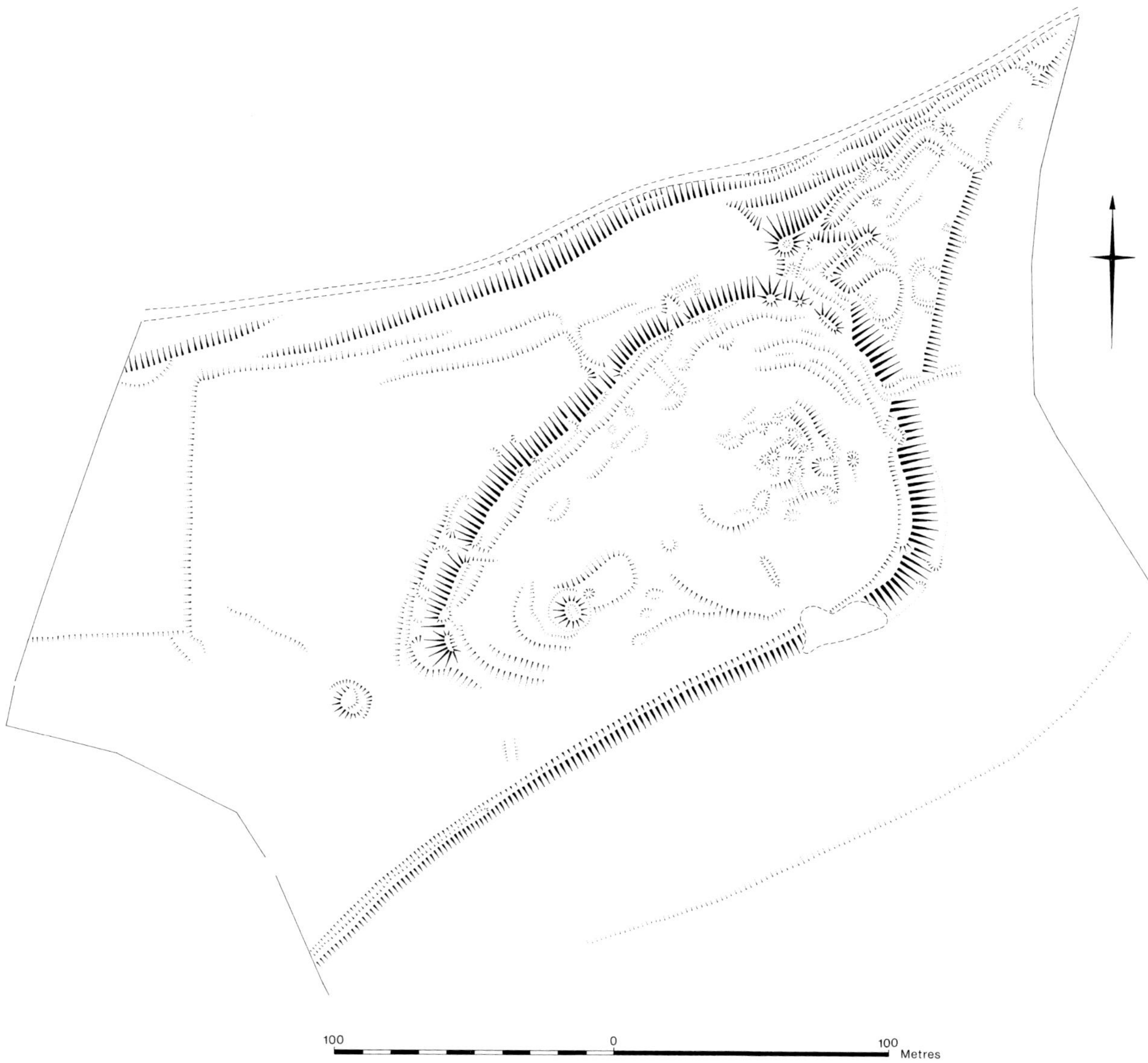

Fig 1:2 Plan of Knap Hill: The prominent summit overlooking the Pewsey Vale is crowned by earthworks of a causewayed enclosure (Oswald et al *2001). The quarrying here is situated in the saddle to the north of the enclosure, where a limekiln may once have existed. The scar ascending the escarpment and utilising the enclosure ditch is a tramway used to haul carts up to the chalk quarries and ease them down to the Vale fully laden. A similar process can be observed amongst the earthworks at Wilmington, Sussex. Pottery and flint recovered from outside the earthwork enclosure when the area was ploughed in the 1970's indicates that, like other causewayed enclosures e.g. Robin Hoods Ball and Windmill Hill, there was extra mural activity during the Neolithic period, though it need not have been contemporary. © Crown Copyright NMR.*

erosion episode is immediately evident where it meets the steep and prominent cliff like escarpment of the Middle and Upper Chalk. From this escarpment, overlooking the villages along the Winterbournes, the Upper Chalk stretches east to the valley of the River Og and beyond.

The western plateau, together with other Lower Chalk outcrops situated either side of the Kennet and the Beckhampton valley, has long been cultivated. The lack of flint cobbles makes it easy on the plough. In contrast, hard deposits that form the base of the Middle and Upper Chalk respectively, was extensively quarried throughout the area. In addition, digging for flint has heavily damaged much of the surface of the chalk and quarries for both materials abound on the higher downs. In some cases, they can be observed to extract preferred seams around the contour, in others such as at Rybury and Oldbury, exploitation is more widely distributed and has damaged or partially destroyed earlier monuments (e.g. Fig 1:1). Chalk was required for cement, for agricultural purposes and for writing. At Rybury, chalk extraction for chimney linings was well under way by the second half of the 19th century (Smith 1884, 115) while Smith also observed the destruction carried out by chalk diggers, at the Oldbury long barrow (*ibid*, 47). In the preceding century Stukeley lamented the destruction caused by chalk diggers servicing a limekiln at Calstone at the junction of Wansdyke and the Roman Road. His illustration of Oldbury hillfort, drawn on 11 July 1723, shows no quarrying within the vicinity of the camp and much of the digging therefore might be assumed to date to the 18th and 19th centuries.

Quarrying then has severely disfigured the landscape, obscuring and destroying archaeological sites in the process. The nature of this quarrying is, however, also of archaeological interest. The quest for chalk may have begun in earnest in Roman times to provide mortar for buildings. Flint, too, was a major construction material used throughout the medieval period in, for example, parish churches, but also in great demand until recent times, not only for building and perhaps flintlocks, but to repair the roads. According to Merewether (1851, 85), flint was often found immediately below the topsoil, where, after extraction it was piled in heaps and the turf replaced. Hectares of ground were turned over in this way and, inevitably, antiquities were encountered and destroyed. Smith (1884, 184) pointed out that at Knap Hill the east side had been so disturbed *'that all traces of the barrow mentioned by Sir R Hoare.... are quite obliterated'*. And it is worth mentioning the earthwork remains of a tramway on the steep scarp to the south of the enclosure which may have been used to lower loads of flint or chalk to the farms in the Pewsey Vale (Fig 1:2). Similarly at Oldbury, Smith lamented that flint diggers had not only destroyed a round barrow outside the hillfort (*ibid* 95), but constantly *`throw up numerous fragments of animal bones and rude pottery'*.

Between Horton and Easton Down, a well preserved series of linear quarries have shaved off the topsoil and chalk to a depth of c1.5m deep. Digging or spoil lines can be seen to form regular units in places, while occasional sarsen boulders have been turned to one side by the diggers. Similar earthmoving is evident on the plateau-like hilltop and covered by extensive quarries on, for example, Bishops Cannings Down. The remains of this are well preserved on the western part of the hill, but elsewhere they are now almost levelled by recent cultivation.

Overlying the chalk in a number of places is a deposit of Clay-with-flints, in part a remnant of Tertiary deposits that once covered the chalk, but which have long since been eroded away (see Geddes and Walkington: Scott-Jackson this volume). Contact between the Reading Beds and the Chalk surface has left a layer of tenacious red clay often containing frost-fractured flint. On the 'Higher Downs' there are numerous shallow quarries amongst the earthworks of the Romano-British villages on Overton and Fyfield Downs that probably relate to extraction of this deposit.

Drainage

Surface drainage across the area is dominated by the west-east flowing River Kennet and its main tributaries, the Winterbourne and Yatesbury streams. In the east, drainage is south-eastwards towards the River Og, which itself flows into the Kennet at Marlborough, and here the dry valleys are sometimes engraved so deeply that they cut through the Upper Chalk and expose the underlying Middle and Lower Chalk. South of the Kennet, the land rises from the valley floor till it reaches Upper Chalk along the escarpment with Tan Hill and Martinsell prominent high points above the Vale of Pewsey. To the west of the Beckhampton valley, local remnants of Upper Chalk survive on Oldbury and Morgan Hills.

Around the foot of the Chalk escarpment, where the permeable chalk meets impermeable marl, and the underlying Upper Greensand meets the Gault Clay, springs, or as they were formerly called, wells, brought water to the surface. There are countless examples within the study area. Many of these are located close to important historic centres and others are associated with earlier settlement. A number are well-known features in their own right. Stukeley (1776, 142) described that at Calstone as *'a most famous spring, or cateract of water, coming out of the chalk-hill, and much talked of*', whilst the Holywell at Stanton St Bernard is mentioned in a charter of AD957 (Smith 1884, 185). Alton, is interpreted by Smith (1884, 186) as the village by the springs (it too has an Anglo-Saxon charter of AD828 referring to the westernmost spring which is called Brodewylle). Sometimes such springs have sapped the escarpment and formed gullies as at Bincknoll, Highway, and Blackwell, Comberwell and Trogwell (Trog = Anglo-Saxon cistern) at Compton Bassett. In places, as at Cherhill and Calstone these form deep gorges in the edge of the chalk. Many of today's villages and farms are placed around these wells and the streams that emanate from them. None of these areas, apart from perhaps All Cannings Cross Farm, have been investigated archaeologically, although St Anne's Well has produced Neolithic and Roman chance finds, while a Roman pavement was discovered at Cherhill.

It is often assumed that the density of archaeological monuments on the 'High Downs' reflects the intensity of past use in comparison to other lower-lying areas. This is misguided. That monuments survive here in profusion is purely a result of less intense agricultural activity on this high and often marginal ground. Of course, the expression as different as 'chalk and cheese' is well known and originates in chalkland areas where there was contrast between pastoral and arable agriculture – between dairy herds best raised on the wetter claylands and well-drained chalk supporting arable cultivation. In fact, it was not that straightforward. The lightest, well-drained soils, those suited to early agriculture, are found on the Upper Greensand, part of the Cretaceous formation, which form a narrow bench at the base of the Lower Chalk into the Vale of Pewsey and around the western edge of the Marlborough Downs plateau. These too have the advantage not only of shelter provided by the Chalk escarpment, but also of two springlines; that of the Lower Chalk marls, and that of the Upper Greensand and Gault clay junction.

On the permeable downland the availability of water was of vital importance for stock and one response to the lack of it was to construct dewponds – excavated cavities were lined with puddled clay and straw to collect rainwater. Most are roughly circular, for example, that close to Wansdyke on Easton Down, or another near Delling Copse on Overton Down, but others are more irregular in outline, or formed with a bank on the downhill side. However, a number are square, and these, constructed to a standard shape, can be seen amongst the Romano-British earthworks on Overton Down and on Bishops Cannings Down overlooking Shepherds Shore. That near Adam's Grave (with sarsens in) is c20m^2 and 2m deep. Smith (1884, 21) noted how such ponds were placed in elevated positions, on Tan Hill, Milk Hill, Barbury Hill, Hackpen, and Cherhill Down, though many can be observed in other locations.

On the lower ground where floodplains were broad enough, floated water meadows were constructed in order to promote an earlier growth of grass for stock. The process is particularly apparent in the Kennett valley either side of Marlborough and alongside the Og to the south of Ogbourne St Andrew. Water meadows were first irrigated here in the early 17th century when the larger landowners and agricultural innovators recognised and capitalised on the benefits that resulted from the method. The floating of the meadows was immensely important to the agricultural economy in this part of the country. Thomas Davis, writing for the newly formed Board of Agriculture, remarked that the value of water meadows here was 'almost incalculable' (Bettey 1999, 185). Unfortunately, what effect this dramatic 'engineering' of the riverine landscape had on the underlying archaeology remains unknown.

Avebury lies at the heart of the North Wiltshire Downs, and its immediate area which includes the monuments of Silbury Hill, West Kennet long barrow, the Sanctuary and Windmill Hill, is designated a World Heritage Site, but beyond that, the Downs themselves are considered an Area of Outstanding Natural Beauty. This study mirrors that of the Rev A C Smith by taking as its area of enquiry both Upper and Lower benches of the Chalk plateau as far as their respective escarpments in the north, south and west. In the east the River Og and Savernake Forest form a rather arbitrary boundary. Just within these limits in the east lies the town of Marlborough, others include Swindon to the north, in the west Calne, and in the south Devizes. All of these centres have, however, been of considerable influence on the activity on the downland at times in the past.

Throughout the area and particularly along the Kennet and its tributaries, small villages and farms nestle in the lee of the hills, their location given away by the clusters of beech trees that surround them, all but obscuring the church towers. On the higher knolls and escarpment edges, rings of beech, planted to provide cover for game, provide landmarks and almost park-like scenic variety for the traveller, while Scots Pine, said to have been planted to guide drovers from water hole to water hole, clusters in places.

Today large swathes of the area are given over to horse racing, the chalk downland has always been a favoured environment for equine pursuits (perhaps from late prehistory, at least, based on evidence from sites such as Potterne (Lawson

2000) and Gussage in Dorset (Wainwright 1979, 157). The military presence on Salisbury Plain was originally a response to the need to provide space for cavalry manoeuvres where there was no danger to horses from rocks or inappropriate terrain (McOmish *et al* 2002). Close to Avebury, stables and practice gallops exist at Beckhampton, Clatford, Wick Down farm, Temple Farm and in the lee of Barbury Castle hillfort. Galtimore Farm at Beckhampton, for example, obtained its curious name from a successful racehorse (Freeman 1983, 100).

Settlement on the warm soils around the fringe of the chalk also allowed easy access to a variety of environments and encouraged the finger-like strip parishes that predominate in the area. Cultivation certainly took place on the chalk, but it was mainly confined to the lower ground around these villages. Stukeley's illustration of a 'Prospect of Heddington' drawn on 18 July 1723, shows the village nestling at the foot of the scarp at the junction of greensand and clays with the chalk, the claylands with their hedged enclosures contrasting with open cultivated fields on the lower chalk slopes (Stukeley 1776). Like the Lower Greensand, the Lower Chalk was easier to cultivate than the Upper Chalk where the multitude of flints present would damage ploughshares. The Clay-with-flints, perched on some of the higher summits, sticky, heavy, difficult to till, however, was left, and even during the Napoleonic Wars was not felt worthwhile cultivating.

The climate is also very different, the Downs are much windier, scoured by south-westerlies from the Bristol Channel and as a result, most farms and settlements are surrounded by some form of windbreak, these days most often conifer. The Downs are, similarly, more prone to frost and snow. It is not unknown for the weather station at Manor Farm in Yatesbury to record frost in June. In contrast to the sheltered positions at the foot of the escarpments, such places are altogether more inhospitable and this is one reason why, until recently, agriculture barely reached the upper chalk plateau.

In the 1930's, however, Piggott saw the lowland areas including the Pewsey Vale, flanking the chalk downs as an impenetrable swampy morass, and used this to explain the apparent cultural differences in the Neolithic remains of Salisbury Plain and the Marlborough Downs. In doing so, he was merely repeating the prevailing view of the times. Smith, for example, had used similar language in 1884 (Smith 1884, 22). But even swamps were useful and cattle, in particular, love the rich grasses: it is interesting that a skull of *Bos Longifrons* was found in Marsh Lane at Cherhill in 1835 (*ibid* 49–50). However, in the centre of this supposedly impenetrable area lies one of the largest and most important Neolithic monuments in the country, the great henge at Marden (Colt-Hoare 1821, 4–6; Wainwright 1971). Within this enclosure lie two large barrows and in close proximity there are two further, recently discovered enclosures, both potential henges (NMR No SU 05 NE 26 and SU 05 NE 39), while clusters of ring ditches can be observed on aerial photographs nearby at Charlton. Concentrations of flint axes in the Vale hint at widespread activity, while more recent work has highlighted the remarkable degree to which Later Prehistoric and Roman activity is present (*pers comm* P Robinson Devizes Museum).

Similarly, recent fieldwalking of some areas of the Bristol Avon valley in the west have produced large quantities of prehistoric flint work (*pers comm* Mike Stone Chippenham Museum), while the area around Swindon is by no means devoid of such activity. Apart from being situated in an area of intriguingly complex geology, Swindon lies at the headwaters of two great river systems, the Thames and the Bristol Avon. Small wonder that aside from its impressive Roman sites the area boasts two stone circles.

In the 1920s that great pioneer of field archaeology O G S Crawford lamented that, whereas the archaeological earthworks on Salisbury Plain were being destroyed by the military, those on the Marlborough Downs were so well preserved that they should be given the status of a National Park. He evidently spoke too soon. Intermittent pleas in local newspapers brought public attention to the effect that local agriculture was having on round barrows, but the words were not heeded, and many monuments were razed to the ground. The negative impact of arable agriculture was being noted long before this, however. In 1849, Merewether returned to Avebury after a gap of 30 years (Merewether 1851, 82). During his reconnaissance across Hackpen Hill to select barrows for excavation he commented that it was difficult to recognise those sites that he had previously dug into simply because of the encroachment of cultivation. One wonders how many disappeared without report? Subsequently, Smith repeatedly bemoaned the '*…greatly more extended cultivation of the downs round Abury….*' and '*…so rapidly do all vestiges of a barrow disappear under repeated ploughings; and so many barrows have I seen thus diminishing year by year on the downs round Abury, until they have become gradually effaced…*' and again '*Unfortunately the downs which surround Abury have been much broken up of late years, and brought into cultivation: and within my own recollection of some half a century, large tracts of these downs have been thus disturbed by the ploughshare…*' (Smith 1884, 1 and 2).

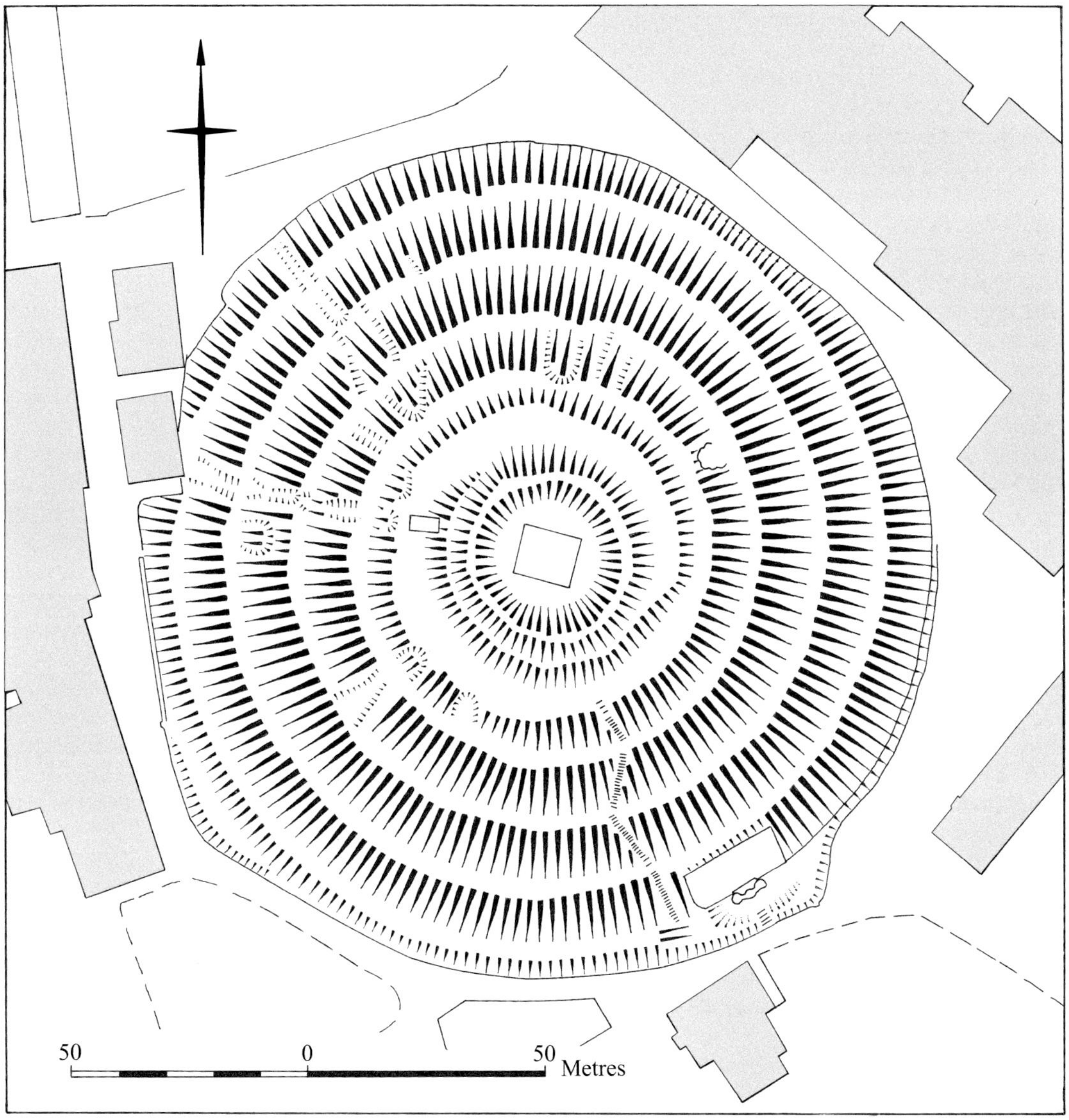

Fig 1:3 Plan of the Marlborough Mound: thought to have been constructed soon after 1066 as a motte with a bailey attached. Excavations into the mound have produced evidence of medieval date from the old ground surface. Being a royal holding during the medieval period there is no lack of documentation and the mound appears to have supported first a wooden and then a stone keep during the medieval period. The mound itself appears to have been landscaped and used as a garden mount at an early stage and the spiral walkway which takes four rising circuits to reach the summit, has been present since at least 1654. A grotto of flint was constructed at the base of the mound before 1726 and the remains of an arched brick feature survive in the east just below the summit. © Crown Copyright NMR.

Crossroads

Avebury lies at a crossroads, literally as well as metaphorically. Leaving aside, for the moment, the contradiction of pagan worship and Christian appropriation, two major routes slice through the henge. That connecting London and Bristol, sweeps east to west, while the south to north routes provide access from south Wiltshire to the northern vales. Both have ebbed, flowed and migrated according to economic fortune, and while former courses can still be traced in the local green lanes away from the henge and village, the later courses became fossilised by turnpiking and were widened by highway authorities. The volume of traffic is heavy now and having arrived at Avebury by these routes, the same roads become a problem to visitors once they are here.

Avebury's spiritual lure seems to have attracted traffic, for the coach road from Marlborough avoided the villages of Manton, Overton, and Fifield. It could easily have avoided Avebury too, but instead took a route across the high ground, where the numerous traffic ruts can still be observed, before being carefully channelled into the east entrance of the great henge. Formerly the Bath to Bristol route passed south of Oldbury Hill generally following the line of the Roman road. Stukeley clearly depicts the Roman road, but illustrated the London road as approaching the east entrance at Avebury and exiting from the south before following the course of the present A4 London to Bristol road as far as Beckhampton. Exactly when the course was diverted through Calne is uncertain, but the approximate course of the present A4 was turnpiked in 1708.

Given the nature of the monumental enclosure one might have expected medieval settlement to be arranged around its perimeter. It might even have adopted the central space as a village green. Instead, the medieval village became firmly established along the east-west route, with dwellings arranged on either side of the road. This route, in places called the *herepath*, is much the earliest of the two that bisect the henge (Pollard & Reynolds 2002, 224–6). Fossilized as a green lane, after making for Yatesbury, it turns northwards rather than continuing to the west, and appears to provide a circuitous route around the Lower Chalk plateau. The reasons for the present road being diverted south at Avebury rather than proceeding straight through, as it previously must have done, are unclear. It is likely that it formerly crossed to Yatesbury and entered Cherhill via Jugglers Lane.

Within this wider area there was a tendency to use the higher ground. The ridgeways, routes like the Pilgrim's Way or the Icknield Way have been, and sometimes still are, considered to be ancient purely on the frequency of ancient monuments, that occur along the false crest of the escarpments. There is, however, absolutely no evidence of the use of such ridges as trackways during prehistory. Much has been taken out of context and elaborated. Smith (1884, 120–1) for example, simply referred to the practice of keeping to the interfluves for more than local journeys, as the alternative, of constantly ascending and descending coombes, although more direct, was more difficult (See also McOmish *et al* 2002; Cossons 1959). Local routes between villages may have followed more direct routes through fields some of which may be fossilised by modern rights of way. For the important routes to market, however, with stock or other goods in tow it may have been easier to use the interfluves. These were not formally defined roads but wide ridgetops along which cattle or flocks could pass unhindered. Thus there are many tracks on the Higher Downs, and at times almost every other interfluve seems to have its 'ridgeway'. Smith referred to a British or Welsh Road (1884, 186) across the downs, a continuation of a route along the edge of the Higher Chalk plateau of Hackpen Ridge, which led south over Wansdyke, and descended the escarpment at Walkers Hill into the Vale of Pewsey. Thus hollow ways ascend the steep escarpment edge at several places as village routes, for example, to Marlborough. And a number of well-scored lanes and paths are referred to as The Vizes or the route to Devizes.

The Dark Side of the Downs

The Downs appear to have been the place for gibbets. Maybe it was the association of wild windswept areas containing pagan barrows and mysterious earthworks that led to this. Stukeley (1779, 142) describes one at the point where the Roman road meets Wansdyke. Another is shown on early maps along Jugglers Lane, between Yatesbury and Cherhill. There, Jugglers Lane was formally the haunt of highwaymen, in particular the Cherhill gang, renowned for highway robbery while they were naked. One 'Judgler's Grave' is marked on a map of 1763 (Bowood House archives).

Conflict

The Anglo-Saxon Chronicle mentions an encounter at East Kennet in AD 1006 (Garmondsway 1975), when the Danes put the Saxons to flight and carried off their booty. The most famous set-piece, however, was probably the battle between the Parliamentarians and Royalists on Roundway Down during the Civil War, but while this appears to have left a mark on the memory, it has left no mark on the ground. The siege of Marlborough resulted in the cutting of trenches on the Common and the defacement of Sir Francis Seymour's house on the site of Marlborough Castle. The motte on which the keep once stood had was converted to garden use (Fig 1:3) though has sometimes been thought to have a prehistoric origin. The Marlborough Mound rises steeply from 83m in diameter at the base to 31m across the top, although post-medieval and recent activities have slightly affected its symmetry. No serious rounding or weathering of the overall profile is observable and if it were not for the spiral walk the sides would be tapered. In terms of shape there is certainly some similarity with Silbury Hill – the spiral even echoes the terrace close to the summit of Silbury – although in size there are considerable differences. The mound at Marlborough is very much smaller, at 19.3 m in height, just half that of Silbury Hill, and excavations around the base have recovered Medieval pottery from the old ground surface (Field *et al* 2001). The mound, however, developed a mythology of its own and despite the weight of evidence to the contrary is still often thought of as a 'mate' to Silbury Hill.

Little is known about Bynknoll Castle on the northwestern scarp, rarely visited, and uninvestigated, it appears to have more in common with the Iron Age promontory forts than Medieval castles.

In more recent times, the Royal Flying Corps chose Yatesbury as a location for an aerodrome. The suitability of this venue was swiftly reconsidered, as the strong winds hindered take off and landing and many aircraft ended up with their nose in the ground. A single scheduled World War I aircraft hangar survives though is crumbling. The remainder of the airfield buildings date to World War II. At this time the camp expanded as a radar training school and Yatesbury Field was covered in wooden huts and occupied by thousands of trainees. During the war too, the Cherhill White Horse, a perfect signpost to enemy aircraft, was camouflaged. In addition, a decoy airfield was established on Bishop's Cannings Down complete with electric lights fed by a huge generator (*pers comm* Mr Frereson, Bishop's Cannings Farm), and designed to distract attention from the RAF radar station. Most of the paraphernalia, including electrical cables, was bulldozed away but an air-raid shelter/mound still remains. Further north, wartime paraphernalia can be detected at Barbury and Liddington, while an airfield was laid out at Wroughton. No substantial earthworks relating to this period appear to survive, although pillboxes can be observed along Juggler's Lane, and another is set into a round barrow on Knoll Down.

The Cold War also left its mark, with the presence on the slopes of Waden Hill of an Underground Monitoring Post, a concrete chamber designed to withstand blast and heat. This allowed a staff of two people to confirm the position of a nuclear explosion and to monitor the fallout for a period of up to 14 days (Wayne Cocroft *pers comm*).

2

Fieldwork in the Avebury area

David McOmish, Hazel Riley, David Field and Carenza Lewis

Analytical surveys of the earthworks of sites that survive within the Avebury World Heritage Site reveal significant chronological depth to the archaeological landscape as well as a spatial extent unexpected and hitherto unrecognised. Summary accounts of a number of surface investigations are presented here.

Introduction

When compared with the surrounding vales, earthwork survival on the North Wiltshire Downs, particularly on the higher slopes and plateaux, remains good. Three causewayed enclosures, 28 long barrows, at least 750 round barrows, many hectares of ancient fields, five hillforts, and of course the massive henge and stone circles at Avebury, mark the area out as one of the most important multi-period prehistoric landscapes in Europe. Alongside this there are the remnants of a wide range of later settlements, ranging in date from the Roman through to post-medieval periods, with their attendant landscape features including roads, tracks and fields. This landscape is, of course, complemented by other non-secular components such as temples, churches and other places of worship. The concentration of archaeological interest has resulted in a good inventory (apparent in the numbers of sites recorded within the National Monuments Record) and many are depicted at small scale on the aerial photograph plots (Crutchley this vol). This chapter deals exclusively with the extant earthworks within the World Heritage Site that were surveyed by the Royal Commission on the Historical Monuments of England (RCHME: from 1999 part of English Heritage) during the final decade of the 20th century and in summary with one integral site investigated since then.

Analysis of surface features in the area has a long pedigree, commencing of course with the plan of Avebury itself made by John Aubrey in September 1668 (Welfare 1989). William Stukeley too, conducted extensive fieldwork investigations and analysis and both men moved beyond the confines of Avebury village to investigate the features generally scattered across the wider downs (Fowles ed 1980; Stukeley 1743; 1776). Amongst the earliest of such explorers, the Very Rev John Merewether surveyed a number of small earthwork enclosures on the Downs in 1849 (Merewether 1851a), some presumably of Bronze Age or Romano-British date, but others that are now thought to be later sheepfolds (Smith, N this volume), while A C Smith's reconnaissance some years later added sites and information to the Inventory at small scale (Smith, A C 1884; 1885). Surveyors of the 1st edition 25inch Ordnance Survey put many of these sites on the map for the first time. Despite encouragement by the Society of Antiquaries to record earthworks before they disappeared, the first half of the 20th century saw archaeological work concentrate on excavations, as at first Gray (1935) and then Keiller (Smith 1965a) concluded large-scale work on the Avebury henge, Keiller on Windmill Hill (*ibid*), Cunnington (1931) at the Sanctuary, and Keiller and Piggott (1936) on the Avenue. After Atkinson's work at Silbury (Atkinson 1967; 1968; 1969; 1970; Whittle 1997a), the latter part of the century saw a renewal of non-invasive investigation coupled with smaller scale, often rescue, excavation. The Archaeological Division of the Ordnance Survey (subsequently merged with the RCHME) surveyed a number of sites, including Wansdyke, as well as individual and groups of barrows at 1:2500 scale, while the RCHME continued the work of investigation at Knap Hill, Rybury, Shaw and West Overton. Excavations at Rybury by Desmond Bonney revealed a flat bottom ditch with large numbers of flint flakes present in the silt, all sealed by an overlying hillfort bank and which seemed to confirm the Neolithic nature of some of the earthworks there (Bonney 1964). The extensive earthworks on Overton and Fyfield Downs were investigated by Peter Fowler and recently

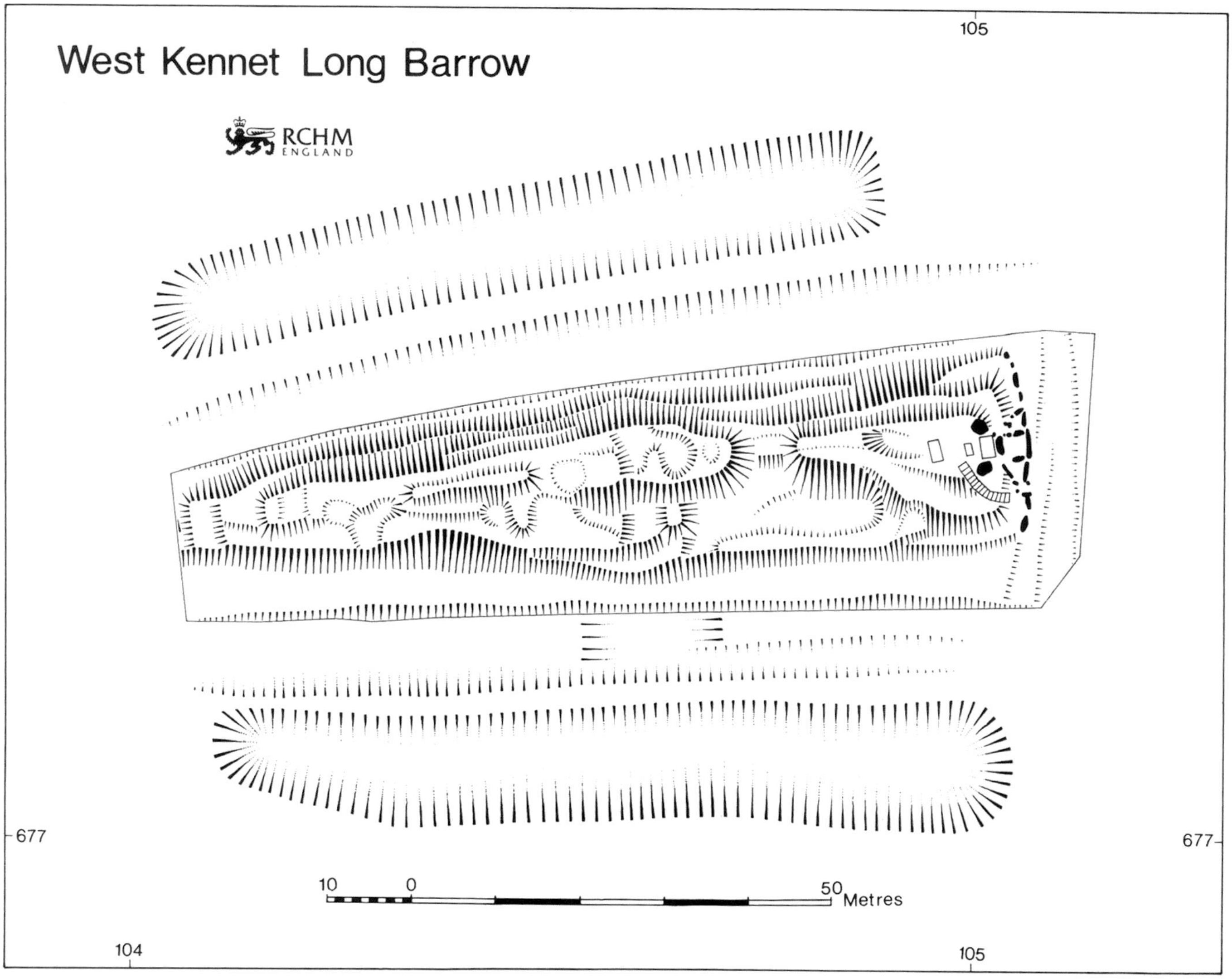

Fig 2:1 Plan of West Kennet long barrow. © Crown Copyright NMR.

admirably published (Fowler 2000). They include a superb 'Celtic' field sequence, presumably chronological, that demonstrates initial stone clearance to boundaries, initial lynchetting, massive lynchetting close to the valley floors, and finally use of the fields for ridge and furrow, while a number of settlements exist of Iron Age and/or Romano-British date. These are all mapped at small scale in Fig 3:9 (Crutchley this volume). During the final decade of the 20th century further ground surveys in the area were carried out including a series of sites within the World Heritage Site itself. Some of these have, in part, been published previously in one form or another (e.g. Oswald *et al* 2001; Whittle *et al* 1999) but are presented here for the first time as a portfolio.

Long Barrows

West Kennet

Even though hardly typical of long barrows in the vicinity (see e.g. Barker 1985; Pollard & Reynolds 2002) the best known and, indeed, most visited long barrow on the Marlborough Downs is that at West Kennet. It is situated at the eastern end of a low interfluve separating two coombes that originate on the higher ground around Wansdyke to the south. Its impressive sarsen and Corallian limestone entrance façade is best viewed from the east rather than from the northern proscriptive route of modern times. Following earlier excavations by Thurnam (1860a), the entrance and associated sarsen chambers were excavated by the Ministry of Works and the chambers conserved and left open to visitors. A full account of the work is presented in the excavation report (Piggott 1962). In contrast with the grand eastern end of the long barrow – the chambered tomb, the mound is considered less often. Aubrey's sketch of three long barrows figured by Piggott (1962, Pl I) left room for doubt concerning the correct identification, though the presence of a façade in the illustration suggests that it is likely to be correct.

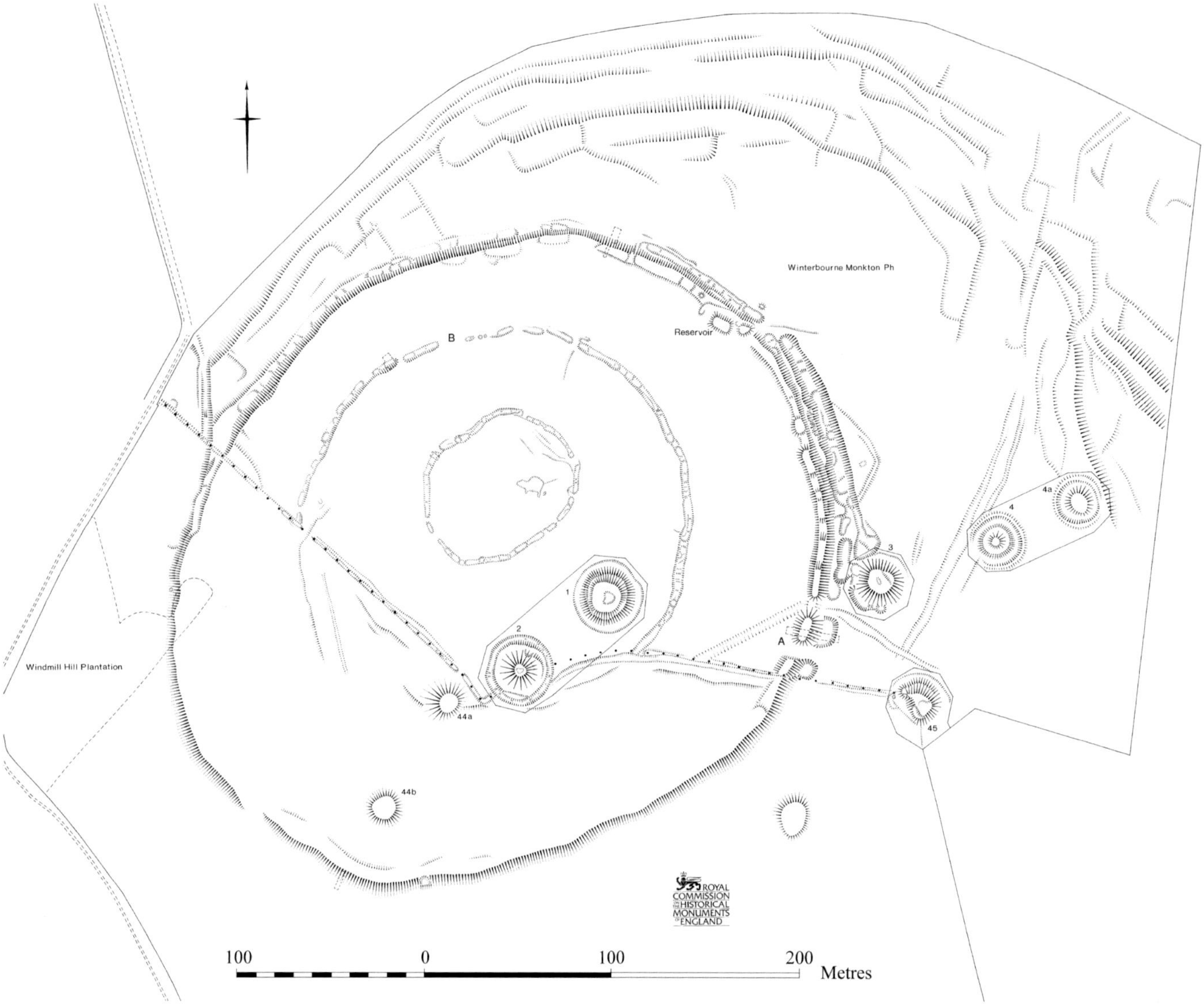

Fig 2:2 Plan of Windmill Hill causewayed enclosure. © Crown Copyright NMR

Of the three illustrated, Millbarrow is named, a second with stones at one end and a peristalith around the mound was described as being 'about a mile westward from Marlborough, towards Hakpin…'. This might be that recently identified by Roger Featherstone from the air overlooking the valley of stones at Lockeridge (NMR 15371/23). The third barrow was said to be 'on the Brow of the hill, south from Kynnet…'. A façade of sarsen is depicted at one end and a peristalith is drawn around the barrow, which is described as being over 'halfe a yard' high. In contrast, Stukeley's sketch (Piggott 1962, Pl II) of the long barrow, which he called the 'Archdruid's barrow', shows a more prominent, almost dramatic, earthen mound extending from the stone chambers.

The survey highlights the irregular nature of the parts of mound (omission of shallow hachures from the mound on the plan serves to emphasise this), some of which appear to be the result of quarrying. These undulations were noted by Piggott and others. In one place a section has been cleared through the mound almost to the ground surface. Merewether (1851a, 97) recorded that the mound had been cut into, while Long (1858, 343) claimed that a farmer had cut a gap as a 'waggon drive' an observation repeated by Thurnham (1860a, 409). Thurnham also noted that individuals had been extracting chalk and flint from the sides.

The survey illustrates one of the most intriguing aspects of the mound construction, namely, the broadening in width of the mound *c* 55m from its west end (Fig 2:1). This appears to be more than an effect created by quarrying, for at this point the orientation of the mound changes slightly. The now almost levelled side ditches also vary in profile and reference to the electrical resistivity survey plan carried out at the time of Piggott's excavation (1962, 10) confirms that a change in direction also occurs in the ditch at this point. At 101m in length, West Kennet is the longest long barrow on the Marlborough Downs. This is intriguing as barrows of this length are rare – a length of around 50m is normal for the larger barrows on Salisbury Plain. In view of this, and taking the change in orientation into account, it seems possible that the West Kennet monument is in fact two contiguous mounds constructed end on to each other.

The ditches, less than 0.10m deep and barely detectable are all but obscured by redistributed ploughsoil and by negative lynchets that cut into the side of the mound. They were present in the 18th century as one of the ditches is visible in one of Stukeley's illustrations (Piggott 1962, Pl II) and were still measurable as earthworks in 1956 (*ibid* fig 2), when contours appear to indicate a depth of some 0.2 or 0.3m. Neither the 1956, nor recent geophysical surveys (David this volume), both of which recorded the ditches, place them in an identical position to that of the present earthwork plan and this can only be reconciled as a result of the movement of ploughsoil on the surface.

Causewayed Enclosures

Generally dated to the second half of the 4th millennium BC, these are the earliest known, deliberately built enclosures in the British landscape, conceivably borne out of the experience of earthmoving in order to create the ditches and mounds of earlier burial monuments. Enclosing space within a formal boundary appears to have been a new concept, though could have been carried out for centuries using vegetation i.e. woodland clearings or hedging and represented a radical departure in a landscape without formal constructed earthen boundaries or barriers. The distinctive morphological signature of these enclosures – ovoid or circular lengths of bank and ditch punctuated by frequent gaps or causeways – suggests that they were not built solely for defensive purposes but that they may have played a symbolic role. Three extant causewayed enclosures are known on the North Wiltshire Downs and a fourth, not visible on the surface, has recently been discovered at Beckhampton by aerial photography (Crutchley this vol), the nature of its ditches confirmed by excavation (Gillings *et al* 2000a). Two of the extant examples are dramatically sited on the chalk escarpment overlooking the Vale of Pewsey and are mentioned elsewhere in this volume (Figs 1:1 and 1:2). The third is on Windmill Hill to the north-west of Avebury and is the only extant example within the World Heritage Site.

Windmill Hill

The survey of the causewayed enclosure at Windmill Hill (NMR No. SU 07 SE 22) recorded three partially concentric circuits of causewayed enclosures; ten round barrows, including a previously undiscovered example; traces of field system, hollow ways and a post-medieval boundary bank (Fig 2:2). Two long barrows are situated close by, one Millbarrow, *c* 1km to the north-east, the other Windmill Hill/Horslip long barrow, *c* 600m further south.

The site lies on the northern edge of a locally prominent undulating chalk ridge whose domed surface rises to a height of 187m above OD and commands extensive views in all directions, particularly to the north which include the lower lying areas of Lower Chalk and clay which form the southern periphery of the Upper Thames Valley in north Wiltshire. The site is roughly bisected by the Avebury – Winterbourne Monkton parish boundary which has had a significant impact on monument survival and destruction. The land included within the Avebury parish has seen more recent and extensive plough damage and, therefore, the earthworks are less well preserved here. The Avebury henge complex is highly visible *c* 2km to the south-west and is separated from Windmill Hill by the Winterbourne valley. To the south, Silbury Hill is a conspicuous landmark, and the horizon is fringed by the steep face of the Upper Chalk escarpment.

The enclosures do not occupy the highest point on the hilltop, with the centre of the inner enclosure lying some distance to the north of the summit. Indeed, they appear to be false-crest sighted on a slope facing north-eastwards. According to Isobel Smith the 'windmill' place name derives from the positioning of such a structure on one of the barrows on the hilltop, possibly Winterbourne Monkton 1 (Smith 1965a, xxvii).

The outer enclosure, 8.45ha in area, measures a maximum 360m in diameter on its longest, north-east – south-west, axis. On close inspection the outer enclosure is polygonal in shape, appears to have been constructed in a series of short straight sections and is now most clearly defined at the north-east, where there has been recent reconstruction. Here, the substantial bank, which is accompanied by an external ditch, appears to be a continuous feature with an undulating profile. It is unclear whether or not the peaks and troughs are original features, however, this seems unlikely in view of the renovation and reconstruction. Although frequent interruptions occur along its course, there are no convincing entrance gaps through the bank.

Slight traces of the bank survive on the south-eastern side of the hill, in an area that has been severely damaged by ploughing but elsewhere the enclosure is marked by a continuous, outward facing lynchet or terrace.

An external ditch survives intermittently around much of the northern part of the enclosure and along its base there are numerous interruptions defining deeper pockets. In places, especially on the north-west, the causewayed ditch is accompanied by an external lynchet and this is either the remains of an outer, though now much damaged, bank, or more likely, given the presence of field system in this area, the remains of a slight negative lynchet.

The middle enclosure is almost circular in plan and encloses an area of 3.32ha. It is of a much slighter construction than the outer enclosure and survives to its greatest height north of the parish boundary, particularly on the east, where it has been excavated and subsequently restored by Keiller. This is visible now as a shallow trench punctuated with deeper ditch or pit segments along its course. Beyond the areas excavated, principally on the north and north-west, the original course of the enclosure survives as a series of irregular elongated pit or ditch segments flanked internally by a slight lynchet, which may be the last traces of a now destroyed internal bank. The southern part of the enclosure survives intermittently and as a slight outward facing lynchet. One possible north-facing entrance into the enclosure was recorded during the survey.

The inner enclosure is sub-circular in outline with a slight indentation on the north-western side and encloses an area of 0.52ha. It is the slightest of the three enclosures and is the one which has been most extensively excavated; only the short section of ditch forming the western side of the enclosure appears undisturbed. Overall the ditch consists of a discontinuous hollow, within which there are numerous deeper segments which tend to be narrower. Occasional causeways are evident, but it is not clear whether those visible in the eastern half of the enclosure are original features or the result of the excavations.

A total of ten round barrows were recorded during the survey. All but one of these, that at NGR SU 08817129, have been previously recorded. The barrow grouping includes bowl, bell, saucer and possible disc variants arranged in a dispersed linear fashion. The largest examples, Winterbourne Monkton 1 and 2, occupy the highest point of the hill and are very conspicuous landscape features. The others, placed on false-crests on the gentle east-facing slope overlooking the Winterbourne valley, are also prominent features when viewed from below. Three of the barrows, Winterbourne Monkton 2 and 3, Avebury 44a, clearly impinge upon the middle and outer circuits of the enclosure.

Slight remains of a field system are present on much of the steep, north-facing slope to the north of the outer Neolithic enclosure within Winterbourne Monkton parish. Here, numerous north-facing lynchets, now spread, generally follow the contour of the hill. Transverse field boundaries at right angles to these are visible as a series of very slight scarps defining small rectangular fields. The overall morphology of this field system suggests that it is of prehistoric or Romano-British origin. It is likely that similar fields also extended across the south-facing slopes of the hill in Avebury parish, but have been destroyed by more recent ploughing. Ridge-and-furrow cultivation of medieval or post-medieval date is visible on aerial photographs, though not surveyed over much of the southern part of the hilltop, this has been truncated by a series of parallel modern drainage features (again not surveyed).

A hollowed trackway approaches the site from the north-west and impinges upon the outer circuit of the enclosure. This hollow-way is in turn bisected by the boundary bank which separates the parishes of Winterbourne Monkton and Avebury. Another slightly hollowed track approaches the site from the east and enters the enclosure through the gap in the outer circuit to the south of round barrow Winterbourne Monkton 3.

The most striking feature of the multiple enclosure complex at Windmill Hill relates to its topographical positioning. All three enclosures have been carefully placed on the hilltop in a location which does not take advantage of the natural topography. The middle and outer circuits in particular, enclose an area well to the north of and below the summit of the hill and the courses of the enclosure boundaries in this area spill dramatically over the well-defined northern edge of the chalk ridge. Indeed, it is clear that these enclosures are false-crest sighted perhaps to provide, or afford, a prospect to or from the lower lying areas to the north and north-west.

Each circuit of enclosure has a slightly different morphology, although this may, of course, relate to the effects of subsequent land-use, damage and the effects of excavation. It is clear though, that moving from the interior outwards, the enclosure boundaries become more substantial, with the outer circuit being the most monumental. There are no banks or ramparts associated with the inner and middle circuits, for instance, and it is unclear whether or not banks originally accompanied all of the ditch segments. Smith has suggested that the asymmetrical silting of the inner and middle ditches does point to the existence of internal banks (1965a, 5).

Although the monument on first impression appears to have been causewayed, survey suggests that the outer enclosure bank may in fact have been continuous. It is unfortunate that the best preserved sections of the bank are those that have been reconstructed by Keiller, so a definitive statement as to their original condition is difficult.

The enclosure complex has at a later stage formed the focus for an extensive grouping of round barrows. As has been stated, at least three of the barrows impinge upon the enclosure circuits, and this general association between Neolithic enclosures and round barrow cemeteries is a commonly repeated one (e.g. Oswald *et al* 2001).

The effect of the later episodes of ploughing on the hilltop undoubtedly contributes to the slight nature of the earlier remains. It is difficult to date the origin of this field system, with any precision, however, Isobel Smith (1965a 12) noted a ploughsoil of Romano-British date in a number of the ditch sections, although she was unaware of the presence of the lynchets of this field system. That this episode of ploughing was long-lived is suggested by the substantial size of the associated field boundaries. They appear to have been over-ploughed, probably in recent times, since much of the survey area retained slight traces of ridge-and-furrow.

In addition, the scatter of Neolithic cultural material collected from the surface of the slopes of Windmill Hill is one of the greatest in the British Isles. Although much of this is contemporary with the enclosures here, there are quantities of earlier as well as later lithics (Whittle *et al* 1999, 347). The implication of this is that the hilltop was of importance to local communities over a considerable period of time. Smaller, though no less significant numbers of finds recovered close to Knap Hill point to extra-mural activity here also. The steep slopes have discouraged cultivation at Rybury, and it is unknown whether similar extra-mural activity is present.

Assuming that arrowhead types imply some chronological separation the arrowheads from the slopes of Windmill Hill (Devizes and A Keiller Museums) hint of at least two and possibly more phases of activity. In fact it is interesting to note how sites elsewhere that foster large numbers of leaf-shaped arrowheads also contain equally large numbers of other arrowhead types. Large numbers of arrowheads have been found at other causewayed enclosures e.g. Carn Brea (Mercer 1981), Crickley Hill (Dixon 1988) and Hambledon Hill (Mercer 1988). In the two former cases they are thought to provide evidence of the enclosures being attacked. It is noticeable that large numbers of arrowheads of very different types and dates occur in precisely the same place elsewhere; leaf, petit-tranchet derivative, and barbed-and-tanged arrowheads all occur at, for example, Limpsfield, and Abinger, in Surrey (e.g. Field & Cotton 1987, 78), Bournemouth, in Dorset (Calkin 1952). One might have regarded such areas as traditional hunting grounds were it not for the presence of the enclosures and other explanations of, for example, traditional places of symbolic conflict might be suggested.

The Avebury Complex

In addition to the well-known henge, earthworks cover a wide area in and around the village of Avebury and extend both sides of the Kennet (Fig 2:3). Many appear to be medieval or later in date, but features of earlier periods may be incorporated.

Avebury henge

The massive Avebury henge with its internal stone settings remains the focus of the World Heritage Site. It is sheltered locally by the higher ground on all sides but the north, by Waden Hill to the south, Folly Hill, Beckhampton, and at a little further distance Windmill Hill to the north-east and Avebury Down in the east. While these hills provide an impression of a dished landscape, the henge itself lies astride a low north to south aligned, Middle Chalk, interfluve, immediately above the valley gravel of the Kennet to the west and a dry valley that may once have supported a winterbourne that runs parallel to it in the east.

The site has a long history of archaeological investigation that commenced in 1648 when it was 'discovered' by John Aubrey and surveyed by him in 1663 (Long 1858; 1862 for facsimiles of his plans). Subsequently William Stukeley (1743) spent a number of years between 1719 and 1724 studying the site and produced a series of extremely valuable and lively illustrations. In turn Philip Crocker produced a plan for Richard Colt Hoare's second volume on *Ancient Wiltshire* (1821; the plan republished with amendments by Long 1858), and Lukis prepared one for A C Smith in 1882 (Smith 1884).

Excavations at Avebury (Fig 2:4) are summarised in Smith's account (1965a, 183; see also Ucko *et al* 1991; Malone 1989; Burl 1979; Pollard and Reynolds 2002). Excluding reports of the earth at the Cove being investigated to a yard deep (Hunter 1829) and the hole dug by Browne (Smith 1965a) in the same place in search of an alter stone, the earliest diggings appear to be those of A C Smith and W Cunnington, operating on behalf of the Wiltshire Archaeological Society (Smith 1867, 209) who *'dug holes in many places, running trenches across certain spots, and tunnelling the large external mound* (bank), *and tapping it at several points...'*. Even where there is some description, no measurements are provided and in most cases

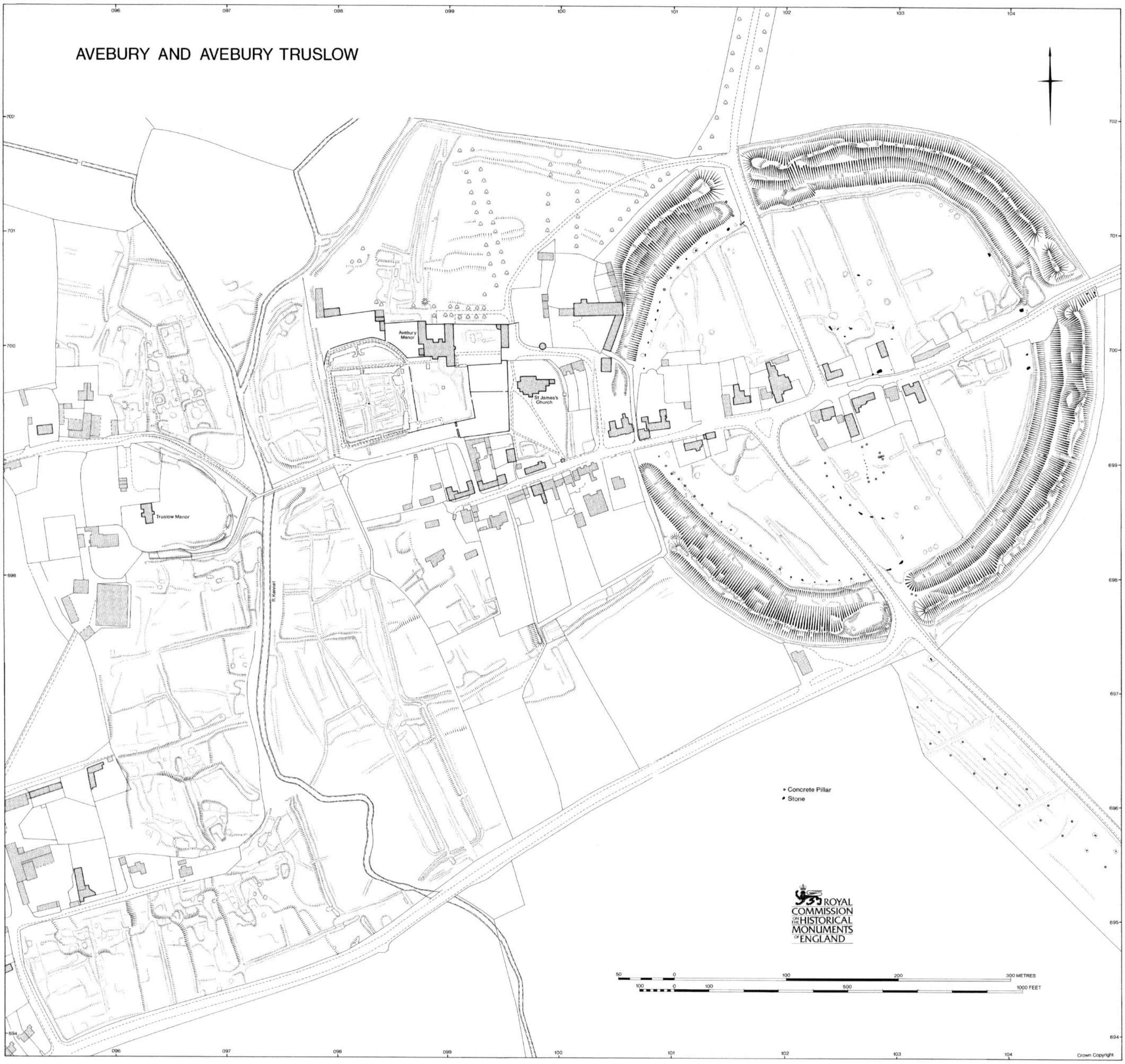

Fig 2:3 Plan of earthworks at Avebury. © Crown Copyright NMR.

the imprecision means that it is only possible to provide approximate locations.

A number of holes were dug in the area of the north circle: to both east and west of the westernmost stone of the Cove next to a tall upright stone ('b' on Long's plan 1857, 18). From the large westernmost Cove stone a large trench was dug in an east-north-east direction for 3m and subsequently this was extended further in an east-north-east direction. *'Here there apparently stood the third stone of the Cove'*. A further trench was dug to the east of the westernmost Cove stone; south-east of the Cove, outside the rickyard, where a recumbent sarsen was recorded, thought to be *'one of the stones of the inner circle surrounding the Cove'*; close by they dug in a *'cavity where an upright stone of the north circle stood north-north-east of the Cove'*. Within the southern circle a trench was cut at the centre and from there a further trench cut nearly due west in a straight line towards the westernmost of the stones standing in the outer circle. Other short trenches were cut to the north, south and east of this. North of the east entrance they cut a deep trench into the west face of the bank; at the south-west end of the bank at a point where a considerable gap had been cut, *'the material having been removed, and the ground levelled flat for the convenience of the village, we selected the centre of the section as the*

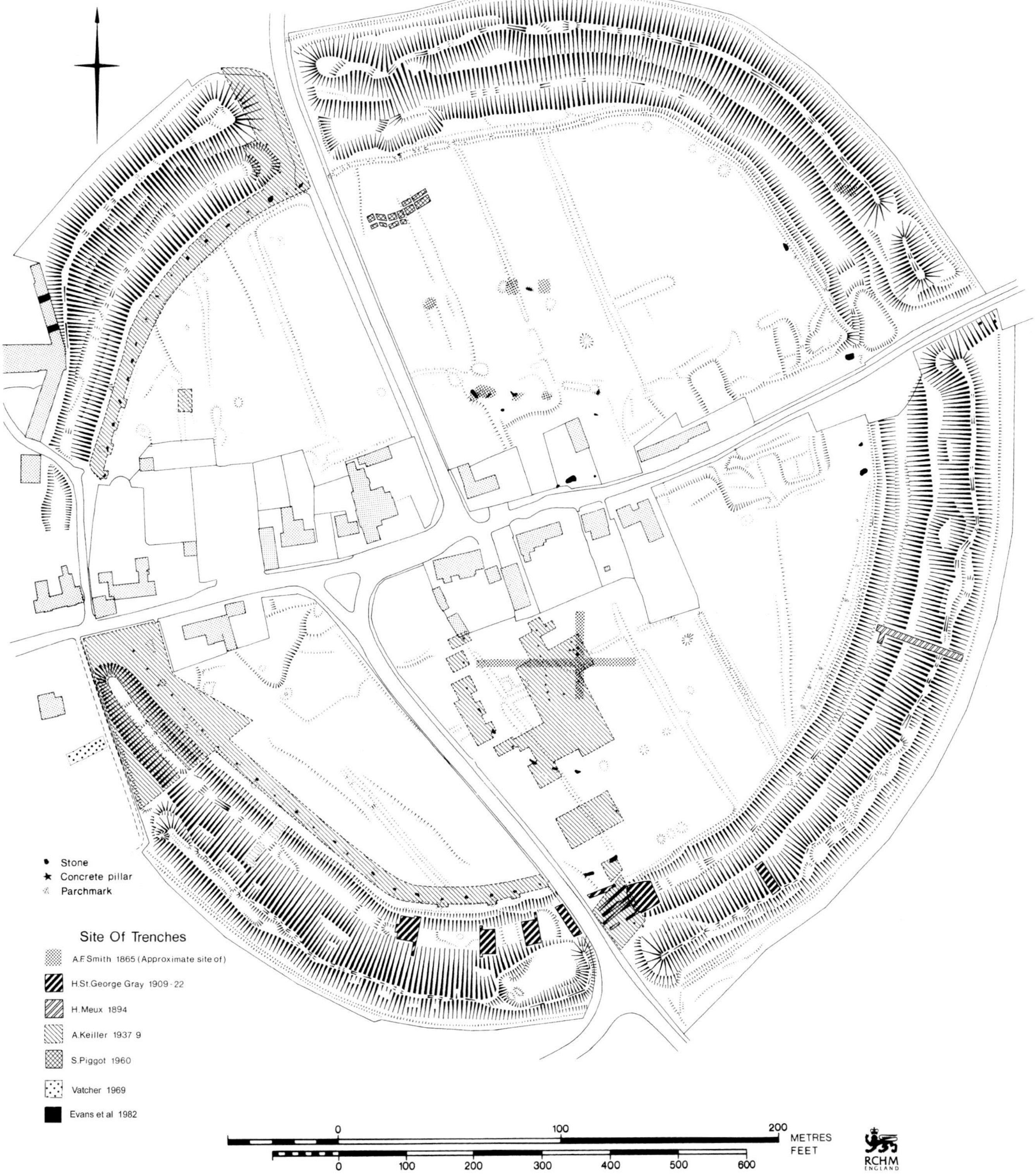

Fig 2:4 Position of excavation trenches at Avebury. © Crown Copyright NMR

point from which to run our trench'; further to the east and on the outside face of the bank '*we dug a small perpendicular hole*'; on '*the WNW side of the gap, behind Mr Kemm's rickyard, in a field called 'Barclose', where the mound bank is thickly planted with trees. Here we made a considerable cutting.*' Further excavations were conducted by Meux in 1894 (Gray 1935; Passmore 1935), or rather E Trepplin and T Leslie on his behalf. Meux cut a trench through the bank in the south-east quadrant, the position of which is still

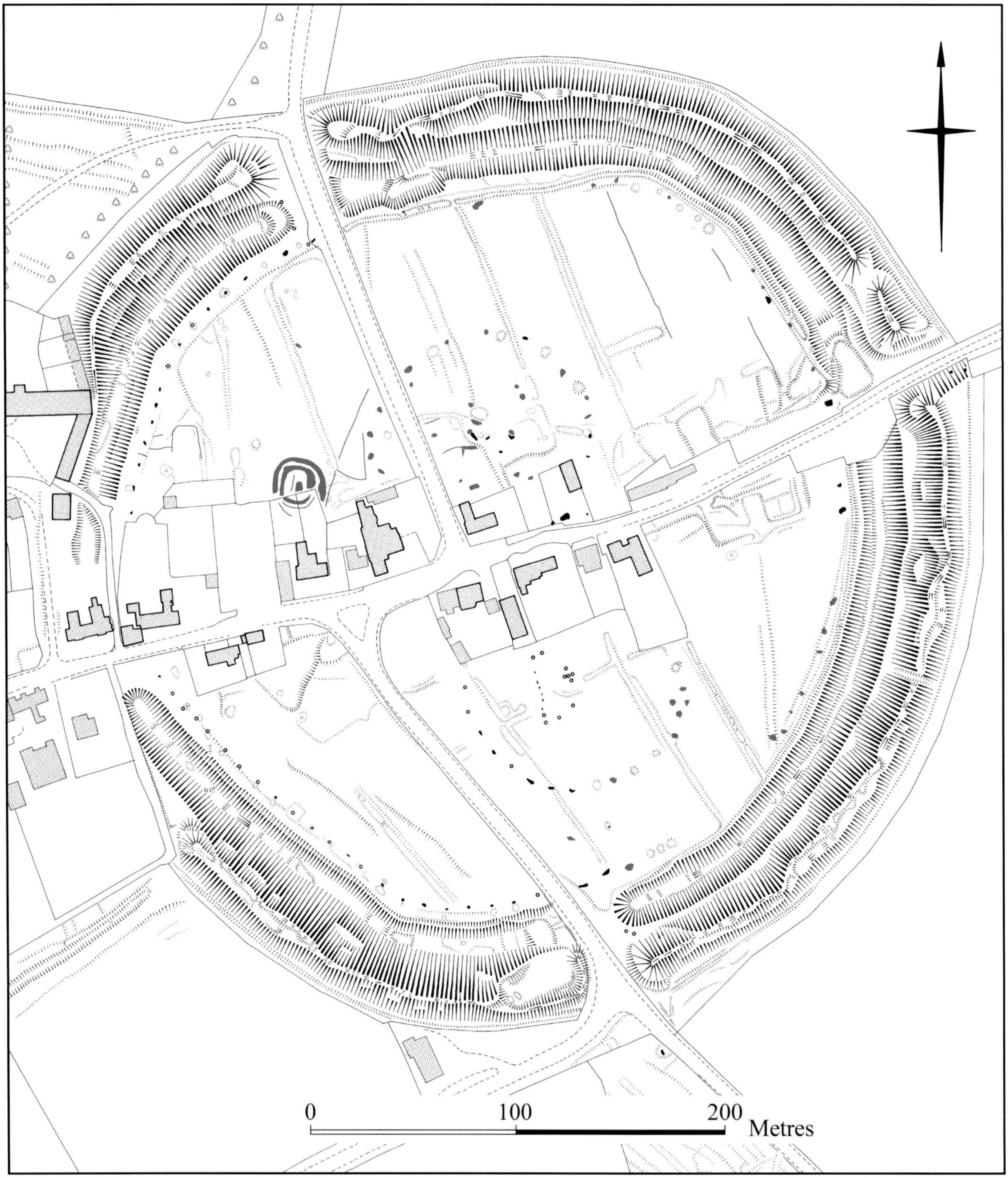

Fig 2.5 Plan of Avebury henge with parch marks. © Crown Copyright NMR.

detectable on the ground as a rectangular depression in the bank (Fig 2:4). Little description of the resulting section has survived, just sufficient to note the presence of a turf line at some 1.5m above the old land surface indicating the presence of an earlier bank. Most important were the extensive investigations by H St George Gray (Gray 1935) and A Keiller (Smith 1965a), who between them excavated considerable portions of the bank, ditch, entrances and stone settings and from which most of our knowledge of Avebury is obtained. Many of Keiller's trenches, particularly those around stones in the southwest quadrant, are still visible as slight earthworks and were planned as such (Figs 2:4 and 2:5). More recently Faith and Lance Vatcher excavated part of the bank in the area of the school (archive in A Keiller museum; Evans 1972), Piggott excavated a series of small trenches in the northern part of the site in search of a putative third inner circle (Piggott 1964), while small scale trenches were placed in the area of the Great Barn (Evans *et al* 1985), behind the craft shop, the Chapel, just outside the henge adjacent to the Workingmens Club and behind Rosemead in the High St (Harrington 1986; Anon 1991, 141).

In essence the site (Fig 2:5) comprises a large henge monument, a massive chalk cut ditch with the spoil dumped to form an external bank, with an integral stone circle that, in turn, encompasses two smaller stone circles, each with their own internal stone settings. In a number of his illustrations, Stukeley depicted the interior of the henge as being divided into a series of closes, most of which can still be traced today, and with an encircling Inclosure bank set around the internal lip of the henge ditch. Gray noted that the earthwork bank was covered in trees and that much household debris had accumulated in the ditch. Most of this was cleared by Keiller after he purchased the Manor in 1934, indeed Keiller's clearances were so enthusiastic, involving the removal of some families, that his admiration in archaeological circles was not matched locally (Rawlins 1999). Apart from these events, and the central west-to-east street along which medieval and post-medieval settlement developed, there appears to have been little damage to the interior of the earthwork. Avebury Manor House and its farm may have had some impact on the earthworks. Landscaping of the park, in particular, appears to have impinged upon the north-western parts of the henge bank.

The earthworks

The massive earthworks of the henge comprise an enormous ditch with an equally massive external bank, *c* 400m in diameter (internally) that encloses an area of 11.5ha. The bank reaches 3m in height above the ground surface and is some 10m wide at its base and has an undulating summit, probably indicative of the dumping of material, though in places may represent collapsed revetting walls and subsequent wear and tear. However, it has seen much disturbance, in particular, it has been severely denuded in the south-west quadrant in the area of Avebury school (not surveyed) and has been partially destroyed for a distance of 100m in the area to the north of this. The internal ditch is now *c* 8.0m wide, narrowing to a width of *c* 1.0 to 3.0m at its base and in places it is separated from the bank by a berm *c* 2.5m wide. Irregularities along the present ditch floor, particularly ledging at the terminals are the remnants of post construction activities including 20th century excavation trenches.

One of the most noticeable features of the plan is that the earthwork is not circular, instead it is constructed as a number of straight sections, each *c* 50 to 65m in length. Although this is not a new observation, it is important to re-emphasise, as even now there is a tendency to talk in terms of the circularity of the henge. Aubrey depicted the shape almost correctly in his plan of 1668, but since then others, including Stukeley, have tended to depict the monument as circular. Despite this angularity there is nevertheless a degree of symmetry to the monument. Whereas the eastern half remains bulbous and curving, the western half is more angular, and in each case the northern arc reflects its corresponding southern counterpart. It is tempting to imagine that there was some purpose behind the shape. If the early Phase 1 bank that was revealed in excavations (Gray 1935, 104; Pitts 2000, 187; Vatcher unpublished archive A Keiller Museum) was a marking out bank (Burl 1979), then there would have been scope to adjust any alteration in planning. At *c* 2m in height, however, the Phase 1 bank would have been imposing, suggesting that there was a greater purpose than simply 'marking out'. The line of the henge bank would therefore not only appear to reflect an earlier enclosure layout, but it may also respect pre-existing restrictions in the west.

While two of the four entrances, the northern and southern, can be accepted as being original, there has clearly been some modification of their form. On both sides of the northern entrance the bank expands outwards. Here, the eastern bank terminal has also been heightened and in view of the emphasis on terminals at other henges, Mayburgh, for example (Topping 1992), this might be considered to be an original feature. Two stone holes now represented by plinths mark the ditch terminal here. The southern entrance is more of a problem. Gray's excavation suggested that the entrance causeway lay between what are now the two massive entrance stones, the Devil's Chair, and its partner to the east of it, stone number 98, while excavations to the west of the road made it clear that the western ditch terminal lay beneath the road. The corresponding bank at the eastern terminal appears to be several metres longer than the ditch, though to a degree this is an impression influenced by the angle of the road, which is not oriented towards the centre of the enclosure.

Why the present road should ignore the solid causeway, and instead use the backfilled ditch is by no means clear, although a former cart route ran perilously close to the ditch in the northeast sector and further afield, it is possibly worthy of note that the Silbury Hill ditch was evidently backfilled to accommodate the Bath Road. The quarried bank to the west of the south entrance may have been used as a source of raw material for the road building at Avebury. Unfortunately the quarry is not depicted on early plans of the henge and it is not clear when it first took shape. Aubrey's plan of the area depicts use of the old Roman road (the A4) between Bath and Marlborough, with an additional route running east to west through Avebury village. If some of Stukeley's illustrations are correct then coaches were using the southern entrance of the henge by *c* 1743, and this would indicate that the road was in its present position at that time and that any change to the morphology of ditch and bank was carried out before that date. The Bath Road had been turnpiked by 1708 and it may be this that encouraged changes in the route of the main highway in order to avoid tolls.

If originally an entrance, the western ditch terminal has been filled in, most probably initially in order to host the former roadway and village street – the *herepath*. There is similar uncertainty regarding the east entrance, which has been heavily damaged. The ditch here has been used to contain a pond to the north of the road, while to the south there are the earthwork remains of a house and garden (both depicted on Stukeley's plan), built alongside the road. Like the northern entrance, the existing bank terminal north of the road is slightly expanded, but in contrast that to the south is slightly inturned. Two further sarsen stones were recorded outside the bank at this point providing a tantalising hint that external stone settings (such as an avenue) may have once existed. Blocking or other modifications to the entrances need not be Neolithic, and may have occurred as a result of re-use at a later period.

A bank, dating to the time of Inclosure, is set around the inner lip of the ditch and while still present in the eastern half of the site, has been removed from the western sectors by Keiller's excavations. In the south-east sector it appears to overlie a considerable deposit of soil, perhaps as much as 1.5m in depth. This may have accumulated partly as a result of cultivation or soil-creep from the interior of the henge. The former land surface is visible considerably lower around the circumference and can be detected as a break in slope or narrow ledge on the upper slope of the ditch. As the soil depth around the stone circle, set at *c* 5m from the edge of the ditch, is nearly 0.5m, there appears to be a considerable chamfer between the outer stone circle and the original edge of the ditch. The build up of soil around the edge of the ditch may in part have derived from cultivation – the soil being shifted from the central areas of the enclosure. If so, the interior of the henge may once have been more dramatically domed than it appears today. Such observations can only be tentative, as there are other possible explanations, including weathering of the ditch edge, but it is conceivable that the convex surface profile of the henge could have been enhanced by chamfering at the lip of the ditch. Similar earth shaping has been suggested for monuments further afield. The henge monuments of the Boyne in Ireland, for example, seem to have been shaped into artificial depressions and domes by shaving off layers of earth (Stout 1991). In the British Isles, the Bull Ring in Derbyshire and the Ring of Brodgar in Orkney appear to display some chamfering or rounding off of the inner lip of the ditch, while the henge at Durrington Walls is constructed in a natural curved depression, which the banks appear designed to enhance.

Like other henges, the position of Avebury is not prominent and when approached the view is of a simple bank that obscures whatever activities are taking place inside. However, even were the bank originally of greater height, the interior can be viewed with ease from the surrounding hills and the purpose of the bank cannot have been simply to prohibit views of the interior. In this respect the monument mimics its landscape, the earthworks focussing attention on the space within, and obscuring though not prohibiting views of the outside world. Attention very much focuses on internal activity, though despite this, it is worth pointing out that Silbury Hill is visible from the northern entrance and parts of the interior.

The siting of the henge is typical of henges elsewhere (e.g. Harding 1987). The low-lying aspect is a common feature, henges often being sited in natural depressions and bowls in the landscape. Set close to rivers and streams, they are not impressive features despite their size, and are often almost hidden from view by the local topography. John Aubrey was aware of the possibility of a connection with water when conjecturing that the 'au' element was a water name that referred to the River Kennet (Long 1858, 318). Passmore claimed that the base of the Avebury ditch reached a level OD similar to that of the nearby Kennet stream and may therefore have formed a wet moat (Passmore mss, Wilts Archaeol & NH Soc library, Devizes). Aware of this possibility Gray plotted the level of the stream against his various ditch sections and concluded that while Passmore may have been correct for the westernmost section, that in the east would not have met the water table. He also noted that there was no evidence of water having lain for long periods in the ditch. While this may be so at Avebury, and must be the case at Durrington and Mount Pleasant as well, Passmore's observation might be true of other henges, particularly Marden and Waulud's Bank, and in this context it is worth recalling that Silbury Hill lies on the floodplain at a confluence of Kennet streams and even with modern watertables, the ditch is wet for much of the winter.

Stone settings

Generally attributed a symbolic importance, the sarsen settings at Avebury consist of a circle of large sarsen orthostats set *c* 5.0 to 7.0m from the inner lip of the ditch. They are placed between 10 and 11m apart and have been considered to have originally constituted a continuous circuit. This circuit is not circular in plan, for it reflects the changes in the alignment of the ditch. In the western half of the monument all the stone settings have been excavated, and the stones either re-erected or concrete plinths put in their place. In the eastern half, only seven stones remain *in situ*, however, the positions of others can be determined from depressions in the ground, which relate either to the original setting, or to the burial or burning pit associated with its destruction. Ground survey at Avebury was carried out during the hot, dry summer of 1990, and one result of this was that buried features were revealed as parchmarks in the grass, while further parchmarks were identified from the air a few years later (Bewley *et al* 1996; Crutchley this volume). Uniquely, the position of a number of hitherto unknown buried stone or stone-burning pits was revealed in the outer stone circle, perhaps some of the stones removed by T Robinson and others (Long 1858). Although the distance between the stones in the outer circle differs, Isobel Smith established that they were set on *average* 11m apart and as a result there were likely to be 98 stones around the circumference. The presence of earthworks or parchmarks provides new information that helps confirm this.

Using Isobel Smith's numbering system (1965a, 175–6) that starts at the southern entrance and works clockwise, the position of stones 47–49 probably lie underneath the Inclosure bank (Fig 2:5). Stone 50 is extant. A local widening of the Inclosure ditch probably marks the position of 51 or 52, while four slight transverse scarps running from the Inclosure ditch to henge ditch may be the result of stones being dragged into the latter. Another scarp, in the area of stone 57, extends from a local depression in the Inclosure ditch, and is likely to mark its setting. Stukeley's plan (see Long 1858; Ucko *et al* 1991) shows two stones lying in the ditch at this point, one either side of stone 50 and it may be that a number of others lay unrecorded by him. Five depressions appear between 59 and 64, while 68 is extant. Parch marks occur in the area of stones 69 and 70 clearly indicating that the stones were not equidistant. A further parch mark, perhaps setting 71 or 72 is a little north of 73 which is still extant and there follows a series of seven parch marks, unevenly spaced, but approximating to the positions of stones 80, 82 to 84, and 86 to 88. No depressions were recorded adjacent to 88 and 91 as was noted by Smith, but three are present very close together adjacent to 94–6. Stones 98 and 1, opposite the southern entrance remain extant. Stukeley showed three large stones present by this entrance. One lay immediately adjacent to the roadway, so close in fact that it comes as no surprise that it has been removed or destroyed since his depiction.

The north and south circles both sit more or less centrally astride the natural ridge that extends across the henge interior. In contrast, the outer stone circle and the henge itself are offset from these. All this suggests that the inner circles may have been constructed at a different time to the henge and outer stone circle. On the basis of artefacts discovered beneath stones, however, Burl has suggested that the north and south circles are earlier in date than the outer circle. Smith (1965a, 248) believed that the outer circle was in place before the ditch was cut, but had not recognised the possibility of an earlier monument.

Both internal stone circles have been damaged by later activities. Nevertheless, much of their respective courses can still be traced. Although only six stones now survive of the north circle, many of the former positions can still be located, three by the presence of depressions in the ground, 10 by parchmarks. Smith assumed an interval of 11m between stones and that there must be 27 stones in the northern circle. The distance appears to be more variable than Smith imagined, though retaining the numbering system: 201 is extant, 202 located as a depression, 203 a parchmark, 204 a depression, 205a and b parchmarks, before 206 which is present. 207 is prone, 208 survives as a fragment, 209 is missing, 210 is prone, 211 a fragment, 212 to 217 are missing, 218 to 220 are parchmarks, 222 probably lies beneath the road, 23 is a parchmark, 24 a depression, 25–6 parchmarks and 27 a depression. These provide evidence of over half of the circle, an arrangement of extremely irregularly spaced stones. Others appear internally and could have been dragged from their positions or have some other purpose. They enclose a circular area 100m in diameter.

The central stone setting, the cove, remains as previously recorded with stones I and II extant. A further 9m to the southwest of stone 'E' another sarsen block was discovered. In addition to the remaining stones, parch marks indicate the presence of three others within the immediate area and five others just beyond. They of course may have been moved from elsewhere but could have formed a setting with the known Cove stones. Stukeley depicts a second, concentric ring here. It remains possible that both Aubrey and Stukeley misinterpreted the internal settings and that something rather different is present. No direct evidence for this either way was recovered during the 1990 survey, but the additional detail of the unaccounted for parchmarks within the northern circle widens the possibility of a setting other than a cove. Two massive existing stones, set at right angles to each other have long been accepted as part of a cove. This is largely based on Aubrey's illustration of a symmetrical setting of three stones (see details and discussion in Ucko *et al* 1991).

Only the southern half of the south circle remains, with 5 stones still standing, four of the stone positions surviving as depressions in the ground and others marked with plinths. In this case the circular area enclosed is slightly larger than its northern counterpart with a diameter of 110m. Isobel Smith believed that there were formerly 29 stones and using her numbering system: 101 to 103 are extant, 104 has a plinth, 105–6 are extant, 107–8 have plinths, 109 is marked by a depression, 110 to 121 are missing, 122 is a depression, 123–5 parchmarks, 126–7 depressions, 128 a parchmark and 129 a depression. Like the northern circle, there is an internal setting confirmed by excavation and marked by re-erected stones, plinths or concrete posts.

Between the southern circle and the southern entrance a parchmark is situated some 15m to the west of the stump of the ring stone. It appears that they may have been a pair. Alternatively it may have been an outlier of the stone row i–x, part of the central setting in the southern circle, with which it shares an alignment. The stump of the re-erected 'Ring-stone' itself is extant. A similar isolated parchmark lies to the north west of the northern circle.

The dramatic photographs of 1996 identified a buried feature in the north-west quadrant. This appears as a sub-circular, double concentric ditched feature, the inner ditch being more square in outline than the inner. A large pit-like feature and small ditch in the interior remain unexplained. The feature has been described as a Neolithic barrow (Bewley *et al* 1996), though it may equally be a feature of Romano-British or Early Medieval date.

The Avenues

Two avenues of paired stones are known in association with the henge at Avebury, namely, the West Kennett (Keiller & Piggott 1936; Smith 1965a; Ucko *et al* 1991) and the Beckhampton Avenues (Gillings *et al* 2000a; 2002). The former extends from the southern entrance of the henge along a sinuous course, it is thought, to the complex structure known as the Sanctuary (Cunnington 1931; Pollard 1992; Pitts 2001). Its course alludes to a complex constructional sequence, which may have incorporated, initially, shorter stretches of stone (and possibly timber) avenues, perhaps as formal approaches to the main and other enclosures.

No contemporary earthworks were recognised along the course of the West Kennet Avenue. Those that were recorded are the scorings of cultivation, parallel with both road and stones at the foot of Waden Hill. The stones themselves are almost equidistant, the maximum error being no more than about a metre. Some are not exactly opposite their partner. The course of the Avenue as it approaches Avebury leads away from the entrance and excavation by Keiller immediately south of the henge entrance indicated that it might make a violent turn to enter the henge. Were it not for this turn, the course of the Avenue leads towards a local hollow or depression situated immediately outside the henge bank. It is difficult to be certain of the nature of this and it is by no means clear whether it has archaeological significance, but its origin might be considered to have resulted from a spring, or swallow hole or some such feature.

There is an assumption, largely based on Stukeley's illustrations, that the Avenue was continuous and provided a link with the Sanctuary at West Overton. However, Aubury's illustration of the West Kennet Avenue differs to those of later illustrators, in that it depicts it as leading to West Kennet rather than the Sanctuary. A second Avenue to which the first abuts, is depicted as leading from the Sanctuary to West Kennet and given the uncertain result of recent excavations along the course of the Avenue at West Kennett (Gillings *et al* 2003), it may be worth keeping an open mind on the matter.

Silbury Hill

Other foci of ceremonial and ritual activity developed in the close vicinity of Avebury and one of them, Silbury Hill, is perhaps the most awe-inspiring of Avebury's monuments, being the largest prehistoric mound in Europe. The first investigation took place in 1776, when Cornish miners were employed by the Duke of

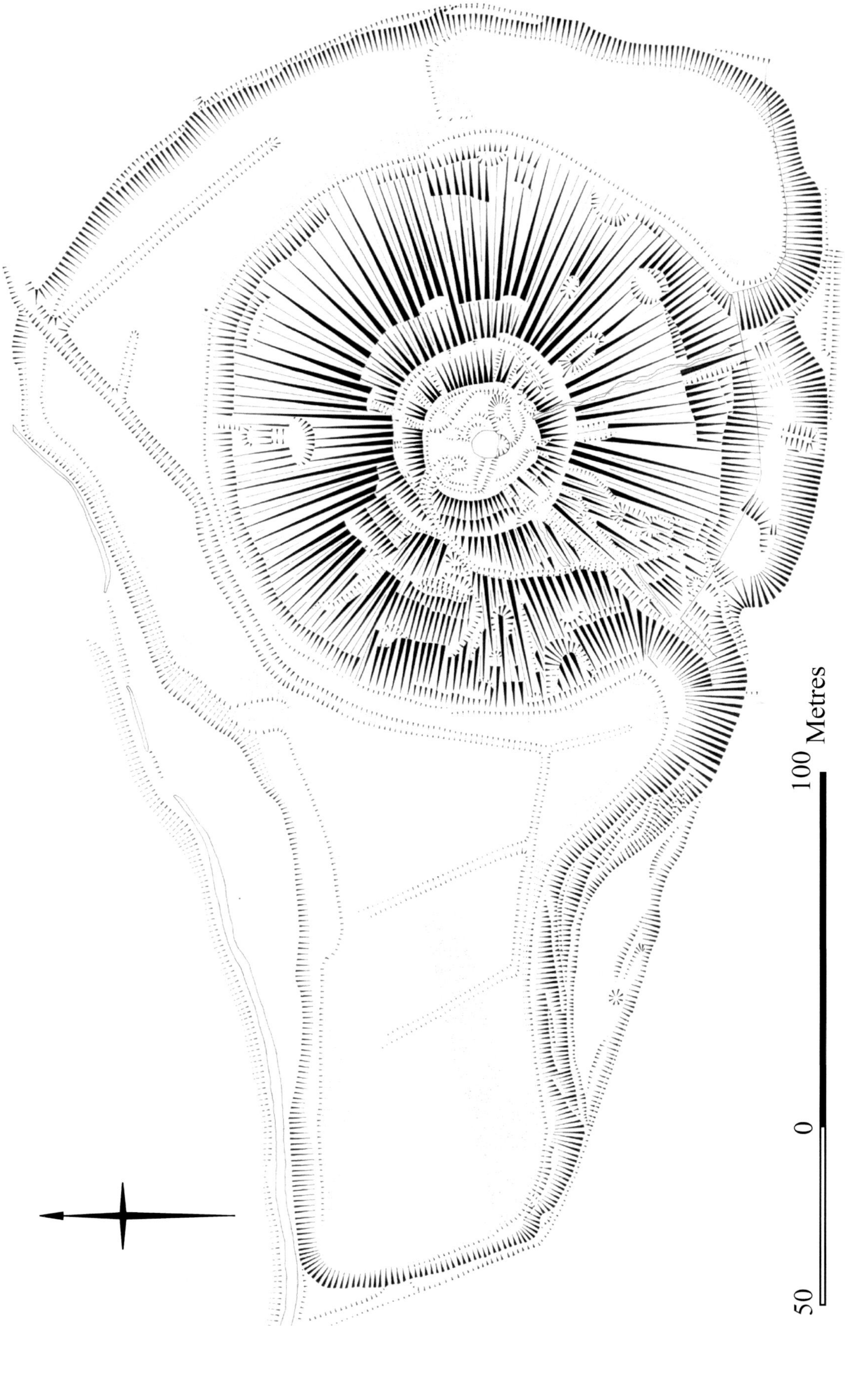

Fig 2.6 Plan of Silbury Hill. © English Heritage NMR.

Northumberland and Colonel Drax to dig a shaft from the summit. Little is known of this work apart from the fact that a thin fragment of wood was found at the base (Douglas 1793, 161; Merewether, 1851b, 74).

In 1849, a civil engineer, Henry Blandford of Rowde who had constructed cuttings and embankments for the Great Western Railway, and Richard Faulkner of Devizes, tunnelled in towards the centre along the old ground surface from the western of the two causeways that breach the ditch (Tucker 1851; Merewether 1851b). At less than 10m from the estimated centre the matrix of the mound appeared to change from chalk rubble to piles of turf, *'containing great quantities of moss in a state of comparative freshness'* with freshwater mollusc shells and insects amongst it (Merewether 1851b, 76; Tucker 1851, 301). Over and around this was a deposit of black earth with a peculiar smell. Having gone 5m beyond the centre, Merewether cut into the tunnel roof and then to the right along the edge of the primary mound. Along this line an unrecorded number of sarsens were revealed evidently forming a peristalith around the central turf feature. Another section cut to the right revealed similar results. Further sections were cut to the left, then in a semi-circular manner at the end of the tunnel though without encountering further features.

Further excavations were conducted in 1886 when trenches were dug in the ditch by A C Pass (Pass 1887, 245–54). The Wiltshire Archaeological Society cut trenches into the mound at the level of the old ground surface to investigate whether the Roman road lay beneath the mound (Wilkinson 1867) while Petrie cut trenches opposite the southeastern causeway searching for a potential entrance (Petrie 1924). Finally the campaign conducted in the late 1960s by Richard Atkinson reinvestigated the original tunnel, trenched the summit, slopes and ditch (Whittle 1997a; Atkinson 1967; 1968; 1969; 1970). Merewether reported that Silbury Hill is surrounded by a peristalith of sarsens, each of the order of one metre across, placed at intervals of about 5.5m, although only eight of these were visible in 1849 (Merewether 1851b, 74). None of these are now visible on the ground surface.

The conical mound rises steeply from a base of 150m diameter, achieving varying angles according to position on the mound, and tapers, sometimes with straight sides, but elsewhere in a slightly cambered fashion, towards its flat summit of *c* 36m maximum diameter (Fig 2:6). Taken vertically from around the perimeter the height differs according to the fall of the natural ground surface – in the north it reaches some 32m, in the east 34m and about 31m at the centre. The mound itself is surrounded by a silted ditch, now up to 53m wide by 6m deep. A full analytical report will be published as part of conservation work on the mound (Chadburn *ed* in prep).

A break of slope several metres above the present ditch floor (Fig 2:6) almost certainly marks the old ground surface and therefore, the real base of the mound. Below this the angle of slope invariably steepens, but it marks the inner edge of the ditch rather than the lower levels of the mound. Although it is difficult to be precise, because continuity of line cannot be traced, the diameter of the mound at this level is generally about 150m, and even taking weathering into account, the diameter of the original final mound must have been of this order.

A contour plan (not figured here) indicates that the form of the mound is not circular but is dictated by a series of radial spines or spokes from which horizontal sections emanate in a similar manner to a spider's web. Some of these 'spines' can be isolated and identified at points where the contours collectively project and disrupt the general curvature. The summit itself is more correctly sub-rectangular, measuring 36m by 32m, and despite containment by a fence that might have influenced shape during recent times, the base may possibly be nine-sided.

A few earthworks survive on the summit, some to over 0.5m in height, but are difficult to interpret, principally because of the lengthy and varied activity known to have taken place during historic times, not least the effects of excavation paraphernalia. Aside from the excavation shaft that is situated almost centrally, the main feature is a circular hollow some 7m in diameter and measuring over 0.5m in depth, set a little to the east of it. A hollowed gully, almost an entranceway, leads into this from the west. Around the lip of the summit are traces of a shallow bank, perhaps remnants of a treeplanting ring. Other earthworks, in particular a bank to the north of the collapsed shaft, may have been a result of past excavations.

At various points around the slopes are traces of horizontal terraces, platforms or breaks of slope, thought by Atkinson to be remnants of his proposed tiered construction. The uppermost of these ledges, a maximum of 2.5m wide on the surface, lies just 4m below the summit. It is better seen on the north and east and barely perceptible in the south and southwest, perhaps because it had been better infilled in that quadrant or, because the prevailing wind from this direction has resulted in greater weathering and erosion. A second ledge can be traced at *c* 10m below the summit, while stretches of breaks of slope that might account for others lie at 15m, 19m and 27m below the summit. If perambulated, the upper ledge completes its circuit at a position below the starting point and implies a spiral arrangement. It is unclear whether this is as a result of the original construction, or of later redevelopment, but assuming that it continued to the base of the mound it suggests that the model of tiered construction proposed by Atkinson may need to be modified and that the 'terracing' could have been a spiral. In the southeast, a ramp, 2m wide, leads prominently from the upper ledge almost to the summit. Again whether this is an original feature is unclear. That it finishes short of the summit may indicate so, if the material above it is later.

In the west are further ledges at a slightly lower level that could represent stages of the 'tiered' construction. They stretch for 12m and provide ledges up to 2m in width. The present path, an important chronological feature, cuts them, but other than this there remains some uncertainty as to whether they are original features.

Other more platform-like features lie around the mound, both on the slopes and close to the original ground level. On the northern slopes a break of angle leads to a prominent crescentic platform or stance *c* 14m by 5m. A trench-like scar leads downhill from this to an apron, while a subsequent scar on the same axis appears to cut the old ground surface.

A similar crescentic platform situated in the south-east is equally prominent measuring 10m by 5m and lying above a considerable apron. Above it, just below the uppermost 'terrace' and on the same axis there is a considerable scar, 13m in length by 5m wide and over 0.5m deep. This may represent trenching, and the hint of a bank to one side could support this view, but it could equally indicate the sort of collapse that has occurred above the Merewether tunnel.

A number of linear features ascending the mound are present. Two of these, each 1.5m in width, situated on the upper north-eastern slopes between the two uppermost ledges mark the position of Atkinson's backfilled excavation trenches. A third situated opposite the westernmost ditch causeway, up to 1m deep and 7m wide, can be traced for 19m up the slope of the mound, is the result of the collapse of the 1849 tunnel.

The present pathway to the summit, eroded and hollowed in places, curves around the western slopes, starting opposite the south-western causeway and ascending to the vicinity of the tunnel entrance, then gradually turning northwards and finally approaching the summit from the north-west. It is easy to assume that this is a feature of recent visitor wear, but the route of the path is visible on early illustrations and dates from at least 1663. Stukeley mentions the construction of a pathway by Richard Holford, then owner of Avebury Manor, which in conjunction with the known tree planting may indicate that some use was made of Silbury as an eye-catcher. Most of the Manor parkland lay to the north, but like the Marlborough Castle mound, there may have been an attempt to incorporate it within a designed landscape.

Situated on a declining spur, the base of the mound will have been placed at an angle and if horizontal construction layers and ditches were intended, more material would consequently need to be placed on the north side of the mound than the south. Similarly, in the southwest and east, the sides of the ditch are steeply cut compared to the

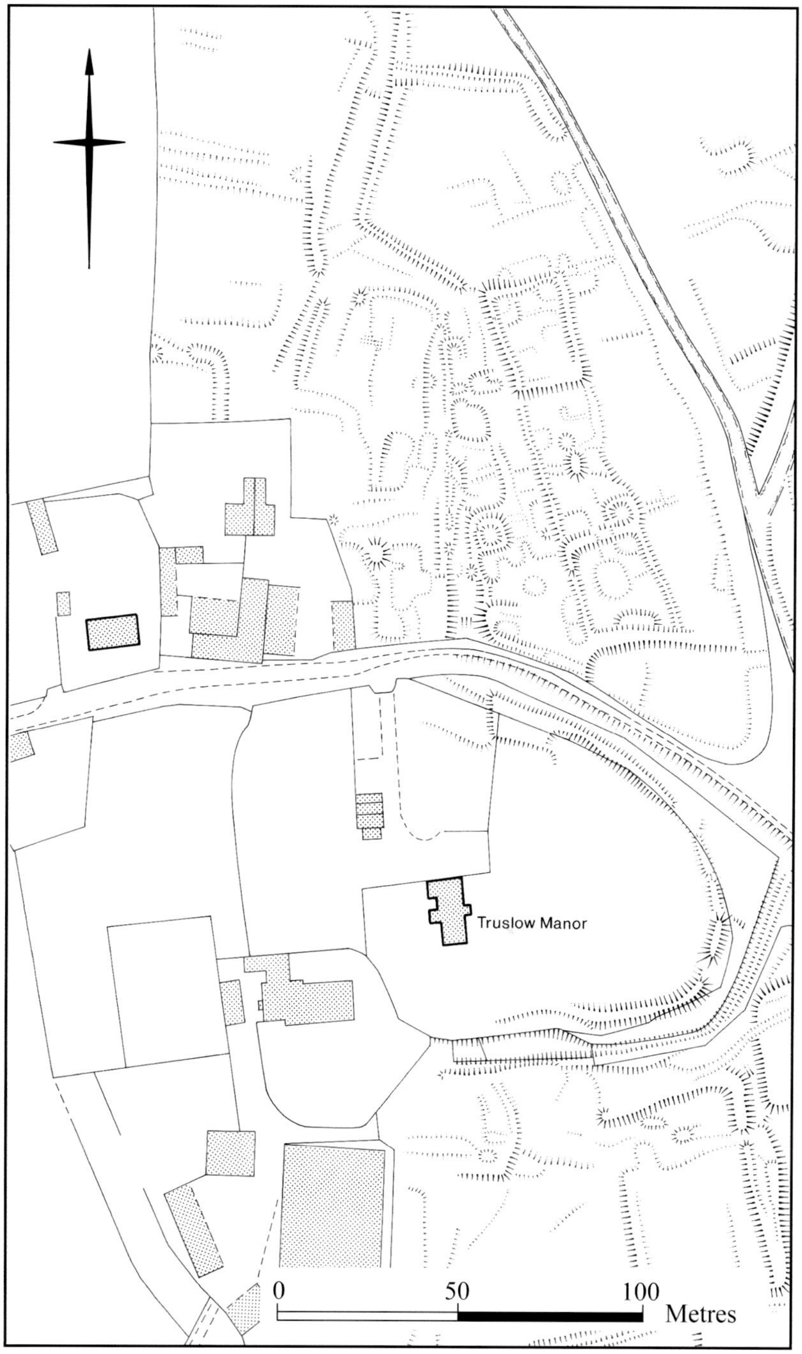

Fig 2:7a) Plan of earthworks at Avebury Trusloe. © Crown Copyright NMR

Fig 2:7b) Plan of earthworks at Avebury Trusloe. © Crown Copyright NMR

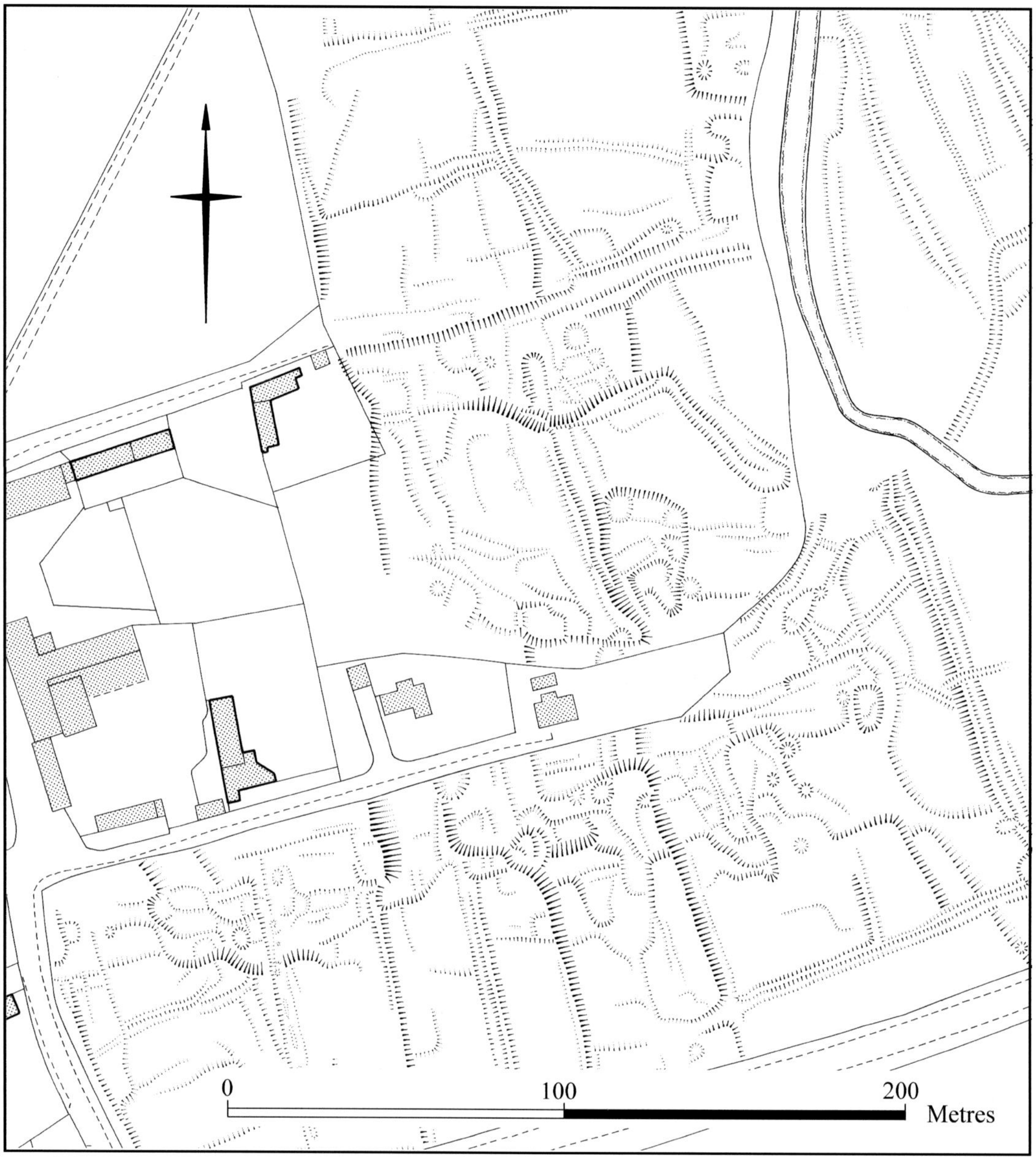

north, where the edge of the visible ditch is quite shallow resulting in a broad flat bottom up to 43m across. At the level of the original ground surface the ditch is between 38 and 53m in width. South of the mound, the ditch, separated from the rest of the circuit by two causeways, appears both narrower and shallower than elsewhere, being 27m wide by 6m deep. However, as Atkinson's excavation trench demonstrated the true edge of the ditch probably lies beneath the A4 road. In the west the ditch has been considerably extended and excavated into an extensive rectilinear quarry, some 85m wide and 165m long, in the direction of the Beckhampton Brook. This extension appears to have been deliberately formed and once waterfilled would effectively provide a cistern or reservoir perhaps as much symbolic or sacred significance as practical (e.g. Ashmore & Brady 1999, 137).

An enigmatic vegetation mark noted in the ditch extension to the west of the mound is difficult to account for. This is some ten metres wide and indicative of a substantial subsurface feature. It appears to extend across the ditch floor for some 50 metres towards the mound. Assuming that it marks a genuine sub-surface feature the darker vegetation suggests that a massive negative feature is present below the surface. Its orientation, however, is curious, running diagonally across the ditch extension leading towards a position that is off-centre of the mound. It may be that a deeper channel, collecting from local

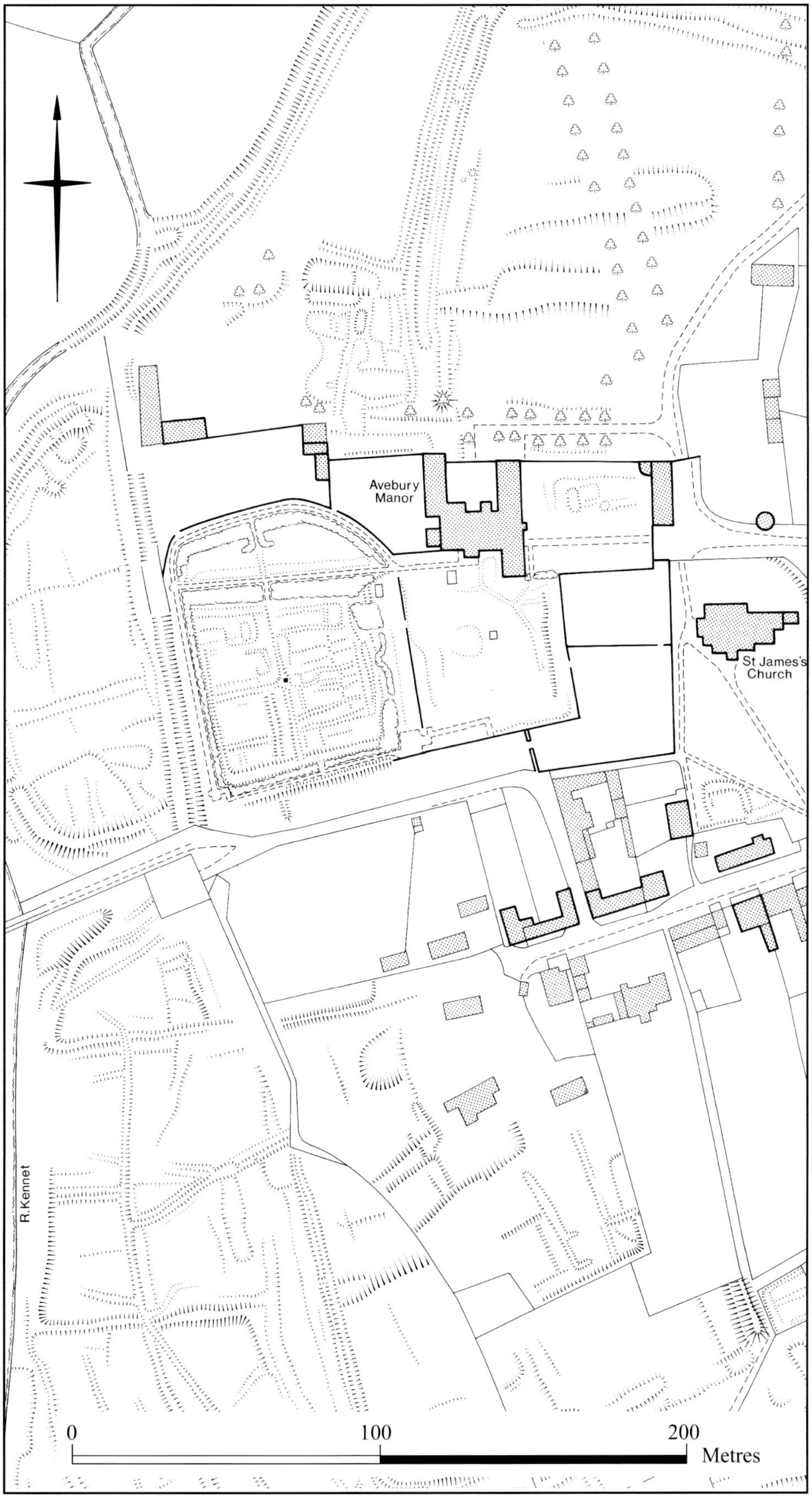

Fig 2:8 Plan of Avebury Manor. © Crown Copyright NMR

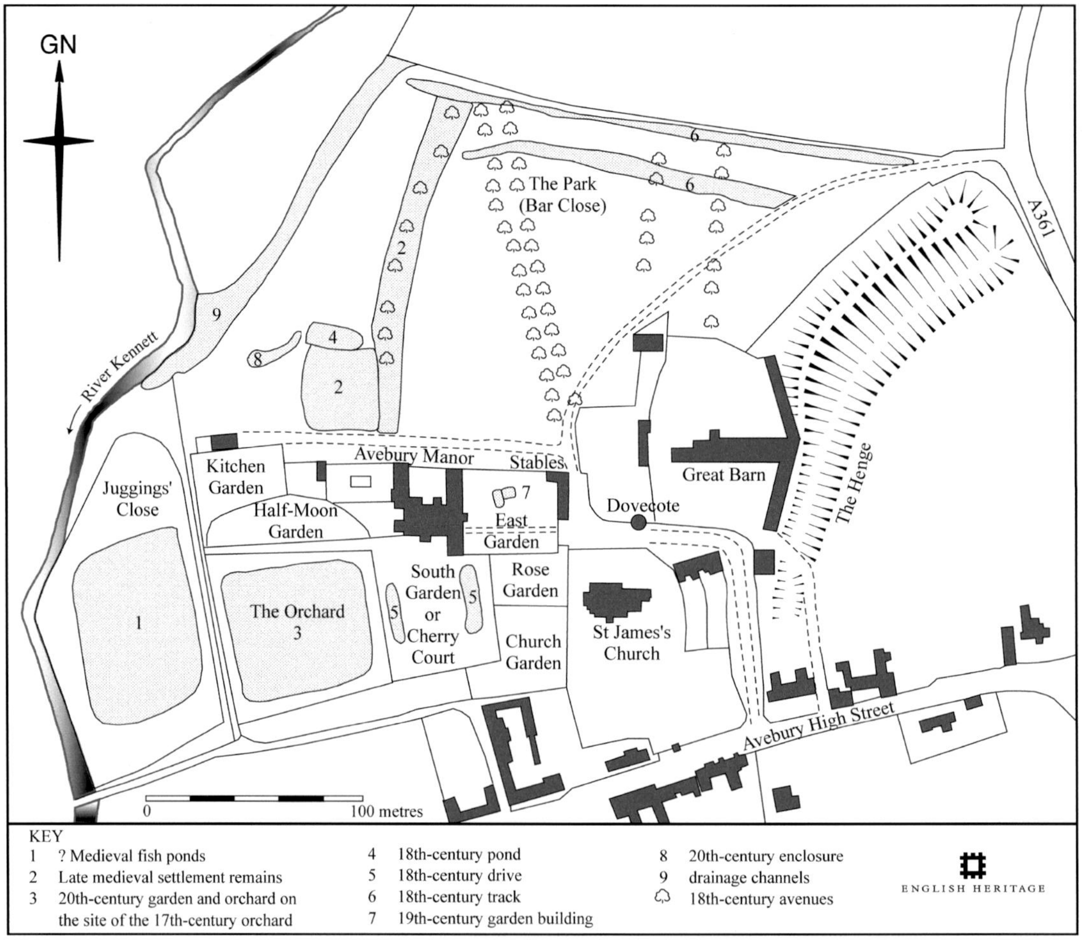

Fig 2:9 Avebury manor interpretation. © English Heritage NMR.

springs, carried run-off together with that of the proto Beckhampton Brook to the deeper ditch around the mound.

Later Earthworks

Earthworks, some perhaps dating to the Anglo-Saxon period, are relatively widespread in the World Heritage Site and occupy several foci. Most of these lie around the village of Avebury itself, both within and immediately west of the henge, while others lie to the west of the Kennet stream in the area of Avebury Trusloe. The plan of the earthworks (Fig 2:3) indicates the location of seven nuclei of activity:

a) West of the Kennet stream, Trusloe Manor (Fig 2:7a) lies within the remains of a partial curvilinear enclosure bordered in the north and east by a road and footpath, its western course is unclear but it probably extended along the curving fence boundary to the south of the Manor towards the road. The wide external ditch to the south, which may indicate the former scale of the enclosure, often holds water, and may have been a remnant of a moat perhaps dating to a period of garden landscaping. The house itself dates to the 17th century (Pevsner 1975, 102), but its location, which is almost central within the enclosure with further settlement beyond its boundary (*below*), may suggest that it is of at least medieval date. In form, the enclosure is similar to that at Raddun, a medieval farmstead on the Marlborough Downs; however, with a diameter of *c* 100m, Truslow Manor is substantially larger. A more plausible interpretation is that it is an Anglo-Saxon enclosure similar to others in the Avebury region such as that at Yatesbury (Pollard & Reynolds 2002).

b) Extending from the northern side of the enclosure is a hollow way with earthworks on either side. Some 15 or so depressions and raised platforms are evident, which are likely to represent the stances of buildings. These building platforms, together with the hollow way, which is aligned precisely on the Manor, may be contemporary with the enclosure. On the eastern side of the meadow, and set back from the hollow way, are at least ten stances enclosed within three small rectangular units, or closes. These earthworks are better defined than those along the hollow way, and probably represent a separate, planned stage of occupation.

c) South of Trusloe Manor, a substantial group of earthworks lies either side of South Street bounded by the A361 road (Fig 2:7b) and a lane at similar distance in the north, both of which probably formed back lanes to the properties. Up to six property boundaries lie to the south of South Street and in at least five cases their boundaries extend south to the A361. These regular property boundaries may represent settlement reorganisation since in places they overlie earlier earthworks. In the west some boundaries lay at right angles and from the staggered nature of the South Street crossroads, and the angled orientation of earthworks nearby, there is a hint that it represents infilling. To the north of the central lane, further building plots with units or multiples of units identical to properties south of the lane still contain structures. At the rear of some, however, further building stances can be traced. The relationship of this settlement to Trusloe is unclear, but the form of the regular rectilinear earthworks would suggest that they are similar in date to the three closes to the east of the hollow way (b *above*). In the east, a substantial bank with a ditch on the eastern side, may be part of a water management system that is more apparent on the eastern side of the river.

To the east of the stream, earthworks lie in three main units and include Avebury Manor itself (Figs 2:8 and 2:9). Properties to the south of the Manor can be considered as one unit with those within the henge. All are set along the west to east routeway, a route that today is disjointed but *may* have formerly continued to the south of Trusloe Manor (along the enclosure). A series of building stances were recorded during the survey, two inside the churchyard, while at least seven properties can be traced at the eastern end of the henge. To the north of the street and south of Avebury Manor, properties are smaller and closely set in groups, with an 'urban-like' character to them. South of the street, they are set within former closes that extend for a similar distance to those across the stream in Trusloe south. To the south they are bounded by a back lane that abuts the henge bank (though the footpath that returns to the village street may be on the line of a former lane).

Within the henge, close boundaries on the same alignment to those to the west of the bank, can still be detected in a number of places and in the eastern part of the henge a series of platforms, scarps and banks flanking the *herepath* route, represent the remains of tofts and crofts of at least three holdings. Close boundaries, within which there are slight traces of ridge and furrow, extent perpendicularly from the roadway. Aubrey's plan shows them as a series of pecked lines but these are depicted as fenced and hedged divisions in Stukeley's plan of 1743. The Inclosure bank, shown by Stukeley in 1724 as hedged and tree-clad, closely follows the inner lip of the ditch, but departs from it in the north-east to follow the stone circle. Keiller removed it from both west quadrants when excavating the outer circle.

d) Much of the area to the west of the henge, which forms a sub-rectangular enclosure, has also been interpreted as a late-Anglo-Saxon *burgh* (Reynolds 2001, 29; Pollard & Reynolds 2002, 202). Evidence of Anglo-Saxon occupation was recovered immediately outside the henge during excavations on the site of the school in 1969 and subsequently in the area of the National Trust car park (Wilson 1970, 200–1; Pollard & Reynolds 2002, 191–210). Like the Romano-British settlement at Silbury (Corney 1997a), the stream may have provided the focus for early settlement, as indeed was the case for so many chalkland villages in Wiltshire. There is just a hint of earlier, prehistoric, activity here too, as Stukeley mentions the recovery of a bronze axe from immediately outside the west entrance of the henge (see Barber this volume).

Avebury Manor

Avebury Manor lies on the northern edge of the village of Avebury, (Fig 2:8). The National Trust purchased the site in 1991 and commenced a programme of research and restoration. It possibly lies on the site of the former monastic alien cell (Brown this volume) and its later history has been charted by Freeman (1983a, 86–105).

The house

Avebury Manor house was rebuilt *c* 1600. Only a small part of the earlier structure survives. Alterations and additions continued in the late 17th and early 18th centuries, but after the mid-18th century little work was done. The Jenner family carried out restoration work in the early part of the 20th century. The National Trust commissioned architectural and archaeological surveys of the house and gardens, which succeeded in detailing their development (Treasure 1992; Fretwell 1992).

The gardens ***(Figs 2:8 and 2:9)***

Documentary evidence suggests that there were four main phases of development to the gardens. A 16th-century survey for Sir William Sharington describes a utilitarian garden around the manor house. Sir Richard Holford improved the house and grounds in the early 18th century, while Mrs Williamson laid out a new garden and pleasure ground in the 1790s. Finally, the Jenner family laid out new gardens in the early 20th century, largely within the existing framework.

Earthworks are preserved in the Orchard, the South Garden and the East Garden. The earthworks in the Orchard comprise a series of slight, regular banks. The most obvious of these features divides the area into four roughly square plots, each measuring some 20m by 20m. They are probably the remains of pathways. The fainter earthworks within each plot may relate to planting. The division into four may well be part of Jenners' garden layout in the 1920s, when a well was created at the centre of the Orchard. The overall pattern of these regular earthworks is similar to that shown in the plan of 1695 (WSRO 184/4), where the Orchard to the west of the house is divided into square plots. The East Garden contains a rectangular platform, 7m by 4m, with a similarly sized rectangular hollow on its eastern side. A slight bank lies to the east, a shallow ditch to the west. The platform and hollow represent the remains of a square building within a square enclosure, depicted on the 1887 Ordnance Survey map (Ordnance Survey 1st edition 25inch map). The bank and ditch are the remains of paths, also depicted on the 1st edition map, but removed by 1924 (Ordnance Survey 3rd edition 25inch map). Some rather irregular slight earthworks, together with a stronger scarp running parallel to the eastern wall of the South Garden, are most likely to be the remains of the oval drive to the south entrance of the house, again depicted on the 1887 map, but removed by 1924. The drive layout may have been altered several times as a circular drive is shown somewhat schematically on the small-scale map of 1779 (Andrews and Dury county map), but the 1794 enclosure map depicts a straight approach from the south (WSRO EA 95).

The landscape park

The formal setting of the manor house did not include a deer park, though a later landscape park was created immediately to the north of the house, bounded by farmland to the north, the farm and henge ditch to the east, the house and formal gardens to the south, and the River Kennet to the west. The estate map of Avebury Great Farm, surveyed for Sir Richard Holford in 1733, is one of the earliest depictions of the wider area around the house and gardens (WSRO 1553/71). This shows three double avenues, all on slightly differing alignments, but running roughly north-south from the northern boundary to the house and farm. By the late 19th century, the western avenue was reduced to a single, rather short, line of trees. The other two avenues remain as double lime avenues, albeit in a depleted state. The area is called 'Back Close' in 1733, 'Bar Close' by the latter part of that century. The current approach to the house from the main road through the park seems to date from some time in the 19th century. Eighteenth-century maps show access to the house and farm from the south (village) side.

The area contains earthworks relating to several phases of activity. Some of the earliest are those to the north of the house, where banks and hollows mark the remains of buildings and garden plots. The 1548 survey, carried out for Sir William Sharington, mentions a close of five acres containing a rabbit warren, 'Hemphey' of two acres, 'pyked close' – half an acre with a pool – in this general area (Fretwell 1992, Appendix 2). A wide linear earthwork feature, comprising a ditch with a bank to the west, runs roughly north to south through the park. It must have functioned as a route to the settlement remains here, but may have its origins in an early approach to the manor house. The western avenue followed its course. A circular mound at its southern end is a tree-planting mound.

The linear features on the northern edge of the park are most likely to be related to the Private Road shown on the 1794 map but out of use by the latter part of the 19th century. A wide ditch in the western part of the park is a drainage channel. A pronounced hollow, 25m by 10m, on the northern edge of the area of settlement is probably the remains of a large pond, perhaps that referred to by the estate steward in 1793 (WSRO 184/6, 271/16). The slight curvilinear feature to the west of the pond corresponds to a small irregular enclosure shown on the map of 1924.

A final area of land lies to the west of the formal gardens. It is low-lying and bounded on its western side by the River Kennet. A ditch on the eastern side separates it from the gardens. A substantial bank curves around the south, west and north sides of the field, enclosing an area of earthworks. These could be the remains of two rectangular fishponds, with a bank or dam separating them. The two pronounced gaps in the enclosing bank may represent sluices. The relationship of these earthworks to the house and grounds is awkward, and they appear to be earlier features. They could relate to the priory, but may also have functioned as fishponds after the priory was dissolved. In 1794 the field was known as 'Juggings Close', an unusual name but present locally further along the same trackway in Jugglers Lane, Yatesbury (Smith 1885). In the early 20th century withy beds were located to the west of Avebury Manor, possibly in this field as the willows along the river suggest (Freeman 1983a, 87).

The Valley Floor

On the eastern side of the Kennet an extensive area of water management is evident (Fig 2:3). In form, the earthworks are different to those of water meadows elsewhere on the Wessex chalk (Bettey 1999, 185), but nevertheless they appear to fulfil a similar function. The principal earthworks are a lengthy ditch, which was probably a 'carrier', and extends along the western side of a substantial bank (this bank is part of the suggested *burgh*). In the south the 'carrier' turns west towards the Kennet. Mid-way along this short stretch a probable collapsed aqueduct marks the point where a 'drain' underlies the 'carrier'. Two cuttings along this carrier allow water to flow west onto the meadow. To the west of the 'carrier' are a series of ditches, which appear to be water 'drains'. The other principal earthworks are the ditches which appear to drain the meadow. Within the meadow some of these appear to cut other, slighter earthworks, suggesting an earlier episode of land-use.

3
Recent Aerial Survey work in the Marlborough Downs region

Simon Crutchley

This paper examines recent Aerial Survey work in the Marlborough Downs region in terms of both reconnaissance and mapping. The Marlborough Downs, taken in its broadest context incorporates parts of the Lambourn Downs to the east. The paper highlights different aspects of reconnaissance, interpretation and mapping and the cyclical nature of aerial survey.

Introduction

The work of the English Heritage Aerial Survey section in the region can be divided into three parts, although as we will see these form part of a feedback process, each of which influences the others. The first aspect is aerial reconnaissance – discovering and recording of sites from the air; the next is small-scale, large area mapping, which normally comes under the remit of the National Mapping Programme (NMP); and finally an occasional programme of large-scale detailed mapping, generally referred to as a Special Project. In the case of each of these activities the Aerial Survey section are continuing a long tradition of research in the region. Some of the earliest aerial photographs of archaeological sites were taken in the Marlborough Downs region. The earliest aerial photograph held by the National Monuments Record (NMR; the archive of English Heritage) was taken only a few miles distant in 1906, from a balloon over Stonehenge. Some twenty years later O G S Crawford, regarded by many as the father of aerial archaeology, collaborated with Alexander Keiller in undertaking a series of flights in the region, which resulted in the publication of *Wessex from the Air* (Crawford and Keiller 1928). Crawford himself carried out little more in the way of active aerial reconnaissance and photography, but he did influence another pioneer who worked in the area, Major G W G Allen. Furthermore, whereas Crawford concentrated to a very large extent on the well preserved earthwork sites, Allen carried out regular surveys of sites that had already been ploughed flat and were only visible from the air (Allen 1984). In a series of surveys between 1933 and 1938 Allen photographed numerous sites in the area including some particularly fines shots taken in low evening sunlight highlighting the field systems on Fyfield and Overton Down. Although it was noted above that Crawford did little flying after his initial collaboration with Keiller, he still had a major contribution to make to aerial survey in the region. For Allen the photograph was the end product, but for Crawford it was only a means to an end. For him the end product was a map, often combining information from a number of photographs with further detail from the ground. As such he was more closely linked with the second aspect of our current work, interpretation and mapping. Almost every plate in *Wessex from the Air* is accompanied by a small plan showing the various archaeological features visible on the photograph, emphasising that our understanding of the features visible requires interpretation. Whilst Crawford produced small area plans he also worked on broader landscapes, much as the Aerial Survey section do today for the NMP. His main work concentrated on the area of Salisbury Plain, just to the south-east of the study region, but the work he began laid the foundations for the current working practices in Aerial Survey today, which I will describe below.

Aerial Recconnaissance

The English Heritage reconnaissance programme is divided into three components. Flying is carried out for the north of England from York and for the south by staff based in Swindon, flying out of

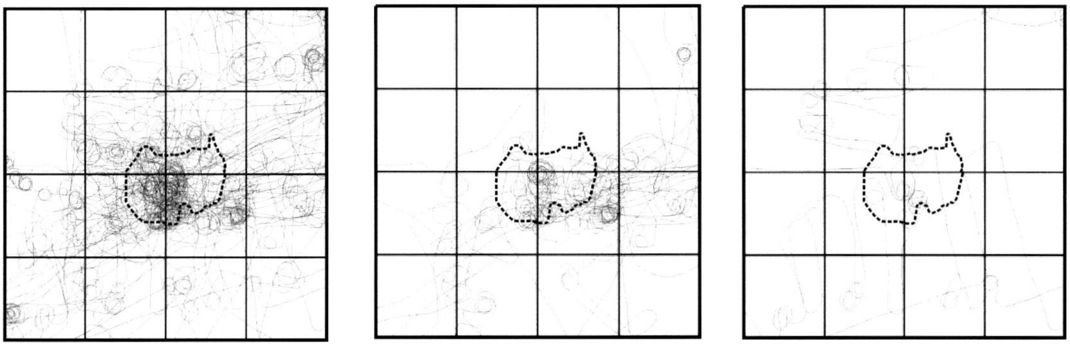

Fig 3:1 Flight traces over the Avebury World Heritage Site – central dotted outline (a) Left all flights 1995 – 2001; (b) centre all flights 1995–6; (c) right all flights 2000 –1. © English Heritage.

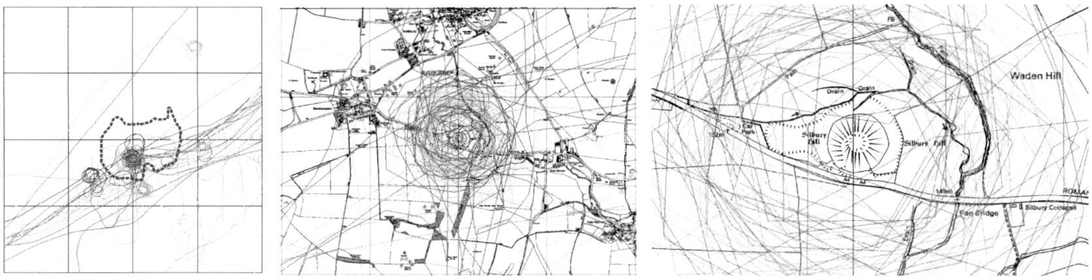

Fig 3:2 (below) Flight traces over the Avebury World Heritage Site – central dotted outline (a) Left – all flights 2001; (b) centre – close-up on 2001 flights; (c) right – extreme close-up showing the cause of concentration of flights – Silbury Hill. © English Heritage.

Fig 3:3 Collapsed shaft on Silbury Hill © English Heritage. NMR (NMR 21034/20) 14-Feb-2001

Kidlington, near Oxford. English Heritage also funds a network of "local flyers" who cover those areas of the country that are difficult to reach for the English Heritage staff. The Marlborough Downs is a busy area of activity as the following flight traces show (Fig 3:1).

These traces cover the area around the Avebury World Heritage Site (the central dotted outline), and show only flights since 1995 by the Royal Commission on the Historical Monuments of England (RCHME), now English Heritage. In the early years, as with other aspects of archaeological investigation in the area, flights tended to concentrate on the known sites in the area, aiming to obtain better pictures rather than specifically looking for new sites. This is particularly noticeable in the trace (1a) from 1995–6 where there is a very clear concentration of circuits around the henge at the centre of the image, partly as a result of the very dry conditions in those years and the first record of the parchmarks within the henge (see below and Bewley *et al* 1996). In more recent years, particularly following the mapping of the area, there has been an attempt at a more systematic approach, aiming to target those areas that appear blank, which has yielded yet more information. It should be noted that the north-west quadrant of the area is relatively blank in terms of flight traces as it lies within the Lyneham Military Air Traffic Zone, which has very restricted terms of access. Since the publication of the Avebury Research Agenda in 2001 (Chadburn & Pomeroy-Kellinger 2001) the reconnaissance programme has also tried to follow some of the priorities highlighted therein (Fig 3:2). In 2001 the focus, however, was very much on Silbury Hill.

The hole, which first appeared in the top of the mound of Silbury Hill over the late May Bank Holiday in 2000 was monitored on a regular basis by the English Heritage reconnaissance team and changes photographed as it grew, and additional collapses occurred (Fig 3:3). The collapse was the result of an excavation that took place in 1776

Fig 3:4 Traces of probable Romano-British field systems and settlement with overlying ridge and furrow on Overton Down. © Crown Copyright. NMR (NMR 15862/28) 11-Dec-1997

(see McOmish *et al* above). The English Heritage reconnaissance programme also records more recent activity such as that by Joshua Pollard and his colleagues at Beckhampton (Pollard this volume) or Mike Pitts at the Sanctuary (Pitts 2000; 2001). The reconnaissance programme continues to survey upstanding earthworks such as the field systems of Overton and Fyfield Downs as changes in lighting conditions and other factors help to highlight previously unrecorded features (Fig 3:4).

Interpretation and Mapping

However, as noted above, although the photographs are a useful record in themselves, they are more effective when integrated with the second aspect of the work of aerial survey: the mapping and interpretation of sites visible on the aerial photographs whether at a large or small scale. The bulk of the work carried out in terms of mapping falls under the National Mapping Programme (NMP). This programme will "map, document and classify, at a common scale and to a common standard, all archaeological sites and landscapes recorded in England on aerial photographs" (Bewley 2001). As such it fits into the broader strategy of the Aerial Survey section of English Heritage, which aims to increase our understanding of past human settlement and land-use. Beginning with pilot projects in Kent and the Thames Valley in the late 1980s, this has progressed through England and by mid 2002 had mapped about 30% of the country. Apart from the more southerly reaches of the Thames Valley project, which extend into the broadest definition of the Marlborough Downs region, there have been four other projects covering parts of the area. The key one is the Avebury World Heritage Site Mapping Project (AWHSMP), but the area is also included at least in part by the Salisbury Plain Training Area (SPTA), the Lambourn Downs Mapping Project (LDMP) and South Berkshire (Small 1999; 2002; Crutchley 2000; McOmish *et al* 2002) (Fig 3:5).

Before going into further detail about the specific projects and their findings it is worthwhile to look briefly at the means by which features on an aerial photograph are transformed into lines on a map. Although the practical application by which this process is carried out has changed dramatically over the past few years, the theory behind it has not. In order to accurately plot features visible on an aerial photograph it is necessary to be able to see a number of "control points" on both the photograph and the base map with which you intend to register it. By comparing the relative position of the control points in terms of distance and angle between one another and the features you wish to map it is possible to plot the features in their true ground position. In the past this was done manually by eye, or using network grids, but with the increased use of

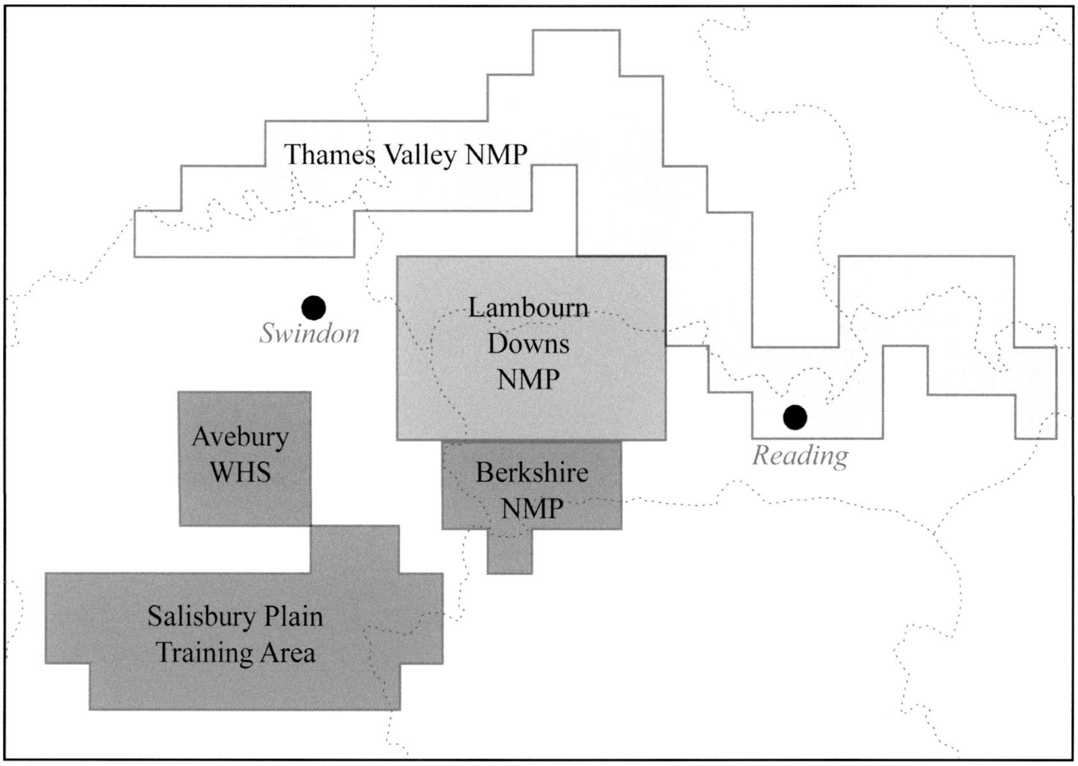

Fig 3:5 NMP projects covering parts of the Marlborough Downs region. © English Heritage.

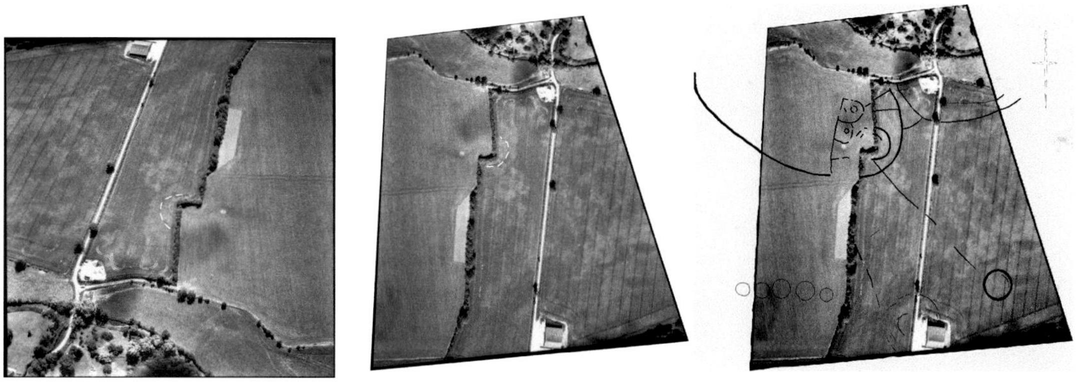

Fig 3:6 The photo rectification process: a) A photograph of West Kennet Enclosure 2 seen as a cropmark and showing evidence of the main enclosure ditch and one of the smaller sub-circular ditch-defined enclosures in the interior (white pecked line). This is a standard scan and shows the photograph with no geo-referencing, b) The same photograph after rectification. This is now correctly referenced with north to the top and, c) The same photograph, this time with the archaeological detail traced off and combined with information from other photographs. © English Heritage.

computers and digital imagery it is now possible to scan an oblique photograph (Fig 3:6a), and using software designed by John Haigh at the University of Bradford (Haigh 1996) rectify it so that it is turned into a plan view with all the effects of perspective distortion removed (Fig 3:6b). Once this rectified image has been created it is then possible to import it into various drawing packages, from where the details of the archaeological features can be copied. These can then be combined with information from other photographs taken at different times to create a composite view of all the archaeological features (Fig 3:6c).

With the move to working in a digital environment it is now possible to create a plot of the landscape as a whole across any given area that has been mapped, at an appropriate scale. This allows the creation of very large-scale maps of entire areas, which give a good impression of the overall archaeological nature and density. The plot below, which covers the Lambourn Downs, illustrates the difference between the prehistoric and Roman banked field systems on the High Downs and the medieval and later ridge and furrow cultivation in the clay vale (Fig 3:7). It is of course also possible to zoom in on a specific area and look at the relationship between specific sites, as here in the area around Alfred's Castle on the western end of the Downs (Fig 3:8).

The same type of analysis can be carried out at Avebury, both with the overall area again showing the separation between the fields on the high downs and those in the vales (Fig 3:9) and more

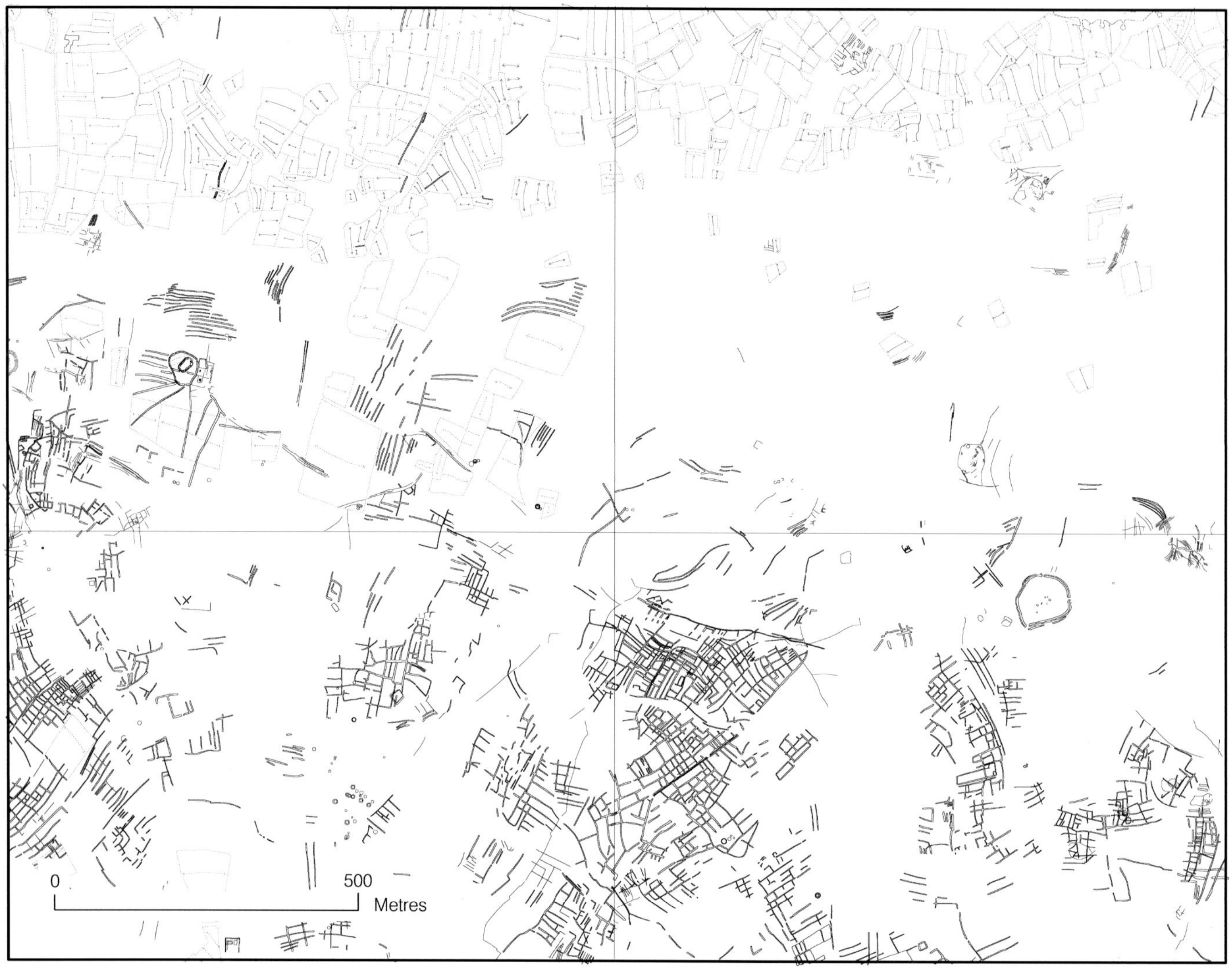

Fig 3:7 The north-western part of the area mapped for the Lambourn Downs mapping project showing the overall distribution and nature of sites. Note especially the difference between the distribution of the small prehistoric and Roman fields on the Downs (black) and the medieval ridge and furrow cultivation in the vale (grey). © English Heritage.

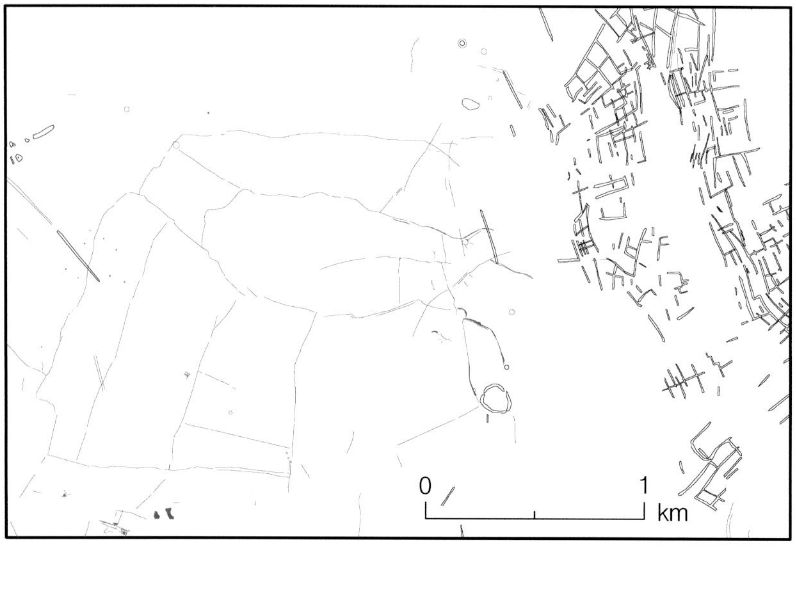

Fig 3:8 Close-up on the area around Alfred's Castle showing the different relationships between the small, banked fields to the right (black) and the large ditched fields to the left (grey). © English Heritage.

detailed analysis of specific recent discoveries (Figs 3:10–3:14).

One of the most exciting finds in the Avebury area was made several years ago, but we are still no wiser as to its function or date. On September 1st 1995 a flight was made with a BBC film crew over Avebury on which some photographs of the henge were taken: the particularly dry weather had revealed traces of a number of the settings for no longer extant stones in the inner circles. When the prints were later examined there was clear evidence of a previously unknown double-

ditched curvilinear enclosure in the north-west quadrant (Bewley *et al* 1996; and see Fig 3:10). This feature was later subject to both resistivity and magnotometry survey, which confirmed its shape and location, but there is still no clear consensus as to what it is and since it is not under threat and lies at the heart of a scheduled guardianship site it is unlikely to be excavated in the near future.

Fig 3:9 Plan of the core Avebury area with the henge at the centre. Extensive traces of 'Celtic' fields on the higher ground to the northeast and south contrast with the lack of such features along the Kennet valley and on the Lower Chalk to the northwest. The latter may be the result of medieval and later cultivation in those areas.

Aerial reconnaissance has also made other exciting new discoveries in the Avebury area. Although there had previously been geophysical

Fig 3:10 Northern quadrants of the Neolithic henge at Avebury showing the feature newly discovered in 1995 in the approximate centre of the photograph and a number of stone holes visible in an arc to the left. © Crown copyright. NMR (NMR 15383/19) 1-Sep-1995.

Fig 3:11 Close-up view of the Neolithic enclosure at Beckhampton first identified by aerial survey in April 1997. The enclosure passes between the two standing stones Adam and Eve that have now been shown to be part of the lost Beckhampton Avenue. The pale area to the upper left side of the image marks the location of the Neolithic South Street long barrow. © Crown copyright. NMR (NMR 15621/16) 7-Apr-1997.

survey in Longstones field it was the discovery of the Neolithic enclosure on 7th April 1997 that led to the excavations in the fields where the Beckhampton Avenue was found (Pollard *this volume*).

More recently still, reconnaissance in the area has added some important new information about yet another key site. The palisade enclosures at West Kennet were first recognised on aerial photographs taken by J K St Joseph of Cambridge University in 1950 and their full extent plotted by RCHME (RCHME 1992; Whittle 1997a). Excavations carried out by Whittle between 1987 and 1992 concentrated very much on Enclosure 2 to the west, largely due to the presence of a number of sub-circular features within it, which turned out to be further post-built structures. Enclosure 1 to the east differed from Enclosure 2 in that it had a double-ditched circuit rather than single, and there was no evidence of any internal features. At least this was the case until April 2000 when a reconnaissance flight recorded the presence of a circular pit-defined feature between the two circuits of the ditches (Fig 3:12), and revealed evidence of greater complexity inside Enclosure 2. The earlier aerial survey had shown that both inside and outside Enclosure 2 were a series of radial ditches. The photographs taken in 2000 showed that the radial ditches at the northern edge of the visible part of the enclosure apparently had breaks in the centre. These could be interpreted as terminals, defined by a clear broadening of the ditch, possibly indicating the presence of an exceptionally large post pipe. There were at least two cross ditches with gaps and the interesting fact is that these gaps appear to lead through to one of the largest of the internal structures, suggesting that this might have been some sort of routeway or avenue.

In 2001 reconnaissance demonstrated that there are still features being revealed through the destructive processes of ploughing. The area of Harestone Down, approximately two kilometres south of the West Kennet palisade enclosures, was plotted as part of the AWHSMP in March 1999 and was seen to be covered in traces of small banked fields typical of the downland (Fig 3:13a). Photographs taken on a flight in June 2001, however, showed that almost all traces of these fields have now been ploughed away revealing the features underneath, in this case a sub-circular enclosure (Figs 3:13b and 3:14). Indeed a second flight in August revealed yet more features, which are discussed in a forthcoming article (Barber *et al* 2003).

Conclusion

This paper has shown how the recent work in the Marlborough Downs region by the English Heritage Aerial Survey section has been representative of its work across the country. Aerial survey

Fig 3:12 Close-up view of the Neolithic palisade enclosures at West Kennet with the newly identified pit circle (centre) and terminal breaks (top right). © English Heritage. NMR (NMR 18747/14) 15-Jul-2000

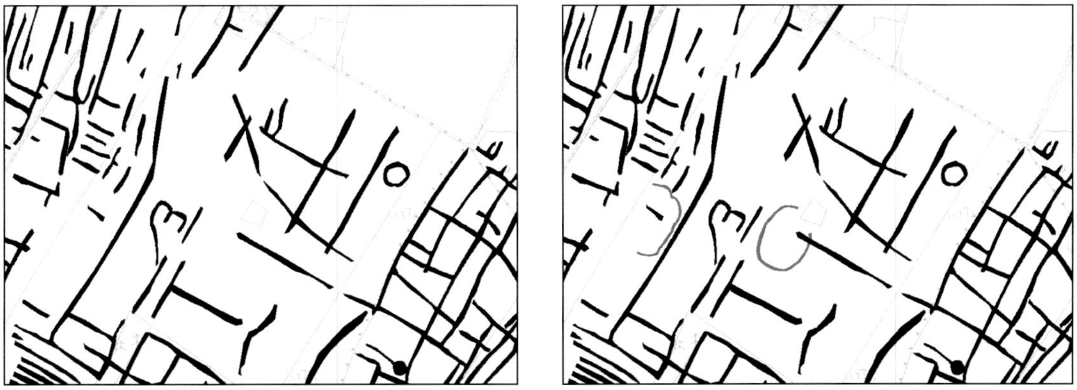

Fig 3:13 Plots of the Harestone Down area showing (a) the traces of banked fields plotted in 1999 (black) and (b) the same with the enclosure revealed by continued ploughing (grey). © English Heritage.

3:14 Newly revealed enclosure on Harestone Down © English Heritage. NMR (NMR 21182/34) 21-Jun-2001.

is a cyclical process, which begins with the finding of new sites and the taking of photographs, but does not end there. The mapping and interpretation of sites whether at large or small scale, helps to build up a picture of ancient settlement patterns and land-use helping us to better understand the past. Although this is an important step in understanding the historic environment, it is only a beginning and further investigation is required on the ground and involving excavation in order to understand the date and function of those sites and landscapes.

Acknowledgements

This paper is based on work carried out by all the staff of the Aerial Survey section at English Heritage in Swindon. Special mention needs to be given to Fiona Small who co-ordinated the AWHS project and wrote the report on which I have drawn for data, and also Damian Grady, Cathy Stoertz and Helen Winton who carried out the mapping. I should also thank Damian again in his role as Head of Reconnaissance for taking a number of the photographs I have used and providing flight traces. I also need to thank his predecessor Roger Featherstone, who took many of the earlier photographs, some of which are reproduced here, but others of which were key for the mapping project. I should also thank the staff at the NMR who processed the photographs and provided them to the mapping team. Finally I wish to thank Bob Bewley for commenting on earlier drafts of the paper.

4
The investigation of sites on the Marlborough Downs using geophysical methods

Andrew David

Together with aerial photographic analysis and earthwork survey the Marlborough Downs and their environs offer marvellous opportunities for the application of geophysical methods of archaeological prospecting. The chalkland soils are highly susceptible to magnetic enhancement and the signatures of former settlements, hilltop enclosures, and ceremonial sites can often be detected and investigated by magnetometers in remarkable detail. Magnetic survey is becoming capable of both greater coverage and sensitivity and will remain one of the most powerful methods of site definition. Earth resistance survey, whilst still more laborious to apply, has complementary potential, especially for focusing upon the definition of structural remains: funerary monuments, buildings and buried monoliths. Integrated with other methods of reconnaissance, these and other geophysical methods have much to offer. This paper will review the use of geophysics in the Marlborough Downs area and will draw attention to its future potential for research and site management.

Introduction

Geophysical survey has an honourable place in the history of archaeological investigations in the Marlborough Downs area. Non-destructive testing, if not exactly geophysical survey, begins at least in the nineteenth century when antiquarians such as A C Smith and W C Lukis probed for buried sarsens at Avebury (eg Lukis 1881) and at Winterbourne Basset (Smith 1885). Later, the same method was applied on the West Kennet Avenue (Passmore 1926), and on Windmill Hill during 1925–9, by Alexander Keiller, who used a specially made skewer to locate pits, noting that the results were 'quite remarkable, and far surpassed thumping in certainty and accuracy' (A Keiller manuscripts held at Alexander Keiller Museum, Avebury). 'Thumping' refers to a genuinely geophysical method, a primitive form of seismics, later termed 'bosing' (Atkinson 1953; Curwen 1930), when archaeologically significant variations in the resonance of the ground were heard as it was walloped with a hammer or crow bar.

The rather more reliable method of earth resistance survey was first applied in archaeology in 1946, and it was at *Cunetio*, near Marlborough, 10 years later, that A J Clark so successfully demonstrated the first transistorised resistivity meter (Clark 1957; 1996). A prototype of the Martin-Clark meter was able to detect the town wall, and bastions, allowing the precise placement of trenches that confirmed their position and character. Rather less successfully, resistivity measurements were made on Silbury Hill in 1959, in an attempt to locate a burial chamber (McKim 1959). And in 1968, Silbury Hill was the site of an early application of seismic survey, which was used to measure the depth of the ditch (Whittle 1997a, 24).

More recently, earth resistance and magnetic methods have come to predominate in archaeological geophysics and have been used to considerable effect in this area, contributing notably to the study of the Avebury henge complex (Ucko *et al* 1990; Bewley *et al* 1996; Gillings *et al* 2000a), and to outlying prehistoric, Iron Age and Roman settlement sites (David 2001; Payne in press). The area also continues to witness experimentation with less familiar methods, such as ground penetrating radar at Adams Grave (C Shell and C Pierce *pers comm*) and, at Silbury Hill again, with recent and novel use of 3D seismic tomography.

A crude attempt at listing all geophysical surveys undertaken within the study area has been made in Table 4:I (which now supersedes that published previously: David 2001). A distribution of these surveys is shown in Fig 4:1. Overall, the methods which have seen the most sustained application, as they have much more widely in the

Table 4:1 Geophysical surveys in the Marlborough Downs area

Location	Grid Ref	Date	By whom	Type	Reference
Avebury Henge	SU 102 700	1975–96	AML	mag, res, EM	Ucko *et al.* 1990; Cole et al 1996
Avebury Cove	SU 1024 7001	1998	Aperio Ltd.	GPR	Dodds and Eddies 1998
E entrance to Avebury Henge	SU 105 701	1990	AML	res	Ucko *et al.* 1990
Avebury Car Park	SU 099 698	1984	AML	mag	David 1984, unpublished
Avebury Manor	SU 099 700	1991	A Bartlett	mag, res	Unpublished: NT archive
West Kennet Avenue	SU 111 686	1990	AML	res, mag	Ucko *et al.* 1990
West Kennet Avenue	SU 108 690	1997–98	Cambridge Univ	GPR, res	Unpublished
Beckhampton Avenue, Longstones Field	SU 090 693	1975–00	AML/CfA	mag, res, GPR	Ucko *et al.* 1990; David 1999, 2000, unpub
Longstones Barrow field	SU 087 691	2002	CfA	mag, res	Unpublished
Beckhampton barrow cemetery (Area A)	SU 092 690	1993	GSB	mag, MS	Powell *et al.* 1996
SW of Beckhampton roundabout	SU 086 688	2001	Leicester Univ	res	Gillings *et al.* 2002, unpub
Devizes Road	SU 083 688	2002	Leicester Univ	res	Unpublished
Falkner's Circle	SU 110 693	2002	CfA	mag, res	Unpublished
Winterbourne Bassett stone circles	SU 093 755	1998	AML	mag, res	David *et al* 2002
Silbury Hill	SU 100 685	1959	F R McKim	res	McKim 1959
Silbury Hill (ditch)	SU 100 685	1968	?Cardiff Univ	seismic	Whittle 1997a
Silbury Hill	SU 100 685	2001	CfA	res, mag, GPR	N Linford 2001; P Linford 2001, unpub
Silbury Hill	SU 100 685	2001–2	Cementation-Skanska	seismic	Unpublished
Silbury Hill ditch	SU 100 685	1968–70	UCSWM	seismic	Whittle 1997a
Waden Hill	SU 105 684	1997	Cardiff Univ	mag	Unpub
Silbury/Waden (Area B)	SU 103 685	1993	GSB	mag, MS	Powell *et al.* 1996
Other foul sewer line sites (Area D)	SU 137 672	1993	GSB	mag, MS	Powell *et al.* 1996
Windmill Hill	SU 087 714	1988–93	AML	mag	Whittle *et al.* 1999

Windmill Hill	SU 090 711	1988, 1993	Cardiff Univ	mag, res, MS	Banham 1995, unpub; Whittle *et al.* 2000
West Kennet Enclosures	SU 109 681	1989	Cardiff Univ	mag	Unpub
West Kennet Enclosures	SU 109 681	1991–2	Cambridge Univ	mag	Unpub
Easton Down long barrow	SU 063 661	1991	Cardiff Univ	mag	Whittle *et al.* 1993, 200; Cardiff Univ archive.
Millbarrow	SU 094 722	1989	Cardiff Univ	mag	Whittle 1994
South Street long barrow	SU 090692	1966, 2000	AJClark; CfA	mag	Ashbee *et al.* 1979; Martin 2001, unpub
Horslip Long barrow	SU 086 705	2000	CfA	mag	Martin 2001, unpub
West Kennet long barrow	SU 104 677	1991, 2001	AML, CfA	mag, res, EM	Martin 2001, unpub
The Sanctuary	SU 118 680	1999	Cambridge Univ	mag	Unpub
The Sanctuary café	SU 118 681	1998	Cardiff Univ	mag	Unpub
Avebury G21	SU 110 692	1997	Cardiff Univ	mag	Unpub
SW side of Overton Hill: barrows G24, G25, G25a		1989	Cardiff Univ	mag	Hamilton 1997, unpub
Avebury G29a, Overton Hill	SU 116 689	1997, 1998	Cardiff Univ	mag mag	Hamilton 1997, unpub Hamilton and Dennis 1998, unpub
Overton Hill, 'causewayed enclosure'	SU 114 684	1989	Cardiff Univ	mag	Unpub
Wroughton Copse(Fyfield Down)	SU 138 707	?	?	mag, res	Fowler 2000, 34, 46
Site X/XI (Overton Down)	SU 132 703	?	?	mag, res	Fowler 2000, 34, 46
North Farm West Overton G16	SU 132 686	1998	Cardiff Univ	mag, res	Hamilton, Dennis and Swanton 1998, unpub
North Farm 'Headlands' enclosure	SU 128 686	1999	Cardiff Univ	mag	Hamilton et al 1999, unpub,; Fowler 2000, 48.
Adam's Grave	SU 112 634	1997–8	Cambridge Univ	GPR, res	Unpub
Oldbury Hillfort	SU 049 693	1996	AML	mag	A Payne forthcoming
Liddington Castle		1996	AML	mag	A Payne forthcoming
Oliver's Castle	SU 001 647	1996	AML	mag	A Payne forthcoming
Martinsell Camp	SU 176 639	1996	AML	mag	A Payne forthcoming

Barbury Castle	SU 149 763	1996	AML	mag	A Payne forthcoming
Burderop Down	SU 168 764	1979	AML	mag	David 1981, unpub
Smeathes Ridge	SU 16288 75704	1998	AML	mag	Bray 1998, unpub
Coombe Down	SU 18230 74470	1998	AML	mag	Bray 1998, unpub
Barrow S of Liddington Castle	SU 21445 78138	1998	AML	mag	Bray 1998, unpub
Dean Bottom	SU 148 741	1977 1978	AML D Bonney & H Welfare	mag mag	Bartlett 1978, unpub Gingell 1992, 159
Foxhill, Wanborough	SU 237 809	1984	AML	res	Unpub
Ogbourne St Andrew churchyard	SU188 723	1999	Cardiff Univ	res	Unpub
Castle Copse, Bedwyn	SU 284 629	1984	AML	mag	Unpublished; Hostetter and Howe 1997
Castle Copse, Bedwyn	SU 284 629	1985	Bradford Univ	res	Hostetter and Howe 1997
Cunetio	SU 216 695	1956	A J Clark	res	Clark 1957, 1996
Tockenham	SU 0388 7971	1994	GSB	mag, res	Harding & Lewis 1997
Compton Bassett		1996–8	Cardiff Univ	mag	Unpub
Yatesbury	SU 071 699 SU 605 715 SU 074 707	1993 1996 1996–8	Cardiff Univ	mag, res	Unpub
Golden Ball Hill	SU 126 640	1997–8	Cardiff Univ	mag, res	Dennis and Hamilton, 1997, unpub
Wansdyke		1970–?	A J Clark	mag, res	Unpub

UK, are earth resistance and magnetic surveys, and it is on the results of these that the following review will concentrate. It has been preceded recently by a similar review included in the Archaeological Research Agenda for the Avebury World Heritage Site (Chadburn & Pomeroy-Kellinger 2001). Although the latter covers a smaller area than that now under consideration it contains much that is deliberately not further duplicated below; however, both accounts will inevitably share some common ground. One point of agreement, worth stressing again here, is that the strength of geophysical survey is best realised when informed by, and informing upon, other means of archaeological prospecting, not least – of course – aerial reconnaissance and field walking, but also coring, geochemical survey, documentary research, and the evidence from metal detecting.

The Surveys

No attempt will be made here to describe in detail the theory or methodologies of geophysical survey. This is already available elsewhere (eg Tite

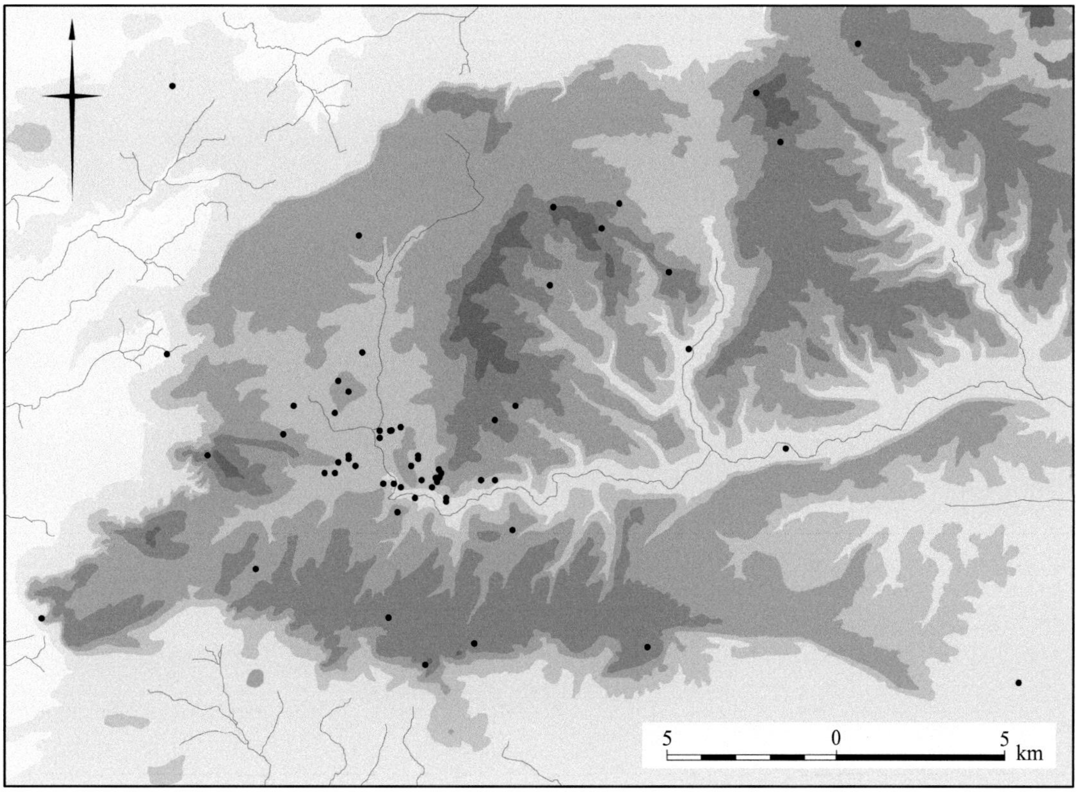

Fig 4:1 Distribution of geophysical surveys. © *English Heritage*

1972; Aitken 1974; Scollar *et al* 1990; English Heritage 1995; Clark 1996). The following will instead be a generalised review of current results, illustrated by a number of individual examples, and including some thoughts on the future potential of the methods for the archaeology of the Marlborough Downs.

Magnetometer survey

The viability of magnetometer survey in the Marlborough landscape is much benefited by the prevailing geology, soils and surface conditions. The solid substrate of much of the area is of course chalk, and the soils developed over this, and its cappings of 'clay-with-flints' are susceptible to magnetic enhancement by activities associated with human settlement. Magnetometer survey has therefore been the foremost geophysical method used in the search for, and definition of, settlements and has also proved valuable in the planning of field systems and ditched burial sites. Results are best over shallower soils, ironically often in circumstances where significant destructive erosion is well progressed and the surface expression of monuments has already been mostly effaced. Where prominent earthworks survive, the underlying magnetic signal can be weakened, and the effect is even more pronounced where sites are more deeply protected by overlying colluvial and alluvial deposits on valley sides and floors. To the west of the downland chalk, there is less experience of magnetic methods to draw upon, but it seems likely that the claylands will be less responsive, whilst surveys over the Greensands and Jurassic calcareous rags and grits are capable of producing excellent results.

From a chronological perspective, the benefits of magnetometer survey are first apparent in the Neolithic. Whilst Mesolithic hearths and pits should be detectable, there are no certain instances yet where this has been demonstrated in our area. However, as soon as ditches came to be dug by agricultural communities, to create enclosures and burial monuments, their traces become detectable. On Windmill Hill, for instance, the fills of all three enclosure ditches provide weak but nonetheless distinct magnetic anomalies, the gaps in which identify the characteristic causeways (Whittle *et al* 1999, figs 16–17). Other anomalies indicate the presence of pits, as well as a previously unrecorded ring ditch and later agricultural features. The identity of Alexander Keiller's excavation trenches was all too clearly demonstrated by the detection of ferrous litter within their backfillings. These results, integrated with those of aerial and earthwork survey, together with more recent excavation, have greatly improved the knowledge of the hilltop (*ibid*).

Other Neolithic enclosures, first identified by aerial survey, have also proved to be detectable magnetically allowing their precise location on the

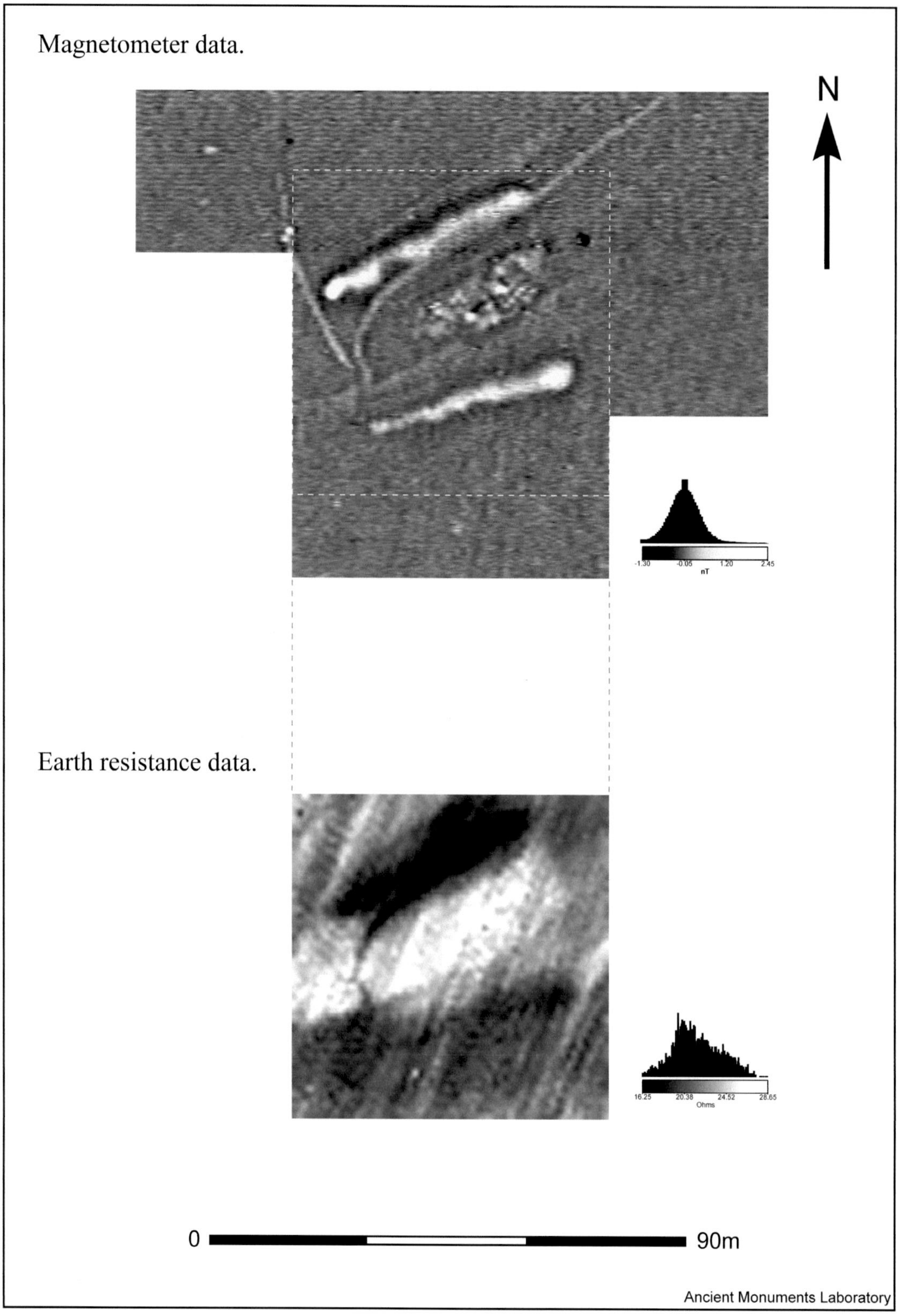

Fig 4:2 Magnetic and resistivity surveys over the Shepherds Shore long barrow. © English Heritage

ground and the recognition of additional detail. The West Kennet palisade enclosures, though largely mapped by aerial photography, were also partly detected by surveys conducted by Cambridge and Cardiff Universities (Whittle 1997a; M Hamilton *pers comm*). Apart from the enclosing palisade ditches, magnetometer survey was able to locate the internal ring features of Structures 1–3 in Enclosure 2 and help guide excavations there (Whittle 1997a, 83–6). At Beckhampton, near the Longstones, magnetometer survey by the Ancient Monuments Laboratory (AML) in 1989 detected traces of the ditched enclosure later fully recognised and identified by aerial photography in 1997 (Gillings *et al* 2000a).

Neolithic burial monuments have also proved very amenable to magnetic survey and fieldwork has been conducted on four long barrows. In each case evidence for the presence of flanking ditches has been detected although only very weakly at South Street and Horslip (Martin 2001a) – but sufficient to define a suitable area over which further cultivation is now suspended. At West Kennet, however, the ditches were clearly detected and shown to survive well outside the area currently protected by fencing (Martin 2001b), although not so far out as indicated by earthwork survey (McOmish *et al* this volume). Some evidence for a scatter of pits was found to the east of the forecourt, and some 60m to the south of the barrow a substantial pit or cluster of pits was located – perhaps a modern feature, but nonetheless provoking speculation on its possible association with the mound (Martin 2001b). The most spectacular results, however, were achieved over the ploughed-down long barrow at Shepherd's Shore, about half way between Devizes and Avebury (SU 0387 6608; Bray 1998a). Although the barrow had been previously investigated by excavation in 1860 and 1927 (Cunnington 1926a), no ditches were then observed. The magnetic data not only reveals with great clarity the substantial flanking ditches, spaced 30m apart to either side of the former mound, but also a central area of disturbance (Fig 4:2). The extent of the latter suggests that archaeological deposits have survived previous interventions, and that perhaps some form of burnt material may be present (despite the fact that Cunnington saw no ashes or signs of fire). The data also defines at least two linear ditches, impinging upon the monument, which are probably later features. Together with earth resistance data, the geophysical survey here has significantly advanced knowledge of a complex and demonstrably quite well preserved site. That such results are not confined just to the odd circumstance, is shown by equally important results from surveys of long barrows further afield at, Tilshead and Rockbourne, Hants (Payne, 2000; Martin and Cromwell 2002).

Coming forward, into the Bronze Age, the most notable contribution of magnetometer survey has been in the location of round barrow ditches. Occasionally, as on Windmill Hill, previously unrecorded ring ditches can be found. More typically, magnetic survey provides corroboration of aerial photographic evidence and can play an important role in the verification (or not, as the case may be) of the positions of recorded, and scheduled, monuments. As part of a project to study plough-damaged examples of the latter, the AML surveyed the apparent sites of three barrows on, respectively, Smeathes Ridge (AM194), Coombe Down (AM618) and near Liddington (AM599). Although possible archaeological anomalies were located in approximately the expected locations, none of these were ring ditches, and doubt therefore remains concerning both the survival and the real location of these monuments – and perhaps many other similarly

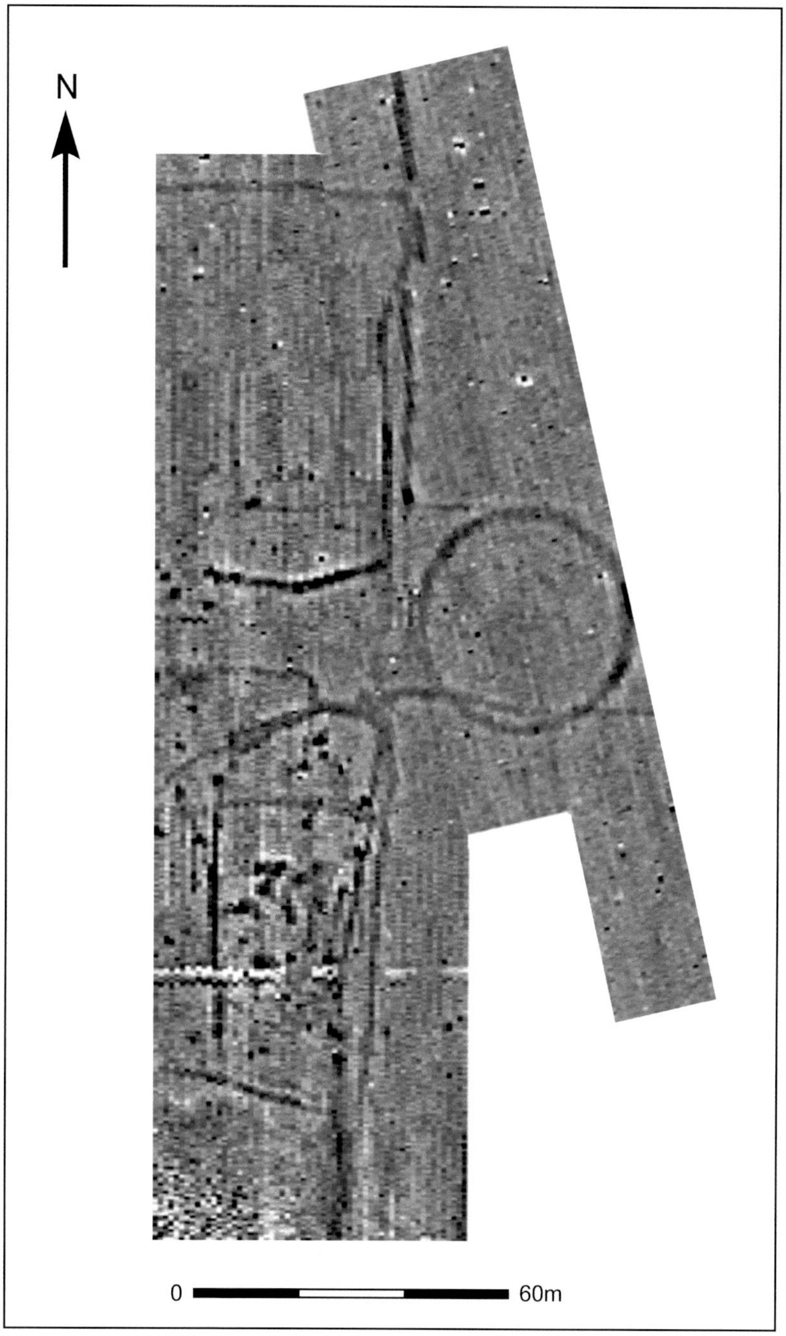

Fig 4:3 Magnetometer survey over a ring ditch (and Roman settlement) at Yatesbury Field. © Cardiff University.

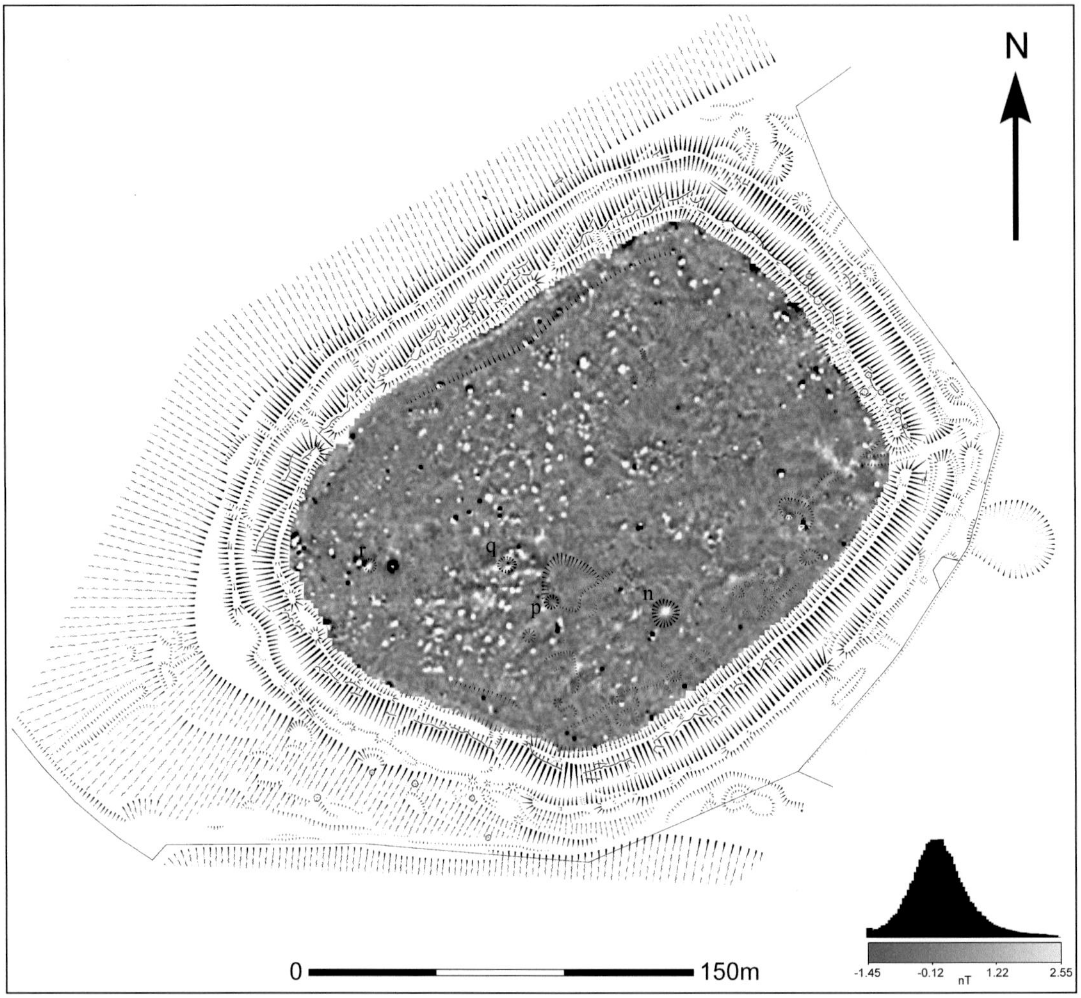

Fig 4:4 Magnetometer survey over Liddington Castle hillfort. © English Heritage.

flattened and insecurely recorded examples (Bray 1998b). Similarly ambiguous results were obtained by Cardiff University, unable to locate a barrow at G21 near Avebury, or a possible ring ditch near barrow G29A on Overton Hill (Hamilton 1997, Hamilton and Dennis 1998). Such ambiguity is difficult to reconcile with the very clear magnetic signatures obtained over other ring ditches elsewhere on Overton Hill (G24, 25 and 25A), and for example at Yatesbury Field (Fig 4:3), over the Beckhampton barrow cemetery (GSB 1992a; Powell *et al* 1966 fig 4), and on the southern extremity of Waden Hill (Hamilton *pers comm*).

So far, magnetometer survey has not yet had much application over known Bronze Age settlements or field systems, both of which are important but still poorly understood constituents of downland archaeology (McOmish this volume). Early AML surveys at Dean Bottom and Burderop Down, in 1977 and 1979 respectively, were probably too limited to be very informative (Gingell 1992), and their indifferent results reflect a relative absence of surviving robust and shallow features capable of providing detectable magnetic contrasts. At other sites, where pits, ditches, hearths and perhaps metal-working might be expected, it can be anticipated that modern surveys, with much expanded coverage, might well be very much more productive. Obvious targets for such survey are provided by concentrations of flints and potsherds located by fieldwalking (eg Horton Down: Wheatley *pers comm* in Pollard and Reynolds 2002).

Features such as those just referred to, if relatively poorly recorded in Bronze Age contexts seem to be more abundant later, in the Iron Age, and no more so than in the defended hilltop enclosures of the Downs. Five hillforts in the area have now been surveyed by magnetometry as part of the English Heritage Wessex Hillforts Project: Oldbury, Liddington, Oliver's Castle, Martinsell Camp and Barbury Castle (Payne in press). In each case the results have been highly informative and well illustrate the contribution that geophysical survey can make towards the furtherance of both academic study and conserv-

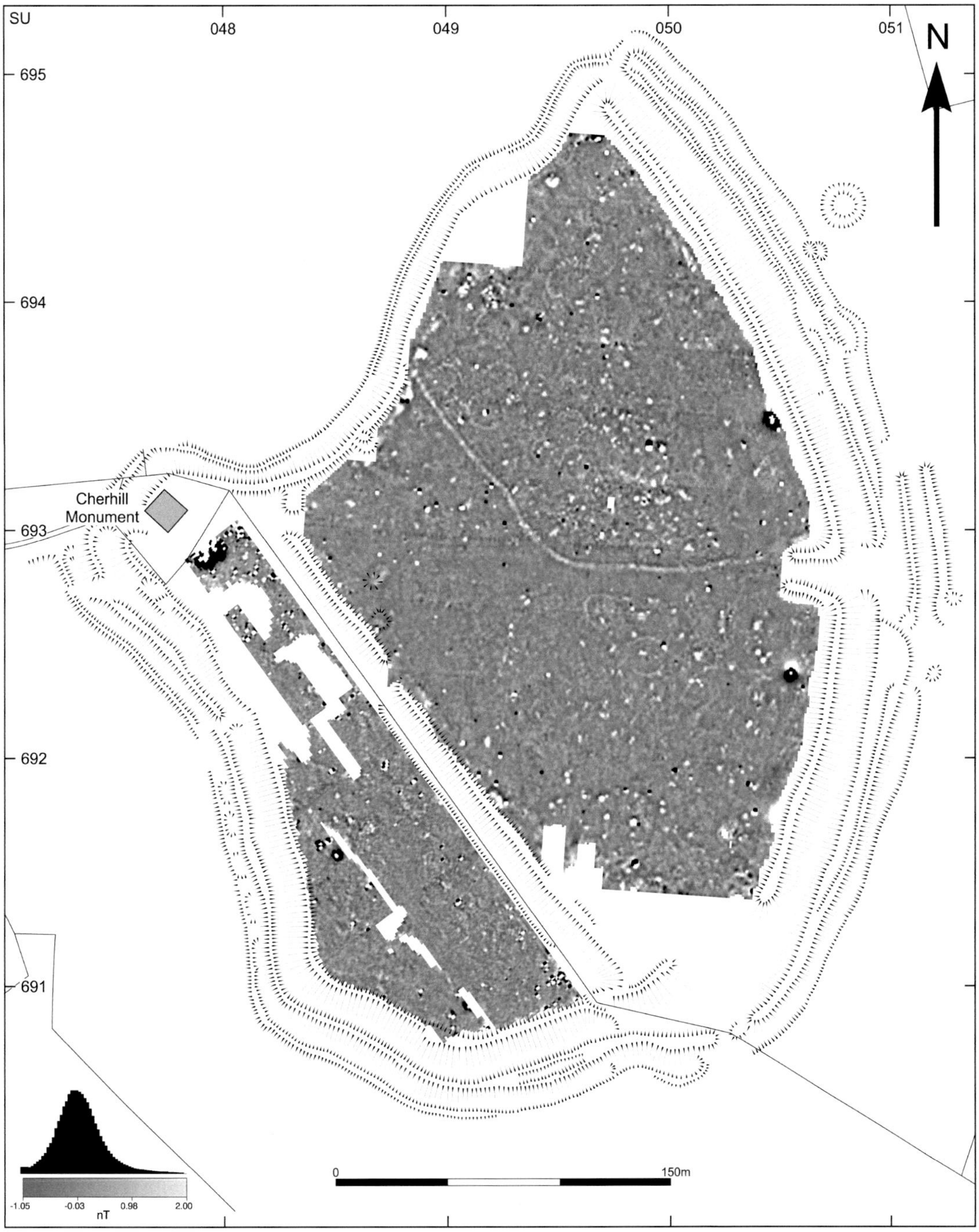

Fig 4:5 Magnetometer survey over Oldbury hillfort. © English Heritage.

ation of a conspicuous category of monument. It is neither desirable nor economic to excavate such sites, yet for these reasons they are relatively poorly understood and information on them must be maximised in other ways to nurture what remains; and geophysical survey provides just such an opportunity.

The hillforts in our study area are each located on the rim of the higher downland, yet there is considerable variation of shape and size and, as the magnetic surveys reveal, in their sub-surface characteristics. Both Barbury and Liddington Castles are shown to contain dense concentrations of anomalies, mostly interpreted as pits. Barbury, especially, is evidently packed from rampart to rampart with pits which, despite WWII activities on the hilltop, are best interpreted as evidence of prolonged and intensive settlement activity. Such is the density of these anomalies that they may have obscured the more subtle magnetic evidence for the house sites suggested by surface survey (Bowden 1998). Together with the evidence of

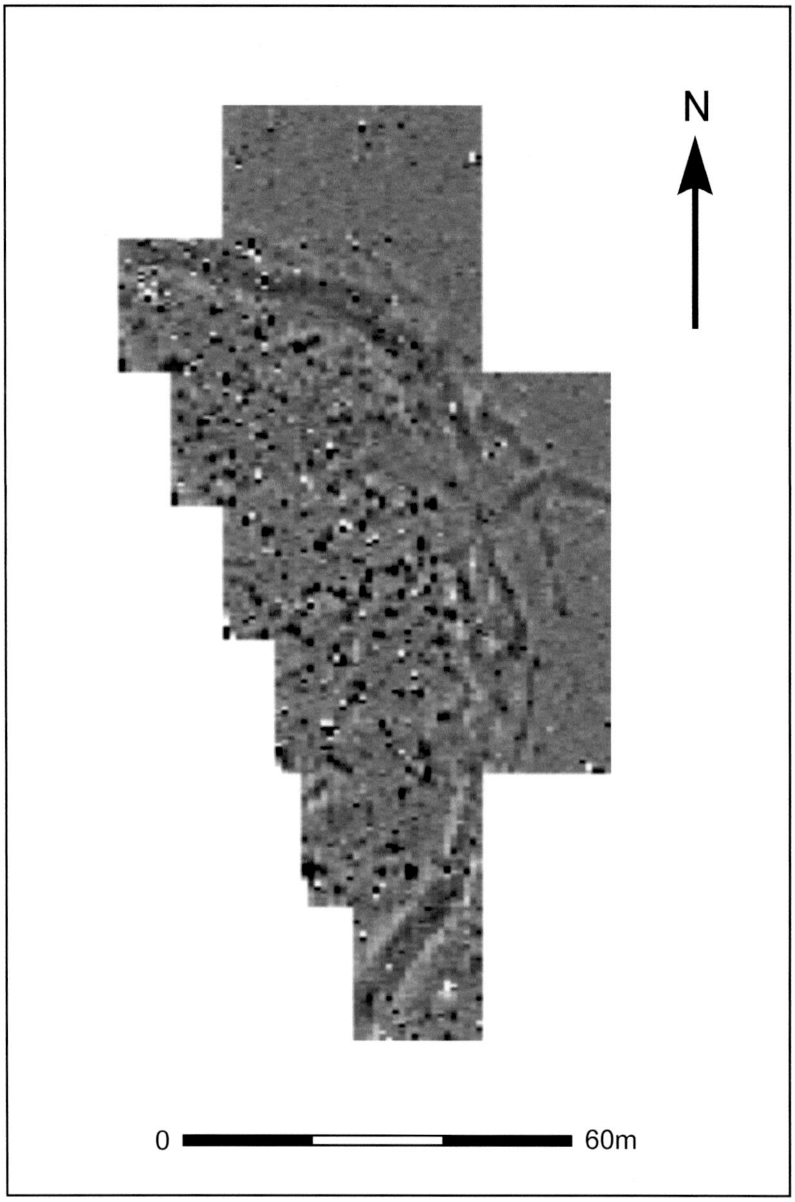

Fig 4:6 Magnetometer survey over part of the Headlands Enclosure, West Overton. © Cardiff University.

substantial and complex multi-vallate defences, Barbury is clearly a developed hillfort of commanding significance then as now. Liddington (Fig 4:4), its slighter but no less prominent neighbour to the north-east, contains fewer pits but these cluster suggestively, within areas of much reduced activity. There are hints of circular hut gullies too, and one clear ring ditch which, if not an earlier barrow may, on account of its unusually large size (18m diameter), be speculated to be a more specialised structure, even a shrine (Payne in press).

Similar results (Fig 4:5) were obtained over the larger fort at Oldbury on Cherhill Hill, except here the magnetometer detected a hitherto unsuspected phase of the site's development, defined by a curving cross-ditch isolating the northern third of the fort from the rest. Whether this represents an early phase or a later retrenchment is not yet clear; pits and ring gullies concentrate within the northern enclosure, but are present to the south of it as well.

By comparison with the foregoing, the results from Oliver's Castle and Martinsell Camp are unspectacular even if the archaeological implications are nonetheless of significance – as neither site showed any clear evidence of occupation. Oliver's Castle was dominated by patterns of ferrous disturbance of recent origin, and an infilled pond, but the intervening spaces demonstrate that the hillfort is devoid of other detectable remains. Martinsell Camp, at 10 hectares the largest of the sample of forts surveyed in the Marlborough Downs area, is defined by relatively slight earthworks. Also in contrast to the interiors of Oldbury, Barbury and Liddington, that at Martinsell seems barren of pits and ring gullies. What magnetic activity there is seems better explained as responses to natural features or flint digging. Whilst occupation cannot exactly be dismissed on such evidence, the strong presumption must be that any such activity was slight, and the site probably radically different to the others in conception and use (Payne in press).

Hillforts are of course rather a special case where enlightenment by geophysical survey is so demonstrable. However, undefended Iron Age settlements are equally if not more amenable to magnetometer survey and should become targets for future fieldwork. The potential has so far barely been exploited in the area but is made readily apparent by the survey of part of the Headlands enclosure on the north side of the Kennet valley at West Overton (Fig 4:6: Hamilton *et al* 1999; Fowler 2000, 56).

Indeed, settlement activity and field systems are just as detectable in the Late Iron Age and Roman periods and there is enormous potential for the detailed mapping of farmsteads, estates and villas – as well as industrial, ritual, military sites, and roads. Taking the example mentioned above, extension of the survey of the Headlands enclosure to encompass the suggested villa (Fowler 2000, 56), as well as many other elements of this landscape palimpsest (*ibid* fig 4.2), would be hugely well repaid (see note). Nearer Avebury, the Waden Hill/Silbury Hill Roman settlement (Corney 1997a) has been shown to be very responsive to magnetometer survey (GSB 1992b; Hamilton *pers comm*) but only small areas have been covered, and more extensive work would no doubt be very well repaid. Further to the west, magnetic survey followed by trial excavations has identified a probable late Roman farmstead (Pollard and Reynolds 157–8, fig 65). And in the

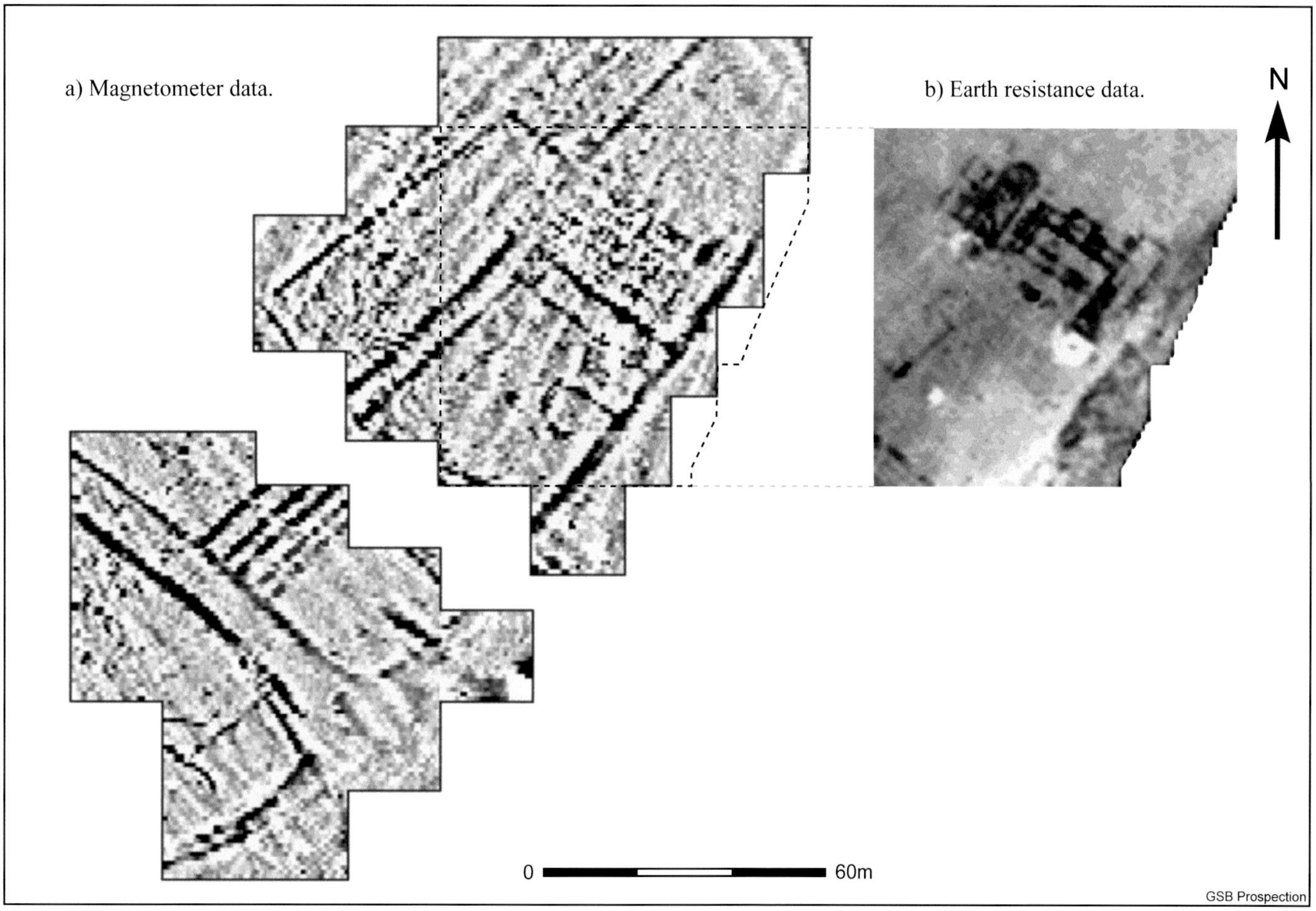

Fig 4:7 Magnetometer and earth resistance surveys over the Tockenham villa. © GSB Prospection.

far north-west of our area a more high-status complex, centred upon a villa, was revealed by magnetometer survey over Jurassic Calcareous Grit at Tockenham by GSB Prospection (Harding and Lewis 1997). The survey clearly identified the enclosures associated with the villa as well as adjoining trackways (Fig 4:7a). The villa itself is not well defined by this data, which should not be surprising, but it was instead mapped in detail by an earth resistance survey (Fig 4:7b; see below).

Once the Romans depart the scene however, the magnetic record has so far made only a negligible contribution to what little evidence there seems to be for post-Roman and early medieval activity. The re-use of Roman sites may not be geophysically distinguishable, and the use of timber construction leaves traces that are only detectable in exceptional circumstances (David 1994). Much medieval settlement is located beneath or intermingled with later towns and villages and the consequent ferrous interference and surface obstruction makes magnetic survey impractical. In fact, magnetometer survey has, as yet, made no demonstrable contribution to the post-Roman archaeology of the Marlborough Downs. A small magnetometer survey in the Glebe Field at Avebury in advance of extending the southern car park was not helpful in defining Anglo-Saxon and medieval features (David 1984). Excavations here and in the main car park have revealed up to four sunken-featured buildings (SFBs) (Pollard and Reynolds 2002), but only one of these was previously surveyed with the magnetometer. The negative results in this instance should not be disheartening, however, as SFBs are often clearly detectable and magnetometer survey ought always to be a consideration when they may be thought to be present (David 1994).

Pagan Anglo-Saxon cemeteries are difficult to detect because of poor magnetic contrasts, although one of the very few instances where the method has worked demonstratively well was at the Blackpatch cemetery, near Pewsey, where the magnetometer located both grave fills and the ferrous signals from iron grave goods (Clark 1996 fig 78). Magnetic survey can be better relied upon to detect ditches, pits and industrial features where these are not contaminated or obscured by later activity. Deserted medieval settlements ought therefore to respond fairly well; and the technique is also applicable to the investigation of roadways, field systems and linear earthworks. Survey alongside critical sections of Wansdyke for instance might be expect to locate impinging features of significance. The magnetometer survey at Tockenham was able to identify ridge and furrow overlying part of the villa site.

Earth resistance survey

Earth resistance survey is no less dependent on geology and soils than magnetometry but has the added complications of a varying seasonal response and the fact that the technique is still relatively laborious to apply. It has therefore rarely been used as a method of reconnaissance, which is more appropriately done with magnetometers, but has been a method of more focused examination of particular monuments with structural components.

Surveys of long barrows at both Shepherds Shore and Adams Grave have shown that the presence of structural features can be implied by resistance data and the method would seem to be well suited to the definition of flanking ditches, and the spread of surviving cairn material (Bray 1998a). Recent conventional resistance survey on the summit of Silbury Hill, however, was not very revealing with little, if any, structural detail being defined (Linford and Martin 2001). Subsequent survey there, using resistance tomography, which seeks to create vertical profiles of resistance variation using multiprobe arrays (Symanski and Tsourlos 1993), was equally disappointing (Linford 2001).

Both buried megaliths and walls have been shown to exhibit resistance anomalies and the method is the preferred choice for locating buried sarsens and the foundations of buildings. In our area it has proved particularly effective in the study of the megalithic sarsen settings of the Avebury Neolithic monument complex (Ucko *et al* 1990). Buried sarsens were first definitively located using resistivity measurements along the line of the West Kennet Avenue, extending immediately southwards from the section of the avenue restored by Alexander Keiller. Here, anomalies corresponding to seven pairs of settings were identified (*ibid* plate 59), although the response was variable and in places indistinct. However, the general efficacy of the method led to an extensive search in 1989 for the alleged Beckhampton Avenue, targeting the area of the Longstones. Although no avenue was certainly found on this occasion, the identification of potentially significant anomalies encouraged a renewed survey in 1999, in advance of a campaign of excavations to test them (Gillings *et al* 2000a). The six earth resistance anomalies that were then identified were found, on excavation, to correspond with buried sarsens (three), stone destruction pits (two) and a stone burial pit from which the stone had been removed. Altogether, these formed three consecutive pairs of stone positions, the northernmost members of which aligned with the Longstones, Adam and Eve, from which they were spaced at an interval consistent with an avenue of settings. Further excavation confirmed the presence of the intermediate settings – shallow destruction pits which proved undetectable beforehand. Additional survey in 2000 located three enormous destruction pits near Adam, the single survivor of the 'Cove'. However, surveys and further excavations to the south-west of the Longstones in 2000 and 2002 have so far failed to identify other stone settings – negative evidence which suggests the avenue may have terminated at the 'Cove'. Further survey might now usefully be concentrated on tracing the avenue in the other direction, towards Avebury, to determine whether or not it did in fact connect with the great henge (see note).

Within the latter, surveys since 1975 have located former stone settings in the north-west, north-east and south-east quadrants (Ucko *et al* 1990: Papworth 2004). Stone settings on the Great Circle and the two inner circles have been found, those associated with the northern inner circle perhaps being most revealing. Here, the positions of at least six stone settings were detected on the perimeter of the circle, in addition to those visible at the ground surface as pits, and including three positions across the road (A361) in the north-west quadrant. The latter were found to be offset significant distances from their presumed locations and the survey therefore throws some doubt on the previously accepted positioning and geometry of the circle. Furthermore, no evidence for an inner circle, as identified by Stukeley within the northern inner circle, was found – although five features were located, including the probable destruction pit of the third cove stone (*ibid* plates 67–8).

Within the north-western quadrant, earth resistance survey was successfully used in 1996 to confirm the presence of a newly discovered and quite unexpected structure, spotted from the air in 1995 (Bewley *et al* 1996). This appears to be a double-ditched, sub-rectangular or sub-circular feature, with dimensions of about 20m x 20m, encircling a possible pit. Although the geophysical anomalies over these marks proved to be very weak, and were interrupted by the course of a garden wall, the general outline was identifiable, even if no further clues about the age and function of the feature were forthcoming.

Outside the Avebury area, and coming forward again in time, earth resistance survey has so far made little contribution to the later prehistoric archaeology of the Marlborough Downs. Whilst the technique is effective at locating ditches, and could therefore detect barrow and enclosure ditches, this is achieved by magnetic survey with much greater economy. For the same reason earth resistance has not been attempted on Iron Age sites, although – once the method becomes speedier and more automated – it will be of interest to survey many more sites, including certain hillfort interiors for the benefit of comparison with their magnetic images. For the time being, resistance survey is best targeted at suspected masonry structures, for instance where hillforts may have been re-used or, indeed, on any site where building foundations are suspected.

In the Roman period, resistance survey has repeatedly proved itself the most effective method of investigating building foundations and the survey of the villa at Tockenham provides an outstanding example (Fig 4:7b). Here the main building complex lies on the north-east side of a large rectangular enclosed area interpreted as a farm yard. The buildings include corridor rooms arranged around a rectangular courtyard to which there is an elaborate entrance structure. The additional wings to either side of the courtyard are composed of very large rooms, one of which has a pronounced apsidal end. Trial excavations revealed robbed wall trenches and mortared surfaces, as well as quantities of tile, pottery, tesserae etc (Harding & Lewis 1994). Taken with the results of fieldwalking, this evidence has resulted in the site being recognised as a nationally significant example of a villa which has therefore been scheduled as an Ancient Monument (SM31660). The only other example of a Roman villa in our area where geophysical survey has been attempted is at Castle Copse, Bedwyn, but here results were much inhibited by the limited area available for survey, and by difficult surface conditions, hemmed in by woodland (Hostetter & Howe 1997). There can be little doubt, though, that both magnetometer survey, and earth resistance survey, as so perfectly illustrated at Tockenham, can jointly make major contributions to the mapping of other Roman sites in the study area.

In post-Roman and later periods, resistance survey – despite success further afield – has not had much application in the Marlborough Downs area. A significant discovery at Avebury is that of a roadway leading into the henge from the east – well to the north of the route of the *herepath* assumed to underlie Green Street (Ucko *et al* 1990, 184–5, plate 58). Within the henge itself, the presence of former 'pasture boundaries' as recorded by Stukeley (1743) and others are confirmed, and several additional linear anomalies suggest a trackway (Ucko *et al* 1990, plate 53), unexplained features (*ibid* plate 67), and other undated, but possibly medieval, enclosure ditches (Bewley *et al* 1996, fig 3). Beyond the henge, the technique has been shown to detect ridge and furrow, in Longstones field, near Beckhampton.

Earth resistance survey, like magnetometer survey, is best applied over larger rather than smaller areas. Results are usually difficult to interpret when the surveys are small and key-hole in nature, as must often be the case when searching for features within the constraints of built-up areas, such as within villages or amongst farm buildings. Whilst the method is undoubtedly capable of locating foundations, for instance of former religious or manor houses, this opportunity is difficult to realise in many circumstances because of the impositions of later activities.

Other geophysical survey methods

Other methods, as stated earlier, have not yet had much application in our area. Electro-magnetic (EM) methods, notably Ground Penetrating Radar (GPR), perhaps have the greatest potential now that powerful computing for data analysis and preparation is increasingly available (David and Linford 2000). GPR surveys have successfully located buried sarsen megaliths, estimating both their depths and morphologies, on both the West Kennet and Beckhampton Avenues. In future such data will be of value in the investigation of the disposition of particular stone settings or suggestive anomalies first detected by other means. A detailed GPR survey of Adams Grave, has for instance, provided valuable indications of the structural composition of the mound (C Shell *pers comm*), but survey of the summit of Silbury Hill was by contrast not very informative (Linford and Martin 2001). Despite such mixed results, one may predict that GPR surveys will contribute increasingly to such focused studies of individual sites; and, with greater spatial application and the use of amplitude time slices (Conyers and Goodman 1997), the possibility of 3D reconstruction of buried sites is now a reality. Apart from buried sarsen structures, buildings are suitable GPR targets, assuming moist clays are not a problem; a potential future case study, for instance, might well be presented by the Roman villa at Tockenham.

Conductivity and magnetic susceptibility survey can each be undertaken with EM instruments, such as the Geonics EM38, but such surveys are rare in the face of the usually more enlightening results obtained by routine methods – as in the case of trial EM38 conductivity survey by the Ancient Monuments Laboratory which detected the ditches of the West Kennet long barrow. Magnetic susceptibility (MS) surveys have a role in the detection of areas of magnetic enhancement of topsoil caused by settlement and/or industrial activities but, again, little application has been seen in our area. The presence of significant enhancement has been demonstrated at Windmill Hill for instance (David *et al* 1999), and also in association with the Roman site at Waden/Silbury Hill (Powell *et al* 1996). However, it is doubtful that sites such as the West Kennet palisaded enclosures would have been detected in this way, and now that detailed magnetometer survey is increasingly capable of rapid and extensive ground coverage, the case for MS surveys seems less pressing than it may once have been.

Mention also needs to be made of the use of seismic survey, as this has been deployed at Silbury Hill, both to profile the ditch in 1968, and most recently in 2001–2. The latter survey, by Cementation Skanska on behalf of English Heritage, was an attempt to explore the mass of the mound itself, following concerns about its stability after a renewed collapse, in 2000, of the 1776 shaft. At the time of writing the results of this 3D tomographic survey, for future publication as part of a wider report on the recent investigations of the Hill, indicate that the mound is a robust structure which is basically stable. Additional limited coring has since taken place prior to deciding what remedial action, if any, may be called for. A low velocity anomaly detected below the northern flank of the Hill seems to be linked with a surface platform and scar, but ground investigation indicates that this area is also stable – even if the anomaly remains unexplained, perhaps representing an undocumented interference with the Hill.

Conclusions

This review has of necessity been brief, but will, it is hoped, have illustrated the uses that have so far been made of geophysical survey in the Marlborough Downs area. Together with other methods of prospection, geophysical survey offers potential both for reconnaissance and for the highly detailed study of particular sites and monuments. Aerial photography (Crutchley this vol) and analytical earthwork survey [McOmish *et al* this volume] are each of prime importance in site discovery and investigation and in the broader embrace of landscape study. Archive study, and the investigation of metal detector finds also provide further impetus for more detailed non-destructive investigations. In such cases geophysical survey provides an extra dimension adding new and detailed information from below the ground surface. Even apparently well-known sites within a World Heritage Site can be shown by these methods to contain previously unknown and major features; and prospecting needs to inform further research, and in its turn, to be informed by excavation itself. Where intrusive investigation must be limited, however, geophysics will provide a vital record for research, conservation and presentation.

The geophysical methods most prominent in their use, and most suited to conditions in northern Wiltshire, are – and must surely remain – magnetic and earth resistance survey. The sites so far surveyed are but a very small sample of the potential that remains. The focus has perhaps understandably been upon the Avebury area, but surveys further afield on hillforts and villas give a taste of a huge untapped potential – especially in the Neolithic, Bronze Age, Iron Age and Roman periods (David 2001). Potential in other periods exists, but is more selective (*ibid*). Magnetometer survey, alone, is capable of achieving great strides over the wide open spaces of the Downs, if only it could be deployed with even greater speed and sensitivity. Automated multi-sensor caesium magnetometer surveys, capable of covering several hectares per day, seem to offer real hope that ground survey can approach the scale taken blithely for granted by photographers aloft. Other technical advances, most obviously with GPR, offer an added bonus of 3D reconstruction to expanded coverage, with surveys of several hectares now feasible. Such optimism needs, however, to be tempered by the caution that geophysical methods still offer relatively little potential in built-up environments, and (more importantly in the Marlborough region) do not yet offer a capability for the discovery and mapping of sites below depths of a metre or more of alluvium or colluvium. Such intractabilities aside, there remain vast areas where survey should in future continue to help open up the horizons of the archaeology of the Marlborough Downs.

Acknowledgements

Thanks are offered to Dr Mike Hamilton for sharing results from surveys undertaken by Cardiff University, and to GSB Prospection for the illustration of their results from Tockenham. Louise Martin of the Centre for Archaeology, apart from helping to conduct some of the surveys referred to, compiled the illustrations; and I am grateful to Andy Payne for supplying figures from the Wessex Hillforts Project.

Note

Since this paper was written, the pace of geophysical survey in the Avebury area has continued, but lack of space precludes presentation of details here. However, it needs to be noted that magnetic and earth resistance surveys by the Centre for Archaeology located several features, later investigated by excavation at Falkner's Circle (Gillings *et al.* 2003; Martin 2004); the Centre for Archaeology has also provided full and detailed coverage of the Headlands Enclosure using a mobile caesium magnetometer array, with particularly clear results (N Linford 2004). And within the Avebury henge, magnetic and earth resistance surveys in the NE and SE Quadrants have located more buried sarsens on the Great Circle as well as other possible features (Papworth 2004); and additional earth resistance survey has been undertaken in advance of excavation of the course of the Beckhampton Avenue (Gillings *et al.* 2002).

5
The Geological History of the Marlborough Downs

Isobel Geddes and Helen Walkington

The geological structure of the Marlborough Downs is outlined and drift deposits described, with special attention being devoted to the nature of sarsen stones.

Introduction

Since the publication of Geological Survey Memoir 'The geology of the country around Marlborough,' which accompanies map sheet 266 (Osborne White 1925), little has been written specifically about the Marlborough Downs, though it has been included in broader accounts of the geology of Wiltshire (*see* Barron 1976; Geddes 2000).

The Marlborough Downs are made up of chalk around 150 metres thick, of Late Cretaceous age, deposited between 72 and 65 million years ago. Variations in the marine environment have made possible a subdivision of this relatively soft, fine white limestone into Lower, Middle and Upper Chalk formations, distinguished not only by the rock's characteristics but also by fossil content, as new species appear and older ones die out with time. Defining the base of both Middle and Upper Chalk are harder 'rock' bands up to 20 metres thick. These 'rock' levels are the only chalk beds hard enough for building, but even they still weather rapidly if exposed to the elements. The best examples of chalk architecture, the barrows and mounds for which the Marlborough country is famous, are today hidden beneath vegetation. Since Prehistoric times the Chalk downlands have provided flint for the manufacture of stone tools, while some quarrying has also occurred for flints for building and on a very small scale for chalk to produce lime, for liming fields and mortar.

In the Early Tertiary (Palaeogene) Period, starting 65 million years ago, uplift and emergence of the region resulted in tilting and partial erosion of the chalk land surface until around 60 million years ago. Then several series of sands, clays and gravels, the deposits of rivers, deltas and the sea, were laid down on top, as sedimentation occurred between pulses of uplift. Few of these sediments can be found today although their remnants are more commonly known on the Marlborough Downs in two residual forms. First are the deposits mapped as Clay-with-flints which cap the Upper Chalk on the summits of the Marlborough Downs and second are sarsen stones, residual lumps of well cemented Tertiary deposits, called silcretes, found lying on the Chalk east and southeast of Avebury. As a result of their durability, they have not been eroded away and appear beyond the limits of the deposits mapped as Clay-with-flints.

The rocks of southern England have been warped or folded by pressures originating in the Alpine mountain region, where the various mountain ranges were forced up by the continual northward push of Africa against Europe during the last 70 million years. This caused the development of a shallow east-west trending trough along the length of the Marlborough Downs dipping to the east; this is the westerly continuation of the syncline known as the London Basin. The remaining younger Tertiary beds fill the centre of the basin and thus thicken eastwards towards London. The Chalk dips beneath the Tertiary beds but crops out at the surface along the north of the basin as the Chilterns and along the southern edge as the North Downs.

The Marlborough Downs landscape is characterised by steep escarpments at the edge of the underlying Chalk outcrop, behind which are open rolling downlands. Such escarpments bound the Marlborough Downs to north, west and south. They are the result of the presence of more resistant bands within the Chalk forming a cap at the top of the scarp where dips are gentle, due to the geological structure. This structure, when combined with the permeable nature of the rocks (which means there is little surface run-off that in time would erode the scarp edge), accounts for the way the downs stand above the surrounding clay vales, sub-aerial erosion by running water being greatly reduced. The top of the undulating northern escarpment has a series of landmarks: northeast of Avebury are the conspicuous beech clumps of Hackpen Hill, leading up to the Iron Age hill-fort of Barbury Castle; to the west, Cherhill Down is topped by the Oldbury hill-fort and the Cherhill monument; and southwest again is Morgan's Hill with the beeches of Furze Knoll. Avebury lies where the valley of the upper Kennet, rising from the Lower Chalk a short distance to the northwest, joins that of the Winterbourne. These streams have cut through the Upper and Middle Chalk and obliterated the scarp. Windmill Hill is a Middle Chalk outlier two kilometres to the northwest, left standing between the headwater valleys of the Kennet and Winterbourne. The Kennet's flow is augmented by springs in the vicinity of Silbury Hill, where the valley turns eastwards to follow the geological structure. It has cut through the Upper Chalk, flowing on Middle Chalk towards Marlborough. The valley sides to the south rise gently through Upper Chalk to the crest along the south-facing escarpment overlooking Pewsey Vale, marking the southern boundary of the Marlborough Downs. This has its own series of hill-forts – Rybury and Martinsell plus the Neolithic causewayed enclosure of Knap Hill between; Milk Hill at 294 metres is the highest point.

The Marlborough Downs are further dissected by many small branching steep-sided dry valleys (coombes) descending to the Kennet valley, which in most cases follow the structural slope. Exceptional are the upper valleys of the Og and the Winterbourne which have subsequently cut along softer beds of chalk to reach headward into the extensive open plain of Lower Chalk stretching from Cherhill to Chiseldon, which they and their tributaries were instrumental in forming. This bench was originally capped by the hard basal Middle Chalk 'rock' band. The dry valley systems are remnants of periods during the Pleistocene when the Chalk was rendered impermeable by permafrost. When this melted, the water seeped down into the permeable chalk, leaving coombes above the present-day water table. The water table reaches the surface where springs appear in the valleys of the Kennet and its tributaries. There is some seasonal variation in level as evidenced by the name 'Winterbourne' (flowing only in winter). Upstream of Marlborough even the Kennet can be reduced to a series of pools during prolonged dry weather.

Environmental changes over time

The late Cretaceous period 97–65 million years bp

Rising sea levels in later Cretaceous time meant there was little land in north western Europe, so deposition of land-derived sediment was minimal, being limited to a little clay. This allowed the accumulation of Chalk on the warm, shallow continental shelves. These conditions persisted for 30 million years. In Britain, the Chalk appears in a wide band stretching from southern Yorkshire to Devon, and thence eastwards into Kent. It is up to 336 metres thick in Wiltshire. This particular type of fine white limestone is distinguished by its softness, whiteness and purity. Unlike most other limestones, the calcium carbonate, which generally makes up over 98% of the rock, was deposited in the form of calcite which is stable at surface temperatures and pressures, so that the original particles are still intact and largely uncemented by regrowth of crystals. The whiteness is a result of its unusual purity and the very small particle size, which increases the rock's reflectivity. Compared with many other limestones, chalk has a low clay content, seldom more than 4%: it contains a very small amount of silica (below 1% usually) and has even less iron (less than 0.1%), which in its oxidised form may give the chalk a yellowish tinge. The Lower Chalk has the highest clay content and hence a greyer colour.

The Chalk is mainly composed of skeletal fragments of golden-brown planktonic algae, of a type which still exist today. These algae secreted simple plate-like crystals of calcite, one thousandth of a millimetre across, inside their cells to produce spheres of overlapping rings of plates called coccoliths (measuring one hundredth of a millimetre in diameter). Each living cell was a globular spherical structure supported by 7–20 coccolith rings embedded in a pliable membrane. The algae were the main food of shrimp-like creatures called copepods. It is now thought that, in order for the plates to sink and accumulate on the sea floor, they first had to be eaten and passed through the copepods. The resulting faecal pellets built up into an ooze on the sea floor and have been preserved as the Chalk. A variety of larger fossils are also present. There are remains of free-swimmers such as ammonites, belemnites and fish (scales and teeth), as well as bottom-dwelling sponges, corals, brachiopods, gastropods, bivalves and sea urchins. Burrows, made by certain crustaceans, bivalves and sea urchins, are responsible for the streaks and mottles commonly visible. Sea depths during deposition have been estimated at 100–200 metres in southern England. Sedimentation rates have also been calculated at 20–40 metres per million years. However, this deposition was not continuous; there were periods of sediment removal and non-deposition. Breaks in sedimentation are marked by the hard, nodular 'rock' bands, which define the base of the Middle and Upper Chalk. These are now designated the Holywell Nodular Chalk Member (previously known as the Melbourn Rock) and the Lewes Nodular Chalk Member (formerly the Chalk Rock) respectively. The finer, soft material was removed in these horizons by the winnowing action of currents to leave behind only the well cemented patches and harder nodules on the sea floor. This increased current activity suggests that a shallowing of the water occurred, either as a result of crustal movements in the Earth, or of sea-level changes.

The Upper Chalk is characterised by the presence of flints, unlike the Middle Chalk, which contains few flints. No flints are found in the Lower Chalk. Flints occur mainly in layers parallel to the bedding, although there is a range of occurrence from continuous sheets (tabular flint) to scattered nodules (nodular flint). Flints are commonly associated with invertebrate burrows, often forming burrow casts, which produce their characteristic shape. Despite their alignment with bedding planes, the evidence indicates that flint formation was not contemporaneous with sedimentation. Indeed it is thought that when sedimentation was halted for a time the boundary between aerobic and anaerobic conditions in the chalk sediment, perhaps 5–10m deep, becomes stationary. Chemical reactions concentrated at this boundary lower the pH, promoting carbonate dissolution and initiating the precipitation of silica from solution as an amorphous gel, which then crystallised (Clayton 1986).

The silica is derived from the siliceous skeletons of animals or plants, such as sponges and plankton, which were subsequently dissolved by the water in the pores of the sediment. Burrowed horizons produced bands of flints, but flints also formed casts of sponges and sea urchins. The silica first filled pores and spaces inside shells and gradually replaced the calcium carbonate of the shell or burrow-fill, to form a cast of the original. Once the silica had been precipitated, there would have been a lower concentration of silica in the water around the site. The result of this chemical imbalance was an influx of more silica into the area by diffusion. This could cause the original flint to slowly grow larger: some flints are well over half a metre across. Flints are 98% crystalline silica, and 1% interstitial water trapped between the crystals. When broken open they can be seen to have a grey-dark brown glassy appearance, which, on microscopic examination, shows a very fine crystalline structure. The cortex (outer surface) of the flint is white or pale grey in colour due to the fact that the water could escape from between the crystals here, leaving microscopic air spaces with different light-reflecting properties.

The Tertiary period 65–2.4 million years bp

The whole of southeast England was uplifted in the early Tertiary period so the chalk-covered continental shelf was subjected to sub-aerial denudation. Pulses of tectonic activity defined the structural downwarps known as the London and Hampshire basins (Jones 1999); the combination of sea level fluctuations and tectonic movements resulted in a broken sedimentary record with deposits being laid down and subsequently being removed by periods of erosion. Palaeocene sediments are the first to lie on the eroded surface of the chalk, belonging to the Reading Formation (previously called Reading Beds, (Ellison *et al* 1994)). These deposits were predominantly fluvial, representing a complex area of lagoons and tidal channels, which lay between rivers draining land to the west into the sea to the east (Anderton 2000).

The warmth of mid-Tertiary times would have resulted in deep weathering of the earlier Tertiary rock mantle, as a low relief land surface formed, only a few tens of metres above the present chalk summits (Jones 1999). The erosion of this sediment cover was accelerated by upwarping along the anticlinal axis following the Vale of Pewsey. This structural line extends along the southern edge of the London Basin and is related to fault movements deep in the earth's crust below. The nearest outcrops of Tertiary sediments in this area are south-east of Marlborough on the southern and eastern fringes of Savernake Forest. The weathered remnants of the former cover of soft, uncemented Tertiary sands and clays are more widespread, however, constituting the thin residual deposits mapped as Clay-with-flints, capping the chalk of the downs, and the sandstone blocks known as sarsen stones which lie scattered on the chalk in this area.

Deposits mapped as Clay-with-flints

The deposits mapped as Clay-with-flints form a patchy cover on higher parts of the Chalk downs, for example on the summits of Totterdown, Clatford Down, West Woods, Tan Hill and Milk Hill, but become more extensive eastwards. The origin of the deposits has been debated for over a century (Catt 1986; Scott-Jackson 2000). However, the combination of uplifted and reworked early Tertiary deposits lying on top of

Fig 5:1 Sarsen stones at Lockeridge Dene.

the eroded chalk surface is thought to be the key to formation. When these overlying Tertiary deposits became sufficiently permeable, the clay within moved downwards towards the junction with the Upper Chalk beneath. The pure Upper Chalk dissolved as a result of the percolating waters being slightly acidic, releasing flints and very small amounts of other insoluble residues. The voids created by the dissolution of the Chalk provided spaces for the deposition of the downward percolating clay. Deep solution hollows and pipes have formed from the variable lowering of the Chalk beneath the Tertiary veneer. Clay-with-flints in the strict sense (*sensu stricto*), is formed from the clay as it moves downward out of the weathering Tertiary deposits combined with the insoluble residues of the chalk below. It forms between the Tertiary cover and the chalk and in places may still be forming today. The highly tenacious nature of the Clay-with-flints *sensu stricto* means that they have undergone only restricted change during the Pleistocene and have had a protective effect on the downlands themselves (Scott-Jackson 2000).

Areas mapped as Clay-with-flints also include windblown loess, waterlain brickearths, Plateau drift, 'clean' clays dug for brick making and flinty deposits worked for gravel. These deposits are generally referred to as Clay-with-flints *sensu lato*. The variety and discontinuous nature of these deposits suggest differing modes of formation and allude to complex landscape histories. However, due to this complexity they have all been grouped within the Clay-with-flints 'catch all' or 'blanket' mapping unit. Clay-with-flints *sensu lato* may often be found overlying Clay-with-flints *sensu stricto*. For example, Codrington (1866) noted a railway cutting north east of Wernham Farm where a section showed the irregular surface of the Chalk covered with Clay-with-flints *sensu stricto* directly overlain by Clay-with-flints *sensu lato* (here brickearth which contained sarsens but no flints). Interestingly, the deposits repeated the general outline of the irregular upper surface of the chalk, indicating the impact of solution as a process for both the formation and retention of deposits mapped as Clay-with-flints. The deposits mapped as Clay-with-flints are of particular archaeological significance as there appears to be a strong association with Palaeolithic, Neolithic and Bronze Age sites (e.g. Barrett *et al* 1991; Wymer 1999; Scott-Jackson 2000 and this volume).

Sarsen stones

Sometimes known as "grey wethers" (wethers are sheep), these isolated blocks of stone are found on the Chalk Downs, particularly on the Marlborough Downs, between Avebury and Marlborough (Fig 5:1 and 5:2). The name "sarsen" is thought to come from either the Anglo-Saxon "sar stan" meaning troublesome stone, or from 'saracen', meaning alien or stranger (Kellaway 1991). Most sarsens are white to greyish or yellowish sandstone, being made of often iron-

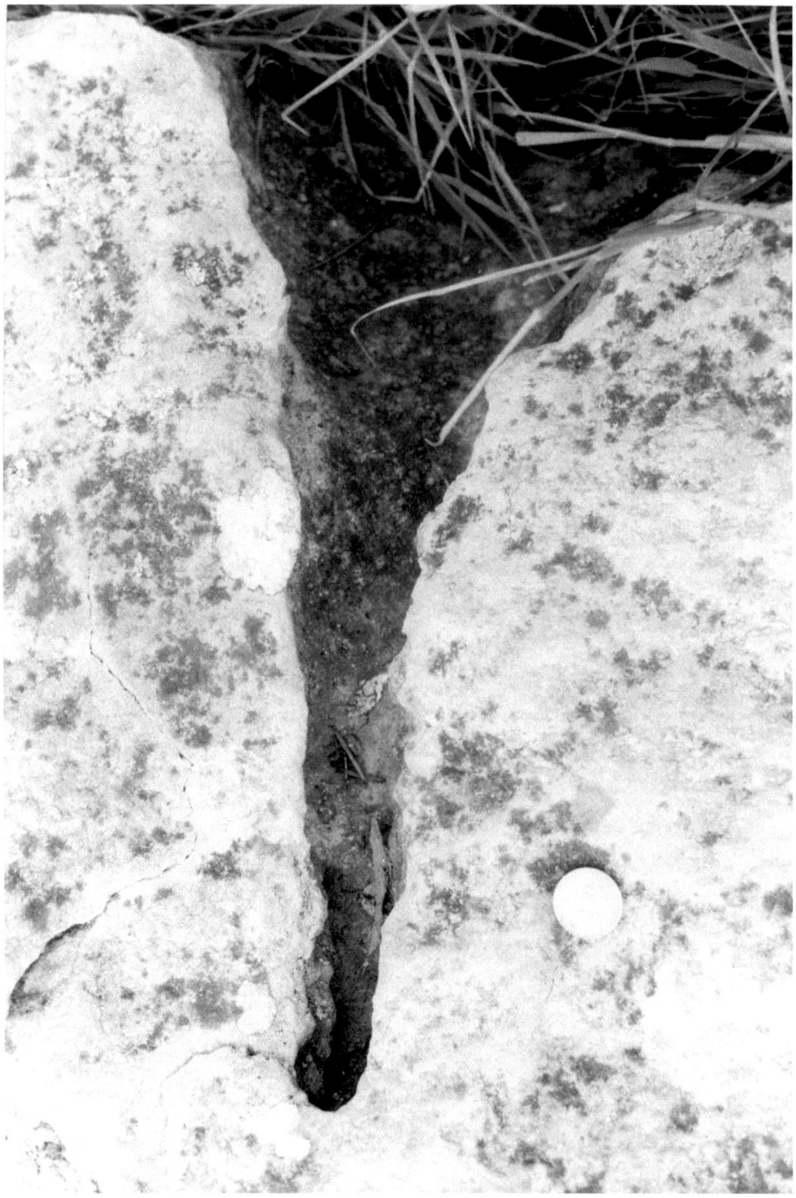

Fig 5:2 Sarsen stone at Avebury showing fossil root-holes.

stained quartz sand with angular grains of various sizes, including flint grains and white feldspar. The stones sometimes contain lenses and thin beds of flint pebbles. Any bedding is generally impersistent, and the shape of the stones appears to be determined by the extent of the uneven cementation, rather than by bedding. Sarsens can be seen in many localities, for example at Fyfield Down Nature Reserve (around NGR SU 130710), Lockeridge (NGR SU 144674) and Pickledean (NGR SU 141690). In addition, beds of sarsen have been found below the surface on local farms. By their nature, their original distribution would have been patchy and coinciding with the Tertiary sedimentary cover. Their hardness means they have even survived the solution and erosion of some of the underlying Chalk as well as the disintegration of the deposits, which originally surrounded them.

Sarsens are thought to be the remnants of locally hardened zones in sands of Tertiary age. Comparison with localities in central Australia (Hepworth 1998) and Botswana (Nash *et al* 1998), where similar recently-formed sandstones have been studied, and also with still-buried Tertiary sands in the Paris Basin in France (Ullyott *et al* 1998) gives clues as to their origin. However, providing a definitive mechanism for sarsen formation is problematic since "silcrete formation may occur in the same landscape by a number of mechanisms in response to different conditions at various stages during the evolution of that landscape" (*ibid* 1998, 266). Some form of landscape depression, such as a valley, appears to be the prime determinant of their formation.

Groundwater can become saturated with silica as it moves through sands. Local changes in the chemistry within the sand deposits may then cause cementation of the loose grains with additional silica, resulting in the development of hard silicified areas beneath the land surface. Changes in acidity can trigger this precipitation from the ground water, probably in zones where there is mixing of waters from different sources. The growth of bacteria and certain plants can also contribute to the process of silicification. Studies suggest that silicification may have been relatively rapid, perhaps taking only 30,000 years for three metre-thick lenses to form (Nash *et al* 1998). The cementation was not of uniform depth or lateral extent, as it depended on local conditions, hence the surfaces of the resulting sarsens are frequently knobbly and pitted, with hollows formed by subsequent removal of softer areas. The sarsens themselves contain many fossil plant roots, which can be seen in the Avebury standing stones. Looking like rusty brown tubes, these roots are up to 3 centimetres in diameter (Fig 5:2), the root itself having frequently decayed away at some point after silicification of the rock, leaving behind tube-like holes. The fossil roots are in the position of growth and have not been distorted by pressure, a further indication of early silicification.

Ullyott *et al* (1998) have studied silcrete formation and recognise two main types: pedogenic silcretes (forming in the soil) and drainage line silcretes (forming in association with ground water). There is some debate about whether the sarsens of the Marlborough Downs were pedogenic, and therefore attest to a hot climate with alternating wet and dry conditions, or whether they represent a ground water phenomenon which provides little palaeoenvironmental evidence. Ullyott *et al* (1998) identify both types in different formations in the Paris Basin. "Sarsen trains," linear distributions of the stones well seen at Overton Down (NGR SU 130709), probably developed as an original feature, silcrete forming along former drainage lines as ground water moved towards the valleys. The drainage line of the Kennet valley was already developing during the Tertiary and silicified areas would follow the water table as it dips towards the valley floor (Nash *et al* 1998). Most of the literature favours the drainage line mode of formation for the Marlborough Downs sarsens.

While there is general agreement that two periods of silcrete formation are represented in southern England, those in the Palaeocene Reading Formation and those in the Eocene Barton Beds (Hepworth 1998), there is debate about which of these the Wiltshire sarsens relate to. Small *et al* (1970) argued that the sarsens of the Marlborough Downs are post Barton Beds age and are indicative of a land surface. The British Geological Survey view (Sumbler 1996) is that sarsens are formed in the Reading Formation and only those found in the heathlands of Surrey are from the Barton Beds.

Sarsens have been used, since pre-historic times, for monuments such as Avebury and Stonehenge as well as for paving and building stone (Tatton-Brown 1998). As a result, their natural occurrence has been greatly reduced over the years, although it has recently been estimated that there are still several tens of thousands left, even after centuries of exploitation. English Nature and the National Trust have bought several areas containing large groups of stones, with the aim of protecting those remaining. The standing stones at Avebury are made from local, naturally weathered, unworked sarsen, revealing the characteristic mammilated growth structures. The protuberances denote what was the upper surface while the underside is flatter and has cavities. At West Kennet Long Barrow the flat sarsens are also presumed to be of local origin. The massive trilithons at Stonehenge are dressed, so formational structures are no longer evident. Mysteriously no sarsens of this size are found at the surface in the UK today, nor are the Eastern Australian silcrete blocks of comparable size (Hepworth 1998). However, Kellaway (1991) records the finding of three large masses of silica-cemented sandstone, similar in size to the Stonehenge Slaughter Stone, during excavations to build the M40 road in Oxfordshire, in red Clay-with-flints filling a complex cavity in the Chalk. It is perhaps significant that here the sandstones were still friable, though silicified, because they had not been exposed to the atmosphere. The trilithons at Stonehenge have been dressed by hand which would have been much easier if they were still relatively soft, although various methods of dressing sarsens have, of course, been developed over the years. Hardening, a common feature of building stone, would have occurred in the last 4,000 years, since they were erected and exposed to atmospheric weathering.

The Quaternary period

The Quaternary period began 2.4 million years ago and continues to the present day (Woodcock, 2000). The Pleistocene Epoch formed the first part of Quaternary time and was characterised by a series of successive glacials (cold stages) and intervening interglacials (warm periods) ending c10,000 years ago at the end of the last (Devensian) cold stage. There was a transition from late Tertiary planation of the land surface to incision and valley development in the Quaternary (Maddy 1997). The initial form of the ground prior to periglaciation had a significant impact upon landscape modification. Quaternary uplift rates resulting from continuing Alpine movement have been estimated in southern England at 7–10 centimetres per thousand years (Maddy *et al* 2000). This resulted from the interaction between crustal movements, sea level changes and climatic oscillations; downwarping of the crust due to the weight of the Pleistocene ice sheets and isostatic rebound on melting would have been an additional factor. There is no evidence that glacial ice ever reached the Marlborough Downs, although they have been affected by periglacial conditions. The result of oscillations in climate was periodic erosion and dissection of the land surface, with the removal of much of the weathered rock mantle, leaving the remainder selectively disturbed by periglacial conditions. However, the effects of periglaciation are not always easy to distinguish from the effects of solution (Williams 1986). Vegetation and animal remains indicate that some interglacial periods, such as OIS stage 5a (Ipswichian), were substantially warmer than today and sea levels were higher. Changing sea levels would have had effects in terms of raising and lowering the base level down to which the rivers erode. This leads to cycles of river valley erosion and deposition and creates problems for determining the relative ages of terrace deposits. Distinguishing the effects of one cold stage from another is also problematic as evidence from previous cold stages may be destroyed by subsequent ones.

Frost shattering (the repeated freezing and thawing of water in rock cracks) of the chalk is a widespread product of periglaciation. It shatters the uppermost levels of the chalk, varying in depth from 0.5 to 2.5 metres, into small fragments. It is possible that the depth of shattering related to the depth of seasonal freezing and thawing, although it is difficult to separate the effects of present day frosts from periglacial ones in creating this phenomenon (Williams 1986). Frost shattering would have also released debris for mass movement downslope.

The formation of dry valleys (coombes) during the Quaternary has puzzled researchers because chalk is permeable and therefore is unlikely to support surface drainage. One explanation has been climate change, which has led to a lowering of the ground-water table, the reason why no rivers flow in the bottom of the valleys today. More likely though is the impact of permafrost during the Pleistocene cold stages. This would have rendered the chalk impermeable, allowing water to flow over the surface, eroding a valley system. Once the permafrost melted, water would once again be able to percolate through the chalk, removing the need for surface drainage unless the water table rose sufficiently to create a stream.

Much of the Quaternary is characterised by erosion but three types of periglacial deposit are found on the Chalk of Wiltshire: windblown, solifluction and meltwater (Evans 1968). All three types of deposit, due to the episodic nature of the processes behind them, have the potential to preserve or destroy archaeological and/or palaeoenvironmental data. Windblown silt and fine sand (loess), which may have been subsequently reworked by water (brickearth) was deposited in dry cold conditions during Pleistocene time, especially the Devensian (most recent) cold stage (Catt 1978). Beneath the Long Barrow at South Street, Coombe Rock overlain by loess has formed involutions as a result of cryoturbation. The molluscan fauna in the loess were indicative of a dry, open, windswept landscape diagnostic of a date between 10,800–10,300 bp (Evans 1968).

Solifluction deposits (also known as Head) such as chalky 'Coombe Rock' resulted from seasonal thawing with solifluction occurring as surface layers melted and moved downslope under gravity. During the Pleistocene cold stages permafrost would have sealed the pores and cracks in pervious rocks such as chalk, making them impermeable. During summer thaws there would have been movement down-slope of a slurry of waterlogged soil and unsorted weathered rock debris by solifluction. The valley floor at Clatford Bottom has around two metres of solifluction deposits – a mixture of chalk and Tertiary material. It has been studied in detail as it has a remarkable concentration of sarsens on its lower northern slopes and valley floor. The theory that sarsen concentration in the lower parts of the valley was the result of downslope movement by solifluction was published by Small *et al* (1970). However, this has since been disputed by Hepworth (1998) who argued that the Clatford Bottom sarsens are a more or less *in situ* disrupted tabular silcrete body. During the wetter conditions of the Devensian there probably was the potential for the downhill movement of sarsen stones into valleys, lubricated by the slippery chalk-mud residue, but the sarsens are regarded by Hepworth (1998) and Nash *et al* (1998) as not having been moved significantly by periglacial processes. Excavation by the Society of Antiquaries (Bowen & Smith 1977) showed that sarsens at Overton Down either rest on a chalk plinth or are found in solution hollows, confirming that they are unlikely to have been transported downhill.

River terraces

During Pleistocene interglacials, melt-water streams would have had strong currents which transported vast amounts of gravel, sand, silt and clay. Relics of extensive gravel sheets are found in Wiltshire south and east of the Marlborough Downs, at levels up to 100 metres higher than present-day valley deposits. For example, there are a few scattered patchy deposits in Savernake Forest (containing Palaeolithic implements) and also on the northern side-slope of the Kennet valley at Mildenhall (Osborne White 1925).

Water-worn gravels occur in the river valleys as terraces along the valley sides, above the present valley floors. Such gravels are found on the terraces of the Kennet and its tributaries. They rise up gently from beneath the recent alluvium of the present-day floodplain, forming a strip on either side of the whole Kennet valley. The lowest deposits consist of marly flint-gravel with detrital chalk, the result of freeze-thaw disintegration in periglacial conditions; chalk content decreases upwards as does the calcium carbonate content of the finer loamy matrix. Tributary valleys have similar deposits, for example, in the dry valleys of Clatford Bottom, Pickledean, Lockeridge Dene and the Og valley. They represent a time when sea-levels were higher, and thus when valleys were not so deeply incised. At that time, the rivers were gradually redistributing surface material on the valley floors. However, it then became colder again, and sea levels fell, as water was stored in the form of ice. The rivers then cut their valleys deeper, leaving earlier gravels and alluvium as terraces on the valley sides. Subsequent rises in sea level, associated with further melting of the ice, caused infilling of these valleys with new river deposits.

River alluvium

Recent alluvium can be found beneath the belts of meadowland bordering the Kennet, Winterbourne and Og. At the present time, the larger streams and rivers of Wiltshire are depositing silt and clay derived mainly from the soil, on the low gradients of their broad floodplains. There may be occasional bands of small gravel and peat plus comminuted shells of freshwater molluscs (of recent age). The lack of coarse material is due to the rivers originating in the Chalk downs and thus lacking great erosive power. Some deposition of alluvium occurs during floods, but most of it is continually built up on the inside of the bends of the meandering rivers. The river flows more rapidly on the outside of a meander, constantly undercutting the outer bank just downstream of the apex of the bend. On the inner bank, flow is slack and it is here that sediment builds up. Thus the whole meander system migrates slowly downstream, leaving behind a layer of alluvium which may bury coarser Pleistocene deposits.

The rocks and deposits which constitute the Marlborough Downs area are all sedimentary in nature. This has preserved environmental indictors, which might have been lost under intense heating or pressure. However, the geology is sufficiently varied to provide great potential for geophysical surveys as the deposits should provide distinctive resistivity signatures. Clearly further geological and sedimentological investigations are required to provide a fuller understanding of the rich landscape which provides the context for archaeological investigation.

6
The Palaeolithic of the Marlborough Downs and Avebury area

Julie E Scott-Jackson

In an attempt to understand the present distribution patterns of Palaeolithic artefacts across the Marlborough Downs, particular emphasis has been accorded here to those factors which have acted on both the downs and surrounding areas since the arrival of Palaeolithic people around 600,000 thousand years ago. Much of the artefact and find-spot/find-site information for this area is well recorded, but inevitably inaccuracies, some serious, have now become incorporated in the existing data. To remove these distortions and to facilitate a detailed analysis of this material a total reassessment of the recorded information is necessary. By combining the updated information with fieldwork, it has been possible to produce a comprehensive gazetteer. Each entry is individually described and discussed with the hope that the compilation and analyses of these data will provide the basis for future investigations and the generation of fieldwork projects.

Background

From around 600,000 to approximately 10,000 years ago, the downlands of southern England provided many opportunities for groups of Palaeolithic hunter/gatherers/scavengers, whose wanderings were spread temporally and spatially in conditions for which there is often no equivalent today.

The only evidence for their presence in the Marlborough Downs is the stone-tools they left behind. From the distribution pattern of these we can conclude that they encamped at both low and high-levels. As no actual camp structures have survived it is not known whether the stone-tools are associated with butchering sites, consumption and resting camps or home bases, but when waste-flakes are present, stone-tool manufacturing can be identified with confidence. On the highest hilltops and plateaux, archaeological and geological evidence suggests that water was held in some of the hollows formed in the clayey capping deposits by tree-throw or solution of the underlying chalk (see Smith 1894; Kendall 1916; Scott-Jackson 2000) and that these hollows may also have provided sheltered areas for the manufacture of stone-tools from the readily available flint or knappable stone. In addition, hilltops and plateau edges may have provided vantage points from which to observe the movements of animals and perhaps other groups of people (Scott-Jackson 2000).

Additional evidence for the existence of campsites may be provided by burnt flint, flora and fauna remains (often of species that are now extinct). Burnt flint, when found in association with stone tools during excavations, is important (surface-finds less so) as it might indicate the presence of campfires and is dateable in certain circumstances. Flora and fauna remains from excavated sites may also be dateable and provide clues to the nature of the camp and the environment existing at that time.

Reconstructing a Palaeolithic Landscape

The determinants of the Palaeolithic landscape of southern England are multi-facetted. Over geological time many changes have occurred, including extreme climatic; the evolution of stone-tool manufacturing techniques and indeed in Palaeolithic people themselves. Reconstructing a specific topographic (or social) Palaeolithic landscape, demands an awareness of the following: the importance of specific areas, the availability of fresh water and knappable stone; the acquisition and the availability of suitable food.

Since Palaeolithic people did not restrict their wanderings to any particular topography, we must consider the landscape as a whole, for no single find-site can provide all the answers. It is necessary therefore, to analyse the interrelationships between the various Palaeolithic stone-tool industries, as represented by the artefacts found in the study area, with the geology and geomorphology of each find-spot/find-site and the area in general. The term *find-spot* refers to a spot where one or more artefacts were found, not necessarily in their original context, whereas *find-site* refers to an area where evidence suggests artefacts may have been made or used – a crucial difference in terms of interpretive significance

Before such research can be undertaken however, the find-spots/find-sites must be positively identified (as far as it is possible), correcting any inaccuracies that may have become incorporated into existing data, and adding, where appropriate, additional geological, geomorphological, archaeological and anthropological information.

Development of the Downland Landscape

Although the geology of the Marlborough Downs has been addressed elsewhere in this volume, it is necessary to briefly consider various processes which are particular to the understanding of the Palaeolithic. The *deposits mapped as Clay-with-flints* referred to in the context of this research are *only* those deposits which *cap* the highest hilltops and plateaux and must not be confused with soliflucted clayey/flints deposits found at low-levels. During the Anglian (OIS 11/12) and subsequent glacial maxima the downlands of southern England capped with Clay-with-flints lay beyond the ice-sheets and above the ensuing meltwaters. This area, alone in Britain, escaped the devastating effects of direct glacial processes. The Clay-with-flints which cap highest downland hilltops and plateaux have therefore, been subjected to only 'restricted change' since OIS 13 (the late Cromerian), a date of a least 600,000 years ago (Scott-Jackson 2000, 5). The use of the term 'restricted change' allows for limited changes within the deposits, in place of the term 'stability', which infers no change and generates misunderstandings as it crosses different disciplines.

The downland landscape as we see it today, is generally thought to have been shaped by periglacial erosion and solifluction processes. Unfortunately, the role of periglaciation and cryoturbation has been over emphasized, with the effects of periglaciation often being confused with those of solution (Williams 1980; 1986; Scott-Jackson 2000). The impact of these data distortions is the archaeological devaluation of Palaeolithic artefacts from high-level sites on Clay-with-flints.

Where downland high-levels are capped by Clay-with-flints, plateau features are evident. Plateaux are by definition relatively flat surfaces, and flat surfaces on top of otherwise typically convex chalk hills imply a modification of the processes of erosion that have produced the usual rounded landform. On these high-levels, the Clay-with-flints (which include brickearths) played a protective role in the development of the Chalk landscape during both warm and cold periods. However, the irregular distribution of these deposits across the downland suggests that they once covered a greater area than they do today.

During very cold/periglacial periods, permafrost would have rendered the underlying chalk and the Clay-with-flints (both *sensu stricto* and *sensu lato*) impermeable. In warm periods, the surfaces that were not covered by these deposits appear to have been lowered more rapidly by dissolution, with the flinty residue being periodically removed by colluviation, particularly from the side-slopes into valleys (Goudie 1988). Slope processes, such as sheet wash, rill wash and solifluction, operating on the downlands in both temperate and cold climates have therefore resulted in large quantities of chalky mud and rubble mixed with whole and/or broken flints and often Palaeolithic artefacts being transported down the hillsides and deposited on the dry valley floors and into the rivers and streams.

Clearly, slopes have changed angle and shape; streams have appeared and disappeared; valleys have been incised and then filled in again with 'sludged in' materials in the form of solifluction deposits, colluvium and alluvium. The greatest topographic changes to the downlands however, took place prior to OIS 13 (the late Cromerian) and the arrival of Palaeolithic people.

Palaeolithic Stone Tool Technology

Stone tools can be categorized as belonging to the Lower, Middle or Upper Palaeolithic periods due to changes in stone tool morphology and technology. However, for the British Lower and Middle Palaeolithic, there is no generally agreed association between various industry types and different species of *Homo*, though it is widely acknowledged that Upper Palaeolithic industries are correlated with modern humans. Although

Fig 6:1 Palaeolithic find-spots/sites in the Marlborough Downs and Avebury area.

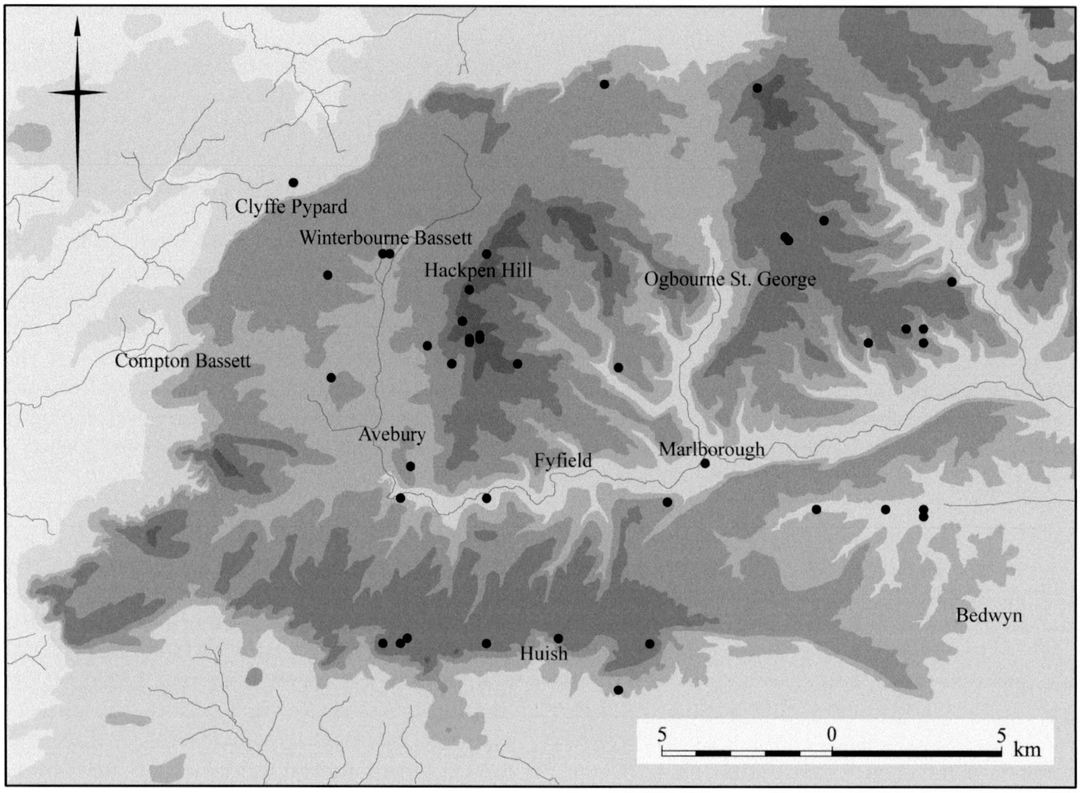

knapping techniques are reasonably well understood, much uncertainty still exists regarding the actual use of the tools.

The majority of the recorded surface-finds in downland areas are of isolated handaxes. A probable explanation for this is collector bias, handaxes being easier to identify in a flint-strewn field. Although a handaxe recovered as an isolated surface-find will provide useful industry-type information, the waste products of stone-tool manufacture have particular value. Traditionally waste-flakes recovered as surface-finds have been considered of limited value and often therefore received little attention, but are of the utmost importance in the construction of Palaeolithic landscapes.

As the main evidence for reconstructing the Palaeolithic landscape is the stone tools, then all are important, whether *in-situ* or re-deposited. Where local data are incomplete, ambiguous, or require interpretation, reference must be made to other Palaeolithic industries/sites – not necessarily in the same county or indeed country.

The Palaeolithic of the Marlborough Downs and Avebury Area

There are 36 Palaeolithic find-spots and three find-sites in the area (Fig 6:1). In the following descriptions, the degree of precision of a provenance is expressed as an abbreviation in brackets after the national grid reference i.e. (A) = accurate; (E) = estimated; (G) = general. There are several reasons why these data must be viewed as a random sample only: extensive field investigations specifically targeting the Palaeolithic have been limited; Palaeolithic artefacts, particularly waste-flakes, are not always recognised for what they are; it is only too likely that many casual finds remain completely unrecorded, and; Palaeolithic sites *per se* are not visible in aerial photographs.

Details of the find-spots, find-sites and associated artefacts listed below were initially complied from Roe (1968), Wessex Archaeology (1993) and the Wiltshire Sites and Monument Record. In an effort to minimise data distortions, the various entries for each find-spot/find-site have been grouped together. Inevitably, over time, inaccuracies and omissions have become incorporated into the record. There are also difficulties in updating taxonomies as, although many of the artefacts are held by Devizes Museum or the British Museum, the whereabouts of others are unknown.

Nevertheless, a number of data distortions have been identified (Scott-Jackson unpublished) and where possible the appropriate corrections or comments made. Much still remains to be done, not the least being a field-based reassessment of all the relevant find-spots and ideally, the compilation of a comprehensive illustrated catalogue of the Palaeolithic artefacts found in the Marlborough Downs, a task beyond the scope of this paper.

The stone-tools in this study area have been found in a variety of geological and geographical contexts, and the archaeological potential within these different environments is now discussed.

Artefacts from the highest hilltops and plateaux

Across southern England, on the highest downland hilltops and plateaux capped with Clay-with-flints, many Palaeolithic stone-tools have been found. Often these have been single isolated surface-finds, however, substantial numbers of artefacts (predominately waste-flakes) have also been found in what appears to be discrete assemblages; that is, they have been discovered as a group of artefacts located close together . Where 'basin-like' solution hollows are present, they are known to be instrumental in retaining, over geological time, both the Clay-with-flints and by association, Palaeolithic stone-tools. Specialist investigations and excavation methodologies are essential to determine the *in situ* or otherwise status of these finds (see Scott-Jackson 2000). Waste-flakes recovered *in situ* from excavated sites and as surface-finds are most important as they are indicative of stone-tool manufacture within the immediate area from readily available flint (*ibid*).

Ridgeway Field, Hackpen Hill – the site of H G O Kendall's excavations

Important finds have come from Ridgeway Field, a high-level site (around 270m OD) on Clay-with-flints, at the southern end of Hackpen Hill. As many Palaeolithic artefacts had previously been recovered as surface-finds in the vicinity of solution features (at SU128 726) not far from Glory Ann Barn, two excavations from around 1909 and in 1912 were conducted (Kendall 1916). In contrast to many excavators of that time, Kendall proceeded with the greatest of care, collecting not only the finest of stone tools but also worked or worn flakes of all sizes. At least six handaxes, ten waste-flakes and one core were excavated from the 1912 site. The integrity displayed by Kendall, combined with his acute observations and the attention to detail in his reports, has made it possible to reassess these data and to determine the *in-situ* status of this Lower and Middle Palaeolithic site (Scott-Jackson 2000, 53–66).

The Ridgeway Field site is of particular importance, being one of the very few excavated Palaeolithic high-level *in-situ* sites on Clay-with-flints. The artefacts excavated from the solution hollow are diagnostically interesting as the presence of waste-flakes, possible hammer stones and burnt flint are indicative of a stone-tool manufacturing site, as yet undated. Evidence of knapping on this high-level clearly substantiates the idea that Lower and Middle Palaeolithic hunter/gatherers/scavengers did not restrict their activities to the valleys, (as intimated by the British Palaeolithic archaeological record) and establishes their dispersal and activity across the landscape as a whole.

Find-spots on Clay-with-flints

Listed below, in addition to the Ridgeway field *in-situ* site, are 14 other find-spots on Clay-with-flints. The archaeological potential within for example, Golden Ball Hill, Alton Barnes, which lies at 193m OD (SU 130 640 (E)) where surface-finds of a handaxe, handaxe fragments and a flake hint at the presence of embedded artefacts and a possible *in-situ* site, is clear.

SU 105 640 (E): Milk Hill, Stanton St. Bernard; (edge of plateau); (312m, OD) – Handaxe.

SU 1070 6415: North of Oxenmere, Stanton St. Bernard; (edge of plateau); (312m, OD) – Flake.

SU 123 731: Berwick Bassett Down, Berwick Bassett; (255m, OD) – Handaxe (crude ovate).

SU 128 726 (A): Ridgeway Field, Hackpen Hill, plateau (265m OD) – At least 6 handaxes, 10 waste-flakes and 1 core were excavated from the 1912 site (Kendall, 1916; Lacaille, 1971; Scott-Jackson, 2000).

SU 128 727 (A): Glory Ann Barn Pit, Hackpen Hill; (265m, OD) – Handaxe (distinctive cream patination) see Kendall, 1916; Lacaille, 1971; Scott-Jackson, 2000).

SU 130 640 (E): Golden Ball Hill, Alton Barnes; plateau; (193m, OD) – Handaxe; Handaxe fragments and Flake.

SU 139 719 (A): Old Totterdown, Fyfield; plateau; (280m OD) – Handaxe (possibly small ovate, Wymer type K, see SU 168 718 below).

SU 1507 6415: Huish Hill, Wilcot; plateau; (287m OD) – Flake.

SU 177 640 (G): Martinsell Hill, Pewsey; plateau; (307m OD) – Handaxe (unfinished).

SU 182 680 (E): Opposite Marlborough College on north flank of Granham Hill, Marlborough; (198m OD) – 1 Handaxe.

SU 216 755: Ogbourne Hill, Ogbourne St.George; plateau; (250m, OD) – Flake (large, with iron oxide staining).

SU 217 754: Ogbourne Hill/Roundhill, Aldbourne; plateau; (250m, OD) – Flake (triangular, heavily rolled [possibly just very weathered] and iron stained).

SU 2272 7596: Woodsend, Aldbourne; plateau; (246m, OD) – Scraper (large sub-circular scraper (75mm x 62mm).

SU 245 685: Veronzoff Lodge, Hens Wood, Little Bedwyn; (165m, OD) – Worked Flint.

SU 251 729 (A): Edmunds Hill, Ramsbury; plateau; (235m, OD) – Palaeoliths.

Artefacts found on the lower hills and slopes

Artefacts found on lower hills and slopes in thin topsoils overlying the Chalk are re-deposited. However, waste-flakes found on such slopes have special importance as they may be indicative of a stone-tool manufacturing site at a higher level, having been moved down hill by various forms of slope processes over geological time. As such, waste-flakes provide useful geomorphological information which may (in particular circumstances) allow not only archaeological links to be made between these artefacts and known high-level find-spots but also the location of previously unknown high-level areas of stone-tool manufacture.

Determining the actual number of find-spots on slopes is somewhat problematical as many surface-finds can only be assigned general (G) or estimated (E) grid references. The various records for the Hackpen Hill area present the greatest uncertainties, for although it is known that many surface-finds were recovered from a number of places (see for example Kendall 1908; 1909; 1914; 1916), details are sometimes obscure.

Find-spots on slopes

SU 074 770: Clyffe Pypard; Gault slope; (140m OD) – Ovate handaxe.

SU 084 744 (A): Wyr Farm, Winterbourne Bassett; Lower Chalk slope; (182m OD) (Wessex Archaeol (1993) record Gravel) – 2 handaxes.

SU 085 715: Windmill Hill, Avebury; Lower Chalk slope; (194m OD) – Handaxe of chert and 2 flakes.

SU 100 640 (G): Milk Hill, Stanton St.Bernard; Middle Chalk slope; (264m OD) – Palaeolith.

SU 100 750 (G): Hackpen Hill, (Field 86), Winterbourne Bassett; Lower Chalk valley bottom; (170m OD) – Handaxe (sarsen), also listed as – at least 3 handaxes and butt of sarsen handaxe). (Note: possibly the same find-spot as SU102 750 (G)).

SU 102 750 (G): Winterbourne Bassett, Lower Chalk slope; (165m OD) – 1 handaxe, also other unspecified genuine artefacts. (Note: possibly the same find-spot as SU100 750 (G)).

SU 105 681 (A): Avebury, (150m north of West Kennet Long Barrow); Middle Chalk slope; (161m OD) – Handaxe (round butted cordate, 89x71x21mm, weighing 140g).

SU 108 690: Beckhampton Ave, Avebury; Middle Chalk slope; (175m OD) – Handaxe (listed as ovate handaxe, Wymer type K).

(Note: This NGR may not be correct for the given find-spot see SU 168 718 in this list).

SU 113 724 (A): Base of Monkton Down, Winterbourne Monkton; Lower Chalk slope; (177m OD) – Sarsen handaxe found at Roman site (944) others by Kendall. (records list as at least 2 handaxes, 1 made of sarsen). (Note: possibly the same find-spot as SU 100 750 (G)/ SU102 750 (G)).

SU 120 719 (E): Winterbourne Monkton Downs, Winterbourne Bassett; Lower Chalk slope; (183m OD) – Handaxe of sarsen found by Kendall 1912. (Note: It is not clear from the records if this (SU120 719) and SU 113 724 are the same find-spot).

SU 125 725: Monkton Down, Winterbourne Monkton; Upper Chalk slope (edge of Clay-with-flints; (255m OD) – Flake (large, striated and abraded).

SU 125 726 (E): Glory Ann Barn Pit, Winterbourne Monkton; Upper Chalk slope; (263m OD) – Handaxe and flake.

(Note: The NGR in this entry is wrong for Glory Ann Barn Pit. The Barn/Pond area is on the Clay-with-flints, plateau, in the area of SU 128 727 (265m. OD). Importantly, although Wessex Archaeology (1993) record a handaxe and flake for this location (the flake listed as being held at Devizes Museum) there is no actual record of a flake being found at the same location as the handaxe in the Glory Ann Barn Pit – the flake found at SU125 725 (Monkton Down) may be the source of the confusion. The handaxe is now lost.

SU 125 740 (E): Hackpen Hill, Berwick Bassett; Upper Chalk slope; (278m OD) – 6 handaxes; 10 flakes; 1 core.

(Note: This entry may to refer to artefacts from Kendall's 1912 excavations although the NGR and geology is not compatible).

SU 130 750 (G): Hackpen Hill; Upper Chalk slope; (280m OD) – 5 handaxes, 3 unretouched Flakes,

(Note: Although this entry may to refer to artefacts from Kendall's 1912 excavations, the given NGR (Winterbourne Bassett, Broad Hinton, Upper Chalk, slope) is not compatible with Kendall's 1912 area of excavation at SU 128 726 – deposits mapped as Clay-with-flints, plateau Hackpen Hill, the Ridgeway Field site).

SU 164 798: Burderop Farm, Chiseldon/Wroughton; Lower Chalk slope; (190m OD) – handaxe fragment.

SU 168 627 (A): NW of Wick Farm, Pewsey; Lower Chalk slope; (154m OD) (Note: the Wilts SMR records a – 'Flint point and scraper'; but Wessex Archaeology (1993) lists a 'retouched flake').

SU 168 718: Manton Down, Preshute; Middle Chalk slope; (170m OD) – Ovate Handaxe Wymer type K. (Note: possible transcription error and data distortions in 2 (maybe 3) recorded entries i.e. SU 168 718; SU 138 718/SU 139 719) and SU108 690 as all have exactly the same (unlikely?) distinctive artefact description).

SU 208 797(G): Liddington Castle, Liddington; Upper Chalk slope; (236m OD) – Handaxe.

SU 240 725 (E): Burney, Ramsbury; Upper Chalk slope; (165m OD) – 2 Palaeoliths.

SU 2642 7424: Aldbourne Common, Aldbourne; Upper Chalk slope (edge of Clay-with-flints); (166m OD) – Scraper (large thick circular 57mm x 70mm x 22mm).

Artefacts found in dry valleys, river valleys and stream channels

Both ancient and modern river valleys, stream channels and (to a lesser extent) dry valleys, have produced a great number of Palaeolithic artefacts. The associated river gravel, alluvium and valley gravel in these low-level downland areas, includes materials (and artefacts) which have been washed down from higher-levels. Colluvium fills the dry-valleys, while much of the river gravel is of Pleistocene age, often overlain and replenished with reworked material (including artefacts) of various origins and ages. Stone tools recovered both as surface-finds and from very shallow gravel deposits, are therefore, almost certainly in a derived context. Although the potential for the survival of *in-situ* sites in river and valley deposits is high, few excavated sites have been found to be *in-situ*, most of the artefacts being derived. Nevertheless, some of the most important Palaeolithic *in-situ* sites in Britain (for examples see Wymer 1968; Roe 1981) have been found in a variety of low-level deposits (frequently gravels, but not specifically in downland areas).

Find-spots in River and Valley Gravels and Alluvium

SU 190 691 (A) Marlborough (Gas Works); Alluvium, floodplane; (132m OD). As this handaxe is recorded as being made from Broom Chert (Lacaille 1971, 82, fig.6, No.3) it may be an import. However, a chert handaxe was also found in the Knowle Farm Pit assemblage downstream at SU 256 676 (A) (see below).

SU 225 678 (E): Ashlade Firs, Mildenhall, (1.5m W of Knowle Farm);Valley Gravel; (165m OD) – Palaeoliths.

SU 256 676 (A): Knowle Farm Gravel Pit , also known as Knowles Farm Pit, Little Bedwyn, Savernake; Head Gravel (mapped as River Gravel) up to 6m deep on valley bottom; (132m OD) – >1600 Handaxes; > 10 Cores; >110 Flakes; > 175 Flakes (unretouched); >50 miscellaneous worked fragments (see below).

SU 256 678 (A): Little Bedwyn, Savernake, (shallow working in valley opposite Knowle Farm), Valley Gravels, valley bottom (132m OD) – 2 Handaxes, 4 Flakes (see below)

Knowle Farm Gravel Pit, Little Bedwyn, Savernake

The old site at Knowle Farm Gravel Pit, Little Bedwyn, Savernake (SU256 676 (A); 132m OD) is 15km east from Avebury, where 2,000 palaeoliths, mainly handaxes (noted for a distinctive silica gloss both on many of the artefacts and natural flints), were recovered from the gravel from around 1901, notably, through the efforts of the Rev H G O Kendall (Cunnington and Cunnington 1903: Dixon 1903: Kendall 1906). Further excavations took place in 1977 (Froom 1983, 27–37). Wymer (in Wessex Archaeology 1993, 57) notes that *'only sporadic finds have been made since'*.

All the Palaeolithic artefacts recovered from the solifluected gravels (Head Gravel, mapped as River Gravel, up to 6m deep on valley bottom) at this site are described as derived, but they vary greatly both in type and condition. Roe (1968, 311) records a total of >1600 Handaxes > 10 Cores; >110 Flakes; > 175 Flakes (unretouched); >50 miscellaneous worked fragments. Froom (1983, 30) states that *'Some palaeoliths have evidently traveled only a short distance, whereas others, heavily battered and rolled, indicate a much greater degree of transportation; the same is true of the unworked nodules which constitute the gravels'* (*op cit* 1983, 30). He also concluded that *'the deposits had accumulated over a considerable period of time, as a result of several processes all relating to cold-climate conditions. Further, these deposits represent the massive and durable residues of strata culled from a wide area.'*

Dating this site remains problematical. Although the main period of activity is thought to have occurred during OIS 8/9 (the Wolstonian), with some reworking during OIS 1 (the later Devensian period), it is also suggested that an OIS 12 *'Anglian rather than a Wolstonian date could not be discounted'*(*ibid*). Froom's observations that the *'Pleistocene deposits remaining undisturbed in modern times can be sub-divided into five units'*(*ibid*), is of particular interest, for within the lowest of these units the 'Lower gravel' Palaeolithic handaxes were found. Further research is needed to determine whether these artefacts are actually associated with the 'Lower Gravel'– if indeed they are, then they may also be pre-Anglian (OIS 13 – Cromerian Complex). Clearly, this site has the potential to provide important contemporary landscape data.

More recently Palaeolithic artefacts have also been discovered in shallow quarrying in the valley opposite Knowle Farm (SU256 678 (A) 132m OD) Little Bedwyn, Savernake.

Geomorphological Links and Archaeological Possibilities

Although the majority of the recorded artefacts can be viewed only as single isolated surface-finds, a number of find-spots appear to have a geomorphological relationship. For example, where one find-spot is on a hilltop and another is on the slope of the same hill (Fig 6:1). This does not of course imply that there is an actual association between the artefacts in question (i.e. from the same assemblage) but that their geomorphological relationship may help explain the processes through which each artefact assumed its present topographic location (e.g. on a slope) relative to its originating location (e.g. manufactured on a hill-top) (Scott-Jackson 2000, 16–18).

Three find-spots: one on a Middle Chalk slope, two on deposits mapped as Clay-with-flints

SU 100 640 (G): Milk Hill, Stanton St.Bernard; Middle Chalk slope; (264m OD) – Palaeolith, – is below:

SU 105 640 (E): Milk Hill, Stanton St. Bernard; Clay-with-flints (edge of plateau); (312m, OD) – Handaxe, which is on the same ridge as:

SU 1070 6415: North of Oxenmere, Stanton St. Bernard; Clay-with-flints (edge of plateau); (312m, OD) – Flake.

Two find-spots: one on deposits mapped as Clay-with-flints, one on an Upper Chalk slope

SU 123 731: Berwick Bassett Down, Berwick Bassett; Clay-with-flints; (255m, OD) – Handaxe (crude ovate), may be associated with:

SU 125 725: Monkton Down, Winterbourne Monkton; Upper Chalk slope (edge of Clay-with-flints); (255m OD) – Flake (large, striated and abraded).

Two find-spots: both on Clay-with-flints

SU 128 726 A: Ridgeway Field, Hackpen Hill; plateau (265m OD) – At least 6 handaxes, 10 waste-flakes and 1 core were excavated from the 1912 site. Kendall (1916:29) records, *'200 yds distant is the barn known as Glory Ann and between the latter and the depression is the pond which resulted from clay-digging for brick making'*, on the same ridge and close to:

SU 128 727 (A): Glory Ann Barn Pit, Hackpen Hill; (265m, OD) – Handaxe.

Two find-spots: both on Clay-with-flints

SU 216 755: Ogbourne Hill, Ogbourne St.George; plateau; (250m, OD) Flake (large, with iron oxide staining), is on the same ridge and close to:

SU 217 754: Ogbourne Hill/Roundhill, Aldbourne; plateau; (250m, OD) – Flake (triangular, heavily rolled [weathered ?] and iron stained).

Two find-spots: both on soliflucted Gravel deposits

SU 256 676 (A): Knowle Farm Gravel Pit , also known as Knowles Farm Pit, Little Bedwyn, Savernake; Head Gravel (mapped as River Gravel) up to 6m deep on valley bottom; (132m OD) – >1600 Handaxes; > 10 Cores; >110 Flakes; > 175 Flakes (unretouched); >50 miscellaneous worked fragments, – is close to:

SU 256 678 (A): Little Bedwyn, Savernake, (shallow working in valley opposite Knowle Farm), Valley Gravels, valley bottom (132m OD) – 2 handaxes, 4 flakes.

Find-spots, slopes and waste-flakes

The following entries record (or elude to) Palaeolithic waste-flake(s) being found on slopes. Such finds have archaeological potential as they may be indicative of stone-tool manufacturing at a higher level.

SU 085 715: Windmill Hill, Avebury; Lower Chalk slope; (194m OD) – Handaxe of chert and 2 flakes.

SU 100 640 (G): Milk Hill, Stanton St.Bernard; Middle Chalk slope; (264m OD) – Palaeolith.

SU 102 750 (G): Winterbourne Bassett, Lower Chalk slope; (165m OD) – 1 handaxe, also other unspecified genuine artefacts. (Note: possibly the same find-spot as SU100 750 (G)).

SU 125 725: Monkton Down, Winterbourne Monkton; Upper Chalk slope (edge of deposits mapped as Clay-with-flints); (255m OD) – Flake (large, striated and abraded).

SU 125 740 (E): Hackpen Hill, Berwick Bassett; Upper Chalk slope; (278m OD) – 6 handaxes; 10 flakes; 1 core.

(Note: This entry may to refer to artefacts from Kendall's 1912 excavations although the NGR and geology is not compatible).

SU 130 750 (G): Hackpen Hill; Upper Chalk slope; (280m OD) – 5 handaxes, 3 unretouched flakes, (Note: Although this entry may to refer to artefacts from Kendall's 1912 excavations, the given NGR (Winterbourne Bassett, Broad Hinton, Upper Chalk, slope) is not compatible with Kendall's 1912 area of excavation at SU 128 726 Clay-with-flints, plateau Hackpen Hill, the Ridgeway Field site).

SU 168 627 (A): NW of Wick Farm, Pewsey; Lower Chalk slope; (154m OD) (Note: Wilts SMR records a – *'Flint point and scraper'*; but Wessex Archaeolgy (1993) lists it as –*'retouched Flake'*).

SU 240 725 (E): Burney, Ramsbury; Upper Chalk slope; (165m OD) – 2 Palaeoliths.

The Artefacts – an assessment

The majority of the recorded artefacts are made of flint. Only four are of other materials – two handaxes made of chert and two of sarsen. One chert and two sarsen handaxes were found on Lower Chalk slopes (i.e. Windmill Hill, 194m OD, chert handaxe; Winterbourne Monkton, 183m OD, sarsen Winterbourne Bassett, 170m OD, sarsen handaxes) and one chert handaxe on alluvium (i.e. from Marlborough, 132m OD).

By reference to the following sources of information (Kendall 1916: Roe 1968: Lacaille 1971: Scott-Jackson 2000) a brief assessment of a number of the recorded Lower and Middle Palaeolithic artefacts has been made possible (there are no Upper Palaeolithic finds). The use of extensive quotations is unavoidable as many terms and description used by Kendall and

Lacaille have in recent years been changed or refined. Without a re-examination of the artefacts, a reinterpretation of their findings cannot be undertaken with confidence.

The following artefact assessments are listed geographically from west to east, with the exception of the Hackpen Hill finds, which are considered last.

(No NGR given) Clyffe Peppard (107m OD) *'an ovate hand-axe was found below the Lower Chalk escarpment'* (Lacaille 1971, 82).

SU 084 744 Wyr Farm (180m OD) a flint hand-axe *'of conventional form found in gravel. Unscathed, sharp and ocherous stained similar to the best specimens of Acheulian workmanship from the gravels exposed in the dry valley in Knowle Farm Pit Savernake'*(*opcit* 1971, 80).

SU 084 744 Wyr Farm (180m OD) a small flint handaxe was also found, *'It is stained ochreous and though its edges are still keen and the flake-ridges dulled, the scars are fairly lustrous on one face but less so on the other. This suggests that the implement had lain near the surface of the soil out of which it was eventually washed' (ibid).*

(No NGR given) *'Windmill Hill a small sharply pointed hand-axe of whitish chert with two remnants of light brown crust [cortex] Acheulian also two Lower Palaeolithic flakes'(opcit.* 1971, 82).

SU 100 750 Winterbourne Bassett (G) a small flat pointed [possibly plano-convex] handaxe much worn [weathered?], irregular shape, and a few reputable implements [not described] (Kendall 1916, 26–48); (Roe unpublished card index):

SU 113 724 Winterbourne Monkton – a handaxe of sarsen, pointed, rough butt, very little weathered, dimensions about 5 inch x 3 1/2 inches x 1 inch (illustrated in W.A.M. LVII 1957/60:400. (*ibid*):

SU 113 724 (168–175m OD) [Winterbourne Monkton] – *'a fine linguate hand-axe, made on a thick flake of fine-grained sarsen, ... It is virtually unaltered except for some rusty streaks and specks. Weak brown staining only serves to emphasize the Acheulian character of the flake-scars and fine trimming'* (Lacaille 1971, 80–82).

(No NGR given) Winterbourne Monkton Down *'an abraded butt-end of a small sarsen hand-axe was found below Winterbourne Monkton Down at (186m OD)'* (*op cit* 1971, 80).

(No NGR given) Winterbourne Bassett *'a small handaxe flint, pale brown, still sharp but slightly pitted and glazed'(ibid)*.

(No NGR given) Winterbourne Bassett *'Unchanged but slightly weathered, irregular four –sided biface almost entirely flaked over in brown sarsen with inclusions of quartz nodules and glassy particles'* (*ibid*).

'Now in the heart of the Wiltshire downland, with its scanty muster of Lower Palaeolithic flint implements, we find a few specimens hewn by characteristic technique to true Acheulian forms in pieces of sarsen-stone. Of all kinds of rock this would be thought the most unlikely to be experimented upon by a practitioner of flaking' (*op cit* 1971 82).

(No NGR given) *'Old Totterdown 'though apparently unaffected by rough transport, certainly did not escape the ravages of climatic alterations after being discarded. Among the surface-finds that exhibit these effects is a hand-axe of cherty flint. Stained deep brown like the implements already considered, and thus resembling many Palaeolithic tools from the Savernake Forest area, this biface was picked up approximately on the 243.8m (800ft) contour near Old Totterdown. ... it has been sadly impaired by thermal action along lines of weakness to the damage of the rather pronounced flake scars. Deep pitting and peeling of the surface are characteristic. Time and weather have contributed to these ancient defacements without seriously dulling the long sinuous edges. Doubtless this palaeolith had lain protected for ages under grass-covered soil or in the capping of fine gravel until eventually dislodged by agricultural operations'*(*op cit* 1971, 79).

(No NGR given) *'northern flank of Granham Hill, which drops to the Kennet River opposite Marlborough College –a small Acheulian flint, flat hand-axe'*(*op cit* 1971, 82).

(No NGR given) Gas-works Marlborough – this flint biface is greatly abraded, a condition very similar to those found at Knowle Farm pit Savernake (*ibid*).

(No NGR given) Gas works, Marlborough – Handaxe, 1 small coarse, medium rolled, pointed type, very comparable with others at Knowle Farm (Roe, unpublished card index).

SU 256 676 (A) Knowle Farm Pit, Savernake A great number of Palaeolithic artefacts both pointed and ovate forms were recovered from the gravel. Roe (1981, 151), who examined an undifferentiated sample from Knowle Farm concluded that the artefacts were mixed and derived from different sources (as discussed above).

Hackpen Hill

The Hackpen Hill plateau has yielded Palaeolithic artefacts both as excavated artefacts and surface finds from Ridgeway Field (SU 128 726) (for a detailed analysis of the excavated artefacts and the site see Scott-Jackson 2000, 62–65). The artefacts from Hackpen Hill all display varying degrees of patination, so much so, that Kendall was able to divide them into two groups.

Group 1 Artefacts: dark brown patina; much abraded and striated. This group had *'course edges and a considerable hump near the middle of the stone, yet they are frequently chipped all over and show a lancelet or sometimes ovate outline'* (*op cit* 1916, 14). (Note: based on typology/condition, group 1 was considered by Kendall to be of a greater age than group 2, this however might not necessarily be so).

Group 2 Artefacts: crimson and sometimes a brown patination: much striation, but less than group 1, and fewer points of impact. This group comprised both pointed and ovate implements and flakes. Lacaille, who visited the area and subsequently examined many of the artefacts, states *'Only a small number of Lower Palaeolithic artefacts have been found by excavation ... they may be put down to the Acheulian culture. They consist of such bifaces as hand-axes and ovates, flakes and cores'* (*op cit* 1971, 84).

Roe records for (SU 130 750 (G) Hackpen Hill). A few reliable finds; a rather oblong ochreous implement with white marking and a small ovate handaxe with variegated white and brown colouring (see for example Kendall 1916, 26–48: Roe, unpublished card index).

Blemished and abraded surface-finds make up the bulk of the Hackpen Hill artefacts, in contrast to the *in-situ* Lower Palaeolithic *'sharp and unscathed implements'* (Kendall 1916, 35) which were excavated from the solution hollow in the Ridgeway Field area. That is, they were found where they had been made or deposited. Lacaille concluded *'As understood today, the Lower Palaeolithic output and the site are, I believe even more interesting than they first appeared'*(1971, 70).

A number of artefacts from the Ridgeway Field area have been described as follows: Handaxes which range in length from 9cm–10.5cm, often exhibit short striations which sometimes cover the surface of these artefacts and *'many of the tools are made on thick flakes, pebbles or small cobbles'*(*ibid*). Ovates and core-tools – are also represented in the assemblage and like the handaxes, may also exhibit striations. Lacaille (*ibid*) gives the following examples: An ovate – *'heavy bulging and scratched with crushed edges and attrite flake-ridges'*.*'Another, less stout and even more abraded apparently ... reduced from normal oval to squarish outlines. Being now so smoothed and bruised of edge, these to implements are hardly distinguishable from water-rolled stones' 'A shapely cordiform tool pocked by thermal fractures, heavily coated, ochreous brown, and better preserved, it exhibits marks of a well-developed Acheulian workmanship''A dihedral and equally well-made form'*.

Roe (unpublished card index) also records the following various worked pieces of uncertain age and type: 1 tiny ovate, fairly flat slight damage and rolled; 1 small ovate type, rather coarse, very rolled, scratched and damaged; 1 small near ovate/ leaf shaped, fairly flat, and neat, much rolled; 1 small coarse ovate type, edges damaged, very rolled.

Lacaille records that as a result of *'Kendall's carefulness, worn or worked flakes and pieces were collected'* and that, *'Among the flakes from Kendall's excavation are several that could be described as Levalloisian'* but adds, *'however, some of these are waste from bifaces, in the making, for example, a number retaining nodular cortex'* (*op cit* 1971, 70). Several of the flakes are also described as showing signs of utilization and trimming. While a number of the small flakes appear to have been retouched to be used as side scrapers. Kendall remarked that *'some bores, scrapes etc. were very small indeed'* (*op cit* 1916, 33).

Lacaille (1971, 73–75) notes that although *'A variety of cores were found but none of the 'tortoise' type'... There are some curious cores among the flints examined from the downland'*. He gives the following examples: *'a small cobble, is so scarred bifacially at one end only as to indicate that the maker intended to use it as an edge-tool....That the implement served as a chopper or heavy scraper appears from the battered condition of the edge'*; *'Of small prismatic pieces from which flakes or blades have been detached, one is particularly noteworthy for its worn convex edge'*; *'Also among the flake-scarred residual lumps of flints, seems to be a sort of plane-scraper'*; *'An easily held, medium-sized, multi-faceted subglobular core. Hardly any part has escaped the alternative flaking that shaped and brought it to a circumferential cutting edge. This mostly retains its pristine keenness, but the flake-ridges are dulled slightly in places and the beds show lustre'*(*ibid*).

The important significance of a handaxe from SU 256 727 (A) Glory Ann Barn Pit, Hackpen Hill is discussed in detail by Scott-Jackson (2000:62–65). Suffice to say here is that its recovery was noted by Kendall (1916:) and referred to by Lacaille (1971:79) thus; *'Found only 200yds (183m) from the principal site* [Kendall's excavation at SU 256 726] .... *a cream-patinated and almost unblemished hand-axe from Glory Ann Barn Pit was picked out of the clay into which it had sunk when the surface was soft. It therefore differs very remarkably from the deeply ocherous-stained worn down pebbled bifaces which have come from these parts'*. There are several reasons to think that this one cream-patinated handaxe may be indicative of a Lower Palaeolithic assemblage that still waits to be uncovered in the Glory Ann Pond area, or elsewhere on Hackpen Hill for that matter (Scott-Jackson 2000:65).

Discussion

Superimposed, as we have seen, one upon the other in time and space, are traces of Lower, Middle, Upper Palaeolithic and later human activity, together with the effects of many varied and diverse climatic changes over geological time. The Palaeolithic landscape itself is, essentially multi-layered. Patterns of Palaeolithic artefact distribution are consistent with that found in other downland counties of southern England. Commonly, many of the find-spots, find-sites and by association, the artefacts, are separated in time by hundreds of thousands of years.

All the artefacts found in the area of study appear to be Lower and Middle Palaeolithic. There are no records of Upper Palaeolithic artefacts being found, indeed such finds are scarce in Britain as a whole. It is just possible however, that in some rare instances Upper Palaeolithic artefacts recovered as surface-finds may have been assigned to Mesolithic collections.

Although the fragmented nature of the surviving data presents an incomplete picture, it is now possible to directly relate this information to the activities of the Palaeolithic peoples who hunted/scavenged/gathered, butchered carcasses, ate and rested and manufacture stone tools, as they made their way across the land we know as the Marlborough Downs.

Even though no actual camp structures survive and it is not known if the stone-tools are associated with seasonal or more permanent butchering sites, consumption and resting camps or home bases, we can be certain that the rivers and streams provided fresh water, whilst on the highest hilltops and plateaux, the hollows which formed in the capping deposits, may well have supplied a source of water or a sheltered area for making stone-tools. Indeed, knappable flint and stone appears to have been readily obtainable for the manufacture of stone-tools from both the chalk and the river gravels.

The Ridgeway Field find-sites and the general distribution of find-spots (in similar geological contexts) on the highest hilltops and plateaux, suggests that the strategic positions of these vantage points were as important to Palaeolithic peoples in their hunting and defence strategies as they were to later inhabitants of the area. These sites, may be described as *'places of continuous occupation'* (Gamble, 1996) for where the Palaeolithic is apparent, often Mesolithic, Neolithic, Bronze Age and indeed evidence of later occupations, may also be found.

From the archaeological data now available we can be certain that Palaeolithic people built fires and manufactured stone-tools on the hilltops and plateaux, but there is less evidence for encampment in the dry valleys and by the rivers and streams. Without doubt many low-level sites have been swept away or are now deeply buried beneath soliflucted deposits.

At Knowle Farm Pit, the numerous Palaeolithic artefacts of all types and conditions, recovered during excavation in the low-level soliflucted gravels are unquestionably re-deposited, being abraded and water worn to different degrees. These artefacts, along with large quantities of material, are generally thought to have been brought down by fluvio-periglacial processes from sites at a higher level into the existing valley and then partially re-sorted by the local streams. The great variability in artefact type and condition certainly suggests that they are mixed and derived from different sources. Just how many sites these stone-tools represent is not known but it is interesting to note that some artefacts display much less abrasion than others and that the gravel from which the Knowle Farm artefacts were extracted is mainly angular and unrolled. Might it be possible that the less abraded artefacts have come from a low-level site (buried, perhaps) near this locale?

The find-spots and find-sites provide both archaeological and geomorphological information, occasionally allowing links to be made between the artefacts from that particular find-spot and known high-level find-spots. As each find-spot on a slope is indicative of Palaeolithic activity at a higher level, then further fieldwork is required to locate previously unknown stone-tool manufacture sites on the hilltops and plateaux.

Sixteen find-spots are situated on high-points capped with Clay-with-flints. As we have seen, a number of these surface-find assemblages from these high-levels may allude to the presence of embedded artefacts and by association therefore, the possibility of *in-situ* sites. As these find-spots attest to Palaeolithic activity we may consider how many of the handaxes recovered as isolated finds were actually lost or discarded by Palaeolithic people, perhaps in the course of hunting, gathering or scavenging across the downlands and into the valleys.

The use of the landscape as a whole can be seen in the distribution of artefacts from the low-levels to the high-levels. Lacaille, writing in regard to the Palaeolithic finds on Clay-with-flints on Martinsell Hill, Pewsey (SU 177 640) states, *'they come from the greatest altitude reached by Acheulian man in the united Lower Palaeolithic province of north-eastern France and southern England. Again, this is a reminder that he did not restrict himself to the river valleys, but ventured up the flanks on to high ground. In this respect one recalls the collection of Acheulian implements from the surface of the plateaux at over 820ft.(250m) above sea-level in the famous Dordogne territory'*(*op cit* 1971, 85).

As Palaeolithic people themselves did not restrict their wanderings to any one area, nor perhaps undertake the same activity at each site, then clearly, we must consider the landscape as a whole, for no single site can ever provide all the answers.

Conclusion

By weaving together this information, a general pattern of Palaeolithic artefact distribution has now appeared, albeit with many gaps. Such a situation is to be expected as these data are much fragmented, being collected by a variety of individuals over many years. However, as each new find is put into place, our archaeological, geomorphological and geological knowledge will be greatly increased.

The finds from the studied area contrast greatly with the very small number of sites in Britain (all at low-levels) which are described as being found in 'primary context'. Although these elusive sites are undeniably invaluable, an over-emphasis on such sites has effectively deterred research in places away from those areas generally considered 'ideal' for the discovery of 'primary sites'. The devaluing of all but the 'finest artefacts' and 'primary context sites' has acted as a serious obstruction, delaying both the discovery and recognition of *in situ* sites (Scott-Jackson 2000) and grossly distorting the value of the Palaeolithic to be found in other conditions and situations. We must work with enthusiasm with what we have, as a plethora of *in situ* sites in primary context is a highly unrealistic expectation – a starving man does not despise a meal because it is not a feast!

It is hoped therefore, that this compilation and analyses of these data will provide a solid basis for future investigations, not the least being the generation of fieldwork projects using appropriate scientific techniques and methodologies. In particular, the investigation of high-level sites on Clay-with-flints (Scott-Jackson 2000, 76–84; 2001b, 5–6, 38, 62–63,74, 80, 84).

Clearly, the problems involved in any study of the Palaeolithic are multitude and complex, but such difficulties should not be a deterrent to the inclusion of the Palaeolithic periods in any landscape study. There is, without doubt, a great need for workers in later periods to be aware of the existence of the Palaeolithic landscape in every area, for as previously noted, where Mesolithic, Neolithic, Bronze Age and indeed later occupations are found – the Palaeolithic may also be evident.

7

Considering Prehistoric Environmental Changes on the Marlborough Downs

Michael J Allen

The concentration of easily recognisable major prehistoric monuments in the 'Avebury landscape' and the Marlborough Downs has lead to a concentration of palaeoenvironmental research. What I wish to explore in this paper is how this environmental analysis, or interpretation, may help us understand social development of communities in this landscape. I address and question some assumptions and perceptions about the physical lived-in landscape which provided the economic basis of the populations who inhabited it.

Introduction

The area of the Marlborough Downs we call the 'Avebury landscape' has deservedly received much archaeological, and thankfully, palaeo-environmental attention. In environmental terms seminal work on the presence of soil pollen, for instance, was presented by Dimbleby from sites in this landscape.

Environmental analyses, and I include my own, have tended to take either just the site of investigation, or the Avebury monument itself, as the centre of the perceived landscape. Although the Marlborough Downs as an entity extends well beyond the Avebury area, our palaeo-environmental database does not. We are, therefore, forced in some way to restrict our discussion to the downland around Avebury that is famous for its numerous and complex prehistoric sites. However, as I will discuss, we will avoid temptation to perceive Avebury as the physical or social centre of this 'landscape', even if it inadvertently lies in the middle of the distribution maps.

Instead of relying on site specific examples we now have enough data to enable an attempt to create more holistic pictures or viewscapes of the actual mosaic of land-use. This is done by visualisation of the mosaic of land-use as I have suggested for the Stonehenge landscape (Allen 1997a). It requires huge environmental databases and the resolution of the large Avebury Area is, surprisingly, not very robust.

Changes not just of land-use, but *patterns* of land-use development allow us to bring another level of interpretation and understanding to the archaeological and monumental record. Perhaps, in retrospect, this is the realisation of the late Bob Smith's approach originally presented 20 years ago.

I do not wish to present a narrative of the development of this landscape here. Rather I wish to use the large database (see Allen 2001a; Table 7:1) to address some specific questions and, perhaps, to challenge some long held assumptions. Before we begin it is necessary to briefly put the Marlborough Downs into a physical, geological and topographical context.

The Marlborough Downs is Upper and Middle Chalk downland to the north of the Kennet Valley between Avebury and Marlborough and encompassing some 20 square kilometres. As an area it is, however, largely an artificial designation. In physiographic terms the area is geologically complex and topographically forms the western extension of the Berkshire Downs. Nevertheless, the geological complexity of this western extremity of chalk downland north of the London basin syncline includes a series of two or three cuestas, prominent lower chalk cuesta north and west of Avebury (Jones 1981) with outliers of Middle and Upper Chalk including Furze Hill (260m), Cherhill Down (259m) and Windmill Hill (186m). The broad inclined chalk plan, separated from Salisbury Plain by the Vale of Pewsey, is drained by the Kennet and its tributary the Og, between which lies a small dissected block of Upper Chalk designated the Marlborough Downs.

	Site	*Grid Ref (SU)*	*reference*	*Late Glacial*	*Mesolithic*	*Neolithic*	*Bronze Age*	*Iron Age*	*Roman*	*Later Saxon & medieval*
1	Cherhill	031 701	Evans 1968	×						
2	Waden Hill	104 685	Evans 1968	×						
3	Cherhill tufa/long barrow	0255 703	Evans & Smith 1983	×	×	×				
4	Beckhampton Rd long barrow	0666 6773	Evans 1968; Ashbee *et al.* 1979	×		×				
5	South Street long barrow	902 6928	Evans 1968; Ashbee *et al.* 1979	×		×				
6	West Overton alluvium	1354 6854	Evans *et al* 1993	×	×					
7	Butler's Field	0979 6982	Evans *et al* 1993		×					×
8	Horlsip long barrow	0860 7052	Ashbee *et al.* 1979							
9	Milbarrow long barrow	0943 7220	Whittle 1994			×				
10	Easton Down long barrow		Whittle *et al.* 1993			×				
11	West Kennet long barrow	105 677	Evans 1972; Piggot 1962			×				
12	Windmill Hill causewayed enc	087 715	Evans 1972; Whittle *et al.* 1999			×				
13	Avebury ditch	101 698	Gray 1935			×				
14	Avebury bank (school)	101 698	Evans 1969; 1972	×		×				
15	Avebury bank (Great barn)	101 698	Evans *et al* 1985		×	×				
16	Avebury Truslow, alluvium	098 697	Evans *et al* 1993	×	×					
17	The Santuary henge	118 679	Cunnington 1931			×				
18	Silbury Hill	100 685	Evans 1972; Whittle 1997			×				
19	Overton Down G6a pit	1193 6834	Smith & Simpson 1964			×				
20	East Kennet Farm/Palisade	111 683	Allen & Carruthers 1989; Whittle 1997			×				×
21	Hemp Knoll round barrow/pit	1024 6788	Roberston MacKay 1980			×	×			
22	G55 round barrow/pit	1024 6788	Smith 1965b			×	×			
23	Roughridge Hill A round barrow	060 660	Evans 1972				×			
24	Pound Field round barrow	1346 6819	Powell *et al.* 1996				×			
25	'Stukeley' barrow, Waden Hill	1072 6838	Powell *et al.* 1996				×			
26	West Overton G6b barrow	1196 6835	Smith & Simpson 1966				×			
27	Fyfield Down I lynchet	SU 141 710	Bowen & Fowler 1962; Evans 1972; Fowler 1967; Fowler & Evans 1967				×			
28	Knap Hill	121 636	Dimbleby & Evans 1974				×			
29	Dean Bottom	147 742	Gingell 1992				×			
30	Burderop Down	169 764	Gingell 1992				×			
31	Waden Hill, lynchet	1072 6838	Wyles & Allen 1996b							×
32	Bishops Canning Down	0580 6660	Gingell 1992				×			
33	Piggledene colluvium	1417 6867	Allen in Fowler 2000				×			
34	Overton Down X/XI	134 702	Fowler FWP 63					×		
35	Overton Down, lynchet	134 702	Bowen & Fowler 1962; Fowler 1967; Fowler & Evans 1967					×		
36	Overton Down XII	133 701	Fowler FWP 65						×	
37	Winterbourne colluvium	1022 6880	Powell *et al.* 1996						×	
38	Winterbourne Roman site	1045/49 6838/43	Powell *et al.* 1996						×	
39	Winterbourne burial	1037 6855	Evans 1966a						×	
40	West Overton, colluvium	1354 6862	Evans *et al.* 1993							×

Table 7:1 Sites on Marlborough Downs around Avebury where environmental evidence has been recovered.

Period	*Environment*
Medieval/Romano-British/ Iron Age	Intermittent cultivation and grassland. Formation of ploughwash deposits.
Bronze Age	Open environment of grassland or arable. Cultivation/ grazing intermittent. Formation of wind-lain material
Late Neolithic	Woodland regeneration. Not at Woodhenge
Late Neolithic	Construction of henge monuments
Neolithic	Long period of grassland, probably maintained by grazing.
Neolithic	Woodland clearance. Ploughing and possibly other forms of tillage. Ploughmarks at Avebury.
(Mesolithic) Atlantic (?)	Dense woodland. Recorded only at Avebury, but probably at most sites.
Mesolithic Boreal (?)	Open woodland. Evidence of fire and possible influence of Mesolithic man (Evans 1972, 219, 256).
(Upper Palaeolithic) Late-glacial	Subarctic environment, probably tundra. Formation of periglacial structures and wind-lain material.

Table 7:2 Main environmental events on the chalk of Wiltshire and Dorset in the late-glacial and post-glacial periods, from Evans and Jones (1979, 209)

More detailed description of its topography can be found elsewhere and relevant summaries found in, for instance, Gingell (1992) and Pollard and Reynolds (2002). What this comment serves to do is to indicate that the Marlborough Downs is not, and should not be considered as, a self contained social entity. Communities in the past who lived in this area were not divorced from the adjacent landscape, indeed this area may be rich in its archaeological heritage because it is a meeting of landscapes, with natural 'corridors' and routeways encouraging communication and a meeting of people passing through.

Understanding the 'Landscape', not just 'Sites'

The interpretation of past human activities in any defined space must be conditioned, or controlled by, the physical parameters within that environment. By this we mean not just the shape and geology, but the transient, and probably more significant, elements such as the soils, the vegetation (forests, plains and fields) and the animals that lived, or could be maintained within that 'environment'. As such, although archaeological interpretations of social action within study areas are presented, often recently with great spatial and temporal resolution, the importance of the natural and maintained vegetative, soil and natural environment is neglected or dismissed with a couple of well-worn, well re-iterated sentences. Yet it is that environment that forms the basis of the nature of the activities those communities perform and the lifestyle they adopt.

Just as the archaeological interpretations have highly localised temporal and spatial parameters, so does the environment. We map human behaviour within a study area and use time to trace development in social activity. The natural environment enveloping those communities is even more dynamic so we must understand and map this too.

Our understanding of the landscape environment is tempered by the manner in which data have been collected and interpreted in the past 40 years and also by the resolution of that data both spatially and temporally. The wealth and diversity of prehistoric monuments in the Avebury area have naturally lead to a long and successful history of archaeological research. This area has also been the focus of significant and informative environmental research, pushing forward in areas of methodology, interpretation and our understanding of this area.

Novel scientific analysis of land snails was undertaken by John Evans for his PhD research at Windmill Hill, West Kennet and Avebury itself in the late 1960s (Evans 1967; 1972). Seminal research into the survival of pollen and land snails was conducted by Geoff Dimbleby and John Evans following that (Dimbleby and Evans 1974). Subsequently most environmental research has been site specific, and the majority has centred on the major Neolithic monumental sites. These provided interpretation of the area of the excavated site, and that of its immediate surroundings. How far that interpretation may be extended from the site is still a matter of debate today, but the application of statistics may provide some aid here (Davies and Wolski 2001).

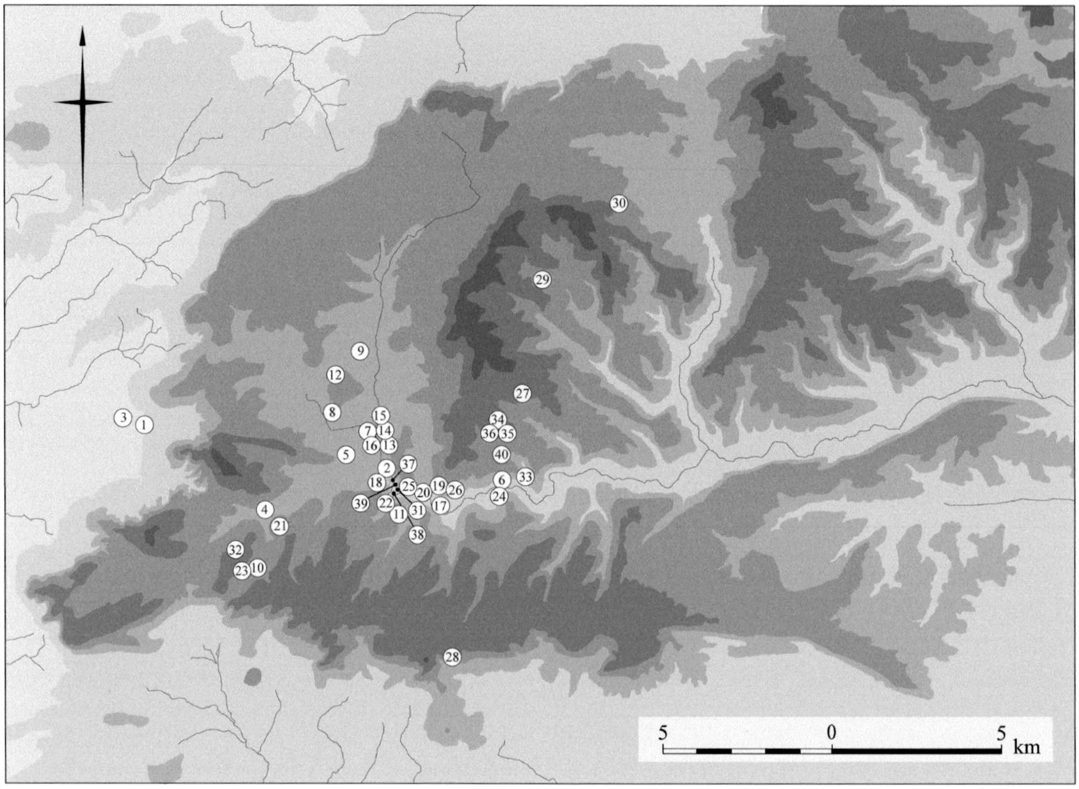

Fig 7:1 Location of sites on the Marlborough Downs surrounding Avebury from which environmental evidence has been recovered (from Allen 2001a, fig 19).

John Evans' work was seminal in the development of our understanding of the chalklands. He was able to summarise general trends which could be detected across the whole of southern England (Table 7:2). These have been tested and modified by his recent work. Certainly his work in studying the sediments in the Kennet valley (Evans *et al* 1988a; 1993) has been influential, but that of his colleagues at Cardiff University on the snails (and other environmental information) from the major Neolithic monuments excavated by Professor Whittle (e.g. Whittle 1997a; Whittle *et al* 1999) and Josh Pollard (e.g. *this volume*) has largely continued on a site-based, rather than landscape-wide interpretation or reconstruction.

Even my own research and analysis in this landscape has, to a certain extent, been site-based. I have, however, attempted to use the data to comment on the wider landscape, and to examine the mosaic of land-use and common, repeated patterns of activity within that landscape. Nevertheless, 10 years ago (in 1992), despite the fact that I thought that I could detect on the Marlborough Downs an emerging, repetitive pattern of neglect in the mid-later Bronze Age (e.g. barrow ditches at least seem to be overgrown), I wrote of the prehistory of the Marlborough Downs that: "It seems unlikely that clearance was extensive over the Marlborough Downs, but we must await a full, structured programme of off-site investigation to provide further interpretation" (Allen 1992, 149). To a large extent we still await that, despite the publication of examples of major research such as the exemplary work by Peter Fowler (Fowler 2000).

Recent environmental landscape reconstruction derived from detailed analyses are more demanding. They appreciate that a landscape is not a uniform entity and that local diversity, and the spatial extent of vegetation and land-use types, is important. In short, they require comment on changes across space. This is exactly what Bob Smith did. He created some of the first scientifically based reconstructions of the pattern of vegetation and land-use for the Avebury Area. His pen and ink reconstructions of the Avebury Area, published in 1984, were based on analytical scrutiny of both the palaeo-environmental and archaeological datasets (Smith 1984). The concept behind these semi-pictoral schematic reconstruction 'maps' was that the examination of the pollen, charcoal, snail and bone databases from each archaeological site to provide an interpretation of the wider countryside. He reviewed all the then current data, evaluated them and used the results to look more holistically at the landscape and to interpret the changing vegetation patterns, or more precisely, the changing and developing patterns of human land-use (see Smith 1984, figs 2, 3, 5 and 6: Fig 7:2).

This combination of data and extent was able

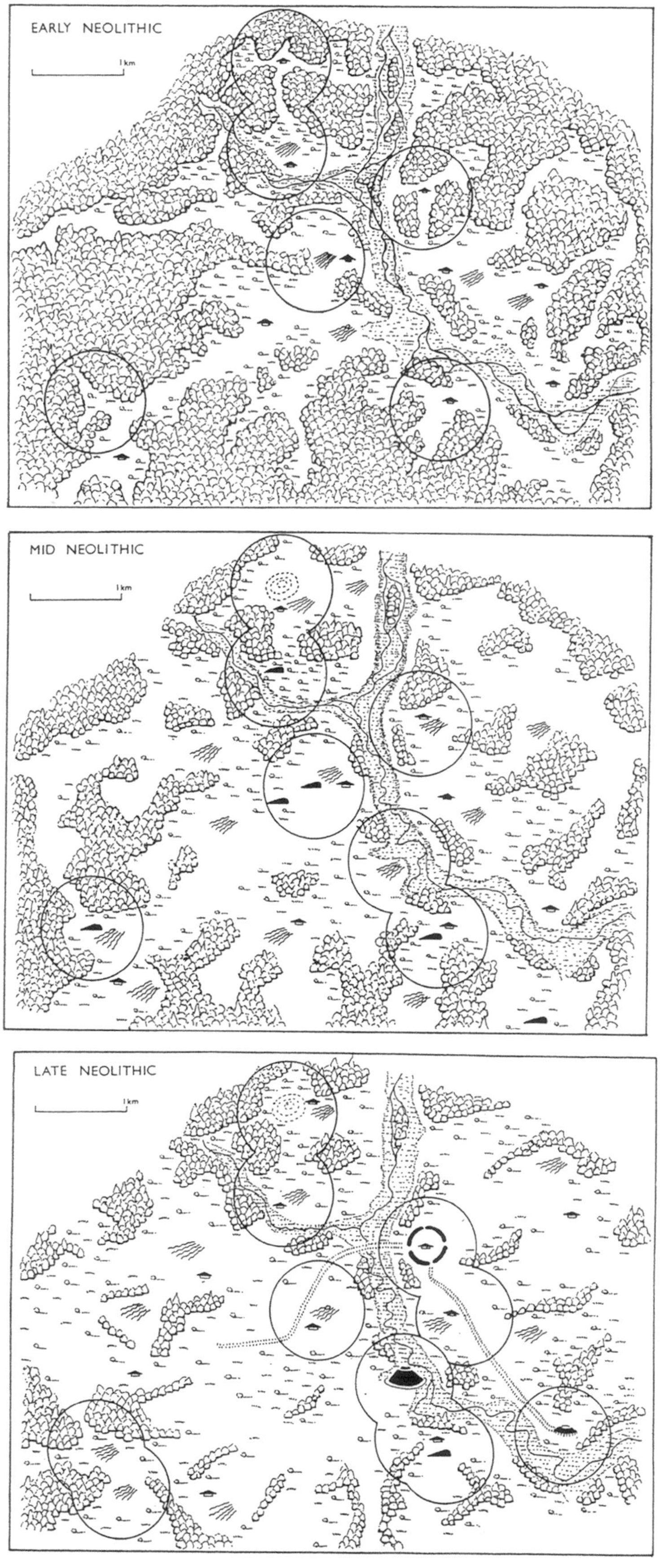

Fig 7:2 Schematic reconstruction of the a) Early Neolithic landscape b) mid Neolithic and c) Late Neolithic of the Avebury region (from Smith 1984, figures 8–10, with permission of the Prehistoric Society).

Table 7:3 Comparison of density of environmental data-sets in chalkland landscapes and the calculation of a 'confidence factor'.

Study area	No of data sets	Km^2 study area	area each data-set represents (A) (data-sets ÷ Km^2)	Confidence Factor (A x 100)
LEWES	9	106	0.085	8.5
ISLE OF WIGHT	9	64	0.140	14.1
STRAWBERRY HILL	1	10	0.100	10.0
STONEHENGE 1	13	54	0.240	24.1
STONEHENGE 2	19	80	0.238	23.8
DORCHESTER	12	35	0.343	34.3
AVEBURY	20	130	0.154	15.4
WINCHESTER	3	16	0.187	18.7
CRANBORNE 1	22	150	0.147	14.7
ALLEN VALLEY/ DOWN FARM	62+	25	2.48	248
KENT	3	1500	0.0002	0.2

to inform us about the nature of both the individual locations in the study area and of the vegetation types which occurred and were exploited within it (Fig 7:1). This analytical approach to reconstruction relies on specific palaeo-environmental datasets and is continually testable and modifiable with new and revised data.

This concept was explored further when I attempted to map vegetation patterns in the Dorchester landscape (in Smith *et al* 1997, figure 120) and the Stonehenge landscape (Allen *et al* 1990, figure 155). Subsequently, more complex, refined and higher resolution mapping has been possible across the Stonehenge landscape by combing environmental datasets and terrain models to map the potential extent of defined vegetation or land-use types (Allen 1997a; 2000a).

These same concepts have lead to the vivid painted landscape reconstructions for the Avebury Area by Jane Brayne, to which I will refer later.

How the developing natural landscape helps us to interpret community action

In order to interpret community action across a defined study area (a stage), it is important that those players are placed within the correct scenery. Many of the older environmental reconstructions are two dimensional statements with little grasp of space, time and the changing dynamics and interpretation of people and the countryside. Descriptive two dimensional interpretations have a place in helping us, as archaeologists, to evolve ideas, but now are often so generalised as to offer only a poor and weak understanding of the landscape. This is not an interpretation you can take to site or any part of the landscape and *visualise.* It is conceptual. What we need to be able to do is to visualise the study area in 3-dimensions, in fact we really need to do this in four dimensions; the fourth dimension being time.

Reviewing all the past evidence (looking back) enables a general consensus to be gathered (Allen 1998), as I have done, for instance, in the Avebury Research Agenda (Allen 2001a). This may allow the isolation of a series of specific or chronological themes (e.g. Allen 2001b; Cleal and Allen 2001), though this is largely abstract. Or we can use that data in any, and for any, one period in an attempt to realise the actual nature of the mosaic of land use (looking forward). This involves scientific reconstruction in three dimensions, and interpretation, and ultimately educated guesswork. This is palaeo-environmental land-use mapping (Allen 2000a).

How does this help interpret community action?

I have used this approach to attempt to *explain* mechanisms of society and communal activities which contributed to the building of Stonehenge (Allen 1997a). There, for instance, I have argued that farming, in terms of cultivation is a high-risk strategy. It is not a life-style that can be adopted instantaneously. Once embarked upon, risks may be shared by communities which may be bonded by shared beliefs, inter-marriage and shared activities in communally built and owned monuments.

Does this precise example work for Avebury? No. The scale, data and concepts are inapplicable here. However exhumation of the datasets and examination of the developing patterns of land-use may allow us to address a number of archaeological issues.

So what of Avebury and the Marlborough Downs? Although sophisticated DEMs (digital elevation models) have been created by English Heritage and Dave Wheatley at Southampton University, the landscape of the Avebury and Marlborough Downs as a single study area is vast. Unlike Stonehenge, however, the environmental database is not as robust. Large though it is, the area over which it extends is much greater, thus severely weakening the extent to which we can interpret between dataset or sites (Table 7:3).

The realisation of the environmental data exists in the series of illustrations by Jane Brayne. Using these data and reconstructions we can start to address a series of specific and generic questions about the Marlborough Downs landscape

The Marlborough Downs; some thoughts, questions, assumptions and perceptions

What I wish to discuss, are a series of points and ideas about the nature of the land-use and the natural environment within the prehistoric Marlborough Downs. I do not attempt to resolve all, if any, of the issues I touch upon, but hope that they will be food for though and considerations within further and ongoing research in this landscape. Some of these points expand on research themes posed in the research agenda for the Avebury World Heritage site (Allen 2001b; Cleal and Allen 2001), while others touch upon themes which can be addressed in this landscape.

1. Landscape perception

Many of the research studies have taken Avebury itself as the centre of the perceived landscape. Why are these foci of our study the centre of the prehistoric lived-in landscape? As I indicated earlier, the Marlborough Downs itself is a small part of a wider chalk downland. If core areas, home territories or community estates existed, there is no need for important monuments to lie physically in the centre of it (*contra* Drewett 1978; 1985). Indeed many, (?such as barrows) may be specifically cited on the periphery and edges of that region. Indeed communal monuments, such as causewayed enclosures and henges, may also lie on margins of adjoining territories, or along know route-ways, valleys. They may have been sites not only for 'the organisation of internal community relationships but also the relationships between communities' (Evans *et al* 1988b, 82), and generally causewayed enclosures are considered as peripheral (e.g. Bradley 1984; Gardiner 1988; 1991; Allen 1997b, 278), and so, perhaps, might henges.

This is a concept we should attempt to avoid. The sites are just points and places within a landscape over which communities travelled and within which they lived. The Avebury area is the confluence of three valleys, it is point on a pathway through the landscape, just as S. Allen indicates in Mesolithic societies (S Allen *this volume.*)

2. How wooded was the woodland; challenging basic concepts

It is assumed that a developing and enveloping cover of woodland mantled the whole of the United Kingdom, almost as a uniform cover by the Neolithic period. Archaeologists have taken the presence of this post-glacial woodland as their assumed starting point when considering the Neolithic countryside.

If we assume this woodland existed, then the first evidence to look for is its the presence, followed by evidence of local clearance. Excellent examples of this typical succession of late glacial tundra, open woodland, the development of post glacial woodland and clearance can be seen in the Neolithic sequences, for instance, from the Avebury buried soil (Evans 1972, 271; Evans *et al* 1985), Cherhill long barrow (Evans and Smith 1983), South Street long barrow (Evans in Ashbee *et al* 1979). the presence of post glacial woodland and its local clearance can also bee seen at both the Easton Down long barrow (Rouse and Evans in Whittle *et al* 1993) and at Windmill Hill (Fishpool in Whittle *et al* 1999). This data tends to confirm our initial assumption, and therefore requires little further examination. Or does it?

I have suggested that there are areas of the chalklands of southern England where the Neolithic woodland may not have existed as a complete blanket. I have postulated such for the Dorchester landscape (Allen 1997b, 278), and recently we have proof that this is also the case in the Allen valley, Cranborne Chase (Allen 2002; Scaife 2000; Scaife in French *et al* 2000). I have also suggested that this may, in part be the reason for concentrated prehistoric settlement in the Dorchester, Cranborne and Stonehenge environs (Allen 2002; forthcoming; in prep.). Can we re-examine the date from the Marlborough Downs with a changed basic assumption? Can we be sure that the woodland was a pre- or post-monument phenomena?

Shaded conditions can be seen in landscapes prior to the construction of both Avebury and Windmill Hill. However in the former open conditions in the buried soil were promoted to create a short-turved grassland for the con-

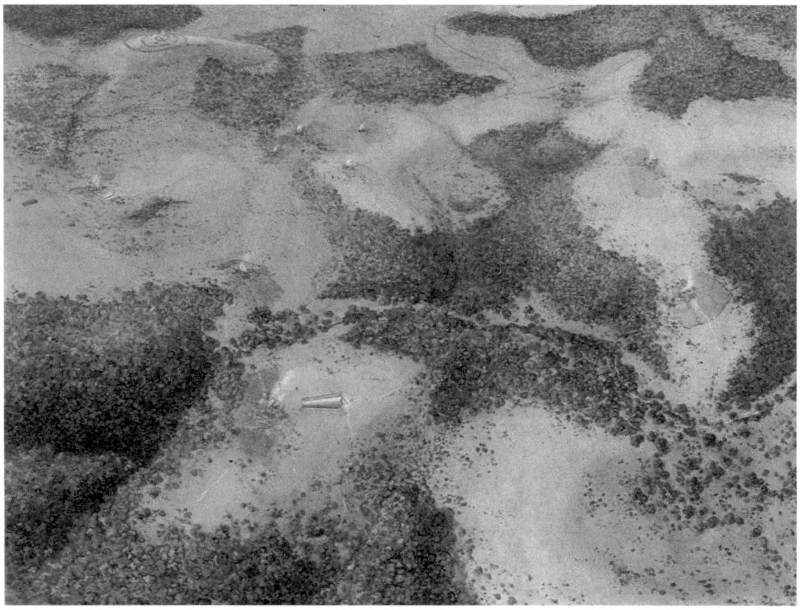

Fig 7:3a Reconstruction of the countryside in the mid Neolithic (c 3400 BC) © J Brayne.

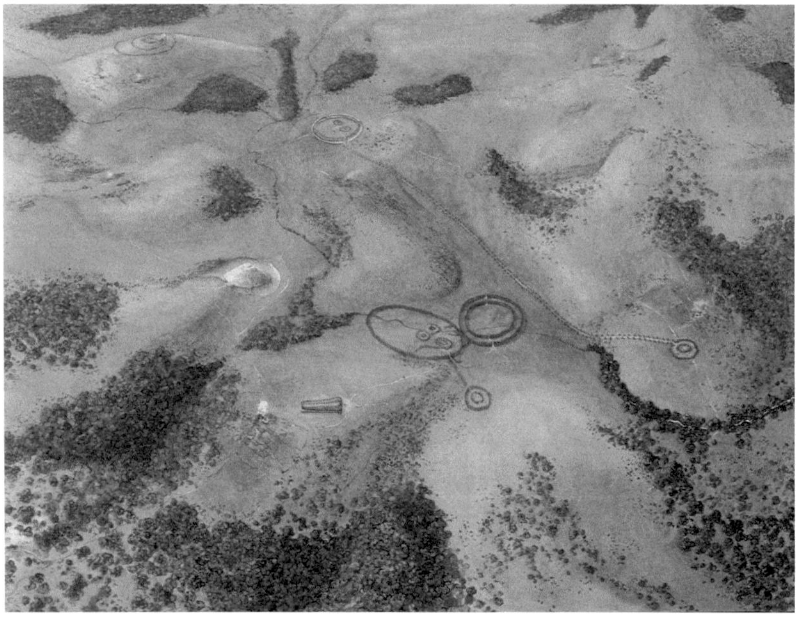

Fig 7:3b Reconstruction of the landscape during the final Neolithic (c 2200 BC) © J Brayne.

struction of the monument. But there is no direct evidence that woodland clearance was associated with monument building. In the latter the nature of the wooded, pre-monument environment can be defined (Fishpool 1999, 131). The nature and occurrence of woodland beneath the numerous long barrows can also be seen to be highly variable.

3. Woodland regeneration

The regeneration of woodland is a common and re-current theme in many monuments in Neolithic Britain. Evidence is primarily from mollusc sequences in ditches, and the Marlborough Downs landscape provides some of the clearest examples (e.g. South Street long barrow). Does this really represent a morass of woodland encroaching into a clearing containing the barrow, the rate and size of which Davies and Wolski (2001) suggest we can measure? Or is this purely the vegetation invasion of the deep ditches – a hypothesis suggested for large Iron Age ditch at Balksbury, Hampshire (Allen 2001c) for instance.

4. Landscape mosaics and what happened between monuments?

It is immediately clear, and indeed obvious, that single vegetation types did not exist uniformly. Patterns and mosaics of vegetation types reflecting land-use and activities that existed. We can see this and start to map this in the Marlborough Downs landscape (see Fig 7:2). The definition of these mosaics can clearly help us understand the development of farming and society. This has yet to be rigorously examined beyond the exemplary work of Bob Smith nearly 20 years ago (Smith 1984).

Clearly areas between monuments (or sites of archaeological investigation) are the most difficult to consider. Yet this is where careful consideration of the topography (*cf* Allen 1997a; 2000a), the addition of pollen evidence (Dimbleby and Evans 1974; Dimbleby 1997), and consideration of species diversity characteristics in land snail assemblages may allow some indication of the nature of the environment beyond the sample location by measuring the level of representation of fauna (species) which may have originated from other local ecologies.

An indication of the nature of the vegetation character and coarseness of vegetation, or ecological, mosaics (*cf* Wiens 1976) may be defined enabling a more explicit interpretation of the extent and pattern of land-use in any given location.

5. Rivers and Streams

Despite the superb research conducted by Evans and Limbrey on alluvial sequences in the Kennet Valley (Evans *et al* 1988; Evans *et al* 1993) which provide an important chronological and ecological framework for the sediment history, we still know little about exactly how the rivers and streams and their valleys looked in prehistory (Cleal and Allen 2001, 60–1). These form the axial routes through the landscape, they are the lines animal of migration, of the first population movements, and we presume some of the first significant modification in this landscape. But can we detect it?

It is suggested (Evans *et al* 1993; Mount 1991) that for most of their post-glacial history both the upper Kennet and Winterbourne valleys contained intermittent streams. The Kennet may only have been a permanent water course early in the post-glacial period (Mount 1991, 219), and Limbrey (1988; 1993) has suggested that may not even have been stream at Avebury in the Late Mesolithic/Early Neolithic and the valley was not subjected to flooding or alluviation (Evans *et al* 1988a, 102). In the Neolithic and Bronze Age we may envisage intermittent, seasonal streams leaving pools in shallow muddy water courses. What Evans *et al* studies have shown is the potentially highly localised nature of the biological and sedimentological data which, therefore, may still question whether we understand the nature of the hydrology of this are in full.

Fig 7:4a Reconstruction of the landscape during the Early Bronze (c 1700–1600 BC) © J Brayne.

6. How open was the Downland?

The upland Downs are characteristically areas for which we have a more secure archaeological understanding. Indeed this is true. But as we have seen above, as the intensity of work in this landscape increases, so does our expectation of the required resolution of interpretation. As with the Neolithic monuments we can define the open downland nature of many Bronze Age sites and burial mounds. But how representative are these location of the surrounding landscape? The presence of prehistoric activity in the form of a settlement, a burial mound or a enclosure, itself should be an indication that the vegetation was cleared locally at least. Should we visualise the area as open downland as today, or as a much wilder countryside (see Fig 7:3a, 7:3b, 7:4a and 7:4b).

The development from a pastoral wildscape to that of a major developed arable landscape and one of animal containment can be seen from the mature Bronze Age onward (see Fowler 2000). This use of the chalk upland, but not highland, provides us with the basis of the character of the landscape we see today. It provided the opportunity for significant settlement (Gingell 1992; Fowler 2000), and field systems. It also unwittingly buried much of the older and still unknown landscape in valley bottoms such as Piggledene where we suspect that Beaker settlement may lie under about a meter of hillwash (Allen 2000b).

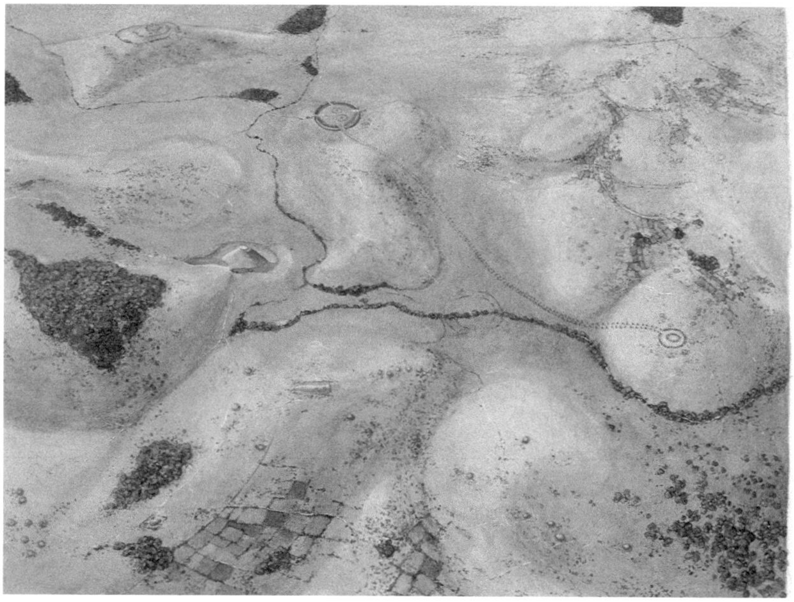

Fig 7:4b Reconstruction of the landscape during the mature Bronze Age (c 1000 BC) © J Brayne.

Concluding comment

As I stated at the onset, I did not wish to provide a narrative of the development of the landscape history. What makes the Marlborough Downs an exciting archaeological prospect is the fact that we have so much palaeo-environmental information, that we realise that we know so little (see Allen 2001b). It is precisely this realisation that should stimulate us to increase the interpretative power and both spatial and temporal resolution across this landscape. In doing so, we will learn not just about the Marlborough Downs, but by inference about prehistoric society from the Mesolithic to the Iron Age, and about the history of chalk landscapes across southern England.

We have the great fortune in this landscape to inherit nearly 40 years of the best analysis from Prof John Evans, it is a landscape where current major research based on renewed fieldwork is being conducted by Josh Pollard and his colleagues (e.g. Gillings *et al* 2000b), it is a landscape which has produced data which still inspires re-analysis and re-examination such as that of woodland regeneration by Davies and Wolski (2001), and it is one in which current bold research programmes are being formulated by Mike Pitts and his colleagues. Long may it continue, and we look forward to the fruition of the ongoing and planned research excavation, and the ensuing debate.

Acknowledgements

I would like to thank Dave Field and Graham Brown for encouraging me to continue to expand my thoughts on this landscape, and to Julie Gardiner for here aid in the production of this paper. Thanks to Rosina Mount for discussing the nature of the prehistoric hydrology. The Prehistoric Society must be thanked for their permission to produced Bob Smiths figures (again), and Jane Brayne for allowing me free use of her excellent reconstruction paintings.

8
Some observations on perception, consolidation and change in a land of stones

David Field

The incidence of sarsen stones on the Marlborough Downs is outlined along with methods of clearance and destruction. Implications of prehistoric removal of stones, the effect on vegetation and the way in which this boulder dominated land might be perceived are also considered.

Introduction

Ever since the 18th century, travellers such as Daniel Defoe have commented on the peculiar nature of the ubiquitous white sarsen boulders that once littered the ground surface between Marlborough and Devizes, the 'Grey Weathers', that from a distance look like grazing sheep (Defoe 1724–6, 265). The phenomenon is one that struck visitors, even geologists such as H J Osborne White, to words of astonishment (Brentnall 1946, 420–1), for such a frequency of such rocks and boulders elsewhere in lowland Britain, at least in recent centuries, was something rarely encountered.

Sarsen is still present across the Marlborough Downs, while beyond the escarpment boulders can be found on the Greensand around Swindon, Calne (e.g. Jones 1949, 131) and to the south in the Pewsey Vale at, for example, Stanton St Bernard. Once the downland was literally covered with them, particularly on the Upper and Middle Chalk around the 'Glory Ann' on the summit of Hackpen Ridge, from where *'they stream off into the valleys'* of Monkton Down, Totterdown and Piggle Dean respectively (Smith 1884). Or in the valleys joining the Kennet from the south around East Kennet, Lockeridge and West Woods. Even the Lower Chalk bench to the northwest of Avebury once appears to have been liberally sprinkled with them and boulders can still be observed in the hedgerows around Yatesbury, Monkton, and Winterbourne Bassett. A pile of sarsen boulders was recently (1999) hauled out of Monkton Field by tractor. According to the farmer, Mr Richard Gauntlett, discovery of sarsen is commonplace and as it damages the plough it is often hauled to the edge of fields. On Boar Down, Compton Basset, numbers of stones occasionally get in the way and are buried in pits or used to build up low ground (Mr Tom Harris *pers comm*). The field name 'Manningstone' near West Nolands, Yatesbury has been interpreted as meaning 'many stones' (Smith 1884, 92). Similarly 'Stanmore' which occurs on the on the Lower Chalk bench west of Winterbourne Bassett as well as to the south of Clatford, is thought to mean stony moor (*ibid* 1884, 82) and despite Smith's (*ibid* 93) view that 'Hailstone Field' means 'neck enclosure', given the amount of sarsen found in the fields the meteorological comparison, or alternatively the application of such names to stone monuments elsewhere, 'Hell Stone' seems more likely.

The earliest documentary mention of sarsen in the area appears to be in the mid-17th century. Brentnall (1946, 420) quotes an entry in the diary of Richard Symons for 1644 as indicating that the people of the area call the stones 'Saracens stones', while Clatford Bottom itself, where a mass of boulders clustered together like a flock of sheep was known as 'Grey wether'. The general view appears to accept that the term 'sarsen', derived from 'saracen' (see also Geddes and Walkington this volume). 'Grey weather' or 'wether', as applied to the sarsens rather than the place, became accepted during the 20th century. John Aubrey, even though astonished on his first visit to Avebury, must have been familiar with the great number of stones that lay across the surface. Writing of a hunt meeting at Christmas 1648 he described how he *'mett with the packs of hounds at the Grey-wethers. These Downes look as if they were sowen with great Stones, very thick; and in a dusky evening they look like a flock of Sheep: from whence it* (i.e. the place) *takes its name: one might fancy it to have been the scene where the giants fought with huge stones against the Gods'* (Jackson 1862, 314).

While the use of both nodular and tabular forms of sarsen (Cunnington 1946, 405–6) for building clearly began in the Neolithic, the stone has been widely utilised in later periods. In the later hillfort rampart at Barbury Castle (Bowen & Smith 1977, 191) and Romano-British house foundations on Overton Down (Fowler 1967, 27–9), for example, while Saxon churches such as Alton Priors and Great Bedwyn were constructed at least in part with sarsen. Use in walling was also widespread, for example, in the boundaries around the medieval grange at Wick Down (Brown this volume). With effect from the post medieval period onwards, ever larger quantities were broken up for building houses and walls at, for example, Berwick Bassett and East Kennet.

Equally, sarsen boulders posed an obstacle within the landscape, both in terms of passage and cultivation. Initial cultivation could only be carried out after clearance, and by moving the boulders to an edge they formed a convenient boundary. The challenge posed in clearing boulders from the land was one recognised as important in initial land-use development, to the extent that it formed a study by the Society of Antiquaries (Bowen & Smith 1977). The point here is not to recount the evidence for such use of sarsen, but to suggest potential new lines of enquiry based on an anthropologically influenced interpretation of the evidence and to acknowledge an interest in how the stones may have been perceived at times during prehistory. Were they, for example, considered simply as economically useful building materials, or in another way entirely. Given ethnographic accounts from around the world such stones are likely to have been perceived rather differently and in essence they might provide an avenue through which investigation of the sacred geography of area could be approached. Among the Zafiminary of Madagascar, for example, to become stone is considered a way of achieving immortality (Bloch 1995, 73): stone is central to origin myths among the Nenet of northern Russia where the first man was considered to be stone and where stone is often considered sacred and forms sacrificial sites (Ovsyannikov & Terebikhin 1994, 57). Among the Inca, along with certain other landscape features rocks are seen as playing an important role in the traditions of origins and in the relationship with the supernatural (van de Guchte 1999, 155), while according to Ingold (2000, 91, 96–7), the Ojibwa of North America believe that people can appear in forms other than human, as animals or stones and that inanimate objects might be perceived as being alive.

Colour too may have been important in this respect and it is readily observed that sarsen boulders occur in shades from red to grey. According to Aubrey (Jackson 1862), the sarsens in Overton Wood, by which he probably meant those along Ox Bottom in West Woods, had lighter colour 'rinds' than those on the open downs. Brentnall recognised that ferruginous staining was common and that the surfaces of some boulders are water polished (Brentnall 1946, 424–8). Free (1948, 339) identified three main types of sarsen based largely on colour, which he assigned to the different parent deposits. First white sarsen, which is widely distributed on the downs; second a red haematite, which he claimed was associated with outliers of the Reading Beds; and third, a brown variety that he associated with plateau gravel. Boulders were encountered during recent fieldwork that appeared to be red below the `water line' and grey above thus indicating that both minerals within the soil and weathering processes had an impact on the surface appearance.

Paths to natural features

The sequence of vegetation cover after the Devensian has been recounted by M Allen (this volume) and it is often thought that the chalk remained forested until eventually cleared by Neolithic agriculturalists, though as Allen has commented, some of these interpretations might be questioned. It may be that vegetation fostered by herbivores ensured a patchy mosaic throughout the Holocene, with shifting clearings as old leys regenerated and new ones developed. The extent and manner in which early humans visited the area after the last glaciation is perhaps unclear. To the south, the presence of three post pits at Stonehenge on Salisbury Plain dating to the eighth and ninth century BC (Cleal *et al* 1995, 43) indicates that the chalk was certainly being utilised by then. Equally there is abundant evidence of early post-glacial activity further along the River Kennet at Thatcham and Wawcott and hunters, scavengers, were evidently finding their way along the stream to its source (S Allen this volume).

Whether these people moved through a forest of pine trees or open glades, one thing is certain, their perception of the area would have been quite different to that of Defoe. Maybe, like him they were seasoned travellers, perhaps nomads following herds of deer and used to different environments and landforms; or perhaps they were rather more sedentary, moving only short distances when the local lack of resources made it necessary. What they thought of the thousands of sarsens that littered the ground will remain unknown. Encountered by such travellers, the boulders might have been treated rather cautiously. Clustering together and partly hidden in coombes that might still contain occasional springs, or lining the route of the proto River Kennet, and containing pebbles or the traces of roots of plants, the unusual stones might be considered objects of awe and wonder and perhaps foster supernatural explanations. Repeated visits might result in the development of legend and mythology, explanations about what the sarsens are and how they came into existence. The forms that natural cup marks and patterns make might easily result in them being identified as former animal or vegetable matter or even humans turned to stone, the kind of belief so commonly found amongst country folk in more recent times. Thus they may have been rocks with their own ancient and living history. Each stone may have been treated as symbolic and to move or damage one might incur the wrath of spirits and perhaps only done with due caution, respect and ceremony. Within certain areas the density of boulders even now impedes movement. Formerly, it was claimed that in some places it was possible to step from one to another for great distances and it may have been difficult to progress in a straight line (Brentnall 1946, 420–21). In such places it may have been necessary to take time and negotiate the stones, procession-like, with considerable care. In some valleys the sarsen trains were so thick that they may have seemed like armies of dead souls. Not only was the area the source of life-giving water, a land of white earth containing a skeleton of flint, but it was also inhabited by petrified beings. The combination here of springs, high places, and unusual boulders is likely to have resulted in perception of the area as an exceptionally symbolic if not sacred place. It was a special land.

Sarsen as architecture

Some twenty-eight long barrows and chambered tombs are known from the area (Barker 1985) many of which contain evidence of having been constructed, at least in part, with sarsen boulders. Sometimes these were simply piled up into cairns. Smith (1884, 180) refers to East Kennet long barrow being composed in this way. The small sarsens 'round and generally flat, which came tumbling so about the men that they gave up the work' of excavation. An almost incidental by-product of the collection of boulders to build cairns would have been creation of a cleared space where different vegetation might flourish. Patches of freshly exposed soil would quickly foster new growth.

Raising stones onto one edge is an early step in moving large boulders. It can dramatically change the appearance of a stone and might be thought of as bringing it to life, perhaps literally so in the perception of the workers. The erection of single standing stones may have been amongst the earliest acts of human interference in such places. A sarsen standing stone was incorporated into a long barrow at Arn Hill, on Salisbury Plain (McOmish *et al* 2002, 29) and it may be that similar depressions and pits beneath such monuments may also, in some cases, have supported uprights. On the Marlborough Downs placing elongated stones on end to create simple peristaliths of standing stones or kerbs may have been a relatively early procedure as at Millbarrow (Whittle 1994) which is dated to the later fourth millennium BC.

In other cases, such as West Kennet long barrow (Piggott 1962), capstones of several tons in weight were placed horizontally on upright boulders. The placing of one stone on top of another was a considerable achievement. It was more than a simple pastime, or piece of sculpture. The raising of such stones provided a cultural signature and although the principles of dolmen construction were recognised across Europe, locally construction must have been a rare enough event and inspired much interest and controversy as well as focussing knowledge and assistance. Why was it necessary to construct such dolmens? The Devil's Den, a massive capstone placed on two uprights situated just above the floor of Clatford Bottom, was not constructed as a prominent feature in the countryside. On the contrary, it was hidden away on the floor of a valley that, records suggest, contained one of the densest concentrations of sarsen boulders in the area; so dense in fact that it was allegedly possible to step from boulder to boulder (Brentnall 1946). The monument would have been largely camouflaged by the sheer concentration of natural boulders. Unfortunately by the middle of the 19th century most of these had been cleared away leaving Merewether to lament that it was then surrounded by nothing but turnips (Merewether 1851a, 74).

Conceivably the process began in imitation of groupings of stones that were present as natural phenomena. Groups of naturally occurring boulders formed into mounds, or even placed boulder on top of boulder by periglacial action. Brentnall (1946, 427), for example, recorded the presence of naturally occurring boulders 'heaped on each other' in a plantation west of Overton Delling. Set amongst such a density of stones, the dolmen could hardly be described as monumental. Apart from surrounding area of removed boulders it would not be distinguished unduly from the naturally placed clitter all around it.

A further example once lay on the valley floor of Temple Bottom, Rockley. This was also situated amongst an enormous accumulation of sarsen, though like Clatford Bottom it has long since been cleared, a process evidently already under way when Smith (1884, 195) visited the site. Hoare regarded it as '*the finest example that we have yet found of this species of internment excepting the one in Clatford Bottom*' (Hoare 1821, 42). Like the Devil's Den, it was thought to have once formed a chamber, for Hoare reports that it lay at the east end of a partly destroyed cairn. According to Smith, excavations here revealed a chamber defined by a circle of upright stones. Within this and between the uprights, he found both burnt and unburnt human bones, parts of two human skulls, bones of a hand and foot, fragments of pottery, a bone chisel and a stone pounder (Smith 1884).

Nearby, on the lower slopes of Manton Down, though set slightly higher above the valley floor than the former, is another example. Like Temple Bottom, Hoare considered it to have been set at the east end of a small long barrow (Hoare 1821), the mound evidently surrounded by a peristalith, a common device for demarcating mounds in the area. When Smith visited, boulders forming what he believed to be part of a mound remained and he reported that some 25 years earlier he had seen the massive capstone that had slipped from the uprights onto the ground. In a subsequent visit he observed that this had been broken in two, presumably to assist removal (1884, 198). All is now completely destroyed, though a considerable number of its components lie jumbled together amongst rank vegetation.

The Shelving Stone, a dolmen or ruined chambered tomb, was first illustrated by Aubrey (Fowles 1980, 822–3) and depicted as two uprights with capstone leaning against them. Merewether (1851b, 93) refered to it as a cromlech at Monkton '*now totally gone*' and until recently the position of the monument was considered to be lost. Grinsell thought that the site lay in the West Field at Winterbourne Monkton, though appears to have confused it with Millbarrow, but the location was recently rediscovered by Chris Barker (1984). An estate plan, *A survey of ye parish of Monkton, Wilts* dated 1774 (WRO39/8), allows the site to be pinpointed with some accuracy. The plan reveals a furlong within the Middle Field to the east of the village referred to as *Shelvenstone*. In the terrier, the furlong is divided into strips, each consisting of an acre, the list beginning at the south end. One of these 'the Stone Acres' is almost certainly the site of the 'Shelvenstones'. This would place the site east-north-east of what is now Middle Farm at NGR SU 104721; a position almost opposite and equidistant from the Winterbourne stream as Millbarrow is to the west. Both sites have forsaken the Higher Downs or even the lower slopes of the escarpment upon which many other monuments are placed. For both, proximity to the winterbourne appears to have been important and their position so close to the historic village made them subject to a constant threat of cultivation. Curiously, the location of the Shelving Stone is at the head of a shallow re-entrant leading to the Winterbourne stream, rather than on the nearby high point of Chink Hill.

Other settings were noted both here and elsewhere. Seven sarsens on the (presumably lower) slopes of Monkton Down were referred to by Smith (1884, 134), placed or rather 'piled' on top of an eighth. He also noted (*ibid*, 122) that three large sarsens situated to the west of Wick Cottages on Winterbourne Down appeared to 'mark either some burial place or other monument of old time'. He referred too, to a small dolmen on the downs above Avebury (*ibid*, 150), a little to the south of the Marlborough coach road, comprising a capstone supported by three smaller stones and surrounded by a 'very low mound of earth' and other potential settings such as those to the south of West Kennet long barrow.

These constructions appear to occur in valleys or re-entrants close to streams or winterbournes. Locations protected from the elements, where temporary shelter might be obtained. Given the density of sarsen clusters, they cannot have marked land useful for cultivation, or even grazing, and were merely the places where there were concentrations of stones. In practical terms, the stones would have got in the way; they obscure the land and deter access and movement through it and given economic considerations such places are not obvious locations in which to settle. Yet the stones themselves provided an attraction. It is not only that they were present, but that these places were *occupied* by stones, where tradition, legend, and myth may have held sway. Was this the land of the dead, a world of spirits or ancestors? A dangerous world where it was taboo to enter, where the living could only visit on certain proscribed occasions? Where it may have been anathema to disturb the surface unless it was done with extreme caution and ceremony?

Apart from small patches of ground the boulder-strewn land would allow little meaningful cultivation, except where boulders may have been collected from the surface to construct cairns leaving areas free of clitter. Clearance here would not only have involved smaller boulders, but necessitated removal of at least some of the larger stones as well i.e. those stones already enshrined with profound meaning. Just as the planting of grain may have involved ceremony, clearance may have too. Removal of each stone may be a ceremonial act – done only with appeasement and permission of the spirits. Ritual may even have involved placing them in straight lines aligned on celestial events.

The importance given to sarsen boulders is reflected in the settings at Avebury itself. A circle of over 300m in diameter, of large sarsen orthostats were placed 10m apart constituting a continuous circuit set several metres from the inner lip of the ditch. As earlier commentators have noticed (Smith 1965a, 208) they follow the course of the henge ditch, and are thought to have been placed in position after the henge was constructed. Internal stone circles to the north and south each enclose c 1.0ha in area, both sit more or less centrally astride the ridge and within each of these are further stone settings. The origin of the stones in the Avebury stone circles is often considered to derive from one of the accumulations that still exist on Overton or Fyfield Downs to the east of the site, each stone being dragged a distance of several kilometres up and over Hackpen Hill. Such suggestions are merely a response to the locations where boulders can be found in abundance today. However, as noted above stone was certainly formerly available around Avebury itself and it is likely that the valleys were once covered with boulders even though only isolated examples now survive. The farmer of land east of the West Kennet Avenue confirmed that a ridge c1.0m high and 30m wide 'consists of a seam of sarsen that runs through the field' (Barker 1985, 21). Thus the land on which the massive henge was constructed would need to be cleared first and any boulders within the immediate vicinity removed. Given this scenario, there is no reason for the stones to have been hauled any great distance. They may well have come from the immediate vicinity of the henge, some potentially from the interior.

Most sarsen boulders that occur naturally on the surface reach two, sometimes three metres across, rarely can examples of larger dimensions be found (e.g. Cunnington 1946, 418). In one case, however, in 1882 the ground was cleared around a massive sarsen on Lerkeley Hill, East Kennet, (Smith 1884, 180–2) of an estimated seven tons, it was found to lie on a number of other stones. Thinking that the latter were deliberately placed to hold a 'capstone', Smith went on to excavate the area and found that the uppermost stone lay on a 'wall' of massive sarsens that formed a rectangle. These evidently overlay a further massive sarsen that occupied the bottom of a pit in which the structure lay. The interstices were packed with flints and smaller pieces of sarsen and beneath the structure a hole c1.5m diameter by 3.5m deep, was lined with red clay and filled with clay, soil and flints. Despite the lack of cultural artefacts, the 'walling' led Smith to believe that the structure was humanly constructed. With the benefit of time it is possible to interpret this as a sinkhole, one of many on the chalk, in which case the sarsen feature would have been entirely natural. More recently three extremely large sarsens (one reported as being over 7m in length) were found in a sink hole at Aston Rowan in Oxfordshire (Bowen & Smith 1977, 189) and it may be these that Geddes refers to as being found in advance of construction of the M40 (Geddes 2000, 70; Geddes and Walkington this volume). The discovery of unusually large sarsen boulders in sink holes might provide a clue to the origin of some of the larger stones at Avebury; those at the Cove or henge entrance, for example. As Geddes and Walkington indicate (this volume) the discovery of sarsens in sinkholes allowed Kellaway to point out that buried sarsen can be relatively soft and that it is the weathering process that hardens it. Such an observation might indicate that the dressed sarsens at Stonehenge were not obtained from the surface and that their origin may be from a local sinkhole.

Other circles were constructed within the vicinity though some of these may have been kerbs retaining barrows (Merewether 1851b, 106; Smith 1884, 134, 177, 173). Faulkners Circle (Smith 1884, 148; Gillings *et al* 2003) comprised just one stone by the time that Smith saw it, but he recognised the position of others and that the circle was constructed in a similar position to the dolmens i.e. on a valley floor. The position of a circle at Winterbourne Bassett has recently been called into question as a result of the discovery of Stukeley's original sketch of the site (David *et al* 2003). The circle comprised two concentric rings of boulders c 30m in diameter, the outer of which comprised some 60 stones. The new identification places the site further south in full view of Silbury Hill and a little distance from the area referred to as Stanmore on early maps.

Merewether reported that Silbury Hill itself was surrounded by a peristalith of sarsens, each about 1m wide, placed at intervals of about 5.5m, although only eight of these were visible in 1849 (Merewether 1851a, 74). A tunnel driven into the mound in 1849 revealed a cluster of sarsens close to the centre. Some of these were described as leaning against what was thought to be a small mound. As Atkinson too encountered boulders in the same area it seems that an early if not original focus of interest here incorporated sarsen boulders though whether these were naturally or artificially positioned is uncertain.

Two forms of sarsen were visually recorded during excavations along the West Kennet Avenue (Keiller & Piggott 1936, 420) and these were often seen to provide contrasting pairings. Type A, tall pillar like stones, differed from type B, broader, diamond shaped boulders. They were initially thought to have been dressed, though Cunnington subsequently rebutted this. In shape two forms could certainly be identified, the first tabular with flat surfaces, often polygon or hexagonal in outline and easily broken up for building purposes; the second nodular. Cunnington suggested that the shapes were an artefact of nature rather than human influence, the polygonal forms being formed in a similar manner to that in which drying mud cracks (Cunnington 1946, 405–6).

Sarsen as memorial

Both Merewether (1851b, 85, 88) and Smith refer to 'countless' unmarked burials or burials marked by sarsen out on the downs, that were initially revealed by flint diggers or farmers during cultivation, including one in Smith's own parish (Smith 1884, 4, 86). A group of nine such burials were found on the downs above Cliff Pypard in 1854 (Smith 1884, 78), when a group of sarsens obstructing cultivation were removed by a team of horses and found to cover graves.

A further series of burials were found in pits beneath sarsens in Monkton Field, Winterbourne Monkton. Thurnam reported that either side of the Monkton/Yatesbury road in the large open fields between Windmill Hill and Millbarrow, ten or twelve large sarsen boulders were removed, at least four of which were found to cover burial deposits. Circular cists were cut into the chalk to a depth of about 4ft; within these over 30 skeletons were recorded (Thurnam in Davis 1865) as being in a crouched or sitting posture, three of them with skulls cleft probably before burial. The upper part of each grave was filled with sarsen fragments and a layer of earth and the whole covered by gigantic sarsens. (Cunnington & Goddard 1934, 29; Smith 1884, 84–5;Grinsell 1957, 126).

One of these pits contained four or five skeletons – Thurnam records five or six, though produced no accompanying finds (Hillier 1854, 303; Davis 1865, 1). Another investigated by William Hillier (1854) was revealed beneath a recumbent sarsen *'about 300 yards west of Millbarrow'*. Beneath this was a large, almost circular pit, seven to eight feet in diameter and four feet deep, the base paved with small 'irregularly shaped' and probably deliberately broken, sarsen stones. On these were placed four to five human skeletons, one evidently a child. Hillier felt that they may have been placed in a sitting position and the weight of the overburden had forced them into a confused state. Thurnam who examined the bones (Davis 1865) referred to twenty-two human burials and claimed to have been present during the excavation of nearly half of them. In turn, the skeletons were covered by some twenty to thirty sarsen boulders, each weighing between ten pounds and ½ cwt, though evidently not placed in any order as on the north-east they reached to the surface of the pit and may have been tipped in from that side. They were covered by soil within which were 'solid masses' of greasy black material of a soap-like consistency that contained small pieces of flint and charcoal. Lying on the surface of this and sealing the pit, lay a huge sarsen boulder, square or lozenge shaped, and measuring almost 3m across and over 1m in thickness. Sherds of coarse black pottery, a sarsen pounding stone, together with bones of dog, pig, sheep and cattle were present in the pit filling. A third pit contained two or three skeletons and a fourth a single skeleton associated with a jet pulley ring, two Beakers, a flint knife and an elongated greenstone pebble. Details are not precise and there is considerable room for caution in the interpretation of the nature of both skeletons and pit, but the finds subsequently deposited at Devizes Museum including V-shaped shale buttons, four urns, at least two of which were Beakers (Anon 1857, 252; Long 1858, 343; Cunnington & Goddard 1934, 26–9) imply a late 3rd or early 2nd millennium date.

Similarly human bones together with a sarsen muller or pounding stone were found under a large sarsen at Down Farm, Pickle Dean Bottom, West Overton in 1894 (Anon 1894, 72; Cunnington & Goddard 1934, 29), while a Beaker associated burial was also found to one side of a sarsen to the south of the Devizes Road at Beckhampton, the sarsen here thought to have once covered the interment (Cunnington 1926b, 399–400). On Morgans Hill *'above Wansdyke'*, discovery of a crouched skeleton found without mound, marker or grave goods was reported by Merewether (1851b, 110) and while this could be of almost any period, a number of other graves marked by sarsen stones are also recorded and are likely to be prehistoric. Although tentative, these examples indicate an association between Beaker burials and sarsen, sometimes as part of the grave, but invariably using large sarsens for sealing or as a marker.

Sarsen as boundary

The clearance of boulders from the Lower Chalk is likely to have been a concerted activity on the medieval and post-medieval fields of the villages of Beckhampton, Winterbourne Monkton, and

Berwick Bassett as well as Yatesbury and Avebury itself. Even though by the middle of the 19th century, according to Merewether (1851a, 74), tens of thousands of boulders still lay scattered over the hills, most of these lay in the more inaccessible parts of the Downs. Smith himself (1884, 180) referred to many sarsens in a valley towards Wansdyke *'being removed to one side and another, having been found great hindrances to the cultivation of the land'*. Stonyfield Bottom, south of East Kennet was cleared *'almost to the last remnant of the great deposit which gave the name to the Bottom...'* (Brentnall 1946, 424). Even in more recent times one local farmer, is reported as saying that in the 1960's the government provided grants to clear fields and he promptly obliged. *'We buried lots of the sarsens. How many? God only knows. I left some of them. I suppose the rest are still down there'* (Kennedy 1998). In two places evidence of more recent clearance episodes exists. A large building stance on Fyfield Down, for example, contains a large number of sarsens that have been dumped into it, while a little to the north a similar collection has been dumped in a small valley. Elsewhere the collection of cleared sarsen was simply placed in heaps on the valley floor. A collection of sarsen formerly lay around the farm buildings at The Firs, Beckhampton, for example, but has now been removed.

To the south of the River Kennet the situation is similar. Accumulations of sarsen on valley floors are slowly being cleared and the process that commenced in earlier times of moving stones to the boundaries of fields creating lines of boulders can still be observed in places. Merewether (1851) and subsequently Smith (1884) thought that sarsen boulders occurred naturally in rows, but some of these observances may have been a result of such clearance. On Overton Down, for example, many have been incorporated in early field boundaries and form lines of stones demarcating prehistoric or Romano-British field boundaries.

Sarsen in industry

Smith noted that most sarsens lying within the vicinity of roads had been long broken up (Smith 1884, 27). Brentnall (1946, 423) quoted Sir Joseph Banks as confirming that by 1767 most of the stones in the area between Marlborough and Silbury Hill had been removed and according to Dr J Stevens by 1873 the sarsen kerbs around local barrows had been used for road repairs or for building (Brentnall 1946, 423). Despite this, good numbers still remain, particularly on Overton, Fyfield and Clatford Downs, where they are protected by the Nature Conservancy. Even here many do not retain their original position and great numbers have been split by wedges and partially removed for construction materials. In one case a small 'kerbstone' workshop can be observed with broken kerbstones and waste pieces present: sarsen being used for kerbstones and as setts for tramways in Swindon (King 1968, 88; Geddes 2000, 80).

Many of the stones from Ox Bottom, West Woods were carted away for road repairs in Swindon (Brentnall 1946, 424). The method of workers at West Woods was to make a small hole in the stone, until a wedge could be inserted and a blow with a sledgehammer was invariably enough to split the stone. During the 1940's, however, explosives were used to break large numbers of boulders in order to metal the Bath road (Free 1948, 338). Many of the sarsens in Hursley Bottom were cleared and used in this way (King 1968, 86). Today the traces of such activity can be traced on the valley floor, as evidence is still present of the clearance process. By Forest Lodge, countless earthfast sarsens remain with trenches dug around their sides to ease removal. A little higher up the valley the removal process is complete, the depressions and trenches themselves being the only indication of where stones formerly lay. The valley floor had been divided into a number of compartments leaving unexcavated causeways at intervals of 50m or so to allow access for vehicles. A concrete base is all that remains of a stone crusher established by the contractors (King 1968, 86).

Much sarsen was broken up and used as building stone. Many were incorporated into buildings in villages on the Lower Chalk, at Winterbourne Monkton, and Berwick Bassett as well as Avebury and West Kennet. As early as 1575 stones were being broken up for buildings and walls, for sarsens were used in the repair of the Marlborough Grammer School in that year (Brentnall 1946, 425) while Stukeley describes methods of breaking stones at Avebury during the 1720's and observed *'At Compton Basset, not far from Marlborough, westward, houses made of stones as big as those at Stonehenge, standing endwise'* (Lukis 1882, 137 – extract from A Common-place book of Dr Stukeley dated 1721, Ormond Street, 1748). In 1673, 1678 and 1702 loads of sarsen were recorded as being carted into Marlborough for building (Brentnall 1946, 425). Merewether (1851a, 74) too recorded the process, noting that stones were being taken annually for building. *'...The stone for the new railway bridge at Windsor is taken from Clatford Bottom'*. Similarly sarsen from both Beckhampton and West Woods appears to have been used for repairs at Windsor Castle (Brentnall 1946, 423; King 1968, 87). Boulders for the latter site being carted to the wharf at Honey Street from where it was taken by barge to Windsor Castle (Free 1948, 339).

Conclusions

Ever since the first boulder was levered on top of others to form a dolmen, humanly influenced change within the valleys was accepted. By their very nature monuments are linked to change, not only in terms of shifting boulders around, but by the effects of vegetation that leap into the surrounding void and foster a new regime. For better or worse the land is effectively reorganised. The metamorphosis of stones from clitter to structure was reflected in the changes of nature. The clearance of boulders may have been a deliberate attempt to harness these changes and to create cultural ground.

The construction of Christian monuments at Avebury, the carved cross and subsequent church is carefully, perhaps respectfully, placed outside the henge. It is possible that material came from the stone circle, but there is no clear evidence of such deliberate re-use at this date. The breaking of stones *en masse* appears to have began in the late Middle Ages either for buildings or roads and this represented a change in views. No longer were sarsen boulders seen as an important component in the character of the area. They were expendable, purely economic.

During historic times the role of stone took on a greater commercial emphasis. Stone was just as convenient a building material as it was inconvenient to cultivators. To those working closely with the material it was the smell of sarsen dust that would linger. Aside from stoneworkers and flint diggers, the valleys containing the sarsen trains were once the preserves of itinerants, of shepherds, tinkers and vagabonds, the notorious Cherhill gang and others. Some sarsens bear their marks. On Overton and Fyfield are boulders with grinding marks, polished and pecked areas, and in one instance, a cup mark, perhaps evidence of an even earlier encounter.

Formal fields were present at least from the Middle Bronze Age and sarsen cleared to straight lines. Once established, field boundaries were consolidated and such alignments were added to over time as more boulders got in way of the plough. Some 'Celtic' fields at Overton and Fyfield developed huge lynchets, the result of continued cultivation on the same spot over centuries using the same boundaries. Such boundaries re-organised space into areas important as places, providing divisions between areas included or excluded and once established it was difficult to destroy or completely obscure the original.

Archaeological interpretation and modern perception of the landscape is in part conditioned by the boulders that lie around on the surface today. The very lack of stones in the wider landscape only enhances the impact and the human achievement of stone monuments. Many of these monuments may originally, however, have been constructed in areas of dense sarsen accumulation and there are implications in terms of the practical engineering involved in monument construction and in the way that these places were thought of by early travellers and settlers. The lack of boulders lying around parts of the landscape is entirely a result of cultural activity over several thousand years. Thus perception of both countryside and and rocks lying around in it has changed dramatically. Metamorphosis from a series of boulders to a humanly made arrangement may have been a great achievement for local people in terms of engineering capability, but the reason behind it was probably more than a physical or intellectual challenge. In a metaphysical sense the stones played an important role in human belief as well as in how the land around was experienced.

To many people today sarsen is just made to sit on. Visitors use these boulders as ready-made picnic tables – nature's furniture. To others, searching for meaning in an increasingly material world, they are a source of energy that can be transmitted and beneficially received when touched, fondled or embraced: or they contain mysterious secrets, shapes of heads, elephants, King Arthur on his throne, and so on. One lady knows that the stones were painted. Only she can see the colours. Perhaps some of them were.

9
Mesolithic hunter-gatherer exploitation of the Marlborough Downs

Stephen Allen

There is widespread evidence of landscape exploitation in the Marlborough Downs by the Mesolithic hunter-gatherers of the early Holocene. The bulk of this evidence are surface finds of lithic artefacts, suggesting activity sites. With the head of the River Kennet close to Avebury, the downland landscape perhaps provides a dual role to Mesolithic groups: that of a resource patch and possibly an arterial route. Further downstream, the Kennet floodplain and valley-sides around Newbury and Thatcham arguably provide one of the richest clusters of hunter-gatherer sites in southern England. The dry-valleys, bournes and rivers such as the Og and Dun are tributaries of the Kennet and seem to have played a pivotal role as exploitation routes, linking the River Kennet valley and the downland. Lithic evidence can often be found following these fluvial features into the Marlborough Downs, often on the summits of valley spurs and heads. Within the downland itself, the location of lithic finds is often on the summit of high points, providing views over the surrounding landscape. The downs clearly played an important part in the subsistence activities of early hunter-gatherers, and perhaps also a cultural role in terms of links with groups travelling into and through the chalkland.

Introduction

The Berkshire Downs forms a large block of high chalk landscape some 50km wide from Reading to the east and the Vale of White Horse to the north and Bristol Avon valley in the west (Fig 9:1). The Marlborough Downs form the western end, characterised by a series of high, steep escarpments and gentler dip slopes, and some of the highest topographical features in the downland landscape, for example, Hackpen Hill at 272m OD. The downs lie between two contrasting geographical zones. Immediately to the west lies the lower ground of the river Avon. The Avon provides access to the coastal resources of the Bristol Channel and the Severn. Centrally within, and rising in the Marlborough Downs, is the river Kennet. The river provides a link with the river Thames at Reading, on the edge of the London Basin, and the area has a high density of hunter-gatherer sites (Fig 9:1) 14km to the east of the Marlborough Downs, between Hungerford and Newbury (Froom 1963, 1965, 1970, 1972a, 1972b, Froom *et al* 1994). Thatcham, 30km east of the Marlborough Downs is of international significance as a dateable early Holocene hunter-gatherer site (Churchill 1962; Wymer and Dimbleby 1958; Wymer 1962). The clearly important role of the river Kennet floodplain and terraces in the subsistence activities of hunter-gatherers is likely to be entwined with activities on the Marlborough Downs.

Within the Marlborough Downs lies Avebury. Its significance as a focus of Neolithic monument activity needs no introduction. Before that activity, the downland landscape was being exploited by perhaps more transient hunter-gatherers. In attempting to examine what hunter-gatherer groups were doing in the downland landscape, I will concentrate on the spatial evidence, albeit somewhat ephemeral, as temporal evidence is elusive.

The eastern downland, the Berkshire Downs, was subject of a survey by Richards (1978). In contrast, the western landscape, the Marlborough Downs, has attracted little large-scale field survey. Wymer (1977) has collated the bulk of both published and unpublished suggested hunter-gatherer artefact findspots. There are inevitable biases and distortions (Smith & Openshaw 1990,

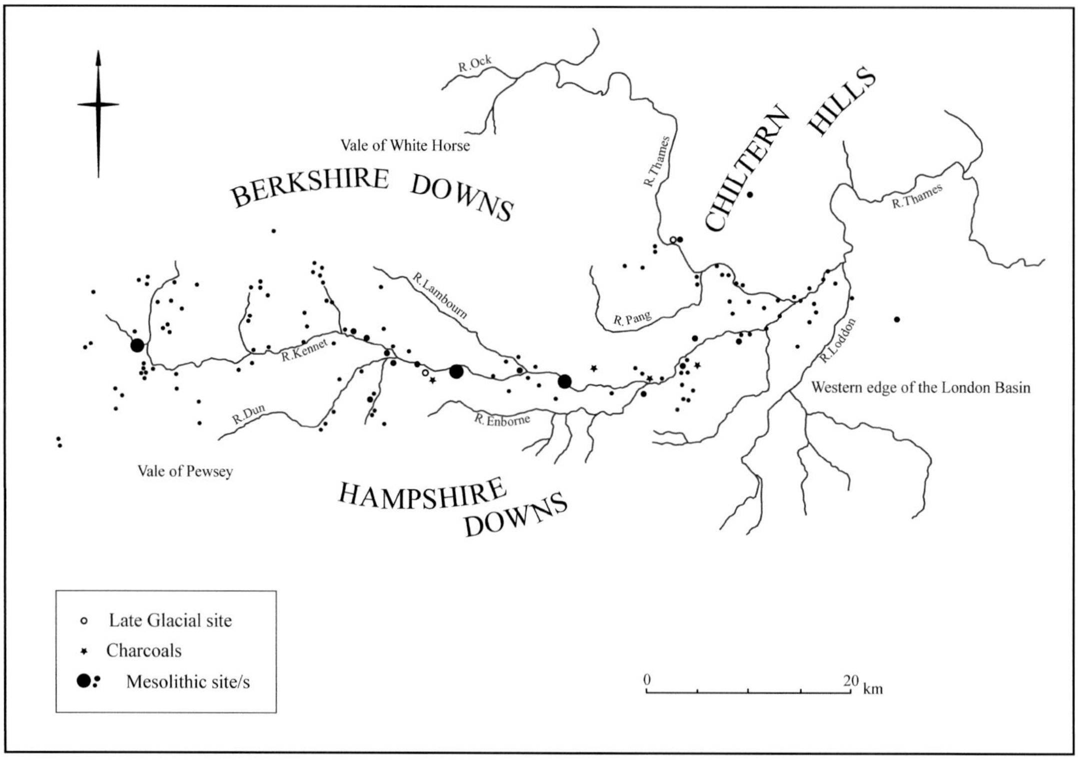

Fig 9:1 Distribution pattern of hunter-gatherer findspots in the river Kennet catchment.

17) in maps based on previous finds, however, an analysis of the location and topography of each findspot reveals a definite spatial patterning to artefact locations. An examination of southwest German sites using the same method (Kvamme and Jochim 1985) demonstrated its importance in understanding site location and its potential for settlement pattern modelling. I would argue that the whole of the downland evidence must be integrated with the landscapes to the north and south, and presented as one whole 'site' (Fig 9:1) to distinguish any traits. Doing this lets us examine any settlement and activity patterns, the role of high places and perhaps the notion of routes, as ways to enter, exploit and travel through the downland landscape.

The Marlborough Downs: Hunter-Gatherer Exploitation

The early Holocene environment

Inevitably the early Holocene environment contrasts with that of today. Avebury is close to what is now the head of the river Kennet. In the early Holocene, environmental evidence suggests that the Kennet was not a flowing river but woodland and marshy ground (Evans *et al* 1993, 185). However, Avebury does sit in a natural valley that travels south to the foot of the Marlborough Downs at West Overton, and now carries the river Kennet. Interestingly, Evans (*et al* 1993, 185) records the environment at West Overton as open country and a permanent stream until around 8400BP, when swamp and woodland established themselves. Both floodplain and wider landscape were likely to be largely woodland, perhaps with some clear patches.

Hunter-Gatherer distribution patterns

Simmons (1996, 197) suggests that there are two basic types of inland settlement: 'base' camps and 'extraction' camps and proposes a number of models based on group size and whether or not groups had access to coastal resources. He argues (*ibid* 204, Fig 5.1b) that a 100-strong band may exploit a 125km river basin, move base camp at times using the river valley as an axis, and spend the winter at the lowest altitude. What unites all of his models, whatever the group size, is that food resource locations are likely to change in response to seasonal fluctuations, and it is likely that hunter-gatherer groups responded accordingly. The distribution pattern of hunter-gatherer findspots in the Marlborough Downs (Fig 9:2) may reflect this, but first that it would be helpful in understanding distribution patterns if we subdivide the landscape into four zones:

- The Kennet valley, from Thatcham and Newbury in the east to Avebury (floodplains,

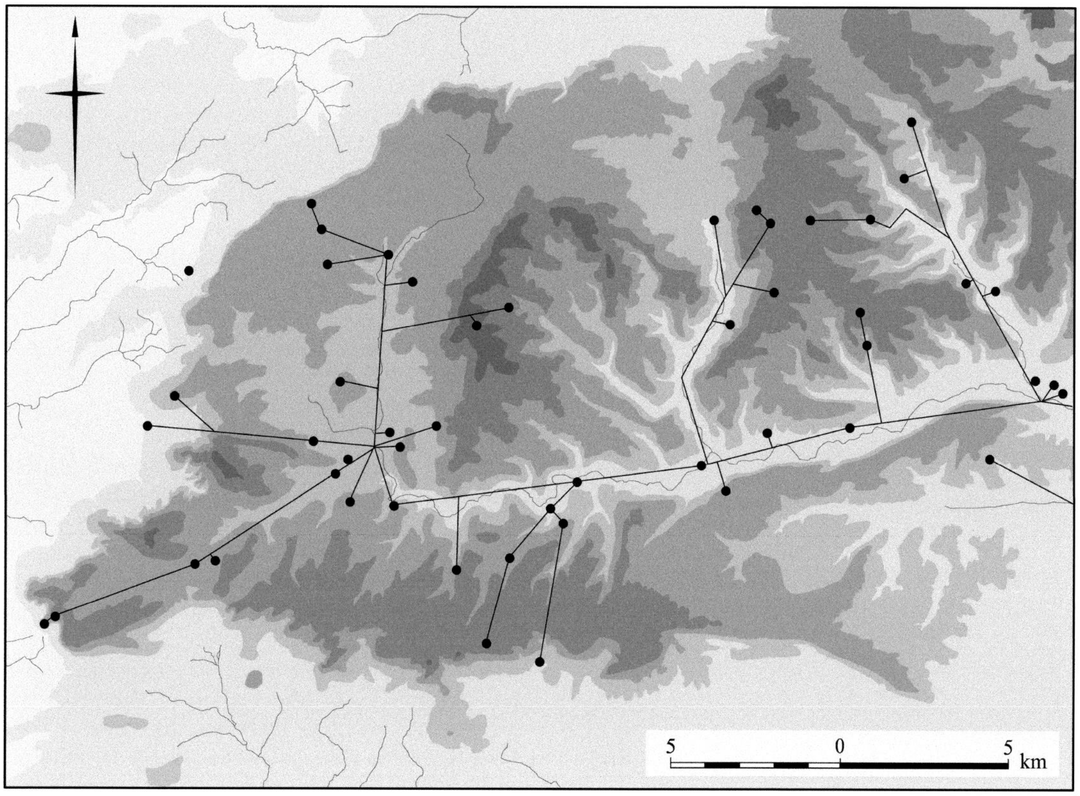

Fig 9:2 Hunter-gatherer distribution pattern specific to the Marlborough Downs. The lines have been added by the author, and simply suggest the way movement may have taken place to exploit the landscape.

valley-bottom terraces, bournes and dry-valleys and tributaries that join the Kennet valley).

- Along the bournes and dry-valleys and tributaries that enter the downland landscape.
- The downland landscape itself, including Avebury.
- The edge of the downland landscape, for example Cherhill.

The purpose of these sub-divisions is to draw out any subtle variations in the lithic compositions and topographical locations between these four zones.

The river Kennet valley and the bournes and dry-valleys entering the higher downland landscape.

With the Kennet providing an arterial route from the Marlborough Downs to the edge of the London Basin it is likely the river valley played a key role in the exploitation strategies of hunter-gatherer groups. This is supported by the dense concentration of findspots in the middle Kennet around Hungerford, Newbury and Thatcham. The river may not however have been exploited as a food resource. Stable Isotope analysis from a dog bone recovered from excavations at Thatcham, within an early Holocene context (Healy *et al* 1992), indicate no firm evidence for the use of either marine resources or riverine fish (Schulting & Richards 2000, 55). Carter (1975–6, 3) reported on the bone recovered from the Mesolithic site at Wawcott, noting that aquatic fauna were 'never much of importance as an article of diet'. Nevertheless, the middle Kennet, although likely to be a palimpset of artefactual evidence, demonstrates the importance of these locations to hunter-gatherer groups for what most have been an abundant resource patch, perhaps without the need to exploit aquatic resources. Binford (1980, 7) suggests that a typical foraging pattern is '*as looking like a daisy, the centre is the residential base, and foraging parties move out, traversing search loops which resemble petals*'. If we apply this model to the Kennet valley findspots (Fig 9:1, Fig 9:2) we can note the following points:

- Artefactual findspots can be noted to 'follow' the river Kennet along its length, from its confluence with the river Thames at Reading to Avebury in the Marlborough Downs, albeit with the highest density in the middle Kennet.
- Along the length of the Kennet it would appear that bournes, streams and physical features such as dry-valleys that meet the Kennet have been used to enter the surrounding higher chalk landscape. It is *very* unusual to find artefactual evidence *not* associated with a clearly recognisable topographical feature that is a possible way of navigating through the landscape e.g. the

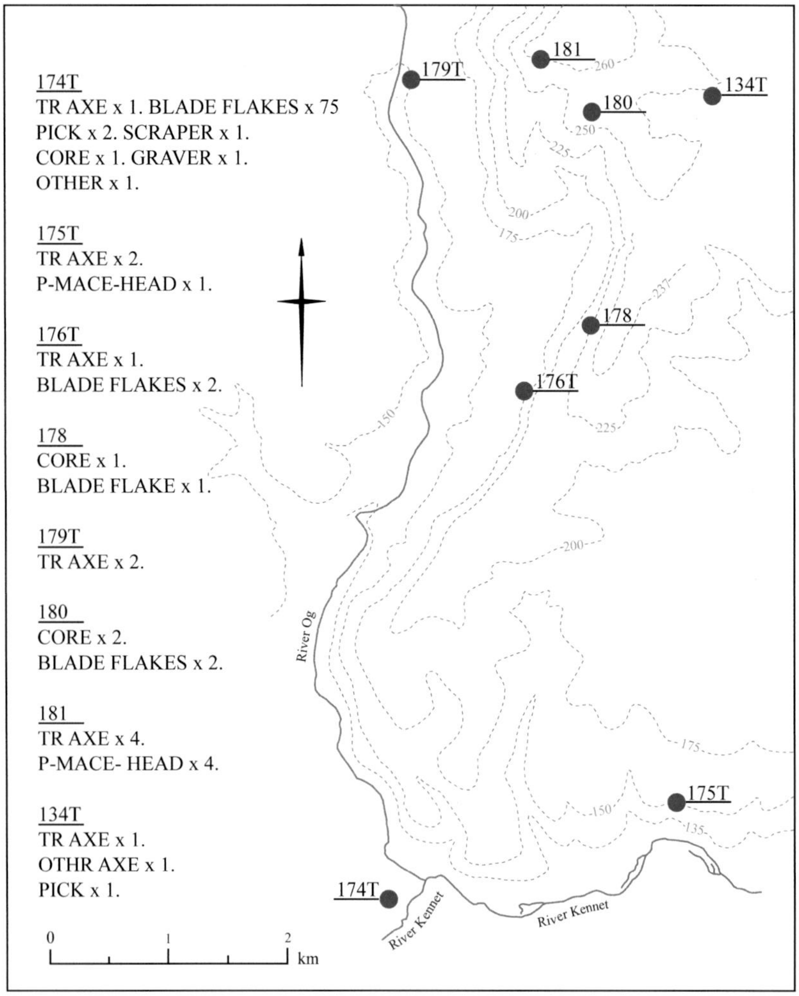

Fig 9:3 The valley of the River Og. Findspots tend to follow the valley, then fan out into the landscape, usually in a situation that overlooks the valley below.

summit of a dip slope or along a valley ridge. This can be demonstrated in the valley of the river Og (Fig 9:3).

- Typically, there tend to be artefactual finds at the confluence of the river Kennet and the topographical features entering the chalk landscape.
- Those finds that are along one these hypothetical 'routes' into the chalk landscape tend to be found at the crest of the valley-side, overlooking the Kennet valley, or as the feature travels into the landscape they are found along the crests, or at the head.

The assemblage compositions and quantity of lithic finds from sites close to the Kennet floodplain and adjacent terraces tend to be of a higher density than the downland landscape. This can be demonstrated by a significant palimpset of occupation evidence in the middle Kennet. These riverside sites perhaps provided locations that offer shelter in cold periods and a rich resource patch, perhaps seasonally returned to time and time again. Healy (*et al* 1992, 58) refers to the sites at Thatcham as a 'home base' with 'a high representation of tools for cutting soft and medium materials'. This is supported throughout most Kennet floodplain and terraces assemblages. Tools and debitage tend to be dominated by blade flakes, microliths, cores and a rich variety of other pieces. What provides an interesting contrast are the tool compositions found on the ridges along features such as the bournes and dry-valleys that enter the downland landscape. Isolated finds of axes, either *one* or several, and rarely with other material, dominate (Fig 9:3). In fact other pieces, mainly associated with perhaps more domestic tasks, are rarely represented at all. This suggests that differing activities are taking place along these hypothetical 'routes'. Remember these findspots tend to be on the crests, edges and the head of features, and generally overlook the valley-where they are situated. The fact the axes are so common suggests that some sort of logistical activity may be taking place, perhaps butchery or kill sites. That the axes have been discarded is perhaps not unexpected. Torrence (2001, 85) argues that such behaviour is likely when tasks and raw materials are likely to occur at the same locations. A field visit by the author to one of these 'edge' sites near Aldbourne revealed an abundance of raw material (clay-with-flints) and a possible Mesolithic hand-axe. It may also be that these 'edge' sites serve a dual role to the hunter-gatherer groups, for both exploitation and navigation through the landscape. These sites are places where visibility over the landscape i.e. the valley where they are situated, is enhanced as the valley side descends below them. It requires very little effort, in terms of minor woodland clearance, to improve this visibility still further. The benefits may have been that an edge habitat is created, which Simmons (1996, 165) notes is important for providing food for deer and aurochs, as well as edible plants and berries.

If this hypothesis is correct, these 'edge' zones also provide places for a viewing platform and can be seen from the valley floor. They may provide 'markers' along the route into the downland landscape, or places that Binford (1980, 9) calls low bulk procurement sites, places where extraction tasks are carried out, but the abandonment of tools is at a very low rate. Kvamme and Jochim (1985, 9) suggest that general (rather than season specific) advantages of ridge tops and plateau edges are:

- Wide views, useful for spotting game and strangers in all seasons.
- Good drainage in all seasons.
- Light forests, which may have offered ease of hunting.

Whatever their role in the lives of hunter-gatherer

groups, these edge sites clearly play a role in the exploitation strategies of groups moving into the landscape of the Marlborough Downs, where once again, high places, with views across the surrounding countryside are favoured.

Onto the downland landscape: distribution patterns from the head of dry-valleys and bournes.

If we treat these dry-valleys and bournes as hypothetical routes into the downland landscape, then a different distribution pattern may be present at the head of these features. Artefact finds tend to fan out into the landscape. What is interesting is that the locations do not wander into the landscape in a seemingly meaningless fashion. They tend to follow clear topographical features that are themselves 'linked' or associated with the dry-valleys and bournes that were used to enter the downland. Find locations tend to follow valley features or ridges, and once again, if a ridge or escarpment is the chosen location, it will be a high point, with a view over the surrounding topography, but always with a clear route through the landscape into the main Kennet valley. This strongly suggests the notion of routes. To exploit the landscape, you need to know where you are going, and how you are getting back. Allowing for what Mithen (1996) calls 'natural history intelligence', familiar physical features in a landscape would probably have to be memorised to navigate and move successfully. This would allow individuals or groups moving away from the main river valley, i.e. the Kennet, to exploit the higher downland landscape. It is very unusual for artefact finds to be found at any great distance from topographical landmarks and this is the case throughout the Kennet catchment (Figs 9:1 and 9:2). Some of these topographical landmarks have a high mean height OD. The downland landscape contains a number of findspots on high places, clearly these places were the preferred location for some sort of activity focus. Spikins (2000, 116) argues that there should be no *a priori* reason to expect upland sites to be for hunting and lowland for base camps. Although that hypothesis may be correct based on lithic composition variability studies, it is possible that at least in the Marlborough Downs, activity on some of the high places may have been for seasonal gatherings. Fowler and Blackwell (1998, 58) suggest that the 'chalk uplands were probably a summer and autumn hunting zone for people who killed and collected but then moved on'. I am not arguing for a wholesale dismissal of downland hunter-gatherer activity during the winter months, simply that the focus of activities may have shifted from the higher downland landscape to the lower river valleys during prolonged periods of poorer, colder weather. It is difficult, in view of the number of sites that are found in the higher downland landscape with a mean height OD of over 200 metres (Fig 9:4) to attribute them to comprehensive all-year round activity.

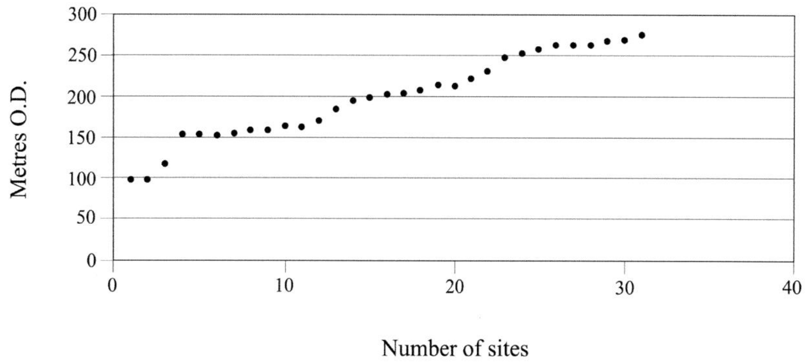

Fig 9:4 Hunter-Gatherer sites in the Marlborough Downs recorded in relation to the height above Ordnance Datum.

I have previously discussed the domination of axe finds along the bournes and dry valleys that dissect the landscape. There is greater variation within the downland sites. Axes are still represented, and again often found without other lithic finds, but the quantity and diversity of other material starts to predominate over axes. Blade flakes become the largest quantity of artefact finds, 72% of all the material represented. Contrast that with the 17% along the bournes and dry valleys. Cores become common, along with gravers, picks, microliths and scrapers. Assemblage compositions reflect a diversity of activity focus quite different from the hypothetical 'routes' that perhaps are the places to enter the landscape. This increasing diversity suggests that a different pattern of activity may be taking place once groups had entered the landscape. Eerkens (1997, 60) suggests that lowland site locations are places where multiple bands nucleated and camped together – whereas upland sites represent the splitting apart of bands into small nuclear families travelling together. It is possible this is what we can see when examining the findspot locations and assemblage compositions in the Kennet catchment and Marlborough Downs. The contrasting lithic compositions between the downland sites and the valleys entering the downland landscape suggests a clear division of landscape zones and their value as a resource to the hunter gatherer groups. There is very little evidence that suggests that groups or individuals left the 'route' taking them into the landscape. Findspot evidence suggests that groups travelled to the head of these features, and then fanned out into the landscape. This pattern is repeated along the river Kennet catchment (Fig 9:1, Fig 9:2). This again hints at 'routes' and the value of differing parts of the landscape to hunter-gatherer exploitation. It suggests that:

- Hunter-gatherer groups may have given the valleys and other features entering the downland landscape a quite different role in their exploitation strategies, compared to the higher downland.

Schofield (*et al* 1999, 46) concludes that when looking at a general distribution of human behaviour in a survey area, the key factor in settlement location was accessibility, both between and within valley systems. It may be that hunter-gatherer groups treated the valleys into the landscape as just that; ways to access the wider landscape. Schofield (1991, 118) argues that settlement within a landscape is not a random process, areas of activity will not appear as a random blur across the landscape, but as specific zones. So these features entering the landscape have perhaps left their own signature in terms of lithic finds, and perhaps played a role in exploitation strategies as both a route and also for extractive activities, presumably after exploitation on the downland landscape itself. It is however, not just topographical features that may have provided 'routes'; the river Kennet itself provided an important communication link for hunter-gatherer groups who may have wanted to move east to west. The land around the head of the Kennet perhaps plays a pivotal role in this argument.

Avebury

Lying as it does in the heart of the Marlborough Downs, Avebury is not only close to the head of the river Kennet but also provides a wide, shallow valley running north-south through the western end of the Marlborough Downs. To the east of Avebury are some of the highest places in the downland landscape, for example, Hackpen Hill and overlooking the valley within which Avebury is situated. Bearing in mind the foregoing discussion concerning high places and the *modus operandi* of hunter-gatherer groups in the rest of the Kennet catchment, then the Marlborough Downs appeal for some sort of hunter-gatherer activity is likely. As a location it provides a route to access the downland from the River Kennet, but perhaps more importantly, access to the west, to the rivers Avon and Severn and perhaps coastal resources. We can be reasonably certain that some movement of hunter-gatherer groups is likely to have taken place across southern England. Wainwright (1960, 201) has examined the microlith industries from Shapwick and Middlezoy in Somerset and Dozmere Pool on Bodmin Moor, both sites to west of the Marlborough Downs, and he compares them to the industries of south-east England, Essex and Thatcham. He concludes that all have close affinities and adds that 'These affiliations suggest a penetration by the Maglemosean immigrants to a much greater extent than has been realized hitherto – a penetration, probably via the Kennet Valley from the east coast across southern England to Cornwall'. Care (1982, 282) has appraised the evidence for the collection and distribution of lithic materials in southern England and concludes that during the Mesolithic period Portland Chert and pebbles from the south-west coast of England 'moved over large areas of southern England', distances of over 100km. Bellamy (forthcoming, 25) argues that the Kennet can be seen as a natural routeway between the chalkland and the East Anglian and Wealdon sites. On balance, it is extremely likely that movement of groups was taking place in and through the Kennet catchment. Movement may perhaps have largely been driven by seasonal resource requirements, nevertheless it is likely to have resulted in a degree of cultural and social contacts with other groups and probably exchange. It is possible to envisage over millennia, the movement of groups along the Kennet from the east, using the river as a guide to entering the chalk south of Avebury. Perhaps one of the keys to understanding the importance of Avebury is surely the significance of the Kennet as a 'route'. I am not implying that the significance of Avebury and the Kennet is just as a route, we have already discussed the evidence for the hunter-gatherer subsistence activities further downstream and in the downland. Bearing in mind the number of hunter-gatherer findspots along the Kennet valley and the surrounding landscape (Fig 9:1) the Kennet valley provides the most prominent way to exploit and move around the catchment. The Kennet and the valley may also have had a symbolic significance to hunter-gatherer groups. Bradley (2000, 35) describes natural places as having an archaeology because they acquired a significance in the *minds* of people. It is perhaps this significance that may have made Avebury a place important to hunter-gatherers as a place to conduct exploitation strategies, to move through the landscape to the east (the Kennet), and to move west, off the downland towards the River Avon. Having previously introduced the concept of movement around the chalk landscape using clear and memorable topographical features, Avebury is situated 6km almost directly east of the western edge of the Marlborough Downs, at the base of which is the town of Cherhill. Running more or less in an east-west direction between Avebury and Cherhill is Cherhill Down, the base of which is a natural route, followed by the modern road, the A4. This follows the course of the River Kennet throughout its length until just south of Avebury, it uses the landscape at the base of Cherhill Down and eastwards to Cherhill. Cherhill Down may then be significant in that it provides a clear topographical feature that links the River Kennet south of Avebury and the edge of the downland at Cherhill. Furthermore there are artefact findspots along this path through the landscape. If we examine the course of the modern road, the A361, which meets the A4 at Beckhampton just south of Avebury and travels southwest to Devizes, it too follows the valley at the base of Bishop's Canning Down and Roundway Hill, until it leaves the downland at Devizes. It too has five artefact findspots along its length. Although the number of findspots may be small, what unites both routes or paths through the landscape are:

- Clear topographical ways to navigate through the chalkland landscape.
- Lithic finds on or very close to these routes or paths.
- The immediate Avebury area being the focus of both routes where another possible path or route, the river Kennet can be utilised if required.

If it is correct that these are paths through the landscape then what is emerging is the importance of Avebury as a *place*, as a possible *focus* in the minds of hunter-gatherer groups. The place with hypothetical paths through the downland , the place where the River Kennet starts its journey to the River Thames, and offers an abundant resource patch between Hungerford and Thatcham. Avebury may have become, along with other sites in the Kennet catchment, what Barton (Barton *et al* 1995) calls a 'persistent place' in the Mesolithic landscape. What perhaps makes Avebury's situation different from other places in the catchment is that if my hypothesis is even partially correct about paths and routes, Avebury seems to be a place where routes and paths and rivers conjoin in a way not found in the rest of the catchment. Bell (forthcoming) argues that perhaps the habitual use of special paths, especially at path intersection places, may have played an important role in structuring settlement patterns over very extended timescales. Barton *et al* (1995, 110) supports the theme of 'persistent place' and goes on further to argue that the physical appearance of the landscape may have influenced settlement patterns. These topographical features would also influence the activity strategies of Mesolithic hunter-gatherer groups.

This combination of natural topographical features providing an intersection of paths, that may have given the western Marlborough Downs increasing symbolic importance to the mobile hunter-gatherer groups as a place in the landscape. This may also provide a hint of why it became a *place* of such important symbolism for the groups that came after the hunter-gatherers. Curiously, although lithic findspots are common around Avebury (Fig 9:2) the quantity of material is not, with cumulatively only 33 individual pieces. In the rest of the higher downland landscape the cumulative total is 2302 pieces, with most sites on the crests of the ridges and nearby summits commonly yielding at least a dozen pieces per site. Hackpen Hill, overlooking the valley within which Avebury is situated, is the highest point in the western end of the Marlborough Downs. The summit seems to have been a focus for hunter-gatherer activity with 81 pieces recorded from this high place. This contrast of low numbers of lithic finds around Avebury and much higher numbers in the immediate higher landscape, may suggest that Avebury was becoming a more symbolic place in the mind of hunter-gatherer groups, not strategic. Exploitation strategies became focused elsewhere in the downland landscape and Kennet valley, Avebury's primary role was perhaps as a significant place as a meeting of paths.

Cherhill

Cherhill lies at the base of the western end of the Marlborough Downs, on the route of the A4. The location is notable because a hunter-gatherer site was excavated there in 1967 (Evans & Smith 1983). The hunter-gatherer horizon at the site was sealed by a layer of tufa, with a piece of charcoal at the base of the tufa giving a radiocarbon date of 5280±140 bc (BM-447). The occupation deposits consisted of a flint industry, animal remains, charcoal and some fragments of sarsen. Based on the lithic industry the site is described as perhaps later Mesolithic (*ibid* 111) with the presence of a major base camp being inferred, although purely on typological grounds, the microliths recovered at Cherhill suggest an earlier Mesolithic date. If the radiocarbon date is correct then occupation at Cherhill provides a contrasting date with the large sites further along the Kennet valley to the east of the Marlborough Downs. Typically, these sites tend to provide an earlier date. Thatcham (Wymer 1962) provided two radiocarbon dates on charcoal, 8080±170 bc and 8415±170 bc (Q658 and Q659). Healy (*et al* 1992) records a date at Thatcham of 9100±80. Elsewhere, at Greenham Dairy Farm, Newbury, Red Deer bone (Sheridan *et al* 1967) associated with hunter-gatherer artefacts provided a date of 6829 ± 110 bc (BM-449). On the whole, and there are some exceptions, the eastern end of the Marlborough Downs, the Kennet valley, tends to suggest earlier Holocene hunter-gatherer activity than the western downland. While only providing one radiocarbon date, the value of Cherhill to the spatial picture is surely its location. It is situated between two resource patches; the coastal resources of the Severn and the inland resources of the river Kennet. It marks a place that faces west, is sheltered, and provides a route to safely enter or leave the higher chalk landscape.

Conclusions

In trying to understand hunter-gatherer exploitation of the Marlborough Downs, the Kennet catchment as a whole has a role to play in defining settlement and activity patterns on the downland landscape. The approach I have taken is to examine the wider spatial picture, whilst not wishing to ignore the temporal evidence, which is somewhat scant. The lack of temporal evidence is somewhat predictable in hunter-gatherer studies and the spatial picture is perhaps the widest source of data available. This demonstrates that a pattern in both lithic compositions and findspot locations can be observed if viewed on this catchment size scale. This synthesis of evidence allows the following points to be postulated

- The most abundant evidence for hunter-gatherer activity is on the western slopes of the Marlborough Downs at Cherhill, and to the east in the middle Kennet valley. These may be home bases from which to exploit the downland landscape, perhaps on a seasonal basis.
- It seems that movement was probably taking place along the river Kennet, with the number of finds in the middle Kennet probably representing a palimpset of artefactual evidence.
- There is enough evidence to suggest that some groups left the main Kennet valley and travelled onto the downland landscape. To do this natural features such as dry-valleys and bournes were exploited, possibly because of there value as a navigable 'path'.
- The lithic compositions along the features travelling into the landscape contrast with material found elsewhere. Axes are commonly found as isolated finds, singly or in groups, on the ridge-lines. This suggests a particular type of activity was taking place, perhaps extractive.
- Once at the head of these 'routes' into the landscape, findspots fan out into the wider downland, but always following topographically distinct features, and usually on ridge-lines or natural summits. The height of these findspots is often over 200m and may indicate seasonal activities.
- The river Kennet itself may have been a route to travel east or west through the catchment. In the early Holocene, the head of the Kennet was just south of Avebury. There are topographically distinct features that offer natural routes or paths off the downland landscape to the west and southwest from the head of the Kennet. This is supported by lithic findspots spread along these features, which are now a route for modern roads. It may be that these routes or paths through the landscape have remained as such throughout the Holocene.

Finally, nowhere in the downland landscape is there a meeting of routes like that at Avebury. From there it would be possible to travel west to Cherhill; southwest to Devizes; or east to move along the river Kennet valley to the river Thames. It may be that this contributed to a growing symbolic importance of Avebury as a persistent place, a meeting of paths and a landscape of sarsens. As a persistent *place*, it may have retained a symbolic importance over millennia. This may hint at a possible reason for Avebury becoming a location for the monuments of those who came after the hunter-gatherers, Neolithic groups.

10
Memory, Monuments and Middens in the Neolithic Landscape

Joshua Pollard

The Upper Kennet Valley is justly famous for the spectacular Neolithic monuments that cluster there. Here it is argued that a focus on the past as comprehended in the past – the significance of history, myth and memory – provides a context for understanding the dynamics of monument construction in the region during the 4th and 3rd millennia BC.

Introduction

Much of the archaeological fame of the Avebury landscape rests on the presence of a series of spectacular Neolithic monuments that occupy the head of the Upper Kennet Valley (Fig 10:1). The most impressive of these constructions date to the early–mid 3rd millennium BC and include the Avebury henge itself, its two megalithic avenues, the Sanctuary, Silbury Hill and the West Kennett palisaded enclosures (Smith 1965a; Whittle 1997a; Gillings *et al* 2002). However, these were not the first monuments in the region. The earthwork enclosures on Windmill Hill, Knap Hill and Rybury (Connah 1965; Smith 1965a; Whittle *et al* 1999), along with around 30 megalithic and non-megalithic long mounds (Barker 1985), belong to the earlier part of the Neolithic of the area, and their building established a tradition of monument construction that was to be long-lived. Recent work has done much to elucidate the sequence of these constructions (e.g. Whittle 1993; 1997a; Gillings *et al* 2002). The earliest (chambered tombs and long mounds) were created in the first centuries of the 4th millennium BC, but the most intense periods of monument building occurred between 3600–3300BC and 2800–2200BC.

While the distribution of earlier Neolithic monuments shows them to be dispersed fairly evenly across the landscape, perhaps a reflection of the extent of contemporary clearings and areas of occupation, by the beginning of the 3rd millennium BC activity was increasingly focussed on the valley floor. By the end of the Neolithic a conscious effort was made, through the construction of megalithic avenues, to draw together disparate components of the cultural landscape (existing monuments and areas of occupation), creating for the first time a formal *monument complex* (Thomas 1999, 216–20).

Why this region should become the focus for such sustained traditions of Neolithic occupation and monument building remains unclear. Perhaps the landscape already held significance during the later Mesolithic, though current evidence points to only occasional, episodic utilization during this period (Whittle 1990). Alternatively, certain physical features of the region could have made it special, drawing Neolithic communities into the area who further enriched its significance through the construction of ceremonial monuments. One aspect of the landscape that must have been striking to its earliest occupants was the occurrence of extensive trails of sarsen stone. As with many other 'stonescapes' (Kahn 1990; Roe & Taki 1999), these spreads of sizable and distinctive blocks could have accrued considerable mythical and symbolic significance (Gillings & Pollard 1999).

These are just speculations, but if beginnings are difficult to define, we can at least chart the emergence of a landscape that became gradually imbued with connotations of the sacred. In this paper, thoughts are offered on this process. In particular, it is argued that the landscape developed as a special region because of the historical and mythological associations that slowly accrued, and that these associations were the outcome of its occupation – in effect, a

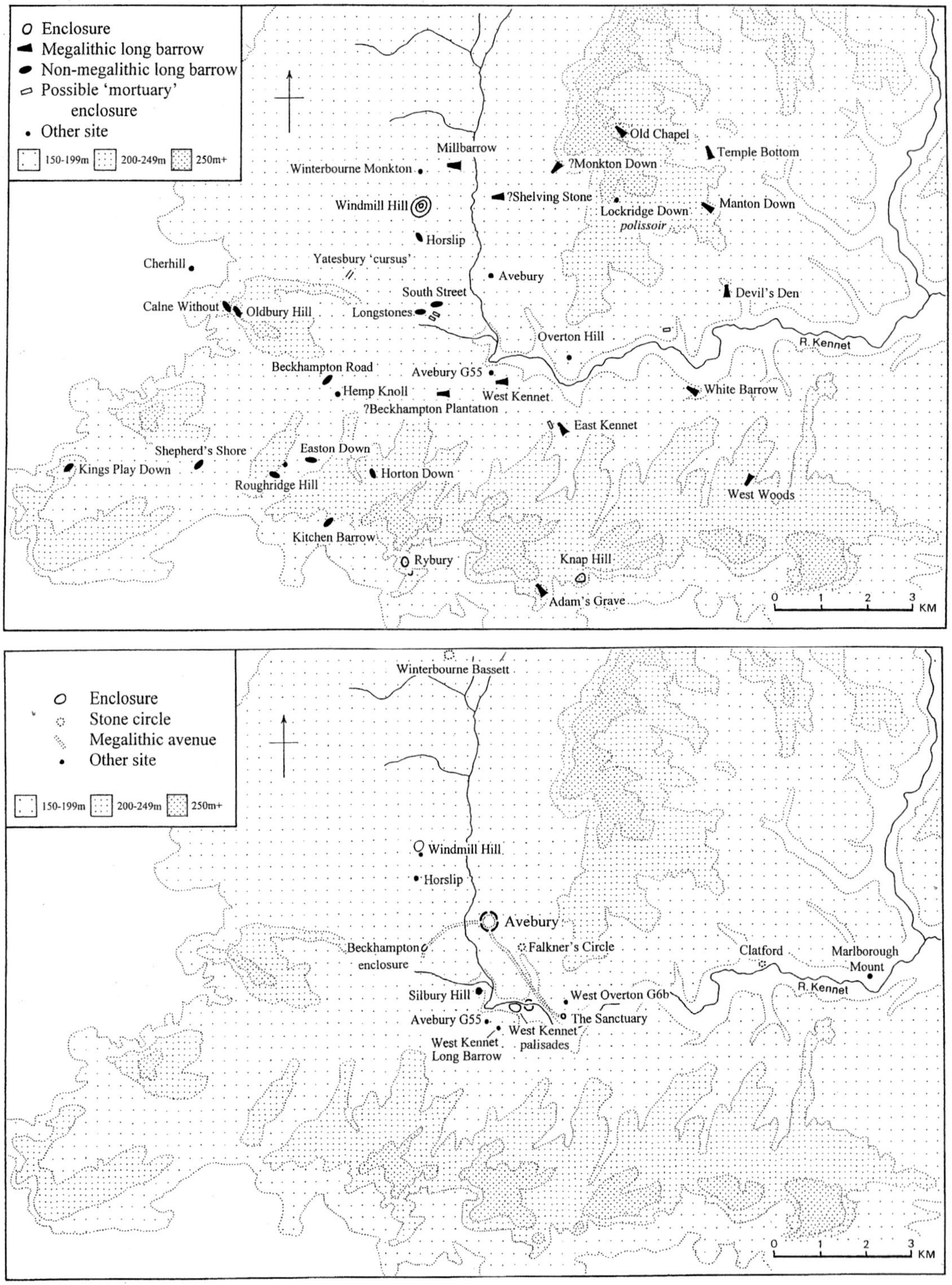

Fig 10:1 Earlier and later Neolithic sites in the Avebury region.

complex interplay existed between occupation, monument building and the creation of place-values. Linked to this is a recognition that perceptions *of the past in the Neolithic* played a pivotal role in the decisions surrounding where communities chose to live, where they built monuments, and the form that these constructions took (see also Bradley 2002). This occurred within a context of mobile or semi-mobile occupation (Whittle 1997b; Pollard 1999), where a tradition of gathering within the region, and participation in monumental projects, became established. Myth and tradition were seemingly important factors, and many monuments seem to make reference to distant times and places, perhaps even to mythic events and origins.

The importance of the past in the past

In a recent paper Gosden and Lock argue that 'all prehistoric societies oriented their actions in the present with the past in mind' (1998, 2). Myth and history mattered to these communities, providing a sense of identity, of belonging and continuity, serving to orientate contemporary activities within the landscape. For these reasons, people would structure the routines of life through a consciousness of the past. Gosden and Lock talk of two types of history: the first genealogical, in which the past is created through links to known ancestors; the second mythical, in which a more distant and less well known past is evoked. The two types may correspond on the one hand to historical events that are the outcome of human agency, and on the other those that resulted from the actions of supernatural forces (*ibid* 1998, 5). Of course, a strict distinction between genealogical and mythical histories is probably too simplistic, since some ancestors may themselves be mythical, and some distant events reinterpreted in genealogical terms (consider, for example, early medieval king lists where both real and mythical individuals were worked into genealogical lines).

Memory

An important aspect of Gosden and Lock's work is the explicit recognition of landscape features as anchors around which the memory of particular stories and events are woven (*see also* Basso 1996; Gow 1995). Features in the landscape, whether 'natural' or humanly-created, acted as memory prompts. This fits with a long-standing Western tradition by which objects (here ranging from small items of portable material culture to static monuments) serve a pivotal role in the transmission of memory. They can be seen to act as analogues of human memory, inasmuch as memories are transferred to objects, which by virtue of their durability preserve and prolong recollection (Forty 1999). According to Kwint (1999, 2), objects serve memory in three distinct ways:

- They furnish recollection. They constitute our picture of the past (they are representations of it).
- Objects stimulate remembering. They are mnemonics (consider Proust and involuntary memory).
- Objects form records. They are analogues to living memory, storing information beyond individual experience, and hence have the capacity to transcend individual time.

Because of their routine encounter and people's engagement with them, landscape features (be they places, elements of natural topography or humanly-constructed features) fulfil the roles of mnemonic devices and records of past events particularly well.

But, of course, objects and topographic features cannot in themselves preserve memory through some form of externalized 'mental storage'. Social or collective memory is sustained through social practices (and decisions are often taken over what is to be remembered and what is to be forgotten (Forty & Küchler 1999)). Bodily performative practices such as ritual, ceremony and re-enactment are central in recollecting and transmitting collective knowledge of the past (Connerton 1989). In Bloch's words, 'it is no accident that long-term evocative social memory makes such great use of visits to sites hallowed by what is believed to have occurred there' (Bloch 1998, 120). Such visits can even facilitate 're-experiencing (of these events) as though one was there' (*ibid*). It is this physical engagement with places, through visits, through ceremony, or through their physical re-working and modification, that keeps them in a socially active state (Gosden & Lock 1998, 5).

We are fortunate in that many of the practices employed in perpetuating the long-term social significance of places often left definable archaeological traces in the form of deposits of artefacts, markers and, most conspicuously of all, monumental constructions. Working through a series of case studies, I would here like to show how the long-term significance of places in the Avebury landscape was maintained and embellished through material practices, and how Neolithic communities in the region represented aspects of their past through monument building. Key to all is the material nature of collective memory, and the intricate relationship between landscape occupation and the creation of monuments.

Assembling monuments from earlier traces: an earlier Neolithic prelude

By the second half of the 4th millennium BC the Upper Kennet Valley had been transformed through piecemeal clearance, limited cultivation and the building of the region's first monuments. The latter include a substantial number of both megalithic and non-megalithic long mounds, quite varied in both their format and location (Barker 1985). On the edges of the region, on Windmill Hill to the north, Rybury and Knap Hill to the south, and perhaps Cherhill to the west, enclosures were created by the digging of circuits of interrupted ditches in woodland clearings

	Occupation	Cultivation	Mortuary ritual	Other
Beckhampton Road	•?	•?		•
Easton Down	•?	•		
Horslip		•?		•
Knap Hill	•			•
Millbarrow			•	
South Street	•	•		•
West Kennet long barrow	•?			
Windmill Hill	•	•	•	•

Table 10:1 Traces of 'pre-monument' activity at selected earlier Neolithic sites in the region.

(Oswald *et al* 2001; Whittle *et al* 1999; Evans & Smith 1983).

Though new creations in this landscape, the very form of these monuments may have embodied complex references to both distant (mythical) and more recent (historical) pasts. Bradley (1998) has drawn attention to the possible origins of these monuments in the *Linearbandkeramik* of Continental Europe. Though considerably separated in both space and time from their prototypical origins, he argues that long mounds referenced longhouses of a kind that were no longer built, while enclosures referred to communal settlements of this distant past (*ibid* 80–1). The very act of building these monuments could have served to materialize a sense of mythic belongings and beginnings far removed from the 4th millennium BC of the Upper Kennet.

At a local level, a deep concern with referencing and 'capturing' something of the past might be seen in the location of these constructions in the landscape. Their siting may in part have been dictated by topography – the enclosures occupy locally prominent vantage points, for example – or the desire on the part of groups to use monumental constructions to define rights of access to particular areas or resources. However, there are grounds for believing their siting was more intimately related to the history and associations of specific places. Julian Thomas has made the critical observation that many of the region's earlier Neolithic monuments were constructed in places of existing significance (Thomas 1999, 203). In fact, of those 4th millennium BC monuments that have been subject to modern excavation, all are in locations with traces of earlier activity (Table 10:1), some of it quite long-lived. In a landscape where the density of occupation was not great, the consistent siting of monuments in locations with existing histories of activity was far from coincidental.

The character of 'pre-monument' activity at each of these sites varied greatly. The construction of the Horslip long barrow was preceded by the digging of a line of pits, the axis of which was later developed by the construction of the barrow mound (Ashbee *et al* 1979). This pit line may, in fact, represent one side of an earlier long mound on the same site (Richard Bradley *pers comm*). Limited cultivation may also have taken place here, as it did at Easton Down (Whittle *et al* 1993), Windmill Hill (Whittle *et al* 1999) and perhaps Beckhampton Road (Ashbee *et al* 1979). At South Street there were at least two episodes of cultivation, limited occupation, and the creation through clearance of a sarsen boulder 'cairn' (Ashbee *et al* 1979) (Fig 10:2). The pre-enclosure occupation at Windmill Hill involved a range of activities, including the digging of pits, the erection of timber structures and the exposure of at least one body (Whittle *et al* 1999, 350–2). A late 5th–early 4th millennium BC radiocarbon date from a hearth under Beckhampton Road suggests the pre-mound activity spanned several centuries; and similar lengthy sequences are represented at Windmill Hill and South Street. Later Mesolithic microliths are also present at the latter site (Ashbee *et al* 1979, 270). Though long-lived, there are not continuous sequences of human occupation and working of these locales. Cultivation is seen as short-lived, and occupation was never of sufficient duration to generate sizeable quantities of refuse. These were places that were periodically visited, to which early Neolithic groups repeatedly returned over several generations. One can argue that it was the traditional significance of these locales that drew people back.

Despite the varied and discontinuous character of such pre-monument activity, it is significant that a number of sites show sequences that suggest a gradual shift from 'routine' to 'special' activities over time. At Beckhampton Road clearance, possibly cultivation, and short-lived occupation characterize the earliest use of the site. However, the immediate pre-mound activity involved the deposition of cattle skulls, one perhaps suspended from a stake setting (Ashbee *et al* 1979, 244–5) (Fig 10:2). The 'cairn' of nine large sarsen blocks under the South Street mound could be interpreted as a pre-barrow shrine (Whittle 1993, 43), its significance being reflected in its subsequent incorporation under the proximal end of the mound. That the sarsens rested *on* the turf line of the buried soil implies their setting pre-dated this part of the mound by only a short interval (Ashbee *et al* 1979, 261). Here the distinction between 'pre-monument' and

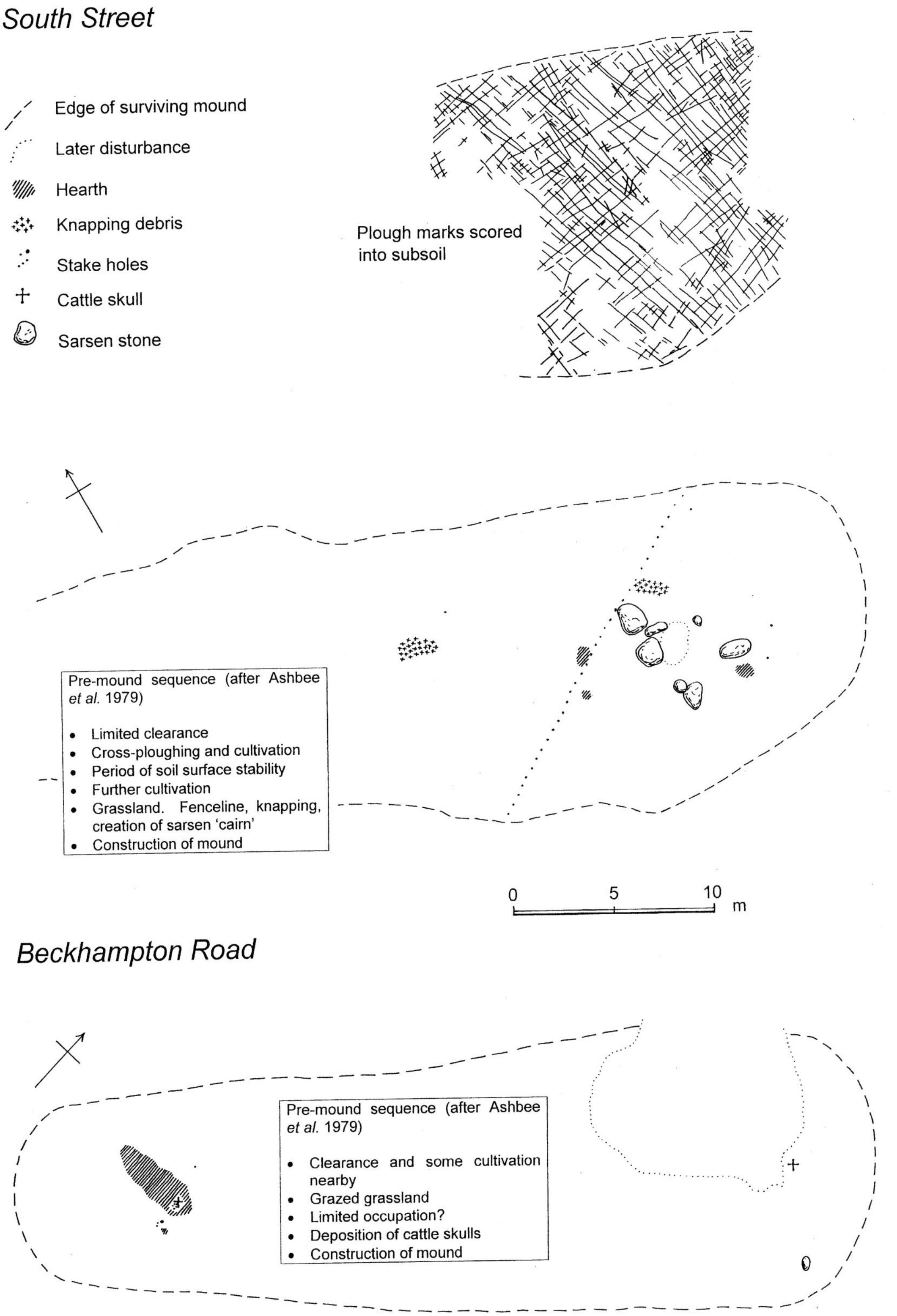

Fig 10:2 Pre-mound features at Beckhampton Road and South Street (after Ashbee et al *1979).*

'monument' phases becomes blurred to the point of being meaningless. At Windmill Hill the long-sequence of pre-enclosure activity may have ended with the construction of post-built structures, deliberate deposits in pits and the enactment of mortuary rituals. The burial of an adult male immediately preceded the construction of the Outer Bank, chalk rubble of the bank in

*Table 10:2 Ceramic sequences at selected sites. * <5 vessels; ** 6–10 vessels; *** >10 vessels.*

	Early Neolithic bowl	Peterborough ware	Grooved ware	Beaker
Avebury	**	**	*	*
Avebury G55	**	***	**	***
Beckhampton enclosure	*	-	*	-
Horslip	***	*	*	***
Sanctuary	*	**	***	**
South Street	*	**	-	*
West Kennet Avenue occupation site	**	***	**	**
West Kennet long barrow	***	***	***	***
West Kennet palisade enclosures	-	*	***	-
West Overton G6b	***	***	***	***
Windmill Hill	***	***	***	***

fact filling the open grave (Whittle *et al* 1999, 79–80). 'The evidence as a whole can be seen as a gradual consecration of a special place' (*ibid* 352).

In each instance it appears as though the specific historical associations of a place led to its ultimate transformation through monument construction. That process of construction occurred within locations with established histories, suggesting a genuine attempt to draw upon the past associations of particular places.

These monuments do not, therefore, represent the imposition of built forms on to an 'empty' landscape, rather they are worked out of places which had slowly accrued considerable significance (Thomas 1999, 203). That process of progressive accumulation of meaning may even have extended to the creation of many of these monuments through a gradual accretion of structural elements – piecemeal and protracted building, rather than their manufacture through single construction events (Lesley McFadyen and Alasdair Whittle *pers comm*). Furthermore, the incorporation of existing features into these constructions, such as the sarsen cairn at South Street and a natural boulder at Beckhampton Road (Ashbee *et al* 1979, 242), also allowed the material remains of earlier practices to be physically incorporated into these sites. Time, process and memory were worked into their very fabric.

Persistent places

The case of earlier Neolithic long mounds and enclosures illustrates how the accumulation of meanings and associations specific to particular places led to their eventual material transformation through monument construction. In another context it was the accumulation of material, in the form of artefacts, soils and animal bone, that led to transformations in the meanings of places.

Thomas has observed that a major theme of the Neolithic landscape of Avebury is 'the enduring significance of place' (1999, 220). A striking number of sites in the region have extremely long histories of activity, sometimes spanning the full Neolithic (Table 10:2). It should be stressed from the outset that these lengthy sequences of activity are interrupted rather than continuous, and frequently involve the repeated return to certain locales after decades or even centuries. Nonetheless, the importance of these places seems to have been retained across periods of temporary 'abandonment'. Avebury is one such location. Several episodes of short-lived pre-monument occupation here are indicated by carinated bowl, plain bowl and Peterborough ware pottery, along with quantities of worked flint (Smith 1965a). Then follows the construction of the first-phase earthwork around 3000BC; various re-workings of the earthwork and stone settings of the henge during the course of the 3rd millennium BC; and finally Beaker-associated depositional activity (Pitts & Whittle 1992; Pollard & Reynolds 2002, 83–91, 125–8).

The enduring lives of monuments

As 'persistent places' (Barton *et al* 1995), monuments are perhaps a special case. They are enduring and conspicuous features in the landscape, and because of their direct association with sacred realms, it is not surprising that the significance of monuments was often perpetuated in collective memory. Even when their original meanings were forgotten, their significance was sometimes re-invented at a later date (Bradley 1993). One mechanism by which the importance of these structures could be maintained and re-animated was through the deliberate deposition of animal and human bone, and selected artefacts. Excavation at a number of earlier Neolithic monuments in the centre of the region has revealed evidence for repeated deposition spanning the 4th and 3rd millennia BC. The list includes the enclosure on Windmill Hill, and the long barrows of West Kennett, Millbarrow, South Street and Horslip. The secondary deposits in the chambers at West Kennett are well known (Piggott 1962, 26–30). Following their use for the interment of human bodies, the chambers were progressively in-filled with layers of chalk rubble, humic soil and sarsen. Mixed in with this matrix were large quantities of pottery (Peterborough wares, Grooved ware and Beaker), worked flint, bone tools and animal bone. Though the excavator saw this secondary filling as a single event involving the re-deposition of material that had accumulated in a nearby 'offering house' (*ibid* 29; and see Case 1995), detailed re-analysis by Thomas and Whittle (1986; and Thomas 1999, 204–6) strongly suggests it accumulated through successive depositional events. On the basis of ceramic evidence alone, the secondary deposits must span nearly a thousand years. What remain unclear are the number of separate depositional events, and the interval at which they were enacted. Piggott's sections show at least ten separate layers of secondary infill (Piggott 1962, fig. 9), which could suggest individual episodes of deposition every 80–100 years. Spanning perhaps three or four generations, this is not too long for recollections of earlier acts to be lost from collective memory.

Though not on the scale of those at West Kennett, the former existence of similar 'secondary' deposits at Millbarrow is hinted at by sherds of Peterborough ware and a fine middle Neolithic polished-edge blade knife (Whittle 1994). The secondary ditch fills of the South Street long barrow contained deliberate deposits of Ebbsfleet pottery, animal bone (including the burial of a young sheep/goat), fragments of human skull and worked flint (Ashbee *et al* 1979). The barrow was covered in scrub and woodland at the time of these deposits, and this activity is unlikely to relate to settlement (Evans 1990).

Substantial assemblages of later Neolithic and early Bronze Age artefacts and animal bone testify to more intensive or protracted later deposition at the nearby Horslip long barrow (Ashbee *et al* 1979, 218–224). The deposits here, which included sherds of Fengate, Beaker and perhaps Grooved ware, along with a range of flint tools and pieces of foreign stone, were focussed on the southern terminal of the eastern ditch (Pollard & Reynolds 2002, fig. 26). Although in close proximity to the zone of later Neolithic occupation on the southern slopes of Windmill Hill (Whittle *et al* 2000), fieldwalking has demonstrated that traces of contemporary settlement are largely absent from the immediate environs of the barrow (Holgate 1987). Material must have been brought down from areas of occupation closer to the summit of Windmill Hill for deposition here.

Through repeated if very episodic acts of deposition the sanctity of these monuments was perpetuated within collective consciousness. Memories of earlier events and a generalized link to the past were thus reinstated through the repetition of depositional acts. This alerts us to the importance of material performances in the transmission of long-term collective memory, whatever those particular representations of the past might be. Here we are looking at the prolongation of the significance of place through staged and highly formalized acts that led to the steady accumulation of material. In other circumstances it was the largely unconsidered and routinized accumulation of exactly the same range of materials that led to the creation of traditionally important places in the landscape. However, those places were settlements rather than monuments.

Occupation and midden creation

Because of the striking nature of the region's monuments it is easy to forget how important occupation must have been in the creation of place-values. There are within the Avebury landscape certain locales that attracted repeated settlement. The list includes Overton Hill (Smith & Simpson 1966), the foot of Waden Hill (Smith 1965a), under the round barrow Avebury G55 (Smith 1965b), and the southern slopes of Windmill Hill (Whittle *et al* 2000). All of these locations have produced ceramic assemblages which include earlier Neolithic bowl pottery, middle Neolithic Peterborough wares and late Neolithic Grooved ware (Table 10:2). The

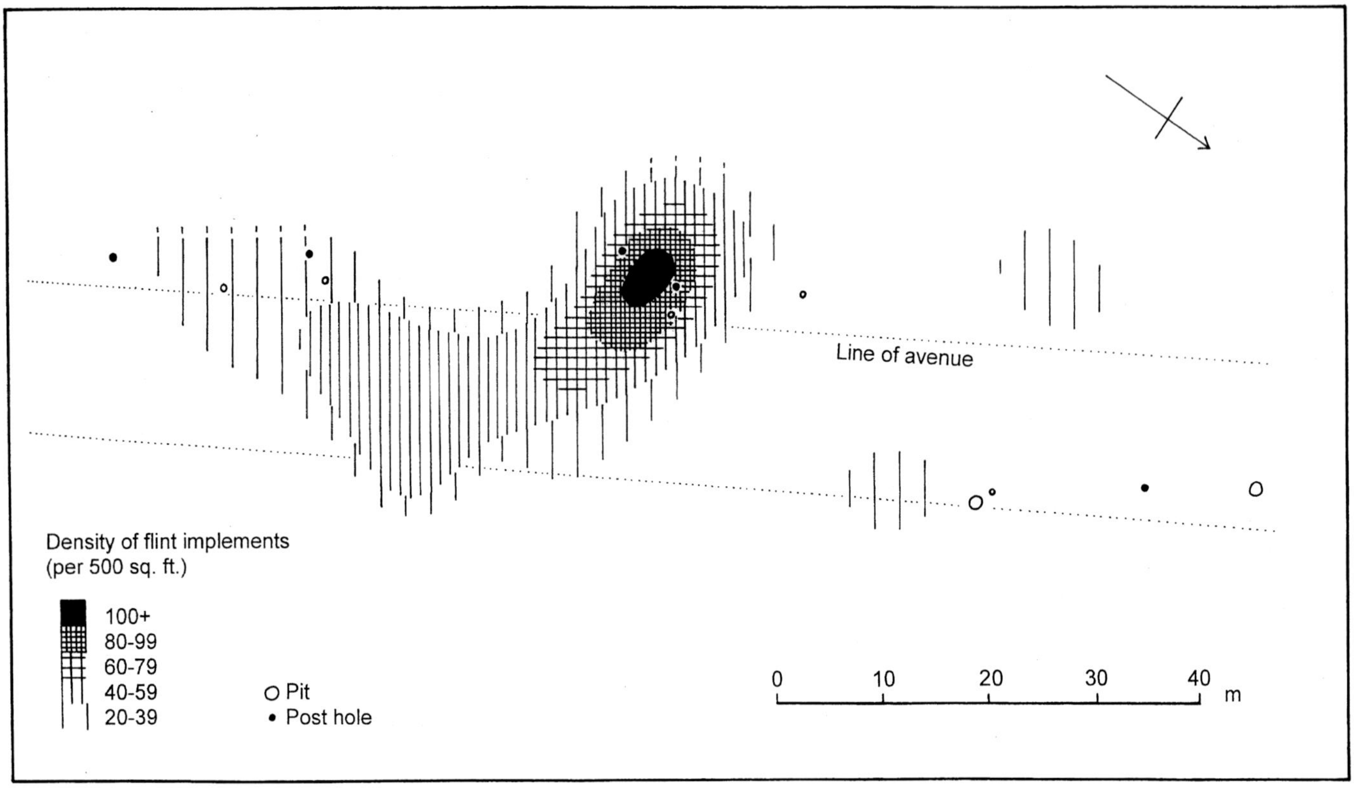

Fig 10:3 The West Kennett Avenue occupation site midden (after Smith 1965a).

absence of definable domestic structures argues against permanent and continuous occupation at these locales; and varying degrees of settlement mobility are in any case the norm for the period (Whittle 1997b; Pollard 1999). So why – operating within a system of tethered mobility (Whittle 1997b, 21) – did mobile or semi-mobile groups repeatedly return to these locations? There is nothing inherently special in terms of topography or the availability of certain resources that might account for the long-term popularity of these locales. But for communities who orientated their lives in relation to the past, and paid respect to that past through the creation and repeated re-working of monuments, it was surely the history of places that made them so important. In the context of shifting settlement, people might be drawn back to particular locations because of genealogical ties with those who had earlier lived there, in order to maintain a sense of ontological stability, or simply because certain places were traditionally sanctioned as auspicious.

In certain instances, as at Avebury G55 and the West Kennett Avenue occupation site, the residues of these occupation events were consciously curated to form middens and discernible refuse spreads (Thomas 1999, 209–10). Middening can be seen to represent more than casual refuse disposal, since it is the product of deliberate strategies of accumulation (Needham & Spence 1997). It can serve a number of purposes: acting as an economic resource, supplying material for manuring or recycling of materials; it can result from specific production and processing activities, such as large-scale lithic working; it can be a form of site management (a means of controlling waste); or middens can operate as symbolic structures, 'assuming connotations of affluence and social success, even becoming marks of territorial dominance' (Needham & Spence 1997, 84–5). In a context where extensive arable cultivation was not practised, and where spatial constraints within loosely structured settlement areas were unlikely to result in elaborate refuse-management regimes, functional explanations for middening are insufficient to explain these features. In one form or another their role must be considered symbolic, providing, in their final form, monumental expression to the process of occupation.

The detail of these unusual sites provides some insight into the dynamics behind their formation. Here consideration is given to the midden spread on the line of the West Kennett Avenue at the base of Waden Hill, examined by Keiller in 1934–5 (Fig 10:3). Excavation revealed a surface scatter of pottery and worked flint spread over an area of *c.*100 by 40m (Smith 1965a, 210–216). That soft prehistoric ceramics survived in quantity in a surface context is remarkable, and hints at the former existence of protecting midden soil deposits. Most of the 600 or so sherds of pottery were of Peterborough ware, with Ebbsfleet, Mortlake and Fengate styles being represented. A small amount of extremely fragile Grooved ware was also recovered; the entire ceramic range potentially spanning several centuries, beginning in the later 4th millennium BC (*cf* Gibson & Kinnes 1997). The lithic assemblage included over a thousand flint implements and an undetermined quantity of debitage. Densities of worked flint approached *c*.50 pieces per square metre, compared with density 'highs' of just over 20 pieces per square metre from test-pitting of the extensive and long-lived scatter on the southern slopes of Windmill Hill (Whittle *et al* 2000).

While there is every reason to assume this material accumulated under conditions of periodic occupation, the character of that occupation needs to be determined. Unusual and fancy implement types are particularly well represented within the lithic assemblage. They include polished-edge knives and scrapers, and a completely polished fabricator (Smith 1965a, 236–242). The working of many pieces is decidedly accomplished, with 40% of scrapers on flakes with facetted platforms, and a number of discoidal cores suggesting on-site manufacture of transverse arrowheads. Excavation records in the Alexander Keiller Museum, Avebury, suggest that scrapers were regularly found in groups of two or more, implying more than just casual discard. Furthermore, many of the implements look to have been deposited whilst in a perfectly usable condition. At the very least, there are hints of profligate use of elaborate material culture here.

No structures were revealed during the excavation, but a scatter of pits and post-holes occurred across the area. All the pits were characterized by formal deposits. One of the larger pits contained a substantial portion of cattle skull set upright with an antler placed next to it (*ibid* pl. 37). Substantial portions of Group VII axes (the only ones from the site) had been placed in holes 1 and 10; while six of the 12 features contained chisel arrowheads. The supports for fairly substantial timber settings, the five post-holes were grouped close to the pits. Associated with Grooved ware, the pits may come late in the life of the occupation site; as might the post-holes given the packing of 'dirty clay', burnt stone and daub (*ibid* 214–6), implying they were dug through midden soils. The position of these features late in, or at the very end of, the sequence of activity here is highly significant. The pits may have acted as closing or 'decommissioning' deposits, while the post settings seem intended to mark and thus memorialize the position of the midden. It is surely not coincidental that two pairs of post-holes occurred within the densest concentrations of material, while another was sited between the two largest pits. The midden may have been 'monumentalized' by the erection of the post settings. (The process is analogous to the marking of Grooved ware pits with flint cairns at Woodlands, near Amesbury: Stone & Young 1948). That process was then taken one stage further during the second half of the 3rd millennium BC when the West Kennett Avenue was laid out in such a way as to incorporate the midden within its course. Significantly, a gap was left in its western line of the Avenue stone settings at the point where it crossed the densest concentration of occupation material (*ibid* 212).

What is the significance of these middens? As deliberate, progressive and inter-generational accumulations of material, broad analogies might be drawn with the Neolithic and Copper Age tells of the Balkans. Like tells, there may not have been any intention at the outset to create large middens, but these features gradually became projects of accumulation. John Chapman has stressed how tell sites became symbols of occupational continuity (Chapman 1997). They embodied collective cultural memory, developing 'place-value' through the gradual process of their formation. In their final stages they stood for a sense of 'deep' or ancestral time, even accumulating associations with specific or generalized ancestors. Quoting Raymond Williams, he suggests these places became 'the materialization of a history', places that incorporated deep historical narratives and stood as a material testimony to, and reminder of, those histories of human dwelling (*ibid* 139–46).

None of the Avebury midden sites approach anything like the magnitude of many tells, but as projects of progressive refuse accumulation that were worked through repeated occupation, and that spanned the lives of several generations, they share striking similarities. Both types of site became landmarks *and* 'timemarks' (*ibid* 145). Perhaps possessing particular kin or group affiliations, on one level their presence may have served to legitimate rights of access and occupation in relation to particular places in the landscape. At another level they provided a sense of ontological stability, of belonging, acting as a material link with the worlds of past generations. As well as providing a physical reminder of recent and distant pasts, middening was a technology that allowed specific genealogies of occupation to be woven into places.

New monuments, old networks

The final case study addresses the way in which the construction of monuments during the later Neolithic of the region was occasionally bound-

Fig 10:4 The Beckhampton enclosure, avenue and cove, Longstones Field, Beckhampton.

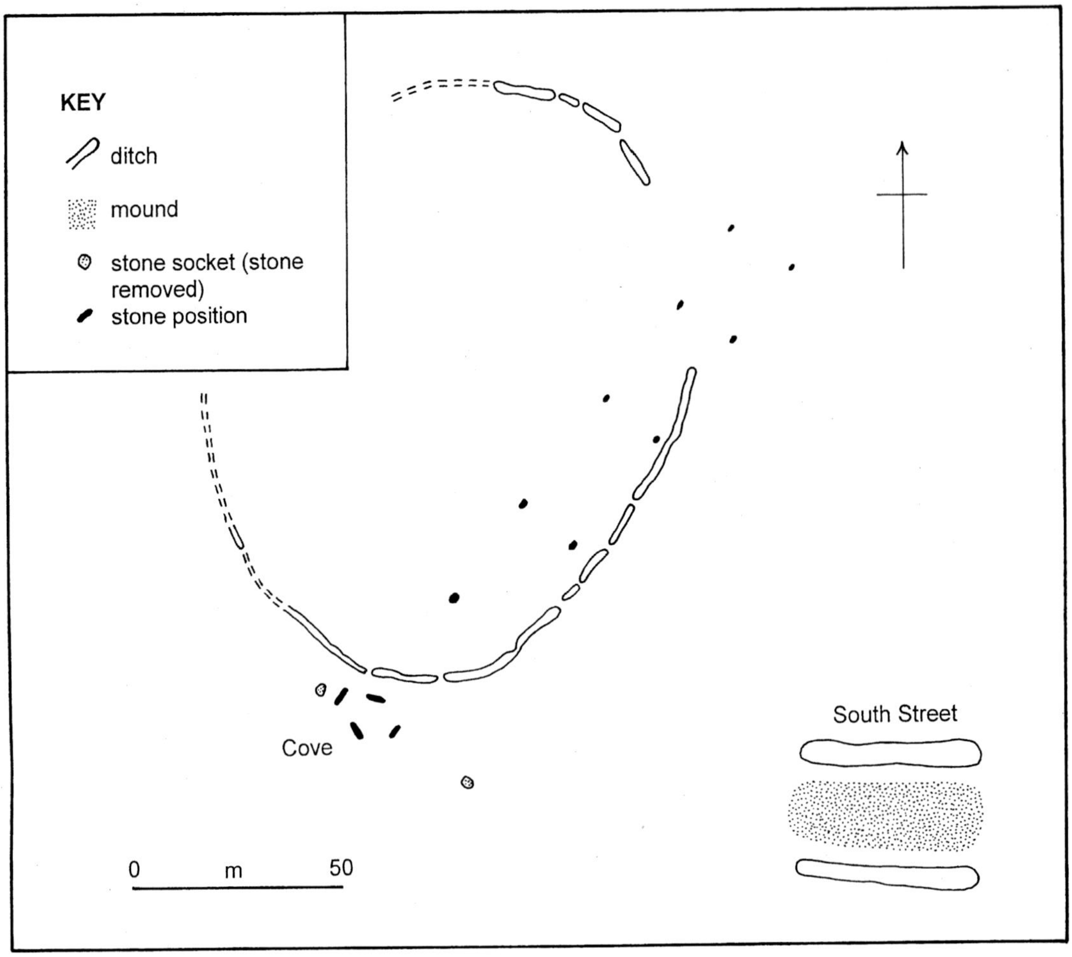

up in the explicit creation of representations of the past. It draws upon the results of recent fieldwork to the west of Avebury at Beckhampton (Gillings *et al* 2000a, 2002) (Fig 10:4).

Since 1999 excavations in Longstones Field have focussed on features belonging to a second megalithic avenue (the 'Beckhampton Avenue'), leading from the western entrance of the Avebury henge monument, and an earlier earthwork enclosure. Dating to *c*2800–2600BC, the enclosure describes a flattened oval, *c*140 by 100m across, with an exceptionally wide entrance to the east. It was created by digging a shallow interrupted ditch, spoil from this being used to form an internal bank. Most likely placed deposits, quantities of animal bone and a few sherds of Grooved ware were found on the base of the ditch, particularly near the main entrance terminals. After an unspecified interval (but long enough for the ditch fills to begin to stabilize), the enclosure was deliberately levelled, seemingly in a single event. The megalithic avenue was then constructed; its course running through the former enclosure entrance, traversing the south-eastern sector of the enclosure, and apparently terminating immediately to the south-west. At some point in the later 3rd millennium BC this terminal was reworked. Two of the stones of the original terminal setting were taken down, and a box-like setting of massive sarsens ('Cove') erected in their place.

The creation of the enclosure, avenue and cove in fact lies at the end of a much longer sequence of Neolithic activity in Longstones Field. The South Street long barrow lies only 70m to the south-east of the enclosure, while the uninvestigated Beckhampton (or Longstones) long barrow is situated only 200m to the west. The enclosure was therefore constructed in a locale with an established history of activity that extended back to the beginning of the Neolithic in the region. In fact, it is quite likely that its siting in this part of the landscape may have been strongly influenced by the particular historical associations of this place.

Lacking the regularity of many contemporary henges and timber circles, the enclosure is an unusual monument. Morphologically, it is rather 'out of time'. The irregular, interrupted ditch and internal bank are more reminiscent of 4th millennium BC causewayed enclosures than later Neolithic henge monuments, though it has affinities (albeit not in terms of geometric regularity) with the slightly earlier Stonehenge 1 (Cleal *et al* 1995). Its form could have been intentionally anachronistic, making quite deliberate reference to earlier enclosure traditions. A direct link to these traditions was perhaps provided by the inter-visibility between this monument and the mid-4th millennium BC enclosure to the north on Windmill Hill. The creation of the enclosure could have stood to some degree in contrast or opposition to the novel values and bodies of sacred knowledge presented by a monument like Avebury. However, its event-like character may imply it was never intended as a lasting statement in the landscape. The alternative is to envisage the construction of such an 'archaic' monument as a deliberate process of re-creation or reenactment – a means of bringing an image of the past to the fore.

The chalk rubble upper fills of the enclosure ditch suggest this monument was deliberately levelled prior to the construction of the avenue. This period (*c*2600–2300BC) is one of particularly frenetic activity in the region, with the construction not only of the Avebury avenues, but perhaps other megalithic settings, the Sanctuary, Silbury Hill and the West Kennett palisaded enclosures (Whittle 1993, 1997a; Pollard & Reynolds 2002, chapter 3). The relationship of the avenue to the enclosure is a curious one. The avenue appears to have been laid out in such a way as to deliberately incorporate the enclosure, and indeed terminates here. However, the levelling of the enclosure appears to have been undertaken as part of that process; so that the construction of the avenue simultaneously involved the 'destruction' and commemoration or marking of the earlier monument. The enclosure was removed from the landscape, but its former presence was worked into collective memory. Furthermore, the bisection of an earlier enclosure by a later linear monument has parallels with the siting of cursus monuments and bank barrows over the causewayed enclosures at Maiden Castle, Etton and Fornham All Saints (Oswald *et al* 2001, 134–5).

Themes of memory, narrative and the biography of place may be deeply rooted in the creation of the West Kennett and Beckhampton Avenues, and the Longstones Cove. Thomas sees the construction of the Avebury avenues as a means of drawing together disparate places of existing significance in the landscape, thus creating a unified monumental complex (Thomas 1999, 220). The Beckhampton Avenue incorporates the earlier enclosure, in the same way the West Kennett Avenue runs through the midden site at the foot of Waden Hill and terminates at a monument (the Sanctuary) built on a site with a lengthy history of activity (Cunnington 1931; Pollard 1992). However, it was not just physical but visual relationships that were created. The laying out of the avenues involved the creation of sight-lines that 'framed' earlier monuments. As the West Kennett Avenue approaches Avebury the stones of the avenue 'enclose' a view of Windmill Hill on the distant horizon in a way that seems wholly intentional (Watson 2001, 300).

It is not inconceivable that the avenues monumentalized existing pathways between these places (Barrett 1994, 15). The avenues provided formalized routeways for procession and movement across the landscape, taking in places of historical significance along their course. Myths and stories relating to particular places were perhaps retold as part of the orchestrated movement of participants along the avenues during major ceremonies, thus perpetuating collective memory of important events and their placing in the landscape. This process of 'bodily remembrance' is particularly potent. As Connerton describes, ceremonies are highly effective mechanisms for preserving *versions* of the past, and it is through prescribed bodily behaviour during such (for example, gesture and formalized patterns of movement) that collective memory is sedimented (Connerton 1989).

Connerton also shows how reenactments of prior, prototypical actions, relating to prototypical events or people of either an historical or mythological nature, are a frequent component of commemorative ceremonies. This is seen with the widespread celebration of New Year and the Christian sacrament as repeated creations of the cosmogonic act (*ibid* 65). Commemorative ceremonies serve to remind a community of its 'identity as represented by and told in a master narrative', providing a form of 'collective autobiography' (*ibid* 70). Did the avenues recreate mythical trails, and was procession along them a reenactment of prototypical journeys into the area by the region's first inhabitants? Perhaps the entire complex of enclosure, avenue and cove at Beckhampton can be seen in the context of reenactment – materializing myth and history. The creation of the anachronistic enclosure referred to earlier acts of monument construction in the area, and perhaps even to more distant realms and communal settlements of a kind that no longer existed (Bradley 1998, 80–1). The avenues monumentalized traditional routes across the landscape; while the cove could be seen as the recreation of an earlier megalithic burial chamber, such as those readily visible in the region at Shelving Stone and Manton (Burl 1988, 7). In one final twist, there may even have been an attempt to replicate the residues of a long occupation history. Vast quantities of knapping debris (in order of 10–15,000 pieces) were found in and around the stones of the cove. Here stone-working was seemingly not directed at the production of usable tools, but was conceivably undertaken with the intention of creating material that resembled debris from long-term occupation – effectively replicating a midden.

Conclusion

There is a tendency to write accounts of prehistoric landscapes in a 'layered' fashion, delineating sequences of change and development in such a way that the slate of the past was periodically wiped clean and activity resumed on a new trajectory. But occupation of the landscape rarely works in such a fashion. Gosden and Lock's assertion that prehistoric communities oriented their actions 'with the past in mind' (1998, 2) is a critical one, and here an attempt has been made to show how Neolithic communities in the Avebury region lived within and transformed a landscape with the past firmly to the fore. The structuring of landscape inhabitation was worked in relation to biographies of place, collective memories and representations of the past, whether historical or mythical. Those memories were sustained as much through occupation and routine practice as through the creation of explicit mnemonic devices, a role that may have been assumed by certain later Neolithic monuments.

The Upper Kennet Valley is justly famous for the spectacular Neolithic monuments that cluster there. These monuments are complex phenomena, embodying multiple meanings, purposes and processes. The motivations that lay behind their creation are not reducible to a single explanation, be it economic, societal or sacred (not that these domains were likely to have been divisible anyway). It would not, therefore, be proper to propose a simple explanation for why so many and so varied a range of monuments were constructed in the Avebury landscape during the 4th and 3rd millennia BC. This acknowledged, a focus on the past as comprehended in the past provides one context for understanding the dynamics behind the traditions of construction represented by these monuments. It is important to understand monuments as events within the context of histories of occupation, and of the way in which dwelling in a landscape leads to its inscription with historical resonance, meaning and myth. These values and qualities provided the driving dynamic for monument building – monuments were worked from the fragments of histories of inhabitation. There is an agency to the past in the past that should not be forgotten.

Acknowledgement

I would like to thank Richard Bradley for providing helpful comments on a draft of this paper.

11
'The small compass of a grave': Early Bronze Age burial in and around Avebury and the Marlborough Downs

Rosamund Cleal

Before great Agamemnon reign'd,
Reign'd kings as great as he, and brave,
Whose huge ambition's now contained
In the small compass of a grave' Horace, *Odes,* trans Francis

Introduction

For more than two hundred years Bronze Age round barrows have held a strong attraction for the antiquarian and archaeologist. As at Stonehenge, the large Neolithic monuments at Avebury drew attention to the many barrows which were, two hundred or more years ago, even more obvious in the landscape than they are now, after decades of cultivation. Early 'barrow digging' left little record, the tantalising accounts in Stukeley (1743) being understandably – because so early – lacking in detail, while those of Dean Merewether (1849), with their greater detail about grave groups combined with a high degree of ambiguity as regards location, are more agonisingly frustrating. Occasional barrow excavations have taken place over the century and half since Merewether, but only in those of the last fifty years or so is the record usually complete enough to be satisfactory. There is, however, useful information to be gained even from this variable record which may shed some light on the society which left us these grass-covered mounds.

Chronology

The 'Early Bronze Age' is usually considered to begin during the second half of the third millennium BC, the date of its inception depending on how the period during which limited copper working took place is viewed (i.e. as metal-using Late Neolithic, as Copper Age, or Early Bronze Age). Here the full Early Bronze Age is taken to be *c*2200BC to *c*1500BC, or, to reflect more accurately the slow nature of these transitions, the 23rd century BC to the 15th and it will be mainly discussed in two parts, an earlier and a later, the division being taken as around the turn of the third and second millennia. In addition the sparse evidence for very late burials will also be mentioned. This gives an overall division into 'early', 'middle' and 'late' Early Bronze Age as shown in the Table 11:1. The table does not include every type of object related to the three phases, but only those occurring within the study area or referred to as comparative material in the text. A wide ranging discussion of Early Bronze Age chronology is to be found in Needham 1996, with which this scheme is largely compatible, as shown, although an earlier inception is assumed here for full Early Bronze Age. These will here be abbreviated as E/EBA, M/EBA and L/EBA, the last two generally being considered together.

Study area

Although it would have been ideal to have included burials in the wider area shown in Fig 11:1, and in particular those to the south-west of Avebury in the 'Beckhampton Road' valley, the number of barrows which have been investigated

Table 11:1 Material culture used to define three phases of the Early Bronze Age for this paper

***c2200–2000 BC*: Early part of the full Early Bronze Age (E/EBA in this paper)** Earlier Beakers (Clarke's 1970 Beaker groups relevant to the area: All-Over-Cord (AOC), European (E), Wessex/Middle Rhine (W/MR), Barbed Wire (BW), Northern/Middle Rhine (N/MR), Northern/North Rhine (N/NR). Equates with Needham 1996 later part of Period 2 (Metal Using Neolithic) and earlier Period 3)
***c2000–1700 BC*: Middle part of the Early Bronze Age (M/EBA in this paper)** Later Beakers (mainly Clarke's Southern tradition, groups S1–S4; the reason why the local N2 Beakers, Developed Northern, which would normally be here are placed in E/EBA are discussed in the text) Earlier Collared Urns (Burgess 1986, Early and Middle) Wessex Culture I assemblages (i.e .Bush Barrow phase): grape cups, gold, Food Vessels. Equates with Needham 1996 Period 3 (EBA)
***c1700–1500 BC*: Late part of the Early Bronze Age (L/EBA in this paper)** Aldbourne cups, Faience beads, Tweezers (?). Equates with Needham 1996 Period 4 (EBA)

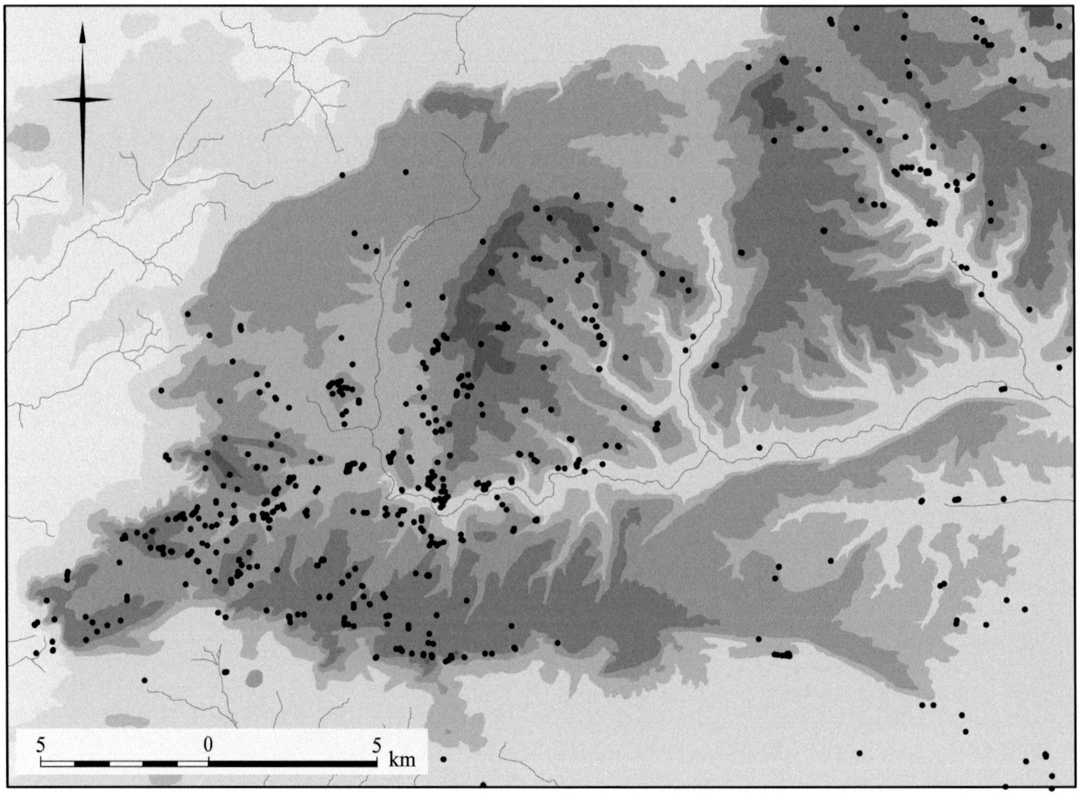

Fig 11:1 Round barrows on the Marlborough Downs

would have resulted in too long a study for this context. Instead, only burials on the Marlborough Downs 'proper' have been considered, along with those of the area around Avebury bounded by higher ground, 'rounded out' to kilometre squares. This is shown by the area of Fig 11:2.

E/EBA Burials

Burials of individuals with or without accompanying grave goods are absolutely rare, although not unknown in Britain, before the second half of the third millennium BC. The appearance of such burials must represent a profound change in the way people viewed death. It seems fairly clear that in the fourth millennium BC on death, or more importantly, on the conversion of the person to dry bone, the individual was subsumed within the collective body of the ancestors. The removal of bones from West Kennet Long Barrow, for instance, and the mixing of bones from different individuals, strongly suggests this (Piggott 1962). During the early third millennium BC this practice seems to have been superseded by another, or others, which have left little trace. Rare instances of probably later Neolithic practices indicate that cremation may have been the favoured rite (e.g. at Stonehenge, or Dorchester on Thames, Cleal *et al* 1995; Atkinson *et al* 1951), the bone perhaps being usually scattered rather than buried, either onto dry land or into water and so leaving no archaeological trace.

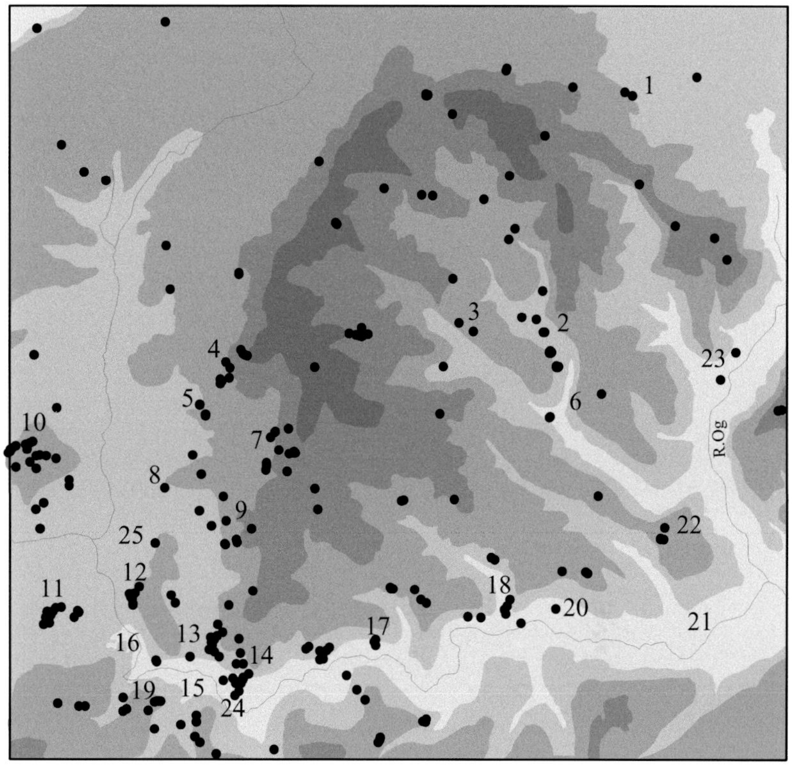

Key:

1. Burderop/Gypsy Lane
2. Rockley Plantation
3. Rockley Down
4. Monkton Down
5. Monkton Down Lower
6. Course of the Rockley Bourne
7. Avebury Down North
8. Avebury Down Barn
9. Avebury Down
10. Windmill Hill
11. Folly Hill
12. Waden Hill North
13. Overton Hill West
14. Overton Hill Seven Barrows
15. West Kennet palisaded enclosures
16. Silbury Hill
17. North Farm East
18. Clatford Bottom
19. Avebury G55
20. Manton Barrow
21. Marlborough Mound
22. Marlborough Common
23. Ogbourne St Andrew churchyard
24. The Sanctuary
25. Avebury G20 and henge
26. Disc barrows south of Beckhampton Penning

Fig 11:2 Round barrows in area referred to in text

Round barrows

The existence of round barrows in the later Neolithic has been thoroughly discussed by Ian Kinnes (1979), but they are not, on present evidence, a feature of north Wiltshire. This may change as the recent excavation of West Overton G19 has revealed a later Neolithic phase (Swanton 1988) and early excavations are likely to have missed any such evidence. But for the most part the earliest mounds in the area belong to the full Early Bronze Age and only one seems convincing as a pre-2000 BC burial. Winterbourne Monkton G9, towards the foot of Monkton Down, nearly 3km north east of the henge was excavated by Dean Merewether in 1849, who describes digging his way down through the mound and into a deep grave beneath it. In the course of this he found, first, and only a foot deep in the mound, which was apparently five feet high, a secondary, Beaker, burial, which will be discussed below. Merewether goes on to describe the composition of the mound and the primary grave (1851b, 105)

> *'The material of which this barrow was composed was chalk rubble, very coarse, and not mixed with other substances, as was generally the case, nowhere were there fragments of bones, urns, or pottery, as observed in others. At the depth of 5 feet were (Y) the heads of two oxen laid side by side and in very perfect condition, but very brittle on removal [measurements of the skulls given]; in each the centre of the forehead had been fractured in a circular hole. Below these the same hollow character of the chalk continued, and the sides of the chamber, 6 feet in length by 4 feet in breadth, had been carefully cut in the natural chalk. The heads of the oxen were laid across the chamber north-east. At a depth of 5 feet below these, and 10 feet from the top, was the skeleton of an adult (Z), in many parts much decayed, but in the crouched position, lying on the left side; behind the head was a small ornamented urn of unbaked clay (aa), or at least only fire-baked, and not in a kiln. The thigh bone was 10 inches in length; at the right foot was a small well-chipped flint arrowhead (bb), and a flint spearhead (cc). A second also was subsequently found near the same spot (dd) though not so well formed.'*

The detail of this is important because it establishes the relationship of the cattle skulls and the primary burial, that is, as placed over the filled-in primary grave at the time the mound was raised and therefore belonging with the primary interment rather than the secondary. It is also reasonably clear from the description that there is likely to have been a ditch from which the clean chalk was derived, and, incidentally, that there was no obvious evidence of previous occupation on that spot, in contrast to many other mounds (notes in Gazetteer). It is interesting to note that material in mounds is often Beaker, which in turn suggests that this mound may pre-date much of that activity, which may therefore be later Beaker period (and therefore M/EBA in the terminology here). The presence of cattle skulls is very reminiscent of the barrow Bishop's Cannings 81, on Hemp Knoll, 7km to the southwest. This is described by the excavator as 'a fairly small barrow' with a ditch 60ft in diameter and a mound covering the whole of the interior (Robertson Mackay 1980, 138); when recorded in 1958 it stood 4.5ft high but was subsequently seriously reduced by ploughing (*op cit* 123). The primary burial comprised a group with a Wessex/Middle Rhine Beaker with an unusual reserved lozenge motif, a very worn and probably re-used belt ring, and a damaged wristguard. The Beaker had a fresh appearance and, in contrast to the other objects, could have been made for the grave (*op cit* 144). Above the inhumation, which was of an adult male, probably in a wickerwork coffin (*op cit* 140), were a cattle skull and four feet, probably from the same animal, which was possibly an elderly cow (Grigson 1980, 165); these were in the south-east corner of the grave pit, outside the coffin and about 2ft above the inhumation. Two radiocarbon dates for this burial were obtained from oak, which lay around one end of the coffin and belonged to an ill-defined object or structure. The two dates obtained are 3540±70 BP (HAR-2998) and 3745±135 BP (NPL-139), calibrating to 1740–1450 BC and 2100–1500 BC (OxCal3, 95.4%) respectively. The range of NPL-139 renders it of little value, while HAR-2998 seems later than would be expected and would place this group in the middle phase of the EBA, as defined here. The vessel from Hemp Knoll, which was not included in the Clarke corpus of 1970, seems best classified as Wessex/Middle Rhine as is also probably the Winterbourne Monkton G9 Beaker. The latter is known only from the Merewether drawing, which shows a vessel with a very restricted neck and mouth, leading Clarke to classify it as N2, a later Beaker group (Clarke 1970 corpus no. 1187). This feature, however, appears to be common to a number of his drawings, and may be in part a fault in the depiction of the vessel, as it is also present in the Beaker from a barrow at East Kennet (G1c) which survives (Clarke 1970, fig. 948) and shows that the Merewether drawing is at fault.

The dating of Wessex/Middle Rhine Beakers is very problematic. On the evidence of the Beaker dating programme there is a wide spread of dates, taking them well into the second millennium (Kinnes *et al* 1991) but this seems at odds with the evidence of the Beakers, and their associated grave goods, which suggests a set of artefacts and funerary practice operating over a fairly short period and associated with sometimes exotic metalwork which is often early. Whittle and Atkinson, in discussing the W/MR burial from Dorchester, Oxon XII which Robertson Mackay considered the closest parallel for the Hemp Knoll group (1980, 146) have reviewed the mixed evidence for W/MR dating. Writing in the early 1990s they point out that 'until recently it would have been normal to accept the Dorchester assemblage without question as early or relatively early in the British sequence, but the question of date has become problematic.', going on to discuss the Barnack, Cambridgeshire group, which is dated by charcoal to the late third early second millennium BC, Smeeton Westerby, which is dated to the early second millennium, and Rotherley, which is dated well into the second millennium BC (Kinnes *et al 1991* gives full details of the dates). Whittle and Atkinson conclude however, that 'all things considered, the exotic character of the Dorchester assemblage and burial supports after all an early or relatively early date in the beaker sequence' (Whittle *et al* 1992, 183) and that is accepted here too, for Winterbourne Monkton G9 and for Hemp Knoll. Although the British Museum dating programme was a huge advance on what had gone before there is clearly a very pressing need for more, and multiple, dates on grave groups. These two graves under barrows, and that at Roundway G8, a rich group under a low mound a further 6km beyond Hemp Knoll to the south west, suggest a tradition of fairly modest barrows developing perhaps towards the very end of the third millennium BC and the beginning of the second. A concern with cattle is suggested by the two burials in which cattle skulls were placed in proximity to the grave group but were not part of it, and a connection with other activities elsewhere is suggested by the very unusual nature of the reserved lozenge motif on the Hemp Knoll Beaker. Although lozenges become common on later Beakers, usually used in different ways, a very similar use, on a similarly typologically early Beaker occurs only 3km from Hemp Knoll, in the blocking of the West Kennet chambered long barrow (Piggott 1962), a vessel for which Case suggests a date of probably no later than the turn of the third millennium (1995, 12–13).

Flat graves

Using the simple but crude division of Beakers into earlier and later, dividing at around the turn of the millennium (Table 11:1), it may be suggested that at least three, and probably six, flat graves within the study area belong to the period before 2000 BC, probably falling into the last quarter of the millennium or around the turn. Three of these, all potentially more clearly earlier Beakers, are closely associated with standing sarsens of the monumental complex (Beckhampton Longstones Cove, West Kennet Avenue (29a) and The Sanctuary (see Gazetteer for details of all burials). Two other Beaker-associated burials, which may also be of similar date, are from graves unassociated with monuments: that of a child at Beckhampton (close to the Grange) and at Lockeridge,). The Lockeridge vessel is squatter than usual and is a rather atypical W/MR vessel (classified by Clarke 1970, fig 179) while the other is noted by Clarke as N2 (Developed Northern, a later group). However, bearing in mind Case's suggestion that in the fourth quarter of the third millennium northern traits are to be found on his Group D Beakers (and he cites the Lockeridge and Beckhampton Beakers as examples of this (Case 1995, 1) these could date from around 2000 BC or the very early second millennium BC at the latest, and I have taken this also to apply to a Beaker from the burial at West Kennet Avenue 25b, classified by Clarke as N2, but similar to the Beckhampton Grange vessel (Clarke 1970, figs 515 and 516). At both Lockeridge and Beckhampton there was the suggestion, made by the excavators, that further, contemporary, graves may have lain undiscovered nearby (Young 1950, 315; Cunnington 1926c, 395). An additional vessel, at West Kennet Avenue, accompanying a burial, has so far defied classification into any of the existing styles of Beaker or Grooved Ware, but may also belong to the late third millennium, as it appears to demonstrate a mixing of Beaker and Grooved Ware traits (Smith 1965b, fig 78 P352). It is apparent then, that by the turn of the millennium complementary traditions of burial had developed: of burial in single flat graves, which could be associated with sarsen and included children; of burial under low round mounds, perhaps mainly for men; and burial next to standing sarsens, again certainly for men and also for adolescents (less certainly only male).

M/EBA Burials

What dating evidence there is suggests that in the early centuries of the second millennium BC, perhaps between about 2000 BC and 1700 BC a great variety of artefacts were in use and were included in burials. Burial rites likewise varied, including flat graves, inhumation under mounds, cremation under mounds and into existing mounds and barrows of various types.

Flat graves

The nature of flat graves, and the low level of construction and other ground disturbing work within this rural area mean that the number known is always likely to be well below that of the actual number in the ground. The extensive excavations at Overton Down (see Gazetteer, Flat Graves, for references) revealed what appears to be a flat grave cemetery of the Beaker period, with at least one child buried with a later Beaker (a paired fingernail decorated Beaker with a long cylindrical neck; not in Clarke; I F Smith in Fowler 1967, 30–31, fig. 5) and others without grave goods. A vessel from Smeathe's Ridge, which, on the grounds of a photograph, may be a coarse Beaker or a Food Vessel suggests another possible location for burials of the early second millennium BC. In these cases the burials were on elevated ground away from the monument complex of Avebury. In Winterbourne Monkton parish, north of Windmill Hill, however, a grave with two fairly late Beakers and other grave goods may be one of several buried under sarsens in that area. Apart from being overlooked by the causewayed enclosure of Windmill Hill and close to the chambered tomb at Millbarrow this is not an area dominated by monuments.

Avebury henge and Avenues, however, cannot be assumed to have been entirely neglected in this M/EBA period. A recently obtained radiocarbon date from a skull fragment found within stonehole 41 in the NW sector raises the possibility that some stone movement and possible re-erection was taking place in the early second millennium BC ((OxA-10109) Pollard and Cleal in prep). The skull and a plain basal sherd probably from a Beaker were found in what Keiller termed the 'lower' stonehole, under some chalk packing which he surmised had been placed in the hole to raise the stone. Whether this was during the original erection of the stone, which seems unlikely given its late date, or a re-erection it must be assumed that the burial had taken place some time earlier and had been disturbed, therefore suggesting the stone re-erection was well within the M/EBA. A similar or slightly earlier date is also likely for a woman buried in the ditch by the southern entrance (often called – incorrectly – the 'dwarf' burial). This burial, which was not accompanied by grave goods but was surrounded by sarsen stones, lay just above a burnt layer which produced a date of 3690±BC (calibrating to 2210–1980 at 1 sigma, 2450–1830 at 2 sigma, published in Pitts and Whittle 1992, 205). Pottery found at the same level appears to belong to a more general Early Bronze Age tradition of grog-tempered coarse vessels, rather than to be identifiable as Beaker (Gray 1935, fig. 7, no. 210, and this writer's own observations). This, then, is unequivocally an Early Bronze Age burial and could belong to the transition between E/EBA and M/EBA. It also shares a position in a left hand (in going out) ditch terminal of a henge with a probably female young adult burial in the henge at Marden (Wainwright 1971). The date of the Marden burial is uncertain, but it was certainly deposited some time after the ditch was dug and is at the junction between a layer with much later Neolithic material and the one above which was sterile so that an Early Bronze Age date cannot be ruled out.

Barrows

The dating of barrows is very uncertain and the vast majority are either undatable because they have not been excavated or have not produced any datable grave goods or material for radiocarbon dating. As the paucity of early barrow burials within the study area seems to be part of a widespread phenomenon it will be assumed that the majority here are of M/EBA and L/EBA date, although it has to be recognised that some uninvestigated barrows may be earlier or be Middle Bronze Age in date.

In the area bounded by the Og to the east, the Kennet to the south and the Winterbourne to the west the frequency of barrows, although high in comparison with most of the county, varies considerably. Fleming notes that his area 2a, which includes the study area plus the area to the south-west, shows a smaller average density than his Everleigh-Stonehenge area (2.2 per sq km as against 7.4 in Everleigh-Stonehenge) but that local concentrations include at least two which are higher than in the latter (those at the Sanctuary and on Bishop's Cannings Down) (Fleming 1971, 152, fig. 7). Special types of barrow (i.e. other than bowl) are of a similar frequency. The majority of barrows are concentrated around the Avebury area and on the western edges of Fyfield and Overton Downs. Less dense distributions occur along the Kennet, around the fringes of the Marlborough Downs and in the combe of the Rockley Bourne running southeast to northwest across the Downs. Locally very dense concentrations occur on Waden Hill just south of the henge, on Overton Hill close to the Sanctuary, around Monkton Down and close to Rockley Plantation. Just the other side of the rivers there are important concentrations on Windmill Hill, Folly Hill and south of West Kennett. Only some of these will be discussed here, but most can be classified by location and show a finite number of recurrent patterns

Barrows and barrow cemeteries overlooking rivers

This is a common location for barrows and barrow cemeteries and one which has been recently highlighted for Salisbury Plain by McComish *et al* (2002). Where monuments are close to rivers, as is the case with the Avebury complex, it can of course be arguable whether it is the river or a monument close to it which is the focus of the barrows and there are many cases within the study area where it is not possible to distinguish between the two. The fact that there are some, however, which are clearly related only to a river or only to a monument indicates that both were important in the siting of barrows.

The cemetery on Overton Hill (Seven Barrows) is an example where both monuments and river may have played a part in determining the location of the barrows. The earliest burial episode known within the cemetery is that from G6b, which is more than a hundred metres from the main concentration of later barrows, including bell barrows as well as bowl. This barrow site probably dates from fairly early in the second millennium, at a time when later Beakers and early Collared Urns were in use. The early phase of G6b is not a barrow at all but what is almost a ring cairn of sarsen, only after the Collared Urn burials being covered by a low mound. To the south, down the slight slope, and towards both the river and the Sanctuary (which would have been at this time a double stone circle), bowl barrow G1 may be fairly early also, if its group of small flat axe, bronze dagger and crutch headed pin is a to be accepted. Annable and Simpson (1964, corpus 299) cast doubt on the association, but Rohl and Needham (1998) have established from manuscript sources that it is likely to be authentic. Needham (2000, 179) suggests that it is likely to be no later than Period 3 (M/EBA here) on the grounds of the form of the axe and the occasional deposition of flat axes in Bush Barrow phase burials. This barrow, and the other extant mounds, form a most striking group when viewed from the river and the slope above it, particularly from the southeast.

To the east, two small cemeteries about which little is known overlook the river at North Farm East and West (Fowler 2000 cemeteries J and K fig 2.4). Only one barrow, G19, in the eastern group, has been excavated and has not yet been published. Here a long history of use was revealed, with inhumations of apparently late Neolithic and very Early Bronze Age date, the latter under a low mound, replaced by a much larger mound over the burial of an adolescent female with beads of jet and amber (Swanton 1988, 181). Further east still there is a scatter of barrows along the north side of the river, particular around Clatford Bottom. Before the next combe, however, and only about 10m above the river and only 300m from it, is the famous Manton Barrow with its apparently elderly female burial with a rich array of Wessex Culture I grave goods. Here, however, it cannot be certain that the river was the focus, as the barrow overlooks what is one possible site for the Broadstones stone circle. The evidence for the circle and its location was summarised by Meyrick (1955), who concludes that it lay below the Manton barrow on the grounds partly of Stukeley's description that it was overlooked by two barrows and partly on a field name. Meyrick was conjecturing more barrows in the area, but the greater concentration of barrows at the entrance to the north side of Clatford Bottom might instead be taken as an indication that the stone circle was further west than Meyrick suggests. Meyrick argues for the river being important in the siting of the Manton barrow by pointing out that the 'Golden Barrow' at Upton Lovell, the other well-known rich female burial from Wessex, also lies very close to a river (*ibid*). Downstream it is not possible to ignore the siting of the Marlborough Mound, which has been regarded as possibly or probably prehistoric at least since the 18th century (Pafford 1965), and is very close to the river.

Barrows overlooking monuments

This is by far the most common location for cemeteries, with Avebury henge, the West Kennet Avenue, the Beckhampton Avenue, Silbury Hill and the West Kennet palisaded enclosures all seeming to have formed a foci for cemeteries in the early centuries of the second millennium BC and perhaps later. The Avebury area is not, as Fleming points out, distinguished by large nucleated cemeteries, which are absent, but small ones are common (1971, 152). Fleming's map of types of barrow cemetery in the Avebury area (*op cit* fig. 3) gives only a general idea of barrow distribution, subsuming the majority of the area under his 'area cemetery' type in which barrows occur in ones and twos at varying intervals (*op cit* 142). Viewed at the local scale, the immediate area around the monument complex is a mixture of very dispersed distributions of barrows, such as along the edges of the downs at Avebury Down, with very concentrated linear or nucleated cemeteries in prominent positions, such as on Avebury Down North, Avebury Down Barn, Overton Hill West, Folly Hill, Waden Hill and part of Windmill Hill. Of these, all but Overton Hill West appear to be focused on the henge, with that cemetery instead focused on the West Kennet Avenue. Elsewhere are cemeteries, which may be focused on still other monuments, such as the disc barrows south of Beckhampton Penning, which may be related to Silbury Hill, and barrows south of West Kennet, which overlook the palisaded enclosures site. There also seems to be a clear pattern of prominent disc barrows which may relate to monuments: in addition to those south of Beckhampton Penning, there was at least one large disc barrow overlooking the henge in the cemetery at the northern end of Waden Hill, illustrated by Stukeley (1743, Pl. 23), one at the southern end which would have overlooked the palisaded enclosures and Silbury Hill (well illustrated during its 'rediscovery' in Powell *et al* 1996, fig. 5, feature 71, and Plate 2), and another, very prominent one also illustrated by Stukeley on what was then called 'Hackpen Hill' overlooking the dry valley in which the West Kennet Avenue and Falkner's Circle lie (1743, Pl. 22). As disc barrows, including two within the study area, have produced L/EBA material and Grinsell suggests that disc barrows may often be late within the Wessex Culture (1974, 90) this would suggest that even late in the Bronze Age the builders of round barrows remained more then ever anxious to place mounds in a clear visible relationship to monuments. This might also explain the siting of Avebury G31 (bowl) or G32 (bell) which are highly visible from the henge bank or immediately outside it and one of which produced a faience bead and therefore is possibly contemporary with the disc barrows, and also the position of the isolated barrow G55 overlooking Silbury Hill (illustrated in Stukeley 1743 pl. 22 and 23), which Smith considered as possibly belonging to the Wessex I/II transition (Smith 1965b). Another potentially late and prominent barrow is Avebury G20, the large bowl barrow lying just to the east of Avebury. This is not recorded as ever having been investigated, although that seems unlikely given its prominence and proximity to the henge. Its situation, close to and east of the henge, on slightly elevated ground and isolated from other barrows, is strikingly similar to that of Amesbury G11, close to Stonehenge, a bell barrow which covered a primary cremation with bone tweezers and a large urn (which does not survive), and might on the grounds of the tweezers potentially be Wessex II.

Barrows associated with winterbournes

As discussed above, there are clearly some barrows and barrow cemeteries which were sited to be close to or overlooking rivers, over and above those which may be also close to or overlooking monuments. There is, however, an additional category, of which there are at least two examples in the study area, where barrows may have been sited not in relation to permanent watercourses but instead to sites where water-courses either sprang or flowed intermittently. The most compelling of these is the Rockley Plantation dispersed linear cemetery, close to Rockley in the heart of the Marlborough Downs (and with outliers up the 'dry' valley). The main concentration of barrows lies at around 155m; all but one are bowls, the exception (Ogbourne St Andrew G9) being a bell. They largely escaped the attentions of Colt Hoare and Cunnington, and of Dean Merewether, but four were excavated in the late nineteenth century (see Gazetteer).

Owen Meyrick drew attention to the fact that an exceptional rising of springs in December 1960 illustrated that the barrows of Rockley Plantation lay clustered around what had become the stream bed (Meyrick 1964). This stream is the Rockley Bourne or Hungerbourne and has historically been noted as a 'seven year bourne', only appearing at long intervals after very wet periods. Its point of appearance has been noted as widely apart as the junction of Rockley Bottom with the Og valley, on the one hand, and a point close to a penning earthwork in Dean Bottom (Osborne White, 1925, 100; not the MBA enclosure) on the other. In January 2003 water was rising for a short period alongside the Plantation barrows, at around NGR SU 165727.

Some points of emergence have also been known as bourne holes, and these may occur in several places along a dry valley, as the ground water in different years rises to different levels. An association between barrows and such bourne holes was noted as early as 1905 by Jukes Brown who notes the Everleigh Barrows as having a similar relation. In the note quoted above Meyrick also recorded that in the same winter he had observed that the Lambourn stream rose within the Seven Barrows cemetery 'where they [the barrows] are most closely gathered at a sharp bend in the road .... this is about 2 miles above its normal rising point, and from the contours of the land it does not appear ever to have flowed from a still higher spring' (*ibid*). Richards (1978, fig. 20) illustrates the layout of the barrow cemetery at Lambourn, noting that it lies close to the 152m (500ft) contour. In recent work on the Salisbury Plain Training Area valley slopes or valley floors close to present or former watercourses have been noted as common positions for barrows (McOmish *et al* 2002, 46–48). The most pertinent question may be whether the watercourses were running more frequently in the Early Bronze Age and that the association was simply with water, or whether there was a particular association between barrows and places where water appeared and disappeared at irregular intervals. McOmish *et al* (2002, 9–10) discuss this in some detail, but the situation remains unclear for the early second millennium BC. It is tempting to consider that places where water came and went might have appeared mysterious, liminal, a reminder of the forces inhabiting the landscape and only intermittently apparent. As a reminder that our own society even in relatively recent times viewed the landscape as rich in signs and symbols is this extract from a publication of 1947 about the Thames Valley: 'After exceptionally wet seasons the water level rises in the Chalk and springs may outflow some distance above their usual positions and in what is normally a dry valley. These intermittent springs are called *bournes* and are known by many other names, including *woe waters* because of a superstition that their flow foretells disaster' (Sherlock 1947, 66).

A small group, of bowl barrows with one possible bell, about all of which nothing is known, overlooks the lower end of the course of the Rockley bourne as it joins the valley of the Og just north of Marlborough, and, according to Osborne White (*op cit*) overlooking its lowest point of emergence. Just outside the study area is potentially another example of this in the Beckhampton Road 'dry valley'. During the wet winters of the 1990s and early 21st century the northern part of the valley had rising ground water extending from south-west of the junction of the Roman road with the present road (approximately SU 072681) to Beckhampton House, that is, emerging at about 160m (524 ft) OD. Lining this stretch of valley are concentrations of round barrows, including linear settings, particularly at Fox Covert and the northern end of Hemp Knoll overlooking the wet area. If this were the only example of such a concentration around a site of seasonal rising ground water it would not be worth comment, but it is clearly part of a wider pattern and one noted from the very heart of the Marlborough Downs as well as from Salisbury Plain.

Burial rites

Of the seven potentially early (pre-2000 BC) inhumations (one barrow and six flat graves: i.e. Winterbourne Monkton G9, The Sanctuary, Lockeridge, the Longstones, Beckhampton near the Grange and West Kennet Avenue adjacent to stones 25B and 29A) there are full details for only three. Two of these (Beckhampton Grange and W. K.A. 25B) have their heads to the north turned to face east and are therefore on their left sides, but the Sanctuary adolescent is on his or her right side, head to south facing east, while the head of the skeleton at the Longstones was to the east. It is therefore not so much in burial rite as in the frequency of flat graves that the area seems to be coherent and distinctive, as it is not a feature shared by, for instance, the Stonehenge area.

This willingness to bury in flat graves seems to have continued into the second millennium BC, as the list in the Gazetteer demonstrates, including bones representing approximately 18 individuals which cannot be shown to be definitely early, and some of these certainly belong to the M/EBA (such as the skull fragments from stone hole 41 in the henge). Proximity to the standing stones of the monuments may still have been sought, although none of the burials associated with them are certainly later than the turn of the third millennium BC (the position of the putative grave for the stonehole 41 burial being unknown). Association between later Beakers and other sarsen stones is demonstrated at Beckhampton (south) and Winterbourne Monkton (flat graves), and it is arguable that the sarsen-associated primary burial at West Overton G6b should be regarded as belonging more to the tradition of flat graves than barrow burial; it may be that to have sarsens in or around the grave was now as appropriate as to have it associated with a standing stone.

In the same centuries in which flat graves with later Beakers were being dug, and the only certainly Beaker barrow of that date (West Overton G6b) was being constructed, we must assume that the earlier non-Beaker associated burials under barrows were taking place and that cremation was also becoming common. West Overton G6b is particularly important here as the structure of the mound and sequence of burials led the excavators to conclude that little more than a few years or a generation at most may have separated the Beaker burial from those with Collared Urns and that all the burials may have happened within that time (Smith and Simpson 1966, 133). There is a sign that cremation was even used within the henge, where an urn full of bones was reported as having been found near the Obelisk in the 19th century (Smith 1965a, 204) but whether earlier or later (i.e. M/EBA or L/EBA) cannot be established.

Because of the restricted nature of most early excavations, in which excavators usually aimed for the centre of barrow mounds, it is not worth while to attempt an estimate of numbers of secondary cremations, and the same excavation technique may also account for the scarcity of Middle Bronze Age cremation burials within the area (West Overton G6b and G19 illustrate what may be recovered under large-scale modern excavation). It should be noted however, that secondary cremation burials are common and generally associated with Collared Urns, and more rarely with Biconical urns and that even on the limited evidence available there are at least 15, excluding those from West Overton G6b and G19.

In terms of primary cremations and inhumations the figures may be a little more meaningful, although it is difficult to be certain from the older accounts whether the excavators certainly encountered primary deposits or misidentified secondary or satellite burials. There would appear to be in the region of ten non-Beaker associated inhumations covered by mounds likely to belong to the early centuries of the second millennium BC. These are widely spread, occurring in the Overton Seven Barrows (G1 and in area: Avebury 23d), Overton Hill West (G25), Avebury Down (G35), Windmill Hill (G46) and Rockley Plantation (G6) cemeteries and Rockley Down (G20), West Overton G19, Preshute 1a (the Manton Barrow) and probably at Ogbourne St Andrew churchyard (where the grave was empty). Although early bone reports cannot be relied upon too heavily, the five skeletons which are aged and sexed in the published reports comprise two 'elderly' females (Manton barrow and Overton Hill West cemetery G25), one young female (West Overton G19), and one adult male (Rockley Plantation cemetery G6). The adult male inhumation and the 'elderly woman' from Avebury G25 (Overton Hill West) were associated with sarsens, the graves at both Rockley and Avebury G25 being partially lined with sarsens, and covered by them. It is worth comment that it is possible that both of these and West Overton G6b could be contemporary, with a pattern of inhumation associated with sarsen followed quite soon afterwards with cremations. In particular both the Rockley barrow and West Overton G6b have Primary Series Collared urns deposited very soon after the primary inhumation, which at the former has no ceramic associations.

Secondary inhumation also appears as a burial type in this period, as do satellite inhumations, probably in the earlier centuries of the second millennium BC. In two cases these are certainly or probably partial child skeletons in pots, one with a later Beaker (Winterbourne Monkton G9) and one in a plain Collared Urn (Windmill Hill G46). One other child inhumation is present, at Avebury G25 (Overton Hill West) probably as a secondary inhumation and an 'elderly' female secondary inhumation was present in the same mound. A satellite infant burial was found close to the primary inhumation at West Overton G19, but an indication that infants might be disposed of less formally during the M/EBA is given by Avebury G55, where the disarticulated partial skeleton of an approximately 6 month old baby was found in a pit which also held material, including Beaker pottery, which did not appear to have been deposited in a formalised way.

There are two cases of possible multiple inhumations within the study area, both reported by Merewether and both associated with grape cups. One is reported as south east of Kennet, and therefore likely to be in the Overton Hill area; the other is on Windmill Hill (see Gazetteer for descriptions). In both cases Merewether was reporting secondhand, although he appears to have drawn the cups, and a battle-axe supposedly associated with the Windmill Hill burials. The cases are so similar, and the cups are almost identical, which suggests either that these are two real cases, the similarity between the vessels perhaps strengthening the likelihood that the same rite occurred twice, or there has been some confusion in the account and there was really only one case (with perhaps Merewether redrawing an earlier drawing and putting it together with his own of the same vessel thinking it was a different one). At Overton Hill there is the possibility that there is an extensive Anglo-Saxon cemetery (graves cut into barrow G6b, Eagles 1986) and a single, apparently extended inhumation from somewhere near the top of Picket Barrow (unpublished material in the Alexander Keiller Museum) indicates that later burials cannot be ruled out on Windmill Hill either. The burials in Monkton Field also seem to have included multiple burials but the dating of these is uncertain; this area clearly demands investigation. In the absence of multiple inhumation emerging as a recognised Early Bronze Age rite from other cases the associations with grape cups must be treated with caution.

Material culture

In comparison to the area around Stonehenge, the Avebury and Marlborough Downs appear relatively poor in grave goods. The 'richest' early grave group lies more than 10km to the south west (Roundway G8) (Annable and Simpson 1964, corpus nos 59–63), and later, in the period of Wessex Culture burials, although the Manton barrow group is striking and one of the most complex in the country it stands in sharp contrast to the rest of the Wessex Culture graves from the study area which generally have only one or two items.

In terms of connections, however, the Beaker graves, in particular, although they are not among the most spectacular of Beaker period graves groups, do suggest some intriguing links outside the study area. As discussed above, the Winterbourne Monkton G9 burial with its two cattle skulls shows a strong local link with Hemp Knoll, and may belong to a much more widespread tradition of male graves with fine, probably early, Beakers and other grave goods, such as the famous new discovery near Amesbury (the 'Amesbury archer') which is not in the immediate environs of Stonehenge, and others further afield, also not associated with monuments (e.g. Winterslow Hut or Mere G6a, Clarke 1970).

The later Beaker group from West Overton G6b belongs to a tradition of rich burials furnished with what may be leather-working equipment. Case identifies three overlapping groups associated with bone/stone spatulae, fire-making equipment, shale or jet buttons and belt rings (Case 1977, 83). West Overton G6b has both spatulae and fire-making equipment, and moreover shows a striking similarity both in the spatulae and the Beaker to a group from Winterbourne Stoke G54 (Clarke 1970, fig 900). The flat grave from Winterbourne Monkton, with its conical buttons, belt ring, flint flake and igneous stone 'hammer' also belongs to this general tradition. It is possible that the exotic hammerstone is related to metalworking.

The ceramic associations other than Beakers are very limited, and rather than exotic contacts there is some hint of local connections. The Collared Urns are almost all certainly or probably Primary Series, although three examples known only from 'near Avebury' are Secondary Series (Longworth 1984, corpus nos 1655–1657) and include two which are very similar in decoration. The Collared Urns from Rockley Plantation also include two with very similar form: (*op cit* Form I, Primary Series, corpus nos 1693–1694) from Ogbourne St Andrew G6, while the two Aldbourne cups from south of Beckhampton (Thurnam 1871, figs 44 and 46) are almost identical.

Conclusion

To revert to the quotation at the beginning of the paper: no-one would argue that the Early Bronze Age had 'kings' but there is no doubt that the men and women buried in the graves and mounds around Avebury and on the Downs were intimately involved in the creation of the landscape we see now and of the impressive funerary monuments within it. As we gain an increasing understanding of the chronology of the Neolithic monumental complex and on what appears to be its enduring influence on the landscape and the way society used it, it becomes clearer that the Early Bronze Age was not separated by radical change from the world of the henge and other monuments of the later Neolithic. With the monuments still influencing the location of barrows well into the second millennium, with perhaps some alteration to the monuments still taking place, and an enduring connection between sarsens and burial, probably sparked by the standing stones but extending beyond that, it would seem that we need to re-evaluate the changes of the Early Bronze Age and perhaps look elsewhere, perhaps to the end of the EBA, for more striking social change. While the introduction of metalworking and the development of a largely individual burial rite cannot be ignored as major changes in themselves it seems clear that they must be have been taking place within a society which, somehow, was still accommodating the monuments into its world-view. Even at the very end of the Early Bronze Age, it may have still been among the 'ambitions' of those members of society who could expect a barrow burial to locate it within sight of one of the ancient monuments.

Acknowledgements

I would like to thank Dave Field for inviting my contribution in the first place and for his subsequent endless patience, all the more impressive as his own knowledge on the subject is wide-ranging and he must often, during the long wait for it, have thought it would be easier to write the paper himself. In particular he drew my attention to references regarding the Monkton Field burials. To Martyn Barber I am also grateful, for coming to my aid with information at short notice. It would also be quite wrong not to acknowledge with gratitude the work of the anonymous compilers of the National Monument Record, who make papers of this sort possible, and to pay a tribute to the late Leslie Grinsell whose work was truly astonishing in its scale and lasting in its value.

Appendix

GAZETTEER OF BURIALS

Entries comprise recorded burials within the study area whether recorded as cremations, inhumations, or as grave goods only. Non-funerary material found in mounds is included, as are Bronze Age or earlier superficial finds except that barrows with superficial, apparently non-funerary finds *only* are omitted. The barrows are arranged under the cemetery names used in the text; not all are historic names as some groups not named by Grinsell have been given names here to ease reference. Numbers used are as listed by Grinsell (1957). These have been used as the primary reference in preference to National Monument Record numbers as they are easier to use in figures and text. Virtually all extant barrows have them, as do most of those excavated (as Grinsell added in many barrows known only from aerial photographs), but NMR numbers are given also. Entries of course draw heavily on the NMR and on the Grinsell gazetteer, but the primary sources have been consulted in most cases; quotations are directly from those sources. The term 'cist' has been retained because it is such a common term in older accounts; if no other detail is given it may be assumed to be simply the hole in the ground dug for the burial. References are given to occasional notes in *Wiltshire Archaeological & Natural History Magazine* (referred to as *WAM* here) by reference to the journal only, but to major articles by author. All National Grid References are SU.

Barrows

West of the Grange

Avebury G19 Bowl
NGR: SU 08096919
NMR: SU 06 NE 55
?Primary cremation.
Goddard 1913, 176. 'A small and slightly elevated barrow', 'at about the level of the down, was a shallow cist, containing black earth and a very few bones' Merewether 1849, 99; Grinsell 1957, 153.

Folly Hill

Avebury G19b Probable Bowl
NGR: 09156907
NMR: SU 06 NE 76 (B)
Damaged mound; no record of excavation. Flat rivetted copper alloy dagger found following recent damage (Soffe 1993, 145, Barrow 1).

Overton Hill area

Avebury G23c Unloc.
Reported (but apparently not excavated) by Merewether 1849, 108, fig. 2, 'small urn, found in a barrow to the south-east of Kennet, round which were twelve skeletons ranged with their feet towards the centre in which the urn was placed'. The 'urn' is a grape cup. Grinsell 1957, 153.

Avebury G23d Unloc.
Probably primary inhumation under cairn. ?Bowl Associated with long and round amber beads and probably faience beads. Stukeley 1743, 44; Grinsell 1957, 153. But could, from a reading of Stukeley, be West Overton G1a.

Overton Hill/Seven Barrows

West Overton G1 Bowl
NGR: 11906797
NMR: Reported by Colt Hoare as containing a primary crouched inhumation in a tree-trunk coffin, head to the east [not clear whether that means facing, or the head was at the east, but Thurnam may have seen the skeleton on re-opening and says the feet were to the west] 'near the head, to which the right hand was elevated, were deposited a small lance [dagger], a long pin with a handle [apparently a crutch headed pin] and a little celt [axe] all of brass' (1812, ii, 90) . Pin illus., possibly, Thurnam 1871, fig. 168; 1860, 329, illus, apparently incorrect objects); Grinsell 1957, 195). Rohl and Needham (1998) examine this association with the aid of manuscript material and conclude that it is a genuine association between a crutch headed pin, a small flat axe and a dagger.

West Overton G1a
NGR: 11906803
NMR: Possible site of a ploughed out barrow, recorded by Stukeley in a figure as well as in describing the source of two faience beads: 'I bought a couple of British beads, one large of a light blue and rib'd, the other less, of a dark blue, taken up in one of the two barrows on Hakpen-hill, east of Kennet avenue. These two barrows are ditch'd about, and near one another. The single barrow next to it toward the snake's head temple [the Sanctuary] is large and beautifully turned, with a ditch about it, at a distance, which throws it into a campanule form'. Grinsell does not suggest that the beads came from this barrow, recording it only as the site of a ploughed out barrow, but it seems possible that they did. (Grinsell 1957, 195), Stukeley 1743, 44 and Tab. 29, where it appears to be shown just south of the Marlborough Road (i.e between what must be G1 to the south and G2 to the north of the road). The identification of this barrow also discussed in relation to the beads by Cunnington (1930, 318–319).

West Overton G2 Bell
NGR: 11936808

NMR: SU 16 NW 155
Colt Hoare number 2, in which Edmund Crocker found 'burned bones, deposited eight inches under the surface of the natural level, and with it a very rude little cup, scratched over with the usual British pattern' (1812, ii, 90). An incense cup with twisted cord impressions probably is equated with this and illustrated in Annable and Simpson (1964, no. 446).

West Overton G3 Bell
NGR: 11956812
NMR: Primary cremation reported by Colt Hoare (1812, ii, 90): 'at the depth of twelve feet eight inches, a simple interment of burn bones deposited within a cist'.

West Overton G3a Bowl (between two bell barrows, G3 and G4)
NGR: 11966814
NMR: Barrow appears to overlie the two bell barrows. Excavated by Thurnam who reported: 'a deposit of burnt bones in a shallow cist, and a rude bone pin nearly five inches in length, which had likewise passed through the fire. The bones were of a small size, probably those of a female'. (1860b, 330).

West Overton G4 Bell
NGR: 11966816
NMR: Colt Hoare barrow 4, in which was a primary cremation: 'at the depth of ten feet, the primary deposit, consisting of a pile of burned bones, had been heaped up on the natural surface. Among them was a small lancehead of brass, similar both in size and pattern to the one before described in no. 1 and a bit of ivory, which probably once belonged to the spear'. A secondary cremation was 'at the depth of two feet under its summit, a large rude urn with its mouth placed upwards, filled with burned bones, and secured on its top and sides by sarsen stones' (1812, ii, 90). Neither the dagger nor the pot appear to survive.

West Overton G5 Bowl
NGR: 12046820
NMR: Grinsell equates with Colt Hoare no. 5, with a primary cremation (1812, ii, 91).

West Overton G6b Bowl
NGR:
NMR: Excavated and fully reported by Smith and Simpson (1966). Inhumation of adult male at least 40 years old, crouched and on left side, head to north [ie facing east]. He had probably been covered by a cloak or hide. The grave was partially sarsen-lined and he had a group of grave goods including a later Beaker and a 'kit' of antler and stone spatulae, a bronze awl, and a flint knife, flake and strike-a-light and a ball of marcasite. Five other inhumations and six cremation burials were made, two of which were accompanied by Primary Series Collared Urns. The inhumations were all children as were three of the cremation burials.

West Overton G7 Bowl (but Grinsell considers may not be a barrow).
NGR: 11936837
NMR: Grinsell notes as probably excavated by Thurnam who found ashes and burnt bones and bits of decayed bronze ; Thurnam 1860b, 330–1; Grinsell 1957, 195.

West Overton G8 Bowl
NGR: 11926849
NMR: Grinsell equates with Colt Hoare no. 6, with a primary cremation and two secondary cremations much higher up, one of which was beneath a coarse inverted urn (1812, ii, 91).

Overton Hill West

Avebury G24 Bowl
NGR: 11556853
NMR: Excavated by Thurnam and by William and Henry Cunnington 1882, but no primary burial found. Secondary cremation with scraper and serrated knife, and another secondary cremation.
WAM 20, 345–7; Grinsell 1957, 154.

Avebury G25 Bowl
NGR: 11526858
NMR: Excavated by Thurnam 1857 and Ponting 1882
Primary crouched inhumation of elderly female in grave partly lined and roofed with sarsens and covered by sarsen cairn 24ft in diameter. 6ft outside base was double retaining circle of sarsens; skeleton on her back, with head to north but lower body twisted onto left side, knees drawn up , left hand against head and right against abdomen.
Secondary crouched inhumation of elderly female, covered with sarsens, head to the west.
?Secondary skeleton of child of 2–3 years.
Also three or fours urns full of burnt bones
Perforated head of bone pin.
A small vessels 3¼ inch diameter in upper part of central cairn. Recent horse burial. Thurnam 1860b, 331; 20, 342–5; 50, 83–88; Grinsell 1957, 154.

Avebury G29 Bowl
NGR: 11676880
NMR: Probably primary cremation and incense up in oblong cist. Colt Hoare 1812, 91, pl. x.

Avebury Down

Avebury G31 or G32 Bowl (32) or Bell (31)
NGR: 11877004 (32) or 11877009 (31)
NMR: Reported by Stukeley (1743, 44) as having produced faience beads. Wessex Grave 43 (Piggott 1938); Grinsell 1957, 154.

Avebury G35 Bowl
NGR: 11347050
NMR: Grinsell equates with Merewether 1(1849, 82–83, fig. A): possibly primary crouched skeleton; above it a coarse urn with burnt bones of a child.

Avebury G35a Bowl
NGR: 11687070
NMR: Grinsell equates with Merewether 10 (1849, 86,

fig. K), which contained two cists with burnt bones, possibly primary; however, Roman finds are reported in the material of the mound indicating that the mound may not have been prehistoric (unless very disturbed).

Avebury Down Barn

Avebury G36 Bell
NGR: 11057093
NMR: Grinsell (1957, 208) equates with Merewether 2 (1849, 83), in which only wood ashes and animal bones were found.

Avebury G37 Bell
NGR: 11257098
NMR: Grinsell (1957, 208) equates with Merewether 3 (1849, 83, figs, B,C, and D.) This contained a possibly primary cremation in a small cist in the chalk and with it two small pieces of bronze. In material a barbed and tanged arrowhead.

Avebury G38 Bell
NGR: 11297101
NMR: Grinsell (1957, 208) equates with Merewether 4 (1849, 83, figs. F and G). this contained a possible primary cremation in a Collared Urn. 2½ft from the top of the mound a rim fragment from another Collared Urn was also found.

Avebury G40 Bowl
NGR: 11417099
NMR: Grinsell equates with Merewether 5 (1849, 84): possibly primary cremation covered in a substance like powdered charcoal.

Avebury G64a Bowl
NGR: 11237127
NMR: SU 17 SW 12
Grinsell equates with Merewether 30 (1849, 106, fig. g,g), as Merewether describes it as a 'short distance on the north of the five barrows on the Avebury Down' (which are probably what is here termed Avebury Down Barn). Merewether noted that it had had a circle of stones around it, with a diameter of about 9ft, but some had been removed. Only 'rude pottery', animal bones, charcoal and teeth of 'deer, oxen and swine' were found, and he concluded that it had probably been dug into earlier. (1849, 106).

Avebury Down North

NMR record for cemetery (includes details of individual barrows 41, 42, 42a and 43): SU 17 SW 53

Avebury G42 Bowl
NGR: 12317112
NMR: as above, 'B'
Grinsell equates with Merewether 8 (1849, 85). Primary cremation overlaid with four layers of sarsens.
Grinsell notes bones and pottery in material of mound; Bronze Age sherds were found by Owen Meyrick on surface but these are now missing (Swanton 1987, 14, site 131).

Avebury G42a Pond – but may not be a burial site
NMR: as above, 'D'
Grinsell equates with Merewether 7, in which Merewether found animal bones, charcoal and pottery; he was convinced that there had been no burial (1849, 85).

Avebury G43 Bowl
NGR: 1297109
NMR: as above, 'C'
Grinsell equates with Merewether 9 (1849, 86, fig. J): ?primary cremation in cist covered by a large sarsen; a secondary cremation higher. In material was an urn with an applied horsehoe handle [Biconical Urn] and Owen Meyrick found Bronze Age sherds including Food Vessel superficially. (Swanton 1987, 13, site 119).

Avebury G44d Bowl
NGR: 12487134
NMR: SU 17 SW 62
Almost certainly Merewether 6 (as adjacent to a surviving linear earthwork described by Merewether) (1849, 84–85). Merewether found an 'oval cist formed in the chalk, about 2 feet by 1½, and 2 feet deep, containing, with burnt human bones, a great quantity of black sooty dust, with which the cist was quite filled up; numerous fragments of bones, teeth of deer, and pottery, were interspersed in the earth forming the mound.'.

Overton Down North

West Overton G9
NGR: 12607104
NMR: SU 17 SW 55
The NMR records that this was excavated for the Ministry of Works in 1960, revealing a primary cremation in a pottery vessel.

Monkton Down (Lower)

Winterbourne Monkton G9 Bowl
NGR: 11677231
NMR: See text for full description. Merewether barrow 28 (Grinsell notes that Goddard probably equated this with W.M. G10), (1849, 105, figs aa, bb and 10). Primary inhumation under mound with Beaker, barbed and tanged arrowhead and two flint flakes; two cattle skulls above grave fill; partial child inhumation in top of mound in later Beaker. Arrowhead is classified by Green as Green Low type (Green 1980, Corpus No. 252, 353).

Monkton Down G10 Disc or saucer
NGR: 11777235
NMR: Grinsell (1957, 220) equates with Merewether 27, in which were 'in the upper mound within the circle and under the sarsens, ox and deer's bones and teeth, sarsens of considerable size, and boar's tusks' (1849, 104).

Monkton Down

Winterbourne Monkton G16 Bowl
NGR: 11977269
NMR: SU 17 SW 15

Excavated by Passmore (WAM 42, 247). Primary not searched for; secondary cremation beneath inverted urn. Beaker and Bronze Age sherds found by Owen Meyrick superficially (Swanton 1987, site 29, 10).

Winterbourne Monkton G17d
Unlocated. Grinsell equates with Merewether 31 (1957, 201). Collared Urn over burnt bones (1849, 107, fig hh).

Windmill Hill

Avebury G46, G46a and G46b
Merewether describes three barrows on the eastern side of Windmill Hill as being particularly interesting (1849, 94). He does not actually state that they formed a linear group rising from east to west, but he begins 'with the lowest on the hill's side' which suggests that they may have run up the slope. If so, they may be equated with, from east to west, Avebury G46b, G46 and G46a which form a line close to the present field boundary. There are, however, other barrows on the eastern flank of Windmill Hill and it is not impossible that they were investigated by Merewether. The NMR accords these 'tentative' identification.

Avebury G46a
NGR: 09057127
NMR: SU 07 SE 51
May equate with Merewether barrow 15 (1849, 94), although Grinsell considered it unlocated and numbered it his G48d (1957, 155). Reported by Merewether as a bowl barrow about 3ft high and probably disurbed by earlier digging. He found no cist or burial deposit 'but fragments of rude pottery were plentiful'; he also found human skull fragments 'of remarkable thickness', two dog or fox teeth, a boar's tusk, a variety of other teeth and bones and a single well-made barbed and tanged arrowhead [illus] classifiable as Green's Green Low type (1980).

Avebury G46 Bowl
NGR: 09147126
NMR: SU 07 SE 50
May equate with Merewether 14 (accepted by both Grinsell (1957, 222), who classifies it as a saucer barrow, and the NMR). As Grinsell notes, Merewether's account (1849, 94) is difficult to interpret: 'This barrow was about eleven paces from the rise at the bottom of the trench, which is much deeper than usual and the mound surrounding the whole is also considerably raised; from out to out of the rise, 30 paces. At 14 inches were the fragments of a small plain urn [illus] containing the *unburnt* [Merewether's emphasis] bones of a child. At something under three feet was the skeleton of an adult in the crouched position [illus] without any urn.' He also notes that the bones of the left wrist and hand were missing, although the burial did not seem to have been disturbed.

Avebury G46b Bowl
NGR: 09287122
NMR: SU 07 SE 15
Grinsell equates with Merewether 13, the furthest down the hillside (1849, 94, fig. O), as does the NMR. 'of a trifling elevation, compared with the depth at which the cist was found – 3feet. Many fragments of early pottery, teeth of red deer and ox, and a bead [illus] of jet or Kimmeridge coal, and nine very smooth gravel pebbles, probably for slinging. The cist, filled with burnt human bones, but without an urn, was 3ft 6in long by 2ft wide and 2ft deep.' (1849, 94) material. Grinsell 1957, 154.

Avebury G48c (could be Winterbourne Monkton)
Unlocated.
Skeleton, flints and sherds found in a grave, probably on the site of a destroyed barrow. WAM 26, 410–11. Grinsell 1957, 155.

Avebury G48e
Unloc.
Grinsell's number for barrow reported by Stukeley (1743, 45, pl. 36) and apparently having contained a Collared Urn inverted over a cremation. Grinsell 1957, 155. The Stukeley illustration shows a tripartite Collared Urn with a well-defined shoulder, plain except for crosshatching around the collar.

Avebury G49
Unlocated.
Grinsell's number for a barrow reported by Stukeley as having contained a 'brass spearhead' by a body, in a barrow between Avebury and Monkton, (1743, 45). Grinsell 1957, 155.

Winterbourne Monkton G1 (bowl) or G2 (bell)
NGR: 086717140 (G1, see below for G2)
NMR: SU 07 SE 21 (A)
Merewether lists and illustrates a grape cup and perforated axe-hammer (Group XII, picrite from Shropshire/Montgomeryshire border) as from a barrow on Windmill Hill. Merewether did not excavate the barrow, only noting that he was told that 'in it were found seven skeletons and a very beautiful little grape urn, according to Sir Richard Colt Hoare's nomenclature, which I have seen and of which I hope to supply a sketch. The skeletons were deposited [he could mean redeposited after excavation] in another barrow, but which I could not learn' (Merewether 1849, 93–4, 108, figs 3, 4; Annable and Simpson 1964, 234–5). The association between the two artefacts is not certain, nor is the association of both or either with the seven skeletons.

Winterbourne Monkton G2 Bell
NGR: 08667137
NMR: SU 07 SE 21 (B)
Known as 'Picket Barrow' Keiller excavated a Biconical Urn inverted over a cremation burial from near the top of the barrow, on the east side (Smith 1965a, 169–170, plate 22); the cremation burial bones do not appear to have been reported on.

Winterbourne Monkton 17d
Unlocated
Grinsell equates with Merewether 31 (1849, 107, fig. h, h): Collared Urn over burnt bones (Longworth 1984, Corpus No. 1732, not classified). Illustration shows vessel in 'cist' but was similar to one with lattice on the collar.

South of Silbury
Avebury G55 Bell (Bowl in Grinsell)
NGR: 10246788
NMR: SI 16 NW 60
Fully excavated by Smith (1965a), revealing a bell barrow with an eccentrically placed mound which had been disturbed on three occasions. The primary cremation had been badly disturbed but had probably had a Collared Urn (only one unclassifiable sherd with twisted cord impressions remaining), and accessory vessel with twisted cord decoration, a 'bronze' awl (not analysed), a horn pendant, three fossil beads and a chalk object which may be a bead. The cremation was of an adult, probably in his or her 20s, but with certain evidence of another individual present: a child probably under one year (Brothwell 1992, 142–143). Of two other cremations, one was probably a secondary and one a satellite, the latter having a bone bead and the former being of a child no more than 10–12 years old and an infant of under one year (*op cit* 143–144); there is no report on the bone from the satellite (unless the satellite and the secondary have become conflated after excavation).

Avebury G56
Unlocated
'A bit of gold and sharp bits of iron' reported by Stukeley in a barrow south of Silbury (1743, 45). Grinsell suggest that the gold could have been the covering of a bead (1957, 155). It is possible that this is G55, excavated in the 1960s (Smith 1965b, 29–30).

South of Beckhampton Penning
All Cannings Cross G23 Disc
Avebury G65 – 67 Disc
Four disc barrows, excavated by Thurnam (1871, 295 (note b), 363–4, figs 44 and 46). All had been dug into earlier; Thurnam found nothing in two, in one a primary cremation with an Aldbourne cup and a bronze awl, the other a primary cremation with only an Aldbourne cup. It is not clear which barrow produced which evidence.

North Farm East
West Overton G19 Bowl
NGR: 13866861
NMR: Like the Manton Barrow, a multi-phase monument. Excavated by G. Swanton (1988). First phase appeared to be a middle or late Neolithic burial site, followed by a small mound over a Beaker period burial. Subsequently a primary young female inhumation was interred with jet and amber beads under a much larger mound. An infant was buried as a satellite.

The 'Manton Barrow'
Preshute G1a Bowl
NGR: 16496912
NMR: SU 16 NE 3
Excavated by Maud Cunnington (1908); Wessex Grave 65 (Piggott 1938). Primary crouched female burial said to be elderly and had been wrapped in a cloth. The body lay south-east to north-west, with the head at the south-east, though bent forward on the chest. Grave goods included over 150 amber and shale beads (one of the latter being gold-bound), a gold-bound amber disc, a chalk bead, an incense cup and a grape cup, a halberd pendant with bronze blade set in gold, a clay stud, a possibly steatite bead, a fossil, three bronze awls, and two knife-daggers, one with an amber pommel). Impressions of a woven cloth, said to be linen, were found around the skeleton (Cunnington 1908 fig. 6 illustrates the position of the skeleton and grave goods). A Collared Urn was found 9ft from the female burial, but it is not clear whether it was secondary or a satellite. The barrow had concentric ditches and so may have been multi-phase.

Rockley Down
Ogbourne St Andrew G20
NGR: 15097312
NMR: SU17 SE 35
The NMR record suggests that this may have been excavated by H. Cunnington in 1879 and reported in the *Journal of the British Archaeological Association* 37 (1881) [not checked by this writer]. If so it had a primary inhumation with secondary cremations, one in an urn and one with a Food Vessel.

Rockley Plantation
Ogbourne St Andrew G1 Bowl
NGR: 16387283
NMR: SU 17 SE 39
Grinsell suggests possibly excavated by H. Cunnington 1879, who found 'marks of cremation only'.

Ogbourne St Andrew G2 Bowl
NMR: SU 17 SE 39
NGR: 16407278
Grinsell notes as excavated by Browne 1889, who found a probably primary cremation beneath an inverted Collared Urn and another urn, perhaps bipartite [?Biconical], about a yard away; primary reference *Report of the Marlborough College Natural History Society* 1889, 107 [not checked by this writer].

Ogbourne St Andrew G6 Bowl
NGR: 16517252
NMR: Grinsell equates with a barrow excavated by H. Cunnington in 1879, with a primary crouched male skeleton in a grave covered by a cairn of sarsen. In the cairn were two cremations in upright Collared Urns and one in a small unclassifiable vessel (Annable and Simpson 1964, Nos 528, 554, 556) of sarsen. (*WAM* 19, 67–69; Smith 1885, L, iv, b.). The primary inhumation was in a grave lined and filled with sarsens

beneath a cairn, 20 ft in diameter, of large sarsens; it was of an older man, lying on his right side, crouched with his head to the south [ie facing east]. All three pots appeared to be integral to the cairn and therefore satellite burials, both were upright and had cremation burials, one of which was a young adult. The small pot appeared to be broken before burial and no cremation is mentioned as from it. Both Collared Urns are Primary Series (Longworth 1984, corpus nos. 1693 and 1694, Pls 58a and 36e).

Ogbourne St Andrew G7 Bowl
NGR: 16317299
NMR: SU 17 SE 37
Excavated by A.C Smith and H. Cunnington 1879, revealing a probably primary cremation beneath an inverted Collared Urn with a flint knife. Secondary burials included a cremation and a skeleton (orientation and position not recorded) with a leaf arrowhead nearby. *WAM* 19, 70–71; certainly Smith (1885) barrow at M.3 a (as Smith's map is cited in report). Collared Urn is Primary Series (Longworth 1984, corpus no. 1695, Pl. 43c).

Ogbourne Sst Andrew G8a Saucer
NGR: 16357305
NMR: SU 17 SE 91
Excavated by Smith and Cunnington 1879 (*WAM* 19, 70–71), who found a primary cremation in a circular cist. Fragments of what were probably Beaker sherds were found in the mound.

Ogbourne St Andrew Churchyard

Ogbourne St Andrew G11 Bowl
NGR: 18877233
NMR: SU 17 SE 31
Probably primary grave 6–7ft long lined with wood but with no interment found. A secondary cremation without ashes wrapped in cloth (PPS 16, 158), flint knife, and parts of a pot. Later burials, Roman or Anglo-Saxon and medieval. Leaf arrowhead found superficially.

Burderop Down/Gypsy Lane

Chiseldon G1 Disc
NGR: 16737642
NMR: SU 17 NE 3
Excavated by Passmore who found a possibly primary cremation which had been disturbed and an urn, and holes filled with wood ash nearby. WAM 44, 242. Ditch and bank section excavated by Gingell (1992).

Ogbourne St George G1 Bowl
NGR: 17597630
NMR: Possibly primary cremation, with leg of pig above. *WAM* 44, 241.

Secondary in a long barrow

Longstones long barrow (Avebury G17)
NGR: 08706914
NMR: SU 06 NE 75
Reported, though not apparently found, by Merewether (1849, no. 11; Annable and Simpson 1964, corpus no. 546), containing bones and a fragment probably of a bronze dagger or knife-dagger (1849, fig. 23). The pot is part of a Biconical Urn with Trevisker-like handles.

Flat graves

Avebury henge, Stone hole 41
Three fragments of skull and two plain, basal, sherds of Beaker in Stone hole 41 of the Outer Circle (Smith 1965a, 204); presumably from a disturbed grave.

Avebury henge, near stone 102 (Southern Circle)
Fragments of ribs and skull in the upper fill of a probably medieval boundary ditch (Smith 1965a, 204); presumably from a disturbed grave.

Avebury henge, near Obelisk
'Urn full of bones found towards the centre of the Southern Inner Circle in the 1880s (Smith 1965a, 204)

Avebury henge ditch
Inhumation of an adult female in the secondary ditch fill, 5.8ft down, of the eastern terminal of the henge ditch at the southern entrance. She is reported as a 'dwarf' and just under 4ft 4ins tall, but Brothwell notes that she could have been as much as 5ft tall (Ucko *et al* 1991, 254, note 2). The burial lay within a rough oval arrangment of 23 sarsen stones, lying north-north-west by south-south-east; the head lay to the south but the skeleton was disturbed by the workmen before the excavator saw it (Gray 1935, 145–146, Pl. 43). A chalk ball, a flint core and flakes, a sheep metacarpus and 19 pottery sherds of more than one vessel were found nearby (*op cit.* 147).

Avebury G55
NGR: 10246788
NMR: SU 16 NW 60
Within the ditch of a bell barrow, on the berm between mound and ditch but probably preceding it, lay a rectangular grave 3ft 4 ins by 2ft 3ins orientated south-south-east to north-north-west. The inhumation was tightly contracted, with the knees drawn up to be close to the forehead. The head was at the southern end and the body on his left side (so facing west, although the report does not say so; the photograph confirms the left side). The right arm was bent across the body, under the right thigh and the left forearm; the left forearm was bent upwards to touch the left shoulder. As there was Beaker material from pits nearby the excavator concluded that this burial is likely to have been contemporary with the Beaker associated use of the site (Smith 1965b, 36). The skeleton was probably male and over 40 years old (Brothwell 1992, 142). One of the pits, 3/3A, which contained later Beaker sherds, also contained parts of the skeleton of an infant, which seemed to represent a dismembered or partly decomposed body. Brothwell ages the skull only, which is all he was able to examine, to about 6 months, and noted the occurrence of evidence which suggest dietary problems during the infant's development. (*ibid.*)

Beckhampton
NGR: 08626877
NMR: SU 06 NE 61
Fragments of skeleton found during a trench to lay water pipes and reported by Mrs Cunnington. The Beaker was in a grave, beside a sarsen stone (Cunnington 1926b, 399–400). The Beaker is of Clarke's type S4 (1970, fig. 982)

Beckhampton, near The Grange
NGR: 08126917
NMR: SU 06 NE 127
Burial of a child of about 5 years old, of unknown sex, in a circular grave about 3.5ft below turf level; at the top the grave was 3.8ft by 3.9ft and at the bottom 2.5ft by 3ft. A sarsen stone had not completely covered the grave, and was 3.5ft by 3.3ft. The excavators were quite sure that there had been no mound over the grave, and also noted other circular depressions nearby which could have been other graves (although there is the possibility of later pits in this area.). The excavator, W.E.V. Young, gives a very full account of the burial (1950, 311–326). The skeleton was on his or her back, with both shoulder blades and pelvis flat to the floor; the head was to the north, turned to face left (east) . The lower legs had been drawn up and appeared to have been tightly bound, so that they were found alongside the femurs. The forearms were crossed on the breast, left over right. A Beaker (Clarke's group N2, 1970 fig. 516) lay at the child's left shoulder, on its side, its mouth pointing east, away from the child. The Beaker was an old vessel, and appeared to have been lain on its better side, leaving holes in its uppermost side as if it may have been holding some liquid. A flat piece of chalk lay at the child's right shoulder, which the excavator was certain was a deliberate inclusion in the grave; he also interpreted it as carved to imitate a child's hand, having five grooves scored into it.Two flint flakes appeared to have been placed under the pelvis, one on either side.

Beckhampton, Longstones
Crouched inhumation, on surface of chalk with no grave cut, next to larger stone of the Longstones, head to the east. Disturbed, but with sherds of a well-made, red Beaker nearby. Beaker classified by Clarke as N/MR (1970 fig. 233); skeleton of an adult of 'about middle age' (WAM 38 (119) 1–7).Excavated by Ben and Maud Cunnington.

Overton Down, Site XI
NGR: 131705
NMR: SU 17 SW 30
Three burials, numbered IA, IB and II by the excavators. IA was of a child of about 7 years, accompanied by an finger-decorated Beaker (Smith 1967). It was disturbed by IB, a male in his twenties, lying crouched with his head to the east facing south and with no grave goods. Eight metres to the north was II, a possibly female adult which had been cut into by a later pit but appeared to be lying in a similar orientation to 1B (ie the surviving feet were to the west (Fowler 2000, 85–86, fig. 6.4). A pit nearby held fragments of a possible cremation burial and other material which the excavator considered indicated a possibly Early Bronze Age date (*op cit* 86).

The Sanctuary
Inhumation of an adolescent male, buried close to the inner side of stone hole 12 of the inner circle, with a small Beaker in front of and just below the knees. (Cunnington 1930 313, 323, Pl.. 9). The Beaker is classified by Clarke as Barbed Wire (1970 fig. 347) but queried by Case (1995). The skeleton lay on his right side, head to the south, i.e facing east. The arms were crossed, the hands enfolding the face, the head bent forward and the legs crossed below the knees. If the stone was standing when the body was buried they would apparently almost have touched and the excavators concluded the stone was put up at the time the burial occurred; however the comment 'the grave and the stone hole cut into one another' may indicate that a stratigraphic relationhip existed but was not recorded. A few cattle and pig bones and a fragment of red deer antler had been placed on the body *(op cit.* 331).

Smeathe's Ridge
NGR: 16597575
NMR: SU 17 NE 5
Crouched inhumation found in a grave 2 feet deep, badly disturbed by workmen who found it. 'The vertebral column lay roughly east and west, with the head to the east', surviving finger bones, which were said to be 'clasping the base of the vessel' were pointing north-east'and were in such a position as to indicate that the skeleton was lying on its right side' [i.e. facing north].Clarke classifies the vessel as European Beaker (1970 corpus no. 1128F); the published account shows base and lower body sherds of a vessel with herringbone cuneiform impressions; it is described in the report as 'the size and shape of a small pudding basin with a projecting ridge 12mm to 16mm below the lip' Passmore (1914) and so could have been a small cordoned Beaker or a ridged Food Vessel. The skull was of an adult male (Keith 1926).

West Kennet Avenue, adjacent to Stone 18B
Grave disturbed by the much later burial of one of the standing stones of the Avenue. The grave was oval, about 3ft by 2ft, and first excavated by Mrs Cunnington, and later by Alexander Keiller. The burial was probably male and had no grave goods.
(Smith 1965a, 209).

West Kennet Avenue, stone hole 5A
Fragment of pelvic bone and two femora heads, belonging to individuals. No grave was found (Smith 1965a, 210)

West Kennet Avenue, adjacent to stone 22B
Intact grave next to stone-hole and upper filling of grave was similar to that of the stone-hole. The burial was of a man, lying on his back with his head to the west, turned to the right (south) and feet to the east.

His legs were drawn up but not tightly contracted. An unclassifiable bowl was behind his shoulders (Smith 1965a, 210, fig. 78, P352)

West Kennet Avenue, site of stone 25A
A small fragment of skull was found nearby (Smith 1965a, 210.)

West Kennet Avenue, adjacent to stone 25B
Grave of an adolescent, apparently an extension of the stone-hole, Smith suggesting that it may have been dug when the stone was in place but propped up. Head probably to north and on left side (so facing east); badly disturbed by cutting of much later stone burial pit but hands probably crossed on chest. Bones belonging to two other individuals were present, one adolescent and one an adult. A Beaker classified by Clarke as N2 (1970, fig. 515) was in sherds and could have accompanied any of the three (Smith 1965a, 209–210, fig. 78, P351).

West Kennet Avenue, adjacent to stone 29A
Very disturbed grave, largely destroyed by the burial of the stone. Bones of an adult male and sherds of Beaker classified by Clarke as European and with cord defined zones of comb impressions; (Clarke 1970, fig. 62) (Smith 1965a, 210, fig.78, P350)

West Overton, Lockeridge
NGR: 14666781 (approx)
NMR: SU 16 NW 49
Crouched skeleton, reported as male, found with a Beaker and a flint dagger. At least one other skeleton had been reported from the same area. The Beaker is of Clarke's Wessex/Middle Rhine group and he illustrates it as close in form and decoration to two from Moravia (*op cit.* figs. 178 and 180.) *WAM* 41, 187–8; Clarke 1970, fig. 179

West Overton – Lockeridge – could be a flat grave or a barrow
A Beaker now in Wiltshire Heritage Museum is reported as coming from Lockeridge (Annable and Simpson 1964, corpus no. 115). It is clearly derived from a grave because of its condition, but whether from a flat grave or a barrow is uncertain. The Beaker is a later type, of Clarke's S2(W) group (1970, fig. 899).

Winterbourne Monkton – Monkton Field
NGR: 091722 (approx)
NMR: SU 07 SE 37
At least one Beaker associated burial, probably with a male skeleton in a circular pit under a large sarsen stone about 300 yds west of Millbarrow long barrow. The grave group appears to have comprised two later Beakers (Clarke 1970 figs. 897, 898, both S2 (W) group), two conical buttons and a 'pulley ring' of shale and a greenstone polishing stone (Devizes Cat. 1934, 26–29; Annable and Simpson 1964, figs. 70–76). Grinsell (1957, 126) notes that there have been as many as 30 burials reported from this area, mostly under sarsen slabs and, it seems, without grave goods; at least one appears to have been multiple (*WAM* 1, 303–304.). It is therefore not at all clear whether all are Early Bronze Age or include earlier or later burials. This is an area rich in buried sarsens, presumably a natural distribution some of which were utilised for burial. Sarsens have been removed in recent years from this area but no burials have been reported.

12
Bronze Age Land Allotment on the Marlborough Downs

David McOmish

Like much of the chalk in central southern England the Marlborough Downs are carpeted by extensive blocks of 'Celtic' fields. First considered as a whole by Chris Gingell some decade ago, recent aerial plots have demonstrated how extensive the systems were and how intensively the Downs may have been utilized.

Introduction

Evidence for cultivation of Neolithic or Early Bronze Age date is clear at a number of locales across the Marlborough Downs. For instance, excavations at the sites of long barrows have, in particular, revealed evidence of episodical cultivation not only on the ancient ground surfaces beneath the mounds (implying here that this cultivation is very early indeed, of 4th millennium BC date) but within the ditches that flank the barrows too. The evidence from South Street is often quoted but the famous criss-cross ploughing is arguably only part of a lengthy, if piecemeal, process of tilling (and cultivation?) (Ashbee *et al* 1979) rather than ritual clearance of turf (Thomas 1999, 24). What is rarely mentioned is that there is at least one other phase of spade digging pre-dating the construction of the long barrow mound. That open grassland was present is beyond dispute given the large quantities of turf, some strips as long as 60cm, that were used to build the long and round barrow mounds on the Marlborough Downs. There are certainly no known physical remains of the earliest fields as we would recognise them but there are structures or features within the barrow mounds, including stone settings and timber alignments, which repay further investigation. For instance, the line of sarsen stones forming the longitudinal axis of the mound at South Street might represent linear clearance either deriving from cultivation or as part of the preparation of the site in advance of the construction. If so, this sarsen then must be seen, *de facto*, as a field boundary. Alternatively, the incorporation of sarsen and ploughsoil within an overtly ritual structure could itself be seen as a symbolic act – a metonymical representation of the earliest field clearance and its alteration of the 'natural' world.

The landscape of the Marlborough Downs had certainly changed significantly by the Middle Bronze Age in that permanent enclosures populated its chalky slopes at a number of locales. These consisted often of small compact settlements enclosed within proportionately much larger banks and ditches indicating that great care was taken to protect or cut-off the domestic setting from the surrounding landscape – a landscape that, significantly, contained good evidence for 'Celtic' fields.

These field systems are composed of small square paddocks, enclosed within embanked or lyncheted boundaries often appearing to form a grid-like pattern. The use of the term 'Celtic' is neither an indication of date nor a pointer to the progenitors of this form of agriculture. Celticism is an increasingly archaeologically challenged concept and is used here simply as a morphological convention, owing its derivation to the work of Curwen and Crawford in the early 20th century. Much variation in form is masked within the catch-all term but it is clear that cultivation, regardless of the date, involves similar processes of laying out, breaking the soil and, possibly crop rotation, which in all cases resulted in the creation of ploughsoils and lynchets. The pattern, location and extent of fields are not solely conditioned or determined by age but where cultivation has been most intensive and long-lived, the field boundaries are often more substantial.

The recognition of this rests with the work of

Owen Meyrick (1973) and Mrs Piggott (1942) but more recently with Chris Gingell (1992). Meyrick and Piggott were fortunate in that they studied the Marlborough Downs before and during the onset of the heavy ploughing that has since destroyed so much of the archaeology in the late 20th century. This work did, however, also allow for more opportunistic assessments through fieldwalking and surface collection outlining spreads of material culture and highlighting the location of settlements both enclosed and open. The landscape history that unfolded was remarkably similar to that witnessed at other Deverel-Rimbury sites (with a date range of 1500 to 1150 BC) where settlement was intimately linked or connected to a network of fields. Piggott and Meyrick looked closely at a cluster of enclosures set within a few kilometres of one another on the Downs to the south of Barbury Castle. The enclosures are similar in terms of morphology and landscape setting and all are associated with 'Celtic' fields. That on Preshute Down consisted of a small D-shaped enclosure with an external V-shaped ditch that produced Deverel-Rimbury ceramics and pre-dated a contiguous field system. The enclosure on Ogbourne Mazey Down which is of a similar date, sliced through fields, although Piggott was not completely sure of their relationship – but this does provide firm evidence for an association between Middle to Late Bronze Age settlement and field systems.

However, it is possible that closer examination of the sequence of earthwork construction might allow the date of the enclosures and fields to be tied down even more closely. There was a mix of open and enclosed settlements, and on occasion pre-existing open sites were enclosed. At Bishops Cannings Down (Gingell 1992, Fig 2) the site remained open but set within the confines of embanked fields and consisted of small circular post-built structures and clusters of paired posts, associated predominantly with Deverel-Rimbury forms of pottery. At Dean Bottom (*ibid*, Fig 14) and Rockley Down (*ibid*, Fig 21), however, enclosing ditches and banks were noted though to varying degrees of completeness. At the former, Gingell found only traces of a slight and incomplete enclosing bank. The settlement here covered an area of 0.5 hectares and at least 5 house platforms had been terraced into the sloping hillside – a favoured location for Middle to Late Bronze Age sites on the Marlborough Downs and, indeed, further afield. Once again the site was associated with 'Celtic' fields, lying, in this instance, close to the edge of a large system. Evidence for earlier activity on the settlement platform came in the form of Beaker 'storage' pits and the bank contemporary with the Middle–Late Bronze Age settlement consisted of 'scraped-up' (and therefore pre-existing) ploughsoil. The ceramics from this site although including Deverel-Rimbury forms were dominated by Post Deverel-Rimbury wares thus implying that the enclosure and its associated settlement dated largely to 1150–850BC.

It is worth speculating that, generally, the act of enclosure belonged to a late phase in the sequence of occupation at a number of sites and it may be that there was a pattern of open settlements set within fields dating to around 1500–1200BC with a subsequent move towards the formal enclosure of a number of the sites before 850BC. This is again supported by the evidence from Rockley Down where a small ditched and banked enclosure was associated predominantly with post-Deverel-Rimbury ceramics. Within the enclosure no postholes were found, instead there were gullies and short lengths of shallow ditch filled up with what looked like midden deposits. Notably, Middle Bronze Age ceramics were found below the bank of the enclosure in a developed ploughsoil – part of a field system that extended well beyond the area of settlement.

It may be significant that the boundaries to the settlements appeared to slight earlier fields and, indeed, incorporated lynchet material in their make-up. Where the banks are accompanied by a ditch it might be plausible to suggest that these were backfilled soon after they were dug. That at Rockley Down was deep and sharply V-shaped in profile but the sides appeared unweathered and a possible interpretation of this is that the ditch wasn't left open for any great length of time. Finds from the ditches also included pottery and metalwork and rather than being seen as casual losses or discard it would seem more appropriate to view these as carefully placed artefacts, selected to symbolically demarcate the boundary between the domestic space and the world around it. Is it also significant that the builders of these enclosures defined their boundaries by scraping up soil from the surrounding fields? By incorporating this sort of dirt it at once anchored the enclosure into a wider landscape that contained good evidence for embanked and lyncheted fields. This may have been an attempt to bind the settlement and the field together in more than a physical sense. By monumentalising the settlement zone, this component was inscribed onto the landscape and enhanced in a lasting way, and would have resembled the remains of heavily embanked and lyncheted fields thus becoming part of the natural order of things. The demarcated settlements became important nodes within a developing structured landscape and one that may also have been 'filling-up' with other enclosed settlements and major land divisions such as linear boundaries.

That extensive arable existed close to the settlements is beyond doubt given the artefactual records witnessed at a number of the excavated sites. The inventory includes good evidence for quernstones and sarsen rubbers all indicative of grain processing. At Dean Bottom quern manufacture may also have taken place. In manufacturing terms a number of the sites on the Marlborough Downs showed evidence of more rounded craft specialisation with metalworking debris being found fairly frequently. Ornaments including pins and bracelets have been found at these places and there is much evidence for implements such as knives and razors as well as awls and tweezers more commonly associated with fabric or textile production.

Six-row hulled barley was a favoured crop during the latter half of the second millennium BC – a single context at Dean Bottom produced most of this grain, here clean and processed and free from weeds. Some wheat was present at this time but it is unclear if this was spelt or emmer. Weeds of cultivation were also present in small quantities including Knot Grass and Cleavers – other weeds pointed to land that had been disturbed in the recent past.

That there were extensive tracts of grassland by the Middle Bronze Age is implied by the animal bone recovered during Gingell's excavations on the Marlborough Downs. At those sites which reached their zenith towards the end of the Bronze Age, sheep/goat dominate the faunal record with smaller species counts for cattle and pig. In contrast at Bishops Cannings Down, with a focus on, earlier, Deverel-Rimbury activity, the main species is cattle. This build up of sheep continues and is reflected again in the faunal assemblages from a number of sites on the Downs and points to extensive tracts of pasture, in all likelihood as part of a mixed agricultural regime.

But what did the layout of these early field systems look like? Unfortunately, we can't make any definitive comment on the extensiveness of the early layout simply because evidence has now been masked by later activity. It is evident, however, that in a number of instances there is a strong correlation between settlements and discrete blocks of fields (*ibid*, Figure 96 – in particular, the area to the south of Barbury Castle). On Rockley Down and at Dean Bottom the enclosures appear to be integrated within a pre-existing spread of 'Celtic' fields. The expanse of fields at Dean Bottom appear to have developed through a piecemeal process of accretion. The complete block of fields here covers an area of approximately 20 ha and lies on a gently north-east facing slope. No overall axial trend is apparent though there seems some bias towards an angle 15° to the east of north. Field size varies greatly from less than 50m^2 to areas in excess of 2 ha –the larger field size probably results from later alteration or enlargement or it may simply be that internal subdivisions were destroyed by subsequent agricultural activity. Field systems of the same nature and extent lie immediately to the north-east of Dean Bottom and although not physically interconnected, the fields share a similar axial configuration and are morphologically similar too. Both ancient field blocks are associated with spreads of Bronze Age pottery and each lacks an overall axial symmetry being composed of fields of varying size with an accreted appearance. Finds of Bronze Age pottery continue to be made within the fields on Preshute Down to the west of Dean Bottom but these are of a substantially different morphology. The fields here have a very pronounced axial layout on a more north-westerly alignment. Two blocks are evident separated by a stretch of uncleared sarsens. The southern block comprises a grid-like layout of fields not dissimilar in size to the Bronze Age fields further east. Major Allen's photograph is now the best evidence we have available on the relationship between fields and settlement in the area of Preshute and Dean Bottom. Two components are visible here – a larger rectangular enclosure and a second smaller enclosure set within a rectilinear field system. The smaller enclosure lies within a field corner and has clearly been overploughed, whether or not this occurred during the lifetime of the field is unknown but there must be a suspicion that this is the case. The larger adjacent enclosure lies outside of the block of fields and, indeed, it appears that one of the lynchets of the system swerves to avoid the boundary. So, it is worth considering that this block of fields, certainly in their latest phase, post-date the Middle to Late Bronze Age enclosure.

The most detailed assessment of the field remains on the Marlborough Downs results from Fowler's work on the Fyfield and Overton Down areas (see Crutchley, this volume, fig. 4) – a large expanse of downland that lies to the east of Avebury and the Winterbourne valley (Fowler 2000). In this survey eleven separate blocks of 'Celtic' fields have been identified by virtue of similarity in size and shape as well as orientation. Many of these field groups are what are termed coaxial fields and a number are associated with later, Late Iron Age and/or Romano-British settlement. On closer inspection it is possible, however, to see traces of earlier layouts subsumed within the later uptake. In addition, there are a number of instances where linear boundaries of

Early Iron Age date slice through fields and points where settlements of presumed Bronze Age date overlie fields.

Fowler has identified three main field system orientations in the relict landscape. A north-south axis which is of Romano-British date; and two other north-west/south-east layouts varying between 15° and 45° to the west of north – these two may incorporate earlier layouts and although Romano-British fields, especially those on Totterwood Down, lie on this axis, Fowler states that they have an origin in the Early to Middle Bronze Age. Excavations across the area of Fyfield and Overton Downs consistently produces evidence for Bronze Age activity but this rarely provides a reliable date for the field remains. Instead, it is presumed that the Bronze Age material is residual and relates to the first phase of arable activity in a landscape that has subsequently been remodelled/remoulded on several occasions.

A similar level of detailed investigation is now required in the chalk downland to the south and east of Avebury – along the escarpment edge that flanks the Vale of Pewsey. Results from the English Heritage survey point to a similarly intense usage of the landscape throughout much of the later prehistoric and subsequent periods but with not quite the same level of survival as on Fyfield and Overton Down. However, this may change given that ground-checking of aerial transcriptions is resulting in 'blank' areas are now being shown to contain the slighted remains of prehistoric and Romano-British fields. Again, fixing the chronology of fields is particularly difficult simply because there has been so little recent excavation and fieldwalking. In addition, the effects of residual artefacts being displaced by the plough and clouding the stratigraphic evidence make it difficult to be precise about chronological context. There are, however, numerous occasions where what we must presume to be 'Celtic' field blocks have been truncated by linear boundaries of presumed Late Bronze Age/Early Iron Age date and other instances where fields are overlain by later prehistoric enclosures. At a superficial level the field blocks do seem to be organised in a different fashion to those further north and east on the Marlborough Downs. Ladder type arrangements appear frequently, often aligned on a north-east – south-west alignment and extend in strips from the edge of the chalk escarpment. The exact date of these fields remains unknown but as elsewhere an Early to Middle Bronze Age origin would be expected with a subsequent massive expansion in the Iron Age and Romano-British periods.

As we have seen there is good evidence on the Marlborough Downs for pre-Bronze Age cultivation but what separates the later bouts of arable activity is the monumental aspect of the resulting fields. This might suggest more settled cultivation and settlement and reflect a desire to 'colonise' the land – a distinct break with earlier traditions of land use (cf Barrett 1994). These are built features, in most cases comprising the remains of clearance and other cultivation debris and some incorporate sarsen walling. The resulting pattern is of a visibly demarcated landscape providing a commentary not only on land use but also perhaps on tenure and related issues such as group conflict, ownership rights and issues of use and access. That the fields were well used is also beyond dispute since so many of the field boundaries are heavily lyncheted and there are, of course, developed ploughsoils underneath the banks of a number of the Middle to Late Bronze Age enclosures. But the level of monumentality that was previously only accorded to the ritual enclosures and barrows was now reflected in what could be termed the secular environment. This transformation is typified by a shift in the locales of social ritual away from major monumental foci towards the domestic setting. The major monuments constructed during the second millennium BC are all related to domestic activity and agricultural production to such an extent that it is plausible to suggest that social standing and power was underpinned by a successful and productive economic regime. The fields and enclosed settlements were landscape markers of these important social changes and many of the activities which took place within the settlements points to things like feasting and special deposition, display and conspicuous consumption.

Conclusion

In summary, we can say that the Marlborough Downs hold the evidence for one of the most remarkable transformations apparent in the archaeological record of southern England. With the rise in new forms of settlement, fields and a change in the associated material culture, we are witnessing the development of intensive agriculture, territorial land divisions and long-lived nucleated settlements. This was played out over a period of three centuries but shaped a landscape that is recognisable to us today.

13
"There wur a bit of ould brass" Bronze Age metalwork and the Marlborough Downs landscape

Martyn Barber

A review of Bronze Age metalwork finds from the region highlights a range of difficulties with the available data, though little is unique to the Marlborough Downs. The principal problem concerns the lack of information available on the depositional context of the overwhelming majority of reported finds. However, some patterns are beginning to emerge from the analysis of the chronological and spatial distribution of certain classes of object.

Introduction

The focus of this brief study is the accumulated assemblage of Bronze Age metalwork recovered from the area around Avebury and the Marlborough Downs in the three centuries or so since the first recorded discovery. The study area is defined quite arbitrarily, owing more to the limits of Ordnance Survey map sheets than to any topographical or administrative boundaries. The resulting gazetteers (Tables 13:2–13:7) cannot yet be regarded as exhaustive, although the information within them is as accurate as possible. Essentially, this is very much a report on work in progress, with an emphasis on raising rather than answering questions.

Thousands of items of Bronze Age metalwork are known from the British Isles, representing an incredible range of objects created to perform a multiplicity of purposes, both utilitarian and otherwise. In recent years, particularly following the remarkable discoveries at Flag Fen (Pryor 2001) and the publication of Richard Bradley's *The Passage of Arms* (Bradley 1990; 1999), it is the "otherwise" aspects that have come to occupy a more prominent place in Bronze Age studies, with the various means by which metalwork might have entered the ground coming under much closer scrutiny than before. This renewed concern with the processes and purposes of deposition has arisen at a time when the more traditional means of studying bronzes – principally typological analyses contributing to broader chronological and cultural frameworks for the period – have declined in popularity, the weaknesses in such approaches having become increasingly apparent (Bradley 1990; Brück 1999a; Barber 2001).

However, to a certain extent there remains a tendency to interpret metalwork in a fairly simplistic manner, overlooking the serious

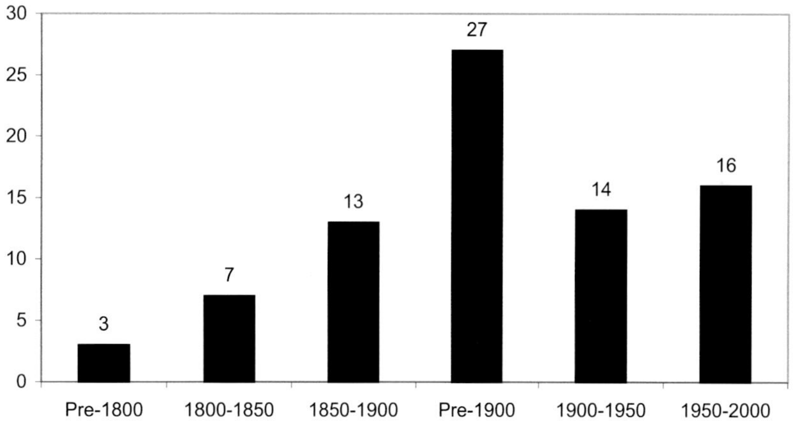

Table 13:1 Frequency of finds by date of discovery. The "pre-1900" column represents items for which no more accurate date of discovery is known. It is, however, likely that most are pre-1850, implying a fairly steady rate of discovery over the past 200-plus years, despite considerable changes in the ways in which objects are found.

Tables 13:2 to 13:7 Gazetteers of Bronze Age metal finds recorded within the study area. Their incomplete nature reflects the fact that data collection is an ongoing process. To prevent these gazetteers being overwhelmed with detail and bibliographic references, the final column in each lists the NMR number for each site or findspot. Further details can be obtained from the National Monuments Record, Great Western Village, Kemble Drive, Swindon, Wiltshire SN2 2GZ by quoting these numbers.

CORPUS NO.	TYPE	CONTEXT	WHEN FOUND	WHERE FOUND	CURRENT LOCATION	NMR NO.
1	Unknown	Round Barrow: Calne Without 2c	1858 or 1871	S of Oldbury	Unknown	SU06NE191
2	Dagger	Round Barrow: Cherhill 9	1849	Yatesbury	Unknown	SU07SE10
3	Awl	Round Barrow: Avebury?	Late 1850s?	Beckhampton Penning	British Museum	SU06NE66
4	Dagger?	Long Barrow: Avebury 17	1830s?	N of Beckhampton	Unknown	SU06NE75
5	Dagger	Round Barrow: Avebury 19b	1992	Beckhampton		SU06NE76
6	Dagger	Round Barrow: Roundway 8	Circa 1855	Roundway Hill	Devizes Museum	SU06SW3
7	Pin	Round Barrow: Roundway 8	Circa 1855	Roundway Hill	Devizes Museum	SU06SW3
8	Dagger	Round Barrow: Roundway 5a	Circa 1855	Roundway Hill	Devizes Museum	SU06SW8
9	Dagger	Round Barrow: Roundway 5b	Circa 1855	Roundway Hill	Devizes Museum	SU06SW8
10	Dagger	Round Barrow: Bromham 1	1928	Oliver's Camp	Devizes Museum	SU06SW44
11	Burnt fragments	Round Barrow: Avebury 37	1849	Avebury Down	Unknown	SU17SW57
12	Dagger	Round Barrow: East Kennet 1c	1840	East Kennet	British Museum	SU16NW62
13	Flat axe	Round Barrow: West Overton 1	By 1810	Overton Hill	Devizes Museum	SU16NW154
14	Pin	Round Barrow: West Overton 1	By 1810	Overton Hill	Devizes Museum	SU16NW154
15	Knife	Round Barrow: West Overton 1	By 1810	Overton Hill	Devizes Museum	SU16NW154
16	Dagger	Round Barrow: West Overton 4	By 1810	Overton Hill	Unknown	SU16NW159
17	Awl	Round Barrow: Preshute 1a	1906	Manton	Devizes Museum	SU16NE3
18	Awl	Round Barrow: Preshute 1a	1906	Manton	Devizes Museum	SU16NE3
19	Awl	Round Barrow: Preshute 1a	1906	Manton	Devizes Museum	SU16NE3
20	Dagger	Round Barrow: Preshute 1a	1906	Manton	Devizes Museum	SU16NE3
21	Dagger	Round Barrow: Preshute 1a	1906	Manton	Unknown	SU16NE3
22	Halberd pendant	Round Barrow: Preshute 1a	1906	Manton	Devizes Museum	SU16NE3
23	Gold/amber disc	Round Barrow: Preshute 1a	1906	Manton	Devizes Museum	SU16NE3
24	Awl	Round Barrow: Avebury 55	1965	West Kennet	Devizes Museum	SU16NW60
25	Awl	Round Barrow: Wilton 5	Circa 1800	Gopher Wood	Unknown	SU16SW177
26	Awl	Round Barrow: West Overton 6b	1962	Overton Hill	Keiller Museum	SU16NW55
27	Dagger?	Round Barrow	Unknown	Windmill Hill	Unknown	
28	Flat axe	Unknown	Pre 1864	Tan Hill	Salisbury Museum	SU06SE24
29	Flat axe	Unknown	Pre 1934	Marlborough?	Devizes Museum	
30	Awl	Uncertain	1988	Windmill Hill	Keiller Museum	
32	Dagger	Unknown	1908	Rockley	Private Collection	SU17SE60
33	Dagger	Unknown	1965	New Town Farm	Devizes Museum	SU16SW43
34	Dagger	Unknown	19th century?	Winterbourne Bassett Down	Devizes Museum	
35	Dagger	Unknown	19th century?	Marlborough?	Unknown	

Table 13:2 Early Bronze Age metalwork from the Marlborough Downs

shortcomings of the available evidence. Bronzes continue to be regarded primarily as invaluable chronological and cultural markers, particularly on excavated sites where their presence is all too often taken for granted, despite their remarkable rarity on settlements of the period. Moreover, recognition of the phenomenon of deliberate deposition in rivers, bogs and lakes has lead to a broad acceptance of a distinction between objects from such places and finds from dry land, something that has helped perpetuate a false distinction between ritual behaviour and more mundane activities (see e.g. Brück 1999b). Thus deposition in wet contexts (such as rivers, bogs, springs etc.) is increasingly accepted as a ritual act, whereas deposition on dry land (for example in enclosure ditches or other settlement-related features) is more often viewed as a result of more straightforward domestic activity, principally temporary storage, deliberate disposal, or accidental loss. However, the available evidence suggests a more complex situation (see e.g. Barber 2001).

Moving from individual finds or sites to the broader landscape, the impact of metal and metalworking remains little explored and poorly understood, often being limited to vague acceptance that the supposedly more efficient bronze axe would have allowed quicker and larger scale forest clearance than the earlier stone equivalent. The difficulties encountered in extrapolating from individual find to landscape are illustrated by the curious statement in the Avebury World Heritage Site Research Agenda (Chadburn & Pomeroy-Kellinger 2001, 43–4) that the LBA socketed axes found at West Wood

Table 13:3 Middle Bronze Age metalwork from the Marlborough Downs

CORPUS NO.	TYPE	CONTEXT	WHEN FOUND	WHERE FOUND	CURRENT LOCATION	NMR NO.
36	Palstave?	Unknown	Early 18th century?	Avebury	Unknown	SU07SE106
37	Palstave	Unknown	19th century?	Windmill Hill	Unknown	SU07SE57
38	Palstave	Unknown	1930	West Stowell	Salisbury Museum	SU16SW42
39	Palstave	Unknown	1797	Pewsey area?	Devizes Museum	SU16SE12
40	Palstave	Unknown	1972	Martinsell Hill	Private Collection	SU16SE29
41	Palstave	Unknown	1894?	"Kennet"	Devizes Museum	
42	Palstave	Unknown	19th century?	Marlborough area	Devizes Museum	
43	Spearhead	Unknown	Early 19th century	SW of Beckhampton	Devizes Museum	SU06NE160
44	Spearhead	Unknown	1886	Tan Hill	Devizes Museum	SU06SE24
45	Spearhead	Unknown	1876	Hemp Knoll	Devizes Museum	SU06NE99
46	Spearhead	Unknown	1910	Bishops Cannings	Devizes Museum	SU06SW58
47	Spearhead	Unknown	By 1978	Morgan's Hill	Devizes Museum	SU 06 NW 79
48	Spearhead	Unknown	1909	Ladies Field, Wilcot	Devizes Museum	SU16SW57
49	Spearhead	Unknown	19th century?	Mill Brow	Devizes Museum	
50	Chisel/palstave	Unknown	19th century?	"Avebury"	Devizes Museum	
51	Tanged knife	Burial?	Circa 1930	Monkton Down	Devizes Museum	SU17SW136
52	Pin	Burial?	Circa 1930	Monkton Down	Devizes Museum	SU17SW136
53	Awl	Burial?	Circa 1930	Monkton Down	Devizes Museum	SU17SW136
54	Pin	Unknown	1911	Shepherd's Shore	Devizes Museum	SU06NW36
55	Rapier	Unknown	Unknown	Ogbourne St George	Devizes Museum	SU17SE80
56	Gold bar torc	Unknown	1814	Tan Hill	Private Collection	SU06SE25

Table 13:4 Late Bronze Age metalwork from the Marlborough Downs

CORPUS NO.	TYPE	CONTEXT	WHEN FOUND	WHERE FOUND	CURRENT LOCATION	NMR NO.
57	Socketed axe	Unknown	19th century?	Coleman's Bottom	Devizes Museum	SU16NW82
58	Socketed axe	Unknown	Pre 1887	Near Oldbury	Devizes Museum	SU06NW100
59	Socketed axe	Unknown	Pre 1984	Bourton	Devizes Museum	SU06SW108
60	Socketed axe	Unknown	Pre 1881	Tan Hill	Salisbury Museum	SU06SE24
61	Socketed axe	Unknown	19th century?	"Temple"	Devizes Museum	SU17SW89
62	Socketed axe	Unknown	1939	Rockley	Salisbury Museum	SU17SE62
63	Socketed axe	Unknown	Pre 1980	Manton Down	Private Collection	SU17SE81
64	Socketed axe	Unknown	Circa 1914	Manton Copse	Devizes Museum	SU16NE139
65	Socketed axe	Unknown	1993	Oliver's Camp	Devizes Museum	SU06SW226
66	Socketed axe	Unknown	1908	"Near Marlborough"	Devizes Museum	SU16NE142
67	Socketed axe	Unknown	Pre 1867	Marlborough Downs	Taunton Museum	SU17SE93
68	Socketed axe	Unknown	Pre 1873	Tan Hill	Cast in British Museum	SU06SE136
69	Socketed axe	Unknown	1978	Dean Bottom	Devizes Museum	SU17SW198
70	Socketed axe	Unknown	1937	Marlborough Downs	Devizes Museum	
71	Tanged chisel	Unknown	Pre 1887	Near Oldbury	Devizes Museum	SU06NW100
72	Gouge	Unknown	Pre 1887	Near Oldbury	Devizes Museum	SU06NW100
73	Razor	Unknown	Pre 1908	Beckhampton Down	Devizes Museum	SU06NE114
74	Tanged chisel	Unknown	Pre 1908	Coleman's Bottom?	Devizes Museum	SU16NW82
75	Awl	Unknown	Pre 1984	Bourton	Devizes Museum	SU06SW108
76	Sickle	Unknown	Pre 1908	Winterbourne Monkton	Devizes Museum	
77	Knife	Unknown	Pre 1911	Near Avebury	Devizes Museum?	
78	Brooch	Unknown	1987	Avebury Down	Devizes Museum	
79	Bracelet	Unknown	1986	Ogbourne St George	Devizes Museum	
80	Bracelet	Unknown	Uncertain	Tan Hill	Salisbury Museum	SU06SE24
81	Pin	Unknown	Uncertain	Tan Hill	Salisbury Museum	SU06SE24

Table 13:5 Currently unphased Bronze Age metalwork from the Marlborough Downs

CORPUS NO.	TYPE	CONTEXT	WHEN FOUND	WHERE FOUND	CURRENT LOCATION	NMR NO.
82	Axehead	Unknown	By 1981	Ridgeway	Private Collection	SU17SW133
83	Awl	Unknown	Pre 1911	Oldbury Hill	Devizes Museum?	
84	Awl/tracer	Unknown	Pre 1908	Beckhampton Down	Devizes Museum	SU06NE114
85	Awl	Unknown	Pre 1911	Wick Bottom	Devizes Museum?	SU17SW91
86	Awl	Unknown	Pre 1911	"Kennet"	Devizes Museum	
87	Awl	Unknown	Pre 1911	Avebury Downs	Devizes Museum?	
88	Awl	Unknown	Pre 1911	Avebury Downs	Devizes Museum?	
89	Awl	Unknown	Pre 1911	Avebury Downs	Devizes Museum	

(presumably a reference to the recent Manton Copse find (Corpus no. 92)) might have been "buried near to where they were utilised" and might thus help to identify the location of woodland, a suggestion that not only offers a remarkably simplistic view of deposition and axe function, but also appears to confuse bronze with pollen and snails.

CORPUS NO.	DATE	CONTENT	CONTEXT	WHEN FOUND	WHERE FOUND	CURRENT LOCATION	NMR NO.
90	MBA	3xpalstaves	Unknown	Pre 1864	Stanton St Bernard area	Salisbury Museum	SU06SE55
91	LBA	9xsocketed axes	Unknown	1914	Manton Copse	Devizes Museum	SU16NE51
92	LBA	7xsocketed axes, 8xpalstaves	Pit	199X	Manton Copse		
93	LBA		Unknown	199X	Nr Bishop's Cannings		

Table 13:6 Bronze Age hoards from the Marlborough Downs

SITE NAME	DATE	EXCAVATED	METAL FINDS
Bishop's Cannings Down	M-LBA	1976-7	Rapier fragment, knife fragment, rivet, awl, ferrule fragment?, casting fragments and casting waste
Dean Bottom	M-LBA	1977-9	Bracelet, ring fragments, palstave fragment, wire fragment, miscellaneous fragments
Burderop Down	LBA	1977-80	Pins, needle, bracelet fragments, tweezers, awls, socketed axe fragment, miscellaneous fragments, casting waste
All Cannings Cross	LBA-EIA	1911-22	Socketed axe fragment, awls, razor, tweezers, miscellaneous fragments
Overton Down ODXI	LBA-EIA	1960s	Socketed axe fragment

Table 13:7 Metalwork from Bronze Age settlements on the Marlborough Downs

The picture emerging from recent discoveries and discussion is that the deposition of metalwork in whatever context requires careful consideration. In addition to the fact that simply discarding a recyclable object appears rather wasteful and demands explanation is the growing evidence that a number of depositional events involving metalwork (as well as other classes of material) were more formal and ceremonial in nature than once believed, being tied in to key events in the lives of people and communities (e.g. foundation and abandonment deposits at settlement sites). However, attempts to integrate the evidence provided by metalwork into a more detailed consideration of Bronze Age life face a number of difficulties, chief among them being the nature and quality of documentary evidence associated with each individual find.

Avebury and the Marlborough Downs: the state of the evidence

The metalwork record from this area is as patchy and frustrating as for any other part of the British Isles. Contextual information is usually lacking, and in too many cases even the stated provenance of individual finds cannot be supported by any reliable documentation. It is unfortunately the case, here as elsewhere, that the overwhelming majority of finds were neither discovered by archaeologists nor recovered in a careful and controlled manner. An account of the circumstances of discovery is a rarity. Nearly all the finds from the area were, until recently, accidental discoveries during the course of agricultural work, building work, road construction, or some form of quarrying. During the 19th and early 20th centuries on the Downs, flint diggers in particular were responsible for a remarkable number of discoveries, and not only of Bronze Age metalwork. Very often, though, little information was recorded. Examples include the socketed spearhead provenanced only to "SW of Beckhampton" (Corpus no. 43), or the socketed gouge "found by flint diggers near the ramparts of Oldbury Camp" (Corpus no. 72). In some cases, the object itself no longer survives (or at least, its current location is unknown). Sadly, this applies to the earliest recorded find from the area, an axehead discovered in the early 18th century at the latest and briefly reported by William Stukeley (Corpus no. 36). The loss of this object is particularly unfortunate given the probable location of its findspot (see below).

More recently the growing popularity of metal-detecting has added a more purposeful element to the search for metal objects, occasionally of Bronze Age date and sometimes with spectacular results, but the majority of such discoveries occur outside of any informed research framework. Furthermore, if the findspot is not accurately recorded and examined archaeologically, such items remain little more than dots on distribution maps, with little indication of their true context. Moreover it is unfortunately the case that although many such discoveries are promptly and reliably reported, there remain others that cannot be taken at face value. Thus we can contrast the recently discovered LBA hoard from Manton (Corpus no. 92), found by a metal detectorist and excavated archaeologically by Gill Swanton, (G Swanton, A Lawson, *pers comms*) with the alleged West Kennet LBA hoard. In the latter case, a socketed hammer, a chisel or graver, and a socketed gouge were initially reported and published as having been found together not far from the West Kennet long barrow. However, the three items proved after further enquiries to represent the unsold residue of two separate discoveries from locations in south Wiltshire (P Robinson, *pers comm*).

Compiling a gazetteer of finds from the area is no more and no less straightforward than for anywhere else in the country. There are a number of invaluable early sources (e.g. Goddard 1908a; 1911; 1917), but no countywide study has been published since Leslie Grinsell's (1957) archaeological gazetteer of Wiltshire, a source that is not without its problems. Some relevant museum catalogues exist (Devizes; Annable & Simpson 1964; Salisbury; Moore & Rowlands 1972), though these are now out-of-date. The National Bronze Implements Index, a card index held at the British Museum, contains additional information on Wiltshire finds, including items in more distant museums and in private collections. Objects from the study area are also considered in a number of more thematic surveys focusing on Bronze Age metalwork (e.g. Evans 1881; Coombs 1972; Rowlands 1976; O'Connor 1980; Needham 1983; Taylor 1993; among others). Some more recent finds have been published in varying degrees of detail in journals such as the Wiltshire Archaeological Magazine. Overall, many hundreds of references to metal objects from the study area have been published since Stukeley's day. Even when satisfactorily tracked down, many are frustratingly brief, some are contradictory, while others offer potentially useful information but provide no apparent source. Based on experience from looking at metalwork from other parts of the country, the situation for the Marlborough Downs can be described as perfectly normal.

Early Bronze Age (circa 2500–1500 BC)

As with archaeology generally, the relative visibility of various phenomena has played a considerable part in structuring our understanding of this phase. The ephemeral nature of short-term EBA settlements contrasts with the more permanent landscape reminders of ceremony and burial – notably the great henge and the numerous round barrows dotting the downland. Both represent phenomena with Late Neolithic origins, although the latter in particular are most commonly associated with the Early Bronze Age. Metalwork of this period is dominated by grave finds, although the reverse is not true. In the study area, as in the British Isles generally, the overwhelming majority of excavated Early Bronze Age graves contained no metal. The other, "stray", finds comprise an awl, some daggers and two flat axes. While the awl and daggers might (but not necessarily) represent further burials, this is unlikely to be the case for the two flat axes. Axes are rare in EBA burials (Needham 1988) and where they do occur in grave contexts (such as West Overton 1 (Corpus nos 13–15): see below; or the Bush Barrow near Stonehenge) they tend to be of diminutive size, unlike the Marlborough and Tan Hill examples (Corpus nos. 29 and 28 respectively). Such a distinction might imply that the distribution of the larger axes could tell us something about the contemporary settlement pattern, in contrast to the better-known distribution of funerary monuments. Unfortunately as has already been noted, away from grave assemblages, the precise provenance of metalwork finds can be hazy at best, while evidence from outside the region suggests that attempts to link metalwork distributions to settlement patterns is to take an over-simplistic view of the means by which bronze and gold entered the archaeological record.

The metal grave goods from the area cannot, for the most part, be considered remarkable. In those few cases where metal is present, daggers predominate, while the awl is the next most common. Only in one case – Preshute 1a, the Manton Barrow (Corpus nos. 17–23) – do awls and daggers occur together. Only two metal-associated graves can be considered exceptional – West Overton 1 with its unusual combination of small flanged axehead, crutch-headed pin and small razor knife (Rohl & Needham 1998, fig 26), all accompanying a crouched inhumation in a tree trunk coffin; and the aforementioned Preshute 1a. This, with its array of "Wessex" finery, is perhaps the best known grave from the area, in part because of an over-emphasis in the literature on "rich" grave assemblages, particularly since Stuart Piggott's (1938) invention of the Wessex Culture. The numerous items of bronze, gold, amber, shale, stone and pottery accompanied a crouched adult inhumation. The skeleton was identified at the time as an elderly female, although the bone report, by Beddoe (in Cunnington 1907a, 1907b) doesn't inspire confidence. The bones were re-interred after the excavation, so confirmation is not possible. Nonetheless, if Beddoe was correct, the association of a woman with two bronze daggers is noteworthy given a tendency to regard such weapons as male items.

Along with the presence of awls in other graves, such associations serve to remind us that understanding the inclusion of grave goods is a far from straightforward affair. The case of awls is particularly intriguing. Fleming (1971, 160–1), saw their inclusion in graves as supporting evidence for pastoralism: "It is impossible to devise a true test of significance in this situation, but it is tempting to recall the traditional ascription of the awl to the leather-working industry. If the people...were mainly pastoralists, they might be expected to display more evidence of leather-working than mixed farmers would". Certainly leather-working represents a plausible use for such tools, but the assertion that leather was more likely to be worked by pastoralists represents a rather simplistic picture of EBA society, craft and exchange. Furthermore, leather-working is far from the only possible use for awls. Clarke *et al* (1985, 86) for example note their potential use for the manufacture of gold and jet items, suggesting their use was "perhaps restricted to the production of prestige objects". The association of awls with craft activities is undeniable, though what their presence in graves tells us about the people with whom they were buried is less clear-cut. Evidence for or against pastoralism is best sought in other aspects of an admittedly sparse archaeological record, while suggestions as to whether, say, leather-working was less important than gold-working are open to debate. Spector (1991), for example, has shown how the awls used in 19th century Minnesota could be viewed as "important material symbols of women's skills and values" (*ibid*, 395), using ethnographic data to show how particular tools could be closely associated with the accomplishments and achievements of their owners, while at the same time the tasks for which awls were used could be equally closely associated with key events in the lives of individual women. That the significance of awls extended beyond simple utilitarian needs is also suggested by deposition patterns from the Middle and Late Bronze Age, with a general absence from the (often tool-dominated) hoards contrasting with their relative frequency from domestic contexts (Needham 1986). Particularly noteworthy during these later phases of the Bronze Age is the recovery of no less than 18 from Flag Fen (Coombs 2001, 287–8, 297, and fig 10.19), Coombs suggesting that their deposition there was linked to important stages in the lives of "craftsmen" such as the completion of apprenticeship or training, or death.

A fuller understanding of graves such as these would require a more detailed appraisal of all excavated grave assemblages in the study area, something that is not possible here. Moreover, it would also face the problem of deficient data. Wiltshire is, of course, rather well known for its numerous excavated EBA grave assemblages, though despite the wealth of information (and surviving finds) presented by the likes of Colt Hoare, Merewether, Thurnam, various Cunningtons and others, the surviving record is far from perfect. Those early excavation "reports" are very much of their time – compared to the best modern standards, they are disappointingly brief and lacking in vital detail. For instance, it is not always possible to assume that any particular object found was contemporary with the excavated burial. Nor is it possible to recognise now exactly what was found. Thus round barrow Calne Without 2c (Corpus no. 1) was dug into by flint diggers during the later 19th century. A Beaker (or parts of one) survives in Devizes Museum, largely because Cunnington went back and poked around after the flint diggers had gone (Cunnington 1887). However, although they had reported finding a skeleton, it is unclear whether it represented a primary or secondary burial. Their statement that near the skeleton "there wur a bit of ould brass" makes a full typological assessment somewhat difficult.

Turning to the less apparent aspects of metal use in the Early Bronze Age, the matter of relative visibility has already been raised, and this is something that applies not just to monuments but to artefacts as well. It has become increasingly evident in recent years that the metalwork available to us today is far from being a random cross-section of the material in circulation during the Bronze Age (see e.g. Barrett & Needham 1988; Needham and Burgess 1980; Needham 1988). The surviving metalwork actually represents the residues of a range of depositional practices rather than a random reflection of routine domestic, industrial and economic activities. If we accept that deposition in the Bronze Age was generally non-random, selective and purposeful, and often occurred at key points in the lives of people and communities, then we have to accept that many aspects of metal use are not directly visible in the archaeological record.

The best known monument in the vicinity is, of course, the henge and its associated structures at Avebury. Equally pertinent to the discussion here are the massive palisaded enclosures at West Kennett (Whittle 1997a). The chronology of the construction and use of the henge is poorly understood (Pitts & Whittle 1992; Whittle 1993) although initial development of the monument appears to have occurred during the first half of the 3rd millennium BC (Whittle's Phase E). The Beckhampton and West Kennet Avenues and their associated monuments (particularly and respectively the enclosure in Longstones Field and The Sanctuary) seem likely to be broadly contemporary, although again, there is some uncertainty. Nonetheless, it seems likely that the whole complex, in its initial phases at least, predates the introduction of metalwork to southern England, something that radiocarbon dating and more traditional approaches would place no earlier than 2500 BC. However, Beaker associations show that these monuments remained in use (as well as remaining a monumental presence in the landscape) for some time. Ceremonial gatherings of whatever purpose would seem obvious arenas for the use and display of prestigious items, including those of metalwork. The lack of such items from the vicinity of the henge – indeed from much of the surrounding area, a couple of graves excluded – need not necessarily imply otherwise. The deposition of material of any kind at such sites was a result of deliberate decisions and careful selection by those who participated in its functions. Furthermore, the abundance of cultural material recovered from the ditches of the earlier causewayed enclosures contrasts with the much lesser quantities placed in the ditches of henges.

Metalwork is of course usually absent from other henges and analogous monuments. Notable exceptions include a single bronze awl from Stonehenge (Cleal *et al* 1995) and a decorated axehead from the ditch surrounding Mount Pleasant (Wainwright 1979, 40 and fig 24). The former was found close to the eastern ditch terminal at the main entrance of the site; the latter in the northern terminal of the henge's west entrance, both contexts suggestive of deliberate and formal deposition. An awl (Corpus no. 30) was also found at the Windmill Hill causewayed enclosure close to a ditch terminal (Hamilton in Whittle *et al* 1999, 343), although the proximity of round barrows may indicate a disturbed burial deposit as a likely source in this case. At this point it is worth returning to the axehead reported by William Stukeley (*see above*). Stukeley's account of the object and its discovery is brief, to say the least:

> "Beside some Roman coins accidentally found in and about Abury, I was informed of a square bit of iron under one of the great stones…They also found likewise a brass ax-head, under an ash-tree dug up in the smith's shop by the church. I understood, by the description they gave of it, it was one of those druid axes or instruments called Celts, wherewith they cut the mistletoe…" (Stukeley 1743, 27).

Assuming Stukeley was indeed referring to a Bronze Age object, and judging by his other writings and illustrations concerning druids and axeheads, this is likely to have been a flanged axehead or palstave (corpus no. 36). The "smith's shop by the church", as depicted on a 1695 plan (WCRO 184/4, reproduced as Ucko *et al* 1991 plate 49) appears to have been located adjacent to the inner edge of the henge ditch, just inside the western entrance to the henge, and on the northern side of the road. The location offers an interesting parallel with the aforementioned flanged axe from Mount Pleasant, which was recovered from the northern terminal of the western ditch. Whether or not the Avebury "brass ax-head" came from within the ditch is something unlikely to be resolved. However, it remains the sole item of (possible) Bronze Age metalwork from the henge itself. The nearest reliably provenanced finds occur more than a kilometre away.

The West Kennet palisaded enclosures appear to be a little later in date than the henge, probably belonging to the second half of the 3rd millennium BC (Whittle's phase F; Whittle 1993; 1997a). Though the enclosures are referred to generally as Late Neolithic, this period actually overlaps with the early stages of copper and bronze use in the British Isles and also, despite its absence from the site, with the use of Beaker pottery. This proposed date range for the sites allows the possibility that some or all of the oak timbers used were cut with axes of metal rather than stone. Clearly this is highly speculative, but serves as a reminder of the difficulties in understanding the early use of metal given that deposition in the Early Bronze Age appears to have been both infrequent and highly selective.

Middle Bronze Age (circa 1600–1000 BC)

In recent years the Middle Bronze Age has taken on a far greater significance than that previously accorded to it. Once the sole domain of palstaves and Deverel-Rimbury pottery, the archaeological record for southern England is now, from the mid-2nd millennium onwards, increasingly dominated by settlements and their associated field systems. It is no longer possible for traditional technological and typological development in metalworking to be seen either as causative of or even closely allied to such broad changes. To a considerable extent, previous assumptions about the importance of technology to social change reflected the importance of bronze as a chronological marker. With the advent of radiocarbon dating and the greater number of excavated sites, the importance of metalwork to the understanding of the Middle Bronze Age has declined significantly. Instead, the occurrence of metalwork at settlements (and other places) is increasingly regarded as deliberate and formal deposition tied to key stages in the lifecycles of people and the places they occupied, possibly reflecting metaphorical connections drawn between people, places, objects and fertility (see for example Brück 1999a; 1999b; 2001). Indeed, the sort of bronzes that might be expected to be in demand among the more settled agricultural communities attested in the archaeological record are noticeable by their absence. There are, for instance, no sickles from the study area, and few from the broader region. This again underlines the deliberate and selective nature of bronze deposition.

With the decline in the practice of depositing metal objects in graves (and the subsequent decline in placing even the deceased in graves: Brück 1995), the metalwork record for the Middle

Bronze Age is disappointingly sparse for the study area, comprising almost entirely of a small number of "stray" finds, the majority of which lack a precise provenance. Only one possible burial deposit is known – from Monkton Down, associated with a tanged knife, pin and awl (P Robinson *pers comm*) though details are scarce (Corpus nos. 51–53). The "strays" are dominated by palstaves and spearheads in almost equal quantities. The possible burial aside, the remainder comprises a pin, a rapier and a gold bar torc.

Unlike the earlier period, however, for the Middle Bronze Age the record is fleshed out a little by the existence of excavated settlement sites (Table 13:7) which have produced small but significant collections of bronze. Sites at Bishops Cannings Down and Dean Bottom were excavated in the late 1970s (Gingell 1992) and produced scraps of bronze, some of which are of pre-1000 BC date. At Bishops Cannings Down, none of the nine items survived in situ – eight were from the ploughsoil while the ninth was contained within the fill of a periglacial feature. A similar situation existed at Dean Bottom, where once again recent cultivation had separated many finds from their original contexts. Consequently it is difficult to be sure whether any of this material represents items deposited or discarded during occupation or after abandonment.

However, one important point to be made concerns the character of these settlement assemblages. Both comprise fragmentary items, the sole possible exception being the twisted rod bracelet from Dean Bottom (Gingell 1992, 107 fig 77.5), part of which was found in a World War Two US Army slit trench. The surviving pieces comprise an almost complete bracelet, the damage perhaps being caused by this recent disturbance. The generally fragmentary nature of these settlement finds can be contrasted with the generally complete nature of "stray" or surface finds of MBA date from the Downs. Compare for example the tiny palstave blade fragment from Dean Bottom (Gingell 1992, 107 fig 77.8) with the complete items that otherwise dominate the MBA assemblage from the Marlborough Downs. Although the sample is admittedly small, this is a picture mirrored elsewhere in the country – stray finds dominated by complete objects, settlement assemblages dominated by fragments. There are a number of possible explanations for this. For example, the dominance of complete objects among stray finds may be due to their relatively greater visibility, particularly to non-archaeologists. Alternatively, very real differences in the treatment and disposal of bronzes may lie behind this – smaller, scrappy fragments may represent pieces not considered worth hanging on to or recycling, whereas the larger, complete items may represent episodes of more formal deposition. This is particularly the case for hoards, the careful arrangement of objects in the ground being an increasingly recognised phenomenon for MBA hoards. The only possible hoard from the vicinity of the study area – the palstaves from Stanton St Bernard (Corpus no. 90) – represent a 19th century find with no surviving record of the circumstances of discovery. With no real context for any of the non-settlement MBA material from the Marlborough Downs, any interpretation remains highly speculative.

This lack of context is particularly unfortunate given the representation of spearheads among the stray finds. Within the study area, such items are absent from the EBA, from MBA hoards and excavated settlements, and from the LBA as a whole (see below). As weapons, they might be taken to imply some form of conflict. The evidence from places such as Tormarton, Gloucestershire and Dorchester-on-Thames, Oxfordshire (see Osgood 2000) where spearheads embedded in human remains have been found shows that we cannot assume that the Marlborough Downs was a tranquil rural idyll throughout the Bronze Age. Nor can we assume that the Middle Bronze Age was any more prone to conflict than preceding or succeeding eras. At the same time however, we cannot be certain that any of the spearheads from the study area were used in anger. Moreover the very fact of their deposition suggests a more complex understanding of the social role of such items.

Thus as with the earlier phase, there are many aspects of metal use likely to remain unrepresented in the archaeological record. As well as ceremony and display, more utilitarian employment of bronzes is also worth highlighting. The Middle Bronze Age is the phase when settlements, enclosed or otherwise, become more visible. These along with attendant field systems and associated earthworks will all have provided opportunities for the use of bronze objects, some more often than others. The limited nature of excavations to date and the nature and quality of the surviving remains means that evidence from the Marlborough Downs is somewhat lacking in this respect. The axe marks on timber at sites on the Somerset Levels and at Flag Fen, for example, highlight the importance of such tools in the everyday lives of people and communities, in terms of woodland management and the construction of features such as trackways, houses and so on. Looking further afield again, axe-blade markings within the Angle Ditch on Cranborne Chase (Pitt Rivers 1898, 103–4) and within the Wilsford Shaft (Ashbee *et al* 1989, 33ff) show that palstaves were more than just woodworking tools.

However, it is the place and manner of

deposition that underlines the possible connections between bronze and the landscape in the minds of the people who used both. Brück (1999a) in particular has recently drawn attention to the metaphorical links being drawn between people, places and things during the Middle and Late Bronze Age. At a time when we begin to see evidence for increasing physical demarcation and division of the landscape in the form of lynchets, enclosure ditches and linear earthworks, deposition of objects including bronzes is increasingly associated with these and other boundaries.

Late Bronze Age (circa 1100–800 BC)

The final phase of the Bronze Age sees a greater array of stray finds from the study area, and a slightly greater variety of objects. A few settlements have also been excavated, yielding LBA metalwork (see Table 13:7), notably the aforementioned Bishops Cannings Down and Dean Bottom plus Burderop Down (all in Gingell 1992), one of the sites investigated as part of the long running Fyfield/Overton Downs project (Fowler 2000; n.d.) and the site at All Cannings Cross (Cunnington 1923). Despite the increase in quantity, the problems and contrasts identified for earlier periods remain. Away from the excavated sites, there is an almost complete absence of information on circumstances and precise location of finds. Furthermore, the distinction between fragmentary settlement finds and complete stray finds largely holds.

In contrast to the MBA, when axes and spearheads appear in almost equal numbers, the latter disappear entirely from the record, the finds assemblage being dominated by socketed axes (14 out of 25 items). Socketed axes also dominate the few known hoards. This abundance and then disappearance of spearheads almost certainly represents a shift in depositional practices rather than a genuine absence of spearheads in the later period, further underlining the extent to which we are dependant on selective rather than random processes when studying Bronze Age metalwork. The extent to which these shifts in practice can be linked to other developments is, given the nature and quality of the available evidence, extremely limited.

What is different about this final phase of the Bronze Age is the existence of apparent evidence for actual metalworking, rather than just the metal itself. Casting droplets and casting waste from Bishops Cannings Down (Gingell 1992, 105–6) and Burderop Down (*ibid* 1992, 109–11) are supplemented by a crucible fragment, whetstone and part of a stone mould piece all found close to or during excavation of the latter site (*ibid*; Needham 1981). Again, these are all ploughsoil finds, making any assessment of their true context difficult. Their presence should imply that metalworking occurred on or close to both sites. However, it is worth pointing out that unequivocal in situ evidence for metalworking in the form of structures and debris associated with smelting and casting is unknown from the British Bronze Age. Furthermore, many Late Bronze Age sites across southern England have produced metalworking debris in the form of crucible or mould fragments and many hoards have contained casting waste without producing any clear indication of metalworking having taken place nearby. An excellent example is provided by Springfield Lyons in Essex, a Late Bronze Age enclosure which yielded a large quantity of clay mould debris from a ditch terminal adjacent to the site's main entrance. The location of this material and the absence of any other metal or metalworking-associated debris from the site strongly suggests that this material represented a deliberate act, perhaps a foundation deposit, rather than the simple discard of waste from an episode of bronze casting (Buckley & Hedges 1987). Nonetheless it may well be the case that by the LBA, many settlements or even individual households were able to manufacture at least some of the items they required. However, this is clearly something that only further excavation of LBA sites can help to confirm.

Discussion

Drawing any conclusions from the available data is fraught with difficulty. The search for finds is far from comprehensive, and as explained above, the quality of the data is far from what it could be. To a considerable extent, the available corpus is also a product of various forms of land-use, changing over time, but as Table 13:1 shows, changes in land-use (including excavation strategies) have not produced marked fluctuations in the discovery or reporting of finds, particularly from 1850 onwards as the publication of archaeological discoveries, however brief, becomes more commonplace. The 19th and early 20th century finds are dominated by excavated grave assemblages and by accidental finds during flint digging on the Downs, both being activities which largely ceased by the early decades of the 20th century. More recently, the majority of new finds are the result of metal detecting, though the quantity of reported finds is nowhere near as spectacular as in other parts of the country. Whether this is due to a lack of metal to be found or a lack of metal detectorists remains to be seen. It is nonetheless clear that land-use and access to

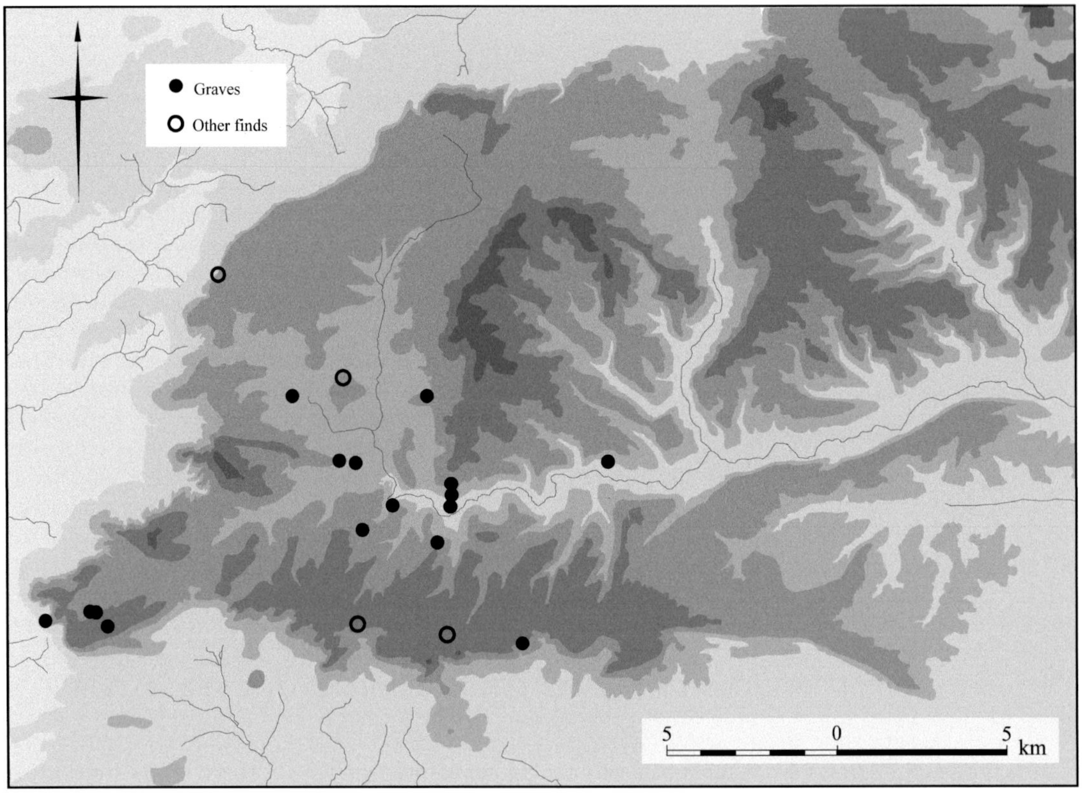

Fig 13:1 The distribution of Early Bronze Age metalwork west of the River Og (see Table 13:2).

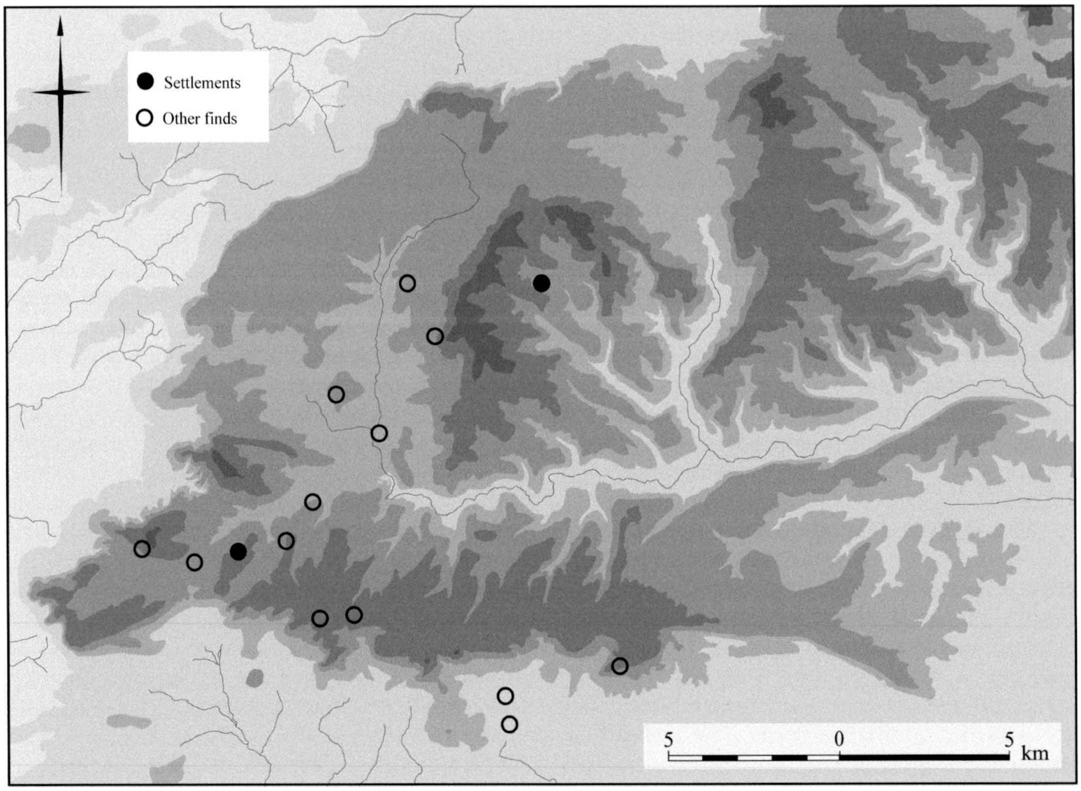

Fig 13:2 The distribution of Middle Bronze Age metalwork west of the River Og (see Tables 13:3, 13:6 and 13:7).

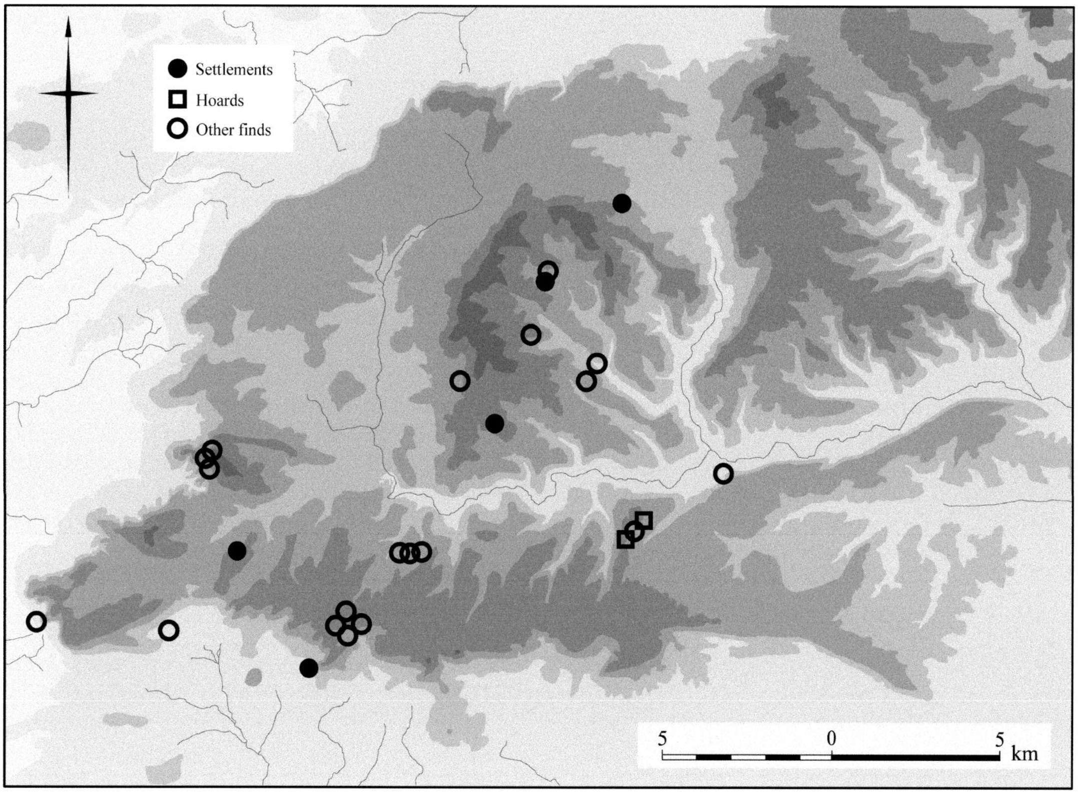

Fig 13:3 The distribution of Late Bronze Age metalwork west of the River Og (see Tables 13:4, 13:6 and 13:7).

the land has had a considerable impact on patterns of discovery. Far less intensive arable agriculture, a lack of urban development, and much more restricted access to metal detectorists are among the factors which make it difficult to compare the Marlborough Downs with other parts of southern England.

As a result, identifying patterns from the distribution maps (Figs 13:1–13:3) is another task fraught with difficulty, a situation not helped by the fact that the process of data collection is incomplete at the time of writing. Thus it is impossible to tell how real some of the observed patterns and gaps in distributions are. For example, Fyfield, Overton and Preshute Downs are, with the exception of a single excavated site (Dean Bottom), entirely devoid of Early and Middle Bronze Age metalwork. There also seems to be a marked preference for prominent landscape features such as hill tops and spurs. The occurrence of objects on or close to later hillforts such as Oliver's Castle, Oldbury, and Martinsell Hill is interesting, given the increasingly common discovery of LBA activity at excavated hillforts in and beyond the general region (e.g. just outside the study area at Liddington). However, other high points unencumbered by contemporary or later hillforts have also yielded metalwork. For example, a noticeable concentration of finds occurs on Tan Hill, the only cluster containing Early, Middle and Late Bronze Age objects within the study area and the only occurrence of gold (Corpus no. 56) apart from the Manton barrow (Preshute 1a). Tan Hill itself lacks a later hilltop enclosure, but is the location of a network of cross ridge dykes and other linear earthworks restricting access in various directions, in addition to earlier round barrows. The hill also overlooks the Neolithic causewayed enclosure of Rybury. It shares with its immediate neighbour Milk Hill the distinction of being the highest point in the area. Sadly, the exact location of most of the findspots is unknown. Many of the grid references assigned by Leslie Grinsell or the Ordnance Survey Archaeology Division relate more generally to the occurrence of the name Tan Hill on published maps rather than to the likely point of discovery. Where any information does survive, it is limited in usefulness. For example, the MBA spearhead (Corpus no. 44) found "N side of Tan Hill, under turf, 1886" (Goddard 1911, 141). More precise, and thus almost unique for the area, is the fragment of gold bar torc (Corpus no. 56) found in 1814 by yet another flint digger "near the highest point of Tan Hill" (Gray 1909/10, 436).

The case of Tan Hill leads us back to the single most pressing problem, identified earlier – the lack of any information on the depositional context of the overwhelming majority of reported finds. The few excavated settlements in the study area suggest that deposition of complete items on such sites was not the norm during the Middle and Late Bronze Age. The plotting of known definite or possible findspots against recorded earthworks and cropmarks might offer some clues, but without the careful excavation of the immediate vicinity of findspots, the significance of much of the surviving metalwork remains unclear.

Of course, none of the problems highlighted here are unique to the Marlborough Downs. However, although important information is emerging elsewhere from excavated sites, from studies of artefact distributions etc, it is important not to generalise too readily. Very real differences in deposition practices, for example, have been identified across space and time within the British Isles. A number of observations from the study area are worth evaluating against a wider geographical background. For example, the relative rarity of axes in the Early Bronze Age; or the absence of weaponry from the Late Bronze Age. The distribution maps need to be considered against the record of earthworks and cropmarks, as well as against a more detailed consideration of past and present patterns of land use. Comparison with the patterns of recovery of other prehistoric material such as lithics and ceramics would also be useful. Most important of all, though, is the need for archaeological examination of reported findspots. Without firm contextual data, we cannot truly begin to understand how this material got into the ground. Without such understanding of depositional practices, we cannot properly make sense of the typological, chronological and distributional data.

14
Prehistoric linear ditches on the Marlborough Downs

Graeme Kirkham

Long linear ditches define a number of large elongated 'territories' on parts of the higher downland. These territories appear to reassert and monumentalise an earlier pattern of land allotment, represented by blocks of fields and traces of settlement activity. Close spatial association between linears and barrows may indicate legitimation of this partitioning of the landscape by reference to an ancestral past. On the south western portion of the Downs there are also instances of short linear ditches set across prominent chalk spurs capped by barrows, perhaps demonstrating that these significant places were incorporated in the bounded landscape. A spur adjoining Tan Hill is enclosed by several ditches and appears to have been a component of a wider 'special' area defined by a clustering of linears. Linear ditch systems are clearly important for understanding the Late Bronze Age – Early Iron Age on the Downs and may also provide insights for earlier and later periods. The traces which survive are evidently the product of complex processes of defining space; further investigation is required specifically aimed at clarifying the 'process' element, identifying the principles underpinning their location and elucidating the degree to which they were functional barriers as well as social or political boundaries.

> *'In tracing these relics of antiquity, particular attention must be paid to the respective situations of the bank and ditch, for by a strict observation of these circumstances can we alone ascertain the continuation of the particular agger we are pursuing; for whenever we find the ditch in a contrary direction, we may conclude that it is not the same object of our research; and in some districts they are so very numerous, that without the nicest discrimination, we shall be frequently liable to error'* (Hoare 1821, 108).

Introduction

Sir Richard Colt Hoare's strictures on tracing linear ditches emphasises the intricacy of the network he found in his explorations on the Marlborough Downs. A very substantial proportion of what he saw has been masked or erased since his time and even then much had already been blurred and altered by well over two millennia of agricultural activity and periodic landscape reorganisation. Now, over much of the Downs, the former linear systems can be traced only from the air; only fragments survive as standing earthworks. Enough can be recovered, however, to indicate that these linear earthworks were important elements, both physical and symbolic, in a later prehistoric landscape of complex conception and associations.

Fig. 14:1 has been compiled from transcriptions of air photographic cover (Gingell 1992, fig. 96; Fowler 2000, fig. 2.1; Crutchley this vol), early editions of large-scale Ordnance Survey mapping and Colt Hoare's published plans of the area (Hoare 1821), supplemented by information from the National Monuments Record and limited field observation. The resulting plan is unlikely to be comprehensive, and other researchers might make different choices over specific features to be added or subtracted. There are acknowledged difficulties in determining whether some linear features are ditches or trackways, for example (Bradley *et al* 1994, 6); some have served as both in different phases. The plan represents a starting point for analysis, however, most particularly in the indications it provides of the broad distribution of linear earthworks across the area of the Downs and their relationship to topography.

Distribution and Form: linears in the landscape

It is clear from the figure that evidence for the former existence of linears is not evenly distributed across the Downs and it is worth considering initially the areas in which they appear to be absent. Wessex-type ditch systems have not been found in the zone between the Kennet and the southern scarp of the Downs, east of the Ridgeway, although in this area much more substantial linear earthworks form important elements in the two Late Iron Age complexes centred on Oare Hill and Forest Hill, Marlborough. Much of this zone is covered by Clay-with-flints and is likely to have been at least partly wooded in prehistory (Fowler 2000, 189; Fowler & Blackwell 1998, 27): elsewhere linears were created in open chalk grassland environments (cf. Ford 1982, 11, 14; Bradley *et al* 1994, 120) and it is possible that they were never present here. It is perhaps significant that concentrations of barrows are also scarce in this area (Fowler 2000, 239).

There are also few traces of linears on the lower portions of the Downs, close to Avebury itself, along the Og and Kennet valleys and on the wide Lower Chalk bench around the north-western and western fringes of the Downs. The lack of evidence in these areas may be a consequence of long-term plough damage and/or colluviation, however, for there are several instances of ditches descending from the Middle and Upper Chalk and apparently fading as they reach the lower ground. Examples include two which run down the western slope of the higher Downs north-east of Avebury, another which descends the north-west flank of Hackpen Hill and several which radiate from the high points on which Barbury, Liddington and Oldbury hillforts are situated. In none of these instances can the linears now be seen to continue for any substantial distance beyond the base of the scarp but it is clearly possible that the network of linear ditches once extended over a much greater area, well beyond the margin of the higher chalk. At the same time, there is little indication that linears ran off the chalk into the greensand and clay vales. Indeed, several of the ditches running south towards the Pewsey Vale terminate very abruptly (and visibly) on the brink of the chalk scarp. An exception may be a bank and ditch which runs off the chalk into the Vale on the boundary between Huish and Wilcot parishes. This is aligned on the barrow group south of Gopher Wood over part of its length but passes just to the east of the spur on which the group is sited. This earthwork could be a medieval or post-medieval boundary but is also plausibly the feature identified as the *Beorh Dic* (barrow dyke) in 10th century charter bounds for the north part of Wilcot parish (Sawyer 1968, 424; Grundy 1919, 187–91), suggesting an earlier origin.

The busiest surviving concentrations of linears on the Downs are in the area extending south and south west from Avebury to the southern scarp and west to Oldbury and in the large block of downland north west of Marlborough. (There is a further substantial group on the east side of the Og valley, not considered here.) Both areas are traversed by linear earthworks running for several kilometres, creating substantial territorial divisions. In the south western block, two long linears lie roughly north-west to south-east across the dip slope (Fig 14:1); both probably originally ran from the southern escarpment, across the wide valley between Beckhampton and Shepherd's Shore, up onto the chalk ridge to the north west topped by Oldbury hillfort. A third linear on approximately the same orientation appears to terminate on the steep scarp on the north side of Morgan's Hill. This survives only fragmentarily and its course to the south is lost, although it appears to have been partly subsumed in the line of the Wansdyke. East of this group, another linear takes a northerly course from the scarp edge east of Tan Hill to a point close to West Kennett long barrow. Two more ditches originate close together on the edge of the scarp above the spectacular combe north of Milk Hill; these run parallel to each other across the ridge behind the scarp and bracket a substantial barrow before descending the dip slope along opposite sides of a dry valley running north east.

With the exception of the last mentioned pair, the linears on this block of upland appear to divide it into large 'territories', roughly 6–7 km in length and up to 2–3 km wide. These are associated with topographically distinctive points in the landscape, particularly the high points and prominent scarp edges on the margins, but cut across the 'grain' established by the general north-east trend of the dry valleys and interfluve ridges dissecting the dip slope. The areas bounded by these linears resemble the 'strip territories' identified on Salisbury Plain (McOmish *et al* 2002, 64), although those on the Downs are on a much larger scale. There are few indications of subsidiary ditches subdividing these areas and it may be that the territories defined by the linear system on this part of the Downs were substantially larger than those on Salisbury Plain.

Individual territories on the Plain are for the most part defined by secondary ditches branching from long 'spinal' ditches which are themselves carefully located to follow significant landscape features, including watersheds, false crests on the flanks of ridges and escarpment edges (*ibid*, 57). In this area of the Marlborough Downs the

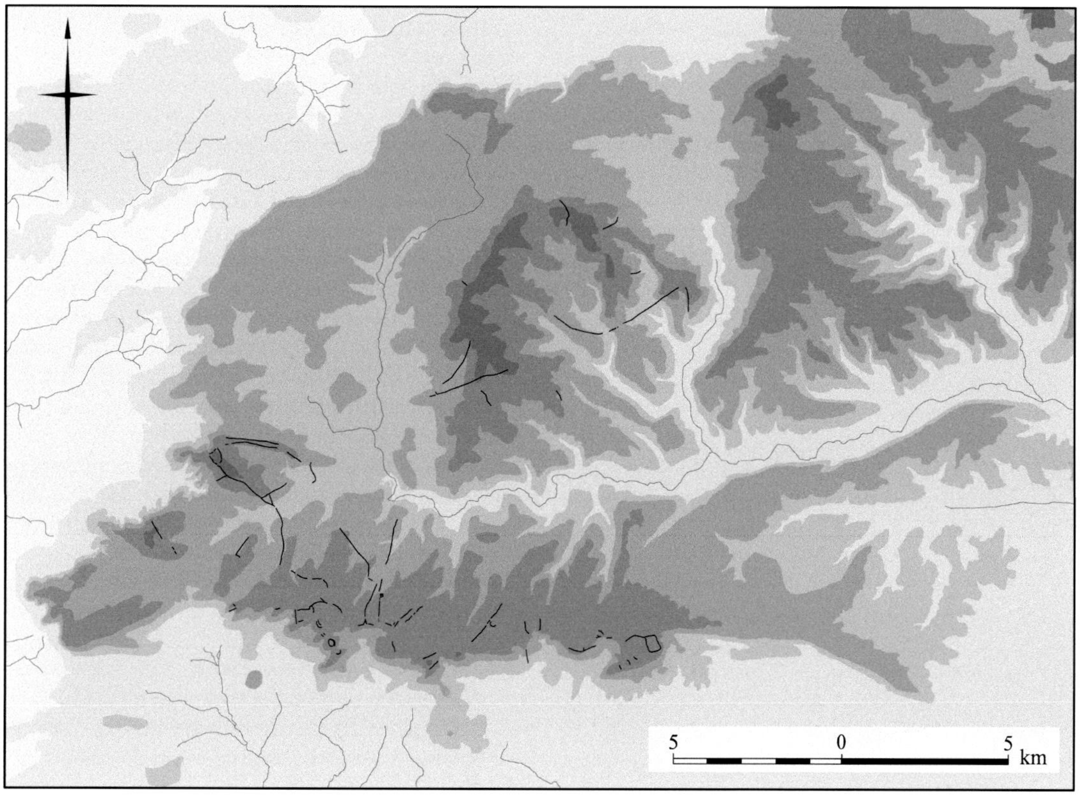

14:1 Map of the distribution of linear ditches west of the River Og. © English Heritage

distinction between spinal and other ditches is largely absent. Some short lengths of ditch running along the contour just below the crest of the scarp can be seen in the area east of Tan Hill where a number of linears terminate; these may have been intended to visually emphasise the presence of the territories beyond the scarp to observers on the lower ground to the south. While these contour-following linears along the scarp edge may once have been more extensive – there are indications that some on steeper slopes have been masked by solifluction – they are not closely comparable with the major landscape divisions represented by spinal linears elsewhere. In this area the spinal element of the linear system is effectively the southern escarpment itself.

On the northern block of the Downs a single 'long linear' can be traced cutting across the whole tract of upland in a way comparable with the ditches on the south western Downs. Its eastern terminal is on Combe Hill, a prominent high point overlooking the Og Valley which is also the focus for at least two other linears and a small barrow group. The linear runs south west to cross the sharply cut valley of the seasonal Hungerbourne stream north of Rockley, slicing through the northern end of the linear barrow cemetery along the valley floor, before turning north west and following the crest of the steep scarp on the south side of Rockley Down. It has not been traced further but appears to be oriented towards Hackpen Hill; a short length of ditch running down the steep north-west escarpment just south of Hackpen may represent its western extent.

South of this, another linear, Fowler's F4 (Fowler 2000, passim), runs roughly west-south-west – east-north-east across the western side of the higher ground. Its course has been plotted between a point about 1.5 km north east of Avebury circle, close to where a small barrow group lies on a spur of Middle Chalk, up the western flank of the higher ground and across Lockeridge Down to Totterdown, from which it may continue south east as a holloway. Fowler (2000, 19, 223) suggests, however, that a short stretch of linear earthwork on Manton Down, roughly at right angles and approximately 2 km to the east of Totterdown, may have been part of the same feature (*cf* Gingell 1992, fig. 96). If this was the case it would have divided a substantial territory to the south west from the area between it and the Combe Hill–Rockley–Hackpen earthwork.

Other linears, possibly subdivisions within these major blocks, survive in very fragmentary form. Only in the area north of the Combe Hill–Hackpen linear is it possible to suggest a series of narrow territories running roughly south west from the north east escarpment between Combe Hill and Barbury. It is not clear whether these territories extended south west across the whole sweep of the upland to meet the western arm of the major linear or perhaps terminated at a strong topographical feature such as the dry valley which bisects the higher chalk between Barbury and Rockley.

Making Spaces and Places: linears, fields and barrows

Perhaps the most striking aspect of the two major linears in the northern block of the Downs is the way in which they relate to prehistoric field systems. These are widespread in the area to the north of the Combe Hill–Hackpen linear while immediately south of it they are almost wholly absent. Similarly, the Lockeridge Down–Totterdown linear, with its possible extension to Manton Down, bounds the area covered by field systems on the southern portion of the Downs north of the Kennet, with the exception of a large block of fields on the northern side of its western terminal (Gingell 1992, fig. 96; Fowler 2000, figs. 2.1, 15.1). The origins of 'Celtic'field blocks on the Downs certainly predate the period in which linear earthworks were constructed (Gingell 1992, 155–6; Fowler 2000), although later expansion or re-organisation of field systems may have been made in reference to linears; this certainly appears to have been the case for the Roman-period field boundaries apparently laid off from the linear F4 on Totterdown (Fowler 2000, 24). It therefore appears that in this area of the Downs the creation of the major linears was effectively a re-assertion of an *earlier* large-scale partitioning of the landscape, dividing substantial areas of settlement activity to north and south from an 'empty' central zone. The divisions may have been utilitarian, with the area void of field systems reserved for grazing, say, or managed woodland; its southern extent may have been partly determined by the presence of an area of Clay-with-flints. It is also possible, however, that political, religious or customary factors underpinned the detailed geography of land use.

In the large area north of the Combe Hill–Hackpen linear, the smaller territories suggested by the pattern of secondary linears also appear to be the focus for settlement evidence – in the form of pottery spreads and 'Ogbourne'-type enclosures – and of apparently discrete blocks of fields (see Gingell 1992, fig. 96). For example, a ditch running roughly east-west divides the three Ogbourne Down enclosures and an accompanying area of surface finds of later Bronze Age pottery from another spread of pottery a few hundred metres to the north; another ditch similarly separates the Ogbourne Maizey enclosure and accompanying fields from another field block and pottery finds to the west. This pattern is repeated, although on a larger scale, in the south western area of the Downs: discrete primary blocks of 'Celtic' fields appear to be centred within the large territories defined by the major linears; there are instances of linears cutting through fields but this tends to occur on the periphery, away from the apparent centres of the field blocks. Again, the linear system in this area of the Downs appears to be giving monumental expression to broad divisions established in an earlier landscape. This interpretation echoes Entwistle's suggestion that the linear-bounded territories on the west side of the Bourne valley on Salisbury Plain were a 'formalisation of territories defined already by the disposition of Middle and Late Bronze Age settlement' (Bradley *et al* 1994, 122). There, it was suggested, the divided landscape subsequently fossilised by the linear system may in itself have been influenced by earlier territorial conceptions given expression in the distribution of Early Bronze Age round barrows (*ibid*).

The association of linear ditches with long and round barrows, well known elsewhere in Wessex, is strongly in evidence on the Marlborough Downs. There are numerous instances in which linears appear to be aligned on barrows or barrow groups, or terminate close to them. In part this association may proceed from coinciding topographic and visibility preferences in the siting of both barrows and linears; barrows may also on occasion have served as convenient sighting points in laying out linear ditches. A stronger link may be implied by instances in which a linear earthwork was routed to incorporate a barrow in its line. One of the two long linears which divide the area between the southern escarpment and the Cherhill Down–Oldbury ridge incorporates two barrows in its line within a distance of about 200m, one of them the formerly prominent multi-period barrow site on Hemp Knoll; when excavated the terminals of the linear ditch were found to have been cut to within less than a metre of the barrow's ring ditch (Robertson-Mackay 1980). The neighbouring long linear to the east (the southern terminal of which lies within a small group of barrows on the escarpment edge) incorporates two adjacent barrows within its line at the point where it makes a right-angled turn to the west as it descends the ridge of a spur on the dip slope; crossing a dry valley it turns roughly north again before making a sweeping curve to the north west around a barrow on the adjacent spur.

Such instances may simply indicate a late prehistoric parallel for the use of earlier, easily recognised and communally defined human or natural features as boundary points which is familiar from late Anglo-Saxon charters. At the same time, the repeated association of linears with barrows clearly offers the additional possibility that the territories defined by ditch systems were being symbolically linked with the legitimacy of earlier occupation and use of the land. This would be of particular significance if the creation of linear ditches was in itself a response to increasing pressure on land. Such a situation may have come about through aggressive expansion of field systems (and hence assertion of 'ownership' by particular groups or settlements) into areas traditionally regarded as communal or valued for other uses such as grazing, or, indeed, on to land seen as 'belonging' to another social group. In that instance, the imposition of a system of linears might be seen as giving monumental expression to community conceptions of how the landscape was ordered at an earlier time; repeated association with and reference to barrows would provide a symbolic expression of the rooting of the system of land division in the ancestral past.

These observations have been primarily concerned with relatively large scale territorial divisions, manifested through systems of major and subsidiary linears and covering wide areas of the Downs. However, linear earthworks were also utilised to define smaller spaces. Pollard and Reynolds (2002, 143) have drawn attention to two sites on the southern escarpment of the Downs where areas of occupation were 'framed' by relatively minor linear features: the Early Iron Age settlement site east of the Giant's Grave promontory fort was enclosed by cross-ridge dykes to east and west and an area of Late Bronze Age occupation on Golden Ball Hill was similarly hedged around with a 'network' of ditches. These sites bear comparison with the Early Iron Age settlement at Swallowcliffe Down in south Wiltshire, also ranged about with a number of short ditches (Fowler 1964).

In addition, the southern escarpment of the Downs has a number of prominent spurs with ditches cut across the 'neck' to create a form of promontory enclosure; several of these spurs have one or more barrows located within or close to the enclosed area. Examples include Easton Hill, where a round barrow lies within the area enclosed by a short ditch, and Kitchen Barrow Hill, where the long barrow is similarly enclosed; here there is also a round barrow immediately outside the linear. At Milk Hill the sites of two barrows are recorded within the area enclosed by the cross ridge ditch and on the northern edge of the south western block of the Downs a narrow spur just west of Oldbury hillfort has a ditch and bank cutting off an area in which four or five barrows are grouped.

Again on the southern scarp, Walker's Hill is spectacularly crowned by the knife-edge profile of Adam's Grave long barrow, which, noted Hoare (1821, 29n), 'differs from all others, in being evidently guarded by a bank and ditch on each side'. A linear earthwork more than 12m across follows the saddle between the hill and the scarp of the Downs to the north; its eastern end was probably close to a small barrow group at the head of the spectacular combe west of Knap Hill. Another bank and ditch *c*11m across runs for 250m roughly parallel to the first across the southern slope of the hill with a probable bowl barrow sited immediately north of it within the enclosed area. The largest barrow group along the southern edge of the Downs is located on a steep sided promontory immediately south of Gopher Wood. Here there is no indication of a ditch across the neck of the spur (the large linear within the wood to the north is most probably an outlier of the Late Iron Age multiple ditch complex centred to the east on Oare Hill) but a short ditch and bank *c*11m across runs across the base of the spur directly below the barrows. Above this there is a marked step or terrace apparently cut into the slope; this may be geological in origin, marking the junction of the Middle and Lower Chalk, but could be a further linear feature.

Here, within a relatively confined area, we have a clustering of topographically distinctive places, previously utilised as the location for highly visible funerary monuments, which are further marked out from the wider landscape by short ditches. Enclosure of these spaces may have been functional, perhaps simply intended to bar access for secular activities such as stock grazing. Alternatively, the primary significance of enclosure may have been to signify that these prominent monuments, clearly visible from the lower ground below the scarp and carrying their own links to an ancestral past, were incorporated into the bounded landscape. It is, of course, only the form of the cross-ridge boundaries which links them to the wider networks of linear ditches and suggests that they may form part of the same conception and process of landscape organisation and are therefore of roughly comparable date. Vyner (1995) has drawn attention to the strong association between cross-ridge dykes and large cairns on steep sided promontories in north-east Yorkshire, and concluded that the linear features may have been contemporary with, or may even have preceded, the Early Bronze Age date for the burial mounds. In the case of the Marlborough Downs, however, the fact that both long and round barrows are treated similarly perhaps indicates a date for their symbolic enclosure in the later prehistoric period, when both types of monument were regarded as equivalent tokens of the past. It is worth noting that cross-ridge dykes in Sussex

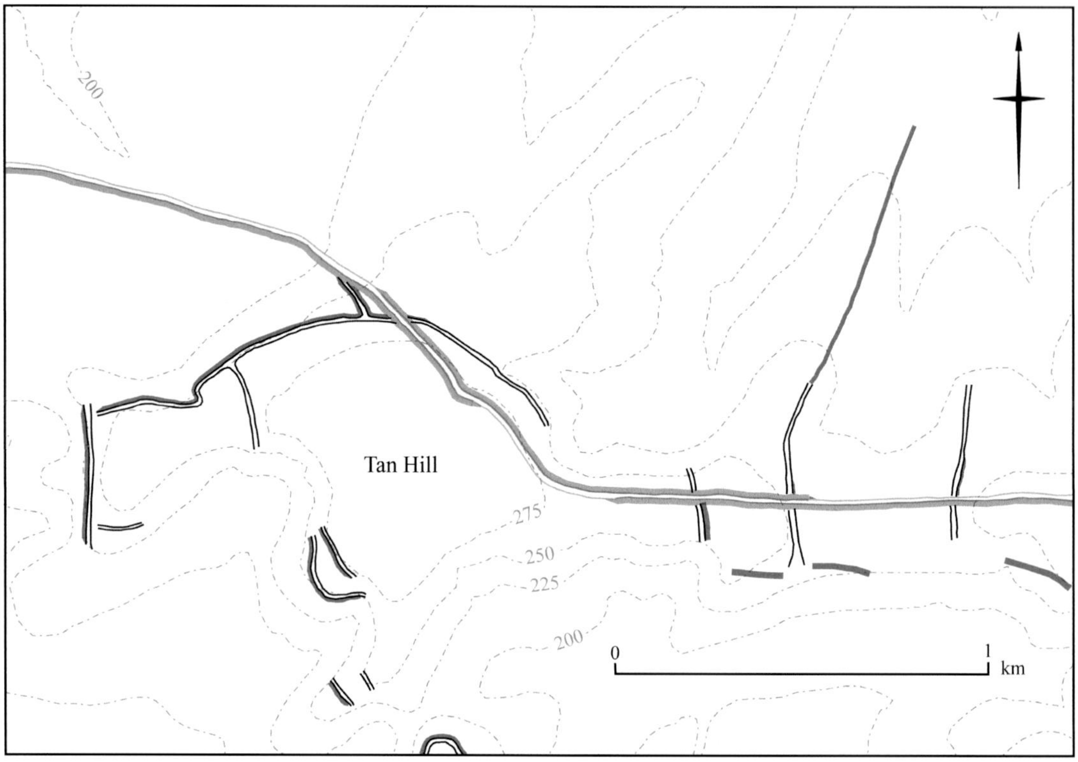

14:2 Linear ditches on and around Tan Hill. © English Heritage

are now placed in the first quarter of the first millennium BC (Hamilton & Gregory 2000, 61, 63) and Fowler (1964; 1965) suggested a possible Early Iron Age date for cross-ridge and spur dykes on the Ebble–Nadder ridge in south Wiltshire; two prominent spurs on the northern scarp of this ridge are the focus of barrow groups, both are cut across by one or more linear earthworks.

The most complex grouping of linear earthworks likely to be of this broad Late Bronze Age – Early Iron Age horizon on the Marlborough Downs is that on and around Tan Hill (Fig 14:2). A number of longer linears terminate on the escarpment east of the hill, an area also marked out by contour-following linears on the upper edge of the scarp and the presence of a number of round barrows. One of the few bivallate ditches in the study area is in the same vicinity, apparently running only a short distance across the narrow ridge but probably descending into the steep sided combe to the north. The summit area, one of the highest points on the southern escarpment and highly visible from within the Downs and from the vale to the south, is partially enclosed by a number of separate, unconnected linear features. Some of these may have been intended to control access but others such as the pair which run almost parallel, one above the other, across the south-west face of the hill are likely to have been aimed at enhancing the visibility of the token enclosure of the hilltop. A ditch runs in a wide arc around the northern flank of the hill; a branch from this running north west is overlain by Wansdyke. This feature could have continued as a long linear, perhaps connecting to an isolated length of ditch identified on Horton Down to the north, but it may be that Wansdyke itself followed and now marks the course of an earlier ditch for some distance, as it appears to have done south of Morgan's Hill. Hoare (1821, 123) noted a section cut through Wansdyke, almost certainly to the west of Tan Hill, which appeared to show an earlier bank underlying the rampart. The dimensions he recorded indicate a substantially larger bank than those accompanying most linear ditches, however, and it is perhaps more probable that Wansdyke itself is of more than one phase here.

Field (2001, 61) has suggested that Tan Hill and a small number of comparable sites may have been 'special' places intended for gatherings of large numbers of people or animals, perhaps earlier forms of the sheep and pleasure fairs which were held there in the later historic period. A number of Middle and Late Bronze Age metalwork finds recorded from the vicinity (Barber, this vol) could relate to such activity but may also hint at deposition associated with ceremonial or ritual activity. The possibility of large-scale communal feasting as an element in the use of such places draws attention to the proximity of the probable Early Iron Age midden site at All Cannings Cross, below the scarp just to the south of Tan Hill (Lawson 2000, 265).

Field also emphasised the significance of deliberate incorporation of references to the past in a variety of sites of the later prehistoric period (2001, *passim*). At Tan Hill, it is notable that the most boldly defined area in the complex is a steep-sided spur to the west of the summit, crowned by a group of at least four barrows (Fig 14:2). This has a ditch across its southern slope, towards the Vale, with another running north – south along the western flank. A third ditch across the northern side of the spur is itself the western end of the earthwork which runs around the whole of the dip slope flank of the Tan Hill summit. A branch running south from this linear cuts across the neck of the spur topped by the barrow group. This subsidiary hilltop, visible a short distance to the west from the summit area of Tan Hill, is therefore marked out on all sides by linear ditches. These are not ramparts and the site is not 'defended' or enclosed in any functional sense: the ditches on the south and west sides approach but do not connect or intersect with each other or with those to the north and north east; at the point where the linear around the northern side of the spur approaches that on the western side there is a vertical interval between them on the hillslope of some metres. These ditches and banks, scarped into the slope, do, however, serve to monumentalise the already distinctive natural feature on which the barrows are located: these linear elements are still highly visible as earthworks and when freshly dug from the chalk would have been conspicuous over a wide area, giving the site a special emphasis within the wider Tan Hill complex.

Conclusion

Linear earthworks are clearly important elements in understanding the archaeology of the Late Bronze Age – Early Iron Age but are also significant across other periods. The territories they define are likely to have fossilised earlier patterns of settlement and land use, perhaps originating from the initial establishment of permanent agricultural settlements on the downland. Elements within these landscape divisions conceivably derive from even earlier perceptions of territoriality manifested in the location of barrows. Subsequently, linears were integral elements of the multiple ditch complexes of the later Iron Age (Ritchie 1971; Corney 1989; 1997b; Barrett *et al* 1991, 232–6); these may themselves represent elaborations of an earlier type of linear-associated site such as Tan Hill. The incorporation of linear components in these monuments (as in the case of the complex of banjo and other enclosures on the northern margins of Aldbourne Chase, east of Ogbourne St George) may in itself have provided them with an important symbolic link to the past. On Salisbury Plain a number of linears were utilised as the 'main streets' of Romano-British villages (McOmish *et al* 2002, 65); this may have been entirely pragmatic but perhaps even here some sense of their earlier significance persisted. In the Anglo-Saxon period some linear ditches were still meaningful as boundary markers and the earthworks could also be significant points in the landscape for the display and disposal of victims of judicial execution, as in the case of a skeleton, apparently with hands tied behind its back, recovered from the ditch of one of the linears on Tan Hill (Anon 1951; Reynolds 1999, 105–6).

This longer perspective offers an oblique reminder that the fragments of linears which can now be identified are likely to derive from a succession of 'systems', created, altered, maintained and abandoned, with potentially fundamental changes in the significance and associations of individual components over that time. Much additional investigation is required in order to see this 'process' element more clearly, understanding the possible significance of morphological differences between linears, identifying sequences and achieving finer resolution on both relative and absolute chronologies. There is also a need for further investigation of the conceptions underpinning the way in which linears were laid out in relation to topography and other monuments; GIS and allied technology are likely to provide significant potential for advances here.

Finally, it is worth remembering that boundaries 'work' in a variety of ways. A churchyard wall, for example, marks the edge of a sacred space in which unnumbered generations of a community's ancestors are buried and where rituals for the newly dead are regularly carried out; the wall also keeps cows out. It is clear that in many situations linears were constructed with particular reference to topography and to earlier landscape divisions and monuments. This is to emphasise their symbolic and social significance, but perhaps at the expense of perceiving that some elements may also have had practical functions as boundaries and physical barriers. The paired linears which frame the head of the steep-sided dry valley which ascends the dip slope between Thorn Hill and Furze Hill, south of East Kennett village, for example, could perhaps have been used to channel herds or flocks driven over the scarp between the Kennet valley and Pewsey Vale. The fact that the two ditches enclose a barrow between them where they converge close to the edge of the scarp, however, suggests that a full understanding of their functions and significance may be more complex.

15
The middle Iron Age on the Marlborough Downs

Mark Bowden

The Marlborough Downs are apparently wealthy in remains of Iron Age date. However, this apparent richness is questioned and instead it is suggested that much of the area may have been peripheral, for settlement and agriculture at least, during the middle Iron Age. If this view is correct and the major Neolithic ceremonial constellation of sites was deliberately avoided in the Iron Age, this has important implications for our understanding of belief systems in that period. A localised and individual historical view of Iron Age social groups is urged and a less rigidly hierarchical view of middle Iron Age society is hinted at.

Introduction

Comparatively little is known of the Iron Age on the Marlborough Downs. This is despite the presence, on the southern edge of the area, of All Cannings Cross – a site pre-eminent in the literature of the period for 70 years or so – of seven hillforts, about fifteen enclosures (some of them well preserved earthworks), numerous linear ditches and acres of 'Celtic' fields.

A glance at the *Map of Southern Britain in the Iron Age* (Ordnance Survey 1967) also suggests that the area is exceedingly rich in chance finds. However, this might be – in part – a 'factoid' resulting from the activities of a few diligent collectors (see, for instance, Swanton 1987). There are concentrations of La Tène *fibulae* to the east of Avebury and west of Beckhampton (Chadburn & Corney 2001a, 22) but the areas adjacent to the major Neolithic ceremonial constellation are distinctly poor in Iron Age material culture. Not a single Iron Age sherd has been recorded in all the excavations at Avebury (Burl 1979, 264 n37). Nevertheless, there is some evidence of Iron Age activity – predominantly late – around Silbury Hill (Chadburn & Corney 2001a, 22), foreshadowing the abundant evidence for Romano-British activity, and indeed settlement, in the same area. This deposition, largely of metalwork, may relate to the watery context (see Fitzpatrick 1984) of the head of the Kennet, rather than to the proximity of Silbury Hill. One could suggest, on the other hand, that these brooches, coins and urn are *not* evidence for Iron Age activity, but that they were curated items, which properly belong with the Romano-British deposits. (Another La Tène I brooch was found in 1897 at West Kennet 'near' a bronze coin of Antoninus Pius (Goddard 1908b)).

While the field systems on the Lambourn Downs to the east were formed largely in the Roman period (Bowden *et al* 1993; Crutchley this vol) those on the Marlborough Downs have a much longer currency, beginning in the Bronze Age (Gingell 1992, 155; McOmish this volume). The well preserved system on Burderop Down, which Gingell states is of Iron Age and Romano-British date (1992, 38), extends westwards towards Barbury hillfort and some scarps outside the north-eastern edge of the fort may be part of it. Fort and fields may be broadly contemporary but no earthwork relationship can be discerned (Bowden 1998, 5, 9) and evidence elsewhere suggests that a middle Iron Age date for the use of such fields is unlikely (Richard Bradley *pers comm*).

Clearly the landscape was not a void in the Iron Age (Fig 15:1). There are the hillforts and enclosures, All Cannings Cross and the other unenclosed settlements. So what is the problem? It is not entirely lack of research, though here that has tended – naturally – to concentrate on the earlier prehistoric periods. None of the hillforts has seen a *major* modern excavation. Two of the enclosures have been excavated, as, of course, has All Cannings Cross. In some cases

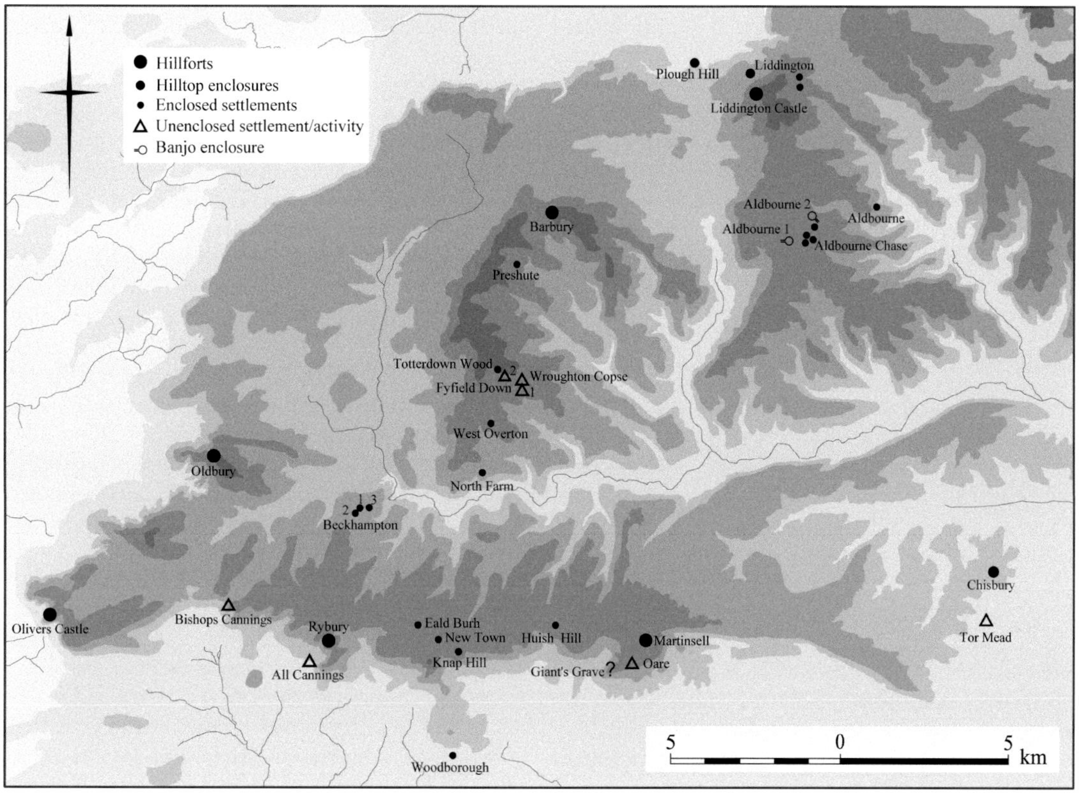

Fig 15:1 Location of Iron Age sites mentioned in the text.

publication has been tardy and less than user-friendly. There is a slightly better record of survey – aerial, geophysical and topographical – but little synthesis has yet emerged. The forthcoming All Cannings Cross research project (D McOmish *pers comm*) will make a major difference here undoubtedly, for the early Iron Age at least.

The main problem, of course, is the paucity or, in some cases, complete lack of dating evidence. How many of those enclosures and field systems are, in fact, of Iron Age origin or use? And if they *are* Iron Age, where within that range do they fall?

Open settlement

The most under-represented and under-studied element in the landscape of the Iron Age, as of the Bronze Age, is unenclosed settlement. Within the study area there are half a dozen known or suspected open sites but there is little understanding of them. All Cannings Cross has received the most attention, but this is known for the pottery style to which it has given its name (Cunliffe 1991, 64–5), rather than for the site itself.

The excavations discovered pits, postholes, ovens and the floors of rectangular buildings. Finds of all types were numerous (M and B Cunnington 1923). The site was occupied in the earliest Iron Age, from the 9th century BC onwards. McOmish has recently suggested that the site is not simply a domestic/agricultural settlement but is akin to the specialised ritual 'midden' deposits of central Wiltshire (1996, 73). Two other sites within the present study area are also included on McOmish's map (*ibid*, fig .1) as 'middens' – Bishops Cannings (Robinson & Swanton 1993) and Martinsell. The latter site lies just to the east of Giant's Grave (Meyrick 1947, 256–7) and is part of a complex with both early and late Iron Age elements. Further work at All Cannings Cross will throw much needed new light on this enigmatic and important phenomenon of the Bronze Age/Iron Age transitional period.

A group of open settlements near Wroughton Copse on Fyfield Down dates to the Iron Age (Chadburn & Corney 2001a, 22) and the same area is part of the Romano-British settlement pattern. Finds indicate activity in the early and mid Iron Age (Meyrick 1947, 258–60), but there may be a hiatus in the late Iron Age. There appears to be some confusion regarding the identity and dating of these sites in the literature; though at least one of them is mentioned by Bowen and Fowler (1963; 1966), Fowler (2000) does not discuss them, perhaps because they have been subsumed within the ambit of the Roman period. Stray finds and isolated features give hints of further open settlement sites, as at Tor Mead,

Great Bedwyn (Grinsell 1957, 73) and Beckhampton Down (H Cunnington 1887a). It has been suggested that there are one or more possible enclosures on Beckhampton Down (NMR: SU 06 NE 124 and 204). It is now well established that during the Iron Age some settlements oscillated between open, partly enclosed and fully enclosed states (Bowden & McOmish 1987, 81; Haselgrove 2001, 56).

Enclosed settlement

There are fifteen or more enclosures of certain or possible Iron Age date within the study area. Two have been excavated – one adjacent to Knap Hill causewayed enclosure (M Cunnington 1911, 49–51, 57–8, 62–5), and Overton Down (Fowler 2000, 'OD XI'). It has been suggested that a rectangular enclosure to the east of Liddington Castle at SU 220 797 (NMR aerial photos SU 2279/3, 4, 5) was also excavated in the early 1970s, but no reliable information about this event is known to the writer. An enclosure which can confidently be accepted as Iron Age, on morphological grounds, is North Farm or 'Headlands' (Bowen and Fowler 1963, 101). Another enclosure, at Aldbourne, which appears to be of 'Little Woodbury' type, has been recorded by aerial photography (NMR: SU 27 NW 27; Knight 2001, 20–1). Of the others, Huish Hill, the Eald Burh, New Town, Preshute Down, and other examples at Aldbourne, might be Bronze Age, Romano-British or, in some cases, medieval rather than Iron Age. David McOmish is of the opinion that the New Town enclosure is probably not of Iron Age date (*pers comm*); see also Smith, this volume. Those on Woodborough Hill (NMR: SU 16 SW 50) and Beckhampton Down are of doubtful existence, let alone date. Fowler (2000, 224) suggests the existence of another enclosure just by the south-west corner of Totterdown Wood and, more tentatively, another south of the Kennet on Lurkeley Hill. These he believes to be analogous to 'OD XI'.

Overton Down XI (Fowler 2000, 82–92, 224) is a 'tombstone-shaped' ditched enclosure lying within a pre-existing field system and over an open late Bronze Age settlement. It contained pits, postholes and hollows, and a succession of circular buildings. It is dated to the 8th–6th centuries BC by the ceramics found. After abandonment the site reverted to arable, and then pasture.

The oval 'Headlands' enclosure has produced surface finds of similar date and Fowler speculates that it could have become the dominant Iron Age settlement of the Fyfield/Overton area with a central role in the control of livestock (2000, 59–60, 224–5). This view is coloured by interpretations of parallel 'Little Woodbury/Gussage All Saints' sites. However, there is as yet no mid-late Iron Age evidence from this site.

There is some suggestion of clustering within the distribution of enclosures but until there is some chronological control the possible significance of this patterning will not be understood. The apparent pairing of oval and rectangular enclosures, which is seen here to the east of Liddington Castle, for instance, is a widespread phenomenon but one which has not been studied in detail.

There are two 'banjo' enclosures within the study area, both at Aldbourne and both now visible only as cropmarks (NMR: SU 27 NW 26 and 53; Knight 2001, 19–20). They are also part of what was apparently a larger settlement complex, including other curvilinear enclosures and field systems, integrated with the linear ditches to the south of Liddington Castle (Colt Hoare 1821, 39; Grinsell 1957, 261). Though late Iron Age linear earthworks are a very different phenomenon from their late Bronze Age predecessors, here it is possible that the earlier linears, discarded in the early Iron Age, have been re-incorporated within a later Iron Age system. There is no secure dating evidence for these sites and, while banjos are usually thought of as late Iron Age phenomena, the dating of the class is not necessarily that tight. Nevertheless, having regard to Mark Corney's work on late Iron Age multiple ditch systems and their affinities (1989), as well as the range of chance finds from the area, one would be happy to assign a late date to this complex.

On the bench of Lower Chalk immediately to the north of Liddington Castle is a large, double-ditched curvilinear enclosure, visible only as a cropmark (aerial photographs 106G/UK/1416/4105–6; RAF 58/3162/0118–0120; NMR SU 2080/6–8, 14). It measures approximately 170m east-west by 120m transversely and is therefore considerably larger than the enclosures mentioned above. Is this a 'hilltop enclosure' or proto-hillfort?

Another interesting, recently discovered site that merits attention is on Plough Hill, Chiseldon (NMR: SU 18 SE 121). A curving ditch, showing as a cropmark, cuts off the end of the hill and possibly extends along the sides. It has a single, south-facing entrance inturned slightly on one side. There are faint indications of a rampart and palisade backing the ditch but no visible internal features. This is a large enclosure, measuring 200–300m across, and might also be classed as a 'hilltop enclosure'. These large enclosures lead us into the consideration of hillforts.

Hillforts

Giant's Grave has usually been listed as a promontory fort (*e.g.* Forde-Johnstone 1976, 213). There seems to be no compelling reason to accept this classification, as the 'Grave' is a cross-ridge dyke and there is little sign of a rampart, no matter how slight, completing the circuit. Nevertheless, it is an important site. The dyke, which is only one of a series of earthworks dividing the ridge, is massive and effectively bars view and access to the spur for anyone approaching from the east. Whatever activities were taking place on that spur were restricted.

The hillforts lying within the study area are, therefore, Barbury, Chisbury, Liddington, Martinsell, Oldbury, Oliver's Castle and Rybury. No two are alike. All that they have in common is a hill or spur location and the presence of substantial ramparts (and the word 'substantial' must be interpreted widely enough to encompass the slight Oliver's Castle as well as the massive Barbury and Oldbury). Martinsell is perhaps the earliest of the series and should perhaps properly be called a 'hilltop enclosure' rather than a hillfort, though it also has signs of later Iron Age and Romano-British activity. It is also the centre of a major complex, including Giant's Grave and the nearby early 'midden' mentioned above, the late 'midden' at Withy Copse, and the linear ditches running along the scarp edge towards Huish Hill. Oldbury is a splendid but poorly understood site. Its curious shape, while it is partly dictated by the topography, seems to owe much to the pre-existing – and presumably late Bronze Age – linear ditches which approach the hill from several directions. These seem to have influenced the line of the ramparts. For a parallel analysis of Casterley Camp see Field 2001, 61; a similar phenomenon has also been demonstrated at Alfred's Castle (Gary Lock, *pers comm*). Finds from cursory excavations (H Cunnington 1887b; W Cunnington 1893) seem to indicate activity mainly in the earlier part of the Iron Age, but the sample is small.

Despite the lack of *major* modern excavation (there was a small excavation at Liddington Castle in 1976), Barbury, Liddington, Martinsell, Oldbury and Oliver's Castle have been subject to recent geophysical survey (A Payne *pers comm*). Analytical earthwork survey has, additionally, been carried out at the first two named.

Barbury Castle (Bowden 1998) is a bivallate fort with a third, outer escarpment (possibly the vestige of a pre-existing enclosure) on the north side. There are two entrances, east and west, and there is a forework outside the east entrance (this forework also possibly formed from a pre-existing enclosure). A small barrow cemetery to the west may originally have extended into the area of the fort – at least one slight mound (Fig 15:2a) survives in the interior. The interior of the fort also exhibits numerous slight earthwork features, and geophysical survey has indicated a considerable density of sub-surface features. Though some of these, both surface and sub-surface, are certainly due to recent activity (especially during the Second World War), many probably relate to the prehistoric use of the site. Up to 35 hut circles can be seen as earthworks and a further six were found by geophysical survey. It is probable that those discovered by geophysics relate to an earlier period of occupation. The possibility that the hillfort as we see it overlies an earlier 'hilltop enclosure' is of interest; similar features have been recorded at other Wessex hillforts, most relevantly in this context Uffington and Segsbury (Lock and Gosden 1997a, 68; 1997b, 76). The enclosures on Plough Hill and below Liddington might be similar sites which never became fully fledged forts. Martinsell, too, as suggested above, might be placed in this category. Barbury ranks as a 'developed' hillfort, both by reason of its bivallation and because of the density of internal features, which contrasts with the neighbours – Liddington, Uffington, Oldbury and especially Oliver's Castle, which has been termed an 'empty' hillfort on the strength of the geophysical evidence (Payne forthcoming). That the defences at Barbury are of at least two phases is demonstrated by the forework, which is cut and overlain by the outer rampart. This confirms what would be expected – that a 'developed' hillfort should show signs of its 'development'. Furthermore, the inner and outer ramparts differ in the width of their crests and the outer rampart has been severely robbed, suggesting that it may have been faced with desirable materials and may therefore have had a very different appearance originally. A few chance finds are datable to the early or middle Iron Age (Meyrick 1947, 260; Grinsell 1957, 94; Anon 1971, 197) but the hoard of ironwork, previously dated to 200–50BC (MacGregor and Simpson 1963) is now thought to be a late Roman votive deposit (M Corney *pers comm*).

Liddington Castle (Bowden 2001) is a univallate fort in a similar location to Barbury. The excavations found evidence for an early date for the first phase of the rampart, in the 7th century BC, with three subsequent phases of uncertain date (Hirst and Rahtz 1996, 29–30, 52). This early date is matched at other 'ridgeway' hillforts, notably Uffington and Segsbury (Lock & Gosden 1997a, 66; 1997b, 76). As at Barbury, there are signs of earlier activity on the site, but here they take the form of linear ditches (Fig 15:3, a, a, a) rather than barrows. These are probably late Bronze Age boundaries. In other cases such boundaries are

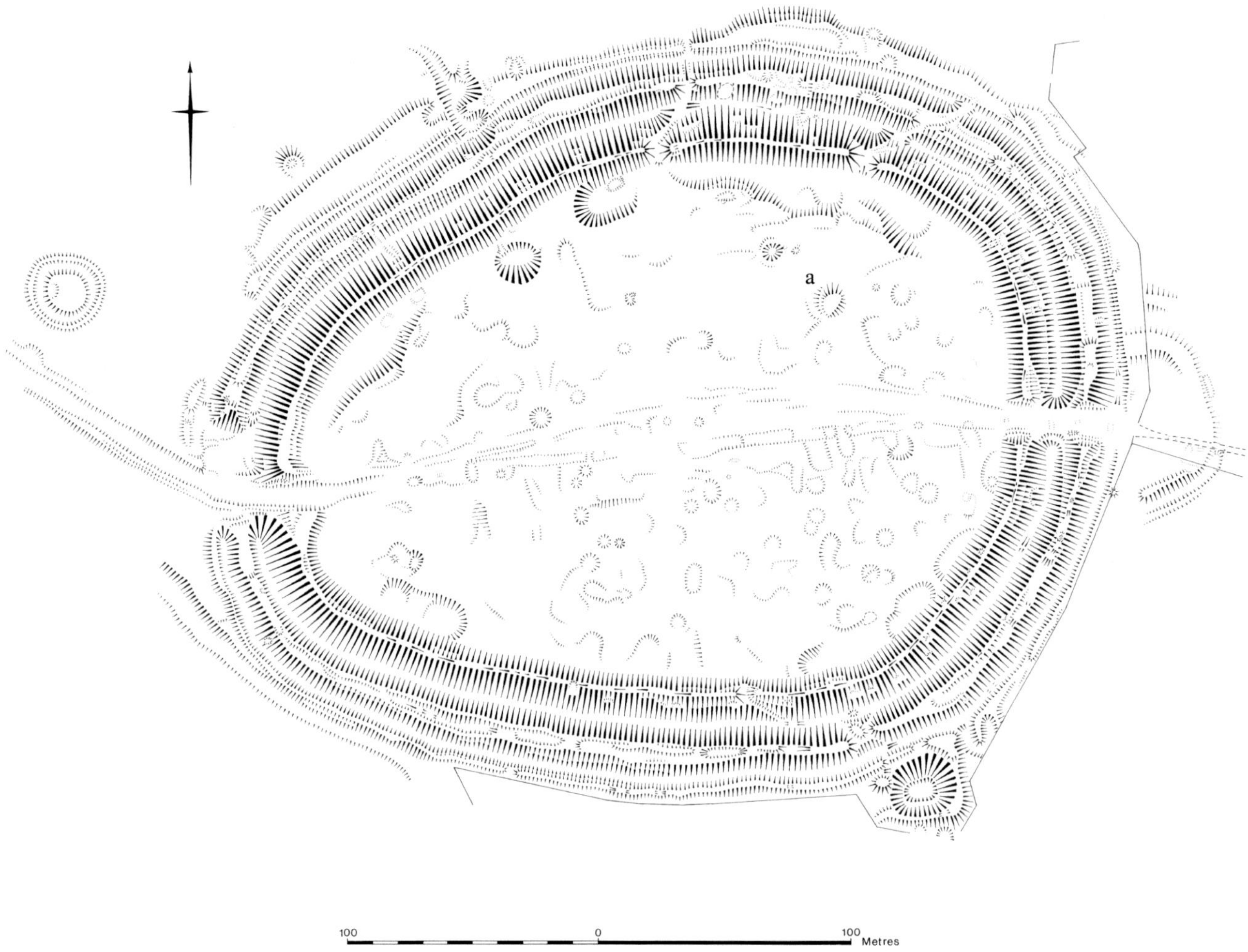

15:2 Barbury © Cropwn Copyright NMR. A full description and inter pretation of the earthworks can be found in Bowden (1998).

contemporary with 'pre-hillfort enclosures' but the sequence is sometimes more complex, as at Quarley where the 'pre-hillfort enclosure' overlies three of the linears (Hawkes 1939). When the builders of hillforts placed their new constructions over the intersections of these boundaries, were they assimilating the boundaries, or trying to 'kill' them? Were they staking claims to larger territories or, more radically, denying that sort of territorial thinking altogether? Were they, alternatively, deliberately placing their forts on the peripheries of territories which continued to exist although the physical markers were allowed to decay?

There is relatively little sign of prehistoric activity in the interior of Liddington, either as visible surface remains or as responses to geophysical survey. This may be partly explained by the intrusive activities of 19th-century flint diggers on the site, but it may also be a true reflection of a lower level, and shorter period, of activity here than at Barbury. Though the rampart was clearly re-built and modified on several occasions the counterscarp bank has the 'lumpiness' characteristic of unfinished earthworks, and this adds to the feeling that the life of this hillfort may have been short.

Barbury had opposed eastern and western entrances. The same was probably true of Liddington, though there the western entrance (Fig 15:3b) appears to have been blocked in antiquity. The eastern entrance at Barbury was covered by a forework while the western one was not. Colt Hoare explained this in military terms – the steep approach from the west negating the need for extra defences (1821, 41). It may be, however, that the east entrance was regarded as the 'principal' entrance – and the same can be argued at Liddington – and had to be screened for symbolic purposes as much as for defensive ones. The orientation of hillfort entrances has been discussed recently by Hill (1996, 110). A symbolic or cosmological aspect to east- and west-facing entrances is likely. This also extends to house entrances but at Barbury the houses, so far as can be ascertained from the surface evidence, do not conform to the expected Iron Age pattern

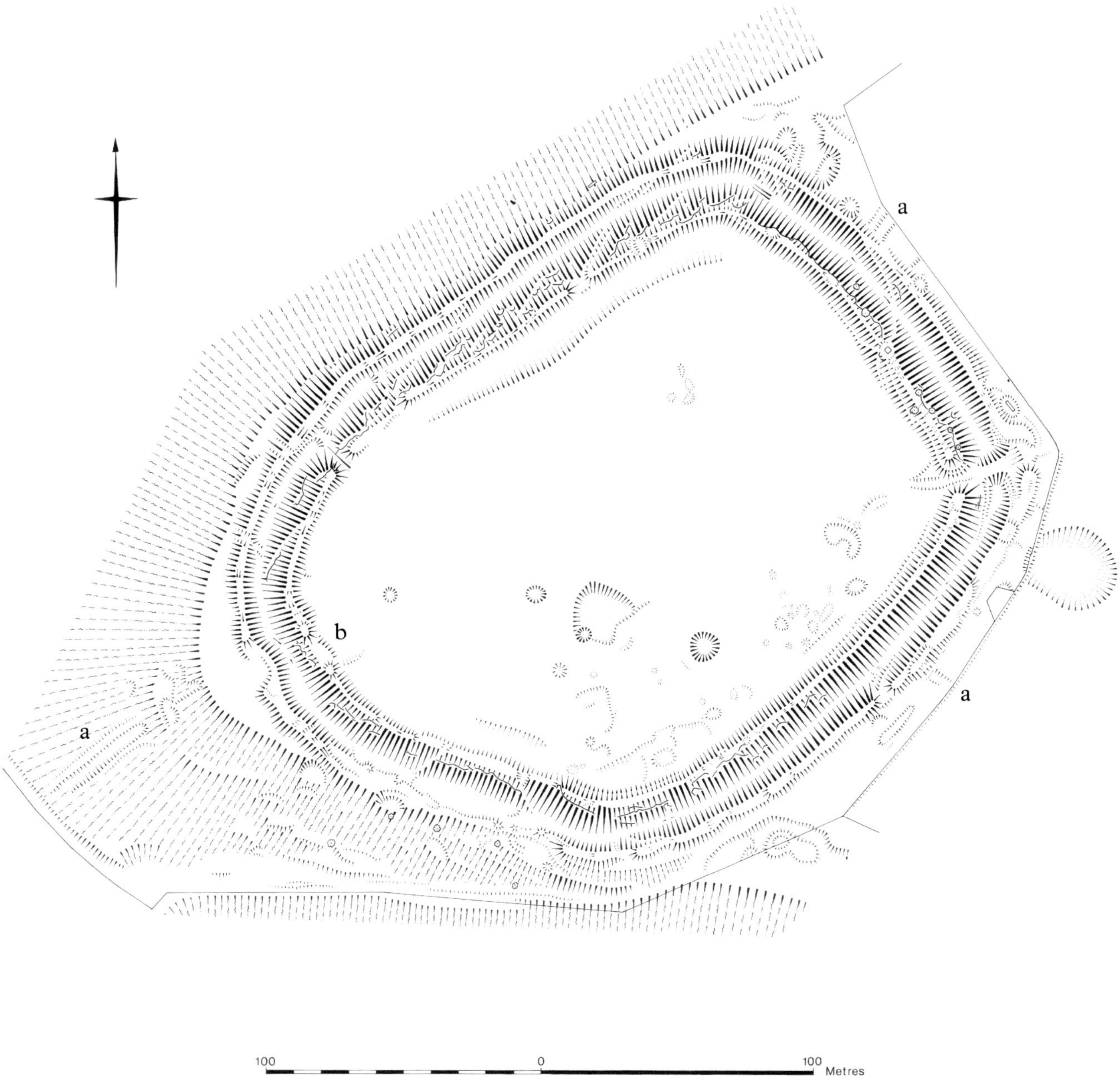

15:3 Liddington Castle © English Heritage. A full description and inter pretation of the earthworks can be found in Bowden (2001).

of orientation to the east or south-east. Instead the entrances seem to face the adjacent rampart so that, while about six houses face south-east, as many as nine face west or north. This is very different from the pattern on most other hillforts and smaller enclosures. However, other sites in Wessex which are exceptional in this way include, perhaps significantly, the 'developed' hillforts of Danebury (Hants), Maiden Castle and Pilsdon Pen (Dorset) (Hill 1996, 104; see also Oswald 1997).

The hillforts appear to be distributed around the edge of the study area. Of course, this is partly an illusion created by the arbitrary boundary – these forts are part of a larger world. Nevertheless, it does reflect a real pattern, that the majority of the hillforts occupy positions on the edges of the high ground, overlooking the vales to either side – Oliver's Castle, small and slight though it is, provides a spectacular example of this. This positioning was appreciated by Stukeley, who described the 'ridgeway' hillforts as 'the eyesore and terror of the plain' (1776, 140). The deliberate choice of this liminal positioning, exploiting and perhaps in some way controlling the resources of both the uplands and the lowlands, does help to explain the distribution of these sites. This is an answer to the question of why Windmill Hill, for instance, has no hillfort. By the same token, however, it fails to explain why Knap Hill has no hillfort. This topographical line of argument runs counter to the view that there is significance in the re-use of earlier significant sites – in this case causewayed enclosures particularly, as at Rybury (Oswald *et al* 2001, 101, 141). Neither geographical determinism nor legitimation through re-use of ancient places fully explains the patterning we observe. One is left with the feeling that we are missing something, and that we have not yet begun to comprehend in any real sense the phenomena of the hillforts. Maybe the search for a 'pattern' is itself the problem. It is important not to think of hillforts in an anthropomorphic way and make facile statements about hillforts 'dominating territories', 'succeeding' and 'developing' or, on the other hand, 'failing'. Instead we might think in terms of community – each hillfort is the response of a social group (or its decision-making part) to local circumstances, hence the variety of form that we observe and the variety of fates. Some communities move on in one direction and find that they no longer need hillforts while others take a different path and aggrandize their ramparts.

Discussion

This is not the time to make statements about the earliest Iron Age on the Marlborough Downs. Current research based around All Cannings Cross would render them redundant in a very short space of time. One outstanding question, among many, concerns the role of the linear ditches, such as those around Tan Hill for instance, and their demise (if that is what it is) at the hands of the builders of the first hillforts (Kirkham this vol). The people of the middle Iron Age in this region, unlike their immediate predecessors and successors, had no apparent use for such physical linear boundaries in the landscape. The lack of evidence for use of 'Celtic' fields in the middle Iron Age as well, here (see below) as in other parts of the country, may be related.

For the early-middle Iron Age, attempts to create a hierarchical model of settlement – hillforts: enclosed settlements: unenclosed settlements – have not worked. Either we cannot recognise the signs of status that were employed – they may not have been fine pottery and metalwork, or large buildings and earthworks, the things that are archaeologically easiest to see – or there was no such hierarchy (though Iron Age society itself is always assumed to have been rigidly hierarchical – but see Hill (1995) for an alternative view).

Peter Fowler has pointed out the irony that areas such as Fyfield Down are constantly cited by archaeologists as survivals of arable farming systems of the past, whereas the arable remains that we see are preserved precisely because these were relatively short episodes in the long, predominantly pastoral, history of the landscape. He suggests that the lack of evidence for activity during the middle Iron Age in the Fyfield and Overton area is related to a change from predominantly arable land use to pastoralism, related to the *floruit* of the hillforts, and cites Salisbury Plain as a possible parallel (2000, 225). It is at least possible, given the paucity of securely dated sites, that this observation is more widely applicable to the study area. However, this needs to be tested. Were the Neolithic and early Bronze Age ceremonial centres deliberately shunned in the Iron Age? As Chadburn & Corney argue (2001b, 67), this is a fundamental question bearing on ideas of the sacred and profane in Iron Age society. Negative evidence is always problematical and it would be both difficult and counter-productive to formulate a project designed not to find anything. A systematic programme of field-walking, however, such as is now being promoted (D Field *pers comm*), to record fluctuating land-use through all periods, will be an important first step towards a clearer view of this issue.

If the area was peripheral in the middle Iron Age this is of some interest for the development of the major late Iron Age centre at Forest Hill (and the complex including the Aldbourne 'banjos'). Haselgrove has argued that important late Iron Age centres often developed in areas on the margins of existing settlement (2001, 44). There is little doubt that there is a major break in the society of Britain round about 100BC, with new forms of settlement and the radically new concepts of coinage and kingship. The late Iron Age is a very different period in every way from the early and middle Iron Age. It has to be treated separately, in relation to the phenomenon of the expanding influence of Rome.

The remarks made in this paper about the current paucity of our knowledge and understanding of the Iron Age, and the unanswered questions, are in no way pessimistic or defeatist. On the contrary, they are intended to be challenging. There is a lot of work to do, in field and library. There is, however, a logical problem with pleas for further data gathering in archaeology. The evidence is fragmentary, by its nature. We will never have 'enough', so it is imperative that we use what we have creatively and intelligently to tell the story of the past. Nevertheless, there is a case to be made for further, targetted, field research. Serendipity is a wonderful aid to archaeology – chance discoveries and chance associations of ideas have given rise to major advances in our understanding – but it would be foolish to rely on such events. That is why Research Designs of the sort that have now been developed for the Avebury World Heritage Site are so important – they should allow us to target our limited resources in the most effective manner. I would endorse the recommendations put forward for the Iron Age in the *Research Agenda* (Chadburn & Corney 2001b), though I would add Oldbury and its environs to the high priority list for earthwork survey.

We have, however, a potentially interesting story to tell, of how the Marlborough Downs were regarded and used in the Iron Age. There was a ring of forts whose occupants, no doubt frequently in conflict with one another, looked out to the surrounding vales at least as much as they looked inward to the high chalk. Some of these forts were built very early in the Iron Age, and their creation implies a changing attitude to the use and division of the land. Some of the forts were occupied for a long time, others hardly at all (in any way that we can recognise at present), perhaps intermittently, perhaps seasonally, each reflecting a separate and distinct history of a local group. The people were predominantly pastoralists, inhabiting also a scatter of farms – none of them very long-lived perhaps – across the Downs; a shifting settlement pattern of small social groups, sometimes enclosing their dwellings within ditches and banks, sometimes not. At the centre lay the Avebury area itself, shunned, perhaps taboo, a silent reserve outside the strident norms of Iron Age life.

Acknowledgements

I am very grateful to Andy Payne for making available the results of geophysical surveys in advance of his own publication. This paper has benefitted from discussions, both general and particular, especially with John Barrett, Mark Corney, David Field, Graeme Kirkham and David McOmish. All illustrations are by Deborah Cunliffe.

16

From *pagus* to parish: Territory and Settlement in the Avebury Region from the Late Roman Period to the Domesday Survey

Andrew Reynolds

The landscape of the Avebury region has long served as a textbook for students of English landscape history. Over the last forty years the work of Desmond Bonney and Peter Fowler, foremost amongst others, has resulted in intense debate about the nature of territorial arrangements from prehistory up to the middle ages and beyond. The origins of the land units that became fossilised as parishes during the twelfth century feature significantly in these debates and the purpose of the present paper is to review and further explore issues of estate development and settlement patterns between the late Roman period and about AD1100. The paper first considers the problem of Roman estate continuity, and then the origins of the hundredal pattern around Avebury, including the nature and distribution of administrative agencies within the Hundred of Selkley in which Avebury lies. The final part of the paper discusses amalgamation and fragmentation of units in the landscape throughout the Anglo-Saxon period based on Anglo-Saxon charters. A case is made for a vibrant and complex trajectory of human reactions to the Avebury landscape that has resulted in much that is tangible today. Overall, it is argued that the territorial framework of the Avebury area by the time of the Domesday Survey of 1086 owed little to the late Roman scene besides a degree of unintential overlap of boundaries utilising major topographical features.

Abbreviations

DB	Domesday Book (Darlington 1955a)
F201	(Finberg 1964b)
OE	Old English
S643	(Sawyer 1968)
TRE	*tempore regis Edwardi* 'in the time of King Edward' (the Confessor)

Introduction

In AD 957 King Eadwig granted 20 *mansae* at *Stantune* (Stanton St Bernard) to Oswulf, Bishop of Ramsbury, 'free of all but the three common dues' (fortress and bridge-work and military service)(S647). The Stanton grant is but one of many made during the central decades of the 10th century by Anglo-Saxon kings that characterise an era so fundamental in English landscape history: the origins of manor, village and estate and the landscape of Domesday Book.

Where early documents have survived, the Avebury area exhibits a long and complex development in tenurial terms and appears to have begun the process of 'manorialisation' somewhat earlier than certain other regions as indicated by a series of land grants of 9th century and earlier date.

This article examines estate and settlement development in the Avebury region with one eye on the issue of continuity from the Roman period and the other on the complex nature of settlement and land tenure during the Anglo-Saxon period. With few notable exceptions, earlier work on the origins of the pattern of estate boundaries in the Wessex region, and more locally in our area, has tended not to differentiate between territorial units of varying size (e.g. hundreds and estates) nor to have considered the possibility that they might have varied origins in chronological terms. Notably, earlier work has taken insufficient account of the level of dynamism and change *within* the Anglo-Saxon period exhibited in the documented histories of estates in our region.

Questions of continuity

Before the various themes identified above are explored, it is worth noting a few of the wider considerations and implications of our topic that ought to be borne in mind throughout the paper. In addition, it should also be noted that the paper is not intended as an exhaustive discussion, but rather as a stimulus to provoke a more dynamic approach to our understanding of the development of the Avebury landscape. Indeed, there is not the space here to enter into a comprehensive review of previous work and current thinking about the emergence of Anglo-Saxon England from late Roman Britannia.

In the first instance, definitions deserve attention particularly as the distinction between continuity of physical elements of the landscape, such as field boundaries, and tenurial arrangements is rarely addressed. The issue of 'continuity' has remained one of the core questions of culture historians of the first millennium AD (see for example the publications of the Transformation of the Roman World Project; *cf* Brogiolo *et al* 2000; Theuws and Nelson 2000). While historians seek continuity in the form of social institutions, the power and influence of individual families and economic arrangements, archaeologists are usually much more concerned with continuity in material culture and social practices. The term continuity is used here in a tenurial sense. Tenurial continuity is almost elusive to the archaeologist, but a careful approach to the evidence in a landscape context does allow the question to be addressed if not solved conclusively. What, then, does the field archaeology of the Avebury region actually have to say about the transition from Roman Britain to Anglo-Saxon England?

In the case of Wessex landscapes there are two distinct schools of thought with regard to the origins of the pattern of medieval parishes. The first, exemplified by the work of Desmond Bonney, Peter Fowler and Jeremy Haslam, argues that there are very long-lived patterns of estates and central places in the landscape of Wessex. Bonney and Fowler have argued for Roman or pre-Roman origins for estates, based on the perceived relationship between burial sites, East Wansdyke and documented estate boundaries and on postulated long-term processes of amalgamation and fragmentation of land units (Bonney 1966; 1972, 169; Fowler 2000, 238–41). Furthermore, Haslam suggests that certain central places, such as Bradford-on-Avon, remained important in the landscape from at least the later Iron Age (Haslam 1984, 89).

A second view sees the creation of what became parish units as a later Anglo-Saxon phenomenon defined in chronological terms by the mass of land grants made by Anglo-Saxon kings to major churches and to private individuals largely during the 10th century AD (Hill 1981, 26; Hooke 1988, 140; 1994, 88; Reynolds 1999, 83).

The term 'continuity' was applied with a degree of abandon during the 1960s, 1970s and 1980s when much interest was directed towards an understanding of how Anglo-Saxon England had emerged from Roman Britain. Some have argued that Anglo-Saxon culture represents a re-emergence of the late Iron Age scene from beneath a layer of Roman material culture and social influence, the so-called 'veneer' model, while others have argued for widespread population movement and take-over (Millett 1990; Welch 1992; Eagles 2001). More recently, interpretations have focussed on elite dominance or a newly dominant ideology alone (Scull 1992; Moreland 2000). Clearly, these models, and the degree of their variance, have as much to say about the difficulties of chronology and character of archaeological material during the 4th–6th centuries as they do about what actually might have happened. In response to these models, it should be noted that there are many fundamental differences between the archaeology of the Late Iron Age and the Early Anglo-Saxon period. There is no evidence for a violent take-over by migrating Germanic peoples (indeed, Germanic material culture of the earliest phase is particularly sparse in our region), while political domination by a small post-Roman elite best fits the available evidence which takes the form of isolated barrow burials of 6th and 7th century date in both north and south Wiltshire. With regard to the adoption of Germanic style material culture, suggestions of a purely ideological change tend to play down the movement of people, which is, of course, a basic necessity for the exchange of ideas.

At the level of individual settlements, Roman villas show a steady increase in number up to the middle of the 4th century AD; a trend which is then immediately reversed in a dramatic and terminal fashion, which Martin Millett, quite justifiably given what comes after, sees as representing '...a basic tenurial discontinuity among the landowning elites...' (Millett 1990, 224).

While it is easy enough to visualise how a Late Iron Age farm might be "Romanised" with few indications to suggest that the basic function of the settlement was different either side of the

Roman conquest, the nature of Early Anglo-Saxon settlements is very different. Evidence for grain storage, for example, is largely absent from Anglo-Saxon settlement sites until the 8th century, a period characterised by the re-emergence of a coin using, surplus producing, mercantile economy. Dominic Powlesland suggests that certain of the Early Anglo-Saxon Sunken Featured Buildings from West Heslerton, North Yorkshire served as grain stores, but it is not until the Middle Anglo-Saxon period that granaries can be more confidently identified, such as the nine-post structure at Wicken Bonhunt, Essex (Powlesland 1997, 106; Wade 1980). A discontinuity in the function and local/regional role of rural settlements between the later 4th and 8th centuries is thus apparent.

During the 1960s, 1970s and 1980s, key excavations, such as those at Barton Court Farm, Abingdon, Oxfordshire, where Early Anglo-Saxon structures and material culture were found in association with and partially superimposed upon a late Roman villa, were hailed as evidence for 'continuity' (Miles 1984, 49). There are many examples of a few sherds of chaff-tempered pottery from villa excavations, both nationally and in the Avebury region, for example at the Cuffs Corner villa, near Clyffe Pypard (Anon 1975–6, 136), but the difficulty of dating this material (let alone its interpretation) between the 5th and 10th centuries is now widely acknowledged (Hamerow *et al* 1994). If anything, it is notable just how many of the most extensive excavations of Early Anglo-Saxon settlements at a national level do not reveal Roman period settlements.

It is appropriate here to mention the process of settlement shift. The concept of continually shifting settlement, from the Neolithic to present, has much to commend it and might account for the general lack of Anglo-Saxon material from abandoned villas. Helena Hamerow (1993, 96–7) has suggested that settlement shift occurred throughout the Early and Middle Anglo-Saxon periods, although individual locales when scrutinised suggest that national modelling is hazardous, especially as the process involved in re-locating a settlement is as likely to be a prescribed tenurial issue as one of individual choice. Indeed, the degree of choice that past populations were able to exercise is of fundamental concern in terms of how we understand the reactions of past populations to their landscapes and thus the issue of 'continuity'.

Recent studies of reactions to ancient monuments and landscapes by past populations have emphasised the role that existing monuments and other landscape features played in the construction of contemporary environments (Semple 1998; Williams 1997). The degree of choice in terms of geographical spheres of influence is a further factor that should accordingly affect the range of reactions to landscape by succeeding populations. In effect, when considering settlement and territorial patterns in the Avebury region we must keep an eye on the issue of constraint of social space, and the degree to which populations reacted to their 'space' in terms of what was freely, or with restriction, available to them. Indeed, the likelihood that patterns of territorial constraint at the level of individual estates remained static from the Roman period up to Domesday is, I would argue, rather slim. Patterns of post-Roman estate morphology provide a significant body of data from which to explore issues of estate development, particularly as certain units are apparently set out as model agricultural parcels in possession of as varied a set of resources as the local topography will allow. Others, like Avebury parish, are more obviously the result of long term fragmentation, or, like Chittoe (see below), perhaps the fortuitous survival of a Roman period land unit. A glance at a map showing estate/parish morphology (Fig 16:1) betrays at once a complex sequence of events and not a view of archaic stability (contra Bonney 1972, 173) or uniform planning.

As noted in the Introduction, issues of territorial scale have suffered much neglect; are units of a certain scale/importance more likely to exhibit continuity than others? Certain scholars have argued for continuity of Iron Age tribal boundaries into Roman *civitates*, which in turn broadly determined the limits of certain English shire boundaries, such as Kent, Norfolk, Devon and Cornwall (Hanson 1988, 55; Millett 1990, 66). It should be noted, however, that the level of topographical determination of administrative boundaries on the macro scale is bound to bring with it a degree of topographically determined overlap, especially as many English shire boundaries utilise major watersheds or river valleys. In the case of Wiltshire, Bruce Eagles has noted that the extent of the Domesday and modern shire probably incorporated parts of four separate *civitates* (Eagles 2001, 212–3), indicating discontinuity of territorial arrangements at this level in contrast to the regions mentioned above (Fig 16:2). A tier of local territorial organisation below that of the *civitas*, and about which we know next to nothing in Roman Britain, is that of the *pagus*, defined by Rivet as a '...unit in which the inhabitants of an area were grouped' (Rivet 1958, 66). Clearly, the fundamental issue is that archaeologists attempting to argue for continuity have explored all too little exactly what it is they are trying to argue for continuity of.

Earlier work by Bonney and Fowler continues to be highly influential. This paper offers a further

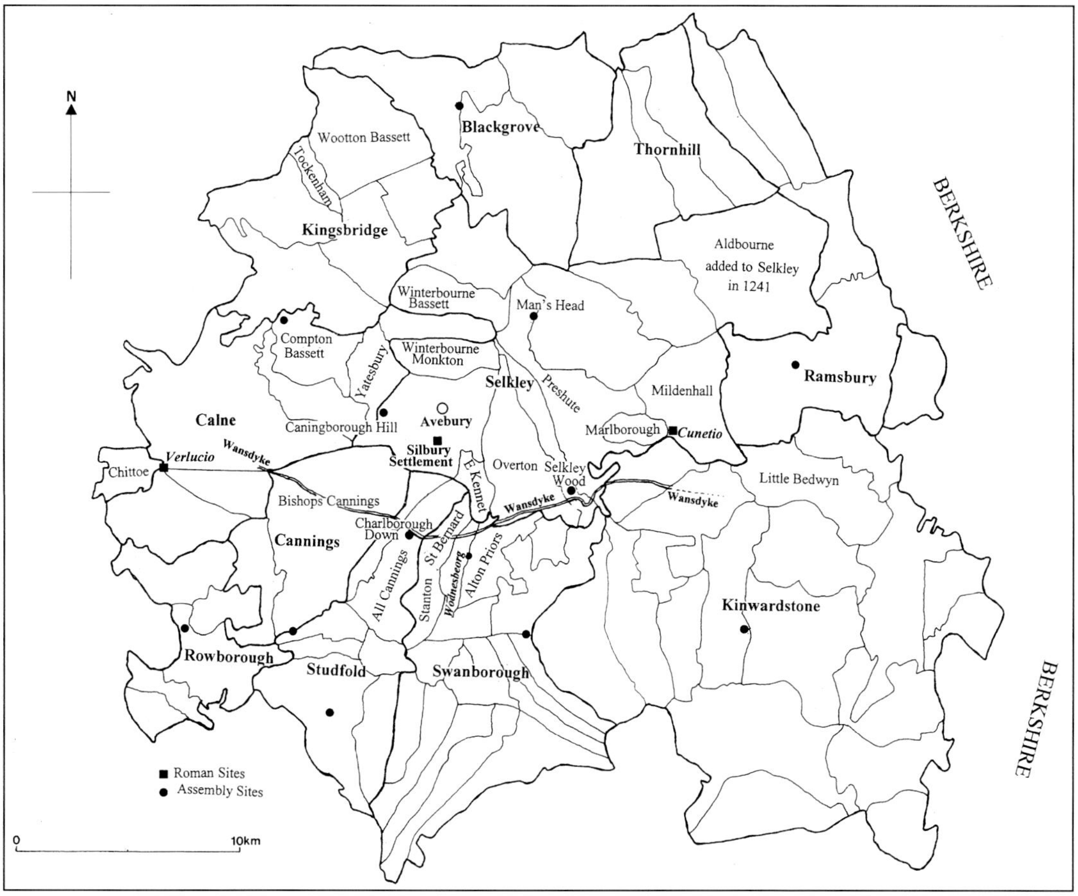

Fig 16:1 Parishes and hundreds in the Avebury region. Hundred names in bold.

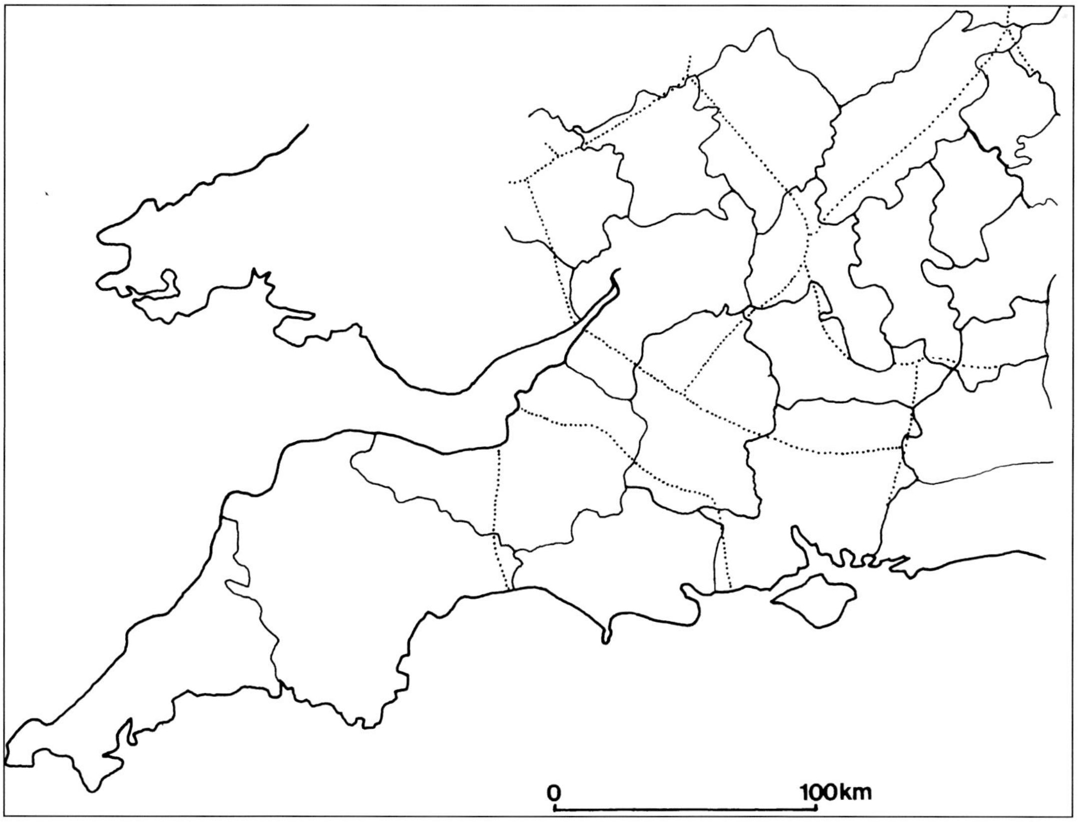

Fig 16:2 Civitas *and shire compared in south western England* (civitas *boundaries (dotted lines) taken from Millett 1990, fig. 16).*

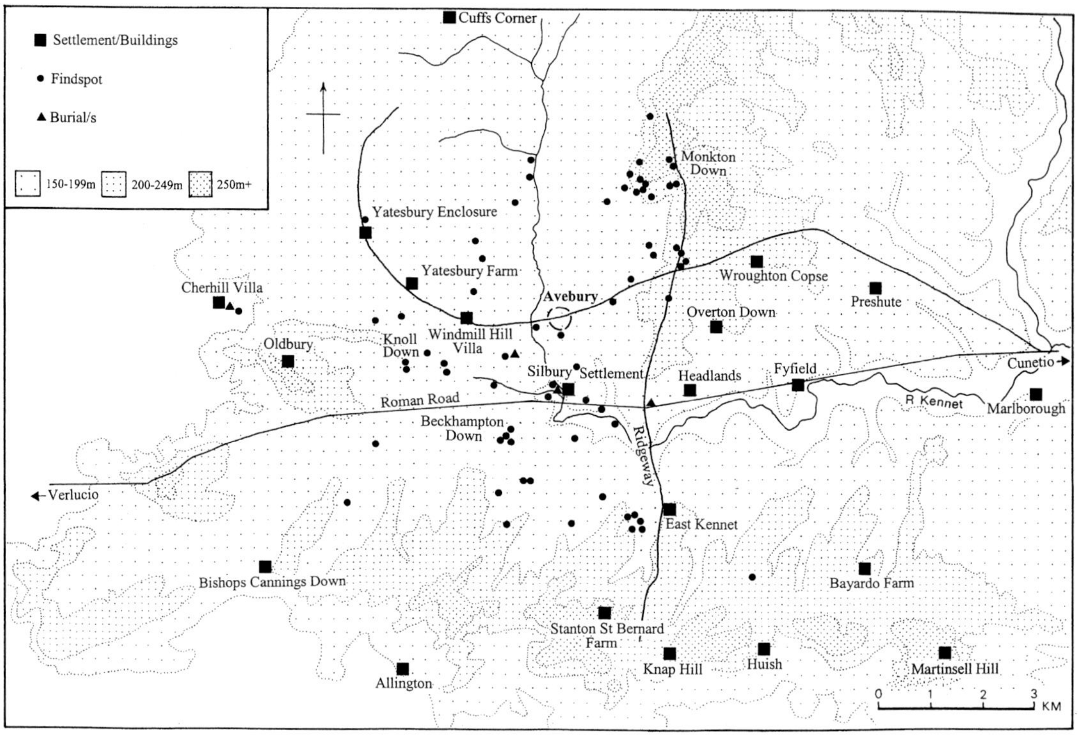

Fig 16:3A Distribution of Roman sites and finds in the Avebury region (after Pollard and Reynolds 2002, fig. 63).

contribution to the debate in attempt to extend its range to consider in particular the difficult period between the highly visible archaeology of the later Roman period and the documented territorial arrangements of the late Anglo-Saxon and medieval periods.

The Late Roman Scene

We cannot map the extent of a single Roman agricultural estate. We do not know much either about the relationships in social and economic terms between individual farms and their lands. What we do know is that settlement in the Avebury area in the Late Roman period was dense and complex (Fig 16:3A), although problems of dating make it difficult to understand the subtleties of Roman occupation in the region often resulting in perceived 'long chronologies' for sites. On the basis of distribution maps, however, it is probably fair to say that the landscape was more extensively exploited during the Roman period than at any time before or up to recent times. We know also that the wealth of individual farms varied considerably, much as it does today. From the lower status collections of timber buildings at Overton Down ODXII and at Yatesbury up to the opulent villa accommodation at Cherhill, with a slightly less well-off neighbour at the foot of Windmill Hill, the view is very much one of a society with a broad spectrum of social conditions (Fowler 2000, 110, fig. 6.21; Pollard and Reynolds 2002, 157–8; Johnson and Walters 1988; Goddard 1923).

A crucial issue for landscape historians is the degree to which these various settlements were autonomous or interdependent (Esmond Cleary 1989, 114). In previous discussions of estate continuity, the assumption has been that the role of the villa was more or less identical to that of the medieval village (Finberg 1964a, 44–5; Fowler 1976). Rivet's classic study of Roman Britain notes the possibility of more complex tenurial patterns and Fowler hints at such, while Walters' recent discussion emphasises the diversity of villa settlements noting that lesser villas '...may well represent subservient tenants or bailiffs controlling divisions of large landholdings' (Rivet 1958, 119; Fowler 2000, 230; Walters 2001, 128). Despite Walters' comments, the 'continuity' view relies on individual farms controlling autonomous estates and within such a world view, the trajectory from villa to village appears a natural progression. Indeed, the rapid growth of the villa during the late third and fourth centuries has been termed the 'manorialisation' of the countryside (Faulkner 2000, 139) and it remains possible that the countryside of later Roman Britain experience a similar process of fragmentation to that which occurred in the later Anglo-Saxon period.

While certain villas probably operated as estate centres for more or less self-sufficient agricultural units, there are strong indications that estates of

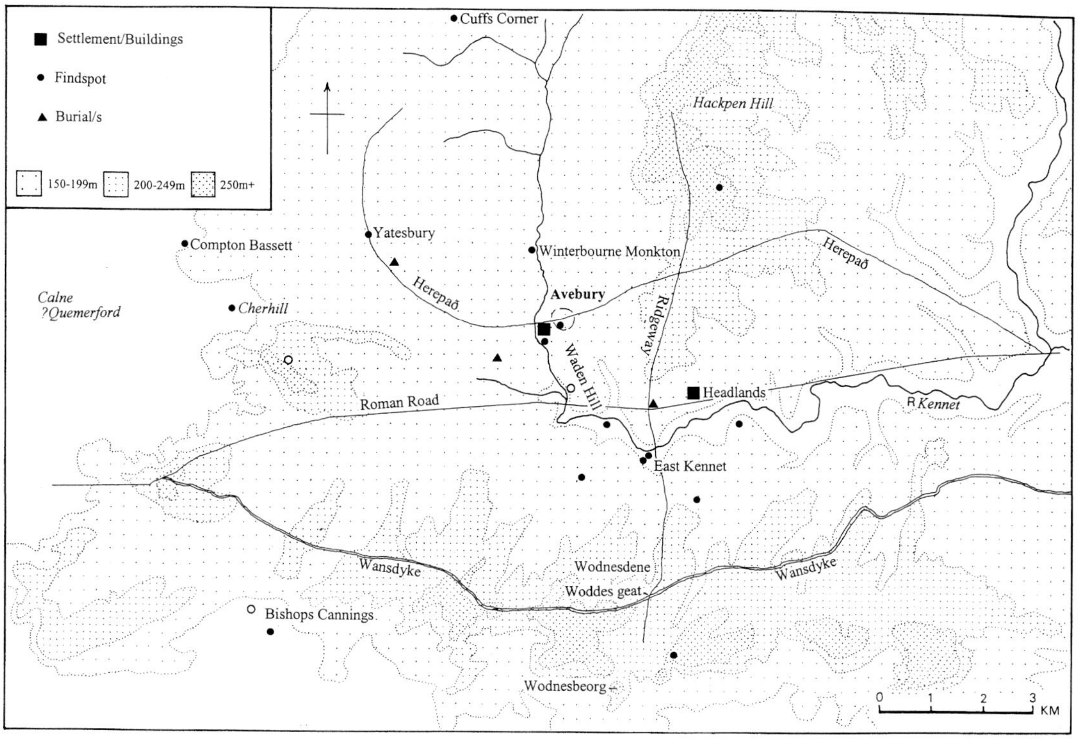

Fig 16:3B Distribution of post-Roman and Early Anglo-Saxon sites and British potential place-names (in italics). Open circles are late Celtic objects (after Pollard and Reynolds 2002, fig. 78).

considerable extent and containing inter-dependent settlements operated alongside smaller units. Examples from our region will suffice to illustrate the point. The recently investigated villa at Tockenham, 10km north-north-west of Avebury, apparently sits within a rectilinear field system aligned on the villa complex (Harding and Lewis 1997). Four pottery scatters to the east of the villa lie amongst less regular fields and are on average only 200–300m apart and 700m from the villa itself (*ibid* 38, fig. 6). These settlements lay on inferior agricultural land and are considered by the excavators to lie beyond the villa fields (*ibid*). An alternative view, given the close proximity of the 'satellite' settlements to each other and to the villa itself, is that they are dependent farms, part of a large 'complex estate' (Fig 16:4). Similarly, within Yatesbury parish at least two Roman settlements are known of a differing character and within 1000m of each other (Fig 16:3); potentially they are part of another 'complex farm' perhaps based on the villa at the foot of Windmill Hill (Pollard and Reynolds 2002, 165).

In addition to the villas are the Roman small towns of the region, *Verlucio*, south-west of Calne, the recently recognised small town at the foot of Silbury Hill, and *Cunetio*, east of Marlborough, which, as Mark Corney notes, are equidistant (12km) from each other along the *Aquae Sulis* (Bath) to *Cunetio* road (Corney 2001, 29).

A further complication is raised by the presence in our region of a settlement type additional to the villa and the small town; the upland village. Expansive settlements of Roman date have long been known on the downland of south Wiltshire at sites like Charlton Down, Chisenbury Warren, Church Pits and Knook Down (McOmish *et al* 2002, 92, fig. 4.7; Cunliffe 1973, 445, fig. 47), but they are present also in the Avebury region. A string of sites on the higher downland following the course of the Ridgeway spaced on average 1.5km apart is evident at Monkton Down, Avebury Down, Overton Down and East Kennet, while similar settlements appear likely on Beckhampton Down and Knoll Down to the south and west of Avebury (Pollard and Reynolds 2002). Were these sites independent settlements? It is suggested here that the upland settlements reflect increasing exploitation of the landscape by existing villa-based farms and that each of the upland settlements was dependent on a 'home' villa. Such a sequence is suggested by the late dating of the ODXII settlement on Overton Down, which Fowler suggests is linked to the potential villa at Headlands a short distance to the west (Fowler 2000, 228). The presence in some quantity of high-status glassware of late 4th and early 5th century date at ODXII suggests that the Headlands villa had lost its importance by this time and this evidence may be read as an archaeological signal of tenurial dislocation. There are known villas that, in spatial terms, are arguably estate centres for the various upland settlements (see Fig 16:3A). If a more complex tenurial

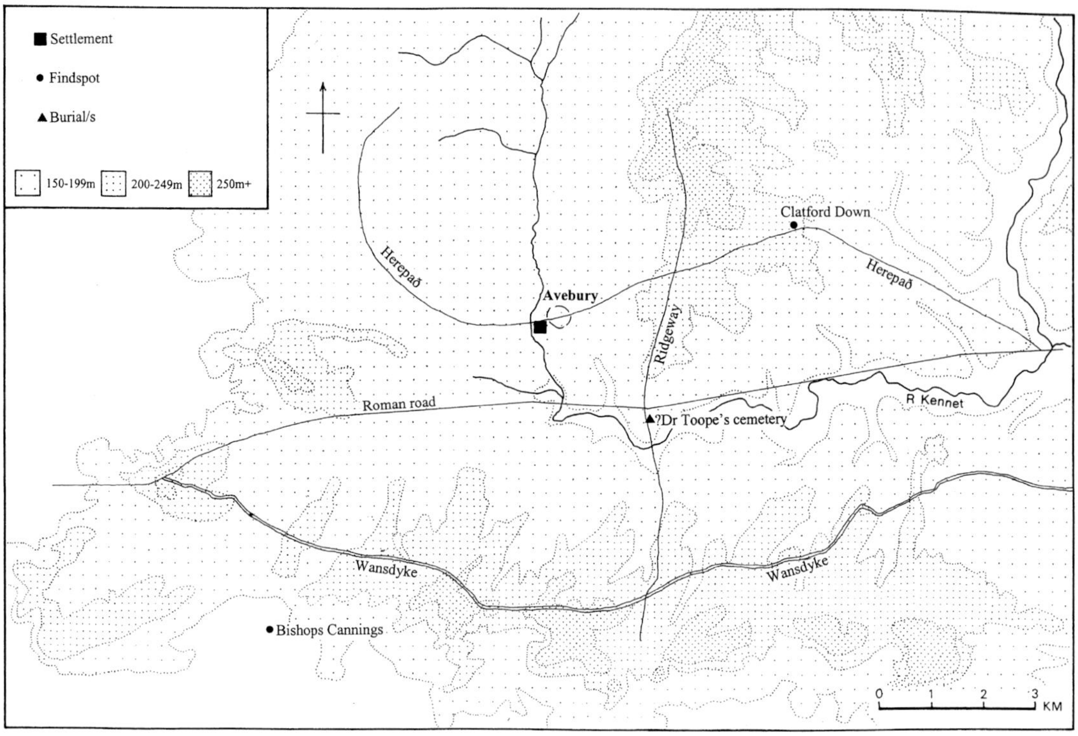

Fig 16:3C Distribution of Middle Anglo-Saxon sites and finds (after Pollard and Reynolds 2002, fig. 96).

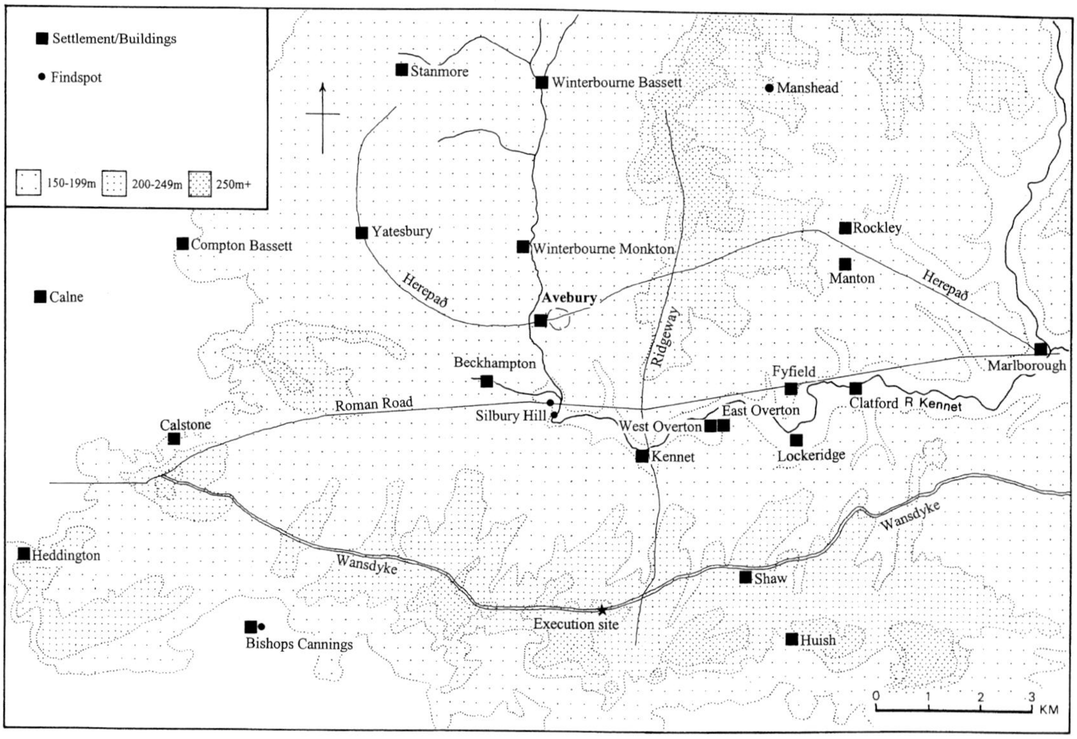

Fig 16:3D Distribution of late Anglo-Saxon sites and finds and Domesday holdings (after Pollard and Reynolds 2002, fig. 97).

pattern is accepted, then the likelihood that administrative boundaries between the various interdependencies within a given 'complex farm' would survive almost total social and economic collapse is arguably very slim. It is much more likely, however, that populations on the ground might have continued to recognise the limit of the *pagus* within which both independent villas and 'complex farms' lay, forming confederacies perhaps based on existing ties and which could, in some areas at least, have formed the basis for the so-called micro-kingdoms considered by

Steven Bassett to represent the building blocks of the larger Anglo-Saxon kingdoms of the 7th century onwards (Bassett 1989).

Although certain scholars have doubted the independence of these small territories seeing them as districts of larger units (Yorke 2000, 82), Bassett and others have shown that certain of these territories correspond to the 7th century and later parishes, or *parochiae*, of major Anglo-Saxon churches, the most notable example being the suggested correlation between the *regio* (Bede's terminology) of the *Stoppingas* and the *parochia* of the minster church at Wootton Wawen in Warwickshire (Bassett 1989, 18–19). The adoption of an administrative framework in a similar style to that observed at the time of the Roman conquest in relation to Late Iron Age arrangements is of considerable interest. A similar process can be observed later in the Anglo-Saxon period, where a correlation between the administrative districts termed hundreds (the Anglo-Saxon equivalent of *pagi*) and the *parochiae* of minster churches is often observed (see below).

Regrettably, we know nothing of the geography of the *pagi* in the Avebury region, but studies elsewhere indicate that they were based on 'central places' in the landscape, including hillforts and towns of varying sizes (see Rivet 1958). We might go so far to suggest three such *pagi* in the Avebury region, centred on *Verlucio*, on the Roman small town at the foot of Silbury Hill (Corney 1997a) and on *Cunetio*. Indeed, Corney has already suggested that Cunetio and *Durocornovium* (Wanborough) might have functioned as *pagus* centres (Corney 2001, 10 and 12). There are interesting implications here, not least for the fact that the places which were to become 'central' in comparable terms during the Anglo-Saxon period, Calne, Avebury and Preshute/Marlborough represent an identical distribution of nodal points in the landscape with each lying only a short distance from its Roman equivalent but separate nevertheless. We will return to this issue below, however, as the shift from Roman to Anglo-Saxon administrative geography in our study area was by no means straightforward. First, it is necessary to set out what is known of the origins of the hundredal geography of the region.

Churches in the landscape: Minster Parochiae *and the origins of Selkley Hundred*

It is now well established that the earliest churches in the English landscape were the 'primary' minsters established in the 7th and 8th centuries following the conversion to Christianity. These 'mother' churches arguably saw to the pastoral requirements of extensive parishes, or *parochiae*, while their physicality and importance varied considerably in terms of scale and influence; distinctions that are documented by the late Anglo-Saxon period in legal terms (VIII Ath 5.1; Robertson 1925). The hundredal set-up as visualised in the Domesday Survey of 1086 indicates that in many cases minster *parochiae* corresponded with hundreds and a simple equation of a minster *per* hundred in Late Anglo-Saxon Wessex is a presumption that has lasted in the literature (see Pitt 1999, 10 for a recent review). Peter Sawyer places an emphasis on the apparently close spatial relationships between minsters and *villae regiae* (royal manors), although Michael Hughes' distribution map of such sites in Hampshire (after Hase 1975) shows only four close associations in this core Wessex shire (Sawyer 1983, 277–8; Hughes 1984, 75, fig. 6). In Wiltshire (as in Devon, Dorset and Somerset) rather more minsters are directly associated with royal manors, for the most part at places that were towns by the late Anglo-Saxon period: Amesbury, Bedwyn, Bradford-on-Avon, Britford, Calne, Chippenham, Downton, Pewsey, Ramsbury, Warminster, Westbury and Wilton.

Within the Hundred of Selkley there are two churches with attributes suggestive of minster status (Pitt 1999, 87–8). The church at Preshute was undoubtedly a minster, for it was the mother church of the late Anglo-Saxon town of Marlborough and probably that recorded in Domesday Book as a holding of William de Belfou with a hide of land and a valuation of 30s (DB I, 26j). The valuation of Avebury church, in the ownership of the powerful priest Regenbald, at 40s and its holding of 2 hides of land compare well with the circumstances of Preshute in Domesday Book (DB I 26d); both churches are listed at the beginning of the Wiltshire DB folios under *Terra Regis*, or King's lands.

The topographical characteristics of Selkley's two minster churches combine well with documentary records of dependent chapels and tithes (Pollard and Reynolds 2002; Pitt 1999, 87–8) to suggest that the hundred is an amalgamation of two territories, one based on each minster, although the territories might potentially pre-date the minsters. A further observation that adds considerable weight to the argument presented here is the hidage assessment provided for Selkley Hundred in the pre-Domesday Geld Rolls for Wiltshire preserved in the Exon Domesday. The total for the hundred is 196 hides and 3 ½ virgates (Darlington 1955b, 199), indicating the amalgamation of two units originally assessed at 100 hides. The shortfall of less than four hides is negligible and is best accounted for through one of the many minor transactions of land observed in the region in the late pre-Conquest period (see Documents and Estates below).

If this scenario is an approximation of the development of the Hundred of Selkley, then the concentration of administrative functions (market town, royal manor and minster church) found in the eastern half of the hundred by the late Anglo-Saxon period suggests that the eastern district, based on Preshute, became dominant, a view borne out by the success of Marlborough and the suggestion that Avebury itself is a failed Anglo-Saxon fortified town with origins as a minster-type settlement initially comparable with Preshute (Reynolds 2001; Pollard and Reynolds 2002, 202–10). The following discussion augments and partially revises the account presented in *Avebury: The Biography of a Landscape* (*ibid*). The location of the meeting place of Selkley Hundred is problematic. The name of the hundred is potentially taken from a meeting place at or near the *'bosco de Selkele'*, Selkley Wood, mentioned in Assize Rolls for 1279 and 1281 and which is located by a further reference to *Selkleye* in the Calendar of Charter Rolls for 1309 between Overton and Fyfield, possibly north of West Woods (Gover *et al* 1939, 291, xl; Stevenson 1983a, 65). This location is on the southern fringe of the hundred and apparently represents the only administrative function left remaining in the western district post-amalgamation. A supposed chapel at '*Selk*', apparently in the northern part of Mildenhall parish, east of Marlborough is also suggested to have given its name to the hundred, but there seems little foundation to this story (Stevenson 1983b, 125). A royal reeve and marketing functions were surely to be found at Avebury itself before the two hundreds were amalgamated.

On closer inspection, and drawing in a wider range of evidence, the appraisal of Selkley Hundred presented here brings about the realisation that the other hundreds roundabout have been subject to changes in extent and organisation that mark them out from the apparently more stable units of South Wiltshire. Broader comparisons are drawn below, but several themes might usefully be explored here, not least the neglected topic of meeting places whose diverse origins perhaps include pre-Christian cult sites and newly constructed late Anglo-Saxon meeting mounds (Meaney 1995; Adkins and Petchey 1984). The Avebury area exhibits features of considerable interest in this respect and new research by the author intends to offer in due course a tentative reconstruction of the administrative macro geography of the region prior to its suggested late Anglo-Saxon re-arrangement (Reynolds *in prep*).

Place-names provide evidence for a number of pre-Christian cult sites in the region, although the material is complex and deserves exposition to a much greater depth than is possible here. The suggested cult-sites potentially relate to a postulated early Anglo-Saxon *regio* (of the *Canningas,* see below), located both centrally and on the northwestern fringe of the unit (Fig 16:4 and see below). Waden Hill south of Avebury is derived from OE *weoh* ('idol, holy place, shrine') and *dun* ('hill') (Gover *et al* 1939, 295; Wilson 1985, 179), while a *weolond* is recorded as a field name in Tockenham parish in the 13th century (Gover *et al* 1939, 295). Adam's Grave, the great neolithic long-barrow beside the Ridgeway north of Alton Priors, was known as *Wodnesbeorg* in a 10th century boundary clause attached to the Alton charter S272 (see below). A silver gilt pyramidal stud with niello decoration and a garnet set into the top has recently been found 'near Adam's Grave' (Robinson 2002, 3). Such items are normally associated with burials of highest-status in late 6th and 7th century Anglo-Saxon society and they are thought to have adorned sword-gear (Dickinson 1974, 27). The ground around Adam's Grave is down to pasture and one hopes that the object has not been removed from a secure context such as a shallow burial. Given that no other objects were reported with the stud, it may represent an accidental loss or, as Robinson suggests, a fitting lost during one of the two documented battles there in AD592 and AD715. A further possibility, if the barrow acted as a focus for cult activity, is that the object is a votive offering; a suggestion that immediately brings to mind the otherwise unaccompanied 6th century sword from the Cunnington's excavations on Knap Hill (Cunnington 1911–12). It is notable that none of these potential cult sites is recorded as a later meeting-place, perhaps further indicating a dislocation of early administrative arrangements in the Late Anglo-Saxon period.

The Man's Head mound, located to the north-west of Marlborough, about 1km before the summit of Hackpen Hill, is a further plausible candidate for the meeting place of Selkley Hundred (Gover *et al* 1939, 291), and probably that of the postulated earlier eastern territory also. There is a Manshead Hundred in Bedfordshire and, further afield, a *Maneshou* (OSw, ODa *manne*, ON *haugr*) 'man's mound' Wapentake in the North Riding of Yorkshire (Mawer and Stenton 1926, 112–13; Anderson 1934, 5). Aside from these more distant parallels, the nature of the Man's Head name requires a brief comment as it compares favourably with other names of a similar type in the region, certain of which, although not recorded as hundred names, arguably represent meeting places prior to the

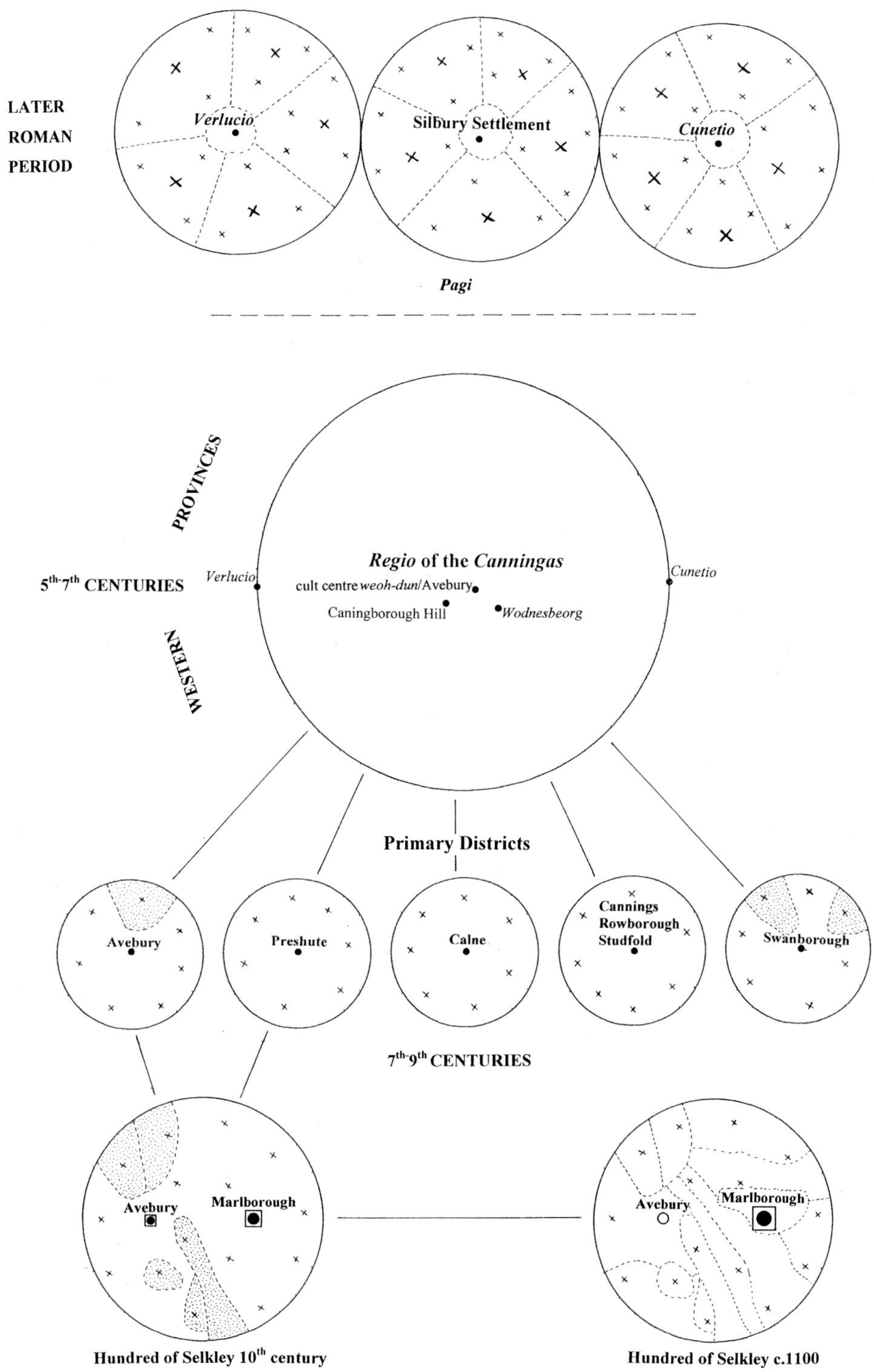

Fig 16:4 From pagus *to parish: a preliminary model.*

suggested reorganisation of hundreds in the area in the late Anglo-Saxon period (Reynolds *in prep*). As a description of a place where the freemen of a district are to meet to consider its affairs, a name like 'Man's Head' is clearly appropriate. The name refers directly to 'the people'. Similarly, Swanborough Hundred to the south of Selkley takes its name from the *swanabeorh* 'hill or barrow of the peasants/common men' recorded in the bounds of Manningford Abbots of AD 987 (Gover *et al* 1939, 320; S865; Semple and Langlands 2001). Two further possible meeting places are of considerable interest. Neither Caningborough Hill, 2km west of Avebury, nor Charlborough Down (site of the medieval Tan Hill fair) are hundred names at Domesday (Smith 1885, 107;

Chandler 1991, 93), although their nomenclature, 'hill or barrow of the *Canningas*' and 'hill or barrow of the *ceorls* (freemen)' strongly suggests that both locations date to an earlier phase of territorial organisation in the region. While Charlborough Down might represent an earlier meeting place for what later became Studfold Hundred, Caningborough Hill lies within Avebury parish but only a short distance north of Bishops Cannings and north-west of All Cannings. The fact that Bishops Cannings and All Cannings lay in different hundreds by Domesday is a prime indicator of territorial reorganisation. As the compilers of the English Place-Name Society volume for Wiltshire note, Cannings is the only example in Wiltshire of an *-ingas* type place name, indicative of 'a folk or small tribe' and, in our case, meaning 'the people of *Cana*' (Gover *et al* 1939, xiv, 250). Peckingell to the north-east of Chippenham potentially preserves a further *ingas* type name, but other explanations of this place-name are much more likely on etymological grounds (*ibid*, 106).

Bruce Eagles has presented a case for the existence of 'British' territories based on late Roman *civitas* boundaries in western Wiltshire into the 7th century (Eagles 2001). Whether one prefers invasion, migration or elite domination (see above), the dating and distribution of archaeological material (Fig 16:3B) presents a case for at least differing identities which, whatever their underlying cause, might well represent the kind of 'quasi-independent' territories, based on *civitates* and ruled by Gildas' *tyranni*, considered by Millett (1990, 228). As noted above, in the context of the rapid decline of an administrative infrastructure, perhaps the most likely context for the survival of group identity is at the level of the *pagus*, a unit which would appear to tally rather better with what we know of the geographical scale and organisation of the earliest 'Anglo-Saxon' territories.

It is plausible to suggest, then, that the territory of the *Canningas* succeeded the Roman territorial pattern in our region incorporating more than one *pagus*, and was itself in turn modified by the creation of smaller proto-hundredal districts with minster churches and royal vills at their centres. It remains an outside possibility, therefore, that certain of the hundreds in our region represent *pagi* grouped together to form the postulated *regio* of the *Canningas,* although *Verlucio* and *Cunetio* appear to lie at the western and eastern limits of the unit. Indeed, the failure of the Roman small towns in our study area to regenerate as early medieval centres may well be due to the 'frontier' nature of the region during the 7th and 8th centuries between the kingdoms of Wessex and Mercia. In our study area, the 'primary minster' districts were further modified in the late Anglo-Saxon period giving us the hundredal geography discernible in the Domesday Survey (Fig 16:4). Peter Fowler, in contrast, suggests a different scenario in the south eastern part of our area with the villas at Fyfield and Headlands and their lands forming the building blocks of the early Anglo-Saxon landscape, with four successive land units, Shaw, West and East Overton and Fyfield, each with its own church, succeeding the earlier pattern before the end of the 8th century (Fowler 2000, 241). In view of the pattern of known minsters in the region (after Blair 1985), it is arguably more likely that the churches in these settlements are later 9th or 10th century at the earliest although chapels are recorded at Fyfield and Alton that were dependent on 'Overton' in the 13th century, which of the two Overton's, however, is not known (Pitt 1999). These chapels perhaps reflect a church of some status at Overton. The postulated territory of the *Canningas* was very likely extensive, subsuming the lands of the Fyfield and Headlands villas, and including much of the Pewsey Vale west of the ancient Hundred of Kinwardstone (itself assessed in the Wiltshire Geld Rolls at 196 hides) (Darlington 1955b, 213). Lands to the north were arguably part of the unit, given the location of Caningborough Hill and the fact that the former parish of Highway was a detached part of Potterne and Cannings Hundred, and also to the east if the detached chapelry of Chittoe can be taken as a guide to the former extent of the territory. To the west and northwest, a series of later 6th and 7th century barrow burials may indicate further the limits of the *regio*. Additional research by the writer will attempt to clarify the picture taking into account additional factors, not least the relationship between the postulated territory of the *Canningas* and East Wansdyke and the chronological implications for both entities (Reynolds forthcoming). Before moving on, the chapelry of Chittoe and its lands require a few additional comments as it exhibits some remarkable features in contrast to other land units in the locality. It is the only estate, for example, along the line of the Bath-Mildenhall Roman road in Wiltshire not to utilise the road as part of its boundary between Monkton Farleigh on the county boundary with Somerset and the start of the Wansdyke on Morgans Hill near Calne. This is a striking observation, especially when combined with the fact that the Roman small town of *Verlucio* lays partly within it (Bonney 1972, 176; Corney 2001, 29). Chittoe itself is a name of British origin, meaning 'yew wood' (Gover *et al* 1939, 252; Eagles 2001, 208, fig. 11.2), and of all the land units considered in this paper it is perhaps the strongest candidate for a Roman survival.

The above observations indicate that the *regio*

of the *Canningas* subsumed the postulated *pagi* based on the Silbury settlement and parts of those based on *Verlucio* and *Cunetio*, thus overall discontinuity of administrative arrangements is again apparent. Whether *Cunetio* took its name from an existing river-name or vice-versa is unknown, although the distribution of 'Kennet' names and Roman central places suggests the former and thus relegates arguments for administrative continuity of the former Roman centre (see Gover *et al* 1939, 8 and Fowler & Blackwell 1998, 130 for contrasting views). Furthermore, the *regio* probably formed the basis for at least four or five hundredal units, although it should be borne in mind that in the south-western part of our study area the hundredal geography is ragged and the units smaller in scale than those to the north and east. Ultimately, the model presented here is tentative with regard to the actual extent of the various units involved.

The issue requires more detailed attention than is possible here, but sufficient evidence has been marshalled to illustrate a territorial complexity that can only have a sobering effect on the continuity debate. All we can assume is that certain locales (as opposed to places) remained central but that the land units they once controlled probably fluctuated both after the collapse of the Roman administration and on throughout the Anglo-Saxon period. As noted above, the hundreds of central North Wiltshire appear to have been subject to an additional stage of modification not immediately apparent in the rest of the county, namely the late Anglo-Saxon amalgamations evident in our study area.

We turn our attention now to the web of agricultural estates that formed the constituent parts of the late Anglo-Saxon landscape and the basis of the Domesday, medieval and modern settlement pattern.

Anglo-Saxon charters and the origins of the manor

Perhaps the most difficult issue here is how to interpret the nature of local territorial arrangements prior to the process of manorialisation. The most likely scenario based on studies elsewhere, and to a certain extent by place-names in our study area, is that large estates equating to what became minster *parochiae*/hundreds operated as multiple estates, or complex farms, in a similar fashion to that proposed above for the Roman agrarian landscape. The date range for this model is likely to cover the 7th–9th centuries, although the quantity of archaeological data for this period is very limited (Fig 16:3C). While an allowance should be made for the possibility that certain estates have a late Roman basis, such as Chittoe, the relationships between Roman estate centres and documented Anglo-Saxon and later boundaries is suggestive of a lost geography of estates. While certain estate boundaries described in charters might well be present in the landscape as tenurial entities well before they were committed to vellum, they are more likely to represent the boundaries between constituent parts of 7th–9th century multiple estates rather than the limits of individual Roman farms. Authentic grants of 8th century date immediately adjacent to our study area arguably describe just such units at Little Bedwyn (S264; AD 778), Tockenham (S96; AD 757; Edwards 1988, 124) and Wootton Bassett (S256; AD 745).

One striking indication that 'manorial' scale agricultural estates are largely early medieval creations are the relationships that can be observed between certain parish boundaries and Roman farms or villas in Wiltshire and in Hampshire, to cite local examples. The parish boundary of Stanton St Bernard cuts through the middle of an enclosed settlement of Roman date to judge by finds of pottery from mole hills and is described as the *'eald burh'* in the various Stanton charters (see below). Further south, the county boundary with Hampshire, at West Dean, cuts in half an impressive villa complex indicating discontinuity at both macro and micro territorial levels. A further Hampshire example is provided by the *'tiggæl beorgæ'*, ('tile barrow') recorded in the bounds of Exton (Meonstoke) of AD 940 (S463), where excavations by Tony King have revealed a substantial villa complex (King 1996). Significantly, for our discussion, the Meonstoke excavations also revealed evidence for Early Anglo-Saxon settlement indicating a 7th century or later origin for the estate boundary on archaeological grounds alone. A number of commentators have noted that, where they are described, the bounds of Anglo-Saxon estates appear to be long established by the time they are documented (Fowler 2000, 238) owing to the detailed nature of the boundary descriptions. I would suggest, however, that the details in the boundary clauses reflect the nature of the landscape which, in England, is one affected by issues of scale whereby neighbours live in immediate proximity and where most, if not all, of the landscape is intensively exploited; a detailed record of where the legal rights and responsibilities of landholders began and ended was, after all, an important issue from the 7th century in Anglo-Saxon England.

Our earliest documented agricultural estates are those recorded in grants of land by Anglo-Saxon kings to religious houses and to private individuals. The creation of *'bocland'*, or bookland, peaked in the central decades of the 10th century, yet our region shows a different pattern to that observed on a national scale. There is a series of grants in the Avebury environs (for Alton Priors, Stanton St Bernard, Winterbourne Monkton and Winterbourne Bassett, Kennet and Overton) and these are listed and discussed below in chronological order of the earliest known grant with Domesday assessments to facilitate discussion (Table 16:1).

Documents and estates

The identification of lands granted by charter in the Avebury region is fraught with difficulties. Although the location of certain estates and their bounds is not in question, such as Stanton St Bernard, there remains a degree of confusion over the secure identification of documented parcels of land in the Kennet Valley and along the course of the Winterbourne to the north of Avebury. The tenurial history of the Upper Kennet valley from Avebury through to Overton has been investigated in considerable depth by Peter Fowler and Ian Blackwell and their identification of the 4 *mansae* at *Ofærtune* granted in S547 as land around West Kennet Farm is accepted here (Fowler 2000; Blackwell unpublished and *see below*). Nevertheless, the pre-Conquest charters and Domesday assessments for Kennet, present a complex picture that will probably remain open to reinterpretation. The Winterbourne estates to the north of Avebury show an equally complex tenurial and settlement history. With simplex place-names of 'Winterbourne' type, like 'Compton' or 'Sutton', it is frequently difficult to be precise about which of several such estates a particular document refers to; the Monkton and Bassett suffixes in the case of the Winterbourne estates are, of course, post-Conquest additions. In view of these observations, it is clear that detailed fieldwork is necessary to solve the Winterbourne perambulations, while the detailed publication of the *Ofærtune* charter bounds by Peter Fowler and Ian Blackwell is eagerly awaited.

The following consideration, then, summarises the various difficulties and disputes over the identification of individual estates together with what is known about them from pre-Conquest documentation and the Domesday Survey.

Alton Priors

A charter dated AD825 (S272) grants of 15 hides at *Æweltune* (Alton Priors) from King Ecgberht to Old Minster, Winchester. The estate has a complex history that has been discussed by Heather Edwards (1988). While the charter itself is a 10th century conflation produced by borrowing material from other documents, Edwards has argued that a grain of authenticity lies embedded within: that Ecgberht gave land to a certain Burhheard about AD825 (*ibid*, 153–4). The subsequent history of the estate is based on an analysis of the witness list and later pre-Conquest documents (*ibid*, 155). The fabricated charter relates how the land reverted to Ecgberht upon the death of Burhheard, although Edwards considers this element dubious preferring a direct passage by sale or gift of the land into the hands of a certain Osmod whose widow Ceolwyn willed the estate to the Old Minster in Winchester about AD900 (S1513; Edwards 1988 153–55). The key to a better understanding of the sequence of events would appear to lie in the identification of the *Aweltune* listed in the Will of King Alfred (873 x 888) as a bequest to his son Edward (the Elder). While Keynes and Lapidge place *Aweltune* in Surrey, Blair omits it from his list of royal vills in that county; Sawyer suggests either Hampshire or Wiltshire (Keynes and Lapidge 1983, 176, Map 5; Blair 1991, 19, Table 1; Sawyer 1968, 422, Cat. No. 1507). If the *Aweltune* in question lies in Wiltshire, then Ecgberht's grant to Burhheard evidently reverted to royal ownership, only to be sold off to Osmod before Alfred's death. The earliest Anglo-Saxon wills have been described as 'reversionary grants of property which royal charters had first bestowed on their donors' (Wormald 2001, 266). The Alton Charter fits this scheme, despite Edwards' disagreement that such a process occurred. Indeed, Ceolwyn's will records how 'a suitable price [for the land] was paid in the presence of King Alfred' (Finberg 1964b, 77, Cat. No. 216) indicating its royal ownership in the later 9th century. By 1086 the Domesday Survey assesses Alton Priors at 20 hides and in possession of the Old Minster (DB II, 30). A late pre-conquest documentary source (S1403) dated 1047 x 52 records the leasing by the Old Minster of two hides and one yardland at Alton Priors to a certain Wulfric for two lives, while the Domesday entry notes 3 hides 'held of the bishop' by a certain William Scudet, which had been granted between 1078 and 1085 (Stevenson 1980, 192).

Stanton St Bernard

To the west of Alton Priors is the classic downland estate of Stanton St Bernard. Although the earliest of three surviving land grants dates to AD903 (S368) and records a gift of 20 *cassati* from King Edward to a certain Ordlaf his '*princeps*', the charter also relates how the land was originally granted between AD839 x 58 by King Athelwulf to his thegn Cenwold, who had himself left the land to his son, though the title deed had been lost (Finberg 1964b, 73, Cat. No. 221, 81, Cat. No. 224). As noted in the Introduction, the estate at

Stanton was the subject of a grant from King Eadwig to Oswulf, Bishop of Ramsbury in AD957 (S647), a transaction confirmed again by charter in AD960 (S685). Domesday Book assesses the estate at 20 hides TRE (DB XIII, 98).

Winterbourne Monkton and Winterbourne Bassett

Land at Winterbourne Monkton was first granted in AD869 when King Æthelred of Wessex gave 25 *cassati* to Wulfhere his '*princeps*' (S341). Wulfhere subsequently gave the land to Glastonbury Abbey and Domesday Book records 25 hides at Winterbourne Monkton in its ownership in 1086 with 3½ hides tenanted to a certain Orgar (Finberg 1964b, 75, Cat. No. 211; DB VII, 63). A further charter, S399, records a grant of 9 '*mansiones*' at *Winterburna* from King Athelstan to his 'lady' Ælfflæd in 928, while the Glastonbury Cartulary relates how she subsequently gave 10 hides at Winterbourne to that Abbey (Finberg 1964b, 81, Cat No 229). There is clearly a problem here with the figures. If the 25 *cassati* of the 869 grant are to be equated with the 25 hides listed in Domesday Book as a holding of Glastonbury's, then where do Ælfflæd's lands fit into the picture given that both Wulfhere and Ælfflæd bequeathed their Winterbourne lands to Glastonbury? It might be that a direct correlation between *cassati* and hide is mistaken in this instance, and that the 25 hides in Domesday Book represent a rounding up of lands granted in 869 and 928. Otherwise, and more likely, is that Ælfflæd's lands lay not in Winterbourne Monkton, as inferred by Finberg and followed by Sawyer (Finberg 1964b, 81, Cat. No. 229), but in Winterbourne Bassett perhaps equating to a block of 10 hides there recorded in Domesday Book (although see below).

At Winterbourne Bassett, a short distance northward again, a grant from King Edgar to Eadric his 'faithful *minister*' records 10 *mansae* at *Winterburnan* (S668; Finberg 1964b 183, Cat. No. 654). Domesday Book lists a holding of 6 hides belonging to Amesbury Abbey in *Wintreburne* identified with Rabson Farm immediately south of Winterbourne Bassett village (DB XVI, 129). The name Rabson is itself a corruption of the earlier '*Abbedeston*' (farm of the Abbess) first recorded in 1242 (Gover *et al* 1939, 309), although the provision in Domesday of values for 1066 and 1086 indicates continuity of pre-Conquest arrangements. Extensive earthworks immediately to the south of Rabson represent further tenurially distinct settlement in the form of Richardson, a site of apparently post-Conquest origin (*ibid* 309–10; Brown this volume). Both Rabson and Richardson retained distinct identities throughout the middle ages as far as the documentary sources are concerned. The pre-Conquest view, therefore, is very much one of complexity. Indeed, a further listing for Winterbourne Bassett describes how land held there in 1086 by Humfrey De Insula was held TRE by two thegns and paid geld for 10 hides (DB XXVII, 274); this land is perhaps the estate given to Glastonbury by Ælfflæd, although why it should have ended up in the hands of Humfrey De Insula would be difficult to acount for and more likely these lands equate to the 10 *mansae* granted in S668.

A further charter of AD949 (S543) records a grant of 1 hide at a *Winterburnan* from King

Estate	Source	Date	Extent	Bounds
ALTON PRIORS				
Æweltune	S272/F198	825	15 *manentes*	yes C10
Aweltune	S1513/F216	c.900	15 hides	no
Aweltune	S1403/F336	1047 x 52	2 hides, 1 yardland	no
Awltone	DB	TRE	20 hides	-
Awltone	DB	1086	3 hides (of above)	-
STANTON ST BERNARD				
Stantun	S368/F201	839 x 58	20 *cassati*	no
Stantun	S368/F224	903	20 *cassati*	yes
Stantune	S647/F286	957	20 *mansae*	yes
Stantun	S685/F290	960	20 *mansae*	yes
Stantone	DB	TRE	20 hides	-
WINTERBOURNE MONKTON				
Winterborne	S341/F211	869	25 *cassati*	yes
Winterburna	S399/F229	928	9 *mansiones*	yes
Wintreborne	DB	TRE	25 hides	-
Wintreborne	DB	TRE	3 ½ hides (of above)	-
EAST OVERTON				
Uferantun	S449/F245	939	15 *mansae*	yes
Ovretone	DB	TRE	15 hides	-
WEST KENNET				
Ofærtune	S547	949	4 *mansae*	yes
Chenete	DB	TRE	13 ½ hides + 2 acres	-
Chenete	DB	TRE	2 hides - 1 virgate	-
Chenete	DB	TRE	1 ½ hides + 1 virgate	-
WINTERBOURNE BASSETT				
Winterburnan	S668/F654	922 for 972	10 *mansae*	yes
Wintreburne	DB	TRE	6 hides	-
Wintreburne	DB	TRE	10 hides	-
WEST OVERTON				
Cynetan	S784/F308	972	10 *mansae*	yes
Ovretone	DB	TRE	10 hides	-

Table 16:1 List of estates granted in Anglo-Saxon charters compared with assessments in Domesday Book. Estates are listed in chronological order of the earliest reference to individual estates.

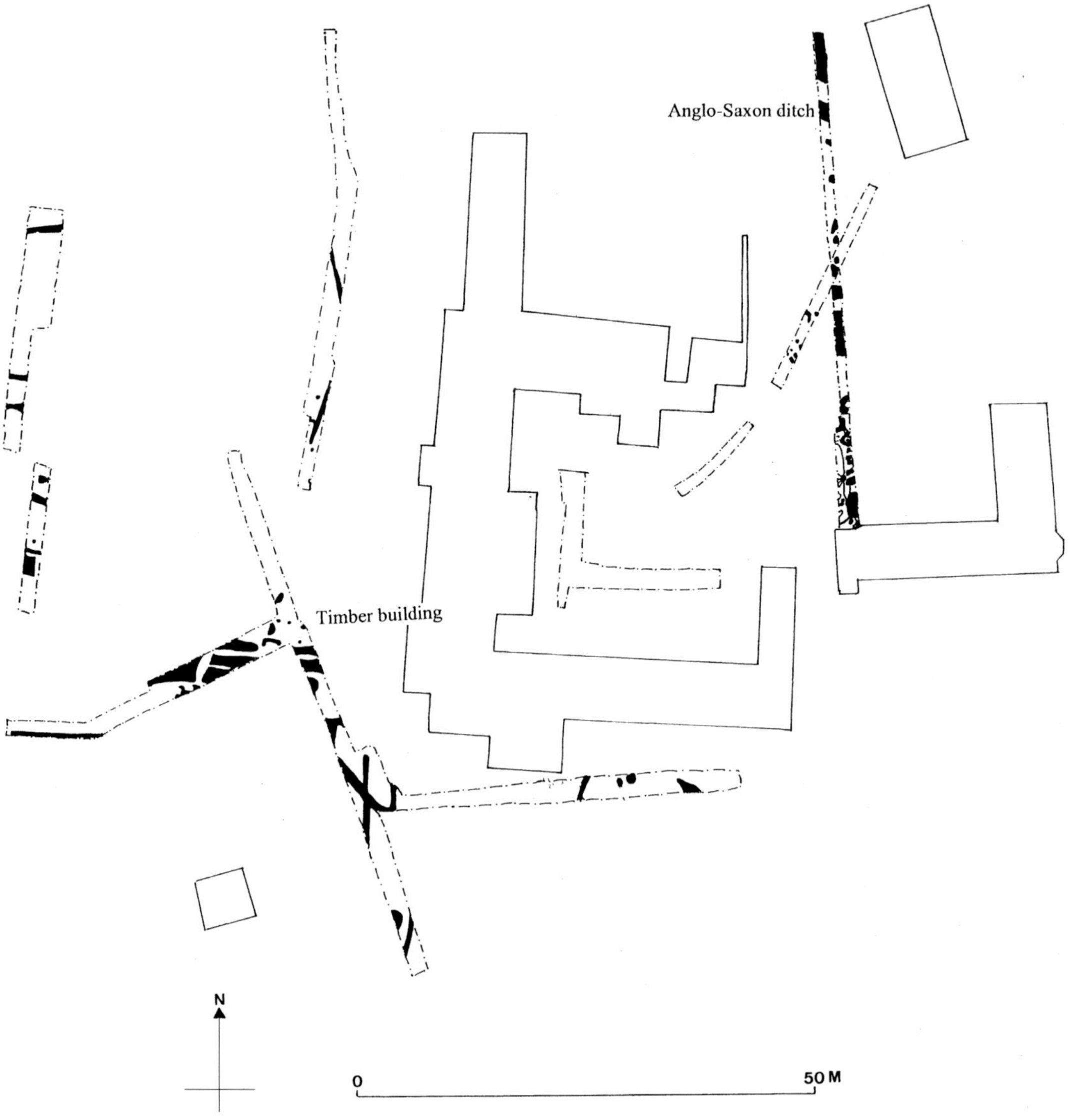

Fig 16:5 Plan of the Anglo-Saxon and later settlement at West Kennet Farm (after Wessex Archaeology 1989; 1997).

Eadred to Ælfsige 'his man' for his services as a goldsmith and silversmith. The location of this grant is not known with confidence, but there are suggestions that it lay in Laverstock near Salisbury (Gover *et al* 1939, xli; Finberg 1964b, 89–90).

East and West Overton

King Athelstan's grant of 15 *mansae* at *Uferantun* to Wulfswith '*ancilla Christi*' in AD939 is to be identified with East Overton and tallies with the 15 hide assessment for *Ovretone* provided by Domesday Book (S449; Fowler 2000, 150; DB II, 37). The story of West Overton, in locational terms is more complex. A grant by King Edgar of AD972 records 10 *mansae* at *Cynetan* (Kennet) given to 'the lady' Ælflæd. H C Brentnall demonstrated that the grant referred more specifically to the tithing of West Overton (Brentnall 1939). The Old English bounds of the charter, however, incorporate a '*chiricstede*', site of a church, on the western boundary of the estate while the (now churchless) settlement lies hard up against the eastern boundary (Fowler 2000, 142); Fowler postulates that settlement shift has occurred (*ibid*). The Domesday Book assessment of *Ovretone* at 10 hides, though, agrees with the extent of the AD972 grant (DB XIII, 105).

Kennet

References to lands at Kennet are also complex. The one pre-Conquest land grant, S547, records a grant of 4 *mansae* at *Ofærtun* to Frithuric 'minister' from King Eadred in AD949. As noted above, on the basis of the boundary clause, the estate is identified with land around West Kennet Farm (Blackwell unpublished). Of particular interest in this case is the recognition of an enclosed middle to late Anglo-Saxon settlement with timber structures found underlying West Kennet Farm during archaeological assessments in 1989 and

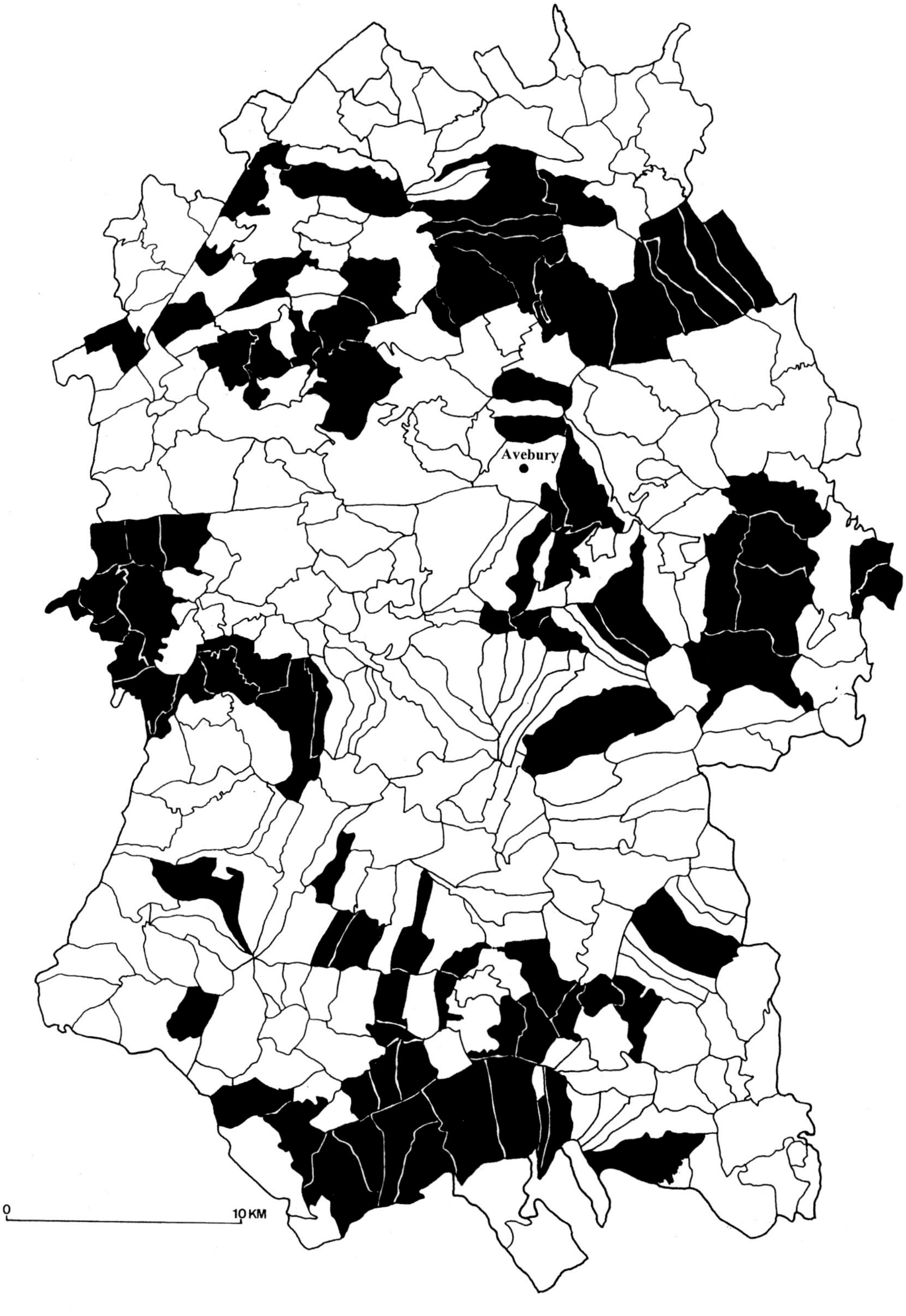

Fig 16:6 The distribution of Anglo-Saxon charters with bounds in Wiltshire (after Pollard and Reynolds 2002, fig. 100 with additions).

1997 (Fig 16:5; Wessex Archaeology 1989; 1997; Pollard and Reynolds 2002, 217, fig. 99). The archaeology, therefore, indicates an earlier origin for the settlement than for the estate recorded in the land grant. Domesday Book contains three references to Kennet; one of 13½ hides, held by five different individuals TRE, and further blocks of 2 hides minus 1 virgate and 1½ hides plus 1 virgate. Darlington suggests that the latter two parcels are to be located in East Kennet (DB XXXVII, 338; DB L, 403) and that the 4 *mansae* lay in East Overton (Darlington 1955c, 85).

Blackwell, however, states a good case that the two small Domesday parcels should be located in West Kennet and that they equate to the 4 *mansae* of the AD949 grant (Blackwell unpublished). In view of the tenurial pattern of the 13½ hides at West Kennet in DB it is quite plausible that the AD949 grant records the passage into *bocland* of one of a group of farms there, very likely that partially revealed by excavation.

Discussion

The earliest grants for Alton Priors, Stanton St Bernard and Winterbourne Monkton chart the first stages in the carving up of royal lands and the emergence of a pattern of landscape and settlement that was to develop and persist into modern times (Fig 16:3D). Estate fragmentation brought with it the demise of the multiple, or complex, estate and, the founding of a new tier of manorial residences and peasant accommodation. Then followed the mass of small parish churches whose success at attaining rights of burial and baptism steadily eroded the role and influence of the ancient minster churches. The morphology of estate units that never became bookland shows a comparable concern for access to a wide range of resources as the booklands. These latter estates, on the basis of Domesday Book show a similar degree of tenurial complexity. To the west of Avebury, estates like Yatesbury represent the classic 5 hide units of the late Anglo-Saxon period, whilst at Domesday the parish of Compton Bassett, further west, comprised three separate holdings each with a third part in two mills illustrating yet further that physical ownership of resources could be less than straightforward (DB LIV, 408; XXVII, 258; XXXII, 314, LXVII, 499).

The geographical distribution of lands granted by charter in Wiltshire shows clear groupings, for the most part concentrated around important central places. Bradford-on-Avon, Malmesbury, Cricklade, Avebury, Bedwyn and Wilton all have concentrated blocks of bookland around them or in close proximity (Fig 16:6). It might be suggested that many of these estates, most of which were granted with the usual conditions of military service, fortress and bridge-work, provided for an effective network of civil defence underpinning and linking the major Burghal Hidage and other fortifications present at the central places listed above. Avebury, as I have argued elsewhere, probably performed a defensive role in the earlier part of the Late Anglo-Saxon period and represents a tier of defensive site immediately below that of the major burghal forts (Reynolds 2001). The concentration of bookland around Avebury is less dense than around the other fortified centres and may in part be a reflection of Avebury's failure as a town. The lack of bookland immediately around Marlborough, whose development potentially hampered that of Avebury is explicable if the growth of the former occurred after the most prolific period of granting land by charter, the mid 10th century.

Conclusions

A series of conclusions can be drawn from the evidence presented in this paper. In the first instance, Avebury displays strong evidence for periodic territorial reorganisation *within* the Anglo-Saxon period. Elements of the landscape preserve early arrangements, but these can only be revealed, if at all, by detailed research, including fieldwork. While the late Anglo-Saxon pattern of settlement and landscape can be reconstructed with some clarity, the situation between the 7th and 9th centuries is very poorly understood indeed. While larger scale territories are more likely to exhibit continuity as recognisable units the Roman legacy, it is argued, is very limited overall and likely to be virtually non-existent in terms of the survival of individual estates into the middle ages and beyond.

Acknowledgements

I am grateful in the first instance to the many friends and colleagues with whom I have discussed the nature of the Anglo-Saxon landscape of the Avebury region. A debt of gratitude must also be paid to those scholars, namely Desmond Bonney, Bruce Eagles and Peter Fowler, whose labours and inspiration make the topic and region considered in this paper such a stimulating pursuit, even though my reasoning and conclusions are in places at variance with theirs. In particular, I should like to mention Sarah Semple and Alex Langlands whose own researches in the region are beginning to reveal yet further subtleties amongst the mass of source materials both archaeological and documentary relating to the Anglo-Saxon period. I should also like to thank the editors of this volume for their patience in waiting for my contribution to arrive and for inviting me in the first place to speak at the day school upon which this collection is based. Richard Reece gave much good and stimulating advice *via* his 'Mobile Library'. Graham Brown, Jonathan Pitt and Sam Turner kindly read through the text and have made it rather more readable than it might have been.

17
Monastic Settlement and Land-use of the Marlborough Downs

Graham Brown

By the time of the Norman Conquest large tracts of the Marlborough Downs were in monastic hands, particularly the area to the north of Avebury and along the Kennet valley. During the 11th and 12th century's further grants of land occurred to the 'new orders' to such an extent that there was hardly a parish that was not influenced in some way by a religious community. Priories were founded and granges established on the downs from where the land was exploited. Although some of the manors and estates were later leased, the land was to remain largely in monastic ownership until their suppression in the mid 16th century. This paper examines the extent of the monastic settlement and land-use on the Marlborough Downs.

Introduction

The monastic institutions of medieval England were amongst the largest landowners in the country. Their wealth was derived from two sources. The first was ownership of land (their temporalities), through cultivation and pasture, the exploitation of its industrial potential, and later by leasing. Temporalities also included the revenues from mills, urban holdings and rents. The second source was the holding of benefices, oblations and offerings at shrines (the spiritualities) (Robinson 1980, 172).

The Marlborough Downs were similar to many regions in the country; by the mid-13th century there was hardly a parish in the region that was not affected in some way by a monastic landlord. Some monasteries held estates on the Downs before the Norman Conquest, but it was not until the 12th century that we see the founding of a number of smaller houses and further exploitation of land by one of the larger Wiltshire houses – the Cistercian abbey at Stanley. The purpose of this paper is to identify the extent of monastic influence on the Marlborough Downs and to assess its impact on the landscape.

Pre-Conquest estates

The Domesday Survey of 1086 provides the first clear indication of monastic presence in the region (Fig 17:1). Although there were no Anglo-Saxon monasteries on the Downs there were, nevertheless, large estates belonging to the great Wessex Benedictine houses of Glastonbury, Amesbury, Wilton, St Swithun's Priory and Hyde Abbey in Winchester. All of these estates were to remain in monastic hands until their suppression in the mid-16th century and formed part of the classic sheep-and-corn husbandry (Smith, this volume) that was so prevalent on the chalk downlands during the medieval period.

The monks of Glastonbury Abbey held the largest amount of land in the region with estates at Winterbourne Monkton, Mildenhall, and Badbury (Thorn & Thorn 1979). These estates, with the possible exception of Winterbourne Monkton, were held directly by the abbot (Abrams 1996, 278) and administered within a bailiwick along with other north Wiltshire estates that included Ashbury in Berkshire (Keil 1964, 61).

Winterbourne Monkton was the earliest recorded acquisition. It was granted to Glastonbury Abbey by the earldorman Wulfere in the late-9th century (Sawyer 1968, *S*341; Freeman 1983d, 194). The settlement itself lay centrally within the parish, and may have been predominantly on the west bank of the river where the church and later manor farm now stand. In 1306 the demesne amounted to a little over 260a

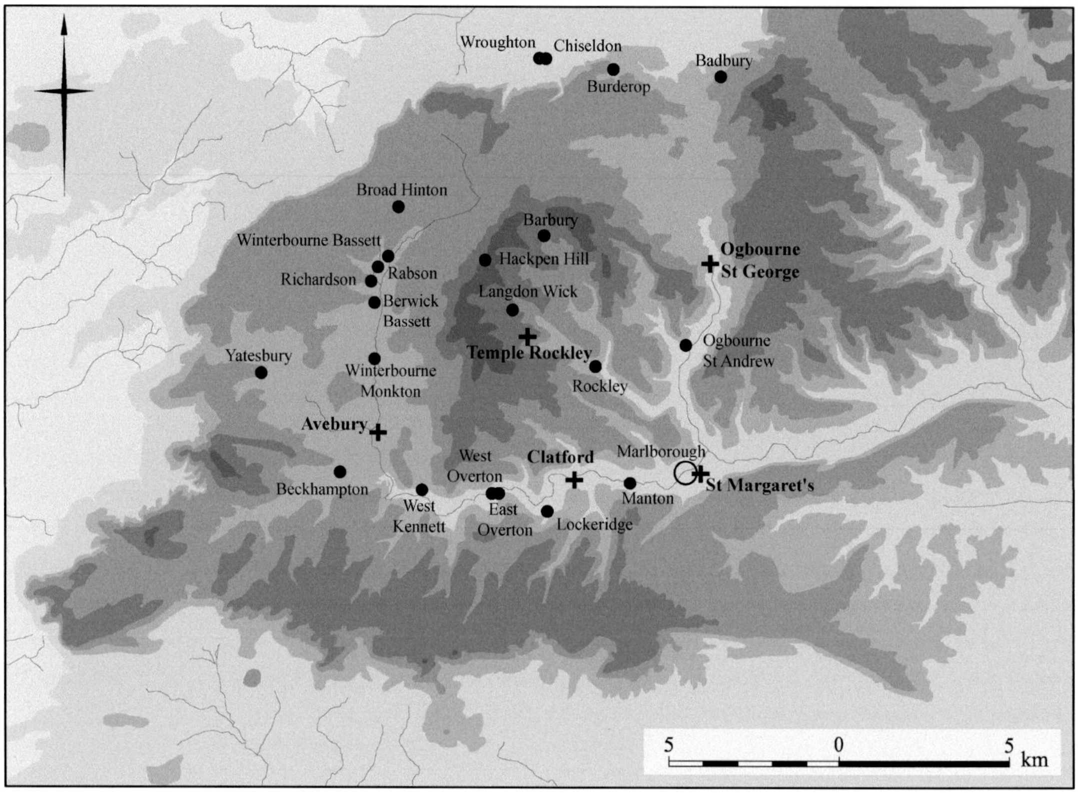

Fig 17:1 Location of sites mentioned in the text.

(*c*169ha) (Keil 1964, 206). The arable lay in the two open fields with pasture, amounting to *c*140a (*c*57ha), on Windmill Hill and in the east on the steeper escarpment of Monkton Down (Keil 1964, 206; Freeman 1983d, 195).

The second estate was at Mildenhall, which lay on the north bank of the Kennet to the east of Marlborough. At the time of the Domesday Survey, Glastonbury Abbey held ten hides here (Thorn & Thorn 1979, 7.7). The value of this estate to the monks, in addition to the arable fields and extensive pasture, was its woodland, which presumably lay on the higher ground on the south side of the Kennet within Savernake Forest. Although the first mention of Mildenhall as a holding of Glastonbury was in the 11th century, it was probably already in the abbey's hands in the later 10th century (Abrams 1996, 176).

The final estate was at Badbury where the monks held twenty hides with over half in demesne (Thorn & Thorn 1979, 7.6). Despite Badbury and Winterbourne Monkton being relatively close they were nevertheless markedly different: Monkton, which was the larger of the two estates, lay predominantly on Lower Chalk, which was eminently suitable for cultivation on the slightly undulating plateau. In contrast, Badbury, which was partly on Lower Chalk, also extended to the north on greensand and clay where a more varied agricultural regime could ensue. Badbury, for example, contained 100a (*c*40ha) of meadow at Domesday compared to Monkton's 6a (*c*2ha), and in the 14th century Badbury had a large herd of cattle unlike Monkton, which specialized in sheep as well as cultivation. It is evident that the monks exchanged both livestock and grain between their manors (Stevenson 1970, 16), thus capitalizing on the particular resources of each estate and supplementing shortfalls whenever they occurred.

Another monastic estate lay near Badbury, at Chiseldon. This estate had been granted to Old Minster in Winchester in the 9th century (Sawyer 1968, *S*354) and later granted to New Minster, which in turn became Hyde Abbey (Sawyer 1968, *S*370; Stevenson 1970, 10). This estate was estimated at forty hides at the time of the Domesday Survey and was the largest single holding in the area. The location is in many respects similar to Badbury, with differing geology and soils when compared to the more southerly estates on the Downs. As well as supporting a large sheep flock, Chiseldon also had a considerable cattle herd in the 13th century. Like the estate at Badbury, it lay within the 'cheese-producing' area of Wiltshire; in 1282–3, for example, 163 cheeses were made, of which fifty-two were sent to Hyde Abbey (Stevenson 1970, 15).

The nuns of Amesbury Abbey held a relatively small estate of six hides at Rabson in Winterbourne Bassett in 1066 (Thorn & Thorn 1979, 16.6). The estate lay to the south of the village of

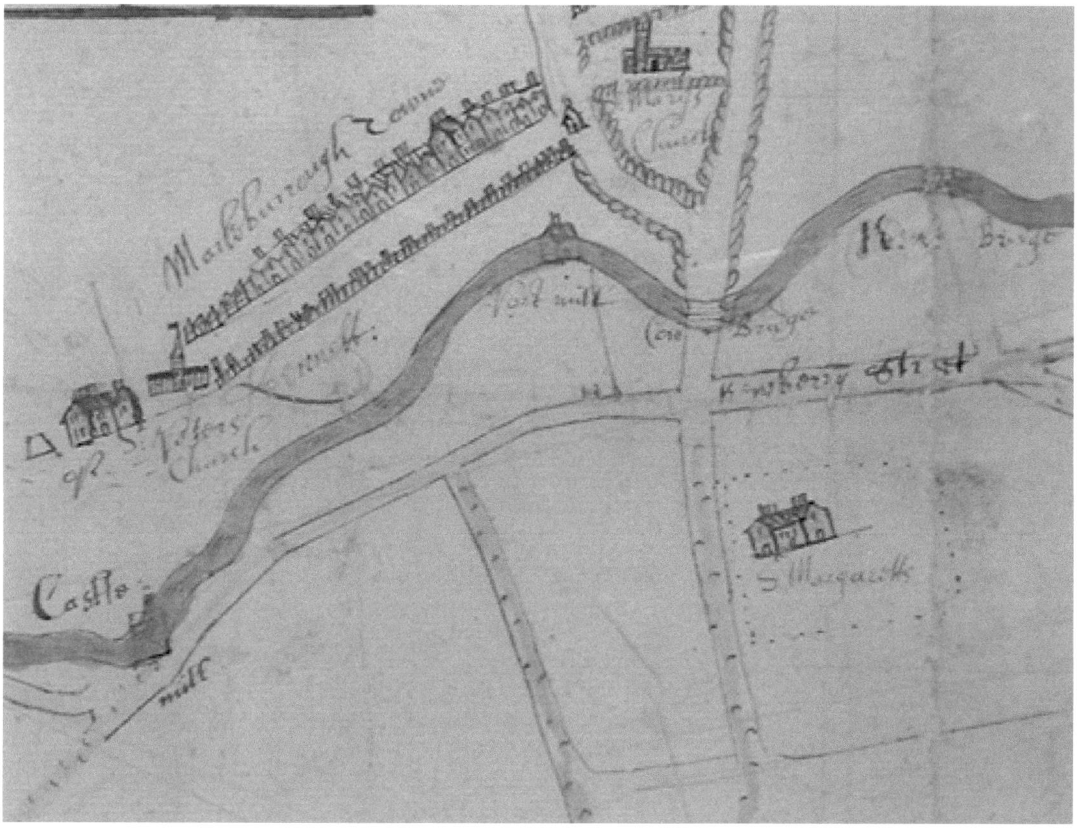

Fig 17:2 The location of St Margaret's priory, Preshute (WSRO: 1300/46).

Winterbourne Bassett with the settlement itself probably in the area of the present farmstead with its fields to the east and west. Pasture, in common with Glastonbury Abbey's estate at Winterbourne Monkton, was on the escarpment of Hackpen Hill (BL: M.T.6.e.1.(1.)).

The cathedral priory of St Swithun's, Winchester, also held land on the Marlborough Downs at the time of the Domesday Survey. It held a thirty-hide estate in the tithing of Wroughton, while along the Kennett valley in the south, it also held East Overton (Crittall 1980, 238; Stevenson 1980, 188). The final pre-Conquest estate was West Overton, which was held by Wilton Abbey (Stevenson 1980, 189).

In addition to these temporalities, a number of monasteries also held spiritualities on the Downs. Two examples are Hyde Abbey and Cirencester Abbey. Hyde Abbey was granted the church at Chiseldon in 903 (Sawyer 1968, S370; Stevenson 1970, 19). The church's land probably lay at Burderop and was coterminous with Parsonage Farm, which was estimated at *c*439a (*c*178ha) in 1781 (Stevenson 1970, 15). Cirencester Abbey held the churches at Avebury and Winterbourne Monkton, as well as the rectory estate that included lands and the rectorial tithes of Avebury and West Kennett and rights in Beckhampton (Freeman 1983a, 92; Freeman 1983d, 196).

Post-Conquest monastic settlement

The two centuries following the Norman Conquest constituted a period of continued and increasing monastic exploitation on the Marlborough Downs. This process can be grouped into two specific categories. First, the establishment of new houses actually on the downland; this was led by the alien priories which were established along the river valleys and the Templars who founded a small preceptory in a secluded position on the higher downs. The Gilbertines arrived rather later, but nevertheless were granted land to the south of Marlborough where they built a small priory. Their principal landholding was to the south of Marlborough, bordering Savernake Forest, and along the Kennet valley. The Carmelites also established a small friary in Marlborough.

The second category is those monasteries that held land on the Downs, but lay some distance away. Foremost amongst these were the Cistercians, who held land on the western Lower Chalk plateau and on the higher central downs.

The Gilbertines

A house of Gilbertine canons was founded on the south bank of the Kennet, just beyond the bounds of Marlborough, by at least 1199 (Knowles & Hadcock 1953, 174; Golding 1995,

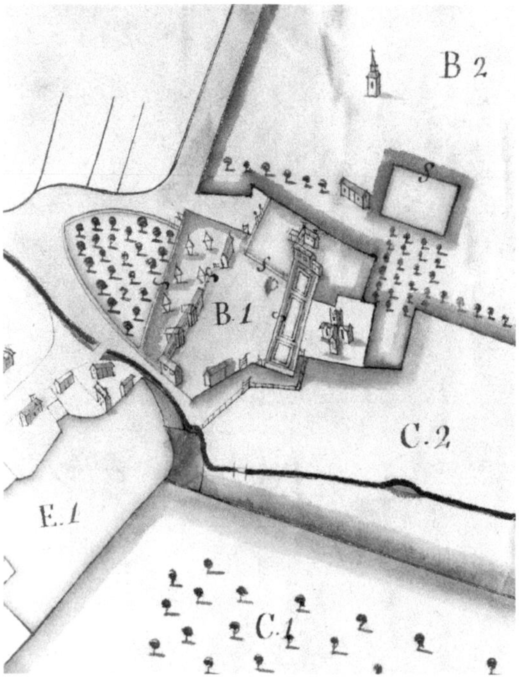

Fig 17:3 The 1751 estate map of Ogbourne by John Doharty. North is to the right (held at King's College Library, Cambridge: OGB /203).

225). The priory, dedicated to St Margaret, was one of two Gilbertine royal foundations (the other being at Newstead, Lincolnshire) and was the most distant from Sempringham, Lincolnshire, the order's 'mother' house. The Gilbertine order, founded by Gilbert of Sempringham *c*1131, was the only English religious order and, unlike other monastic congregations, it had both double houses of canons and nuns as well as single houses.

St Margaret's priory, which was a single house of canons, enjoyed close ties with the Crown, particularly Henry III who was to prove their greatest benefactor. His gifts included pasture rights for sixteen oxen and four cows in Savernake Forest; timber from the forest for building and repairs to the priory; and a fair to be held on the vigil and feast of St Margaret (20th July). They also had the right to the toll on brewing beer in Marlborough Barton and other rights in Marlborough Castle (Chettle & Kirby 1956a, 316). The relationship between Crown and priory was assured in 1265 when a canon celebrated mass in the castle chapel for an annual stipend of 50*s* (Golding 1995, 226).

The priory does not appear to have been particularly wealthy and at its suppression in 1539 there was a prior and only four canons. The precinct, including its orchards and gardens, is known to have covered an area of *c*1.2ha (Chettle & Kirby 1956a, 318 quoting PRO: E 315/400). Although no evidence of the priory buildings survives, its location can be identified from an estate map of 1668, which shows a post-Suppression house, known as St Margaret's, set within a rectangular enclosure (WRO 1300/46; Fig 17:2). This observation is supported by the parish Tithe map that shows a rectangular field in the area of the former mansion house measuring *c*2ha known as 'Priors Croft and Fair Close' (WSRO: Preshute TA map).

No archaeological investigation has been carried out on the site of the priory apart from a small-scale excavation undertaken by Marlborough College in 1938 (Sewell, 1938, 12). The area where three skeletons and a quantity of floor and roof tiles were found was thought to be part of the cloister garth. The floor tiles included several with a *fleur-de-lis* design that dated to the 13th century and were amongst the earliest from the site (*ibid*, 15). The limited nature of the excavation, however, coupled with stone robbing and the remains of 17th century brickwork, makes a meaningful interpretation difficult.

Much of the canon's land lay close to the priory, in Marlborough Barton, with tenements in Marlborough and along Newbury Street on the south side of the Kennet. In 1542 there was 80a (*c*32ha) in demesne distributed in Estfeld, Middelfield, Westfeld, and Brechhorne near Savernake Forest (WSRO: 9/2/129; 9/2/392). The first element 'Brech' in the field name Brechhorne, meaning the 'breaking of land' (Gelling 1984, 233; Gover *et al* 1939, 423) indicates asserting on the fringes of the forest. The sheep pasture was in the common of Marlborough and meadow lay along the Kennet riverbank and included Castle Meadow below Marlborough Castle. There was also a water mill, known as the Portmill, situated on the southern boundary of Marlborough.

The Gilbertines, or White Canons, had nine manors in Wiltshire, the most valuable being East Kennet where they may have established a grange. The others were at Marlborough, Winterbourne Monkton, Yatesbury, and along the Kennet valley at Lockeridge, Clatford, and Manton. The latter holding was at Flexborough, which lies along the western side of Manton, next to Clatford. Elsewhere in Wiltshire they held land in Burbage, Puthall, East and West Grafton, and Allington (Chettle & Kirby 1956a, 318).

The Gilbertines were influenced by the Cistercians in their Rule and their attitude to estates and regarded a grange (which was essentially a monastic farm managed by lay brothers) as a spiritual and economic imperative (Golding 1995, 394). There may have been a grange at East Kennet, possibly near the church. Grants by local landowners to them included three messuages, a cottage, five virgates of land and a meadow (WSRO: 9/2/392). They also held the spiritualities of the rectory (Chettle & Kirby

1956a, 318), which presumably implies that they held the glebe. With this accumulation of land, perhaps consolidated into blocks and outside manorial control, and the interest in the church, we may be seeing either a grange estate, or at least the process of its formation.

There may have been another grange at Lockeridge where the Canons had 100a (*c*40ha) in the late-13th century. This estate included two messuages and may have been centred at Upper Lockeridge (Fry 1908, 203; Stevenson 1980, 190).

The Carmelite Friars

Marlborough was also the site of a small Carmelite friary. The 'White Friars' were established in the town *c*1316 when their two principal benefactors, the merchants William de Rammeshulle and John Godhyne, granted them a messuage and 2a (*c*0.8ha) of land to build their friary with a garden (Waylen 1854, 82; Galbraith 1956, 333). Six years later they gave further land adjoining the newly founded friary, which was situated near the town centre between the High Street and the river. At its suppression in 1538 the friary comprised a church, cloister, chapter house, dormitory, prior's lodging, kitchen, orchards, a dovecote, and ponds called 'Fish Garthe' (Galbraith 1956, 333; Stevenson 1983c, 206). No structural evidence of the friary survives; however, its location can be identified from a 1843 map, which shows 'The Priory' near the High Street (WSRO: 2027). The precinct boundary may have been contained between the High Street and the river, and between a side street and drain in the south and another smaller stream and property boundary in the north.

The Alien Priories

There were three alien priories on the Marlborough Downs: Ogbourne St George, Avebury and Clatford. An alien priory was essentially a small Benedictine house that was dependent on a monastery in Normandy or one of the new Norman abbeys built in England. There were also others that were dependent on former Anglo-Saxon houses (Aston 1993, 65). Nearly thirty Norman monasteries held land or spiritualities in England (Matthew 1962, 29). Although some of these houses founded conventual priories on their newly acquired land, the majority did not, and simply regarded the land as outlying estates, which were administered by perhaps only a few monks who acted as bailiffs for the Norman monastery (*ibid*, 51). Many dependent houses were little more than manor houses comprising perhaps a hall, barns, and other outbuildings. These minor houses, or cells, had a chequered history and were taken into the hands of the Crown at various times during the wars with France. In the 14th century some of their land was confiscated and used to endow new colleges and the founding of some Carthusian monasteries (*ibid*, 118). The alien priories were finally suppressed in the early 15th century, which enabled Henry V to endow two religious houses and Henry VI two colleges (*ibid*, 118).

The largest alien priory in the region was at Ogbourne St George where a daughter house of the abbey of Bec-Hellouin was founded *c*1149 (Knowles & Hadcock 1953, 87). It was to become the estate centre for a number of widely dispersed manors of the abbey in the south of England (Morgan 1946, 22). Ogbourne St George was clearly of some considerable economic importance since it was also the administrative centre for the Honour of Wallingford (Freeman 1983c, 152).

The village of Ogbourne St George lies on the west bank of the River Og some 6km north of the market town of Marlborough. An estate map, dating to 1751, shows the manor house and church detached from the remainder of the village (Fig 17:3). The house is set within a walled enclosure with a regular row of buildings to the south. A long formal garden extends from the manor house along the south side of the church and a dovecote lies isolated in a field to the west. This complex is, in all probability, on the site of the former cell. An inventory dating to 1324 of the chattels at Ogbourne describes the manor house as comprising a hall with five trestle tables, four forms and two washbasins. There was also a storeroom, a bake house, brewhouse, kitchen, larder, and dairy (Morgan 1939, 149). The present house dates to at least 1619 (Anon 1942, 1228; Pevsner 1975, 366), but in the absence of any detailed architectural analysis, the possibility of an earlier core in the structure should not be ignored.

The abbey of Bec-Hellouin's estate on the Downs was extensive and covered much of the parishes of both Ogbourne St George and Ogbourne St Andrew. At the time of the Domesday Survey, Ogbourne was a large estate of some thirty hides held by the Crown (Thorn & Thorn 1979, 1.22), which later passed to Maud of Wallingford, who conveyed it to the abbey of Bec-Hellouin some time after 1122 (Freeman 1983c, 154). It is not clear when the estate was subdivided, but in 1294 Ogbourne St George was one of the largest of Bec's manors with a value of £82 13s (*ibid*, 155). The open fields lay principally to the north of the village, with meadow on the lower ground near the river. The demesne arable covered an area of 558a (*c*363ha) and there was enough pasture for 1,450 sheep; this pasture was probably on the downland to the south and west of the parish. Cattle were pastured on Rough Hill where there was also a windmill (*ibid*).

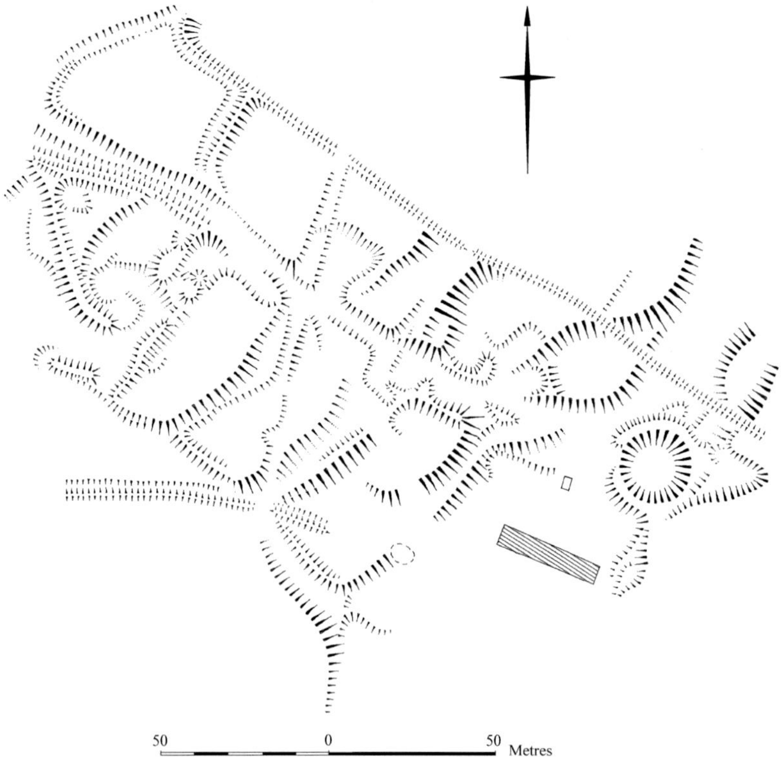

Fig 17:4 The deserted settlement at Barbury (NMR: SU 17 SE 6, © Crown copyright NMR).

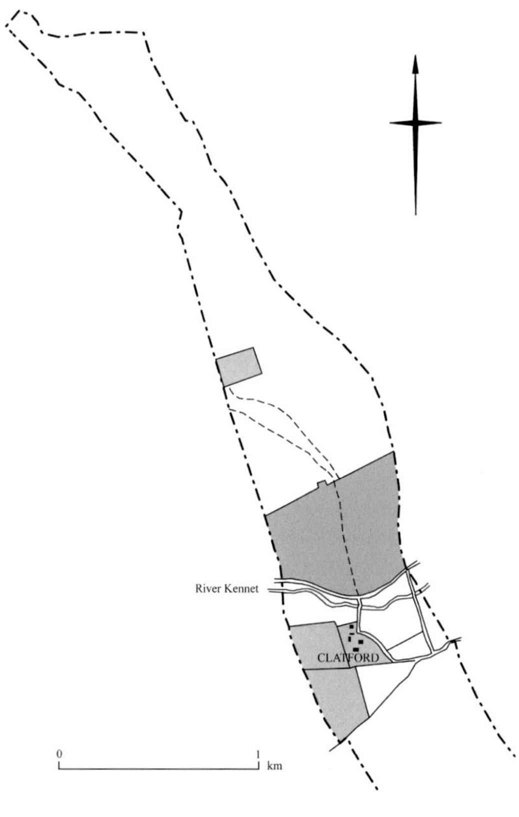

Fig 17:5 Lands of Clatford Priory (re-drawn from Preshute Tithe Award map).

The second Bec-Hellouin holding lay nearby at Ogbourne St Andrew. The village lay on the west bank of the River Og, *c*2km south of Ogbourne St George. The open fields were probably on both sides of the Og with pasture beyond on the downs. A late-13th century survey records 352a (*c*146ha) of arable in demesne and common pasture for 1,000 sheep. This land was known as Poughcombe Farm from the 17th century (Freeman 1983b, 145–6).

The second alien cell was at Avebury, which was founded during the reign of Henry 1 (1100–1135) (Knowles & Hadcock 1953, 83). It was one of two cells in England belonging to the abbey of St George de Boscherville, near Rouen (Kirby 1956b, 392). Although the present manor house dates to *c*1557, it conceivably lies on the site of the former cell (NMR: SU 07 SE 18). A survey, dating to 1324/5, describes the house as comprising a hall, kitchen, bakehouse, brewhouse, cellar and dairy (TNA:PRO: E.106/8/26). Another survey conducted some thirty years earlier indicated that the cell incorporated a dovecote and garden (TNA:PRO: E.106/2/2). A chapel is also mentioned at this time, but whether this was a separate building is unclear since, in 1142, the monks were granted licence to have an oratory in their court; it was to be used only by the monks and other religious (Kemp 2000, 51), thus maintaining the autonomy of the church at Avebury.

The monks' holding at Avebury amounted to 322a (*c*130ha) of land in demesne and 15a (*c*6ha) of meadow. There was also a water mill and a windmill (perhaps on Windmill Hill). They had pasture for 500 sheep, twenty-four oxen, six bullocks and six cows. The population of Avebury in 1294 was sixty-seven households including four free tenants with six virgates, thirty-six villeins holding one virgate, five villains with ½ virgate, and twenty-two cottagers (TNA:PRO: E. 106/2/2).

Avebury Priory held two other estates on the Marlborough Downs with a third at Catcombe in Hilmarton. The largest of the downland estates was at Barbury where, in 1294, they held a messuage and 120a (*c*41ha) of land in demesne valued at 4d. This value suggests that the arable land lay predominantly on the Middle Chalk to the south, with pasture on the higher slopes and within Barbury hillfort where there was sufficient for 300 sheep and eight oxen. There were also five villeins who held four virgates of land as well as two cottagers, each with an acre (*c*0.4ha) of land (TNA:PRO: E.106/2/2).

Situated between Barbury Castle and Barbury Castle Farm are earthworks that have been interpreted as a deserted medieval settlement (NMR: SU 17 NE 6; Fig 17.4), which may have been Avebury's holding. The earthworks cover an area of *c*1.5ha and lie in a south-east facing

Fig 17:6 An aerial photograph of the deserted medieval settlement at Richardson (NMR 15208/37. © Crown Copyright NMR).

coombe; they include a well-defined hollow way with several small rectilinear building platforms and closes. Pottery sherds dating to the 12th and 13th century have been found (*ibid*).

A third alien cell was situated at Clatford. This was the smallest in the region. It was one of two properties in Wiltshire (the other one being at Hullavington) granted by Hugh de Mortimer in the late-11th or early 12th century to the abbey of St Victor en Caux (Seine Maritime) (Stevenson 1983d, 173). In 1337 the demesne arable amounted to 60a (*c*24ha) divided into equal areas of wheat, barley and oats. There were also 279 sheep, eight cows and twelve oxen (*ibid*, 178). Little is recorded of the buildings apart from a chapel that was mentioned some time before 1443 (Blakiston 1956, 394).

The cell probably lay in the area of the present Clatford House, which apparently dates to the early 17th century (Butterworth 1999, 95; Stevenson 1983d, 173). Earthworks to the east of the house probably represent additional settlement desertion.

The cell's landholding can be identified from the tithe award and map where it is described as ancient demesne and had a negligible tithe value – it amounted to 163a (*c*66ha) (WSRO: Preshute Tithe Award). It lay in consolidated blocks on the northern side of the tithing, the largest of which was on rising ground to the north of the London to Bath road (Fig 17:5). There were also three closes beside Clatford House and a detached enclosure, probably a sheep enclosure, on the higher downs. Apart from this land, the monks also had a mill on the Kennet (there was also one here in 1086), which was ruinous in 1416 (*ibid*, 179), but the millrace can still be seen.

Soldiers of Christ

The Knights of the Temple of Solomon of Jerusalem, more commonly known as the Knights Templars, held four estates on the Marlborough Downs. The Templars, in common with the other military orders, combined a military with a religious way of life. They originated in the Holy Land during the early 12th century (Forey 1992, 1). Their principal estate on the Marlborough Downs was the manor of Temple Rockley, which was situated on the higher downs and granted to them by John FitzGilbert, brother-in-law of the Earl of Salisbury, by 1159 (Lees 1935, 206). The estate lay to the south of the tithing of Langdon Wick in the parish of Preshute and was probably coterminous with the area of the present tithing of Temple Rockley (WSRO: Preshute Tithe Award). In 1185 the demesne amounted to a carucate (which was probably equivalent to 40–50a (*c*17–21ha) (Lees 1935, cxxx); there were also eight tenants each holding 5a (*c*2ha) of land, while a ninth held a croft (*ibid*).

A second estate was in neighbouring Rockley in the parish of Ogbourne St Andrew where the Templars were granted a hide by Robert of Ewias in the 12th century (*ibid*, 206; Stevenson 1983d, 145). The largest of the Templar 'outliers' however, was a manor at Lockeridge, which was granted to them by the Earl of Hereford sometime between 1141 and 1143 (Stevenson

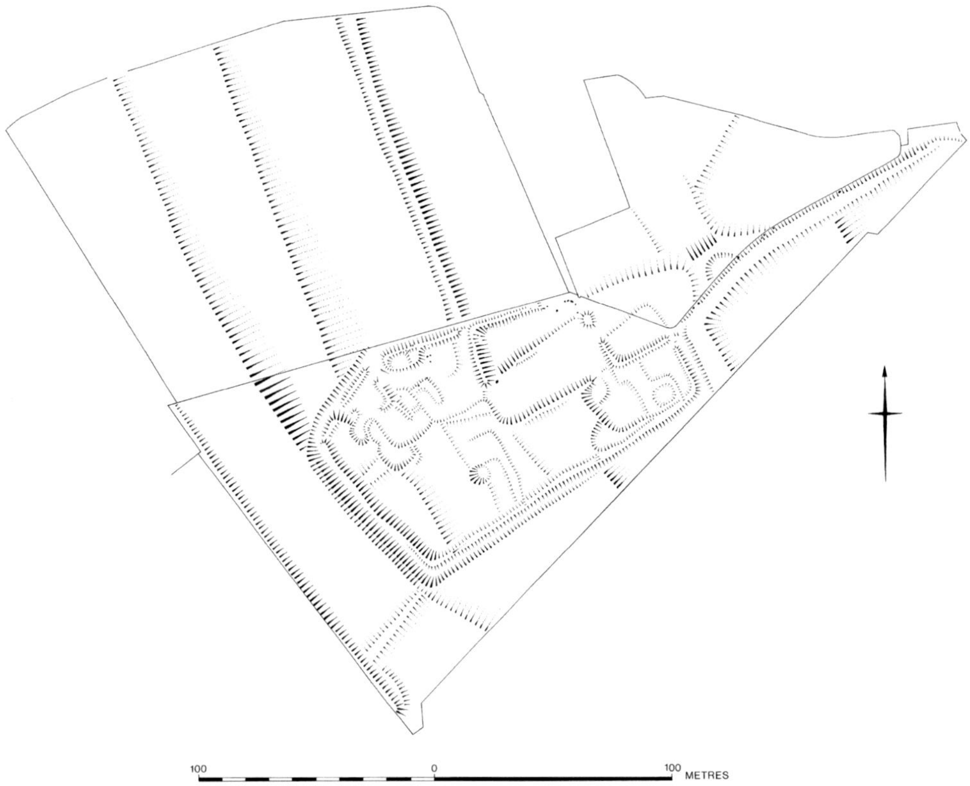

Fig 17:7 Earthwork plan of the grange at Wick Down Farm. © G Brown

1980, 189). Further land at Lockeridge was added in the later-12th century (*ibid*, 196). The fourth estate was at Berwick Bassett where they held a virgate of land (Lees 1935, 53).

The Templar's land on the Downs probably lay within a bailiwick that included other estates in Wiltshire, Berkshire and Oxfordshire (*ibid*, xxxii). It was administered from a preceptory, which was probably similar in form to an alien priory. The location of the preceptory at Temple Rockley is unclear; although Chandler (2001, 190) suggests that it may lie at 'The Beeches' copse, at the southern extremity of the tithing, where a midden containing 12th and 13th century pottery was found. However, no structures were identified here (NMR: SU 17 SW 23). It has also been suggested that it lay near Wick Down Farm, within an earthwork enclosure (Fowler & Blackwell 1998, 138; Fowler 2001, 169); however, this enclosure lies in the tithing of Langdon Wick, which was a holding of Stanley Abbey and therefore probably their grange (*below*). Perhaps a more plausible location would be in the area of the present Temple Rockley Farm, which lies in a wide valley closer to a source of water and where gravels provide more fertile soil.

Following the suppression of the Templars in 1308 their estates passed to the Knights Hospitallers in 1314 (Gilchrist 1995, 68). In 1338 Rockley contained a messuage with a garden and dovecote, valued at 10*s*. There was also 320a (*c*129ha) of arable land valued at 4*d* an acre (the same as Avebury's Badbury estate), pasture for 900 sheep and a several pasture for twenty-two large animals. Meadow, amounting to 6a (*c*2.4ha), was the most valued land at 12*d* an acre (Larking 1857, 187). At the Lockeridge estate there was a messuage and pasture for 300 sheep, but no arable land was listed (*ibid*). At this time the estates were administered from a larger preceptory at Sandford, Oxfordshire (Stevenson 1983d, 179).

Downland esteates

Apart from these new post-Conquest foundations, only one other monastery held any appreciable amount of land on the Downs – the Cistercian monastery at Stanley. Founded in 1151 (Knowles & Hadcock 1953, 115) on the northern edge of the Royal Forest of Chippenham, Stanley Abbey lay within easy reach of the Downs. By the mid-16th century Stanley held thirty estates in Wiltshire and neighbouring counties, four of which were on the Marlborough Downs: at Richardson, Berwick Bassett, Broad Hinton, and Langdon Wick, as well as additional pasture on Hackpen Hill (Birch 1875; Chettle & Kirby 1956b, 273). The abbey also held a small meadow at Avebury and tenements in Marlborough.

Henry VIII's survey of ecclesiastical property in 1535, the *Valor Ecclesiasticus*, lists a grange of Stanley Abbey at Richardson. It is referred to as *Berwick Bassett cum Richardson et Langeden* (Caley & Hunter 1814, 114), which suggests that these estates were grouped together for administrative purposes at this date. The settlement of Richardson itself lies to the south of Rabson in Winterbourne Bassett. Here, earthworks covering an area of *c*12ha, lie on the southern edge of the parish and represent the remains of at least fifteen house platforms and other irregular closes. On the northern side of Richardson Wood, the southern half of a dry moat survives. Ridge and furrow is also present to the north-east and south of the settlement. A post-medieval house and gardens also overlies part of the site and fragments of medieval tile, pottery, post-medieval brick and stone rubble have been found. (NMR: SU 07 SE 23; Fig 17:6).

Although it is not entirely clear where the grange was actually located, it is tempting to identify it with the moated site within the wood. It lies at the western end of the settlement and detached from the other properties. By the mid-18th century a grand house had been built near the moated site (BL: M.T.6.e.1.(1)). At this time Richardson was divided into two farms, Upper Richardson (which can be equated with Whyr Farm) and Lower Richardson, which included the area of the deserted settlement.

Land in Richardson had been acquired by Stanley Abbey in small parcels sometime in or before the 13th century. The amounts varied from as little as an acre to one of 24a (*c*16ha). In common with Cistercian estates elsewhere, the land was probably consolidated by exchange and further purchase to form a compact block along the southern edge of the parish extending up to the downs and probably into adjacent Berwick Bassett. The actual estate holding is difficult to reconstruct since none of the land is shown as tithe-free on the Tithe Award map; although documentary sources refer to it possessing a drove and a sheep pasture on Hackpen Hill (Birch 1875, 260).

A further holding of Stanley Abbey was at Langdon Wick, which was originally part of the Barton of Marlborough before the Crown granted it to the abbey in 1194 'for pasture' (*ibid*, 284). Little is known about this estate in the medieval period, although it was clearly an important resource in the monastic economy in the later-13th century since it was the abbey's fourth highest valuation in Pope Nicholas' taxation of 1291, higher even than the neighbouring grange at Richardson (Caley 1802, 193).

Langdon Wick lies on the higher downs to the north of Temple Rockley and at the northern extremity of the parish of Preshute. It covers an area of *c*310ha and, apart from a small parcel of land on its southern boundary, was tithe-free (WSRO: Preshute TA; WSRO: 1780/4) and therefore undoubtedly represents Stanley's estate.

This large expanse of land was farmed from a grange, which was probably the rectilinear earthwork enclosure that lies 200m to the south-west of Wick Down Farm. The enclosure covers an area of *c*1ha and overlies a 'Celtic' field system. In the north-western corner there are at least three building platforms with their attendant yards. To the east of these platforms are two large rectilinear enclosures, which were probably stockyards. Other closes and building platforms lie along the southern side (Fig 17:7; Brown *forthcoming*). A medieval date for this enclosure is indicated by the pottery that was recovered from the enclosure bank (Goddard 1913, 309); however, an earlier pedigree should not be dismissed since only the bank has been investigated. Two large closes, which may originally have been part of the 'Celtic' field system, abut the grange on the southern side. The closes are on the same general alignment as the grange and may have been utilized as further stock enclosures.

Although the initial grant to Stanley Abbey was for pasture, there is also evidence of possible medieval cultivation (NMR: SU 17 SW 44 & 153) to the east and north of the grange (and significantly outside the two possible stock enclosures). The cultivation extends over the rising downland towards the tithing boundary and in the west as far as a drove that leads north from the grange towards Hackpen Hill.

In addition to these holdings, Stanley Abbey held additional pasture on Hackpen Hill, including another sheep-drove (Birch 1875, 260). Since the Cistercians farmed their land outside manorial control, it is likely that the pasture was a consolidated block, perhaps defined by ditches or fences, and that the droves provided access across the downs and a link between their estates.

Conclusion

A glance at the ecclesiastical map of Wiltshire at the time of the Suppression of the Monasteries in the mid-16th century shows that, after the Salisbury area, the Marlborough Downs had the highest concentration of monastic settlement in the county (Crittall 1956, 154). Even by the time of the Domesday Survey, monastic influence in the region was substantial, particularly along the Lower Chalk plateau in the west and north, and along the Kennet. All these estates functioned within a much larger network supplying the needs of a monastery and also supplying and exchanging resources between estates.

Sheep-and-corn husbandry were the mainstay of medieval agriculture on the Wessex Chalk, and the Marlborough Downs was no exception; it was an ideal area for large sheep flocks and extensive cultivation of the lighter Lower Chalk soils, which had first attracted the Anglo-Saxon monasteries. The 'new orders', who settled here in the 12th century, continued this exploitation and established themselves along the Og and Kennet. This largely riverine siting is of interest, and may have been influenced more by their proximity to the great medieval powerhouse of Marlborough, with its castle and market, which undoubtedly had an effect on their fortunes (as well as that of the region as a whole) than to any other single factor. The priories were also sited relatively close to the London to Bristol road, which would have provided good communication to other markets.

The importance of Marlborough in this new 'monastic landscape' should not be ignored. Apart from the two monastic houses in or near the town, it also played host to a number of others: Bradenstoke Priory, Maiden Bradley Priory and Stanley Abbey all had tenements here. These properties may have been used as a commercial 'base' for business transactions in the town and a ready access to the market, as well as providing a source of revenue.

A final point about the siting of these new houses, which by its very nature is lost to the archaeological and historical record, is the possibility of a conscious effort to further 'Christianise' this former pagan 'ritual' landscape and impose a new 'order'. It is interesting, for example, that Avebury was chosen as the site of an alien priory, which was sited beside the former Anglo-Saxon minster, and also just outside the bounds of the henge. Could the granting of land here by a Norman lord be seen as an imposition on the former Anglo-Saxon regime, as theirs was on the pagan? Another local example is at Ogbourne St Andrew, where the present 12th century church is beside a large bowl barrow, thus emphasizing the re-use of a sacred pagan site. When excavated, as well as the primary deposits and finds of Romano-British and medieval date, an Anglo-Saxon secondary inhumation dating to the 10th century was found in the barrow (Freeman 1983b, 139).

What 'physical' effect of the ownership of such a large tract of land by the monastic community had on the landscape is not entirely clear. For example, apart from two notable exceptions, it is unclear whether the monastic demesne was distributed amongst the common fields or whether it was held in severalty (it is interesting to note, however, that the glebe of Beckhampton chapel lay in small strips in Stanmore, an area of common land to the west of the village of Winterbourne Basset (WSRO: Winterbourne Basset TA). The exceptions were the Cistercians and Gilbertines who pursued a deliberate policy of land acquisition that enabled them as far as possible to consolidate their land into blocks and farm it outside manorial control (this perhaps implies that their land was enclosed in some way). This would presumably have enabled them to farm their land as they wished, with little or no recourse to their neighbours. The Cistercians were particularly active in this respect, acquiring land on the lower ground in the west and central downland, but also extensive pasture on the higher ground.

This brief essay has highlighted the extent of monastic involvement on the Marlborough Downs and assessed its influence on the landscape. It has also inevitably highlighted a number of gaps in our understanding of this period. Further research, for example, is needed to identify the specific land holdings of some of the monasteries, and for the moment the effect on the landscape of the leasing of monastic land, so prevalent by at least the 15th century, remains unclear.

Acknowledgements

I would like to express my thanks to David Robinson, Andrew Reynolds and David Field who commented on an earlier draft of this paper. Deborah Cunliffe re-drew Fig 17:4 and 17:7 for publication.

Primary Sources

The National Archive:Public Record Office (TNA:PRO)

E. 106/2/2 – Extents of lands of Alien Priories in Gloucestershire, and Wiltshire 22Ed.1 [1293/4]

E. 106/8/26 – Extent of lands of Alien Priories 6 Feb 1324/5

British Library (BL)

M.T.6.e.1.(1.) – A survey of Winterbourne, Rapson, Richardson, Upper Richardson alias Whyr, Summers's Hand alias Trotman's Farms [1760]

Wiltshire and Swindon Record Office (WSRO)

9/2/129 – Letters patent giving St Margaret's Priory, Marlborough dated 1543.

9/2/389 – Miscellaneous papers concerning lawsuits about St Margaret's Priory, 1763

9/2/392 – Copies of records used to prepare cases in disputes with the Duke of Marlborough 1236–1762 including the bailiff's account of the priory in 1540.

1300/46 – Preshute, Savernake Forest, 1668

1780/4 – The Manor of Langdon and Wake in the Parish of Preshute 1779

2027 – Map of Marlborough, Wiltshire 1843

TA Preshute – Tithe map of Preshute 1845

TA Winterbourne Basset – Tithe map of Winterbourne Basset 1843

18
Medieval and Later Sheep Farming on the Marlborough Downs

Nicola Smith

Sheep have been one of the most important influences in shaping the landscape around Avebury. A mixed economy of corn growing and sheep rearing dominated the chalk areas of Wiltshire from at least the medieval period onwards and its impact could clearly be seen until recently in vast areas of old chalk grassland on the downland sheep-walks. Within living memory much of this distinctive historical landscape of the Marlborough Downs has been lost to intensive arable farming or to racehorse gallops. Even so, it is still possible to find traces of the sheep, and their shepherds, who inhabited the hills for so many centuries. Some old chalk grassland survives in steep-sided dry valleys, while place-names recall long forgotten activities, and despite its transient nature, some interesting and distinctive features connected with sheep husbandry are also still to be found. This paper will consider the methods of sheep farming practised on the Marlborough Downs and identify some of the archaeological remains.

Introduction

Sheep were among the earliest semi-domesticated animals kept by prehistoric communities. Excavations have demonstrated that they were kept at settlements on the Marlborough Downs from at least the late Bronze Age, when they formed part of a mixed economy with cattle and arable (Gingell 1992, 142, 156). The earthwork remains of numerous Bronze Age settlements and 'Celtic' field systems found on the downs to this day demonstrate prehistoric use of the chalk hills for both settlement and agriculture. By 500–1000AD, however, most of the downland was used largely for sheep grazing (Fowler & Blackwell 1998, 136). Many valley settlements became the centres of long thin land units, townships, stretching up onto the hills to encompass their share of the upland grazing land as well as meadow and arable closer to home.

Little has been written about the sheep husbandry of the Marlborough Downs, although detailed and informative accounts for Wiltshire as a whole have been published (Crittall 1959, 21–29; Davis 1811; Hare 1994). There was in fact very little interest in the archaeological remains of sheep farming until recent times. When Crawford and Keiller published their plan and an aerial photograph of a 'perhaps medieval' sheep enclosure on Cherhill Down (NMR SU 06 NE 50) they commented that 'the earthworks on this plate are none of them of any particular interest' (Crawford & Keiller 1928, 234). Sheep-keeping enclosures were occasionally excavated in the belief that they may be prehistoric settlements, but usually very little was found. Archaeological evidence has, however, come from two excavations in particular. A rectangular enclosure (NMR SU 06 NW 42) near Morgan's Hill was excavated by M Cunnington. From pottery and other evidence (*see below*) found at the site, it was interpreted as a probable medieval fold or penning for sheep. More recently, excavations of an earthwork complex at Raddun found it to be a farmstead whose economy was based on sheep husbandry and which began life as a sheep house in about 1220 (Fowler 2000, 120–128). Specific area studies have also added to our knowledge of sheep husbandry on the Marlborough Downs. Most relevant is Fowler's study of Fyfield and Overton Downs (Fowler 2000; Fowler & Blackwell 1998) but work in adjacent areas such as Salisbury Plain (McOmish *et al* 2002, 115–117) and the Cotswolds (Dyer 1995) is also significant.

Sheep and corn

During the medieval period the usual farming practice on the north Wiltshire Downs was cultivation in open fields and sheep keeping. Corn was usually the most important product of manors but revenue was gained from otherwise unproductive land by maintaining large sheep flocks. This is seen clearly at Ogbourne, an estate held by the French monks of Bec Hellion, where in 1282 there was pasture for *c*1,000 sheep but most of the estate's income, £87 out of £114, came from corn sales (Elrington 1983, 145). Similarly on the Barton estate of Marlborough corn growing was most profitable but flocks of over 1,000 sheep were recorded in 1196 and 1279 (*ibid*, 174). Arable was also of prime importance on the estates of Glastonbury Abbey, but their accounts for 1333–4 record the sale of 245 sheep's fleeces and 202 lamb's fleeces from their estate at Winterbourne Monkton, and 337 sheep's fleeces and 61 lamb's fleeces from their estate at Badbury. Meat and skins were also sold (Keil 1964, 80).

Sheep keeping for wool became increasingly profitable during the medieval and early post-medieval periods due to the rising wool and cloth industries. Soon after 1210 the scale of sheep farming at the Overton estate of St Swithun's Priory, Winchester, was transformed. In 1210 a tax assessment for the manor records 300 sheep but by 1248 the manor reached a peak of 2,256 sheep, making it one of the most important sheep farming manors of the cathedral priory estate at that time (Fowler 2000, 156–7). The Overton sheep were kept in three enclosed shelters during the winter months, including the sheep house at 'Raddun'. Fowler's excavation of the remains at Raddun demonstrated that the type of sheep found there were primarily used for their wool (*ibid*, 127). It was further believed that sheep housed in such 'sheepcotes' produced better fleeces than those kept outside (Dyer 1995, 152).

On large monastic estates, of which there were several on the Marlborough Downs (see Brown, this volume), sheep flocks were often managed centrally and on an inter-manorial basis. Wool and stock for slaughter produced at Overton, for example, were sent to a central store at Barton Priors outside Winchester (Fowler 2000, 157). St Swithun's Priory also held an estate at Alton Priors. There was considerable inter-change of stock between this estate and other priory manors, and because it was almost entirely on chalk it depended on Patney, which lay at the foot of the chalk escarpment of Salisbury Plain, for meadow and hay. In 1261 there were 464 ewes on the estate, 100 of which were sent to Overton, and of 380 lambs raised there 121 were sent to Overton after shearing (Elrington 1980, 197). By the mid 14th century five sheep flocks were also kept by Glastonbury Abbey on its north Wiltshire downs manors of Badbury, Winterbourne Monkton and Ashbury (Berks). These manors frequently exchanged stock. In 1333 118 wethers (castrated males) from Badbury went to Ashbury and 80 to Winterbourne Monkton (Crittall 1970, 16). Customary duties of cottagers at Winterbourne Monkton in the 14th century included driving beasts to Badbury and Christian Malford, and once a year to Glastonbury (Elrington 1983, 197).

Some specialisation in sheep husbandry also occurred on these estates. This can be seen in the composition of sheep flocks. All Cannings, in monastic hands until the Dissolution, had a demesne flock of 874 wethers in 1450 (Crittall 1975, 26). This lack of breeding stock suggests specialisation for wool. Wethers were said to be the most important producers of wool (Dyer 1995, 152), while ewes were kept for wool, lambs, milking and apparently produced the best manure (Davis 1811, 68). In Temple Rockley the duties of tenants' wives included washing, shearing and milking sheep (Elrington 1983, 179). Glastonbury Abbey also kept some sheep on its estates for dairying until 1333–4, when it sold lactage on all manors with milking ewes (Keil 1964, 132). When no longer of use for these purposes sheep of all types were culled for meat.

From the 1490s onwards, manorial income relied increasingly upon rents as demesnes were leased out. Sheep flocks still remained large on many manors on the Marlborough Downs. By the early 16th century there was pasture for tenantry flocks of 690 and 570 sheep on West and East Downs in All Cannings (Crittall 1975, 26). During the Civil War Sir Edward Baynton kept 1,000 sheep on his tenement in the tithing of Cannings in Bishops Cannings, 644 of which were carried off by the Royalists to feed the Oxford garrison (Pugh & Crittall 1953, 195).

The movement of sheep between upland and lowland grazing and the extent to which transhumance played a part in sheep rearing on the Marlborough Downs seems to have varied from manor to manor. Transhumance in the hills of northern England meant seasonal movement of livestock onto upland pastures over distances of more than half a day's journey and for a whole summer season (Winchester 2000, 92–3). On the Marlborough Downs, where conditions were relatively less harsh, the downs were often used for sheep during the winter and cattle grazed there in summer. At Winterbourne Monkton, for example, part of Windmill Hill and Monkton Down was common grazing for cattle in summer but used for the lord's sheep in winter during the 13th and 14th centuries (Elrington 1983, 195). At Ogbourne St Andrew also there was sheep pasture on 480a of Coombe Down, 409a of which was summer pasture for cattle but grazing for Ogbourne St George's sheep in winter (*ibid*, 146). At All Cannings, however, some sheep were over-wintered on lowland pasture, since in 1540 common winter pasture for 108 sheep lay in 'Farifield' south-west of the village (Crittall 1975, 6). This may have been used for ewes and yearling lambs, while wethers may have spent at least part of the winter on the downs. In both systems movement of people to live with the sheep would have been necessary for herding, and for milking if any were ewes. The presence of sheep houses or 'sheepcotes' on the Marlborough Downs indicates some seasonal settlement, since one of their uses was to accommodate itinerant shepherds, and perhaps dairymaids (Dyer 1996, 31). Their main function, however, was to provide winter shelter for sheep and shepherd in bad weather (Dyer 1995, 151, 161).

Many sheep droves existed across the Marlborough Downs. Some are documented for the first time in the medieval period but could well be much earlier in origin (Fowler 2000, 256–7). 'La Drave', recorded at Winterbourne Bassett in the 13th century (Gover *et al* 1939, 500) may have been a sheep drove. Numerous examples are mapped for the first time during the 19th century. Examples include 'Sheep Drove' north of Ogbourne St Andrew, 'Sheep Drove' north-west of Rockley and 'The Wide Drove' from Ogbourne Maizey onto the downs (Smith 1884). Those from villages to the downs were local routes to watering places or to night folds on the fields, while others were long distance routes for droving, leading to the great abbeys or sheep markets of medieval England.

Sheep's manure was a valuable by-product, indispensable in maintaining the productivity of cornfields on the manors of the Marlborough Downs. Although wool sales were profitable, even when wool prices were highest, in the mid-16th century, the number of sheep it was possible to keep over winter was strictly limited due to shortage of winter food (Crittall 1959, 54–5). The usual practice in sheep and corn husbandry was for sheep to feed on the downs (or later the water meadows) during the day and be folded at night on next year's arable field. Hurdle pens were used to confine sheep to manure the ground (*ibid*, 22). These pens were moved every night, with the usual rule that 1,000 sheep could manure a 'tenantry acre' (3/4 statute acre) in one night (Davis 1811, 110). By the 16th century the Wiltshire Horned Sheep (Fig 18:1), which was slow to fatten and had a light fleece, had been bred for their ability to climb between field and down and to drop manure only at night. Valuable accumulations of manure also came from sheep houses, which needed to be accessible to carts to bring straw in and take manure away to the fields (Dyer 1995, 154–5).

Fig 18:1 A Wiltshire Horned sheep depicted by Davis, 1811 (reproduced courtesy of Wiltshire County Library).

Sheep and corn husbandry did not suffer from early agricultural changes, but benefited from them. The floating of water meadows in the valleys provided early grass for ewes and their lambs and yielded a better hay crop meaning that more sheep could be kept over winter. More fodder crops were also produced.

Changing times

Davis wrote in 1811 with regret at the recent passing of the sheep and corn husbandry of the Wiltshire downs. Instead the "first and great object" in sheep farming on the Wiltshire downs had become, or was becoming, the improvement of the carcass of both ewe and lamb. The Wiltshire Horned sheep had fallen victim to such improvement and had been selectively bred out of existence. The only flocks to survive were at Broad Hinton (Davis 1811, 207). For most of the 18th-century flock management on the Wessex downs had seen an emphasis on wether flocks kept on open fields by common shepherds, but after 1770 these were replaced by flocks of breeding ewes and a rapid turnover of lambs for early slaughter (Bowie 1990, 119). Sheep types introduced, such as the Southdowns and Hampshires, were not hardy enough to live on coarse grass or to walk far from the fold for their food. Farmers were thus induced to plough up the downs for sheep feed and the land soon became exhausted (Davis 1811, 139–40). Better feed, although increasing the weight of the sheep, made their wool coarser and less valuable.

From 1874–5 wet weather and American

competition created more problems for sheep and corn farmers (Crittall 1959, 94). From the late 18th-century onwards the movement towards enclosure had accelerated. From the 1880s onwards wire fencing was put up on hitherto unfenced downs in Wiltshire. Dew ponds were also constructed, so a daily walk down to the river Kennet was no longer part of the herdsman's routine. These innovations cut labour costs and provided for the new breeds of sheep which remained permanently on the downs (*ibid*, 109). Labour shortages from 1920 onwards caused the hitherto linked corn acreage and sheep numbers to diverge sharply as corn growing was no longer dependent upon other parts of the farming system, but upon large amounts of artificial fertiliser (Crittall 1959, 110–112). Mop makers, sheep-bell makers, hurdle makers, reddlemen and other traders dependent upon the old sheep and corn economy also disappeared from the north Wiltshire Downs.

Sheep enclosures

Most of the activities of sheep husbandry were transient and their effects subtle, in creating and maintaining the chalk grassland characteristic of the downs. However, permanent enclosures, with or without associated buildings, were used to keep different types of sheep apart, to keep sheep in, or perhaps for activities such as milking and lambing. Where flocks were large it was also usual to maintain three permanent sheep folds – one for ewes, one for wethers and one for hogasters or yearlings – with a shepherd in charge of each (Crittall 1959, 21).

Numerous enclosures of various shapes and sizes exist on the Marlborough Downs; most only survive as crop-marks, but a few earthwork sites remain. Many of the enclosures are known to date from prehistoric times, others have clearly been superimposed upon, and so post-date, prehistoric or Romano-British field systems, but a large number are undated. Some early enclosures were evidently re-used as sheep pens in later times, for example Barbury Castle, which has a dew pond inserted into its rampart. Others are undoubtedly sheep enclosures created during the medieval and later periods.

The sheep enclosures of the Wiltshire Downs are typically sub-square or sub- rectangular in plan and surrounded by a small bank and outer ditch. The banks may once have been surmounted by hedges. The enclosures vary enormously in size, the largest being about 200m by 200m, while smaller examples tend to be around 30m by 30m, presumably reflecting the different sizes of the flocks kept within or their different uses. There seems to have been no particular advantage in any one shape and they often appear to have been laid out by rule of thumb being more or less square or rectangular, but some turning out to be rough trapezoids. In other areas of Britain such as Exmoor and Wales circular or oval sheepfolds were used and similar enclosures may have been used for sheep keeping on the Marlborough Downs. Indeed, the Raddun excavations showed that a simple curvilinear stock enclosure, predominantly for keeping sheep in overnight, was first constructed at the site in the early- to mid-13th century. A timber-framed building, probably for milking and lambing, was later erected at its entrance, and two more irregular enclosures were subsequently added to the complex (Fowler 2000, 123).

Original entrances to sheep enclosures are difficult to identify without excavation. Simple gaps in the banks and ditches of many appear to be later breaches. The bank of the sheep enclosure on Morgan's Hill had a large number of gaps in it, which appeared to have been made after the enclosure was constructed. Excavation confirmed that the ditch had also originally been continuous (Cunnington 1910, 592). In other examples entrances curiously appear to be absent (eg NMR SU 06 NE 30, 208 and SU 16 SW 34). Flanking banks extending beyond enclosures, which were probably used to assist in herding sheep into the enclosures, are another common feature (eg NMR SU 06 NE 31, 12 and SU 16 NW 223).

The identification of sheep enclosures can be assisted by their location. Most were situated in sheltered spots in dry valley bottoms, or in combes between the hills, sometimes at the head of re-entrant valleys where sheep could be funnelled in between the steep hillsides. Lamb folds in particular needed to be sheltered from the weather and this may have been the purpose of some of the smaller enclosures in dry valley bottoms. A few sheep enclosures are to be found on hill slopes, for example, a rectangular enclosure, 70m by 45m, overlying a dyke below Adam's Grave long barrow. For stock on the move locations close to drove roads would have been advantageous. At West Overton two 'Pennings' are separated by a droveway heading east. There was a sheep-house and a washing pool in the north-east corner of the lower penning (Fowler 2000, 62).

The best dating evidence we have for medieval sheep enclosures on the Marlborough Downs comes from Cunnington's excavations of the enclosure in a chalk combe below Morgan's Hill. This large, roughly square enclosure (Fig 18:2) measuring 190m by 185m, is defined by a single bank and ditch. Although a total of 176ft (53.6m) of the ditch was entirely cleaned out during the excavations, and sections were cut through the bank, very little evidence was found for its date or purpose. Within this enclosure a smaller oblong enclosure measuring 45m by 25m was excavated. Pottery of 13th and 14th century date was found at varying depths to within a few inches of the bottom of its ditch, along with more or less complete sheep skeletons, scattered sheep's bones and teeth, a few ox bones and those of at least three dogs. Further fragments of medieval pottery were found in another slight bank within the larger enclosure. The inner enclosure was believed to be contemporary with the larger enclosure around it and the complex as a whole was interpreted as a sheepfold, with the inner enclosure affording additional protection for weak and sickly animals and perhaps for shepherds' shelters (Cunnington 1910, 596). A remarkably similar complex, lying in a similar position, in a chalk combe on Avebury Down below Hackpen Hill was recorded as an earthwork in the 19th century (Fig 18:3) (Merewether 1851b, 102, No 5). It had been noted earlier by Stukeley and had been the subject of excavation but no clues as to its date or purpose had been found (Colt Hoare 1821, 94). The complex has now been ploughed out, but aerial photographs show that it overlay and post-dated a field system of probable prehistoric or Roman date (Fig 18:4). Medieval pottery was also found at a rectangular cropmark enclosure north-west of Barbury Castle. This enclosure had double walls and a smaller enclosure on its southern side. It was interpreted as a pen for small cattle (Passmore 1943, 194), but could be a sheep pen.

By the 19th century the term 'penning' first appears on maps of the Marlborough Downs, although it had been mentioned in 18th-century writings (Smith 1884, map, 40). It indicates the presence, or former presence, of a sheepfold (RCHM(E) 1979, xxi). 'Penning' enclosures were described as being of 'double square plan'

Fig 18:2 An enclosure on Morgan's Hill, excavated by M Cunnington in 1909. © Crown copyright (NMR 4221/15).

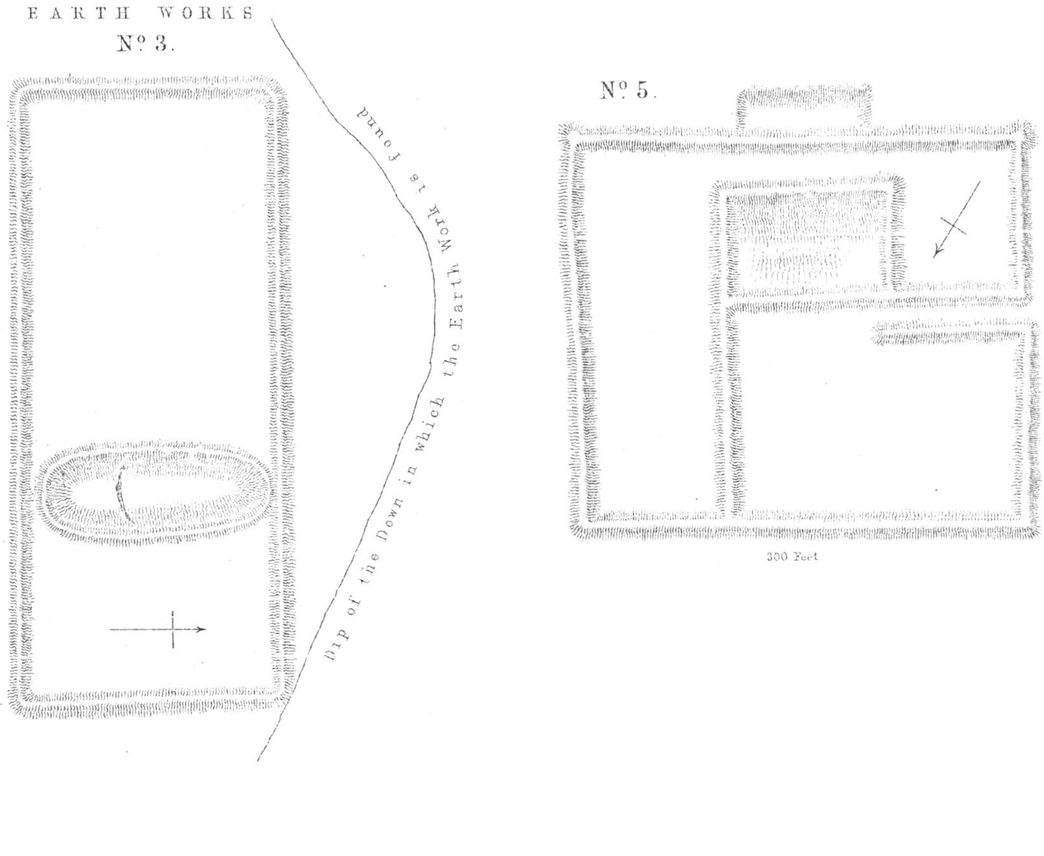

Fig 18:3 Mereweather's survey of earthworks on Hackpen Hill (No 5) and in All Cannings (No 3), 1849, for the Archaeological Institute.

Fig 18:4 The Hackpen Hill earthworks visible as cropmarks. © Crown copyright (NMR 210/173).

surrounded by a bank surmounted by a hedge of whitethorn and a ditch (Merewether 1851b, 109). They may have been yards or folds distant from the farm. By the late 19th century they had been disused for a long time, but they were still remembered and their positions were sometimes marked by the belts of trees originally planted to provide shelter for them (Smith 1884, 39–40). Two such enclosures on Overton Down lie adjacent to manorial pasture and close to major routes from Avebury, Bath and East Kennet, showing a continuing need for livestock enclosures on the edge of manorial pasture and the importance of communications and movement (Fowler 2000, 62–3).

In addition to the simple sheepfold enclosures, two more complex earthwork sites on the Marlborough Downs may be connected with sheep farming. In Alton Priors parish an unusual enclosure complex (NMR SU 16 SW 27) (Fig 18:5), close to Newtown Farm, overlies a field system and a possible Bronze Age round barrow. While the size, shape and general layout of the two main trapezoidal enclosures is consistent with that of sheepfolds and the building platforms inside could be the sites of sheepcotes, there is clearly more than one phase to the remains. The antiquity of the name 'Newtown' here would also merit further investigation as it could well indicate permanent settlement at the site. A further complex earthwork site, from which sheep rearing may have been managed, was a probable grange on Wick Down, belonging to the Cistercian abbey at Stanley (see Brown this vol).

Occasionally enclosures associated with sheep fairs can be found, although none have yet been identified on the Marlborough Downs. Sheep fairs were important events in a shepherd's year, second only to lambing time. They were rowdy and colourful gatherings attracting shepherds, gypsies with children, piebald ponies and dogs, as well as shady dealers and pick-pockets from far and wide. The sites of ancient fairs were remote and difficult to reach by modern transport. For this reason most died out during the 20th century. In earlier periods shepherds walked for days with their sheep across the hills guided at night by white stones known as 'shepherds' lanterns' which marked the downland tracks (Gurney 1985, 19). On Salisbury Plain traces of pens for the annual sheep fair held within the ramparts of Yarnbury Iron Age hillfort are still to be seen, although it lapsed at the turn of the 20th century. The most famous sheep fair on the Marlborough Downs was that held at Tan Hill every August, until 1932 when it was moved to a site adjoining the Bath road near Silbury Hill. There is a small earthwork, possibly the site of a building, set into the back of the Wansdyke bank where it passes over Tan Hill. This could be a shepherd's hut or something to do with the fair (D Field *pers comm*).

Sheep houses

Sheep houses, otherwise known as 'sheepcotes' or '*bercarie*', clearly existed on the Marlborough Downs from at least the 13th century when detailed documentary records first appear. In the reeves' accounts for the Barton of Marlborough in 1281, for example, two sheepcotes are mentioned – 'the west' sheepcote was repaired following wind damage, while 'the east' sheepcote was moved to 'Blakingrove' at the cost of 4s (Brentnall 1923, 80). It is not known when sheepcotes were first constructed, but a small earthwork enclosure on Overton Down, measuring 40m by 55m and associated with a pond, has been suggested as possibly the site of an Anglo-Saxon sheepcote (Fowler 2000, 80–82). On the Cotswolds the prevalence of these expensive structures in documentary records coincides with the large-scale English wool export trade in the 12th century and the continuing boom of the 13th and 14th centuries. Although English wool exports declined in the late 14th and 15th centuries there was increasing home demand for raw material as the English cloth-industry expanded (Dyer 1995, 156). Their presence on the Marl-

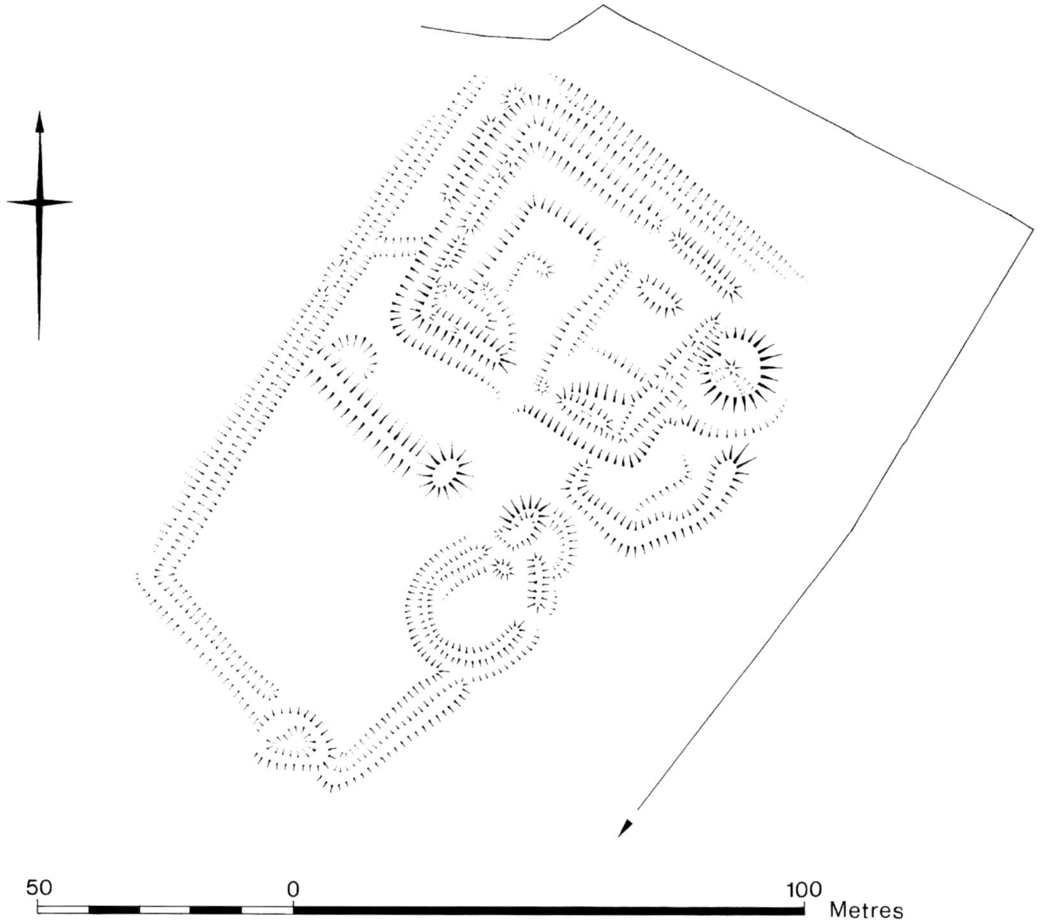

Fig 18:5 A complex of enclosures and other features near Newtown Farm (surveyed by D McOmish, G Brown & V Wilson. © Crown Copyright.

borough Downs therefore almost certainly reflects the growth of sheep rearing for the wool trade.

In addition to providing winter shelter these buildings were used as fodder stores and sheltered ewes at lambing time (Dyer 1995, 152). On the Cotswolds they are usually found on upland pastures in slight dips for shelter and isolated from settlement (*ibid* 1995, 147) but accessible by carts. On large estates various parts of a flock had distinct pastures and their own sheep house. Ewe flocks were sometimes kept in a sheepcote close at hand for milking or lambing while the wethers, who required less labour, were kept further afield (Hare 1994, 161). Overton manor had three sheepcotes from 1248, including the one excavated at Raddun (see above). The others were at Attley (Audley's Cottage/Hillside Farm) and Hackpen. The site of Hackpen sheepcote is possibly represented by an earthwork enclosure at Down Barn (NMR SU 16 NW 31). This lay beside a pond, on marginal land between arable and pasture and close to an intersection in local tracks and regional routes (Fowler 2000, 99), including a 10th-century 'Lambs' Path' (Fowler 2000, 157, 242). A further sheep house and two sheep 'pennings' separated by a drove-way were situated at the junction between arable and pasture in West Overton, close to the boundary with East Overton (Fowler 2000, 62). Place-names such as 'Petticoat Down' on the east side of Winterbourne Down (Smith 1884, HII) and 'Shipton Piece' west of Bishops Cannings point to further examples. The demesne of Bourton manor also included a 5a meadow called the 'Shiphouse Mead' (Pugh & Crittall 1953, 195), indicating the presence, or former presence, of a sheep house there. Documentary references provide further examples, such as "... a certain close round the Abbott's sheepcote" given by Gregory Delamere of Winterton Monachorum to Robert of Pederton, Abbot in *c*1270. The acts of Abbot Robert also record that he erected a kitchen with offices, a sheepcote covered with stone and a windmill. These were probably the buildings of which the traces were visible in 'Gregories Close' (Jackson 1862, 342).

A number of features within the sheep enclosures on the Marlborough Downs are undoubtedly the typically long and narrow, but substantial, footings of sheepcotes. Those on the Cotswolds are known to have varied in length from 23–65m and were usually 6–8m wide (Dyer

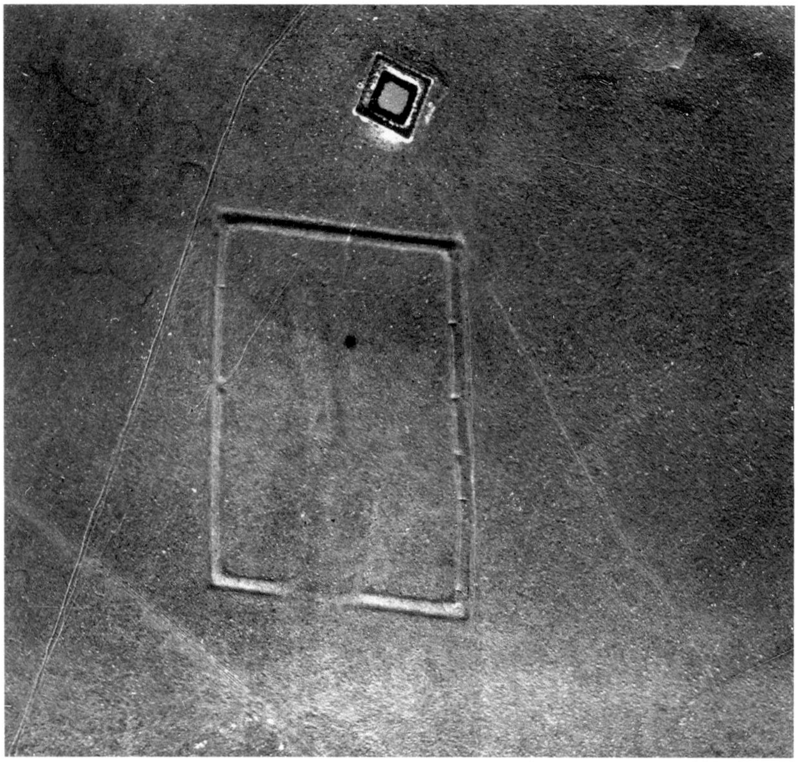

Fig 18:6 An enclosure on Horton Down. The cropmark of a long thin depression inside may be the site of a sheepcote. © The Keiller Collection (reproduced courtesy of Mr G Currie).

Fig 18:7 An enclosure with a rectangular inner feature, possibly a sheepcote site, on All Cannings Down. © Crown Copyright (NMR 15836/31).

1995, 139). On Horton Down a roughly rectangular earthwork enclosure (NMR SU 06 NE 28) (Fig 18:6) has a crop-mark of a long thin depression inside it. This could be the site of a building, possibly a sheepcote. The presence of a dew pond just outside the enclosure shows that it was almost certainly in use during the past 200 years, but could well have medieval origins. A very similar enclosure (Fig 18:7) in a dry valley on All Cannings Down has a rectangular inner feature 20m by 10m, which would be compatible with the dimensions of known sheepcotes. A smaller enclosure, 35m by 25m (NMR SU 06 NE 32) lay close by, but has since been levelled by cultivation. The enclosures may have been sheepfolds belonging to the Abbey of St Mary, Winchester, who held All Cannings manor until the 17th century (Crittall 1975, 23). A further, elongated, enclosure (NMR SU 06 NE 30) (Fig 18:3) straddling the bottom of a dry valley in All Cannings parish had an internal feature 40m by 10m, again consistent with the dimensions of a sheepcote. This enclosure has now been ploughed out, but it formerly overlay a prehistoric field system and its earthworks were surveyed in the 19th century (Merewether 1851b, No 3).

Water

Sheep were washed annually ready for clipping or shearing and until recent times washing was carried out in a deep pool or stream. On the hills of northern England flocks were gathered in sub-circular stone-built wash folds on the stream bank, with an opening facing a pool (Winchester 2000, 59–61). No such folds have been found on the Marlborough Downs, but enclosures astride streams may have been used for folding sheep before and after washing. On Salisbury Plain enclosures astride the Imber Brook may be evidence of sheep washing (McOmish *et al* 2002, 117), while at Elmont on the Cotswolds there are earthworks suggesting a sheep wash (Dyer 1995, 154). Sheep washes could be privately owned but were often shared between parishes. For this reason they are often to be found on parish boundaries, sometimes close to a road or track, such as the Washing Pool at Overton Hill, close to the boundary between the Anglo-Saxon estates of East and West Overton (Fowler 2000, 51, 62). In the 1930s a major wash pool lay at Washpool Bottom, Calstone to which hundreds of sheep and their shepherds travelled from a 20 mile radius every May and June. At a spot where a spring entered and left the pool it was dammed and diverted into two spouts through which water rushed at pressure. The down-hill side was bounded by a stone wall from which sheep were heaved in. After washing they exited through a wooden gangway (Gurney 1985, 121–5). The site is marked as 'Wash pool & Plots' on Smith's map of 1884. Several enclosures to the east of this wash pool, in Ranscombe Bottom and on the hills above are of uncertain date or purpose, but some may have been for sheep using the pool, for example a sub-rectangular enclosure (NMR: SU 06 NW 90) overlooking Ranscombe Bottom. A further sheep wash site is indicated by the name 'Washpool Cottage' close to Chiseldon church (Crittall 1970, 14). Locations within villages, such as this, or alongside farm buildings were also common. Wash pools were abandoned in recent times because there are fewer sheep and wool buyers developed more satisfactory ways of cleaning fleeces (Cotswold Sheepwash Project).

The chalk hills of the Marlborough Downs are generally free draining and so enclosure ditches were probably dug to provide material for the banks rather than for drainage. Two sheepfolds nevertheless appear to be attached to systems of ditches. On Cherhill Down two concentric rectangular enclosures (NMR: SU 06 NE 50) defined by narrow ditches and slight up-cast banks are linked to an extensive herringbone drainage system of probable 19th century or later date. The inner enclosure, at least, appears to be a typical medieval or post-medieval sheepfold, with a pond lying just outside it. (A photograph of this site appears in Crawford & Keiller 1928, plate XLIV). A probable sheep enclosure (NMR: SU 06 NE 105) abutting the ditch of the Wansdyke is also attached to a system of later drains.

Numerous ponds built for watering livestock are visible across the Marlborough Downs and associations are frequently found between sheep enclosures and ponds, the ponds usually lying just outside the sheepfolds. The prominent big, square earthworks, the so-called 'dew ponds', were built within the last 200 years. They are lined with clay, concrete, pitch, or rammed chalk and are made up on their sides to protect the lining from damage by animals and to give a greater surface area for water collection. Many were made by the Smith family of Market Lavington and by the Cruse family of Imber, but they by no means had a monopoly. Although true dew ponds were not filled by springs or water run-off, they were filled by rainfall rather than dew (Pugsley 1938, 8, 57–8). Their existence close to sheep enclosures indicates that, although some may have medieval origins, these enclosures were in relatively recent use for 'grass sheep'. These new breeds of sheep introduced onto the Wiltshire Downs during the 19th century (see above) were kept permanently on the hills and fattened for meat, often on pasture improved by ploughing. It was not desirable for them to lose weight by walking long distances to water. A few ponds associated with sheepfolds, however, are definitely medieval, such as the excavated 13th-century example at Raddun (Fowler & Blackwell 1998, 42; Fowler 2000, 123–4). Other small round ponds associated with probable sheep enclosures on Overton Down and at Down Barn (Fowler 2000, 80–81, 99) may also be of an early date.

Conclusions

Although sheep rearing has made a significant impact upon the landscape of the Marlborough Downs its remains have received relatively little attention. The fact that the ancient sheep and corn method of farming continued relatively unchanged for many hundreds of years gave the impression that it would always continue and so it was taken for granted. Only now, after the landscape has been virtually transformed by modern agriculture, is the nature of medieval farming beginning to be understood. This paper has brought together some of the archaeological evidence for sheep husbandry on the Marlborough Downs, but there is still much scope for study. Detailed examination of the documentary records for individual townships, accompanied by further fieldwork would undoubtedly determine the true date and purpose of some of the enigmatic enclosures and other features on the Marlborough Downs, as well as revealing the sites of further sheepfolds and sheep houses. We may also learn more about how sheep rearing changed over time and how the remains on the Marlborough Downs reflect these changes.

Gazetteer

Gazetteer of medieval and post-medieval sheep enclosures on the Marlborough Downs. A provisional list based upon information held by the National Monuments Record. More examples undoubtedly remain to be discovered, while others may be subject to re-interpretation in the light of further information.

Parish	Place	Shape/size	Topography	Associated Features	National Monuments Record No	References
All Cannings	All Cannings Down SU 09636580	Rectangular 38m x 25m	On side of ridge between two valleys	West and eastern sides extend beyond for 35 m	SU 06 NE 31	VCH I,pt 1, p261 AP RAF 540/958 4204 1952
All Cannings	All Cannings Down SU 09436663	Rectangular 140m x 60m	Across valley bottom	Overlies fields. Internal feature 40m x 10m	SU 06 NE 30	Mereweather No 3 AP RAF CPE/UK/1821 2082 1946
All Cannings	All Cannings Down SU 09556522	Square, small 20m x 20m	Bottom of combe		SU 06 NE 208	AP RAF CPE/UK/1821 2082 1946
All Cannings	All Cannings Down SU 09166529	Quadrangular 35m x 25m	Valley Floor		SU 06 NE 32	AP RAF CPE/UK/1821 2082 1946
All Cannings	All Cannings Down SU 09066522	100m x 85m	Valley floor	Internal feature 20m x 10m Dew Pond	SU 06 NE 32	VCH I, pt 1,p261 AP NMR SU 1163/3 1933
Alton	South of Adam's Grave SU 11256327	Rectangular 75m x 45m	Hill Slope	Overlies dyke and possible round barrow	SU 16 SW 34	Smith 1884, p115 AP NMR SU 1163/3 1933
Alton	Newtown Farm SU 11586408	Complex of enclosures		Overlies fields Building platform(s)	SU 16 SW 27	VCH I, pt 1, p261 AP NMR SU 1664/18 1993
Alton	SU 12306389	Rectangular 15m x 10m		Internal enclosure	SU 16 SW 138	AP NMR SU 1263/37 1982
Alton	SU 10676350	Rectangular 40m x 25m	Bottom of steep slope	Dew pond overlies corner	SU 16 SW 139	Aps NMR RAF/CPE/UK/1821 6152-3 1946
Avebury	Avebury Down SU 11546938	Rectangular 100 x 80 yds.	Sloping ground	Small enclosure in SW angle. Overlies fields.	SU 16 NW 66	WAM 38, p183 Mereweather V Excavated by Colt Hoare Aps NMR SU 1169/9-1- 1949
Avebury	Horton Down SU 08306750	Oval 84m x 60m	Level shelf on hill slope		SU 06 NE 122	AP CUCAP ACS55-8 1961 VCH I, pt1,p272
Berwick Bassett	Berwick Bassett Down SU 11957363	Rectangular	Foot of slope		SU 17 SW 171	AP NMR OS/73072 286 1973
Berwick Bassett	Berwick Bassett Down SU 11887320	Two rectangular. Concentric	Foot of slope		SU 17 SW 170	AP NMR OS/73072 286 1973
Berwick Bassett	Berwick Bassett Down SU 12237245		West facing slope	Adjacent to a hollow-way	SU 17SW 178	Aps RAF 106G/UK/1415 4142-3 1946
Berwick Bassett	Berwick Bassett Down SU 12277362		West facing slope	Adjacent to above enclosure and hollow-way	SU 17 SW 178	Aps RAF 106G/UK/1415 4143-3 1946
Bishops Cannings	Bishops Cannings Down SU 05606615	Square 70m x 70m	East facing hill slope	Associated with field system	SU 06 NE 12	SAM 21868 VCH I, pt 1, p262 AP NMR SU 0566/5 1993
Bishops Cannings	Bishops Cannings Down SU 060667	Sub-rectangular		Another earthwork leads from it		Smith records oval & square enclosures here
Bishops Cannings	North of Shepherds Shore SU 07306562	Large and square 120m x 115m	Hill slope	Attached to a later ditch system.	SU 06 NE 105	Smith; WAM 38 pg202 Mereweather No 2?
Bishop Cannings	SSW Beckhampton SU 06936714	Sub-square 50m x 50m			SU 06 NE 86	VCH I, pt1, p262 Aps NMR SU 0667/21-4 1995
Bishops Cannings	Horton Down SU 07756608	Rectangular 144m x 103m		Cropmark of long thin depression inside Dew pond.	SU 06 NE 28	Hare 1994 Aps NMR SU 0765/8-9 1982, Su 0766/2 1967
Bishops Cannings	Morgan's Hill, North Down SU 040670	Square 190m x 185m	In chalk combe	Internal features including 45m x 25m enclosure	SU 06 NW 42	Excavated by Cunnington 1909
Bishops Cannings	North Down SU 04176773	Rectangular – complex 120m x 120m & 60m x 30m		Enclosure inside 50m x 50m Overlies barrow cemetery	SU 06 NW 59	AP NMR Su 0467/34 1988
Bishops Cannings	SU 04946754	Square 56m x 56m			SU 06 NW 60	Aps NMR SU 0567/1/494 1969, SU 0467/35 1988
Bishops Cannings	Roundway Hill SU 026648	Rectangular 160m x 120m			SU 06 SW 23	VCH I, pt 1, p263 APs RAF CPE/UK/1821/2065-6
Broad Hinton	Hackpen Hill Below White Horse SU 12927517	Rectangular	Hill slope	Depression in NW corner. Ponds.	SU 17 NW 12	Smith 1884, p121 VCH I, pt1, p263
Calne Without	Ranscombe Bottom Calstone Down SU 044682	Sub-rectangular/oval	Bottom of combe		SU 06 NW 90	Smith 1884 Section III C6(d) AP NMR SU 0468/25

Cherhill	Cherhill Down SU 05326959	Rectangular – two concentric and one attached	Bottom of combe	Dew Pond	SU 06 NE 50	Smith 1884 Crawford & Keiller p234
Fyfield	Fyfield Down SU 141707	Rectangular	Bottom of combe	Connected by hollow-way to md farm at Raddun	SU 17 SW 98	SAM 33951
Fyfield	Wroughton Mead Fyfield Down (Raddun) SU 138577077	Complex	Hill slope		SU 17 SW 63	Fowler 2000, 118-128 SAM 33951
Huish	South-east of Huish Farm SU14676371	Rectangular 60m x 55m		Small enclosure inside 35m x 35m	SU 16 SW 62	
Huish	SU 14966420	Rectangular 65m x 50m	Edge of escarpment	Dew Pond	SU 16 SW 19	OS 6" 1889 VCH I,pt1,p266 Colt Hoare 2 p11? AP RAF 540/9583195 1952
Ogbourne St Andrew	Dean Bottom SU 15007400	Square 9a	Hill slope	Overlies field system	SU 17 SE1	VCH I,pt1, p268 AP NMR SU 1474/9
Ogbourne St Andrew	Upper Herdswick SU 157758	Sub-rectangular				AP NMR SU 1575/3 1967
Ogbourne St Andrew	Ogbourne Maizey Down SU 171726	Rectangular 62m x 50m	High level ground	Next to 'the Wide Drove'	SU 17 SE 41	AP VCH 1, pt 1, p268 Smith 1885, 198 WAM 38,p301
Preshute	Wick Down Farm Rough Hill Su 135733	Polygonal-complex 160m x 96m	Lower hill slope	Internal sub-divs 7 bldg platforms, sarsens. Possible sheep drove from it to Hackpen Hill.	SU 17 SW 44	WAM 38, p309 1913 md/Pmpot.under bank Grange of Stanley Abbey? See Brown – this vol.
Preshute	Manton Down SU 151714	Sub-square				AP NMR Su 1571/2 1954
Stanton St Bernard	North of Wansdyke SU 10606505	Square 103m x 105m			SU 16 NW 11	
Stanton St Bernard	Stanton St Bernard Down	Very large oblong		Double bank and ditch. Projections		Smith 1884, 0181 XII Gviiib WAM 38,p322
West Overton	Down Barn SU 13046978	Trapezoidal 53 x 13 x 30 x 53 yds	Bottom of small combe	Low platform on one side. Pond	SU 16 NW 31	Fowler 2000,99 SAM 33951 WAM 58 p346
West Overton	White Hill SU 14466727	Irregular		NE of trackway Parallel ditches and building platform inside	SU 16 NW 225	AP NMR 14809/22 1997
West Overton	White Hill SU 13207052	Sub-rectangular 30m x 50m	Brow of hill	Ponds. Cut by trackways	SU 17 SW 30	Fowler 2000, 80-2,Hackpen Sheepcote? Crawford & Keiller 1928 p124-5, ABCD
West Overton	White Hill SU 14426748	Rectangular 30m x 25m1		Continuations beyond	SU 16 NW 223	
West Overton	Totterdown	Small rectangular ditched		Over lynchet		Crawford & Keiller p125, GHIJ Fowler 2000,p78
Winterbourne Bassett	White Horse Hill SU 12507455	Oblong 1.5a	At foot of down	Cut by a ditch	SU 17 SW 2	WAM 38, p356
Winterbourne Monkton	Su 101727	Sub-rectangular		Beside Road		APs NMR SU 1072/2,6
Wroughton	Below Barbury Castle SU 14907676	Rectangular 110m x 100m	Level ground at foot of downs	Shallow terraces inside Dew Pond	SU 17 NW 5	Part excavated C19 AP NMR Su 1476/33 1956
Wroughton	NW of Barbury Castle SU 147769	Sub-rectangular 220ft x 150ft	Level ground at foot of downs	Small annexe 100ft x 100ft	SU 17 NW 6	Excavated by Maskelyne AP NMR Su 1476/22
Wroughton	SU 14247668	Square ¼ a	Level ground		SU17 NW 18	OS 6" 1960 AP RAF 106G/UK/1415 3297 1946
Wroughton	Below Barbury Castle SU 147771	Sub-square	Level ground		SU 17 NW 20	AP NMR SU 1477/5 1953
Wroughton	East of Barbury Castle SU 15757650	Sub-square	Bottom of slope from downs			AP NMR SU1576/30 1996

19
'New myths at Swallowhead: the past and the present in the landscape of the Marlborough Downs'

Jon Cannon

Swallowhead Spring, near Silbury Hill, is a new ritual site in the landscape of the Downs, the direct result of a book, The Silbury Treasure, *published in 1976. As such it poses a range of challenges to the project of archaeology, questioning established ideas about the validity and significance of ritual sites; providing living evidence for the processes by which such sites are created; and suggesting a significant cultural dimension to a range of other modern and early modern features in the landscape.*

Swallowhead Spring

There is an hitherto unpublished ritual site in the Marlborough Downs. It includes a stone circle, which has only recently been destroyed by farming, and a rich assemblage of objects, including carvings, vessels and other artefacts, all deposited in and around water (Fig 19:1).

The site is clearly part of the 'sacred landscape'

Fig 19:1 Swallowhead Spring: rag-dressed Willow tree, the Kennet in full flood, September 2000 © Jon Cannon.

Fig 19:2 The tree at ground level, with the small 'stone circle' beside it, March 1996 © Jon Cannon.

of the Downs, situated as it is between Silbury Hill and the West Kennett Long Barrow. Its neglect in the literature is all the more remarkable because we have a reasonably precise date for it, and a body of evidence which helps interpret its meaning, purpose and significance.

The site is Swallowhead Spring, at NGR SU101681, which runs from a distinctive single opening in a dry valley and runs for about 65 feet before joining the Kennet at the point where that river turns from running south to running east. Stukeley called it 'the true fountain of the Kennet' (Stukeley 1743), and many others have agreed (eg Pollard & Reynolds 2002, 14), saying that the river before this point is called the Winterbourne. A C Smith called Swallowhead 'the reputed and very picturesque, but not actual, source of the Kennet, though the springs there are abundant and largely increase the infant river' (Smith 1878–9, 323; note 1). Ritual activity on the site began in the last 20–25 years, and is almost certainly the result of the publication in 1976 of Michael Dames's *The Silbury Treasure*, one of the classics of 'New Age' archaeology (1976).

The Silbury Treasure argued that this spring is key, not only to Silbury Hill itself, but to the entire Avebury landscape. It suggested that the distance from the spring to the Kennet forms a measurement unit from which the proportions of the Hill are derived; and that the Hill itself is a colossal sculpture of the pregnant belly of the 'Great Goddess', the goddess of the spring, with her body delineated in the outline of the surrounding 'quarry ditches'. His subsequent publication, *The Avebury Cycle* (Dames 1977), found references to Swallowhead in the design of West Kennett Long Barrow and other sites, and saw the image of the Great Goddess replicated in the entire landscape of the Downs, traced by the Neolithic and Early Bronze Age monuments within it, with the Spring her vulva.

This is a structure built on flimsy evidence: Dames does not try to defend it by citing any specific traditions associated with Swallowhead Spring itself – unless one counts the beguiling name 'Swallowhead', which is recorded by Stukeley (note 2) – and the only known cultural association of the Spring is that cited by both Stukeley and A C Smith: 'Fairgoers on Palm Sundays [the date of an annual fair at Silbury Hill] used to come to the springs to get water in which they dissolved sugar to make the traditional sugar-and-water drink – which they would take up Silbury Hill and drink on the summit' (Smith 1860–1; note 3). Swallowhead is the most convenient nearby source of fresh spring water.

Although there may indeed be significance in the proximity of several sites of different periods – the West Kennett Long Barrow; Silbury Hill; the palisaded enclosures; a Roman settlement and associated wells (Pollard & Reynolds *op cit* 119, 178) – to the Spring, Dames's theory stretches even the most vaguely-considered elision of archaeology, art history and wishful thinking to its limits. But whether or not the idea has any credence as a defendable theory about the past,

Fig 19:3 The spring mouth in an unusually dry year, January 1996 © Jon Cannon.

Fig 19:4 Dressings at the tree.

what it does do is continue a process followed by a thousand myth-makers down the ages – create a new series of stories about a place by claiming to have discovered the 'truth' about its past.

This approach would have been familiar to, for example, the medieval monks who 'discovered' Arthur's tomb at Glastonbury; it may even have not been unfamiliar to those who 'closed' West Kennett Long Barrow around the time the henge was built (Thomas & Whittle 1986).

And it *is* an evocative idea. A map of Silbury Hill, including the quarry trenches which surround it, looks a little like a section cut through, say, some of the images of women found in other

Neolithic cultures: Dames illustrates a 7th century BC clay statue from Çatal Hüyük, Turkey and a figurine from Hamangia, Rumania (Dames 1976, 50, 52). More than this, Dames's ideas fills the landscape with significance, imagery and meaning; as a creative contemporary cultural response to landscape, rather than a piece of archaeology, it has a certain power.

Certainly, the image has struck a chord: At some point, presumably after the book was published, people started visiting the spring and dressing it. There is good evidence to suggest that this activity is a direct result of Dames's book (note 4), which thus takes on a new significance as the foundation text for a new ritual site.

Deposits and Structures at Swallowhead

I have been visiting Swallowhead since 1994 (note 5), making an informal record of the ritual interventions being made there. I have only twice encountered other people – usually others who have read Michael Dames's book. Even around the Summer Solstice, when there are usually a couple of tents and the remains of a campfire, their occupants have never been present when I arrive.

Visiting Swallowhead, trying to record the history of the monument and understand the culture of those who are dressing the spring, but never actually meeting them, I find myself somewhere between participant/observer and archaeologist. The people who are dressing Swallowhead Spring are creating just the kind of

Fig 19:5 Artefacts at the tree, March 1996 © Jon Cannon.

Fig 19:6 Artefacts at the tree, Summer Solstice 1997 © Jon Cannon.

Fig 19:7 Offerings at the spring mouth, October 1996; previous offerings here are already becoming 'archaeology' © Jon Cannon.

archaeology we find in the Marlborough Downs: a small stone circle (Fig 19:2); layers of ritual deposits created at specific times of year; the fragile footings of temporary dwellings. They are so far invisible to me, yet they are part of the present, with all the immediacy of cultural context that implies.

The dressing is focused on a Willow tree that grows in the middle of the path of the water (Fig 19:2), just before it meets the Kennet; and around the spring mouth itself (Fig 19:3). The objects left usually reflect a range of Pagan and New Age beliefs in a non-specific way – rags, wind chimes, crystals – but occasionally are more ambitious and culturally specific (Figs 19:4, 19:5, 19:6, 19:7). The activity is focused around the Solstices and, to a lesser extent, the equinoxes and other key dates of the 'ritual year', such as 1 May. The general character of objects left appears not to have an overall pattern, implying that much of the activity there – at least, the activity which leaves an archaeological record – is not planned in advance, but is spontaneous and individualistic.

This is confirmed by enquiries in February 2003 among three informed observers of the site (note 6). There is now apparently a reasonably established practise for those who spend key nights at West Kennett Long Barrow of walking to Swallowhead around dawn; many then continue to Silbury Hill and the henge. These observers confirm that activities at the Long Barrow are not formally organised and people attending may have a wide range of beliefs, united simply by their feeling about the place itself or their interest in some of the rituals that take place there. In spite of this there are clearly a small number of people carrying out more organised rituals at the spring, as evidenced by the tents there around the Summer Solstice and the circular route between spring and tree sometimes found trampled into the undergrowth. Considering this, it is surprising how little known the site is (note 7).

Most of the items at Swallowhead are rags tied to the trees, or to the bushes around the spring mouth, but there are usually small, carefully-made objects, too. After 21 December 1995, for example, a figure made of wicker, arms outstretched with a prominent erection, was hanging from a branch high up on the willow; after 1 May 1996, a home-made wickerwork pouch with bells tied to the bottom, containing a face made of earth, its face, hair and eyes picked out in plastic 'crystals', coloured stones and wood shavings, hung from the willow; on 21 June of that year, there was a whole picnic area around the willow, with people's bags, a campfire, and a plastic sheet for shelter. I have also found runes, and once a dead bird in the hollow of the tree – though this was so out of character it may have been a landowner's jape.

Until 2001, between the willow and the river, there were five small lumps of Sarsen arranged into a stone circle; this has now been broken up during a period of consolidation work carried out on the Kennet bank, perhaps by a local farmer. Some heavy plant was used, and the actions imply (at the very least) that the landowner or his contractors think little of the site. Prior to this a 'ritual path' – a circular pathway in the undergrowth between tree and spring, passing either side of a prominent Sarsen that lies midway between them – was becoming a permanent feature, perhaps reflecting a more communal dimension to the practises of some of those visiting the site.

Swallowhead and Archaeology

So what does all this amount to? Is a handful of hippies at the edge of a field of any interest to archaeologists? I would contend it is. Not merely because the whole story reminds us that we are dealing with a place that matters to people – not just because of its history – but in the present. For some of those people at least, this landscape is still sacred.

The site also has implications for our thinking about the project of archaeology. Here we are trying to understand those who lived here in the Late Neolithic, to get to grips with their rituals and beliefs through the medium of the monuments they left, while around us today, people are doing the same thing: believing something about the landscape, and creating monuments as a result of those beliefs. Here we are trying to understand the Marlborough Downs as a *landscape*: a series of interconnected monuments, and again someone is creating their own contemporary mythology which does just that. Most powerfully of all, Michael Dames and others are creating myths that have the persuasive power to make people feel spiritually connected to the Downs and their former inhabitants, engaging people with the Avebury landscape at a deep level. A kind of public engagement some archaeologists would give their back teeth for, reflecting (sometimes destructively (note 8)) a depth of feeling about place that motivates many of us, even if our resulting actions are different.

The cultural/ritual dimension of the Avebury landscape occurs in many of the papers in this book. The implication is that from the late Palaeolithic to Roman times, various sites on the Marlborough Downs have played a vital role in people's cultural and ritual lives. Of course this story does not cease with the closing of the prehistoric era, it simply becomes more complex because we have more information. We know about the building histories of churches, and the economic and cultural context in which they were set. We know that people come to some of the sites on the Downs to worship today – because we can see them, and talk to them – and because they are creating an archaeology of their own (see note 13).

Observing these processes at work – alive, created by contemporary human beings – brings to life the processes which led to a site like Avebury being constructed. Ideas being generated and disseminated, taken up by communities and turned into something new: these are key aspects of the processes which fill a landscape with monuments. It is not, after all, our role to decide whose religious beliefs have validity; it is simply to observe, conserve and interpret the material results of those beliefs.

And archaeology is being created. The traces of ritual paths in the flattened grass are one kind of archaeology; while the deposits around the spring mouth, which have usually been dispersed by the elements a few months after having been left – but which include insoluble objects such as small statuettes (Fig 19:7) – will already have created a stratigraphy of their own in the marshy ground around it.

The site could be seen as playing a role complementary, if rather more theoretical, to that of the Experimental Earthwork (Bell *et al* 1996) on Overton Down: whereas that project is designed to explore the erosional and depositional realities of an earthwork, Swallowhead offers a living laboratory for investigation of the processes – sociological and cultural as well as depositional – which surround the creation of a monument itself.

Studying sites like Swallowhead can thus inject a vital human dimension into archaeological practise, addressing key underlying questions: How do belief systems rise and fall? How do these changes reflect wider changes in society? What moves people to create monuments, especially monuments with little 'practical' function? How does the form of such a monument reflect or develop the beliefs that inspired it?

Monuments Revisited

Certainly, a key theme of almost every phase of monument-building in the Avebury landscape is the way in which new monuments respect or adapt the older monuments they replace, extend or relate to. A review of this process shows just how widespread it is, how spread out in time, and how it can occur in unexpected ways. It is too early to claim that Swallowhead is a less valid or influential reinvention of a past archaeology to validate a current purpose.

Some of the older relationships within the landscape are well attested. Looking at the remnants of the middle Bronze Age landscape in the area around Avebury, we see hundreds of round barrows dotting the scarps, a massive and much older complex of stone monuments on the Kennet floodplain, and the remains of older monuments still upstanding on isolated hills – the causewayed enclosures – and alongside valley routes through the chalk – the long barrows. Clearly the builders of each of these monuments was aware of those preceding them: what they thought about them is less clear. The evidence exists for conservation and reuse, in some cases, and for closure and abandonment, in others. Either way the actual beliefs held about older monuments could be complex and contradictory.

Such patterns exist in modern times, and have impacted on the landscape too, as Swallowhead shows. St James's church is an unusually 'archaeological' work of architecture (Pevsner 1963): in addition to its structural eloquence it carries its own history of fitting, repainting and addition, each layer of this 'stratigraphy' reflecting both practical and ideological demands. Post-Reformation iconoclasms left only thefont and the rood loft, the latter shorn of its crucial context in the shape of the Rood itself, like a scheduled barrow sitting alone in a field of Rape. Later ritual changes are evidenced in the remains of seventeenth-century stalls and the nineteenth-century pulpit (*ibid*, 101–2). One could suggest from this that moving objects around within a structure is more likely to reflect internal debates within a belief system – in this case the tension between 'High' and 'Low' church, between Laudianism and Nonconformism. The same may be just as true as the evidence for making and re-making of stone settings that may have occurred at Avebury, and is well documented at Stonehenge.

One could go on to suggest that it is only when a new structure is created that can we discern a defining moment in the history of a belief system, and at Avebury this is suggested in the modern period just as eloquently as it is in the disjuncture between, say, causewayed enclosure and henge. When the established church finally split in the seventeenth century, one of the earliest Nonconformist chapels in Wiltshire was built at Avebury (Redvers Higgins & Hiller 2002; Stell 1991, 207), the dissenters' chapel, in existence by 1707 and today with a United Reform congregation. One is tempted to observe cultural dimensions to the site of this structure in the landscape: unlike the ambivalent approach to the

Fig 19:8 Worshippers gather by Stone 1, Avebury Summer Solstice 1995 © Jon Cannon.

Fig 19:9 New stone circle at East Kennett, January 1996 © Jon Cannon.

henge embodied by medieval foundations, all of which are outside the circle, this chapel is built firmly in the centre of the stones itself.

Similar relationships may even be encoded in the plan of medieval Avebury, which relates interestingly to the course of the recently discovered Beckhampton Avenue, with the High Street leaving the henge through one of its 'gates' (Gillings *et al* forthcoming) and running roughly towards the Avenue site discovered in 1999 and the settlements' two main religious structures, the parish church (a Saxon foundation) and the priory (now the Manor House, founded early in the twelfth century), both on the North side of it (note 9).

If – and it is an 'if' – these patterns are appropriating, or neutralising, or reflecting the power of the remains of former belief systems, they provide one simple but powerful model for similar previous relationships in the landscape. The fact that the belief system which actually motivated the construction of the henge and its avenues was dead thousands of years before the village was planned and the church was built alters, but does not reduce, the significance of the question of how one relates to the other. The question of whether the stones continued to have some superstitious association in the medieval period likewise tells us little about their 'original' meaning but is valid as an investigation in its own right (e.g. Chadburn & Pomeroy Kellinger 2001).

Cultural dimensions to modern Avebury

As well as providing many comparitors between known developments in people's beliefs and the structures they built, the Avebury landscape of the modern and early modern period contains other monuments with a little-explored cultural dimension. It is well known that the seventeenth and eighteenth centuries saw the birth of archaeology, or at least antiquarianism (Piggott 1989); and that – starting with William Stukeley – commentators of the mid- to late- eighteenth century saw in the 'druidical monuments' evidence for a native civilisation that, while primitive, had nobility and made significant cultural achievements. These ideas eventually became underlying assumptions of much late eighteenth and early nineteenth century Romantic culture (Piggott *op cit* 136–152; Piggottt 1976, 121–2).

Via the work of the Bath architect John Wood, these ideas also had a direct impact on the monuments of the period, giving national and local significance to the revival of Classical architectural styles. Key parts of Georgian Bath are the result of this: thus the architecture of the Circus and Royal Crescent at Bath (from 1754) is based on Roman examples, although the plan is a copy of the henge-and-stone-circle complex at nearby Stanton Drew (Mowl & Earnshaw 1988, 179–206; and Piggott *op cit* 146–147); combining 'architectures' of the Classical world with those of native British civilisation.

These ideas may have directly impacted on the landscape of the Downs. A series of landscape interventions was made in the late eighteenth and early nineteenth centuries by landowners, most of which survive to this day. The fashion for cutting new White Horses on and around the Marlborough Downs began c 1780, perhaps with the recutting of Westbury White Horse. Almost all appear to have been either carried out or supported by a member of the local farming gentry; almost all post-date the creation of a turnpike road from which they are positioned to be seen (Newman 1997, 197–209; note 10). These monuments are, therefore, a highly cultural act; they were surely inspired by the Romantic vision of British prehistory which was part of the legacy of investigations on the Wiltshire chalk by Aubrey, Stukeley and others, evoking a 'native' culture embodied in such 'druidical' monuments as Uffington and the Cerne Abbas Giant.

The planting of copses, often on barrows or other circular earthworks, also appears to have begun in the late eighteenth century. Many such copses remain distinctive features of the Downs. Chanctonbury Ring in Sussex, for example, was planted with a copse of trees by local landowner Charles Goring in 1760, partly as a way of making a landscape that was seen as too open and featureless more appealing in aspect. The Ring became an influential and much-visited picturesque spot (Brandon 1998; Field *et al* 2002; note 11). For landowners of this period, the Downs were, as they have remained, excellent riding and hunting country, and such copses were and are partly covers for game, but this does not obviate the possibility – as the South Downs evidence implies – that their creation had a significant cultural dimension. Indeed both the cutting of white horses and the planting of copses on barrows arguably both evoke the past and visually 'improve' the landscape by breaking up the empty grassland. Antiquarians had suggested horseracing and other sporting activities as explanations for the cursus at Stonehenge (note 12): perhaps the local gentry were partly evoking the authority of their noble if primitive hunting and horseriding forebears, in a kind of rural parallel to the more urbanised vision of John Wood.

While the truth is likely to be more complex than the above generalised suggestion, it is hard not to see both the barrow copses and the white horses as cultural monuments that relate to past monuments, and the evidence for this vital cultural dimension to 18th and 19th century 'layer' of the landscape may still exist in the letters and estate records of the period, as well as in study of their visibility *vis à vis* their sponsors' estates or key roads and settlements.

So Swallowhead is only the most recent phase of a history of monumentalising the Avebury landscape, partly in response to its own past, that can be observed several times in the historic period as well as the prehistoric one. It is also not alone. Deposits are left at Avebury itself, and at West Kennett Long Barrow, on a regular basis. Elaborate rituals, involving considerable numbers of people, regularly take place at both sites – in Christian and New Age as well as a range of Pagan traditions (Fig 19:8; note 13). A local householder has built a medium-sized stone circle in a plot of land by the road in East Kennett (Fig 19:9; note 14). The crop circles are another dimension to this, their ephemeral nature a stark reminder of how much is now invisible that may once have been startling. Yet even the crop circles are generating some permanent monuments (note 15).

At the Summer Solstice the shape of the stone circles at Avebury are echoed by the rings of people holding hands among them. It is a sight that somehow brings the monument to life: after all, the structure is presumably built for ritualised gatherings of some kind. Other sites on the Downs – from White Horses to hilltops – now also have deposits left at them on a regular basis. In another case of the influence of Michael Dames's work, in 1994 I found a fragment from a perfect miniature plaster model of the font of Avebury church sitting on top of the Triangulation Point on Tan Hill (note 16).

Historic and Prehistoric textuality

If the relationship between Swallowhead Spring and the Dames book reminds us of one thing, it is the importance of texts to understanding this landscape. It is perhaps the greatest challenge of prehistoric archaeology that we know absolutely nothing of the stories and names which explained the monuments these people built. Monuments like this start with belief, or at least with practical requirements – death, protection, gatherings of people – that have a significant cultural dimension: the structures that survive are merely emanations or expressions of that culture, that belief; we are lucky that we now tend to put our myths in writing.

As we move forward in time, the archaeology – the stratigraphy if you like – of this vital invisible textural layer on the landscape begins to become legible. By the time we get to early medieval sites like Wansdyke – 'Woden's Dyke' (note 17) – place names provide some clues to the cultural associations of monuments that still exist. By the time we reach the medieval period, we have entire texts – in the form of the Bible and the liturgy – to explain the form and meaning of structures like St James's church, while place names such as Adam's Grave (note 18) tell us something about a culture's reaction to the older monuments in its landscape. In both these cases the place-names themselves reflect changing cultures: the 'dyke' in 'Wansdyke' may be an antiquarian influence; 'Adam's Grave' replaced an older 'Woden's Barrow' (see above notes). Other associations – such as the idea of a 'King Sil' beneath Silbury Hill, may be all that remains of folklore traditions that have now disappeared (note 19).

The landscape is thus layered, not only with the physical remains of past societies, but with the ghost-like stratigraphy of the belief systems which encoded their most deeply-held understandings about the nature of the world. This layering can be as challenging a palimpsest as any stratigraphy, but it is crucial to understanding a monument, and – writing or no writing – the ideas and stories which Neolithic monuments expressed would have been as rich and complex as any since.

At Swallowhead Spring we are in the unique position of having the text to accompany a new, if diminutive, ritual site in the Avebury landscape. Archaeology, of course, is creating a larger and more methodologically exacting body of texts on the subject of the same sites.

So archaeology is itself therefore not immune from these processes: perhaps all we are doing with our stratigraphy, our survey, our GPS and our typologies of pot is trying to stay in touch with our ancestors. Before we mock those who hug the stones and dress up the springs at Avebury, we should remember that our own motivation – to stay in touch with the past by engaging with places – may not be so different from that of those who built West Kennett Long Barrow.

Notes

1. I am grateful to Katy Jordan and her Wiltshire Folklore Database for the reference.
2. The Wiltshire County Council Sites and Monuments Record contains nothing.
3. I am grateful to Katy Jordan and her Wiltshire Folklore Database for the reference. Stukeley is quoted by Dames as saying the same thing; *The Silbury Treasure*, *op cit* p 43.
4. Pete Glastonbury (whose website is at http://www.users.myisp.co.uk/~gtour/index.html) lives in Avebury and has been observing the landscape since the 1970s. He believes he first saw rags being left around the well in 1981 (11). More circumstantially, the extent to which Dames's ideas are now part of the mythology of Swallowhead is indicated by the following quote from a letter to the magazine *Source* in Spring 1995. The letter expressed sadness at the drying up of the flow at Swallowhead that year, saying' Something that mattered can never be the same again. The source has dried up and *the centre from which Avebury grew has gone* [my emphasis].' (Smith, J 1995, letter to *Source* **3**, 28; I am grateful to Katy

Jordan and her Wiltshire Folklore Database for the reference.) By the early 1980s, groups of women perhaps associated with the Women's Peace Camp at Greenham Common near Newbury were visiting the top of Silbury Hill for a 'women's gathering' on Lammas Day, 8 August, presumably inspired by Dames's contention that the Hill was designed for Lammas Day rituals. It is possible that these women began the dressing at the Spring, although I have not noted the survival of any special activity at Swallowhead around that date.

5. Evidence, mostly photographic, for subsequent observations by myself at Swallowhead and other sites can be found in my personal archive, from which most of the illustrations to this article were taken
6. Pete Glastonbury (*pers comm*); Jenny Blain of Sheffield Hallam University (ww.sacred sites.org.uk); the Avebury discussion group (http://groups.yahoo.com/group/Avebury_uk_/messages, and Katy Jordon (*pers comm*).
7. Philip Shallcrass of the Gorsedd of Bards of Caer Abiri told me in a letter of 21 February 1996: 'I… haven't been there… although several people have suggested I should go … other members of the Gorsedd do visit.' Christopher Gingell of the National Trust was unaware of activities at Swallowhead in 1998 (*pers comm*).
8. Activities also take place at Avebury stone circle itself and inside West Kennett Long Barrow (see footnote 13 below): in the latter case, the frequent leaving of burning candles etc against the Sarsens of the burial chamber may well be damaging the very monument the worshipper holds so dear.
9. Paul Everson, *pers comm*
10. Suprisingly, the earliest 'modern' hill figure is The White Horse of Strichen, Aberdeenshire, cut in 1773 by the local laird. The fashion may have been begun locally by the recutting by a local aristocrat of the existing horse of uncertain origin at Westbury in 1778 (Newman 1997, 36–45), adjacent to a Turnpike enacted 1757–8. The first 'new' White Horse in the area was that on Cherhill Down, overlooking the London-Bath road, cut in 1780, adjacent to a Turnpike enacted 1706–7, from the west and 1742–3 from the E, by a Doctor Christopher Alsop and subsequently regularily scoured by the Lord of the Manor; followed in 1785 by Pewsey, (adjacent to Devizes-Ludgershall and Swindon-Everleigh turnpikes, both enacted 1761–2) by a local farmer; and then by Marlborough in 1804 (nearby turnpike enacted 1742–3), by the teacher and pupils of a local academy; and Alton Barnes, again by a local farmer, in 1812 (turnpike not enacted until 1840). Later horses in the area included Broad Hinton (1835; by the parish clerk, turnpike 1809), Devizes (1845; by 'shoemakers' turnpike 1706–7), Broad Town (1864, by a local farmer, turnpike 1809) and Inkpen Beacon (1868), by a local house owner. There was also an undated, uncredited (and no longer extant) horse at Rockley (Turnpikes 1809 and 1761–2). Turnpike date from The *Victoria History of the Counties of England: A History of Wiltshire*, volume IV.
11. Brandon (1998) and (Field *et al* 2002) describe the attempt by the Lord of Avebury Manor, Richard Halford in 1723, to plant trees on the summit of Silbury Hill and cut a path to its summit, perhaps to form an eyecatching feature in the landscape.
12. A suggestion of William Stukeley's, quoted in Legg (1986)
13. The vicar of Avebury takes his congregation on an annual circuit of the Henge, with a cross at the head of the procession, on each Good Friday. Examples of the many activities in the New Age and various Pagan traditions that are creating a – currently small-scale – archaeology at Avebury include the following, observed on 1 February 2003 ('Imbolc', in the ritual year). Ashes, probably human, scattered in a circle around Stone 14 of the West Kennett Avenue; coins and other deposits in many of the root holes that occur naturally in the Sarsens; a daffodil bulb, presumably planted the previous year, sprouting at the foot of Stone 41 of the stone circle.
14. in a small field at SU119664. The southern extension of the Ridgeway passes along the adjacent road.
15. For example, the image of a particularly famous crop circle carved on the gatepost on the nearest road to the Alton Barnes field where it appeared, by the village church at SU107620.
16. Dames (1977, 185–6), cites Tan Hill as another key location – Rybury and Clifford's Hill are the head of the Great Goddess; the escarpment of which Tan Hill is the peak is her arms and shoulders. He also refers to the font in the church in passing, as an image of Christianity defying Paganism, (*ibid* 106).
17. Gover *et al* (1939). The 'Woden' is first mentioned in 903 ('wodnes dic') and remains consistent throughout the medieval period. As a neat example of the 'stratigaphic' effects of place names, the Editors suggest that the change from 'Woden's ditch' to 'Woden's dyke' is an Early Modern one, perhaps influenced by Stukeley.
18. Adam's Grave is of course a Long Barrow; Gover *et al* (1939, 318) gives no date for its earliest use, but suggests it was called Wodnesbeorge – 'Woden's Barrow' in 925. An 'Adam's mere' in south Wiltshire is first mentioned in the thirteenth century.
19. In the seventeenth century, both Aubrey (Aubrey J 1695 *Monumenta Britannica*, vol 2) and Pepys (Pepys S 1854 ed *Diary*, vol 3 466) reported the local tradition that a King Sil, or Zeal, or Zel, or Seall was buried in Silbury Hill, as cited in Dames, M *The Silbury Treasure op cit*, 14.

Bibliography

Abrams, L 1996 *Anglo-Saxon Glastonbury: church and endowment* Woodbridge: Boydell Press

Adkins, R A and Petchey, M R 1984 'Secklow Hundred Mound and Other Meeting Place Mounds in England'. *Arch J* **141**, 243–51

Aitken, M J 1974 *Physics and Archaeology* Oxford: Clarendon Press, 2nd edition

Allen, G W G 1984 'Discovery from the Air' *Aerial Archaeology* **10** East Dereham: Aerial Archaeology Publications

Allen, M J 1992 'Landscape history: the molluscan evidence', in C J Gingell *The Marlborough Downs: a Later Bronze Age Landscape and its Origins* Devizes: Wilts Archaeol & Nat Hist Soc Monograph **1**, 145–149

Allen, M J 1997a 'Environment and land-use; the economic development of the communities who built Stonehenge; an economy to support the stones', in B Cunliffe and C Renfrew (eds) *Science and Stonehenge*. Oxford, Proceedings of the British Academy, 115–144

Allen, M J 1997b 'Landscape, land-use and farming', in R J C Smith, F Healy, M J Allen, E Morris, L Barnes and P Woodward *Excavations along the route of the Dorchester by-pass, Dorset, 1986–8*. Salisbury: Wessex Archaeology Report No. **11**, 277–283

Allen, M J 1998 'Landscape and landuse reconstruction: looking forward or looking back?', in Woodward, A and Gardiner, J (eds) *Wessex Before Words: some new research directions for prehistoric Wessex*, 15–17.

Allen, M J 2000a 'High resolution mapping of Neolithic and Bronze Age chalkland landscape and land-use; the combination of multiple palaeo-environmental analyses and topographic modelling', in A Fairbairn (ed) *Landscape and Environment, Economy and Society: Plants in Neolithic Britain* Neolithic Studies Group, Oxford: Oxbow Books, 9–26

Allen, M J 2000b 'Piggledean Bottom: dry valley', in P J Fowler *Landscape Plotted and Pieced; landscape history and local archaeology in Fyfield and Overton, Wiltshire*. London: Report of the Research Committee of Society of Antiquaries of London **64**, 209–211

Allen, M J 2001a 'Resource assessment, palaeo-environmental data', in A Chadburn and M Pomeroy-Kellinger (eds) *Archaeological Research Agenda for the Avebury World Heritage Site*. English Heritage & Avebury Archaeological and Historical Research Group, 34–38

Allen, M J 2001b 'Research agenda, palaeo-environmental', in A Chadburn and M Pomeroy-Kellinger (eds) *Archaeological Research Agenda for the Avebury World Heritage Site*. Wessex Archaeology and English Heritage, 54–57

Allen, M J 2001c 'Land snail evidence for landscape and land-use change' in C J Ellis and M Rawlings Excavations at Balksbury Camp, Andover 1995–97, *Hampshire Studies* **56**, 54–67

Allen, M J 2002 'The chalkland landscape of Cranborne Chase; a prehistoric human ecology' *Landscapes* **3**, 54–68

Allen, M J and Carruthers, W J 1989 'Environmental assessment of the alluvial deposits (trench H)', in *West Kennet Farm, West Kennet, Marlborough, Wilts. Archaeological evaluation, 1989*. Salisbury: Wessex Archaeology, 40–48

Allen, M J Entwistle, R and Richards, J. 1990 'Molluscan studies' in J C Richards *The Stonehenge Environs Project*. English Heritage Archaeological Reports No **16**, 253–256

Anderson, O S 1934 *The English Hundred Names*. Lund: Lunds Universitets Årsskrift. N.F. Avd. 1 Bd 30. Nr 1

Anderton, R 2000 'Tertiary Events: the North Atlantic Plume and Alpine Pulses', *in* Woodcock, N and Strachan, R (eds) *Geological History of Britain and Ireland*. Oxford: Blackwell science

Annable, F K and Simpson, D D A 1964 *Guide catalogue to the Neolithic and Bronze Age Collections in Devizes Museum* Devizes: Wilts Archaeol & Nat Hist Soc.

Anon 1857 'Contributions to the Museum and Library' *Wilts Archaeol & Nat Hist Soc Mag* **3**, 252

Anon 1894 'Additions to the Museum and Library' *Wilts Archaeol & Nat Hist Soc Mag* **28**, 72

Anon 1917 'Skeleton find on Liddington Hill' *Wilts Archaeol & Nat Hist Soc Mag* **39**, 501–2

Anon 1942 'The Manor House, Ogbourne St George, Wiltshire' *Country Life* **92**, 1226–29

Anon 1951 'A Skeleton on Tan Hill', *Wilts Archaeol & Nat Hist Soc Mag* **14**, 228.

Anon 1964 'Excavation and fieldwork in Wiltshire 1963' *Wilts Archaeol & Nat Hist Soc Mag* **59**, 185

Anon 1971 'Accessions to the Museum 1970' *Wilts Archaeol & Nat Hist Soc Mag* **66**, 196–2000

Anon 1975–6 'Wiltshire Archaeological Register for 1974–5' *Wilts Archaeol & Nat Hist Mag* **70/71**, 132–8

Anon 1991 'Excavation and fieldwork in Wiltshire 1989' *Wilts Archaeol & Nat Hist Soc Mag* **84**, 141

Ashbee, P, Bell, M, and Proudfoot, E 1989 *Wilsford Shaft: excavations 1960–62*. English Heritage Archaeological Reports **11**. London: English Heritage.

Ashbee, P, Smith, I and Evans, J 1979 'Excavation of three long barrows near Avebury, Wiltshire'. *Proc Prehist Soc* **45**, 207–300

Ashmore, W and Brady, J E 1999 'Ideational landscapes of the ancient Maya', in W Ashmore and A Bernard Knapp (eds) *Archaeologies of Landscape: Contemporary Perspectives* Oxford: Blackwell

Aston, M 1993 *Know the Landscape: Monasteries* London: Batsford

Atkinson, R J C 1953 *Field Archaeology* (second edition) London: Methuen

Atkinson, R J C 1967 Silbury Hill *Antiquity* **41**, 259–62

Atkinson, R J C 1968 *Silbury Hill* BBC:London

Atkinson, R J C 1969 The date of Silbury Hill *Antiquity* **43**, 216

Atkinson, R J C 1970 Silbury Hill, 1969–70 *Antiquity* **44**, 313–4

Atkinson, R, Piggott, C and Sandars N 1951 *Excavations at Dorchester, Oxon Part 1.* Oxford: Dept of Antiquities Ashmolean Museum.

Banham, A J 1995 *A methodology for geophysical surveys in archaeology. Windmill Hill, 1993: a case study* Undergraduate project report, University of Wales College of Cardiff. Unpublished

Barber, M 2001 A Time and a Place for Bronze, *in* J Brück (ed.) *Bronze Age Landscapes: Tradition and Transformation*, 161–9. Oxford: Oxbow Books.

Barber, M, Grady, D and Winton, H 2003 'From Pit Circles to Propellers: Recent Results from Aerial Survey in Wiltshire' *Wilts Archaeol & Nat Hist Mag* **96**, 148–60.

Barker, C T 1984 'Millbarrow and Shelving Stone – finally at rest?' *Wilts Archaeol & Nat Hist Soc Mag* 78, 115–7

Barker, C T 1985 'The Long Mounds of the Avebury Region' *Wilts Archaeol & Nat Hist Soc Mag* 79, 7–38

Barrett, J C 1994 *Fragments from Antiquity: An Archaeology of Social Life in Britain, 2900–1200 BC.* Oxford: Basil Blackwell.

Barrett, J C and Needham, S P 1988 Production, Circulation and Exchange: problems in the interpretation of Bronze Age bronzework; *in* J C Barrett and I A Kinnes (eds.) *The Archaeology of Context in the Neolithic and Bronze Age: recent trends*, 127–140. Sheffield: Dept of Archaeology and Prehistory, University of Sheffield.

Barrett, J C, Bradley, R, Green, M, 1991 *Landscape, Monuments and Society: the Prehistory of Cranborne Chase* Cambridge: Cambridge Univ Press

Barron, R S 1976 *The Geology of Wiltshire: a field guide.* Bradford-on-Avon: Moonraker Press

Bartlett, A 1991 *Report on geophysical survey at Avebury Manor, Wiltshire, 1991.* Unpublished

Barton, R N E Berridge, P J Walker, M J C and Bevins, R E 1995 'Persistent Places in the Mesolithic Landscape: an Example from the Black Mountain Uplands of South Wales' *Proc Preh Soc* **61**, 81–116

Bassett, S 1989 'In Search of the Origins of Anglo-Saxon Kingdoms' *in* Bassett, S (ed) *The Origins of Anglo-Saxon Kingdoms.* Leicester: Leicester University Press, 3–27

Basso, K H 1996 'Wisdom Sits in Places'. In S. Field & K.H. Basso (eds), *Senses of Place*, 53–90. Santa Fe: School of American Research Press

Bell, M forthcoming 'Wetland-dryland relationships in the Severn Estuary and surroundings during the Mesolithic and Neolithic', *in* Haughey, F and O'Sullivan, A (eds) *Neolithic archaeology in the intertidal zone of rivers and estuaries.* Oxford: Oxbow

Bell, M, Fowler, P J and Hillson, S W (eds) *1996 The Experimental Earthwork Project 1960–92* Council for British Archaeology Research Report **100** York: Council for British Archaeology

Bellamy, P S forthcoming 'An interpretation of the Lambourne Valley Mesolithic Site Based on an Analysis of the Flint Artefacts', in Macphail, R I and Allen, M J (eds) *Archaeological Investigations on the A34 Newbury Bypass, Berkshire/Hampshire, 1991–97* Salisbury: Wessex Archaeology

Bernard Knapp (eds) *Archaeologies of landscape* Oxford: Blackwell

Bettey, J 1999 'The development of water meadows in the southern counties' in H Cook and T Williamson *Water Management in the English Landscape,* Edinburgh: Edinburgh University Press, 179–95

Bewley, R Cole, M David, A. Featherstone, R, Payne, A and Small R 1996 New features within the henge at Avebury, Wiltshire: aerial and geophysical evidence *Antiquity* **70**, 639–46

Binford, L R 1980 'Willow smoke and dogs' tails: hunter-gatherer settlement systems and site formation'. *American Antiquity* **45,** 4–20

Birch, W de G 1875 'Collections towards the History of the Cistercian Abbey of Stanley, in Wiltshire' *Wilts Archaeol & Nat Hist Mag* **15**, 239–307

Blackwell, I W unpublished 'Saxon Charter S547; West Kennet', *Fyfield Working Paper 11a.* HTTP://www.ads.ahds.ac.uk/catalogue/, accessed 13/12/01

Blair, J 1985 'Secular Minster Churches in Domesday Book' *in* Sawyer P (ed) *Domesday Book: A Reassessment.* London: Edward Arnold, 104–42

Blair, J 1991 *Early Medieval Surrey. Landholding, Church and Settlement before 1300.* Stroud: Alan Sutton

Blakiston, H N 1956 'Priory of Clatford or Hullavington' *in* Pugh, R B and Crittall, E (eds) *A History of Wiltshire* **3**, Oxford: Oxford University Press, 393–4

Bloch, M 1995 'People into places: Zafimaniry concepts of clarity' in E Hirsch and M O'Hanlon (eds) *The Anthropology of Landscape: perspectuives on time and space*, 63–77 Oxford: Clarendon Press

Bloch, M 1998 *How We Think They Think: anthropological approaches to cognition, memory and literacy.* Boulder & Oxford: Westview Press

Bonney, D 1964 'All Cannings: Rybury Camp' *Wilts Archaeol & Nat Hist Soc Mag* **59**, 185

Bonney, D 1966 'Pagan Saxon Burials and Boundaries in Wiltshire', *Wilts Archaeol & Nat Hist Mag* **61**, 25–30

Bonney, D 1972 'Early boundaries in Wessex', *in* Fowler P J (ed) *Archaeology and the Landscape.* London: John Baker, 168–86

Bonney, D 1979 'Early boundaries and estates in southern Britain', *in* Sawyer (ed) P H *English Medieval Settlement.* London: Edward Arnold, 41–51

Bowden, M 1998 *Barbury Castle: an archaeological survey by the Royal Commission on the Historical Monuments of England* RCHME archive Report AI/3/1998

Bowden, M 2001 *Liddington Castle: archaeological earthwork survey* (version 2). EH Survey Report no. AI/4/2001

Bowden, M and McOmish, D 1987 'The required barrier' *Scot Archaeol Rev* **4:2**. 76–84

Bowden, M, Ford, S and Mees, G 1993 'The date of the ancient fields on the Berkshire Downs' *Berks Archaeol J* **74** (1991–3). 109–33

Bowen, H C and Fowler, P 1963 'The archaeology of Fyfield and Overton Downs, Wilts (interim report)' *Wilts Archaeol and Nat Hist Soc Mag* **58**. 98–115

Bowen, H C and Fowler, P 1966 'Romano-British rural settlements in Dorset and Wiltshire' *in* Thomas, C (ed) *Rural Settlement in Roman Britain* CBA Res Rep **7**. 43–67

Bowen, H C and Smith, I F 1977 'Sarsen stones in Wessex: the Society's first investigation in the evolution of the landscape project' *Antiq J* **57**, 185–96

Bowie, G 1990 Northern Wolds and Wessex Downlands: Contrasts in Sheep Husbandry and Farming Practice, 1770–1850, *Agric Hist Rev* **38**. 117–126

Bradley, R 1984 *Social Foundations of Prehistoric Britain.* London: Longman

Bradley, R 1990 *The Passage of Arms. An archaeological analysis of hoards and votive deposits.* Cambridge: Cambridge University Press.

Bradley, R 1993 *Altering the Earth: the origins of monuments in Britain and Continental Europe.* Edinburgh: Society of Antiquaries of Scotland

Bradley, R 1998 *The Significance of Monuments: On the shaping of human experience in Neolithic and Bronze Age Europe.* London: Routledge

Bradley, R 1999 *The Passage of Arms. An archaeological analysis of hoards and votive deposits.* 2nd edition. Oxford: Oxbow Books.

Bradley, R 2000 *An Archaeology of Natural Places* London: Routledge

Bradley, R 2002 *The Past in Prehistoric Societies.* London: Routledge

Bradley, R, Entwistle, R, Raymond, F 1994 *Prehistoric Land Divisions on Salisbury Plain: The Work of the Wessex Linear Ditches Project* London: English Heritage.

Brandon, P 1998 *The South Downs* (reprinted 1999) Chichester: Phillimore & Co

Bray, E 1998a *Long barrow 495C, Shepherds Shore, Wiltshire: report on geophysical survey, November 1997* Ancient Monuments Laboratory Reports Series **3/98**. Unpublished

Bray, E 1998b *Wessex Bowl Barrow project: report on geophysical surveys, April 1998* Ancient Monuments Laboratory Reports Series **40/98**. Unpublished

Brentnall, H C 1923 'Barton Farm in the Thirteenth Century' *Report of the Marlborough College Natural History Society* **72**. 69–82

Brentnall, H C 1939 'The Saxon Bounds of Overton' *Report of the Marlborough College Natural History Society* 87, 116–36

Brentnall, H C 1946 'Sarsens' *Wilts Archaeol & Nat Hist Soc Mag* **51**, 419–39

British Geological Survey 1:50,000 map, Sheet 266, Marlborough. HMSO

Brogiolo, G P, Gauthier, N and Christie, N 2000 *Towns and their Territories between Late Antiquity and the Early Middle Ages.* Leiden, Boston and Koln: Brill

Brooke, J W 1910 The excavation of a Roman well near Silbury Hill, October 1908 *Wilts Archaeol & Nat Hist Mag* **36**, 373–75

Brooke, J W and Cunnington, B H 1896 'Excavation of a Roman well near Silbury Hill' *Wilts Archaeol & Nat Hist Mag* **29**, 166–171

Brothwell, D 1992 'The human remains from Avebury Barrow G55, with special reference to the further evidence of a childhood deficiency disease in the Bronze Age', *Wilts Archaeol& Nat Hist Soc Mag* **85**, 141–144.

Brown, G forthcoming *A Cistercian Grange on Wick Down. Wilts Archaeol & Nat Hist Soc Mag* **98**

Brück, J 1995 A place for the dead: the role of human remains in the Late Bronze Age. *Procs Prehist Soc* **61**, 245–277

Brück, J 1999a Houses, lifecycles and deposition on Middle Bronze Age settlements in southern England. *Proc Prehist Soc* **65,** 145–166

Brück, J 1999b Ritual and Rationality: some problems of interpretation in European archaeology. *European Journ Archaeol* **2**(3), 313–344

Buckley, D G and Hedges, J D 1987 *The Bronze Age and Saxon Settlements at Springfield Lyons, Essex. An Interim Report.* Essex County Council Occasional Paper No. **5**. Chelmsford: Essex County Council

Burgess, C 1986 "Urnes of no small variety": Collared Urns reviewed ' *Proc Prehist Soc* **52**, 339–51

Burl, A 1979 *Prehistoric Avebury* New Haven and London: Yale University Press

Burl, A 1988 'Coves: structural enigmas of the Neolithic'. *Wilts Archaeol & Nat Hist Mag* **82**, 1–18

Butterworth, J 1999 *Monastic Sites and Monastic Estates in Somerset and Wiltshire in the Middle Ages: A Regional Approach* unpublished Phd thesis, University of Bristol

Caley, J (ed) 1802 *Taxatio Ecclesiastica Angliae et Wallae Anctontate P. Nicholais IV, c1291* London: Record Commission

Caley, J and Hunter, J (eds) 1814 *Valor Ecclesiasticus temp. Henr. VIII auctoritate regia institutus* **2**, London: Record Commission

Calkin, J Bernard 1952 'The Bournemouth area in Neolithic and Early Bronze age times' *Proc Dorset Nat Hist & Archaeol Soc* **73**, 32–70

Care, V 1982 'The Collection and Distribution of Lithic Materials during the Mesolithic and Neolithic Periods in Southern England'. *Oxford Journ of Archaeol* **1**(3), 269–285

Carter, H H 1975–6 'Fauna of an area of Mesolithic occupation in the Kennet Valley considered in relation to contemporary eating habits'. *Berks Arch Journ* **68**, 1–3

Case, H 1977 'The Beaker culture in Britain and Ireland' 71–100, in R. Mercer (ed) *Beakers in Britain and Europe Oxford:* British Archaeological Reports (International Series) 26

Case, H 1995 'Some Wiltshire Beakers and their contexts' in *Wilts Archaeol & Nat Hist Soc Mag* **88**, 1–17

Catt, J A 1978 'The Contribution of Loess to Soils in Lowland Britain', *in* Limbrey, S and Evans, J G (eds) *The Effect of Man on the Landscape: The Lowland Zone.* Council for British Archaeology Research Report No. **21**, 12 – 20

Catt, J A 1986 'The nature, origin and geomorphological significance of Clay-with-Flints', *in* Sieveking, G de G and Hart, M B (eds) *The Scientific Study of Flint and Chert.* Cambridge: Cambridge University Press

Chadburn, A and Corney, M 2001a 'Resource assessment: Iron Age' *in* A Chadburn and M Pomeroy-Kellinger (eds) *Archaeological Research Agenda for the Avebury World Heritage Site.* Wessex Archaeology and English Heritage. 19–24

Chadburn, A and Corney, M 2001b 'Research strategies: Iron Age' *in* A Chadburn and M Pomeroy-Kellinger (eds) *archaeological Research Agenda for the Avebury World Heritage Site.* Wessex Archaeology and English Heritage. 67–8

Chadburn, A and Pomeroy-Kellinger, M (eds) 2001 *Archaeological Research Agenda for the Avebury World Heritage Site* Wessex Archaeology and English Heritage

Chandler, J 1991 *The Vale of Pewsey.* Bradford on Avon: Ex Libris Press

Chandler, J 2001 *Marlborough and Eastern Wiltshire* Hobnob Press: Salisbury

Chapman, J 1997 'The origins of tells in Eastern Hungary'. In P Topping (ed.), *Neolithic Landscapes*, 139–64. Oxford: Oxbow Books

Chettle, H F and Kirby, J L 1956a 'Priory of St Margaret, Marlborough' *in* Pugh, R B and Crittall, E (eds) *A History of Wiltshire* **3**, Oxford: Oxford University Press, 316–19

Chettle, H F and Kirby, J L 1956b 'Abbey of Stanley' *in* Pugh, R B and Crittall, E (eds) *A History of Wiltshire* **3**, Oxford: Oxford University Press, 269–75

Churchill, D 0 1962 'The stratigraphy of the Mesolithic Sites III and V at Thatcham, Berkshire, England' *Proc Preh Soc* **28**, 362–370

Clark, A J 1957 The transistor as the archaeologist's latest tool *Illustrated London News* **230**, 900–1

Clark, A J 1996 *Seeing Beneath The Soil* London: Batsford 2nd edition

Clark, M J, Lewin, J and Small, R J 1967 *The sarsen stones of the Marlborough Downs and their Geomorphological Implications* Southampton Research Series in Geography **4** Southampton: Southampton University

Clarke, D L 1970 *Beaker Pottery of Great Britain and Ireland* Cambridge: Cambridge University Press

Clarke, D V, Cowie, T G, Foxon, A 1985 *Symbols of Power at the Time of Stonehenge.* Edinburgh: National Museum of Antiquities of Scotland/HMSO

Clayton, C J 1986 'The Chemical Environment of Flint Formation in Upper Cretaceous Chalks', *in* G de G Sieveking and M B Hart (eds) *The Scientific Study of Flint and Chert.* Cambridge: Cambridge University Press

Cleal, R M J and Allen, M J 2001 'Towards a research framework for the Avebury landscape', in A Chadburn and M Pomeroy-Kellinger (eds) *Archaeological Research Agenda for the Avebury World Heritage Site.* Wessex Archaeology and English Heritage, 57–62

Cleal, R, Walker, K & Montague, R 1995 *Stonehenge in its landscape: twentieth-century excavations.* London: English Heritage Archaeol Report **11**

Codrington, T 1866 The geology of the Berkshire and Hampshire extension and the Marlborough Railways *Wilts Archaeol & Nat Hist Mag* **9**, 167–193

Connah, G 1965 'Excavations at Knap Hill, Alton Priors, 1961'. *Wilts Archaeol & Nat Hist Mag* **60**, 1–23

Connerton, P 1989 *How Societies Remember*. Cambridge: Cambridge University Press

Conyers, L B and Goodman, D 1997 *Ground-Penetrating Radar: an Introduction for Archaeologists* California: Altamira Press,

Coombs, D 1972 *Late Bronze Age metalwork in the south of England. Typology, associations, distribution, chronology and industrial traditions*. Unpublished PhD, University of Cambridge Dept. of Archaeology

Coombs, D 2001 Metalwork, *in* F Pryor *The Flag Fen Basin. Archaeology and Environment of a Fenland Landscape*, 255–317. Swindon: English Heritage

Corney, M 1989 'Multiple Ditch Systems and Late Iron Age Settlement in Central Wessex', *in* M Bowden, D Mackay and P Topping (eds) *From Cornwall to Caithness – Some Aspects of British Field Archaeology: Papers Presented to Norman V Quinnell* British Archaeol Reports **209**, 111–28 Oxford: British Archaeol Reports

Corney, M 1997a 'New Evidence for the Romano-British Settlement by Silbury Hill' *Wilts Archaeol & Nat Hist Mag* **90**, 139–41

Corney, M 1997b 'The Origins and Development of the 'Small Town' of *Cunetio*, Mildenhall, Wiltshire'. *Britannia* **28**, 337–50

Corney, M 2001 'The Romano-British nucleated settlements of Wiltshire' *in* Ellis, P (ed) *Roman Wiltshire and After*. Devizes: Wiltshire Archaeological and Natural History Society, 5–38

Corney, M and Walters, B 2001 'Romano-British' in A Chadburn and M Pomeroy-Kellinger (ed) *Archaeological Research Agenda for the Avebury World Heritage Site* 24–27 Salisbury: Wessex Archaeology and English Heritage

Cossons, A 1959 'Roads', *in* Crittal, E (ed) *A History of Wiltshire* **4**, Victoria County History. London: OUP, 254–271

Crawford, O G S, and Keiller, A 1928 *Wessex from the Air* Oxford: Clarendon Press

Crittall, E (ed) 1959 *The Victoria History of the Counties of England: Wiltshire* **4**. Oxford: Oxford University Press

Crittall, E (ed) 1970 *The Victoria History of the Counties of England: Wiltshire* **9**. Oxford: Oxford University Press

Crittall, E (ed) 1975 *The Victoria History of the Counties of England: Wiltshire* **10**. Oxford: Oxford University Press

Crittall, E 1956 'The Religious Houses of Wiltshire: Introduction' *in* Pugh, R B and Crittall, E (eds) *A History of Wiltshire* **3**, Oxford: Oxford University Press, 150–55

Crittall, E 1980 'Wroughton' *in* Crowley, D A (ed) *A History of Wiltshire* **11**, Oxford: Oxford University Press, 235–52

Crutchley, S 2000 *Salisbury Plain Training Area: A report for the National Mapping Programme*. Unpublished report, Swindon: English Heritage

Cunliffe, B 1973 'The Period of Romanization, 43–c250' *in* Crittall, E (ed) *The Victoria History of Wiltshire* **1:2**. London: Oxford University Press, 439–52

Cunliffe, B 1991 *Iron Age Communities in Britain* 3rd edition. London: RKP

Cunnington, H 1887a 'Description of the opening of a British dwelling-pit at Beckhampton' *Wilts Archaeol and Nat Hist Soc Mag* **23**. 65–8

Cunnington, H 1887b 'Relics of ancient population on Oldbury Hill, Wilts' *Wilts Archaeol and Nat Hist Soc Mag* **23**. 213–22

Cunnington, M E 1907a 'Notes on the Opening of a Bronze Age Barrow at Manton, near Marlborough'. *The Reliquary and Illustrated Archaeologist* **13**, 28–46

Cunnington, M E 1907b 'Notes on the Opening of a Bronze Age Barrow at Manton, near Marlborough'. *Wilts Archaeol and Nat Hist Soc Mag* **35**, 1–20

Cunnington, M E 1908 'Notes on the opening of a Bronze Age barrow at Manton, near Marlborough' *Wilts Archaeol & Nat Hist Soc Mag* **35**, 1–20

Cunnington, M E 1910 'A Medieval Earthwork near Morgan's Hill' *Wilts Archaeol & Nat Hist Mag* **36**. 590–598

Cunnington, M E 1911 'Knap Hill Camp' *Wilts Archaeol & Nat Hist Soc Mag* **37**. 42–65

Cunnington, M E 1911–12 'Knap Hill Camp' *Wilts Archaeol & Nat Hist Mag* **37**, 42–65

Cunnington, M E 1913 'Interment near Old Shepherd Shore' *Wilts Archaeol & Nat Hist Mag* 38, 106

Cunnington, M E 1923 *The Early Iron Age Inhabited Site at All Cannings Cross Farm, Wiltshire. A description of the excavations and objects found, by Mr and Mrs BH Cunnington, 1911–1922*. Devizes: George Simpson & Co. Ltd

Cunnington, M E 1926a 'Barrow near Shepherds Shore' *Wilts Archaeol & Nat Hist Mag* **43**, 397–8

Cunnington, M E 1926b 'Bronze Age Beaker from Beckhampton' *Wilts Archaeol & Nat Hist Soc Mag* **43**, 399–400

Cunnington, M E 1926c 'Notes on Recent prehistoric finds' *Wilts Archaeol & Nat Hist Soc Mag* **43** (145), 395–400

Cunnington, M E 1931 'The "Sanctuary" on Overton Hill, near Avebury', *Wilts Archaeol & Nat Hist Soc Mag* **45**, 300–335

Cunnington, M E and Cunnington, B 1923 *The Early Iron Age Inhabited Site at All Cannings Cross Farm, Wiltshire*. Devizes: George Simpson & Co

Cunnington, M E and Goddard, E H 1934 *Catalogue of Antiquities in the Museum pt 2* Devizes: *Wilts Archaeol & Nat Hist Soc*

Cunnington, R H 1946 'Tabular sarsen and mud cracks' *Wilts Archaeol & Nat Hist Soc Mag* 51, 405–418

Cunnington, W 1893 'Notes on food-vessels from Oldbury Hill' *Wilts Archaeol and Nat Hist Soc Mag* **27**. 291–3

Cunnington, W and Cunnington, WA 1903 The Palaeolithic implements and gravels of Knowle Farm, Wiltshire. *Wilts Archaeol & Nat Hist Soc Mag* **33**. 131–138

Curwen, E C, 1930 Neolithic Camps *Antiquity* **4**, 22–54

Dames, M 1976 *The Silbury Treasure* reprinted 1992 London: Thames & Hudson

Dames, M 1977, reprinted 1996 *The Avebury Cycle* London: Thames & Hudson

Dames, M 1992 *The Silbury Treasure* 2nd ed London: Thames & Hudson

Dames, M 1996 *The Avebury Cycle* 2nd ed London: Thames & Hudson

Darlington, R R 1955a 'Translation of the Text of the Wiltshire Domesday' *in* Pugh, R B and Crittall, E (eds), *A History of Wiltshire* **2**. The Victoria History of the Counties of England. London: Oxford University Press, 113–168

Darlington, R R 1955b 'Text and Translation of the Wiltshire Geld Rolls' *in* Pugh, R B and Crittall, E (eds), *A History of Wiltshire* **2**. The Victoria History of the Counties of England. London: Oxford University Press, 178–217

Darlington, R R 1955c 'Introduction to the Wiltshire Domesday' *in* Pugh, R B and Crittall, E (eds) *A History of Wiltshire* **2**. The Victoria History of the Counties of England. London: Oxford University Press, 42–112

David, A 1984 *Avebury Car Park* Ancient Monuments Laboratory Reports Series No 4449. Unpublished

David, A 1994 'The role of geophysical survey in early medieval archaeology' *Anglo-Saxon Studies in Archaeology and History* **7**, 1–26

David, A 2001 'Geophysical survey', in A Chadburn and M Pomeroy-Kellinger (eds) *Archaeological Research Agenda for the Avebury World Heritage Site* , 71–9 Salisbury: Wessex Archaeology and English Heritage

David, A and Linford, N 2000 'Physics and archaeology' *Physics World* **13**: 5, 27–31

David, A, Field, D, Fassbinder, J, Linford, N, Linford, P and Payne, A 2002 'A family chapel .... to an archdruids dwelling': an investigation into the stone circle at Winterbourne Bassett, Wiltshire *Wilts Archaeol & Nat Hist Soc Mag* **96**, 195–205

David, A, McOmish, D and Whittle, A 1999 'The lay-out of the enclosure: earthwork and geophysical survey', in A Whittle, J Pollard, and C Grigson *The Harmony of Symbols: The Windmill Hill Causewayed Enclosure* 7–23 Oxford: Oxbow Books

Davies, P and Wolski, C 2001 'Later Neolithic woodland regeneration in the long barrow ditch fills of the Avebury area: the molluscan evidence', *Oxford Journ Archaeol* **20**, 311–317

Davis, J B 1865 *Crania Brittanica: delineations and description of the skulls of the aboriginal and early inhabitants of the British islands: with notices of other remains ... Vol 2 plates and descriptions, plate 58, 1–6.* London

Davis, T 1811 *A General View of the Agriculture of Wiltshire*, London: Richard Phillips

Defoe, D 1724–6 *A tour through the whole island of Great Britain* (Penguin *ed* 1979) Harmondsworth: Penguin Books

Dennis, I, and Hamilton, M A 1997 *Exploratory excavations and survey of Mesolithic, Late Bronze Age and Iron Age sites at Golden Ball Hill, near Alton Barnes, Wiltshire: an interim report for 1997* Cardiff Studies in Archaeology, Specialist Report Number **7**. Unpublished

Dickinson, T M 1974 *Cuddesdon and Dorchester-on-Thames*. Oxford: British Archaeological Reports **1**

Dimbleby, G W 1997 Pollen, in A Whittle *Sacred Mound Holy Rings; Silbury Hill and West Kennet palisade enclosures: a Later Neolithic complex in north Wiltshire*. Oxford: Oxbow Monograph **74**, 29–32

Dimbleby, G W and Evans, J G 1974 'Pollen and land-snail analysis of calcareous soils'. *Journ Archaeol Science* **1**, 117–133

Dixon, P 1988 'Neolithic settlement on Crickley Hill', in C Burgess, P Topping, C Mordant and M Maddison (eds) *Enclosures and defences in the Neolithic of Western Europe*, 75–87 Oxford: Bri Archaeol Report Int ser 403

Dixon, S B 1903 On the Palaeolithic flint implements from Knowle, Savernake Forest. *Wilts Archaeol & Nat Hist Soc Mag* **33**, 139–44

Dodds, G S H and Eddies, R 1998 *The Cove, Avebury: investigation to determine the depth of two standing stones* Aperio Ltd, Project No 2057. Unpublished

Douglas, Rev J 1793 *Nenia Britannica: or a sepulchral history of Britain* London: Benjamin & John White

Drewett, P L 1978 Neolithic Sussex, in Drewett, P.L. (ed.), *Archaeology in Sussex to AD 1500*. London: CBA Research Report No 29, 23–29

Drewett, P L 1985 *Settlement, ceremony and territorial organisation in Sussex, 4th–2nd millennium BC*. Unpubl. PhD thesis Univ. Lond

Dyer, C 1995 'Sheepcotes: Evidence for Medieval Sheep Farming' Med Arch **39**. 136–164

Dyer, C 1996 'Seasonal Settlement in Medieval Gloucestershire' *in* Fox, H (ed) *Seasonal Settlement*, 25–33 Vaughan Paper **39**. Leicester : University of Leicester

Eagles, B N 1986 'Pagan Anglo-Saxon burials at West Overton' *Wilts Archaeol & Nat Hist Soc Mag* **80**, 103–19

Eagles, B N 2001 'Anglo-Saxon presence and culture in Wiltshire *c.* AD 450 – *c.* 675' *in* Ellis, P (ed) *Roman Wiltshire and After*. Devizes: Wiltshire Archaeological and Natural History Society, 199–233

Edwards, H 1988 *The Charters of the Early West Saxon Kingdom*. Oxford: British Archaeological Reports **198**

Eerkens, J 1997 'Variability in Later Mesolithic Microliths of Northern England'. *Lithics* **17–18**, 51–65 Lithic Studies Society

Ellison, R A, Knox, R W O'B, Jolley, D W and King, C 1994 'A Revision of the Lithostratigraphical Classification of the Early Palaeogene Strata of the London Basin and East Anglia'. *Proc Geol Assoc* **105**, 187 – 197

Elrington, C (ed) 1980, *The Victoria History of the Counties of England: Wiltshire* **11**. Oxford: Oxford University Press

Elrington, C (ed) 1983 *The Victoria History of the Counties of England: Wiltshire* **12**. Oxford: Oxford University Press

English Heritage 1995 *Geophysical Survey in Archaeological Evaluation, Research & Professional Services Guideline No 1* London: English Heritage

English Heritage, 1998 *Avebury World Heritage Site Management Plan*, London: English Heritage (currently being revised)

Esmond Cleary, S 1989 *The Ending of Roman Britain*. London: Batsford

Evans, J 1881 *The Ancient Bronze Implements, Weapons, and Ornaments of Great Britain and Ireland*. London: Longmans

Evans, J G 1965 'Land Mollusca, in Smith, I F Excavation of a Bell Barrow, Avebury, G.55', *Wilts Archaeol & Nat Hist Soc Mag* **60**, 44–45

Evans, J G 1966 'A Romano-British interment in the bank of the Winterbourne, near Avebury' *Wilts Archaeol & Nat Hist Soc Mag* **61**, 97–98

Evans, J G 1967 *The stratification of Mollusca in chalk soils and their relation to archaeology*. Unpubl. Ph.D. thesis, Institute of Archaeology, University of London

Evans, J G 1968 'Periglacial deposits on the chalk of Wiltshire' *Wilts Archaeol & Nat Hist Soc Mag* **63**, 12–26

Evans, J G 1969 'Further periglacial deposits in North Wiltshire' *Wilts Archaeol & Nat Hist Soc Mag* **64**, 112–113

Evans, J G 1972 *Land Snails in Archaeology* London: Seminar Press

Evans, J G 1990 'Notes on some Late Neolithic and Bronze Age events in long barrow ditches in southern and eastern England'. *Proc Prehist Soc* **56**, 111–116

Evans, J G and Jones, H 1979 'Mount Pleasant and Woodhenge: The land Mollusca', in Wainwright, G J *Mount Pleasant, Dorset: Excavations 1970–1971*. London: Society of Antiquaries Research Report 37, 190–213

Evans, J G and Smith, I F 1967 Cherhill. *Archaeological Review* (Dept. Extra-mural studies, Univ. Bristol) No. 2, 8–9

Evans, J G and Smith, I F S 1983 'Excavations at Cherhill, North Wiltshire, 1967'. *Proc Preh Soc* **49**, 43–117

Evans, J G Rouse, A and Sharples, N 1988 'The landscape setting of causewayed camps: recent work on the Maiden Castle enclosure', in J C Barrett and I A Kinnes (eds), *The Archaeology of context in the Neolithic and Bronze Age: recent trends*. Sheffield: J.R. Collis, 73–78

Evans, J G, Limbrey, S, Maté, I and Mount, R 1988 'Environmental change and land-use history in a Wiltshire river valley in the last 14,000 years', in J C Barrett and I A Kinnes (eds) *The Archaeology of context in the Neolithic and Bronze Age; recent trends*. Sheffield: J.R. Collis, 97–103

Evans, J G, Limbrey, S, Mate, I and Mount, R 1993 'An Environmental History of the Upper Kennet Valley, Wiltshire, for the Last 10,000 Years'. *Proc Preh Soc* **59**. 139–195

Evans, J G, Pitts, M W and Williams, D 1985 'An Excavation at Avebury, Wiltshire, 1982' *Proc Prehist Soc* **51**, 305–310

Farley, M E, 1971 *The Roman evidence from Silbury Hill, Wilshire* unpub undergraduate dissertation University College Cardiff

Faulkner, N 2000 *The Decline and Fall of Roman Britain*. Stroud and Charleston SC: Tempus

Field, D 2001 'Place and Memory in Bronze Age Wessex', in J Brück (ed) *Bronze Age Landscapes: Tradition and Transformation*, 57–64 Oxford: Oxbow Books

Field, D and Cotton, J 1987 'The Neolithic: a survey of the evidence' in J G Bird and D Bird (eds) *The archaeology of Surrey to AD1540* Guildford: Surrey Archaeol Soc

Field, D, Brown, G and Crockett, A 2001 'The Marlborough Mound revisited' *Wilts Archaeol & Nat Hist Mag* **94**, 195–204

Field, D, Brown, G with Thomason, B 2002 *An Investigation and Analytical Survey of Silbury Hill* English Heritage Archaeological Investigation Report AI/22/2002, Swindon: English Heritage

Finberg, H P R 1964a 'Roman and Saxon Withington' *in* Finberg, H P R (ed) *Lucerna.* London: Macmillan and Co Ltd, 21–65

Finberg, H P R 1964b *The Early Charters of Wessex.* Leicester: Leicester University Press

Fishpool, M., 1999 'Land Mollusca', in A Whittle, J Pollard and C Grigson *The Harmony of Symbols; the Windmill Hill causewayed enclosure.* Oxford: Oxbow Books, 127–138

Fitzpatrick, A 1984 'The deposition of La Tène Iron Age metalwork in watery contexts in southern England' *in* B Cunliffe and D Miles (eds) *Aspects of the Iron Age in Central Southern Britain* Oxford University Committee for Archaeology. 178–90

Fleming, A 1971 'Territorial patterns in Bronze Age Wessex' *Proc Prehist Soc* **37**(1), 138–166

Ford, S 1982 'Linear Earthworks on the Berkshire Downs', *Berks Archaeol Jour* **71**, 1–20

Forde-Johnstone, J 1976 *Hillforts of the Iron Age in England and Wales* Liverpool University Press

Forey, A 1992 *The Military Orders from the Twelth to the Early Fourteenth Centuries* London: Macmillan

Forty, A 1999 'Introduction'. In A. Forty & S. Küchler (eds), *The Art of Forgetting*, 1–18. Oxford: Berg

Fowler, P J 1964 'Cross-Dykes on the Ebble-Nadder Ridge', *Wilts Archaeol & Nat Hist Soc Mag* **59**, 46–57

Fowler, P J 1965 'The Cross-Dyke on Buxbury Hill, Sutton Mandeville', *Wilts Archaeol & Nat Hist Soc Mag* **60**, 47–51

Fowler, P J 1967 'The archaeology of Fyfield and Overton Downs, Wiltshire. Third Interim Report' *Wilts Archaeol & Nat Hist Soc Mag* **62**, 16–33

Fowler, P J 1976 'Agriculture and Rural Settlement' *in* Wilson, D M (ed) *The Archaeology of Anglo-Saxon England.* Cambridge: Cambridge University Press, 23–48

Fowler, P J 2000 *Landscape Plotted and Pieced. Landscape History and Local Archaeology in Fyfield and Overton, Wiltshire.* London: Reports of the Research Committee of the Society of Antiquaries of London **64**

Fowler, P J 2001 *The Fyfield and Overton project 1959–1998; FWP 63; FWP65.* Archaeological Data Service Internet Publication http://ads.ahds.ac.uk/catalogue/exc_arch/Fyfod/

Fowler, P n.d *Excavation within a later prehistoric field system on Overton Down, West Overton, Wiltshire: land-use over 4000 years.* FYFOD working paper FWP 63; at http://ads.ahds.ac.uk/catalogue/ (consulted 15 November 2001)

Fowler, P J and Blackwell, I 1998 *The Land of Lettice Sweetapple: An English Countryside Explored.* Stroud and Charleston SC: Tempus

Fowler, P J and Evans, J G 1967 'Ploughmarks, lynchets and early fields' *Antiquity* **41**, 289–301

Fowles, J (ed) 1980 *Monumenta Britannica* by John Aubrey (1626–97) annotated by R Legg Dorset: DPC

Fowles, J *ed* 1980 *John Aubrey's Monumenta Britannica* Dorset: DPC

Free, D W 1948 'Sarsen Stones and their origin' *Wilts Archaeol &Nat Hist Soc Mag* 52, 338–44

Freeman, J 1983a 'Avebury' *in* Crowley, D A (ed) *A History of Wiltshire* **12**, Oxford: Oxford University Press, 86–105

Freeman, J 1983b 'Ogbourne St Andrew' *in* Crowley, D A (ed) *A History of Wiltshire* **12**, Oxford: Oxford University Press, 138–51

Freeman, J 1983c 'Ogbourne St George' *in* Crowley, D A (ed) *A History of Wiltshire* **12**, Oxford: Oxford University Press, 151–60

Freeman, J 1983d 'Winterbourne Monkton' *in* Crowley, D A (ed) *A History of Wiltshire* **12**, Oxford: Oxford University Press, 192–98

French, C, Lewis, H, Allen, M J and Scaife, R 2000 'Palaeo-environmental and archaeological investigations on Wyke Down and the upper Allen Valley, Cranborne Chase, Dorset, England: interim summary report for 1998–9', *Proc Dorset Nat. Hist & Archaeol Soc* **122**, 53–71

Fretwell, K 1992 *Avebury Manor, Park and Garden Survey* National Trust report

Froom, F R 1963 'The Mesolithic around Hungerford: parts I, II and III'. *Trans Newbury and Dist Field Club.* **11**, 62–87

Froom, F R 1965 'The Mesolithic around Hungerford: parts IV and V'. *Trans Newbury and Dist Field Club* **11**(3), 45–51

Froom, F R 1970 'The Mesolithic around Hungerford: part VI'. *Trans Newbury and Dist Field Club* **12**(1), 58–67

Froom, F R 1972a 'Some Mesolithic sites in south-west Berkshire'. *Berks Archaeol Journa.* **66**. 11–22

Froom, F R 1972b 'A Mesolithic site at Wawcott, Kintbury, Berkshire'. *Berks Archaeol Journal* **66**, 23–44

Froom, F R 1983 Recent Work at the Lower Palaeolithic Site at Knowle Farm, Bedwyn. *Wilts Archaeol & Nat Hist Soc Mag.* **77**, 27–37

Froom, R, Cook, J, Debenham, N, Ambers, J 1994 'Wawcott XXX(30): An Interim Report on a Mesolithic Site in Berkshire', *in* Ashton, N and David, A (eds) *Stories in Stone.* Lithic Studies Soc Occas Paper. **4**. 206–212

Fry, E A 1908 *Abstracts of Wiltshire Inquisitiones Post Mortem 1242–1326* London: British Record Society

Galbraith, G R 1956 'Carmelite Friars of Marlborough' *in* Pugh, R B and Crittall, E (eds) *A History of Wiltshire* **3**, Oxford: Oxford University Press, 333–4

Gamble, C S 1996 Hominid Behaviour in the Middle Pleistocene: an English Perspective, in C S Gamble and A J Lawson (eds) *The English Palaeolithic Reviewed Salisbury:* Trust for Wessex Archaeology Ltd

Gardiner, J P 1988 *The composition and distribution of Neolithic surface flint assemblages in central southern England.* Unpubl. Ph.D. thesis, University of Reading

Gardiner, J P 1991 'Flint procurement and axe production during the Neolithic on the South Downs; a re-assessment', *Oxford Journ Archaeol* **9**, 119–140

Garmonsway, G N1975 *The Anglo-Saxon Chronicle* trans 1955, rep. London: Dent

Geddes, I 2000 *Hidden Depths: Wiltshire's Geology and Landscapes.* Bradford-on-Avon: Ex Libris Press

Gelling, M 1984 *Place-Names in the Landscape* London: Dent

Gibson, A and Kinnes, I 1997 'On the urns of a dilemma: radiocarbon and the Peterborough problem'. *Oxford J Archaeol* **16**(1), 65–72

Gilchrist, R 1995, *Contemplation and Acton – The Other Monasticism* London: Leicester University Press

Gillings, M and Pollard, J 1999 'Non-portable stone artefacts and contexts of meaning: the tale of Grey Wether (www.museum.ncl.ac.uk/Avebury/stone4.htm)'. *World Archaeol* **31**, 179–93

Gillings, M, Peterson, R and Pollard, J 2003 *Other interesting Avenues of Research: an interim report on excavations carried out by the Longstones Project on the line of the West Kennet Avenue and the Faulkner's Circle* Universities of Leicester/Newport/Southampton

Gillings, M, Peterson, R, Pollard, J and Wheatley, D 2002 *Surface collection and geophysical survey in Beckhampton Field, Novenmber 2001* Unpublished

Gillings, M, Pollard, J and Wheatley, D 2000a 'The Beckhampton Avenue and a 'new' Neolithic enclosure near Avebury: an interim report on the 1999 excavations'. *Wilts Archaeol & Nat Hist Mag* **93**, 1–8

Gillings, M, Pollard, J and Wheatley, D 2000b 'The Rev. Stukeley's lost megalithic avenue', *Past* **34**, 8–9

Gillings, M, Pollard, J and Wheatley, D 2002 'Excavations at the

Beckhampton Enclosure, Avenue and Cove, Avebury: an interim report on the 2000 season'. *Wilts Archaeol & Nat Hist Mag* **95**, 249–58

Gillings, M., Pollard, J. Wheatley, D. & Peterson, R forthcoming: *The Beckhampton Avenue and Enclosure: a report on the 1999–2002 excavations*

Gingell, C 1992 *The Marlborough Downs: a later Bronze Age landscape and its origins* Devizes: Wiltshire Archaeological and Natural History Society Monograph/Trust for Wessex Archaeology

Goddard, E H 1908a Notes on Objects of the Bronze Age found in Wiltshire. *The Reliquary and Illustrated Archaeologist* **14**, 242–9

Goddard, E H 1908b 'Notes on objects of 'Late Celtic' character found in Wiltshire *Wilts Archaeol & Nat Hist Soc Mag* **35**, 389–407

Goddard, E H 1911 Notes on Implements of the Bronze Age found in Wiltshire, with a list of all known examples found in the County. *Wilts Archaeol and Nat Hist Soc Mag* **37**, 92–158

Goddard, E H 1913, 'A list of prehistoric, Roman, and Pagan antiquities in the county of Wilts arranged under parishes', *Wilts Archaeol & Nat Hist Soc Mag*, **38**, 153–378

Goddard, E H 1917 Bronze Implements of the Bronze Age found in Wiltshire, not previously recorded. Supplementary List (Feb. 1917). *Wilts Archaeol and Nat Hist Soc Mag* **39**, 477–484

Goddard, E H 1923 'Roman Pavement near Avebury', *Wilts Archaeol & Nat Hist Mag* **42**, 359–61

Golding, B 1995 *Gilbert of Sempringham and the Gilbertine Order c1130–c1300* Oxford: Clarendon Press

Gosden, C and Lock, G 1998 'Prehistoric histories'. *World Archaeol* **30**(1), 2–12

Goudie, A I 1988 *Landforms of England and Wales* Oxford: Blackwell

Gover, J, Mawer, A and Stenton, F 1939 *The Place-Names of Wiltshire*, English Place-Name Society **16**. Cambridge Cambridge: The University Press

Gow, P 1995 'Land, People and Paper in Western Amazonia'. In E. Hirsch & M. O'Hanlon (eds) *The Anthropology of Landscape: perspectives on place and space*, 43–62. Oxford: Oxford University Press

Gray, H St G 1909/10 Notes on the Allington Gold Torc. *Wilts Archaeol and Nat Hist Soc Mag* **36**, 435–8

Gray, H St G 1935 'The Avebury Excavations, 1908–1922', *Archaeologia* **84**, 99–162

Green, C P 1997 'The provenance of rocks used in the construction of Stonehenge', *in* B Cunliffe and C Renfrew (eds) *Science and Stonehenge*. Oxford: Oxford University Press

Green, S 1980 *The Flint Arrowheads of the British Isles Oxford:* British Archaeological Reports 75

Grigson, C 1980 'The animal bones', 161–171, in Robertson Mackay 1980

Grinsell, L 1957 'Archaeological Gazetteer' *in* Pugh, R and Crittall, E (eds) *A History of Wiltshire* **1:1** London : VCH/Institute of Historical Research/Oxford University Press. 21–279

Grinsell, L V 1974 'Disc barrows' *Proc Prehist Soc* **40**, 79–93

Grundy, G B 1919 'The Saxon Land Charters of Wiltshire', *Archaeol. J.* **76**, 143–301

GSB: Geophysical Surveys of Bradford 1992a *Report on geophysical survey: Kennet Valley Foul Sewer Improvements* Report No 92/37. Unpublished

GSB: Geophysical Surveys of Bradford 1992b *Report on geophysical survey: Kennet Valley Foul Sewer Improvements Survey II* Report No **92/62**. Unpublished

Gurney, P 1985 *Shepherd Lore*, Avebury: Wiltshire Folk Life Society

Haigh, J G B 1996 'Another member of the AERIAL software family' *AARGnews* **12**, 26–33

Hamerow, H 1993 *Excavations at Mucking. Volume 2: the Anglo-Saxon Settlement.* London: English Heritage Archaeological Report **21**

Hamerow, H Hollevoet, Y and Vince, A 1994 'Migration Period Settlements and 'Anglo-Saxon' Pottery from Flanders', *Med Arch* **38**, 1–18

Hamilton, M A 1997 *A geophysical exploration for two round barrows, Avebury* Cardiff Studies in Archaeology, Specialist Report Number **6**. Unpublished

Hamilton, M A. and Dennis, I 1998 *A geophysical exploration for Avebury G29a* Cardiff Studies in Archaeology, Specialist Report Number **10**. Unpublished

Hamilton, M A, Dennis, I, and Swanton, G 1998 *A geophysical survey at North Farm, Wiltshire, 1998* Cardiff Studies in Archaeology, Specialist Report Number **8**. Unpublished

Hamilton, M A, Dennis, I and Swanton, G nd (but 2000) *A geophysical survey at Snail Creep Field, North Farm, Wiltshire, 1999* Cardiff Studies in Archaeology, Specialist Report Number **15**. Unpublished

Hamilton, S and Gregory, K 2000 'Updating the Sussex Iron Age', *Sussex Archaeol Colls* **138**, 57–74

Hanson, W S 1988 'Administration, urbanisation and acculturation in the Roman West', *in* Braund, D (ed) *The Administration of the Roman Empire (241BC–AD193).* Exeter: Exeter University Press, 53–68

Harding, A F 1987 *Henge monuments and related sites of Great Britain* Oxford: British Archaeol Report **175**

Harding, P A and Lewis, C 1997 'Archaeological invesitgations at Tockenham, 1994' Wilts Archaeol & Nat Hist Mag **90**, 1997, 26–41

Hare, J 1994 'Agriculture and Rural Settlement in the Chalklands of Hampshire and Wiltshire' *in* Aston, M and Lewis, C (eds) *The Medieval Landscape of Wessex*, Oxbow mon **46**, 159–169, Oxford: Oxbow Books

Harrington, P 1986 'Excavations at Avebury 1982' *Wilts Archaeol & Nat Hist Soc Mag* **80**, 217–21

Hase, P 1975 *The Development of the Parish in Hampshire, Particularly in the 11th and 12th centuries.* Unpublished University of Cambridge PhD thesis

Haselgrove, C 2001 'Iron Age Britain and its European setting' *in* Collis, J (ed) *Society and Settlement in Iron Age Europe.* Sheffield: JR Collis Publications. 37–72

Haslam, J 1984 'The Towns of Wiltshire', *in* Haslam, J (ed) *Anglo-Saxon Towns in Southern England.* Chichester: Phillimore, 87–147

Hawkes, C 1939 'The excavations at Quarley Hill, 1938' *Proc Hants Field Club* **14**, 136–94

Healy, F, Heaton, M and Lobb, S J 1992 'Excavations of a Mesolithic site at Thatcham'. *Proc Preh Soc* **58**, 41–76

Hepworth, J V 1998 'Aspects of the English silcretes and comparison with some Australian occurrences'. *Proc Geol Assoc* **109:**4, 271–288

Hill, D 1981 *An Atlas of Anglo-Saxon England.* Oxford: Basil Blackwell

Hill, J D 1995 'How should we understand Iron Age societies and hillforts? A contextual study from southern Britain' *in* Hill, J and Cumberpatch, C (eds) *Different Iron Ages: studies on the Iron Age in temperate Europe.* BAR IS **602**, 45–66

Hill, J D 1996 'Hill-forts and the Iron Age of Wessex' *in* Champion, T and Collis, J (eds) *The Iron Age in Britain: recent trends.* Sheffield: JR Collis Publications. 95–116

Hillier, W 1854 'Discovery of an Ancient Tumulus at Winterbourne Monkton' *Wilts Archaeol & Nat Hist Soc Mag* **1**, 303–4

Hirst, S, and Rahtz, P, 1996 'Liddington Castle and the Battle of Badon: excavations and research 1976' *Archaeol J* **153**, 1–59

Hoare, R C 1812 *The Ancient History of Wiltshire* 1 London: Miller/Luckington, Hughes, Harding, Manor and Lepard (and facsilimilie edition 1975 Wakefield: E P Publishing)

Hoare, R C 1821 *The Ancient History of Wiltshire* 2 London: Luckington (rep 1975 E P Pub: Wakefield)

Holgate, R 1987 'Neolithic settlement patterns at Avebury, Wiltshire'. *Antiquity* **62**, 349–53

Hooke, D. 1988 'Regional Variation in Southern and Central England in the Anglo-Saxon Period and its Relationship to Land Units and Settlement', *in* Hooke, D (ed) *Anglo-Saxon Settlements*. Oxford: Basil Blackwell, 123–51

Hostetter, E and Howe, T N (eds) 1997 *The Romano-British villa at Castle Copse, Great Bedwyn* Bloomington and Indianapolis: Indiana University Press

Hughes, M 1984 'Rural Settlement and Landscape in Late Saxon Hampshire' *in* Faull, M (ed) *Studies in Late Anglo-Saxon Settlement*. Oxford: Oxford University Department for External Studies, 65–79

Hunter, J 1829 'The present state of Abury', Wilts *Gentleman's Mag* **II**, 1–7

Ingold, T, 2000 *The Perception of the Environment: essays in livelihood, dwelling and skill* London & New York: Routledge

Jackson, J E, (ed) 1862 *Wiltshire: the Topographical Collections of John Aubrey FRS* corrected and enlarged by John Edward Jackson Devizes: Wilts Archaeol & Nat Hist Soc

Johnson, P and Walters, B 1988 'Exploratory Excavations of Roman Buildings at Cherhill and Manningford Bruce', *Wilts Archaeol & Nat Hist Mag* **82**, 77–91

Jones, D K C 1981 *The geomorphology of the British Isles: Southeast and Southern England*. London: Methuen

Jones, D K C 1999 'Evolving models of the Tertiary evolutionary geomorphology of southern England, with special reference to the Chalklands', *in* Smith, B J, Whalley, W B, Warke, P A and Ruffell, A (eds) *Uplift, Erosion and Stability: perspectives on long-term landscape development*. London: Geological Society Special Publication No.162, 1–23

Jones, J B 1949 'Wiltshire's oldest sarsens' *Wilts Archaeol & Nat Hist Mag* **53**, 131–3

Jukes Brown, A J 1905 *The geology of the country south and east of Devizes* HMSO

Kahn, M 1990 'Stone-faced ancestors. The spatial anchoring of myth in Wamira, Papua New Guinea'. *Ethnology* 29, 51–66

Keil, I 1964 *The Estates of the Abbey of Glastonbury in the Later Middle Ages* unpublished PhD thesis, University of Bristol

Keiller, A, and Piggott, S 1936 'The recent excavations at Avebury' *Antiquity* 10, 417–27

Keith, A 1926 'Report on human remains received from Mr. A.D. Passmore' *Wilts Archaeol & Nat Hist Mag* **43** (144), 311–312

Kellaway, G A 1991 *The Hot Springs of Bath*. Bath: Bath City Council

Kemp, B R 2000 *English Episcopal Acta 18: Salisbury 1078–1217* Oxford: Oxford University Press

Kendall, HGO 1906 Investigations at Knowle Farm pit *Wiltshire Archaeol and Nat Hist Soc Mag*. **34**, 299–307

Kendall, H G O 1908 Excursions to Avebury and Winterbourne Bassett. *Proc Geol Assoc*. **20**, 536–539

Kendall, H G O 1909 Palaeolithic Implements, *etc. from* Hackpen Hill, Winterbourne Bassett, and Knowle Farm Pit (Wiltshire). *Quarterly J Geol Soc* (London). **65**, 166–168

Kendall, H G O 1911 Palaeolithic periods at Knowle Farm Pit. *Proc Socf Antiqs (London)* 2nd series, **23**, 453–464

Kendall, H G O 1914 'Flint implements from the surface near Avebury: their classification and dates' *Proc Soc Antiqs (London)*, 73–88

Kendall, H G O 1916 Excavations on Hackpen Hill, Wilts *Proc Soc Antiqs (London)* 2nd series, **28**, 26–48

Keynes, S and Lapidge, M 1983 *Alfred the Great*. Harmondsworth: Penguin

King, A C 1996 'The South-East Façade of Meonstoke Aisled Building' *in* Johnson, P (ed) *Architecture in Roman Britain*. York: Council for British Archaeology Research Report **94**, 56–69

King, B 1879 'Avebury – the Beckhampton Avenue' *Wilts Archaeol & Nat Hist Mag* **18**, 377–83

King, N 1968 'The Kennet Valley sarsen industry' *Wilts Archaeol & Nat Hist Soc Mag* **63**, 83–92

Kinnes, I 1979 *Round Barrows and Ring ditches in the British Neolithic* London: British Museum Department of Prehistoric and Romano-British Antiquities Occasional Paper No 7

Kinnes, I, Gibson, A, Ambers, J, Bowman, S, Leese, M and Boast, R 1991 'Radiocarbon dating and British Beakers: the British Museum programme' *Scottish Archaeol Review* **8**, 35–68

Kirby, J L 1956a 'Preceptory of Temple Rockley' *in* Pugh, R B and Crittall, E (eds) *A History of Wiltshire* **3**, 327–8

Kirby, J L 1956b 'Priory of Avebury' *in* Pugh, R B and Crittall, E (eds) *A History of Wiltshire* **3**, 392–3

Knight, D 2001 *Liddington Environs Project, Wiltshire*. English Heritage Aerial Survey unpublished report

Knowles, D and Hadcock, R N 1953 *Medieval Religious Houses England and Wales* London: Longmans

Kvamme, K L and Jochim, M A 1985 'The Environmental Basis of Mesolithic Settlement', *in* Bonsal, C. (ed) *The Mesolithic in Europe, 1–12*. Edinburgh: John Donald

Kwint, M 1999 'Introduction: the physical past'. In M Kwint, C Breward and J Aynsley (eds) *Material Memories: design and evocation*, 1–16. Oxford: Berg

Lacaille, A D 1971 Some Wiltshire Palaeoliths, *Prehistoric and Roman studies, The British Museum Quarterly* **35**, 1–4

Landon, J R 1991 *Booker Tropical Soil Manual*. Harlow, Essex: Longman Scientific and Technical

Larking, L B 1857 *The Knights Hospitallers in England: being the report of Prior Philip de Thame to the Grand Master Elyan de Villanova for A.D. 1338* London: Camden Society

Lawson, A J 2000 *Potterne 1982–5 Animal husbandry in later Prehistoric Wiltshire* Salisbury: Wessex Archaeology

Lees, B A 1935 *Records of the Templars in England in the Twelfth Century. The Inquest of 1185* London: The British Academy

Legg, R 1986 *Stonehenge Antiquaries*, Sherborne: The Dorset Publishing Company

Limbrey, S 1992 'Micromorphological studies of buried soils and alluvial deposits in a Wiltshire river valley' in S Needham and M G Macklin (eds), *Alluvial Archaeology in Britain*. Oxford: Oxbow Monograph **27**, 53–64

Linford, N 2004 *Headlands Enclosure, West Overton, Wiltshire: report on geophysical survey, November 2003* Centre For Archaeology Reports Series **19/2004**

Linford, N and Martin, L 2001 *Silbury Hill, Wiltshire: report on geophysical survey, February 2001* Centre For Archaeology Reports Series **21/2001**. Unpublished

Linford, P 2001 *Silbury Hill, Wiltshire: report on geophysical survey, June 2001* Centre For Archaeology Reports Series **65/2001**. Unpublished

Lock, G and Gosden, C 1997a 'Hillforts of the Ridgeway Project: excavations on White Horse Hill, 1995' *South Midlands Archaeol* **27**. 64–9

Lock, G and Gosden, C 1997b 'Hillforts of the Ridgeway Project: excavations at Segsbury Camp 1996' *South Midlands Archaeol* **27**. 69–77

Long, W 1858 'Abury' *Wilts Archaeol & Nat Hist Soc Mag* **4**, 309–363

Long, W 1862 'Facsimilies of Aubrey's Pland of Avebury' *Wilts Archaeol & Nat Hist Soc Mag* **7**, 224–227

Long, W 1878 'Abury Notes' *Wilts Archaeol & Nat Hist Mag* **17**, 327–35

Longworth, I H 1984 *Collared Urns of the Bronze Age in Great Britain and Ireland*. Cambridge: Cambridge University Press

Lukis, W C 1881 'Report on the prehistoric monuments of Stonehenge and Avebury' *Proc Soc of Antiqs* 2nd Series **9**, 141–157

Lukis, W C ed 1882 (ed) 1887 'The family memoirs of the Rev William Stukeley MD' *The Publications of the Surtees Society*

MacGregor, M and Simpson, D 1963 'A group of iron objects from Barbury Castle, Wilts' *Wilts Archaeol & Nat Hist Mag* **58**. 394–402

Maddy, D 1997 'Uplift-driven valley incision and river terrace formation in southern England'. *J Quaternary Science* **12**: 6 539–545

Maddy, D, Bridgeland, D R and Green, C P 2000 'Crustal uplift in southern England: evidence from the river terrace records'. *Geomorphology*, **33**, 167–181

Malone, C 1989 *English Heritage Book of Avebury*, London: English Heritage/ Batsford

Martin, L 2001a *Two long barrows near Avebury, Wiltshire: report on geophysical survey, December 2001* Centre for Archaeology Reports Series **20/2001**. Unpublished

Martin, L 2001b *The West Kennet long barrow, Wiltshire: report on geophysical survey, January 2001* Centre for Archaeology Reports Series **78/2001**. Unpublished

Martin, L 2004 *Faulkner's Circle, Wiltshire: report on geophysical survey, 2002 and 2003* Centre for Archaeology Reports Series **4/2004**

Martin, L and Cromwell, T 2002 *Tenantry Farm, Rockbourne, Hampshire* Centre for Archaeol Report Series **74/2002**

Matthew, D 1962 *The Norman Monasteries and their English Possessions* Oxford: Oxford University Press

Mawer, A and Stenton, F M 1926 *The Place-Names of Bedfordshire and Huntingdonshire.* Cambridge: Cambridge University Press

McKim, F R 1959 'An attempt to locate a burial chamber in Silbury Hill' *Wilts Archaeol & Nat Hist Mag* **57**, 176–8

McOmish, D 1996 'East Chisenbury: ritual and rubbish at the British Bronze Age-Iron Age transition' *Antiquity* **70**. 68–76

McOmish, D Field, D & Brown, G 2002 *Field Archaeology of the Salisbury Plain Training Area*, Swindon: English Heritage

Meadon, T 1999 *The secrets of the Avebury stones* London: Souvenir Press

Meaney, A L 1995 'Pagan English Sanctuaries, Place-Names and Hundred Meeting-Places' *Anglo-Saxon Studies in Archaeology and History* **8** 29–42

Mercer, R 1981 'Excavations at Carn Brea, Illogen, Cornwall, 1970–73' *Cornish Archaeol* **20**, 1–204

Mercer, R 1988 'Hambledon Hill, Dorset, England', in C Burgess, P Topping, C Mordant and M Maddison (eds) *Enclosures and defences in the Neolithic of Western Europe*, 89–126 Oxford: Brit Archaeol Report Int ser 403

Merewether, Rev J 1851a 'The excavation of Silbury Hill, in Memoirs illustrative of the History and Antiquities of Wiltshire…' *Proc Archaeol Inst of Great Britain and Ireland 1849*, 73–81 London: Bell

Merewether, Very Rev J 1851b 'Diary of the examination of Barrows and other earthworks in the neighbourhood of Silbury Hill and Avebury' *Memoirs illustrative of the history and antiquities of Wiltshire* Proc Archaeol Inst Gt Britain & Ireland, 82–112 London: George Bell

Meyrick, O 1947 'Notes on some early Iron Age sites in the Marlborough district' *Wilts Archaeol and Nat Hist Soc Mag* **51**. 256–63

Meyrick, O 1955 'The Broadstones', *Wilts Archaeol & Nat Hist Soc Mag* **56** (203), 192–193

Meyrick, O 1964 'Siting of barrows round springs' *Wilts Archaeol & Nat Hist Soc Mag* **59**, 182

Meyrick, O 1973 'Notes on some Beaker habitation sites in N Wilts' *Wilts Archaeol & Nat Hist Soc Mag* **68**, 116–118

Miles, D 1984 *Archaeology at Barton Court Farm, Abingdon, Oxon.* Oxford and London: Oxford Archaeological Unit Report **3**/Council for British Archaeology Research Report **50**

Millett, M 1990 *The Romanization of Britain.* Cambridge: Cambridge University Press

Mithen, S 1996 *The Prehistory Of The Mind* London: Phoenix

Moore, J N and Rowlands, M 1972 *Bronze Age Metalwork in Salisbury Museum.* Salisbury: Salisbury and South Wiltshire Museum

Moreland, J 2000 'Ethnicity, Power and the English' *in* Frazer, W O and Tyrell, A (eds) *Social Identity in Early Medieval Britain.* London and New York: Leicester University Press, 23–51

Morgan, M 1939 'Inventories of Three Small Alien Priories' *Journ Brit Archaeol Assoc* 3rd Series **4**, 141–49

Morgan, M 1946 *The English Lands of the Abbey of Bec*, Oxford: Clarendon Press

Mount, R J 1991 *An environmental history of the upper Kennet valley, and some implications for human communities.* Unpubl PhD thesis, Univ Wales, College Cardiff

Mowl, T and Earnshaw, B 1988 *John Wood: Architect of Obsession* Bath: Millstream Books

Nash, D, Shaw, P and Ullyott, S 1998 'Drainage-line silcretes of the Middle Kalahari: an analogue for Cenozoic sarsen trains?'. *Proc Geol Assoc* **109**: 4, 241–254

Needham, S 1981 *The Bulford-Helsbury manufacturing tradition: the production of Stogursey socketed axes during the Later Bronze Age in Southern Britain.* British Museum occasional paper no. **13**. London: British Museum Press

Needham, S 1983 *The Early Bronze Age Axeheads of Central and Southern England.* Unpublished PhD, University College, Cardiff

Needham, S 1986 Late Bronze Age Artefacts, *in* I M Stead, and V Rigby *Baldock: the Excavation of a Roman and Pre-Roman Settlement*, 141–3 Britannia Monograph Series **7** London: Society for the Promotion of Roman Studies

Needham, S 1988 Selective Deposition in the British Early Bronze Age. *World Archaeol* **20**, 229–248

Needham, S 1996 'Chronology and periodisation in the British Bronze Age' 121–140, *in* K. Randsborg (ed) *Absolute Chronology Archaeological Europe 2500–500 BC, Acta Archaeologica* 67

Needham, S 2000 'Power pulses across a cultural divide: cosmologically driven acquisition between Armorica and Wessex' *Proc Prehist Soc* **66**, 151–207

Needham, S and Burgess, C 1980 The Later Bronze Age in the lower Thames Valley: the metalwork evidence. In J Barrett and R Bradley (eds) *Settlement and Society in the British later Bronze Age* 437–469. British Archaeological Reports (British Series) **83**. Oxford: British Archaeological Reports

Needham, S and Spence, T 1997 'Refuse and the formation of middens'. *Antiquity* **71**, 77–90

Newman, P 1997 (first pub 1987 by Robert Hale Ltd) *Lost Gods of Albion: the Chalk Hill-Figures of Britain* Stroud: Sutton Publishing Ltd

O'Connor, B 1980 *Cross-channel relations in the Later Bronze Age: relations between Britain, North-Eastern France and the Low Countries during the Later Bronze Age and the Early Iron Age, with particular reference to the metalwork.* British Archaeological Reports (International Series) **91**. Oxford: British Archaeological Reports

O'Brien, W 2002 'Megaliths in a mythologised landscape: southwest Ireland in the Iron Age', in C Scarre (ed) *Monuments and landscape in Atlantic Europe* London: Routledge

Ordnance Survey 1967 *Map of Southern Britain in the Iron Age* revised edition. OS: Chessington

Osborne-White, H J 1925 *The geology of the country around Marlborough.* Memoir of the Geological Survey: explanation of Sheet 266. HMSO

Osgood, R 2000 Northern and Western Europe, *in* R Osgood, S Monks, and J Toms *Bronze Age Warfare* 9–36. Stroud: Sutton Publishing Ltd

Oswald, A 1997 'A doorway on the past: practical and mystic concerns in the orientation of roundhouse doorways' *in* Gwilt, A and Haselgrove, C (eds) *Reconstructing Iron Age Societies.* Oxford: Oxbow Monograph **71**. 87–95

Oswald, A, Dyer, C and Barber, M 2001 *The Creation of Monuments: Neolithic Causewayed Enclosures in the British Isles.* London: English Heritage

Ovsyannikov, O V and Terebikhin, N M 1994 'Sacred space in the culture of the arctic regions', in D L Carmichael, J

Hubert, B Reeves and A Schanche (eds) *Sacred sites, sacred places*, 44–81 London & New York: Routledge

Pafford, J H P 1965 'Marlborough Castle' *Wilts Archaeol & Nat Hist Soc Mag* **60**, 129

Papworth, M 2004 *Report on the geophysical survey of parts of the SE and NE Quadrants of Avebury Henge: October–December 2003* National Trust

Pass, A C 1887 'Recent Explorations at Silbury Hill' *Wilts Archaeol & Nat Hist Soc Mag* **23**, 245–54

Passmore, A D 1914 'On some Bronze Age pottery of 'Food Vessel' type', *Wilts Archaeol & Nat Hist Soc Mag* **38**, (122), 585–586

Passmore, A D 1926 'Avebury: a new stone in the Kennett Avenue' *Wilts Archaeol & Nat Hist Mag* **43**, 341–3

Passmore, A D 1935 'The Meux Excavation at Avebury' *Wilts Archaeol & Nat Hist Mag* **47**, 288–9

Passmore, A D 1943 'Medieval Enclosures at Barbury and Blunsdon' *Wilts Archaeol & Nat Hist Mag* **50**, 194

Payne, A (in press) *The Wessex Hillforts Project: new perceptions of 1st millennium BC monumental earthworks in central southern England* English Heritage Archaeological Report

Payne, A 2000 *Whitebarrow, Tilshead 4 long barrow, Tilshead, Wilts: report on geophysical surveys May 1997* Ancient Monuments Laboratory Reports Series **70/2000**

Petrie, W F 1924 'Report of diggings in Silbury Hill, August 1922' *Wilts Archaeol & Nat Hist Soc Mag* **42**, 215–8

Pevsner, N (revised by Cherry B) 1963 (revisions and reprints 1975, 1981, 1985) *The Buildings of England: Wiltshire*, London: Penguin Books

Pevsner, N 1975 *The Buildings of England: Wiltshire* London: Penguin Books

Piggott, C M 1942 'Five Late Bronze Age Enclosures in North Wiltshire', *Proc Prehist Soc* **8**, *48–61*

Piggott, S 1938 'The Early Bronze Age in Wessex' *Proc Prehist Soc* **4**, 52–106

Piggott, S P 1962 *West Kennet Long Barrow: excavations 1955–56*. London: HMSO, Ministry of Works Archaeol Rep 4

Piggott, S 1964 Excavations at Avebury 1960 *Wilts Archaeol & Nat Hist Soc Mag* **59**, 28–9

Piggot, S 1976 *Ruins in a Landscape: Essays in Antiquarianism* Edinburgh: Edinburgh University Press

Piggot, S 1989 *Ancient Britons and the Antiquarian Imagination: ideas from the Renaissance to the Regency* London: Thames and Hudson

Pitt Rivers, A H L F 1898 *Excavations in Cranborne Chase, near Rushmore, on the Borders of Dorset and Wilts 1893–1896*. Vol 4. Farnham: Privately Printed

Pitt, J M A *1999 Wiltshire Minster Parochiae and West Saxon Ecclesiastical Organisation*. Unpublished University of Southampton (King Alfred's College) PhD thesis

Pitts, M 2000 *Hengeworld* London: Century

Pitts, M 2001 Excavating the Sanctuary: new investigations on Overton Hill, Avebury *Wilts Archaeol & Nat Hist Soc Mag* **94**, 1–23

Pitts, M W and Whittle, A W R 1992 'The development and date of Avebury', *Proc Prehist Soc* **58**, 203–12

Pollard, J 1992 'The Sanctuary, Overton Hill, Wiltshire: a re-examination'. *Proc Prehist Soc* **58**, 213–226

Pollard, J 1999 'These places have their moments': thoughts on settlement practices in the British Neolithic'. In J Brück and M Goodman (eds) *Making Places in the Prehistoric World: themes in settlement archaeology*, 76–93. London: UCL Press

Pollard, J and Reynolds, A 2002 *Avebury: the biography of a landscape*. Stroud & Charleston, SC: Tempus

Potter, J F 1998 'The distribution of silcretes in the churches of the London Basin'. *Proc Geol Assoc* 109, 289 – 304

Powell, A B, Allen, M J and Barnes, I 1996 *Archaeology in the Avebury Area, Wiltshire: recent discoveries along the line of the Kennet Valley Foul Sewer pipeline, 1993*. Salisbury: Wessex Archaeology Report No. **8**

Powlesland, D 1997 'Early Anglo-Saxon Settlements, Structures, Form and Layout' *in* Hines, J (ed) *The Anglo-Saxons from the Migration Period to the Eighth Century*. Woodbridge: The Boydell Press, 101–24

Pryor, F 2001 *The Flag Fen Basin: archaeology and environment of a fenland landscape*. London: English Heritage

Pugh, R and Crittall, E (eds) 1953 *The Victoria History of the Counties of England: Wiltshire* **7**. London: Oxford University Press

Pugsley, A 1938 *Dewponds in Fable and Fantasy*. London: Country Life

Rawlins, M 1999 *Butcher, Baker, Saddlemaker: Village life in in Avebury from 1920 to 1974* printed Chippenham, Wilts

RCHM(E), 1979 *Stonehenge and its environs* Edinburgh, Edinburgh University Press

RCHME, 1992 *West Kennett – East Kennett: Archaeological Survey in the vicinity of the Avebury World Heritage Site*. Unpublished report, Swindon: RCHME

Redvers Higgins, N and Hiller, J 2002 *United Reform church, Avebury, Wiltshire: report on archaeological investigations – excavations and building survey*. Oxford: Oxford Archaeology

Reynolds, A J 1999 *Later Anglo-Saxon England: Life and Landscape*. Stroud and Charleston SC: Tempus

Reynolds, A J 2001 'Avebury: a Late Anglo-Saxon burh?', *Antiquity* **75** 29–30

Reynolds, A J in prep 'Assembly sites in central North Wiltshire from the Early Anglo-Saxon period to Domesday'

Richards, J C 1978 *the Archaeology of the Berkshire Downs: an introductory survey* Berkshire Archaeological Committee Publication No. 3, Reading

Ritchie, A 1971 'Settlement Archaeology – Methods and Problems', *in* M Jesson and D Hill (eds) *The Iron Age and its Hill-Forts: Papers Presented to Sir Mortimer Wheeler,* 91–95 Southampton University Archaeological Society

Rivet, A L F 1958 *Town and Country in Roman Britain*. London: Hutchinson University Library

Robertson MacKay, M E 1980 'A 'head and hooves' burial beneath a round barrow, with other Neolithic and Bronze Age sites, on Hemp Knoll, near Avebury, Wiltshire', *Proc Prehist Soc* **46**, 123–176

Robertson, A J 1925 *The Laws of the Kings of England from Edmund to Henry I*. Cambridge: Cambridge University Press

Robinson, D M 1980 *The Geography of Augustinian Settlement in Medieval England and Wales* **1** Oxford: British Archaeological Report 80(1)

Robinson, P 2002 'The Treasure Act', *Trilithon* **46**, 3

Robinson, P and Swanton, G 1993 'On Blagan Hill' *Current Archaeol* **12**(2). 73–4

Roe, D A 1968 *A Gazetteer of British Lower and Middle Palaeolithic Sites*. Council for British Archaeology Res Rep **8**. London

Roe, D A 1969 An Archaeological survey and policy for Wiltshire. Part 1. Palaeolithic *Wilts Archaeol & Nat Hist Soc Mag* **64**, 1–18

Roe, D A 1981 *The Lower and Middle Palaeolithic periods in Britain* London: Routledge and Kegan Paul

Roe, D A Unpublished Card Index of British Palaeolithic artefacts and sites

Roe, D and Taki, J 1999 'Living with stones: people and the landscape in Erromango, Vanuatu'. In P.J. Ucko & R. Layton (eds) *The Archaeology and Anthropology of Landscape*, 411–422. London: Routledge

Rohl, B and Needham, S 1998 *The Circulation of Metalwork in the British Bronze Age. The application of lead isotope analysis.* British Museum Occasional Paper **102**. London: British Museum Press

Rowlands, M J 1976 *The Production and Distribution of Metalwork in the Middle Bronze Age of Southern Britain.* British Archaeol Reports (British Series) vol. **31**. Oxford: British Archaeol Reports

Ryder, M 1984 Medieval Sheep and Wool Types. *Agric Hist Rev* **32**, 14–28

Sawyer, P H 1968 *Anglo-Saxon Charters: An Annotated List and*

Bibliography London: Royal Historical Society Guides and Handbooks **8**

Sawyer, P H 1983 'The Royal Tun in Pre-Conquest England' *in* Wormald, P Bullough, D and Collins, R (eds), *Ideal and Reality in Frankish and Anglo-Saxon Society.* Oxford: Basil Blackwell, 273–99

Scaife, R G 2000 Pollen analysis of the R. Allen Valley at Wimborne St. Giles, Dorset, Unpubl Research MS

Schofield, A J 1991 'Artefact distributions as activity areas: examples from south-east Hampshire', *in* Schofield, A J (ed) *Interpreting Artefact Scatters* Oxbow Monograph **4**, 117–128. Oxford: Oxbow Books

Schofield, J, Millet, M, Keay, S and Carrete, J M 1999. 'Prehistoric Settlement in the Tarragona Region of North-East Spain: Results from the Ager Tarraconensis Survey'. *Lithics* **20**, 33–48

Schulting, R J and Richards, M P 2000 'The use of stable isotopes in studies of subsistence and seasonality in the British Mesolithic', *in* R Young. (ed) *Mesolithic Lifeways: Current Research from Britain and Ireland* Leicester Archaeology Monographs **7** University of Leicester

Scollar, I, Tabbagh, A, Hesse, A, and Herzog, I (eds) 1990 *Archaeological Prospecting and Remote Sensing* Cambridge: Cambridge University Press

Scott-Jackson, J E 2000 *Lower and Middle Palaeolithic Artefacts from Deposits Mapped as Clay-with-flints: A New Synthesis with Significant Implications for the Earliest Occupation of Britain* Oxford: Oxbow Books

Scott-Jackson, J E 2001 'Lower and Middle Palaeolithic', in A Chadburn and M Pomeroy-Kellinger (eds) *Archaeological Research Agenda for the Avebury World Heritage Site* 5–6. Salisbury: Wessex Archaeology and English Heritage

Scott-Jackson, J.E. Unpublished. *A Gazetteer of Lower and Middle Palaeolithic Artefacts from Deposits Mapped as Clay-with-flints on the Chalk Downlands of Southern England*

Scull, C J 1992 'Before Sutton Hoo: Structures of Power and Society in Early East Anglia', in M. Carver (ed.), *The Age of Sutton Hoo.* Woodbridge: The Boydell Press, 3–23

Semple, S 1998 'A fear of the past: the place of the prehistoric burial mound in the ideology of middle and later Anglo-Saxon England' *World Archaeology* **30:1**, 109–26

Semple, S and Langlands, A 2001 'Swanborough Tump', *Wilts Archaeol & Nat Hist Mag* **94**, 239–42

Sewell, E R A 1938 'Excavations at St Margaret's Priory, Marlborough' *Report of the Marlborough College Natural History Society* **87**, 12–16

Sheridan, R, Sheridan, D and Hassel, P 1967 'Excavations at Greenham Dairy Farm, Newbury, 1963'. *Trans Newbury Dist Field Club* **11 (4)**, 66–73

Sherlock, R L 1947 *London and Thames Valley* HMSO

Simmons, I G 1996 *The Environmental Impact of Later Mesolithic Cultures: the Creation of a Moorland Landscape in England & Wales*, Edinburgh: Edinburgh University Press

Small, F J 2000 *The Lambourne Downs: a report for the National Mapping Programme* Aerial Survey Report Series **AER/13/2002** Swindon: English Heritage

Small, F J 1999 *The Avebury World Heritage Site Mapping Project, Wiltshire.* Unpublished report, Swindon: English Heritage

Small, R J, Clark, M .J and Lewin, J 1970 'The Periglacial Rock-Stream at Clatford Bottom, Marlborough Downs, Wiltshire'. *Proc Geol Assoc* **81**: 1, 87–97

Smith, A C 1860–1 'Silbury', *Wilts Archaeol & Nat Hist Soc Mag* **7**, 180

Smith, A C 1867 'Excavations at Avebury' *Wilts Archaeol & Nat Hist Soc Mag* **10**, 209–16

Smith A C 1878–9 'A sketch of the Parish of Yatesbury *Wilts Archaeol & Nat Hist Soc Mag'* **18**, 319–359

Smith, A C 1884 *British and Roman antiquities of North Wiltshire* Marlborough: Marlborough College Natural History Soc

Smith, A C 1885 *Guide to the British and Roman antiquities of the North Wiltshire Downs in a hundred square miles around Abury* Second edition, Devizes: *Wilts Archaeol & Nat Hist Soc*

Smith, C and Openshaw, S 1990 'Mapping the Mesolithic' *Contributions to the Mesolithic in Europe*, 17–22. Leuven University Press

Smith, I F 1964 'Excavation of three Roman tombs and a prehistoric pit on Overton Down', *Wilts Archaeol & Nat Hist Soc Mag* **59**, 68–85

Smith, I F 1965a *Windmill Hill and Avebury: Excavations by Keiller 1925–1935* Oxford: Clarendon Press

Smith, I F 1965b 'Excavation of a bell barrow, Avebury G55', *Wilts Archaeol & Nat Hist Soc Mag* **60**, 24–46

Smith, I F and Simpson, D D A 1966 'Excavation of a round barrow on Overton Hill, north Wiltshire'. *Proc Prehist Soc* **32**, 122–55

Smith, R W 1984 'The ecology of Neolithic farming systems as exemplified by the Avebury region in Wiltshire', *Proc Prehist Soc* **50**, 99–120

Smith, R J C Healy, F, Allen, M J, Morris, E L Barnes, I and Woodward, P J 1997 *Excavations along the route of the Dorchester by-pass, Dorset, 1986–8.* Salisbury: Wessex Archaeology Report **11**

Smith, W G 1894 *Man, the Primeval Savage: his haunts and relics from the hilltops of Bedfordshire to Blackhall London:* Stanford

Soffe, G 1993 'A barrow cemetery and other features recorded by air photography at Beckhampton, Avebury', *Wilts Archaeol & Nat Hist Soc Mag* **86**, 142–157

Spector, J D 1991 What this awl means: towards a feminist archaeology, in J M Gero and M W Conkey (eds) *Engendering Archaeology: Women and Prehistory*, 388–406. Oxford: Blackwells

Spikins, P 2000 'Ethno-facts or ethno fiction? Searching for the structure of Mesolithic settlement patterns', *in* Young, R (ed) *Mesolithic lifeways: Current Research from Britain and Ireland,* 105–118. Leicester Archaeology Monographs **7** University of Leicester

Stacy, N E 2001 *Surveys of the Estates of Glastonbury Abbey c1135–1201* Oxford: Oxford University Press

Stell, C 1991 *Nonconformist Chapels and Meeting Houses in South West England*, London: Royal Commission on the Historical Monuments of England

Stevenson, J H 1970 'Chiseldon' *in* Crittall, E (ed) *A History of Wiltshire* **9**, Oxford: Oxford University Press, 6–23

Stevenson, J H 1980 'Overton', *in* Elrington, C R (ed) *A History of Wiltshire* **11**. The Victoria History of the Counties of England. London: Oxford University Press, 181–203

Stevenson, J H 1983a 'Selkley Hundred', *in* Elrington, C R (ed) *A History of Wiltshire* **12.** The Victoria History of the Counties of England. London: Oxford University Press, 62–6

Stevenson, J H 1983b 'Mildenhall', *in* Elrington, C R (ed.), *A History of Wiltshire* **12.** The Victoria History of the Counties of England. London: Oxford University Press, 125–38

Stevenson, J H 1983c 'The Borough of Marlborough' in Crowley, D A (ed) *A History of Wiltshire 12,* Oxford: Oxford University Press, 199–29

Stevenson, J H 1983d 'Preshute' *in* Crowley, D A (ed) *A History of Wiltshire* **12**, Oxford: Oxford University Press, 160–84

Stone, J F S and Young, W E V 1948 'Two pits of Grooved Ware date near Woodbridge'. *Wilts Archaeol & Nat Hist Mag* **52**, 287–304

Stout, G 1991 'Embanked enclosures of the Boyne region' *Proc Royal Irish Acad* **91**c, 245–64

Stringer,C B 1996 The Boxgrove Tibia; Britain's Oldest Hominid and its Place in the Middle Pleistocene Record in C B Gamble and A J Lawson (eds) *The English Palaeolithic Reviewed,* 52–56. Salisbury: Trust for Wessex Archaeology

Stukeley, W 1743 *Abury, a temple of the British Druids with some others described... Volume the Second.* London: Privately printed.

Stukeley, W 1776 *Itinerarium Curiosum*. London: Baker & Leigh, and facsimile ed 1989 Gregg: Farnborough

Sumbler, M G 1996 *London and the Thames Valley*. British Regional Geology 4th edition HMSO, London

Swanton, G 1987 'The Owen Meyrick Collection' *Wilts Archaeol & Nat Hist Mag* **81**. 7–18

Swanton, G 1988 'West Overton' in 'Excavation and fieldwork in Wiltshire, 1987', *Wilts Archaeol & Nat Hist Soc Mag* **82**, 181–182

Szymanski, J E and Tsourlos, P 1993 'The resistive tomography technique for archaeology: an introduction and review' *Archaeol Polona* **31**, 5–32

Tatton-Brown, T 1998 'Building with stone in Wessex over 4000 years'. *Hatcher Review* **5**: 45, 1–60

Taylor, R 1993 *Hoards of the Bronze Age in Southern Britain. Analysis and Interpretation*. British Archaeol Reports (British Series) vol **228**. Oxford: Tempus Reparatum

The Royal Commission on Historical Monuments (England) 1979, *Stonehenge and its Environs*. Edinburgh: The University Press

Theuws, F and Nelson, J (eds) 2000 *Rituals of Power: From Late Antiquity to the Early Middle Ages*. Leiden, Boston and Koln: Brill

Thomas, J 1999 *Understanding the Neolithic*. London: Routledge

Thomas, J and Whittle, A 1986 'Anatomy of a tomb – West Kennet revisited'. *Oxford J Archaeol* **5**, 129–156

Thomas, K D 1985 'Land snail analysis in archaeology: theory and practice', in N R J Fieller, D D Gilbertson and N G A Ralph (eds) *Palaeobiological Investigations: research design, methods and data analysis*. Oxford: British Archaeol Reports, Int. Series 266, 131–175

Thorn, C and Thorn, F 1979 *Domesday Book – Wiltshire*, Chichester: Phillimore

Thurnam, J 1860a Examination of a Chambered Long Barrow at West Kennet, Wiltshire *Archaeologia* **38**, 405–21

Thurnam, J 1860b 'Examination of barrows on the downs of north Wiltshire in 1853–57, *Wilts Archaeol & Nat Hist Soc Mag* **6**, 317–336

Thurnam, J 1871 'On ancient British barrows, especially those of Wiltshire and the adjoining counties (Part II Round Barrows)' *Archaeologia* **43**, 285–544

Tite, M S 1972 *Methods of Physical Examination in Archaeology* London and New York: Seminar Press

Topping, P 1992 'The Penrith henges: a survey by the Royal Commsission on the Historical Monuments of England' *Proc Prehist Soc* **58**, 249–64

Torrence, R 2001 'Technology: macro-and microscale approaches', *in* Panter-Brick, C Layton, R H and Rowley-Conwy, P (eds) *Hunter-Gatherers. An Interdisciplinary Perspective*, 73–98. Cambridge: Cambridge Univ Press

Treasure, D 1992 *Avebury Manor, Vernacular Building Survey*National Trust report

Tucker, C 1851 'Report of the examination of Silbury Hill' *Memoirs illustrative of the History and Antiquities of Wiltshire and the City of Salisbury* Proceedings of the Meeting of the Archaeological Institute at Salisbury 1849 Archaeol Inst of Great Britain and Ireland

Ucko, P J, Hunter, M, Clark, A J, and David, A 1990 *Avebury Reconsidered; from the 1660s to the 1990s* Institute of Archaeology, London: Unwin Hyman

Ullyott, J S, Nash, D J and Shaw, P A 1998 'Recent advances in Silcrete research and their implications for the origin and palaeoenvironmental significance of sarsens'. *Proc Geol Assoc* **109**: 4, 225 – 270

Van de Guchte 1999 'The Inca cognition of landscape: archaeology, ethnohistory and the aesthetic of alterity', in W Ashmore and A Bernard Knapp (eds) *Archaeologies of Landscape: contemporary perspectives*, 149–168 Oxford: Blackwell

Vatcher, F de M, and Vatcher, L 1968 'Avebury: School Site' *Archaeol Rev* **3**, 6

Vyner, B 1995 'The Brides of Place: Cross-Ridge Boundaries Reviewed', *in* B Vyner (ed) *Moorland Monuments: Studies in the Archaeology of North-East Yorkshire in Honour of Raymond Hayes and Don Spratt* CBA Research Report **101**, 16–30. York: Council for British Archaeology

Wade, K 1980 'A Settlement Site at Wicken Bonhunt, Essex' *in* Buckley, D (ed) *Archaeology in Essex to AD 1500*. London: Council for British Archaeology Research Report **34**, 99–104

Wainwright, G 1979 *Mount Pleasant, Dorset: excavations 1970–71*. London: Society of Antiquaries

Wainwright, G J 1960 'Three Microlith Industries from South-west England and their Affinities'. *Proc Preh Soc* **26**, 192–210

Wainwright, G J 1971 'The excavation of a Late Neolithic enclosure at Marden, Wiltshire' *Antiq J* **51**, 177–239

Wainwright, G J, 1979 *Gussage All Saints: an Iron Age settlement in Dorset* DoE Archaeol rep *10* London: HMSO

Wakefield, J D 1999 *Legendary landscapes: secrets of Ancient Wiltshire revealed* Marlborough: NOD Press

Walters, B 2001 'A Perspective on the Social Order of Roman Villas in Wiltshire', *in* Ellis, P (ed) *Roman Wiltshire and After: Papers in Honour of Ken Annable*. Devizes: Wiltshire Archaeological and Natural History Society, 127–46

Watson, A 2001 'Composing Avebury' *World Archaeol* **33 (2)**, 296–314

Waylen, J 1854 *A History of Marlborough* London: J Smith

Welch, M 1992 *The English Heritage Book of Anglo-Saxon England*. London: Batsford

Welfare, H 1989 'John Aubrey – the first archaeological surveyor?' *in* M Bowden, D Mackay & P Topping (eds) *From Cornwall to Caithness: aspects of British field archaeology* Oxford: British Archaeol Report **209**, 17–28

Wessex Archaeology 1989 *West Kennet Farm, West Kennet, Marlborough, Wilts. Site Code W300. Project Code 32731. Archaeological Evaluation 1989*. Unpublished MS

Wessex Archaeology 1993 *The Southern Rivers Palaeolithic Project Report No.1, 1991:1992, The Upper Thames Valley, the Kennet Valley and the Solent Drainage System. Salisbury:* Trust for Wessex Archaeology

Wessex Archaeology 1997 *West Kennet Farmhouse, Wiltshire. Summary Report of 1997 Excavations and Assessment Document*. Unpublished MS

Whittle, A 1990 'A Model for the Mesolithic-Neolithic Transition in the Upper Kennet Valley, North Wiltshire'. *Proc Prehist Soc* **56**, 101–110

Whittle, A 1993 'The Neolithic of the Avebury area: sequence, environment, settlement and monuments' *Oxford J Archaeol* **12**, 29–53

Whittle, A 1994 'Excavations at Millbarrow Chambered Tomb, Winterbourne Monkton, North Wiltshire' *Wilts Archaeol & Nat Hist Soc Mag* **87**, 1–53

Whittle, A 1997a *Sacred Mound Holy Rings; Silbury Hill and West Kennet palisade enclosures: a Later Neolithic complex in north Wiltshire*. Oxford: Oxbow Monograph **74**

Whittle, A 1997b 'Moving on and moving around: Neolithic settlement mobility'. In P Topping (ed.), *Neolithic Landscapes*, 15–22. Oxford: Oxbow Books

Whittle, A W R, Atkinson, R J C, Chambers, R and Thomas, N 1992 'Excavations in the Neolithic and bronze Age complex at Dorchester-on-Thames, Oxfordshire 1947–1952 and 1981' *Proc Prehist Soc* **58**, 143–201

Whittle, A, Davies, J J, Dennis, I, Fairbairn, A S, Hamilton, A and Pollard, J 2000 'Neolithic activity and occupation outside Windmill hill causewayed enclosure, Wiltshire: survey and excavation' 1992–3 *Wilts Archaeol & Nat Hist Soc Mag* **93**, 131–180

Whittle, A, Pollard, J and Grigson, C 1999 *The Harmony of Symbols: The Windmill Hill causewayed enclosure, Wiltshire.* Cardiff Studies in Archaeol. Oxford: Oxbow Books

Whittle, A, Rouse, A J and Evans, J G 1993 'A Neolithic downland monument in its environment: excavations at the Easton Down Long Barrow, Bishops Cannings, north Wiltshire'. *Proc Prehist Soc* **59**, 197–239

Wiens, H A 1976 'Population responses to patchy environments', *Annual Revue Ecol. System* **7**, 81–120

Wilkinson, The Rev Prebendary 1867 'A report of diggings made in Silbury Hill and in the ground adjoining' *Wilts Archaeol & Nat Hist Mag* **11**, 113–118

Williams, H 1997 'Ancient landscapes and the dead: the re-use of prehistoric and Roman monuments as early Anglo-Saxon burial sites', *Med Arch* **41**, 1–32

Williams, R B G 1980 The weathering and erosion of Chalk under periglacial conditions, in D K Jones (ed) *The shaping of Southern England,* 225–248 London: Academic Press

Williams, R B G 1986 'Periglacial phenomena in the South Downs', in G de G Sieveking and M B Hart (eds) The Scientific Study of Flint and Chert *Proceedings of the Fourth International Flint Symposium,* 161–167 Cambridge: Cambridge University Press

Wilson, D 1985 'A note on O.E. *hearg* and *weoh* as Place-Name Elements Representing Different Types of Pagan Worship Sites', *Anglo-Saxon Studies in Archaeology and History* **4**, 179–83

Wilson, D 1970 'Medieval Britain in 1969' *Medieval Archaeology* **14**, 200–1

Winchester A 2000 *The Harvest of the Hills: Rural Life in Northern England and the Scottish Borders 1400–1700.* Edinburgh: Edinburgh University Press

Woodcock, N H 2000 'The Quaternary: history of an ice age', in Woodcock N and Strachan, R. (eds) *Geological History of Britain and Ireland.* Oxford: Blackwell Science

Wormald, P 2001 '*On þa wæpnedhealfe*: Kingship and royal property from Aethelwulf to Edward the Elder', in N Higham and D Hill (eds) *Edward the Elder 899–924.* London and New York: Routledge, 264–279

Wyles, S F and Allen, M J 1996 'Land Mollusca from Bronze Age features', in A B Powell, M J, Allen, J and I Barnes *Archaeology in the Avebury Area, Wiltshire: recent discoveries along the line of the Kennet Valley Foul Sewer pipeline, 1993.* Salisbury: Wessex Archaeology Report No **8**, 19–26

Wymer J J 1962 'Excavations at the Maglemosian site at Thatcham, Berkshire, England'. *Proc Preh Soc* **28**, 329–361

Wymer, J J 1968 *Lower Palaeolithic Archaeology in Britain* London: John Baker Publishers Ltd

Wymer, J J 1977 *Gazetteer of Mesolithic sites in England and Wales* York: Council for British Archaeology

Wymer, J J 1999 *The Lower Palaeolithic Occupation of Britain Volume 1 Text.* Salisbury: Wessex Archaeology and English Heritage

Wymer, J and Dimbleby, G W 1958 'Excavations on the Mesolithic site at Thatcham'. *Berks Archaeol Journal* **57**, 1–24

Yorke, B 2000 'Political and Ethnic Identity: A Case Study of Anglo-Saxon Practice', *in* W O Frazer and A Tyrell (eds) *Social Identity in Early Medieval Britain.* London and New York: Leicester University Press, 69–89

Young, W E V 1950 'The Beaker interment at Beckhampton' *Wilts Archaeol & Nat Hist Soc Mag* **53,** 311–327

Young, W E V 1959 'The West Kennet Avenue' *Wilts Archaeol & Nat Hist Mag* **57**, 229–30

Young, W E V 1961 'The West Kennet Avenue' *Wilts Archaeol & Nat Hist Mag* **58**, 30